T5-BAG-165

STUDIES IN ISLAMIC PHILOSOPHY AND SCIENCE

Published under the auspices of
the Society for the Study of Islamic Philosophy and Science

# A MUSLIM THEOLOGIAN'S RESPONSE TO CHRISTIANITY

IBN TAYMIYYA'S

*AL-JAWAB AL-SAHIH*

EDITED AND TRANSLATED BY

THOMAS F. MICHEL, S.J.

CARAVAN BOOKS
DELMAR, NEW YORK, 1984

**For Fazlur Rahman,**
**who introduced me to**
**the thought of Ibn Taymiyya**
**and generously directed my research**

Published by Caravan Books
Delmar, New York 12054, U.S.A.



**Library of Congress Cataloging in Publication Data**

Ibn Taymīyah, Ahmad ibn ʻAbd al-Halīm, 1263-1328.

A Muslim theologian's response to Christianity.

(Studies in Islamic philosophy and science)

Translation of:
Jawāb al-sahīh li-man baddala dīn al-Masīh.
1. Christianity—Controversial literature.
2. Islam—Apologetic works.
I. Michel, Thomas F., 1941- .
II. Title. III. Series.
BP170.I18913 1983 297'.293 83-15430
ISBN 0-88206-058-9

# CONTENTS

# FOREWORD

In 717/1317[1] the Hanbali scholar Taqi al-Din Ahmad ibn Taymiyya, residing in Damascus, received a treatise sent to him by Christians in Cyprus. The work was an enlarged version[2] of an apology for Christianity composed about the year 1150 by Paul of Antioch, the Melkite bishop of the Crusader see of Saida. In response, Ibn Taymiyya composed *Al-Jawab al-Sahih li-Man Baddal Din al-Masih* [The correct answer to those who changed[3] the religion of Christ], a work whose length and scope have never been equalled in Muslim critiques of the Christian religion and whose depth of insight into the issues that separate Christianity and Islam sets it among the masterpieces of Muslim polemic against Christianity.

*Al-Jawab al-Sahih* is far more than a rebuttal of Paul of Antioch's 25-page treatise, and it cannot be viewed simply as containing Ibn Taymiyya's attitude towards Christianity. In this work his concern—as always in his writings—was Islam. Ibn Taymiyya was essentially a dialogical type of thinker; among his voluminous writings[4] there exists hardly any extended work in which the polemical element is missing. He seemed best able to say what Islam is (or should be) by pointing up its contradistinction to what Islam is not (or must not become).

Ibn Taymiyya viewed Christianity as an example instructive for Muslims on how the recipients of the one and eternal divine message, delivered to them by their infallible prophet Jesus, went astray by substituting their own teachings and practices for those commanded by their prophet. Hence the title of *Al-Jawab al-Sahih*. Ibn Taymiyya's concern was that he saw the same tendencies in the practices and teachings of Muslims of his time. He observed world views and theologies current among many Muslims of his day which he considered parallel to and sometimes even farther from the truth—embodied in the Qur'an and hadith rightly interpreted by the *salaf*—than what was held and practiced by Christians.

The crucial difference is that whereas the Christian community *as a whole* had departed from the teachings of Jesus, the earlier prophets, and Jesus' right-believing early followers, the Islamic *umma* still retained the correct teaching of Muhammad and the other prophets. It was destined to remain on the right path, because it had been promised that there would always remain a small core of believers who would in every age profess and teach the undiluted and unadulterated religion of Islam.

Ibn Taymiyya saw himself as representative of this body of proponents of the truth. This belief is the basis of the polemical nature of so many of his writings. He was constantly on the watch for deviations from the right path and ready to oppose error within the Islamic community with all the considerable learning in the Islamic tradition which he possessed and all the force of his considerable argumentative powers.

Christians are, of course, outside the Islamic *umma*. An attack by one of their number on the universal nature of Muhammad's prophetic mission and ultimately upon the necessity of Islam within God's eternal plan for human salvation was a challenge which Ibn Taymiyya could not pass up. However, his interest was always in the Islamic community, and by pointing up the falsity of the Christian's argumentation and indicating the errors into which Christians as a people had fallen, he hoped to call back Muslims from their dangerous tendencies in the same directions.

Thus, as a background for understanding Ibn Taymiyya's basic concerns in *Al-Jawab al-Sahih*, I have chosen to place the work in the context of his polemical theology as a whole. By understanding Ibn Taymiyya's polemical reactions to *wahdat al-wujud* theology, popular Sufism, the peripatetic philosophical movement in Islam, Mu'tazili and Ash'arite *kalam* theologies, and Shi'ism, one can better appreciate the principal interests underlying his argumentation against Christianity.

It must be further noted that although *Al-Jawab al-Sahih* was certainly the most important work which Ibn Taymiyya directed against Christianity, it did not include everything which he wrote on the subject. Earlier works of his against Christianity provide a survey of the development of his thought concerning the Christian religion, and I have consequently included a treatment of these other, earlier works.

Finally, there needs to be a note concerning the text itself. *Al-Jawab al-Sahih* has been printed twice.[5] The second edition is basically a reprint of the first with typographical errors corrected. The few changes in wording are based on sense rather than on consultation of the manuscripts. The manuscript evidence gives a conflicting witness to the original state of the text. For reasons I explain in the Appendix to this study, I believe the present printed edition of 1,400 pages to have been originally two works: the first,

*Al-Jawab al-Sahih*, a response to Paul of Antioch, found in the first 1,000 pages of the printed edition, the second, an unnamed work of approximately 400 pages intended to prove the prophethood of Muhammad to whomever might deny that. In this study I am concerned with the former work, to which I will refer by the title *Al-Jawab al-Sahih*. For lack of a better title available, I will refer to the latter work by the (probably spurious) title given it in one manuscript: *Takhjil Ahl al-Injil* [Putting to shame the people of the gospel].

# PART ONE
# THE THEOLOGY OF IBN TAYMIYYA AND HIS CRITIQUE OF CHRISTIANITY

## INTRODUCTION

The central and overriding concern which underlies all of Ibn Taymiyya's controversialist writing is the problem of the relationship between God and the Universe; that is, the question of God's transcendence and immanence. The proper goal of rational reflection upon the sources of religion—the Qur'an and the sunna—is the affirmation of *tawhid*, the assertion of God's oneness. True *tawhid* means the elaboration of God's nature as He is in Himself and as He is vis-à-vis the universe as Creator (*al-khaliq*) and Commander (*al-amir*).

For Ibn Taymiyya, in declaring God to be the one creator, he affirms the essential separateness and dissimilarity of God from the universe and avoids *tashbih*. By declaring Him commander, Ibn Taymiyya maintains the religious and ethical connection between God and the universe and rejects *ta'til*.

Viewed another way, the assertion of true *tawhid* means following the narrow thread between, on the one hand, so associating God with His creation that the real distinctions between them are compromised, and, on the other, making Him so transcendent that the divine Power and Will which are the essential bases for religious life become irrelevant. Ibn Taymiyya describes this endeavor in characteristically Qur'anic imagery—that of the Straight Path. Following pure *tawhid* means describing God only as He has described Himself in the Qur'an and sunna, and responding to Him in obedience only as He commanded men in these sources of divine information. Any deviation from this Straight Path inevitably leads to error, and the farther a sect strays from this path, the more severely they are in error.

True Islam expresses at the ontological level the median path between *ta'til* and *tashbih*, and thus those views which are most strongly opposed by Ibn Taymiyya in his controversialist writings are those of the Muslim philosophers, particularly of the peripatetic school, and of the *wahdat al-wujud* school of Ibn 'Arabi. Of these two, the former represents to Ibn Taymiyya pure *ta'til*—the description of God as self-centered First Principle who neither creates nor speaks nor wills nor acts nor knows the *particularia* of His universe; the latter, Ibn 'Arabi's *wahdat al-wuhud* school, represents pure *tashbih*—the existential identification of God with the universe, union of God with the whole of creation, and the oneness of all that exists.

In questions of metaphysics, these two positions are the logical extremes into which men's errors lead them when they depart from the Qur'an and the sunna. Other errors are dangerous as well, not only as deviations in themselves from the Straight Path, but because they lay the groundwork of principles which logically conclude in the two great errors of pure *ta'til* and pure *tashbih*. From this standpoint Ibn Taymiyya takes issue with the Ash'arite school on matters of divine power and human freedom and with the Mu'tazilis on questions of the divine nature and attributes. This viewpoint further serves as the basis for his criticism of tendencies and practices within Sufism, Shi'ism, and—outside the Islamic *umma*—in Christianity. He sees all these as manifestations of *ghuluw*—exaggerated conceptions of God's immanent presence, which result in a specified or limited form of divine *ittihad* and *hulul* with individual creatures.

Although Ibn Taymiyya's controversialist writings are mostly concerned with what he sees as errors in the area of theodicy, his point of view is the same when he is attacking errors in the ethical sphere. If at the ontological level *tawhid* means affirming the reality of God's being creator and carefully defining that according to the norms of the Straight Path, at the ethical level it means the believer's affirming God's nature as commander and walking the narrow Way between antinomianism and formalistic legalism. For Ibn Taymiyya the ethical counterparts of the peripatetic school of philosophy are the Batinis—Durzi, Qarmati, and Nizari Isma'ilis—whom for their antinomian beliefs he labels apostate and renegade (*murtadd, mulhid*).

At the other extreme are the *mutafaqqihun*, the would-be jurists, whom Ibn Taymiyya accuses of turning Islam into a soulless legalism. Ibn Taymiyya's criticism of Ash'arite *kalam* has strong ethical implications in that he accuses them of destroying the ethical basis of religion by making morality dependent upon the arbitrary will of God. This, in ethical terms, is *ta'til* and gives religious support for the peripatetic philosophers' reduction of God to the Unknowing and the Unwilling.

That Ibn Taymiyya's theological language abounds in technical terms for the relationship between God and the universe underlines its importance in his thought and allows for his subtle precision in delineating this relationship. The problem, according to Ibn Taymiyya, is how to achieve *tanzih* without *ta'til*, *tamthil* without *tashbih*, personal devotional piety without *hulul*, *ittihad*, or *mulamasa*.

The accomplishment of this goal is impossible for man through his own powers. Left to his own devices, man inevitably strays into one or another deviation. It is only revelation from God that can permit man to understand and follow the truth—that is, to affirm the relationship as God Himself has described it. This accounts for Ibn Taymiyya's strict reliance upon the Qur'an and prophetic sunna and upon the authoritative interpretation of it by the *salaf*—the pious ancestors.

The only valid source of knowledge about God is what He Himself has revealed. Those who stray farthest from the truth are those who, like the peripatetic philosophers both inside and outside Islam, try to construct a natural theology on purely rational bases. Others, like Christians, Shi'i *ghulat*, and many Sufis, who began with a sound basis of revealed truth, preferred to follow their own whims (*ahwa'*) and inventions (*bida'*), and fell inevitably into unbelief. Still others, like the Mu'tazila and the Ash'arites, while basically holding to God's revealed truth, have allowed human reason to sit in judgment upon it and be the arbiter of its limits and prescriptions, and thus they have ended up in error.

The only valid theological argumentation, therefore, is exegetically sound reflection and elaboration upon the evident (*zahir*) meaning of the Qur'anic text.[1] Human reason has an associative and systematizing role to play in delineating the relationship between God and the world, but, because of its limitations, it is unable to offer any original insights into the nature of this relationship.

The relationship between creator and creation which Ibn Taymiyya is at such pains to define is basically one of absolute freedom and independence on the part of God towards creation (constrained only by His own *sunna*—His customary mode of acting, which is consistent with His nature as He has revealed it) as contrasted with the total need and dependence of all else upon Him as its creator and commander. It is the implied interdependence of God and creation that makes the *wahdat al-wujud* philosophy appear so blasphemous to Ibn Taymiyya, and the Christian doctrine of the incarnation of the Word of God in a creature a particularly repellent form of unbelief. For Ibn Taymiyya, God is best characterized by one of His names—*Al-Samad*—the eternal, unchanging, self-sufficient Rock to which all else turns (*yasmud*) for existence, guidance, and salvation.

I hope to do two things in this introduction to *Al-Jawab al-Sahih*. In Chapters 1-5 I would like to present Ibn Taymiyya's application of his basic theological concern to errors which he opposed in the Islamic community. Chapters 6-8 will show his application of this same insight to his critique of Christianity.

# CHAPTER 1

## THE POLEMIC AGAINST *WAHDAT AL-WUJUD*

Ibn Taymiyya sees the central problem which faces Muslim thinkers as follows: how can one affirm divine unity and avoid the dualism of God and the universe without compromising the essential separateness of God from His creation. Islam is preeminently the religion of unity, and the divine oneness is the subject of the first *shahada*. From this emphasis on the oneness of the divine it can be but a short step in logic to the oneness of Reality, the oneness of Existence itself.[1] Ibn Taymiyya's speculative writings can be seen as a comprehensive argument that this step cannot be taken if the conclusions are to remain consistent with reason and the divinely revealed message.

He perceives that a rationalist tends towards what is in essence atheism, while a religiously oriented person is inclined towards pantheism. The former, having no sense of God or worship in his heart, tends to describe God by attributes of lifelessness, non-existence, and distance, and concludes by worshiping nothing. By contrast, the religious person, who has a sense of God and worship, tends to direct that to the existent creation which he sees and thus concludes by worshiping everything.[2] It is this latter person who is attracted by the views elaborated by the proponents of *wahdat al-wujud*.

While the crippling limitations which the peripatetic philosophers place upon the nature of God expose their view as the more corrupt and blasphemous,[3] the theories of *wahdat al-wujud* present a far greater practical challenge to Islam. The minimalist religion of the philosophers by its nature can appeal only to an intellectual elite, while many ignorant but religious Muslims, impressed by the facile argumentation and often genuine piety of the proponents of *wahda*, will follow them seeking faith, but will be led instead into rejection of the religion of the prophets.

> They invite people to drink the potion of unbelief and apostasy in the vessel of God's prophets and friends; they dress in the garments of those striving in the way of God while they are in secret among those

waging war against God and His messenger; they expound the message of unbelief and apostasy in the patterns of expression of God's friends who affirm Him. Thus a man enters among them so that he might become a believer, a friend of God, but becomes a hypocrite and an enemy to God.[4]

Ill-informed Muslims often follow those who preach the unity of existence—and Ibn Taymiyya claims to have known many personally who have been impressed by *wahda* shaykhs; usually they do not realize that the teachings they follow are opposed to what God has revealed through His prophets, nor do they know what is held by the true friends of God. It is for this reason that the account of the origins, beliefs, and implications of *wahdat al-wujud* within Islam was a recurrent subject of Ibn Taymiyya's controversialist work.[5] It was a primary concern for him not only in essays directed specifically against *wahdat al-wujud* but also in those works written against other errors in Islam and in his polemic against Christianity.

Much of his polemic is a presentation of the principal themes of *wahdat al-wujud* and argumentation to show their incompatibility with the data of revealed prophetic religion. True *tawhid*, he states, is based on two statements which are expressed in the Surat al-Ikhlas; belief in the unity of existence concludes in denying both.[6] The first is a denial of any imperfections or deficiencies in God. God is *al-Samad*—the supremely independent, self-sufficient being endowed with all the attributes of perfection to which all else turns in need (for existence, life, guidance, help, forgiveness, etc.). Ibn Taymiyya will endeavor to show that belief in the unity of existence introduces elements of change, imperfection, non-existence, and temporality into the nature of God, and rather than affirming the divine independence, it makes God and the universe mutually dependent.

The second principle of *tawhid* is the total dissimilarity of God to anything else, and more specifically, to His creation. The attributes of perfection are unique to God, and nothing else participates in them. Ibn Taymiyya claims that the theory of *wahdat al-wujud* denies this radical dissimilarity by predicating existence univocally to God and creation, and thus establishes an identity and unity (*wahda*) of existence.

> The basis of the error of these people is that they do not apprehend the dissimilarity of God to creatures and His transcendence beyond them (*'uluwwuhu 'alayhim*). They know that He is existent, and they therefore think that His existence is not other than (*la yakhruj 'an*) their existence, in the manner of someone who sees the rays of the sun and supposes that they are the sun itself.[7]

This dissimilarity between God and the universe is clearly enunciated in the sacred books of the Jews, Christians, and Muslims; any denial of it can have no foundation in revealed religion. Neither is there any basis in reason, he states, for the identification of divine existence with that of limited, temporal beings. Ibn Taymiyya takes the theological and poetic expressions of the leading proponents[8] of *wahdat al-wujud* and attempts to show that their views are either internally contradictory, that they are gratuitously asserted, or that they actually disprove the unity of existence they claim to affirm.[9]

Ibn Taymiyya rejects the major philosophical premises of a monist view of existence. These premises, he states, are two:

> 1) All things subsist in non-being (*al-'adam*), independent in themselves. This is similar to the view of one who holds that the non-existent is a thing; but in this case one does not distinguish between the essence (*dhat*) of the creator and the essence (*dhat*) of the creature because He does not have an essence which necessitates that His existence be distinguished from contingent essences.
>
> 2) The existence belonging to these established essences is the very existence of Necessary Truth (*al-Haqq al-Wajib*).[10]

Here Ibn Taymiyya is referring to Ibn 'Arabi's view that all essences are pre-subsistent in the mind of God before descending to participate in the one state of existence. God's absolute existence is therefore in need of the universe that His glory be manifested. From Ibn Taymiyya's point of view, his opponents replace the belief in a sovereign creator and commander with a divinity identifiable with the universe whose activity becomes a series of self-manifestations. He further tries to demonstrate, as will be seen below, that the *wahdat al-wujud* school is merely building upon the notion of God as the sole and universal actor in the universe developed by Jahmite and Ash'arite theologians in their writings on *qadar*.

He accuses them of applying to external reality concepts which refer only to mental existence. It is possible to conceive of unlimited, absolute existence, but in reality this is not found as such outside the mind. Existence can never be applied univocally both to limited beings-in-time and to the eternal being who stands outside created reality.

> These people hold that God is absolute existence, for they specify Him as existence without non-being (*al-'adam*). Then they say that He is absolute. But the absolute on the condition of being free from every affirmative or negative restriction is only in minds, not in external real-

ity. These people hold that universal existence is divided into necessary and contingent, and this the philosophers have made the subject of divine knowledge. They call it the High Wisdom and First Philosophy, but it is universal only in minds and not in [external] existents.[11]

These views Ibn Taymiyya traces back to Mu'tazili theses which deny God's attributes and refuse to describe Him by positive qualities.

Ibn Taymiyya points out that the spectrum of views held within the orbit of *wahdat al-wujud* is wide. Variations exist within various schools and significant differences of opinion occur among the most important shaykhs. The most important distinction which must be made is that between belief in the absolute oneness of existence on the one hand and, on the other, in the union of God with some creature.

The former, which Ibn Taymiyya refers to as "general union" (*ittihad 'amm*), indicates an identification of God with the whole universe at an existential level. The second is either "specific union" (*ittihad khass*) or divine indwelling (*hulul*). In specific *ittihad* God enters into union with holy individuals, such as some later Sufis believed about Al-Hallaj, some Shi'a about one or more of the Imams, or Melkite and Jacobite Christians about Jesus. In *hulul* God takes up residence in some person or designates that person as the *locus* of His activity and presence in the universe. This, according to Ibn Taymiyya, is what many Sufis claimed for their shaykhs, Nestorian Christians for Christ, and Ibn 'Arabi and his followers for themselves.

However, the positions of specific *ittihad* and *hulul* are incompatible with that of general *ittihad*. Specific *ittihad* and *hulul* presuppose multiplicity and differentiation in reality, which is denied by general *ittihad*. This latter view is expressed by Ibn Sab'in: "A perishing Lord and a reigning servant; that you are. There is only God, and multiplicity is a delusion."[12]

Ibn Taymiyya's criticism is that if this is their position, then they are both dishonest and inconsistent when they praise persons like Al-Hallaj who claim specific *ittihad*. The more astute among them, like Al-Tilimsani,[13] have recognized this; for him, anyone claiming specific *ittihad* like Al-Hallaj or *hulul* like Ibn 'Arabi is as much an unbeliever as were the prophets who taught multiplicity of being. According to them, Christians are not unbelievers for believing in the divine union in Christ, but for specifying such union to one individual. Idol worshipers are not unbelievers for worshiping the divinity present in their statues and images, but for limiting the divine presence to some creatures in preference to others. Al-

Tilimsani, whom Ibn Taymiyya calls "The rebel, the most outrageous of all people, the most profoundly unbelieving of them,"[14] is at least consistent and states openly the blasphemy which others like Ibn 'Arabi and Ibn Sab'in use sophistry to avoid. For al-Tilimsani, the only ones professing *tawhid* are people like Pharaoh, who said to Moses "Am I not your highest lord?" and Iblis when he refused to specify any object of honor or worship.

Ibn 'Arabi, whose many admirable qualities Ibn Taymiyya notes, cannot be taken seriously in argument because of the internally contradictory nature of his writing. He notes that Ibn 'Arabi's theology is nevertheless no unnuanced pantheism, and that any argumentation from reason against the views of Ibn 'Arabi will ultimately turn on questions of epistemology.

> The existence of beings created in the time is the very existence of the Creator—not other than Him and not outside Him. It is this which they innovated and by which they have departed from all the shaykhs and *'ulama'* who preceded them. This is the view of the rest of the Ittihadiyya. But Ibn 'Arabi is the nearest of them to Islam, the one whose speech is best in many places. He distinguishes between the One manifesting and what is manifested. He affirms the divine commanding and forbidding as well as the revealed religions against what is brought against them. He has commanded the following of much of what the shaykhs have prescribed by way of moral and religious duties. Many religious people have thereby taken their path from his teaching and have benefited from it, although they do not know its true nature.[15]

Ibn Taymiyya criticizes Ibn 'Arabi for claiming the indwelling of the divine presence within him and for alleging the reception of a kind of inspiration which equals and even exceeds the revelation, *wahy*, given to prophets. The first statement is incompatible with the rest of his philosophy, claims Ibn Taymiyya, while the second is blasphemous.

> If he means specific *hulul* as the Christians claim about Christ, this necessitates that this indwelling be established in him from the time of his creation—as the Christians say about Christ. This is not something resulting for him from his gnosis, his religious practices, his realization or perception of God. In that case there would be no difference between him and other humans. Why should *hulul* be established in him without others? This is worse than the view of Christians, for Christians claim that about Christ, but he was born without father. The shaykhs do not excel in the very manner of their creation, but have only excelled in religious practices, *tawhid*, knowledge and realization (*tahqiq*) of God. This is something that happened for them after it had not been. If this were the cause of *hulul*, it would necessitate that *hulul* be something occurring in time among them unrelated to their creation.[16]

Thus he accuses Ibn 'Arabi of redefining *hulul* and of tailoring the concept to his own purposes. If specific *hulul* is regarded as a religious state which can be achieved through religious practices or gnosis, then the relationship between God and the believer expressed by it is, on the one hand, incompatible with a view of absolute universal unity of existence and, on the other, in need only of several careful distinctions to be acceptable to *Sunni* Islam as Ibn Taymiyya envisions it. In fact, as will be clear in Chapter 8, Ibn Taymiyya speaks more than once of a sense of divine *hulul* in the believer which he finds acceptable.

It is the attitude of Ibn 'Arabi and those like him towards the relative status of the prophet and the mystic to which Ibn Taymiyya takes exception more strongly. For Ibn Taymiyya, religion is preeminently prophetic religion. Not only Islam, but the religions of the Book before it—in fact all revelatory messages which mankind has received from God—have been delivered through his messengers and prophets. Ibn Taymiyya is unsympathetic to natural religion and natural theology, and he firmly states that without the guidance of the prophets, mankind will inevitably stray from the true path. Moreover, those within Islam who have most directly attacked the institution and prerogatives of prophecy, like the peripatetic philosophers and the proponents of *wahdat al-wujud*, and those outside of Islam who have least known its teachings and guidance are the people found to be farthest from the truth.[17]

Ibn 'Arabi declares the Seal of the Friends of God, whom he identifies with himself, to be superior to the prophets—and more specifically to the Seal of the Messengers (Muhammad)—in knowledge of God and of the true nature of the universe.

> The real nature of what he states is a denial of the Creator so that there is found nothing save creatures. This is actually the view of Pharaoh. He made the one who knows the highest in knowledge of God so that even all the prophets and messengers would benefit from this knowledge . . . He made the Seal of the Friends [of God] superior to the Seal of the Messengers in respect to truth and knowledge of it. He took from the source whence the angel inspired (*yuhi*) the Seal of the Messengers. The Seal of the Messengers is only master in intercession, and his mastery is only in this particular area, not of a general nature.[18]

By claiming that prophetic inspiration, or that which is equivalent or superior to it, is available to those who are not of prophetic status, Ibn 'Arabi makes the nature of prophetic revelation relative. Anyone could claim inspiration or immediate divine knowledge, and the purpose of revelation, which is to channel God's guidance and command to men, would be thwarted. That Ibn Taymiyya was not merely reacting to an academic danger will be seen in the treatment of his writings against teachings of Sufi masters and popular preachers. In all these phenomena, as preeminently in *wahdat al-wujud*, he saw the revelation given through the prophetic line—the only true and certain source of knowledge about God and His will—become merely one of a number of "ways" of knowing.

They claim that "the ground of reality is the ground of imagination,"[19] and that that which contradicts sound reason can be perceived and affirmed through immediate perception (*kashf, dhawq, wajd*) and that there can be known by *kashf* that which others believe to be contrary to revealed information. They claim that just as the prophets brought divine information which could not otherwise be humanly known, so have those who have attained the gnosis—knowledge that existence is one.

Ibn Taymiyya's response is that the prophets could not bring a divine message that contradicts reason; although revelation brings information unattainable by reason, both forms of knowledge are always in accord. If *kashf* is contrary to sound reason, then it is certainly opposed to revelation and is untrustworthy.[20]

Ibn Taymiyya holds that Ibn 'Arabi reverses the process. It is creative imagination which passes judgment upon that which is learned from reason. Moreover, it is this imagination which he identifies with the channel of revelation. For Ibn 'Arabi there can be no dispute between what is learned through *kashf* and information revealed through the prophets, for both ultimately refer back to the same source. Reason then becomes the weakest of the three, and is only acceptable if it is in accord with what is learned through immediate perception and revelation.

> Ibn 'Arabi accepts from reason that which imagination accepts from it. Imagination for him is the angel from whom the prophet drew. To this end he said that he drew from the same source from which did the angel who inspired the Prophet. He said, "If you know this, there will derive to you beneficial knowledge." The point here is the teaching about prophecy. A prophet is one whom God informs, and who then bears the message of what God informed him.[21]

Ibn Taymiyya is thus at pains to assert the priority of prophecy in obtaining knowledge about God and to remove it from human control. The prophet is one whom God chooses as a messenger; prophetic inspiration is by its nature not something which can be sought and achieved through religious practices and knowledge. If the conclusions of *wahdat al-wujud* are accepted, prophecy is superseded and made irrelevant, and so too are the beliefs and practices of Islam, which were revealed through prophecy. The divine creative imagination, according to Ibn 'Arabi, manifests itself immediately to, in, and through one who knows the secret of the oneness of reality, and the prophetic religion is relegated to being a secondary guide for those who are not yet spiritually adept. Thus in Ibn 'Arabi's treatment of prophecy, Ibn Taymiyya sees an attack on the nature of Islam itself.

Their diminution of the role of prophecy, he asserts, was not the only error into which their belief in the unity of existence led them. In identifying all creation with God, they have committed *shirk*—in fact the greatest *shirk* which is possible to commit.[22] Idol worshipers, popular Sufi movements, Christians, and Shi'i *ghulat* commit *shirk* by claiming that God has united with or taken up residence within some creature, and thus they make that creature participate in the worship due God alone. However, the followers of *wahdat al-wujud*, by denying any multiplicity or differentiation in the universe, have committed universal *shirk*, for they have excluded nothing from participating in divine worship.[23]

Conversely, from their point of view, that which is presented in the Qur'an and the sunna is *shirk*, for it denies the universal oneness of existence. According to them, only they themselves follow the true *tawhid*, which consists of the realization and affirmation of the oneness of reality. Al-Tilimsani stated it provocatively but accurately, "The whole Qur'an is *shirk*; there is no *tawhid* in it."[24]

It is the nature of God to grant and sustain life, to command, dispose, judge, and forgive His creatures; it is the nature of mankind to worship, thank, seek, and obey their Lord.[25] By positing an existential identity between God and the universe, the followers of *wahdat al-wujud* have in effect denied God through their rejection of His essential and distinguishing characteristics. They have destroyed the basis of religious life by denying man's nature as worshiper, seeker, and obedient servant.[26] In their view the worshiper is the one worshiped, and both are in mutual need of the other. The belief in the unity of existence leads therefore to pure *ta'til*, where God is not denied in theory, but in practice becomes inoperative and irrelevant.[27]

The three essential qualities of God which are effectually denied by holding the unity of existence are His role as creator, His sovereignty as Lord of the universe, and His supreme independence from all that is other than Him.[28]

The real nature of the belief of the Sufi renegades like Ibn 'Arabi and Ibn Sab'in is that this world has been necessarily and pre-eternally existent. It has no maker other than itself. They say that existence is one, and the real nature of their view is that there is not in existence a creator as another existent being. Their teaching on the afterlife and on prophecy is worse than the teaching of Jews and Christians and idol worshipers, for they make possible the worship of every idol, and do not specify some idols for worship.[29]

In the view of the Ittihadiyyun, God is no longer Lord and Commander of the universe, but rather its existential absolute. In this their view is equivalent to that of the materialists (*Dahriyya*) or the naturalists (*Taba'i'iyya*), who deny the existence of any Maker for the world or the existence of any necessary being but the universe.[30]

Ibn Taymiyya accuses those who teach the unity of existence of undermining individual and social morality. He had noticed tendencies among Sufis to deemphasize the moral and cultic prescriptions of the *shari'a* in favor of works of supererogation. He finds the theoretical basis for this in the theories of *wahdat al-wujud*. For those to whom the veil has been pulled back, and who understand the oneness of all reality, all things are licit, for all are one. Sins, crimes, and forbidden things presuppose a differentiation in reality, and once this is seen as an illusion, sin is impossible.

The rebel Al-Tilimsani does not distinguish between existence and subsistence as does Ibn 'Arabi, nor between the absolute and the particularized (*al-mu'ayyan*) as does al-Rumi[31]. . . . For this reason he used to permit all forbidden things (*al-muharramat*) so that reliable people related about him that he said, "A daughter, a mother, and a foreign woman are one thing. For us there is nothing *haram* in that. But those behind the veil [i.e., those who do not realize the secret of unity] say '*Haram!*' We say, 'It is *haram* for you'."[32]

For these reasons Ibn Taymiyya sees the philosophy of *wahdat al-wujud* as the greatest danger to Islam in his time. Its proponents, he states, are the "precursors of the *Dajjal* (Antichrist),"[33] and the enervating effect their influence had upon the Islamic community he believes to have been partly responsible for the triumph of the Mongols. Their danger arises from the insidious nature of their errors. He claims to have known many personally who joined them through ignorance of the true nature of their teachings and admits that he himself had previously been impressed by Ibn 'Arabi, until he came to realize the real import of his doctrine.

To those following the spiritual path they misrepresented the *tawhid* which God revealed in His books through His prophets by an *ittihad*

> (divine union) which they called *tawhid*. Its true nature is *ta'til* of the Maker and denial of the Creator. Long ago I was actually among those who held a good opinion and extolled Ibn 'Arabi when I read worthwhile things in his books like his teaching in much of the *Futuhat*, the *Kunh*, the *Al-Muhkam al-Marbut*, the *Al-Durra al-Fakhira*, *Matali' al-Nujum*, and the like. But when I perceived the true nature of his intent, I did not study the *Fusus*.[34]

Their teachings, asserts Ibn Taymiyya, are opposed to all revealed religions. Pagan idol worshipers admit that there is a creator who fashioned a world distinct from Him, and the generality of Christian, Jewish, and Sabaeans affirm that even more strongly. But these people, who in effect deny that, and who make God's existence dependent upon the created universe, are worse than those idol worshipers. Ibn Taymiyya does not hazard a guess as to whether they will find a pardon like believing Muslims on the Resurrection Day.[35]

According to Ibn Taymiyya, the philosophy of *wahdat al-wujud* did not develop as an isolated phenomenon among Muslims. On the contrary, he sees it as the most eclectic of beliefs and a mixture of all errors.[36] He traces several currents within theological and philosophical thought and in practices of popular piety and preaching which served as bases from which *wahdat al-wujud* theses were developed or which showed similarities with some aspect of monist thought.

In Chapters 2 through 5 I will study the movements and schools of thought against which Ibn Taymiyya wrote controversialist works. In addition to giving an outline of his objections to these movements within Islam, I hope to give special attention to the factors which he sees as having predisposed many to adopt the stance of *wahdat al-wujud*. By this I intend to show the common thread which for Ibn Taymiyya links these phenomena of error. This, I believe, can enable one to understand better the particular viewpoint from which Ibn Taymiyya was working in his controversialist writing on Christianity.

# CHAPTER 2

## THE POLEMIC AGAINST THE PHILOSOPHERS

Ibn Taymiyya lists three principal sources for the belief in the unity of existence already present in unorthodox formulations of Islam. These are the negative formulation and exaggerated transcendence (*ta'til*) of the Jahmites, the ambiguous expressions of the Sufis, and the free-thinking irreligion (*zandaqa*) of the philosophers.[1] Of these groups the one he considers most seriously in opposition to true Islam is that of the peripatetic philosophers.

It must first be determined to whom Ibn Taymiyya is referring by the term "philosopher" (*faylasuf*). Usually this term is applied, often further qualified by "peripatetic" (*mashsha'i*), to Islamic philosophers of the neo-Platonic and Aristotelian tradition, principally to Al-Farabi and Ibn Sina, but occasionally also to Ibn Rushd and Nasir al-Din al-Tusi. On rare occasions he applies the term to al-Suhrawardi and the philosophers of the Ishraqi school. However, Ibn Taymiyya usually reserves for these latter the term "philosophizers," or "would-be philosophers" (*al-mutafalsifa*). He likewise distinguishes those individuals in the later Ash'arite and Mu'tazili *kalam* traditions—such as Al-Shahrastani, Al-Ghazali, Fakhr al-Din al-Razi, and Al-Amidi—whose terminology, conceptual categories, and conclusions were influenced by the peripatetics as "the philosophizing *kalam* theologians," or "the philosophers among the Mu'tazila" (*al-mutakallimun al-mutafalsifa, al-mutafalsifa min al-mu'tazila*). However, because these individuals are never referred to as "philosophers" per se, we can understand Ibn Taymiyya's polemical writings against the *falasifa* as being directed at the tradition of Al-Farabi and Ibn Sina, and occasionally at the Ishraqis.

Ibn Taymiyya's judgment upon the philosophers is severe. Time and again he calls them apostates and renegades, "the dregs of those adhering to Islam," as well as free-thinking irreligionists. At one point in his polemic against them he states that they deny every element which constitutes Islamic faith. They are, in fact, farther from this faith than are the Christians, who, although they are unbelievers and have corrupted elements of the prophetic revelation, continue to argue their beliefs from the Qur'an and the earlier books and hold to the universal principles brought by the prophets.

> They [the Christians] hold the universal principles upon which the messengers have agreed, such as faith in God, the creator of everything, who is omniscient and omnipotent, and faith in His angels, His messengers, the Last Day, the Garden and the Fire and more—[all of] which you [philosophers] reject.[2]

Ibn Taymiyya's criticism, then, is that the philosophers reject God as creator by teaching the eternity of the world and by positing its emanation from God in place of the creation *ex nihilo* expressed in the sacred books. They reject the omniscience of God by claiming that the First Principle knows only Himself and does not know the particulars of the universe. They reject God's omnipotence by denying that he can break natural laws—the natural sunna—by an act of creation. They reject angels by identifying them with the intelligences of the neo-Platonic cosmology and by identifying Jibril with the demiurge. By making prophecy a natural phenomenon and by making the prophets inferior to the philosophers in some respects, they deny the unique prerogatives of the prophets, and thus deny the messengers. They reject heaven and hell as mankind's final ends and replace this with salvation for the enlightened through personal knowledge and, in the case of Ishraqis, ascent through personal enlightenment to the divine. In short, they reject all the universal principles of faith taught by the prophets and stated in the divine books. Some of the elements of Ibn Taymiyya's criticism of the philosophers' views deserve a more thorough treatment, insofar as they bear on his criticism of other intellectual and religious movements within Islam and upon his attitude towards Christianity.

First of all, Ibn Taymiyya entirely rejects the neo-Platonic cosmology elaborated by the philosophers. He claims that since they have never offered either a religious or rational proof for the system, it is simply a gratuitously asserted hypothesis.[3] He takes each element of the cosmological structure and attempts to show its incompatibility with reason and with the religion of the prophets.

The concept of emanation is a type of generation on the part of God. It is admittedly an intellectual generation rather than something physical, but nevertheless implies that there is something of the essence of God which is emanating from Him. Through the mediate levels of the intelligences, the souls, and the celestial spheres, it is that emanation of the divine essence from which the universe is derived, and thus in a certain aspect is begotten from God.[4] The clear distinction and differentiation between the essence of God and that of the universe which is affirmed by the concept of creation *ex nihilo* is in the philosophers' system denied. Moreover this "begetting" introduces an aspect of change and multiplicity into God which is incompatible with His absolute unity.

In fact the type of intellective generation which the philosophers posit for God is even more unreasonable and impossible than the kind of physical generation (*tawallud hissi*) affirmed by pagan Arabs and Christians.

> These philosophers are farther from resembling understandable generation than that generation which is claimed by the pagan Arabs and the generality of Christians and Jews. For this intellective generation is more impossible than the physical generation of the others. Physical generation is understandable concerning separate self-subsisting substances, but intellective generation is not understandable in terms of substances at all. The latter group affirm generation from two principles, and this is reasonable; but these [philosophers] affirm generation from one principle. The others affirm generation by separation of a part; and this is understandable; but these hold for a generation without that, and that cannot be imagined . . . Thus it is understood that the view of those others—although it is false and God has made its falsity clear and has rejected it—is nearer to being reasonable. But the view of these people is of greater falsity.[5]

According to Ibn Taymiyya it is clear that the procession of intelligences, souls, and celestial spheres in the neo-Platonic system amounts to a form of *shirk* and angelolatry, whereby the angels are identified with the neo-Platonic intelligences and become participants in divine qualities. Their emanation from God makes them parallel to the "daughters of God" worshiped by the pagan Arabs.[6] This is particularly clear in the case of the demiurge (*al-'aql al-fa''al*), to whom they attribute the divine prerogative of fashioner of the sensible universe.

> These people claim that from the First Intelligence proceeded everything which is under Him. Thus from Him proceeded intelligence, soul, and sphere, and from the intelligence, another intelligence, soul, and sphere on to the Active Intellect. From it proceeded all which is under it by way of matters and forms which they call "the minor lords" (*al-arbab al-sughra*), and the "minor gods" (*al-aliha al-sughra*). But it is conclusively known from the religion of the people of the three religions—Muslims, Jews, and Christians—that nothing of angels was the

> maker (*al-fa'il*) of all things which were produced and the inventor (*al-mubdi'*) of everything beneath the sphere of the moon.[7]

It should be noted that Ibn Taymiyya never accuses the philosophers of making the demiurge "the creator" (*al-khaliq*) of the sublunar universe, for as Ibn Taymiyya perceives the cosmology of the philosophers, the act of creation (*khalq*) is denied. In this, and in the fact that the essential dissimilarity and separateness of God to the universe is diminished,[8] is found the greatest affinity between the cosmos as envisioned by the philosophers and that described by the monist school of Ibn 'Arabi. In either system, when true creation is denied, there results that lack of sharp differentiation in act and substance between God and the universe which had been demanded by the act of creation.

God's role as Commander, which forms the basis for religious obligations, is made even more strongly inoperative in the cosmological system of the philosophers than it is by the monists. For among the philosophers, according to Ibn Taymiyya, God neither wills, nor acts, nor loves, nor commands, nor knows anything other than Himself. He finds the philosophers' thesis that God knows only universal ideas—and not the *particularia* of the universe—a view particularly disruptive to religious life. Here also can be seen a connection between the philosophers and the proponents of *wahdat al-wujud*.

> The would-be philosophers—Aristotle and his followers—hold that He does not do anything, will anything, know anything, or create anything. For what, then, should He be thanked? Or for what is He praised and worshiped? The Batini Shi'a and the Sufis like Ibn Sab'in and Ibn 'Arabi are secretly like that. But they say that existence is one: the existence of the creature is the existence of the creator. Thus each existing being ought to be worshiping himself, thanking himself, praising himself.[9]

The effect of the philosophers' *ta'til*, states Ibn Taymiyya, is that God has no effect on the life of the believer, who in turn is not motivated to advert to God religiously. The philosophers have thus described God much as did the pagan Arabs, for whom God was too distant and exalted, and they approached Him through intermediaries.[10]

Moreover the omnipotence of God is also put into question by the philosophers. Ibn Taymiyya opposes the view of Al-Suhrawardi[11] that God's consistent manner of acting demands the eternity of the world, for creation would be a breaking of His habitual state and thus imply change in God. This defense for the eternity of the universe was not limited to Al-Suhrawardi, and Ibn Taymiyya's objection is that in manners of customary occurrences and laws of nature God has no necessary sunna, and thus He is free and omnipotent in His dealings with the universe.[12] It is in the religious realm in His role as revealer, commander, and judge, that God's customary sunna has meaning. Even here, God's sunna places no limitation on His omnipotence, for it only means that God always acts according to His nature; that is, God is not self-contradictory.

Nowhere is Ibn Taymiyya's criticism of the philosophers more harsh than on the subject of their treatment of prophecy. To him the philosopher's view of prophecy robs the prophets of their special status as messengers of revelation from God. He quotes Al-Farabi as holding that the special characteristic of prophecy consists in "excellence in imagizing spiritual realities,"[13] that is, the ability of turning spiritual realities into images. Prophecy thus becomes a natural function in mankind, and the difference between the prophet and others is merely one of degree. It is true that Al-Farabi takes a far more minimalist approach to prophecy than does Ibn Sina, but even the latter severely delimits the prophet's prerogatives.

> Ibn Sina . . . has posited three characteristics of the prophet: first, that the prophet obtains knowledge without being taught. This—the power of intuition—he calls the Holy Faculty. Secondly, the prophet's imagination symbolizes this intellectual knowledge and thus he sees in his own soul psychic (*ruhani*) forms and also hears in his own mind voices . . . but so does the melancholic according to them. Thirdly, the prophet has a mental power whereby he can influence the matter of the world, and produce strange events which they regard as miracles . . . These people do not admit that transcending the highest sphere there may be something which can act or produce. So there is nothing beyond which speaks or moves in any way—not even an angel let alone the Lord of the World.[14]
>
> Elsewhere he says:
>
> Prophecy is an overflowing upon souls from the Active Intellect of the same nature as that which is seen by a sleeper. They hold for some of the attributes of prophets without others, and some of what they brought without the rest. They do not hold for all of what the prophets have brought.[15]

Ibn Taymiyya holds that on the matter of prophecy the philosophers are worse than Christians and Jews, who, although they do not accept all the prophets, at least accept all the attributes of prophecy. His point is that the philosophers' views wage an attack on the very institution of prophecy and thus upon the one and universal religion which is brought solely by prophets. Those who in turn reject prophecy on rational or any other grounds are thereby depriving themselves of the only source of information from or about God.[16]

Thus in his criticism of the philosophers' formulation of prophecy he is actually taking issue with the world view of the philosophers, which he judges to be directly opposed to that of the Qur'an. The philosophers, informed by the ideals and the methodology of classical humanism, begin with observation of what is known and proceed to theorize about the unseen. The Qur'anic approach, as Ibn Taymiyya sees it, is the reverse of this. The most certain knowledge comes through the prophetic revelation, and this in turn directs the study into the human sciences.

> Ibn Taymiyya, so far as I know, is the only medieval Muslim who seeks to formulate clearly the ultimate issues at state between the cognitive approach to reality of the Greeks and the "anticlassical" attitudes of the Koran.
>
> According to Ibn Taymiyya, the goal of human life is neither the philosophic contemplation of God nor the mystic type of love of Him—for each of these leads to the doctrine of the Unity of Being, of the identity of the world and God and so to the absolute inanity of both God and man—but the active concept of *'ibada*, a knowledge of God's will and its fearless implementation in life.[17]

The philosophers' methodology, Ibn Taymiyya states, has made them the most knowledgeable and informative of people in some areas of life, but the most ignorant and misguided in others. On issues dealing with sense perception and natural processes their method of observation serves them well. In areas of the unseen (*al-ghayb*), however, they are helpless, and because they do not seek instruction from the prophets—who alone bring clear and certain knowledge of the unseen—they are doomed to error.

> The teaching of the philosophers on divine matters and general intellective principles is extremely limited and there is much confusion in it. They only speak well on matters of natural sense perception, and on the general principles pertaining to that, their teaching is for the most part good. However, the unseen, of which the prophets bring information, and universal intellective principles which are general to all existent beings—about those things they know nothing at all.[18]

Ibn Taymiyya criticizes the philosophers for applying their methodology to the Qur'anic revelation. Working from the assumption that whatever they do not know or cannot prove cannot be true, the philosophers, he claims, have performed *tabdil* and *tahrif* on the Qur'an, both in concept and in terminology.

> When they hear the information of the prophets about angels, the Throne, the Chair, the Garden, and the Fire, they presume that nothing exists except that which they know, and becoming confused they interpret the teaching of the prophets according to what they know—even though there is no proof for that and they have no knowledge in this denial of theirs. For absence of knowledge is not knowledge of an absence.[19]

They identify the Throne mentioned in the Qur'an with the ninth celestial sphere, the Chair with the eighth, the angels with the intelligences and celestial souls, and Jibril with the Active Intellect, the Demiurge.[20] In this way, they are attempting to interpret the Qur'an within a conceptual frame essentially foreign to the sacred books.

He claims that the philosophers employ vague and general terms not taken from the sacred books, which can admit of various types of proper and improper meanings. They deceive people by claiming that this essentially ambiguous language expresses the truth known by reason or immediate perception and that it agrees with what has been revealed, if its incompatibility with what was revealed is not evident.[21] In this Ibn Taymiyya takes a strong position against the innovation of terminology. He holds that only the terms used by the early Islamic community can be known to adequately express divine matters. A new term may or may not be accurate in describing the sunna, but since it is by its nature ambiguous, it may not be used in theological argumentation.

> The whole point is that they depend on these general ambiguous terms, and if they were made to specify their statements, then the truth would be distinguishable from error. Every view which does not go back in expression and meaning to the Book and the sunna and the speech of the *salaf* of the community has no bearing on the heavenly proofs and applies neither to the sunna nor to innovation, neither by agreeing with nor opposing them, much less by applying to faith of unbelief. But the sunna is only that which agrees with the religious proofs, and innovation is that which opposes them.[22]

The influence of the peripatetic tradition upon other movements and individuals in Islam is incontestable. Among those whom Ibn Taymiyya lists as being particularly affected by the ideas of the philosophers are the later *kalam* theologians such as Al-Ghazali, Al-Razi, and Al-Shahrastani, as well as Nizari Isma'ilis and the authors of the epistles of the Ikhwan al-Safa'.[23] Although the particular influence varied in type, Ibn Taymiyya saw it in every case as negative.

Most important to Ibn Taymiyya is the influence which the philosophers had upon the school of Ibn 'Arabi. The philosophers, in depersonalizing God by transforming the active Qur'anic concept of the sovereign creative God into a passive one of a First Principle from which all existence flows and whose only activity is eternal self-contemplation, have thereby laid the philosophical bases for Ibn 'Arabi's view of Absolute Existence contemplating preexistent essences within Himself, so that from Him flows the unique existence which actualizes all that is in the universe.

Ibn Taymiyya realizes that the philosophers and the proponents of the unity of existence are poles apart in some respects. The philosophers can be said to represent pure *ta'til*—an extreme transcendence whereby God is conceived of as so distant and ineffectual that His role as a religious force is eradicated. At the other extreme, the *wahdat al-wujud* school represents pure *tashbih*. God's immanent presence in the world is exaggerated among them to the point that His distinctness and dissimilarity is compromised. However, for Ibn Taymiyya the result of both errors is the same; in either case God ceases to be the transcendent One who stands outside the universe but who is in constant interplay with its destiny through His freely chosen activity as creator, commander, and judge.

Ibn Taymiyya reports a correspondence between Al-Nasir al-Tusi[24] (whom he calls "The Sabaean Philosopher," and "Minister of the Apostates"), and Sadr al-Din al-Qunawi[25] (whom he calls "The Christian Ittihadi philosopher"). His treatment is instructive in indicating Ibn Taymiyya's evaluation of the relative degrees and forms of *kufr* expressed by the philosophers and the *wahdat al-wujud* teachers.

> From the correspondence between Al-Sadr and Al-Nasir, in which Al-Nasir affirms the being whose existence is necessary and Al-Sadr makes that to be Absolute, Unlimited Existence—and that this is God—can be known the truth of what I have said [about the resemblance of what they hold] and the nature of their agreement on error and unbelief may be understood. Al-Nasir is nearer [to the truth] in respect to his admission of the Lord as the Maker who is distinguished from the universe. But he is more unbelieving by reason of his remoteness from prophecy, religions (*shara'i'*), and religious practices, Al-Sadr is nearer by reason of his extolling religious practices, prophecies, and a sense of God in the manner of the Christians, but he is more unbelieving by reason of the fact that there is no reality to his object of worship. He worships only Absolute Existence, which has no reality outside mental concepts.

> Thus Al-Sadr was more unbelieving in formulation, less unbelieving in act. Al-Nasir is more unbelieving in act, less so in formulation. Each of them is an unbeliever in both his formulation and in his action . . . But Al-Nasir is nearer to the *'ulama'* because of what is true in his teaching, just as Al-Sadr is nearer to practicing [Muslims] because of what there is of service of God in his actions.[26]

These two philosophical-theological systems—that of *wahdat al-wujud* and that of the peripatetic philosophers—represent to Ibn Taymiyya the opposite extremes of error to which mankind could deviate from the Straight Path. For him, however, in addition to these two extreme heterodox systems, there are intermediate stages of error which predispose a believer for greater deviations from the truth.

As stated at the beginning of this chapter, Ibn Taymiyya mentions two errors among Muslims which serve to lay the groundwork for *wahdat al-wujud*: these are the ambiguous expressions of the Sufis and the negative formulation of the Jahmites. Each of these will be studied in turn in Chapters 3 and 4.

# CHAPTER 3

## THE POLEMIC AGAINST SUFIS

It is commonly accepted, both among Muslims and in Western scholarship, that Ibn Taymiyya is the "irreconcilable enemy of Sufism."[1] This conception is often supported in Western scholarship by a negative characterization of Ibn Taymiyya as an inflexible and possibly unbalanced[2] opponent of every religious expression within Islam except a soulless legalism which he derived from the early teachers through the Hanbali tradition. Related personal characteristics, seen from another perspective, have made him a spokesman and hero for modern Islamic reformers; his devotion to the *salaf*, his defense of free will and the *shari'a*, his conscientiousness and willingness to suffer for his belief, his conviction that Islam is to be taken seriously and practiced sincerely—these qualities have made him an instructive model toward whom Muslims of this past century have gravitated.

On one point, however, Muslim and Western scholars have generally agreed—his unrelenting opposition to Sufism.[3] There have been only a few voices which have mentioned the need for greater precision in defining Ibn Taymiyya's relationship to Sufism. Laoust pointed out the influences of the mystical tradition upon Ibn Taymiyya, particularly in the voluntarist rather than rationalist nature of their religious systems and in his adoption of the Sufi terminology of human affectivity for describing religious experience.[4] He also stressed that it was principally the school of Ibn 'Arabi against which Ibn Taymiyya exerted his efforts.

Fazlur Rahman calls Ibn Taymiyya a "neo-Sufi" and notes that he tried to integrate as much as possible of the Sufi legacy into his synthesis of orthodox Islam. He states, "He was not only not inimical to Sufism as such, but considered it necessary, a part of religion of law."[5]

Recent studies by George Makdisi take the situation a step further. On the one hand he has given ample evidence of the close historical and ideological connections between the Hanbali tradition and Sufism,[6] while on the other he has shown that Ibn Taymiyya was very probably a self-acknowledged member of the Qadiri *tariqa.*[7] His evidence for this is two quotations from Ibn Taymiyya in which he affirms his own membership in Sufi orders. Moreover, Professor Makdisi has uncovered a *silsila* in which Ibn Taymiyya's name appears. Ibn Taymiyya's first statement is taken from his *Al-Mas'ala al-Tabriziya* and he declares his affiliation with 'Abd al-Qadir al-Jilani:

> I wore the blessed Sufi cloak of 'Abd al-Qadir [al-Jili], there being between him and me two [Sufi shaykhs].[8]

In a stronger statement of mediate transmission, and hence more doubtful authenticity, Ibn Taymiyya is quoted as confirming his membership in more than one *tariqa* and his preference for the Qadiri.

> I have worn the Sufi cloak of a number of Shaykhs belonging to various *tariqas*, among them that of the Shaykh 'Abd al-Qadir al-Jili, whose *tariqa* is the greatest of the well-known ones.[9]

Confirmatory evidence of the first statement is offered by the *silsila* in which Ibn Taymiyya is mentioned in the chain of initiation of 'Abd al-Qadir with two shaykhs separating them.[10]

While an undisputed judgment on Ibn Taymiyya's membership in a Sufi *tariqa* is still awaited in scholarly circles, an examination of the writings of Ibn Taymiyya confirms beyond question the views of Laoust and Rahman and gives strong support for the thesis of Makdisi. Ibn Taymiyya praises Sufism as one of the ways by which believers go beyond the legislated performance of religious duties to come closer to God.

> The lawful is that by which one approaches near to God. It is the way of God; it is righteousness, obedience, good deeds, charity (*khayr*), and fairness. It is the way of those on the Path (*al-salikin*), and the method of those intending God and worshipping Him; it is that which is traveled by everyone who desires God and follows the way of asceticism (*zuhd*) and religious practice, and what is called poverty and Sufism and the like.[11]

In a commentary on the *Futuh al-Ghayb* by 'Abd al-Qadir al-Jilani, eponym of the Qadiri *tariqa*, Ibn Taymiyya makes the same point. True worship is not completed by fulfillment of obligatory duties (*wajibat*), but includes also the performance of praiseworthy supererogatory works (*mustahabbat*); this, he declares, has been the consistent teaching of all the great Sufi shaykhs.

> The great shaykhs like Shaykh 'Abd al-Qadir encouraged people to follow the path of those approaching God who go beyond what is necessary—to avoid the reprehensible as well as the forbidden, to perform the commendable as well as the obligatory.[12]

In the same commentary he quotes 'Abd al-Qadir approvingly for his advocating an ascetic path, which moves the believer beyond the state of those who will be on God's right hand on Judgment Day to a path in which the religious goal is perfection. This is achieved by a voluntary response to God's command as expressed in the Qur'an and in the teaching and example of Muhammad elucidated in the sunna.

> Shaykh 'Abd al-Qadir—may God sanctify his spirit—taught asceticism in the intention and desire of the soul so that a person does not act according to the judgment of the will (*irada*) and the soul (*nafs*). This raises him beyond the state of the Just of the Right Hand (*ashab al-yamin*) . . . Whoever attains this and behaves according to the Qur'anic Muhammadan *shari'a* command, he is the most perfect of creation.[13]

Other statements by Ibn Taymiyya show his attitude towards Sufism to be other than uncompromisingly negative. He says that the love for God which comes from faith necessitates a "faith-informed intuition" (*al-dhawq al-imani*) and a "religious ecstasy" (*al-wajd al-dini*).[14] The adjectives "faith-informed" and "religious" indicate the perspective from which Ibn Taymiyya will criticize Sufi statements and practices. His point will continually be that mystical experience is by its nature ambiguous, and the only way of discerning whether the experience is from God or a *shaytan* is to examine whether it is in accord with Qur'anic revelation and the sunna.

One cannot dismiss a religious practice merely because it was developed in recent times, he states, for some practices, like the retreat (*khalwa*), resemble actions performed and commanded by the prophet.[15] Extreme care is necessary, however, because of the ambivalent nature of any practice not explicitly commanded in the sunna; each practice must be individually examined by that sunna, and failure to do this has allowed demons to lead many well-intentioned believers astray.

It is significant that Ibn Taymiyya does not see his position as that of an outsider critically judging Sufi practice. He continually cites earlier Sufi writers as authorities confirming his statements. Thus, in defining the nature of true *wajd* which is in accord with the Qur'an and the sunna, he cites Al-Tustari's judgment: "Every ecstatic experience (*wajd*) to which the Book and the sunna do not bear witness is false."[16]

For Ibn Taymiyya, the correct distinction is between the true followers of the Sufi path, which is in accord with the sunna—whom he calls "Sufis who are people of knowledge" and the impostors of the Ibn 'Arabi tradition, whom he declares renegades from the true path. He thereby disqualifies those of the school of Ibn 'Arabi from any true claims to Sufism; rather, for Ibn Taymiyya, they are backsliders from the tradition and usurpers of the title.

> Ibn 'Arabi and those like him, although they claim that they are Sufis, are actually among "renegade philosopher Sufis," not the Sufis who are people of knowledge. Much less are they among the shaykhs who are the people of the Book and the sunna—like Fudayl b. 'Iyad,[17] Ibrahim b. Adham,[18] Abu Sulayman al-Darani,[19] Ma'ruf al-Karkhi,[20] Al-Junayd b. Muhammad, and Sahl ibn 'Abd Allah al-Tustari and those like them.[21]

He calls the true Sufis "the people of uprightness," and the feature which characterizes them most and distinguishes them from the "pseudo-Sufis" (*al-mutasawwifa*) is their insistence on the necessity for abiding by the divine "command and prohibition" (*al-amr wal-nahy*). So long as the legal aspect of Islamic life remains central to the mystical striver, the ethical challenge of the Book and the sunna is fulfilled.

> The upright (*al-mustaqimun*) among the followers of the path—like the majority of the early shaykhs (*shuyukh al-salaf*), such as Fudayl ibn 'Iyad, Ibrahim ibn Adham, Ma'ruf al-Karkhi, Al-Sari al-Saqati,[22] Al-Junayd ibn Muhammad and others of the early teachers, as well as Shaykh 'Abd al-Qadir, Shaykh Hammad,[23] Shaykh Abu al-Bayan,[24] and others of the later masters—do not permit the followers of the Path to depart from the divinely legislated command and prohibition, even were that person to have flown in the air or walked on water. He must do what is commanded and avoid what is forbidden until he dies. This is the Truth which the Book and the sunna have indicated.[25]

It is particularly Al-Junayd and 'Abd al-Qadir al-Jilani to whom Ibn Taymiyya refers as exponents of true Sufism. The renegades, he says, in the *wahdat al-wujud* tradition disdain the praiseworthy shaykhs like Al-Junayd, for whom *tawhid* meant "the differentiation between the eternal and the temporal, between the creator and the creature";[26] at the same time they extol the reprehensible masters like Al-Hallaj.

Ibn Taymiyya esteems 'Abd al-Qadir al-Jilani highly, and references to his person and to his teaching abound in Ibn Taymiyya's writing. He uses a pious story about 'Abd al-Qadir to elucidate the wariness proper to a believer in crediting a divine or a diabolical origin to a mystical experience; by the same story he illustrates that the true shaykh sees God's command and prohibition as an indispensable element of Islamic worship.[27] He upholds 'Abd al-Qadir and his teacher Hammad al-Dabbas as two masters who defended human responsibility for actions and a believer's obligation of obedience to God's religious will.[28] This is in contrast, he states, to some Sufis who did not hold for *al-amr wal-nahy*, and thus endangered the ethical bases of religious life. Moreover, the true shaykhs like 'Abd al-Qadir and Hammad al-Dabbas are to be praised in contrast to compulsorists of the *kalam* school like Al-Razi whose predestinarian position also led to the destruction of moral values.

Finally, it is the Sufis' emphasis on the love of God, and their voluntarist approach to religion rather than a rationalist emphasis on speculative knowledge of God and revelation that shows their greatest affinities with Ibn Taymiyya. Once again, the impression which Western scholarship has handed on about Ibn Taymiyya is misleading, for his writings on God's love for mankind and a believer's love for God are voluminous, and the concept of love is not something extraneous or peripheral to his appreciation of Islam. His criticism of the Ash'arite *kalam* school and the Mu'tazila is always that by allowing human reason to sit in judgment on what God has handed down, the dynamic religious call of the Qur'an has been allowed to dessicate into man-made negative systems. To this he contrasts the consistent Sufi priorities of love and will, which he sees to be in direct line with the religious perceptions of the *salaf*.

> The denial of the vision, love, and speech of God is also something well-known in the teaching of the Jahmites, the Mu'tazila, and those who agree with them. The Ash'arites and those who follow them agree with them on the denial of [God's] love,[29] but they are opposed to them in affirming the Vision [of God]. However, the vision which they affirm has no reality to it . . . As for the Sufis, they affirm the love [of God]—this is even more evident among them than all [other] issues. The basis of their Way (*tariqa*) is simply will and love. The affirmation of the love of God is well known in the speech of their early and their recent masters, just as it is affirmed in the Book and the sunna and in the agreement of the *salaf*.[30]

In short, there is too much in Ibn Taymiyya's own approach to religion which is similar to that of the Sufis for him to be considered an unmitigated enemy of the movement in Islam. However, he saw serious dangers to the purity of Islamic belief and practice in many of the popular manifestations of Sufism. He saw elements of superstition, evidence of ***shirk***, effects of innovation, and an easy starting point for moving, on the one hand, towards an identification of God and the believer, and on the other to a monist view of existence—an identification of God with His creation. At the same time, most Sufi practices, terminology, and teaching could be interpreted in a way consonant with the Qur'an and sunna and its understanding by the *salaf*. The problem, as Ibn Taymiyya saw it, was one of the ambiguous nature of Sufism, which could always bear a true meaning as well as one which was inimical to Islam.

> There are found in the teaching of some of them imprecise and ambiguous statements, just as the Christians have gone astray in a similar way in what they hold concerning Christ. They follow ambiguity (*al-mutashabih*) and reject the clear and precise (*al-muhkam*). Also, [one can find] statements of those whose minds are overwhelmed who speak in a state of spiritual drunkenness.[31]

The Qur'an and the sunna, the statements of the Companions and their followers, and the unanimous consensus of the early imams have all affirmed the dissimilarity of God to the universe, that nothing of the essence of God is found in His creatures, nor is anything created found in the essence of God.[32] This crucial distinction, however, is blurred and often denied by the statements of Sufi masters, particularly in their *shatahat*. The principal danger of Sufism lay in that its imprecision could lead believers by imperceptible degrees into a monist view of existence of the type taught by Ibn 'Arabi. This process in fact occurred in the lives of many Sufis.

Ibn Taymiyya acknowledges that mystical language is intrinsically ambiguous because it is describing an experience which by its nature is ineffable. It is an unanswerable question whether, when mystics speak of striving for union with the divine, or of passing away in the overwhelming presence of God, or when, in a state of mystical transport, they declare "There is no one in my clothes but God," they are claiming that a true union—an identity—with God is possible and sometimes achieved, or whether their words should be interpreted as necessarily inaccurate attempts to approximate a description of their experience.

Ibn Taymiyya's approach is to say that since this language is by its nature imprecise and general, any statement may bear a meaning either compatible with or contrary to the message of the Qur'an and the sunna. For this reason he treats the whole gamut of Sufi terminology and practice in an attempt to delineate the true Islamic meaning from false interpretations.

Some recently developed practices like retirement (*khalwa*) resemble those of the prophet, such as the times he retired to the cave at Hira' to pray.[33] It is therefore not novelty itself that makes a practice unlawful. However, many Sufis surround this practice with a number of details connected with prophetic inspiration (e.g., they may make their *khalwa* extend over a period of forty days in imitation of Moses on Sinai or Jesus in the desert on the assumption that at the end of their *khalwa* they will receive a revelation analogous to that of the prophets). This is an innovation and opposed to the teaching of the Qur'an and the sunna.

What happens is that they often do have extraordinary experiences of a mystical nature. They may see visions, hear voices, and learn things through immediate insight. If their practices have had any aspect of innovation connected with them, one can be certain that such experiences are of demonic origin. What is said about the *khalwa* applies as well to other mystical practices.

> Some of what they [the Sufi shaykhs] command in a *khalwa* by way of hunger, sleeplessness, and silence—is beyond the limits of the *shari'a*. Even the absolute sleeplessness, hunger, and silence in the *khalwa* was mentioned by Ibn 'Arabi and others. These things beget for them Satanic states.[34]

Even if their practices have been within the bounds of the *shari'a*, they cannot be certain that the extraordinary experiences they have in these states are from God (as the story about 'Abd al-Qadir al-Jilani's vision showed). The experience itself is always ambiguous; it is only by examining it against the certainty of the Qur'an and sunna that its validity can be learned.

The most common Sufi practice, *dhikr*, is of this nature. It can be either lawful or unlawful depending upon its agreement with the Qur'an and sunna. The best *dhikr*, he states, is the first *shahada* because there is no possibility of *shirk* in that.[35] As individuals begin to be included in the *dhikr*—even praying for the prophet—the practice becomes "farther from the sunna, entering more into innovation, and closer to the seduction of Satan."[36] Even the use of the pronomial name for God, so popular a form of *dhikr*, is dangerously close to *shirk*; the pronoun refers back to whatever is pictured in the heart, and the heart in turn is easily led astray and is thus untrustworthy.

In *dhikr*, as in all mystical practices, the believer cannot trust his sensibilities concerning what is proper or improper, for all such practices presuppose some loss of control of personal powers. While these practices can be beneficial to some, they are limited in their value, and certainly not to be compared with the value of the great obligations of Islam like *salah* and *zakah*. His criticism of the Sufis is that they tend to exaggerate these less valuable supererogatory practices like *dhikr* to the detriment of essential religious obligations.

> Being content with a simple lawful *dhikr* like saying "There is no God but God" may sometimes benefit a person, but this *dhikr* alone—without that which goes beyond it—is not the way to God. The best bodily act of worship is the *salah*, and then recitation [of the Qur'an], and then *dhikr*, and then private prayer (*al-du'a'*).[37]

Even more than their practices is the terminology of the Sufis ambivalent and imprecise. There is usually a sense in which their terms can be in agreement with the Qur'an and the sunna, and Ibn Taymiyya wrote at length to distinguish between the lawful and the unlawful meanings in religious concepts such as *zuhd* (asceticism), *sabr* (patience), *wara'* (piety), *taqwa* (reverential fear),[38] *hulul* (divine indwelling),[39] *mahabba* (love),[40] *faqr* (poverty),[41] and particularly *fana'* (passing away, extinction).

In all of Sufi teaching there is no concept more problematic than that of *fana'* (annihilation). This notion, which implies a passage out of the usual state of awareness and consciousness into some type of union with God, has carried different connotations in the individual teachings and experiences of Sufi masters.

Ibn Taymiyya points out several dangers connected with striving for the state of *fana'*. It can become the ultimate religious goal, with the resultant limitation of a person's response to the Qur'anic call in its fullness. Secondly, in that state an individual is particularly susceptible to delusions of demonic or psychological origin and can easily become convinced of something contrary to the prophetic message. Finally, in this kind of state the separateness and dissimilarity of the believer and God seems to the mystic to have disappeared. This prepares him for deluded convictions of his oneness with God and the unity of all creation.

On the other hand, there is a sense in which the state of *fana'* is a true and even ultimate goal of a believer's path towards God. For this reason Ibn Taymiyya carefully distinguishes between three types of *fana'*.[42] The first is that of the proponents of *wahdat al-wujud*; for them *fana'* is the annihilation of the experience of multiplicity "whereby it is seen that the existence of the creature is the very existence of the creator, and that existence is one."[43] For them the goal of religious striving is the intuitive realization of the unity of all that is, and the false sense perception of the multiplicity of existence is extinguished. Ibn Taymiyya declares the absolute existence which remains and is worshiped to be merely a mental concept which does not exist in external reality. According to him, this type of *fana'* is an exercise not only in unbelief but in futility.

The second type of *fana'* is *fana' al-rububiyya*. It occurs at the level of religious experience and happens to a believer who greatly desires that there be nothing separating him from the God he loves. Its causes are natural and psychological, affirms Ibn Taymiyya, and the experience is certainly not the goal of religious striving—not even a necessary station on the Way—and instead usually proves to be an actual obstacle on the believer's path to God.

> This [state] very often presents itself to someone to whom some matter has suddenly occurred—e.g., love, fear, or hope. The person's heart becomes separated from everything else except that which he loved, feared, or sought, so that in his total absorption with that, he does not have feeling for anything else.[44]

In this state, says Ibn Taymiyya, the believer thinks that a type of union with God has been attained and that no difference in existence remains between the lover and the Beloved.

> This is an error, for the creator does not unite with a thing at all. Moreover, one thing does not unite with another unless the two undergo change or corruption or unless there result from the union a third thing which is neither the one nor the other.[45]

Ibn Taymiyya's objection to this type of *fana'* is parallel to his criticism of the divine union with individuals held by Sunni and Shi'i *ghulat* and is similar to his refutation of Christian explanations of the incarnation of the divine Word in Christ. All of these beliefs, he states, demand change, corruption, and temporality in God, as well as a sense in which God goes out of existence in the formation of a new thing.

According to Ibn Taymiyya, the moderates among the Sufis have always realized and taught that this union through *fana'* never occurs in external reality, but only appears so to the mystic while he is experiencing that state. Upon "returning" from the intoxicated mystical state (*sukr*) he realizes that what he has experienced was a transient illusion which did not affect the essential dissimilarity and transcendent nature of God.

It is in this sense that the ecstatic utterances (*shatahat*) of mystics like Abu Yazid al-Bistami are to be understood. Their desire for intimacy with God is so great that it overcomes their mind, and they become like those who are drunk, dreaming, swooning, or insane—that is, people who are not in control of their senses.[46]

Rather than seeing this as an elevated mystical state, Ibn Taymiyya views it as a phenomenon which occurs due to the weak-mindedness of some mystics. Their stronger counterparts,[47] he asserts, never lose consciousness, self-control, knowledge, or the ability to differentiate in their mystical states, and it is these individuals who are in the tradition of the *salaf.*

Finally, there is a sense of *fana'* which is commanded by God and brought by the prophets.

> It is that one passes away in worship of God from the worship of all else other than Him. He passes away in obedience to Him from obedience to whatever is other than Him, in trust from trusting in anything other than Him, in hope in Him and fear of God, from hoping and fearing whatever is not Him. Thus he is with the Truth rather than with creation. It is as Shaykh 'Abd al-Qadir said: "Be with the Truth without creation, and with creation without the self."[48]

True *fana'* consists in the believer's stripping himself of desire to do other than what God commands and in directing the whole complex of religious drives—hope, fear, trust, love, obedience—only to God.[49] This includes the state where the believer takes his guidance only from God in what He has clearly revealed in the Book and the sunna.

It is in this sense that Ibn Taymiyya can be called a "neo-Sufi." In taking not merely Sufi terminology but also the concepts of mystical consciousness, by interpreting them in a manner consistent with the Book and the sunna, and by tracing the origins of these concepts to the early shaykhs and the *salaf,* he shows that the striving for God, the need to go beyond the minimum worship of God which is strictly prescribed, and the desire of the believer for a close individual relationship to God in love is all not a novel or peripheral activity in Islam, but finds its roots in the prophetic message itself and the consistent tradition of the community. However, he stresses that this Path to God is not an unregulated spiritual domain where each teacher and student is free to search out individual methods and beliefs, but they must constantly refer everything back to the Book and the sunna; any departure from that is a deviation into error.

To see the mystics' search for God as the single or ultimate goal of Islam, as some Sufis do, is to distort the message of the prophets and to constrict the fullness of the Qur'anic call. This conviction leads Ibn Taymiyya to another, still more serious criticism of Sufism.

He holds that by accepting non-*shari'a* religious practices in addition to those prescribed in Islam, and by making these supererogatory and sometimes innovative practices of prior importance to imposed obligations, the Sufis are in effect revising the goal of religious life. The goal is no longer obedience and gratefulness to the Creator and Commander of people's lives, but rather a union of love with the divine Lover. If this union were attainable and sometimes actually achieved, then the importance of religious and ethical obligations would be lessened and could even be discarded. In this way the antinomian tendencies attributed to popular Sufi preachers are in direct parallel to the theoretical antinominanism of *wahdat al-wujud* philosophers like Al-Tilimsani; both arise from a blurred distinction between God and the universe and effect a collapse of values in religious practice and ethical behavior.

Ibn Taymiyya criticizes many Sufis for not responding fully to the implications of God's message about Himself in the Qur'an. He holds that God has revealed Himself as the creator, and man's response is one of gratefulness, worship, and love. The Sufis, he claims, are intent on fulfilling this religious duty to the detriment of all else. God has also revealed Himself as the Commander, Omnipotent (*al-qadir*). Man's response to this is obedience, fulfilling the cultic and moral applications of the law. To be content with worship and love of God as the final goal of religious life, without realizing that that implies the building of life on earth in accord with God's will, is to achieve the *tawhid* of pagans, not Islamic *tawhid*. His criticism, then, is that to follow the path to annihilation (*fana'*) in union with God, and to make this the ultimate goal of *tawhid*, is a goal that is incomplete and inconsistent with an appreciation of Islam as authoritatively interpreted by the *salaf*.

> For certain groups of Sufis, and those who adhere to gnosis, union with Truth (*tahqiq*) and *tawhid*, their goal in *tawhid* is the experiencing of this *tawhid*. They experience that God is lord over everything, the governor and creator of all . . . By this one enters into *fana'* of union with the deity, whereby he who was not passes away and He who has never ceased to be remains. Among them this is the goal beyond which there is no other. It is obvious that this is an affirmation of the *tawhid* held by idolaters, and a person does not become a Muslim simply by this *tawhid*. Much less does he become a friend of God, or one of the masters of His friends.[50]

Ibn Taymiyya's opposition to many Sufi practices and teachings had a less theoretical side to it. He was appalled at the non-*shari'a* practices he saw which had come to be accepted as part of Islamic life. Many of these practices he considered pure innovations opposed to the spirit of the *salaf*, and he felt that in many cases they were actually expressions of *shirk*. Moreover, it was more often than not Sufi teachers who were the propagators of these inventions. To fight this danger to Islam from within its midst, Ibn Taymiyya wrote many treatises; as the details of his life show, he did not limit his criticism of these practices to writing, and it is certain that much of the suffering and imprisonment he endured was the direct result of his campaign against popular mystical practices.[51]

The great failing of Sufism, he claimed, was that because so much of its terminology and so many of its practices were general and imprecise, the Sufis tended not to distinguish between what God commanded as obligatory and unchangeable and what they personally desired and seemed good to them. He says, "They did not distinguish between a religious desire in accord with the command of God and His prophet and an innovated desire."[52] This, he holds, is merely playing into the wiles of the demons, whose purpose it is to turn men away from the practices which come from God and lead back to God. These practices are made to seem distasteful and onerous by the demons, who at the same time picture innovated practices as attractive and beneficial.

> Satan beautifies those religious practices for the people of innovated worship and he makes the lawful path seem hateful to them, so that he makes them dislike learning, the Qur'an, and the hadith. Thus they do not love to hear the Qur'an and hadith nor to make remembrance (*dhikr*) of it. Books in general may be hateful to them, so that they do not love any book or have any book with them, even a copy of the Qur'an or the hadith.[53]

The anti-intellectual tendency among Sufis Ibn Taymiyya sees as being directly inspired by the demons who want to foster ignorance among well-intentioned believers. He declares that this distrust of learning was opposed by the great Sufi masters and quotes from statements by Al-Sari al-Saqati, Al-Tustari, and Al-Junayd to the effect that study of the Qur'an and the traditions is essential for each Muslim.[54] Finally, he declares that it is this ignorance that has led to the sectarianism of Sufi groups, each of which has a small corner of the truth and is embattled against all other groups.

There is much *shirk*, he states, in these innovated practices. Pilgrimages to tombs of holy men and even prophets detract from the uniqueness of the Hajj and associate those dead persons whose tombs are visited in the worship due God alone.[55] Practices which occur in the context of the visits are often dangerous to the purity of religion. For example, people often make circumambulation of a tomb in imitation of the great circumambulation of the Ka'ba. They seek intercession from the dead person, although the Qur'an declares that there is no intercessor between God and the believer except Muhammad, whose exercise of that function will be restricted to Judgment Day.[56] They make vows to others than God, which Ibn Taymiyya sees as a clear form of *shirk*.[57] They engage in practices which have no relationship to Islam either in origin or in belief and which in reality are expressions of pure superstition[58] or actual service of the demons.[59] They employ techniques like *sama'* (*dhikr* accompanied by musical instruments)[60] and dancing at the shrines and tombs to induce states in which the participant loses control of his mind and becomes susceptible to Satanic deceptions.

They disseminate stories of fabulous miracles which occur at these unlawful places of pilgrimage. Sometimes the dead man is seen or heard by the visitors, and sometimes healings, favors, and secret messages are granted to those seeking them.[61] Most often these accounts are fraudulent, states Ibn Taymiyya, and when they are not, one can be sure that they are feats of the demons. A true miracle, he asserts, is wrought only by God at the hands of the prophets and those who scrupulously follow them and will never be performed by God in circumstances of innovation and *shirk*.

It is some of the most popular shrines in Islam which are the sites for some of the most extravagant excesses. Particularly, the shrine of Al-Husayn in Cairo and the Shi'i shrines of the Imams are the occasions for diabolical perversions of Islam. The shrine of Al-Husayn, he asserts, is a fraud and does not contain Al-Husayn's head at all. "It is probably the head of some Christian monk," he concludes with a touch of irony.[62] The Shi'i institutionalization of pilgrimages to the tombs of the Imams is one of the most reprehensible aspects of Shi'ism.

Ibn Taymiyya is not unaware of the natural desires of the family and friends of deceased persons to pay visits to their loved ones' graves. This visitation in itself is not opposed to the *shari'a*, but the majority of traditional practices associated with the custom are merely forms of *shirk*.[63]

> The visit of the followers of *tawhid* to the graves of Muslims includes the *"salam"* upon them and private prayer for them. But the visit of the people of *shirk* includes their making a creature resemble the creator. They make vows to him, they prostrate themselves before him, they pray to him, and they love him like they love the creator. Thus they will have made him a rival to God and will have made him equal to the lord of the universe.[64]

The danger of *shirk* is not so serious a possibility for members of family and friends, but its likelihood is greater on the occasion of the deaths of holy persons and Sufi masters. It is here that abuses and innovations—such as *mawlids*, the building of mosques on their tombs, and entreating these "friends of God" as intercessors—creep in.

In fact, Ibn Taymiyya sees in the exaggerated respect which many Sufis have for their masters, living and dead, a danger to the institution of prophecy and thus to the religion of the prophets. They treat their masters as though they were both impeccable and infallible, although the clear teaching of Islam has been that only the prophets have infallibility (and even the prophets are not entirely preserved from sin).[65] Sufi masters, delighted with the adulation of their disciples, often give teaching and example which is opposed to the *shari'a* and neglect to inform their disciples of the difference between their teaching and that of the prophets.

> Many people err in this matter, for they think that a certain person is a friend of God and suppose that a friend of God receives from Him everything which he says. So they accept all that he says and all that he does, even if that person opposes the Book and the sunna. They agree with him and oppose that with which God has sent His messenger, and they oppose the information and the command which God has made obligatory for all mankind to believe and obey.[66]

Some of the Sufi teachers, like Al-Hallaj, actually believe that they are superior to the prophets and thus become renegades from Islam and are deserving of death. For Ibn Taymiyya, Al-Hallaj represented the worst aspects of a Sufi who because of his mystical experiences rejected both the beliefs and the commands of the prophets.[67]

From Ibn Taymiyya's point of view, it was proper and necessary for the *'ulama'* to demand his death.

> He [Al-Hallaj] displayed various kinds of *kufr*, several of which necessitated his being killed. He was not a God-fearing friend to God, but his religious practices, exercises, and efforts were sometimes demonic, sometimes of his own invention, and sometimes in agreement with the *shari'a*. Thus he overlaid truth with falsehood.[68]

It is an essential point with Ibn Taymiyya that only the prophets be recognized as infallible. This is one of the distinguishing characteristics of prophecy and one integral to its nature. What distinguishes a prophet from every holy person—no matter what that person's credentials in terms of mystical experiences or good deeds—from every religious thinker and leader, from every member of the family of the prophet, is that one can place absolute and certain confidence in the truth of what the prophet has brought from God.[69] The statements, teachings, and views of all other people may be either correct or in error, and it is only by measuring what they say with what is known to be true from the prophets that the reliability of their teaching can be ascertained.

Ibn Taymiyya sees the lack of appreciation of this unique characteristic of prophecy as the basis for a common error of Christians, Shi'a, and Sufis. They exaggerate in the natural respect people have for those who have "come close to God" and consider these people infallible. Thus the Christians make their church leaders superior to the prophets by following their teachings rather than those revealed in the Books. The Shi'a declare the Twelve Imams to be both impeccable and infallible and make this one of the bases of their religion. Many Sufis believe that their shaykhs have had experiences which equal or transcend those of the prophet and that their teachings are based on a quasi-prophetic experience which they in turn can teach to others.[70] Ibn Taymiyya accuses Al-Ghazali as being among those who advocate the attainment of "revelations."

> Abu Hamid [al-Ghazali] and those like him who command this Way do not think that it leads to unbelief, but it should be known that innovations are the messenger (*barid*) of unbelief. Nevertheless they command the disciple (*murid*) to empty his heart of everything. They may even command him to sit in a dark place, to cover his head, and say "Allah, Allah." They believe that if his heart becomes empty, he is then ready and the sought-for knowledge descends upon his heart. They might even say that there happens to him something of the same type as that which occurred to the prophets. Some of them claim that there occurs to him something greater than what happened to the prophets. Abu Hamid constantly praises this Way in the *Ihya'*[71] and elsewhere. This is one of the remnants of philosophy in his thought. The would-be philosophers like Ibn Sina and those like him claim that all the knowledge which occurs in the prophets and others is only the Active Intellect. Therefore they say that prophecy is acquired when, according to them, one's heart becomes serenely undisturbed, and something like what flowed upon the prophets flows over upon one. According to them Moses ibn 'Imran was addressed from the heaven of his own mind and did not hear a voice from outside him. Therefore they say that there occurs for them what occurred for Moses and greater than what occurred to Moses . . . All this serves to diminish their faith in the messengers. Thus they have disbelieved in some of what the messengers brought and have believed in some.[72]

The danger of the Sufis' exalting the mystical experience of the shaykhs to the level of prophecy or beyond it is that this results in their advocating a way to God other than what the prophets have handed on.[73] He notes tendencies among many of the Sufi masters to make claims of by-passing the teaching of the prophets by what they have learned through intuitive, immediate knowledge. If knowledge of divine realities is sought and if certitude were able to be achieved through such techniques, then the nature of the Qur'an as *furqan* would be effectively denied and all religious teaching and experience would become relative. God's nature as Creator could not be affirmed with certainty, nor His role as commander of human destiny sustained, and in the human path to God there would be only the juxtaposition of divergent religious experiences. This is the antithesis of the one Straight Path, the path of the *shari'a* known with certainty to be from God through the mediation of His messengers.

It is the implications of the Sufi Way upon prophecy which Ibn Taymiyya sees as most seriously challenging Islam. So long as the goals, methods, and techniques of Sufism are constantly judged and measured by the certain knowledge obtained through prophetic revelation, they can be beneficial in assisting believers to "approach most closely" to God. When, on the other hand, the knowledge and experience of the divine obtained through Sufism is what judges the validity of the prophetic message, then its claimants have rejected Islam for unbelief.

# CHAPTER 4

## THE POLEMIC AGAINST THE SPECULATIVE THEOLOGIANS

Ibn Taymiyya inherited a long-standing Hanbali mistrust of speculative theology, particularly in its Ash'arite and Mu'tazili manifestations. This mistrust was in the early centuries directed by Hanbalis towards both the method and the conclusions of ***kalam***. The commonly accepted position seems to have been that expressed by Al-Barbahari (d. 329/941) that ***kalam*** was a forbidden innovation.

> Be aware that doing ***kalam*** about the Lord is innovation and damnation. One cannot speak about the Lord except by using the description which He gives Himself in the Qur'an and the explanations of that presented by the prophet to his companions.[1]

Al-Ash'ari attempted unsuccessfully to convince the Hanbalis of the legitimacy of speculative theology, and it was for this reason that he wrote two major treatises.[2] He rejected strongly the Hanbali position that the method of rationalist theology was itself ***bid'a*** and argued convincingly that they themselves, as well as Ibn Hanbal and his predecessors before them, were engaging in ***kalam***.

> There is no sound tradition from the Prophet to the effect that the Qur'an is uncreated or created. Why, then, do you hold that it is uncreated? They may say: Some of the companions and the Followers held that. One should say to them: The Companion, or the Follower, is subject to the same constraint as you are, namely, that he is a deviating innovator for saying what the Apostle did not say. And another may say: I suspend my judgment on that, and I do not say created, nor do I say uncreated. To him one should say: Then you, in suspending your judgment on that, are a deviating innovator. For the prophet did not say: "If this question should arise after my death, suspend my judgment on it, and say nothing." Nor did he say: "Regard as deviating and unbelieving him who affirms that it is created, or him who denies that it is created."[3]

Although the methods as well as much of the terminology of speculative theology subsequently came to be part of the Hanbali tradition, its principal conclusions were not accepted by the generality of Hanbali thinkers. There were exceptions—Hanbali scholars who adopted Ash'arite or more rarely Mu'tazili, conclusions—and Ibn Taymiyya frequently includes Hanbali predecessors like Abu Ya'la and Ibn 'Aqil among those holding Ash'arite or Mu'tazili positions.[4]

Even some later Hanbalis, such as Muwaffaq al-Din ibn Qudama (d. 620/1223) reaffirmed the early opposition to the science of *kalam* as a whole. Ibn Qudama's basic position was that the *kalam* theologians rejected the certainty of the divine sources of knowledge—the Qur'anic revelation and the prophetic sunna as known through hadith reports—in exchange for the necessarily relative judgments of reason.

> It is strange that these speculative theologians—may God blind their faculties of understanding even more than He has already done!—claim that they are not satisfied except by decisive proofs and convincing arguments, and judge that the traditions—which they assert to be traditions transmitted by a single traditionist—do not convey certain knowledge;[5] then they adduce arguments such as this, which does not prove anything at all, neither manifestly nor by way of certainty.[6]

On justifying speculations as being in accord with the methodology and terminology of the *kalam* theologians, Ibn Qudama states:

> This is very far from what is right and much closer to what is wrong. For you people have cast away the Book and the sunna, and have become aloof from God and His apostle; you are in nowise assisted by God towards the right, nor directed towards the truth; what you say is not accepted, nor is your terminology heeded.[7]

Ibn Taymiyya, however, accepted the basic position of Al-Ash'ari on the legitimacy of *kalam* as a divine science. He states that its original intent was both valid and praiseworthy. Speculative theology developed as an apologetic science whose purpose was to argue the case for Islam convincingly in the terminology and conceptions of its opponents. As such, it was analogous to translating the Qur'an so that it be understood by non-Arab speakers, which practice Ibn Taymiyya also strongly approves. However, this dialectical argumentation (whose presence in the Qur'an he confirms)[8] as practiced by the *salaf* was strictly governed by the Qur'an and sunna. The error of the later speculative theologians, as represented both by the Mu'tazili and Ash'arite traditions, was to reverse the process by allowing the judgments of reason to determine the content and the message of the Book and the Wisdom.[9]

> Whoever speaks the truth which God permitted as a judgment (*hukm*) and an argument (*dalil*) is among the people of knowledge and faith, for God speaks the truth and it is He who guides along the path. As for preaching to the people who follow a certain terminology in their own terms and language, there is nothing reprehensible in that when that is required and when one's meanings are correct. It is like preaching to non-Arabic-speaking Byzantines, Persians, and Turks in their own language and custom. This is permissible when the need for it is great; the imams were only adverse to it when there was no need for it.[10]

Ibn Taymiyya distinguishes between the innovation of opinions and acts (*bad' al-aqwal wal-af'al*) which do not render someone an unbeliever and the innovation of beliefs (*bad' al-'aqa'id*) for which *takfir* is pronounced.[11] A new formulation of the content of the prophetic message is permissible if it corresponds exactly to what is meant in the Qur'an and the sunna.

Certain terms like *jawhar* (substance), *jism* (body), and *hayyiz* (place) imply categories which are incompatible with the teaching of the Qur'an and sunna. Both the affirmation and negation of such terms leads to error, and the correct course, which was followed by the *salaf* and the great imams like Ibn Hanbal, was to suspend judgment on such terms, refusing either to confirm or reject them.[12] It was here that the speculative theologians strayed into error. Confident that a valid judgment of reason could be made on any given question relating to God and the universe, a school of thought would affirm a philosophical question— e.g., "Is God a substance?" "Is God a body? (If not, how does He see, speak, etc.)." Others, seeing the errors into which the first school had fallen, would deny the statements which the other had made and thus develop new errors.

Ibn Taymiyya points to the case of Al-Ash'ari, who, when he rejected Mu'tazili theses, was driven by his need to affirm the opposite of what they held to adopt positions which were farther from and more destructive to the teaching of the Qur'an and the prophetic sunna than those espoused by the Mu'tazila:

> Al-Ash'ari had been one of the Mu'tazila and continued for forty years to follow their *madhhab*, which he learned from Abu 'Ali al-Jubba'i. When he departed from their *madhhab*, he became an expert in their principles—in refuting them and in showing their contradictions. That which he retained from the sunna was not any of the specific characteristics of the Mu'tazila but was rather a type of predetermination (*qadar*) shared with the Jahmites. Al-Ash'ari did not support the characteristic teachings of the Mu'tazila in anything; on the contrary he contradicted them in all their principles and inclined on matters of justice, the names, and the judgments of God to the *madhhab* of Jahm and many of the

groups like him such as the Najjariyya—the followers of Husayn al-Najjar,[13]—and the Dirariyya—the followers of Dirar ibn 'Amr.[14] Thus they opposed the Mu'tazila on predetermination, the names and judgments of God, and deliverance from the divine threat.[15]

In short, although Ibn Taymiyya accepts *kalam* as a discipline not only permissible but even beneficial to Islam, he remains highly critical of the conclusions of the theologians, both Ash'arite and Mu'tazili.[16] He criticizes both groups for following their rational methodology to conclusions which contradict the teaching of the Qur'an and the sunna.

The basic error of both Ash'arites and Mu'tazila is that of negative formulation (*salb*), although the two opposing parties apply this to different subjects. When the Ash'arites deny human causality, or indeed all causal agency but the divine, Ibn Taymiyya attempts to introduce a modification of the Mu'tazili position in which he affirms the reality of human agency. On the other hand, he rejects the Mu'tazili denial of the hypostatization of the divine names and the omnipotence of God.

Ibn Taymiyya sees in both Ash'arite and Mu'tazili theologies a common error leading to a common danger to Islam. Their error is in allowing human reason to be judge of what is contained in revelation.[17] They work from the premise that what is revealed in the books must be in agreement with reason, and so for them it is no longer revelation, but rather reason, which is the ultimate criterion of truth.

The danger which this produces is a limited form of *ta'til*, whereby the concrete reality of God is diminished and made inoperative in human life. This occurs with a "compulsorist" Ash'arite view of predestination, where if all actions are performed by God, and He wills and therefore loves both good and evil, then the commands of the *shari'a* become irrelevant. Similarly, if one follows the Mu'tazilis in refusing to speak of the knowledge of God, the love of God, the power of God, and the like, then the divine reality recedes from human life.

It is significant that Ibn Taymiyya regularly uses a common pejorative term for these two groups, who considered one another to be mutually contradictory. He deems both "Jahmites," a term which carries for him the basic meaning of *mu'attila*—those who exaggerate the transcendence of God to the point where His relationship with mankind as Creator and Commander becomes irrelevant. The application of the term "Jahmite" to Ash'arites is somewhat surprising inasmuch as its more common significance in Islamic religious history indicates views more commonly associated with the Mu'tazila.[18] Earlier Hanbalis considered the Mu'tazila to be committing *ta'til* by denying anthropomorphic expressions in the Qur'an and hadith and by denying God's causal agency over human acts; they termed the offenders "Jahmites." Ibn Taymiyya, whose attitude towards *qadar* was a break with earlier Hanbali statements, considered Jahm to have represented an extreme form of determinism and held that the Ash'arites were the closest group to Jahm by their denial of human causal agency. Thus, he extended the term to them.

Because Jahm ibn Safwan, the 2nd/8th century eponym of this sect, left no writings, nor any recognizable group of disciples who identified themselves as Jahmites, it is impossible to know the original tenets of Jahm and his followers. What is noteworthy is that at a later date (after the 3rd/9th century) the term "Jahmite" referred, especially in the Hanbali tradition, to a number of clearly enunciated heretical theses.[19] Ibn Taymiyya's use of the term is, while always pejorative, ambiguous, and except for the basic meaning of proponents of "negativizing extreme transcendentalism," the term always raises the question of what group is intended.

> Jahmiyya sometimes is applied with a general meaning, and by it is intended the general denial of [divine] attributes. Sometimes it is applied with a specific meaning and by it is intended the followers of Jahm ibn Safwan in his opinions; the most important of these are the denial of attributes, a compulsorist view [on *qadar*], and a view holding the extinction of the Garden and the Fire.[20]

Ibn Taymiyya extends the meaning of the term customary in earlier Hanbali tradition to include all views of divine will and human freedom where man is no longer the performer of his own actions and God's will is absolute and arbitrary. Within this complex of views which exalt the divine Actor at the expense of human ownership of action lie Al-Ash'ari and the important school of *kalam* which followed him.

> The later Ash'arites are frequently mentioned by Ibn Taymiyya in connection with teaching ascribed to the Jahmites. Admittedly it appears that Ibn Taymiyya's *bête-noire*, the equation "love equals will," was held in common by the true Jahmites, thorough-going predestinarians; by the Mu'tazilites, free-willers; and probably by the original Qadarites as well. But it is clear that the doctrine reached Ibn Taymiyya primarily through Ash'arite channels and with Ash'arite corollaries.[21]

Ibn Taymiyya's writing covers the gamut of questions and concerns treated by the *kalam* theologians. His works treat not only of the celebrated question of predetermination and free will but also the nature of the essential attributes and names of God, those of his active attributes, particularly willing, knowing, loving, and speaking. He writes of the uncreatedness of the Qur'an and yet denies its eternity. He treats epistemological questions and balances the relative status of revelation, reason, and intuition as modes of knowledge. He treats of the nature of revelation and faith, the role of the califate and the imamate, and eschatology. Because of the extent and the depth of these writings he could be called the greatest Hanbali *kalam* theologian.

Volumes could be written concerning Ibn Taymiyya's refutations of specific points of *kalam* theology, and a study needs to be made in which Ibn Taymiyya's own responses to the issues of speculative theology are systematized and elucidated. The purpose of this chapter is much more limited; it is intended to treat only the salient issues on which Ibn Taymiyya's criticism of Ash'arite and Mu'tazili theology rests. These issues are the problems of *qadar* (predetermination and free will, or the relative influence of divine and human causality on human actions) and *al-sifat* (the hypostatization of the names of God, i.e., His attributes). From Ibn Taymiyya's perspective, it is their positions on these questions which have led the theologians of both schools out of the bounds of orthodoxy (the Straight Path), and while never becoming unbelievers, they have paved the way for those who—like Ibn 'Arabi and his followers—would apostatize from *tawhid* itself.

Ibn Taymiyya claims his position on *qadar* to be a restatement of the consensus of the *salaf* which they formulated from teachings in the Qur'an and the traditions.

> God is the creator, the Lord, and the possessor (*al-malik*) of each thing. Whatever He wills occurs, and what He does not will does not occur. He is Powerful (*al-qadir*)[22] over each thing. It is He who created man anxious, fretful when evil befalls him and grudging when good befalls him.[23] But man is truly an agent, and has will and power.[24]

If one's principal reference in argumentation is reason, the apparent contradiction in this formulation encourages further delving into the question. It is here that both Ash'arites and Mu'tazila have erred. The Ash'arites have attempted to establish God's unique and sovereign role in creation and have concluded by making His religious role as the Commander of the *shari'a* irrelevant. The error of the Mu'tazila was the opposite; concerned with the affirmation of the necessity for a free response in obedience and love to the divine command at the religious and ethical level, they compromised the universality of His creatorhood.

Of these two positions, that of the Mu'tazila is closer to the truth and that of the Ash'arites more destructive of religious practice. The Mu'tazila not only affirm the importance of the *shari'a* by declaring a person's responsibility for his acts, but they hold for the purposiveness of God's works as being directed by His providential wisdom (*hikma*). By positing a real distinction between the intrinsic evil of others, they affirm that God's will is not arbitrary and reassert true ethical bases for religion.

Ibn Taymiyya's criticism of Ash'arite theology is that in their attempt to establish the universality and supremacy of God's will they devised an ethical *tawhid*[25] whereby God becomes the only true actor in the universe. The effect of this view is that the divine will is identified with divine love, and this will becomes absolute and arbitrary. Good and evil are what God has willed to be so, not because of any quality inherent in the acts.[26] The ethical bases are thus cut from religion. Furthermore, if true human causality were denied, then the universe, instead of being a creation ordered in wisdom towards the good out of love of its Commander, would become the predetermined activity of a single divine will.[27]

On two levels the Ash'arite position on *qadar* prepares the way for *wahdat al-wujud*. If all things are performed by the divine Will uninformed by His wisdom, then the distinction between inherently good and bad acts is destroyed[28] and the way is paved for the antinomianism—at an intellectual level—of *ittihadi* writers like Al-Tilimsani,[29] and at a popular level of the wandering Sufi *qalandars* and *malamis*.

> For if on the doctrinal level it is primarily against the Ash'arite equation of God's love with his creative will that the Hanbalite doctor directs his rebuttals, it was still essentially in the in the antinomian mystics, the *malamis* and the Qalandaris, that he was able to observe the practical consequences of this Ash'arite teaching.[30]

At the ontological level the distinction between God and the universe is endangered. While not accepting a Mu'tazili position that man is an independent creator of his acts, Ibn Taymiyya sees that by eliminating all causality and authorship of action from creatures, the resultant atomism leads directly to the universe being considered as a constantly reenacted manifestation of the divine will—in the terminology of *wahdat al-wujud*—a *tajallin* or a *tanazzul*.

> Ibn Taymiyya reinstates into Muslim theology the doctrine of the purposiveness of the Divine behavior, a doctrine so strenuously denied by Ash'arism, Maturidism, and Zahirism as compromising the omnipotence of God's will and His dissimilarity to His creation.[31]

Ibn Taymiyya sees the affinities between the Ash'arite position on *qadar* and *wahdat al-wujud* monism as follows: in both, action is one, and the Actor is one.[32] The apparent diversity and multiplicity of actors in the universe is deceptive and in reality only manifests the single activity of the divine Will. The individual believer can neither do nor change anything in life, and the highest wisdom is for him to come to this knowledge. The *wahdat al-wujud* philosophers take the final step into unbelief which the Ash'arites refused to take; if all is one and multiplicity merely a deception, then all activity, which demands differentiation between a cause and that which is acted upon, is denied.

> They say that God does not give anyone anything. He does not make someone prosperous or bring him happiness or trouble. Rather, His existence flows over upon essences. Thus you praise only yourself; you rebuke only yourself. They say that this is the secret of *qadar*, and that God only knows things in respect to His vision of them while they subsist in non-being outside His holy Mind. They say that God is not able to change even one of the atoms in the universe.[33]

Their position on *qadar* led the Ash'arites, states Ibn Taymiyya, to a position on matters of worship and morality analogous to that of the pagan idolaters who opposed Muhammad. They opposed his preaching with the statement, "Had God willed [otherwise] we would not have ascribed partners [to Him], nor would have our fathers, nor had we been forbidden anything" (Qur'an, 6:149). They were claiming that they could not be held responsible for their *shirk* and unbelief, for if all power were truly with God who truly hated their unbelief, He would not have permitted it. Ibn Taymiyya held that the Ash'arites, by placing all causal agency in God, and by identifying the divine love with the divine will, must hold that whatever occurs is willed and hence loved by God. How is this compatible, asks Ibn Taymiyya, with Qur'anic teaching that God commands some actions and forbids others, loves some and hates others, rewards some and punishes others?[34] If a person were not responsible for his disobedience nor praiseworthy and beloved by God for his obedience to God's command, then what is the basis on which God could reward and prefer some individuals to others?

If Ash'arites hold a position similar in many respects to that of the pagans of the Jahiliyya, the Mu'tazila, on the other hand, are the Magians among Muslims. By affirming that there is in creation something which was not the creation of God (i.e., human acts) they are positing a second agency distinct from God and in effect they propose a dualism.

These people[35] agree with the idolaters in some part of their view, but not in all of it, just as the Qadarites in the community (*umma*)—who are the Magians of the community—agree with the pure Magians in some of their view but not in all of it. This is inevitable, for the prophet called them to the worship of God alone, permitting no one to share in the worship due Him, to the love of God alone in exclusion to anything other than Him, and that God and His prophet be more beloved to a person than anything other than them. Love follows upon reality, so that if what is loved is not in itself deserving that it be loved, then His command to love him[36] is not possible, much less that He be more loving to us than all others.[37]

Ibn Taymiyya admits that the Mu'tazili denial of the universality of divine agency is based on positive goals—the affirmation of God's transcendence by declaring him beyond willing unbelief or reprehensible actions, the definition of true human responsibility for obedience or disobedience to the *shari'a*, and a confirmation of a wise purposefulness in all the acts that God performs. Thus they deny divine omnipotence by declaring that God only wills what is best for mankind, and therefore some things occur contrary to his will (e.g., unbelief and criminal actions). Rather than merely affirming what is stated in the Qur'an and the sunna on the matter of the purposiveness of the divine plan—that is, that God *does* act according to a wise purpose rather than arbitrarily—the Mu'tazila elaborate this to say that God by His nature *must* act according to this divine wisdom. In this they place a limit on his sovereign freedom by placing him under the law of purposeful action. Their error on this matter arises from their making an argument from human activity and nature and applying it to God. Human love demands that the lover will the good for the beloved insofar as that good is known and the lover is capable of effecting it.

Ibn Taymiyya claims that the Mu'tazila argue that since God loves perfectly and knows the good absolutely, were His power over human action absolute and unlimited, he would have to will what is good for man in a way that man must perform it. But since man does disbelieve and act wrongly, God's absolute power or will must be limited by human freedom. This predication of the necessary consequences of the divine nature by argument from analogy with human nature is, according to Ibn Taymiyya, illogical and invalid, and will inevitably lead to erroneous conclusions.

The free-will party of the Mu'tazila and others intend to extol the Lord and to declare him beyond those actions which they think repugnant and wrong. Thus they deny the universality of His power and will and do not make him creator over everything; they do not hold

> that whatever He wills occurs and what he does not will does not happen. Then they impose upon their Lord a law (*shari'a*) of what He ought to do or what is forbidden Him—and this by analogy with themselves. They speak of establishing justice and [human] potentiality by this false analogy in which they make the creator resemble the creature. In this way they have erred and have caused others to err.[38]

Ibn Taymiyya strongly affirms the hypostatization of the names of God as opposed to the Mu'tazili denial of the attributes. He states that the Mu'tazila perform *ta'til* on God by their refusal to admit the concept of the speech of God, His knowledge, power, etc.[39] He endeavors to show that there can be no justification for this from the *usul al-din*, and that such a refusal is contrary to reason and self-contradictory.[40]

The question was not, in Ibn Taymiyya's time, the burning one which it had been three centuries earlier, and except that the Mu'tazili denial of attributes had been incorporated into Shi'i theology,[41] it did not present an active danger to the community which needed a specific refutation. He states that many excellent refutations of the Mu'tazili position have preceded him, and he refers his readers to these.[42] He explicitly approves the Ash'arite position which affirmed the divine attributes, and he places it—along with similar *kalam* theologies like the Kullabiyya, the Karramiyya, and the Hishamiyya[43]—squarely within the consensus of the community on this matter. (This is in contrast to his judgment of earlier Hanbalis like Ibn 'Aqil and Ibn al-Jawzi, whom he identifies as following a Mu'tazili position of denial of the attributes).[44] He gives an historical account of how the denial of divine attributes entered the Muslim community and of its historical links with the neo-Platonic cosmology taught by the Greek and Sabaean philosophers and adopted by Jahm ibn Safwan and Al-Farabi.[45]

Ibn Taymiyya rejects a number of theses and practices identified with Mu'tazila. Against a Mu'tazili denial, he affirmed the intercessory role of Muhammad for believers at the Hour of Judgment.[46] He restated belief in the uncreatedness of the Qur'an, although unlike Ibn Hanbal, he denied the eternity of the Qur'an. That is, the uncreatedness of the Qur'an must be positively affirmed, but its eternity must not be accepted as the consequent of that. The Qur'an is eternal only in its genus, not as an individual manifestation of God's speech.[47] He defended the validity of sound hadith reports against Mu'tazili objections.[48] He criticized Mu'tazili intolerance and *takfir* of Muslims opposing their views.[49] He rejected Mu'tazili apologetic works and refutations of Christianity as being rationalist exercises and lacking in any religious force.[50]

He objected strongly both to a Mu'tazili denial of anthropomorphic expressions in the Qur'an as well as to their usage of allegorical interpretation to explain them. This position earned him the accusation of anthropomorphism (*tashbih, tajsim*) and subsequent imprisonment both early and late in his life.[51]

In an attempt to avoid the anthropomorphic implications of the Qur'anic expressions of the *Umm al-Kitab* and the *al-Lawh al-Mahfuz*[52] and to reject the eternal and universal attribute of God's knowledge, Mu'tazili theologians were led to conceive of all beings before their creation as subsisting in a void—or non-being. God brought them out of non-being into existence by His act of creation. However, in refusing to include all created beings in the preeternal knowledge of God, they were forced to hold the subsistence of the non-existent in non-existence.[53] This, according to Ibn Taymiyya, is extremely close to the proposition of Ibn 'Arabi that the essences of all things preexist in the eternal absolute Existence, whence that Existence flowed into them and a manifestation of that Existence occurred in the universe.

> This [the unity of existence] is based on the principle that the non-existent (*al-ma'dum*) is a thing subsisting in non-being (*al-'adam*) as many of the Mu'tazila and the Rafida [Shi'a] claim. These people err in that they do not distinguish between the knowledge of God of things before their being, in that they subsist with Him in the *Umm al-Kitab* on the *Lawh Mahfuz*, and their subsisting external to the knowledge[54] of God. The belief of Muslims—the people of the sunna and consensus—is that God wrote on the *Lawh Mahfuz* the measures of created things before He created them. Thus they distinguish between intellectual existence (*al-wujud al-'ilmi*) and real existence outside [the knowledge of God] (*al-wujud al-'ayni al-khariji*).[55]

In evaluating Ibn Taymiyya's critique of speculative theology, several points are noteworthy. Firstly, Ibn Taymiyya considers Ash'arism and Mu'tazilism as expressions of the same procedure—that of including "the reasonable" among the bases for religion. As such, he became a staunch opponent of the Ash'arite tradition, whose proponents were striving during the 6th/12th-8th/14th centuries to establish Ash'arite theology as the orthodox response to the speculative questions raised by heterodox Mu'tazila.[56] Ibn Taymiyya's answer to them is that delving into divine matters with rational categories and terminology is an effort which is necessarily futile because of the inadequacy of the instruments employed. *Kalam* in the sense of rational arrangement and argumentation from the material of the Qur'anic revelation and the prophetic sunna is permissible, sometimes even praiseworthy, and ultimately inevitable, but on certain questions the only response which is proper is *tafwid*—suspending judgment and entrusting the solution to God.

It is worth noting, moreover, that Ibn Taymiyya does not consider his position original to himself. He traces it back most directly to Ibn Hanbal and claims it to be the attitude of the *salaf*. That the opposition to both the methodology and the conclusions of speculative theology was a constant element within the Hanbali tradition has been confirmed by modern scholarship.[57]

In Ibn Taymiyya's rebuttal against the Ash'arite teaching on *qadar*, however, there is a dramatic extension of the traditional Hanbali disapproval of *kalam* into an important new area. The strength of Ibn Hanbal's (d. 241/855) attack on the Mu'tazila and the Jahmiyya was directed against the denial of anthropomorphisms, the divine attributes, and a consequent defense of the uncreatedness and eternity of the Qur'an.[58] On the other hand, Ibn Hanbal's judgment on human causal agency was determinist.[59]

Abu al-Husayn al-Malati[60] (d. 377/987) supports Ibn Hanbal's accusations against Mu'tazili and Jahmite theses, but cites the traditionist Khushaysh ibn Asram in support of determinist *hadith*.[61] Al-Malati describes six sects of "Qadariyya," the common factor among them being their assertion of forms of human agency for evil and unlawful acts. At one point, however, Al-Malati mentions a hadith report which could be interpreted as proposing a position on *qadar* very similar to that later adopted by Ibn Taymiyya, "May God curse the people of *qadar*—those who reject [one kind of] *qadar* and those who believe in [another type of] *qadar*. Does not creation and command belong to Him?"[62] For Ibn Taymiyya it is God's role as Creator of the universe and Commander of the *shari'a* that is the essential element which must be preserved in any formulation on *qadar*.

Ibn Batta's position on *qadar* gives no evidence of any development on the statements on *qadar* by Ibn Hanbal in his creeds. Even Ibn Batta's wording seems but a paraphrase of Ibn Hanbal.[63]

> Next there must be faith in *qadar*—its good and its evil, its sweet and its bitter, its little and its much are all determined (*maqdur*), occurring from God for His servants at the moment He wills it to occur, neither preceding the time nor delaying that which was fixed in God's presence.[64]

The difficulties encountered by Abu Ya'la al-Farra with the Ash'arites had nothing to do with *qadar*. In a lost work, *Ibtal al-Ta'wilat li-Akhbar al-Sifat*, Abu Ya'la attacked the Ash'arite usage of allegorical interpretation upon the divine attributes, and the

Ash'arites in turn accused him of *tashbih*.[65] Among Abu Ya'la's extant works mentioned by his son[66] are refutations of Ash'arites and Mu'tazila, but in the *Kitab al-Mu'tamad*, Abu Ya'la's conclusions are consistently in agreement with the Ash'arite position of the universality of divine agency. He states that whatever God creates has already "preceded in His knowledge and wisdom." After delineating the various possible meanings for *qada'* (divine decree) and *qadar*, Abu Ya'la states:

> By the *qada'* and the *qadar* in the statement of the Prophet "We believe in the *qada'* and the *qadar*" is meant the creation of what has preceded in His knowledge and His wisdom—that He creates it. As a proof there is the statement of the Prophet: "We believe in His judgment and His setting the measure; its best and its worst He created." "Acts" are among what is meant by that.[67]

As stated above, Ibn Taymiyya criticized Abu Ya'la and his more famous student Ibn 'Aqil for adopting the views of the speculative theologians on issues involving the divine attributes. It is noteworthy that when Ibn 'Aqil was forced to retract the Mu'tazili theses he had adopted in his youth, his stance on *qadar* was not an issue. The affair once again centered on questions of the createdness of the Qur'an and the interpretation of anthropomorphic expressions in the Qur'an and the Traditions.[68] Laoust states that in his later years Ibn 'Aqil wrote a treatise attacking Ash'arite theses which is now lost;[69] this is unfortunate, as its contents would very probably clarify Ibn 'Aqil's views on *qadar*.

It was stated above that Ibn Taymiyya cites with approval the teaching on *qadar* of the famous Hanbali mystic 'Abd al-Qadir al-Jilani (al-Jili). Ibn Taymiyya writes that 'Abd al-Qadir, like al-Junayd before him and like the generality of orthodox Sufi shaykhs, "warned against holding for *qadar*."[70] This statement of Ibn Taymiyya's, however, cannot be supported by an inspection of 'Abd al-Qadir's great work, *Al-Ghunya li-Talibi Tariq al-Haqq*. In this work 'Abd al-Qadir's explanation of what the Muslim must believe about *qadar* is strongly determinist. Nothing ever has occurred or will ever occur except by the foreordained judgment and decree of God. Those destined to be people of the Garden will act accordingly, while those destined for the Fire will act in such a way to deserve it. A person's actions are created by God before his birth. 'Abd al-Qadir supports his explanation with a series of determinist hadith reports.[71] I have not been able to find, either in the *Ghunya* or in the *Futuh al-Ghayb*, any statement by 'Abd al-Qadir which would confirm Ibn Taymiyya's claim that the Shaykh "warned against holding determinism."

The writings of two 7th/13th century Hanbali authors confirm the view that the traditional Hanbali opposition to *kalam*, and specifically to Ash'arism, did not include rejection of the Ash'arite formulation of *qadar*. The first of these is the work written by Ibn Qudama against speculative theology.[72] Islamic literature has possibly never produced a treatise so totally opposed to the conclusions of speculative theology, and Ibn Qudama's work can be said to epitomize the Hanbali rejection of *kalam*. An inspection of this work reveals, however, that not a single reference to *qadar* is made by Ibn Qudama, whose attack once again centers upon the methodological procedure of speculative theology, the use of *ta'wil* to interpret anthropomorphisms, and the Mu'tazili rejection of divine attributes.

The final piece of information comes from a book of sects written by the Hanbali 'Abbas ibn Mansur al-Saksaki (d. 683/1284), who died the same year in which Ibn Taymiyya began teaching at the Sukkariyya madrasa in Damascus. In form, his work *Al-Burhan fi Ma'rifat 'Aqa'id Ahl al-Aydan*[73] follows the traditional structure for this type of literature. Before elucidating the orthodox belief of "the people of the sunna and consensus" the author presents the seventy-two heterodox sects, which are grouped according to the similarity of their errors. As an appendix he adds the non-Islamic religions.

In Al-Saksaki's treatment, the Islamic sects are arranged under four headings, to each of which a chapter is devoted: Khawarij, Murji'a, Mu'tazila and Qadariyya, and Rafidiyya (Shi'a). In the second chapter, which concerns the sects of the Murji'a, after treating the Jahmiyya, the Karramiyya, and the Marisiyya, Al-Saksaki describes the belief of the Kullabiyya of which he sees Ash'arism as a subgroup. He accuses the Ash'arites of *ta'til*, based on their view of divine speech, but their position on *qadar* is nowhere criticized.

> He [Ibn Kullab] and his sect used to hold that God does not have speech which is heard, that Gabriel did not hear from God a thing of that which he conveyed to His messengers, and that which he sent down upon the prophets was a figurative expression (*hikaya*) of the speech of God in which there was neither command nor prohibition, neither information (*khabar*) nor that from which information could be sought (*istikhbar*). But that is only known from it in another meaning. They held that God did not have words (*kalimat*), nor are there suras and verse in the Qur'an nor any of the languages; rather it [the Qur'an] is one single thing which all these express. Abu al-Hasan al-Ash'ari came to hold this view, and his sect the Ash'arites trace their origins to the same Abu al-Hasan al-Ash'ari. In our day they are numerous—more than can be counted—and spread throughout the [Is-

> lamic] countries. They work their deception upon the masses and the ignorant that [their belief] is the declaration of God's transcendence (*tanzih*), but in reality it is stripping Him of religious relevance (*ta'til*). I take refuge in God from the wickedness of their belief.[74]

The purpose of this brief survey of Hanbali objections to *kalam* has been to point out that there is a consistency within the tradition. It accused the speculative theologians, Ash'arites as well as Mu'tazila of professing *ta'til* rather than *tawhid*, that is, elevating God beyond the point where He is the genuine object of worship for mankind. To the earlier Hanbalis, the Mu'tazila were the more serious offenders because of their denial of God's attributes, their allegorization of Qur'anic statements, and their rejection of hadith reports. On the matter of divine agency of human acts, the Hanbalis either expressly agreed with the Ash'arite position or else were silent on the matter while they repeated the same argumentation and hadith citation against the Mu'tazili position as did the Ash'arites.

From Ibn Taymiyya's point of view, there was an essential element missing in the traditional Hanbali opposition to Ash'arite *kalam*. God is not only to be worshiped alone as the Creator of the universe, but He is the Commander of the *shari'a*, to whom complete obedience is owed. Earlier Hanbalis had rightfully perceived that the speculative theologians had performed *ta'til* on an ontological level by stripping God of those qualities of speech, knowledge, love, etc., which are essential to mankind's response in belief and worship of Him, and by eliminating the religious force of the Qur'anic statements with which God has described Himself. Ibn Taymiyya saw that equally important to this first *ta'til* was the theologians' *ta'til* upon the ethical and legal bases for religion. In this case it was the Ash'arites who were the primary offenders. Their solution to the problem of human freedom and divine omnipotence was purely formalistic and formulaic; it provided an intellectual solution to a question raised by themselves. However, Al-Ash'ari's God was not such that He could be truly worshiped, obeyed, or loved, for all these actions presuppose free human agency, an ability on the part of the servant to believe or disbelieve, obey or disobey, love or refuse to love.

Ibn Taymiyya's contribution, then, is to reassert primary religious needs and goals in the face of what he saw as a powerful movement to formalism, against a theological formulation which attempted to be intellectually satisfying while at the same time it failed to preserve the spirit agreed upon by the early generations of Islam. Thus the second great principle which guides Ibn Taymiyya's polemical writings is established. Against the partisans of *wahdat al-wujud*, the peripatetic philosophers, Sufis, and Shi'i *ghulat* Ibn Taymiyya found it necessary to defend the essential dissimilarity of God to the universe so that His role be preserved as Creator of the universe to whom worship is owed and the Commander of the good and Prohibitor of the bad to whom obedience is due. Ibn Taymiyya's second principle which he develops in these polemics is that both aspects of mankind's response to God—worship only of Him and obedience only to Him—require, along with assertion of the universality of divine power, a free human response. Human reason, by delving into this apparent contradiction in search of a logical solution, can only end in error, and the question must ultimately be referred back to God (*tafwid*) in faith.

# CHAPTER 5

## THE POLEMIC AGAINST THE SHI'A

In addition to extreme *tashbih* in the form of *wahdat al-wujud* monism, which Ibn Taymiyya considered absolute *shirk* (*al-shirk al-mutlaq*), and its limited expressions in the errors of Sufism and popular Islam, and in addition to the absolute *ta'til* of the philosophers and its limited forms of Ash'ari and Mu'tazili speculative theology, Ibn Taymiyya directed a number of polemical writings against what he saw to be another complex of deviations within Islam. These are his polemical writings against the Shi'a. Many of the beliefs and practices in Shi'ism which Ibn Taymiyya considered aberrations are parallels to deviations within Sunni Islam against which he inveighed. Moreover, many of these errors are analogous to ways in which Christians deviated from the one religion of the prophets.

Ibn Taymiyya's earliest writings against the Shi'a were occasioned by the unsettled political situation in Syria at the time of the Mongol incursions (697/1297-704/1304).[1] The inhabitants of the predominantly Shi'i mountain area of Kasrawan were accused of assisting the Mongols, and Ibn Taymiyya wrote a lengthy *fatwa* to show the permissibility of *jihad* against them. The account given by his biographer al-Mar'i (d. 1033/1623) is as follows:

> He set out in 704 to combat the mountain people, accompanying Aqqush al-Afram, the viceroy of the province of Damascus. They did not cease to fight until they had taken the mountain and driven out its inhabitants. He then engaged in debate with the shaykh of the Shi'a, who proclaimed the infallibility of 'Ali.[2]

Ibn Taymiyya's argument in his treatise in which he declared the unbelief of the Shi'a is based on the nonconformity of Shi'i beliefs and practices to the *shari'a*. Any people who do not follow the *shari'a* exactly are in innovation, and if they prove any danger to Muslim life and property they must be opposed.

> If they say "we pray but we do not pay *zakah*," or "we pray the five prayers but not the Friday or the congregational prayer," or "we are

grounded on the five principles of Islam but do not forbid shedding Muslims' blood or taking their properties," or "we do not abstain from *riba* or alcoholic drink or gambling," or "we follow the Qur'an but not the Messenger of God; we do not act upon the established hadith reports," or "we believe that the Jews and Christians are better than the majority of Muslims, and that those who pray to Mecca have disbelieved in God and His Messenger and only a small group of them remain believers," or if they say "we do not wage *jihad* with Muslims against unbelievers," or other matters opposed to the Law of the Messenger of God, his sunna, and what the consensus of Muslims holds—*jihad* must be waged against all these groups.[3]

There is precedent for this in the action of the Prophet himself and in that of the Companions, who declared the necessity of opposing the Kharijites by force.

But many of these people, such as the Khurramiyya,[4] the Qaramita, and the Nusayriyya, are worse than the Haruri[5] Kharijites. All who believe about a man that he is God or about someone other than a prophet that he is a prophet or who fight against Muslims over such things are worse than the Haruri Kharijites.[6]

Shi'a, he says, are the most deceitful, the most gullible, and the most hypocritical of all the people who call themselves Muslims.[7] In fact, he says, they are hardly Muslims at all; they more closely resemble Jews and Christians in their beliefs and associate with the People of the Book more than they do with (Sunni) Muslims.

They have resembled the Jews in numerous matters, especially the Samaritans among the Jews whom they resemble more than other types. They are similar to them in their claim of the imamate in a person or hidden within himself, in their rejecting all those who brought the truth other than him who they claim [to be imam], in their following whims and in corrupting [God's] message from its contexts, in delaying the breakfast[8] and the sunset prayer, and in forbidding the animals slaughtered by others than them. They resemble the Christians in going to excess concerning a man, in innovated practices, and in *shirk*.[9]

This *fatwa* naturally displays the hyperbolic accusations typical of wartime propaganda; however, this early treatise set the basic lines of opposition which Ibn Taymiyya would follow in his later, more thoughtful attacks on Shi'ism. He mentions their deceitfulness and gullibility in inventing and accepting spurious hadith reports, the hypocrisy attendant upon a *zahiri-batini* dichotomy in religious profession and interpretation, the infallibility of the imam and the consequent threat to prophecy and the glorification of the state, in excessive honor given to humans in the forms of divine indwelling and union, and innovated and idolatrous practices of worship.

In an even earlier writing, a letter sent to the Mamluk sultan Al-Malik al-Nasir, Ibn Taymiyya encouraged the sultan to wage *jihad* against the Mongols and the Shi'a. In this letter he presents an objection which lies at the heart of his criticism of Shi'ism—their *takfir* of the *salaf.*

> Their belief is that Abu Bakr, 'Umar, 'Uthman, the people of Badr and the allegiance at Hudaybiyya, the majority of the emigrants and the Ansar, those who followed them in uprightness, the Imams of Islam and their scholars of the four law schools, the shaykhs and worshipers of Islam, the rulers and armies of Muslims, the Muslim masses and individuals—according to them all of these are apostate unbelievers, more unbelieving than Jews and Christians. According to them they are apostates, and the apostate is worse than the unbeliever by origin. For this reason they give preference to the Franks and the Tatars [Mongols] over the people of the Qur'an and faith.[10]

Ibn Taymiyya's criticism was directed most strongly against Shi'i "extremism," Nusayris, Druzes, and Qarmati, Fatimid, and Nizari Isma'ilis. This opposition is based not only upon the incompatibility of many *ghulat* beliefs to Sunni Islam, but also reflects the political situation of Ibn Taymiyya's time which saw almost constant warfare in the Mamluk attempts to reconquer and pacify Syria and the Lebanon against Druze and Shi'i opposition.[11]

Ibn Taymiyya's basic criticisms against these sects are these: they have declared the *shari'a* abrogated and do not admit the divine command and prohibition; by elevating an individual beyond the status of the prophets and admitting a type of divine *hulul* or *ittihad*, they commit the same type of *shirk* as Christians and pagan idolators; by declaring infallibility for their *imams*, they challenge the institution of prophecy. This last criticism is applied by Ibn Taymiyya to Twelver Shi'ism as well, and forms one of his principal arguments against them.

Upon the *ghulat* Ibn Taymiyya pronounces *takfir*, and his judgment against them is always severe.

> These Druzes and Nusayris are unbelievers by the agreement of Muslims. It is not permitted to eat their butchered meats, nor to marry their women. They do not even admit of the *jizya*, for they are apostates from the religion—neither Muslims, nor Jews, nor Christians. They do not hold for the necessity of the five prayers, the Ramadan fast, nor the pilgrimage to Mecca, nor do they prohibit what God and his prophet have forbidden by way of dead meats, alcoholic drinks, and the like.

With these beliefs, even if they manifest the *shahadatayn*, they are unbelievers by consensus of Muslims.[12]

Muslims may have no social relations whatsoever with these people, and they must be totally ostracized by Islamic society. For Ibn Taymiyya this is not a question which permits a variety of opinions. Anyone who even doubts their status as unbelievers is an unbeliever himself.

> The unbelief of these people is something upon which Muslims cannot differ; even he who doubts their unbelief is an unbeliever like them. They are not of the same status as the People of the Book nor that of pagans. They are apostate godless people (*zanadiqa murtaddun*) whose repentance will not be accepted. They should be killed wherever they are found and cursed even as they are mentioned. It is not permissible to employ them as guards, doorkeepers, or watchmen. Their scholars and their pious should be killed so that they do not lead the others astray. It is forbidden to sleep with them in their homes, to give them sustenance, to walk with them, or to take part in their funerals if one of them is known to have died.[13]

One of Ibn Taymiyya's best known polemical works is written against the Nusayriyya. Ibn Taymiyya's objections to this sect can be summarized under three headings. Firstly, as in the letter to the Sultan al-Nasir, he accuses them of being inimical to all things Islamic. He repeatedly refers to them as "apostates," people who had known Islam, who then left it and developed an intense hatred for it. It is this hatred for the Islamic community which explains their constant support of the military enemies of Islam, as well as their mockery and scorn for all the practices and personages held in respect by Muslims. For them 'Umar ibn al-Khattab, the second successor to Muhammad as Commander of the Faithful, is "the Iblis of all Iblises, and just behind him in the measure of devilry is Abu Bakr."[14]

The second great objection which Ibn Taymiyya brings against the Nusayris is their challenge to the notion of prophecy. They have pieced together a prophetology, he charges, from non-Islamic and even anti-Islamic sources, which they follow in preference to the message of the true prophets. He describes their distinction between the seven "Asma'"—men like Adam, Noah, Moses, Jesus, Muhammad, who were the bearers of an exoteric, imperfect revelation, and the "Ma'ani" such as Seth and 'Ali. These Ma'ani represented the inner meanings of the Asma', their hidden counterparts who bore and personified the secret and real meaning of the revelation.

Not only does this formulation challenge the Islamic belief that there is no one closer to God than the prophets, nor anyone other than they through whom God's message is delivered, but the *zahiri-batini* dichotomy would make all belief and all revelation subjective. This, he claims, is what has happened in their esoteric interpretations of the Qur'an and the pillars of religion. For them the five prayers mean the five names of 'Ali, Hasan, Husayn, Muhsin, and Fatima. Recollection (*dhikr*) of these five names takes the place of the five prayers for those who are spiritually adept.

The *zahiri* meaning of Qur'anic words and verses and religious practices is inoperative for those who have attained degrees of gnosis, and the moral behavior commanded by the *shari'a* is not obligatory. In fact, the *shari'a* itself is abrogated, and an antinomian society which they claim to be that of the resurrection obtains.

Finally, they adopt from the pagan and Magian philosophers other beliefs, like transmigration of souls and the eternity of the world, which are incompatible with the message of all the prophets. These beliefs lead them to deny God's role as creator, as their antinomianism led them to deny His nature as religious commander. Thus, according to Ibn Taymiyya, the real nature of their belief is a godlessness inimical to revealed religion.

> The apparent form of their religion is Shi'ism (*al-Rafd*), but its hidden nature is pure unbelief (*al-Kufr al-Mahd*). The reality of their concern is that they do not believe in any one of the prophets or messengers—neither in Noah nor Abraham nor Moses nor Jesus nor Muhammad—nor in a single thing from the Books handed down from God, neither in the Torah nor in the Gospel nor in the Qur'an. They do not hold that the world has a creator who created it, that God has a religion which He commanded, or that there is a place other than this world in which people are repaid according to their deeds.
>
> Sometimes they build their opinion upon the beliefs of the naturalist[15] and Platonist[16] philosophers as the authors of the Epistles of the Brethren of Purity[17] have done. At other times they have built it upon the view of the [peripatetic] philosophers and that of the Magians who worship light. To all that they add Shi'ism, and they argue for it from the message of the prophecies either by a forged statement[18] . . . or by a wording established as being from the prophet which they have distorted from its context, just as do the authors of the Epistles of the Brethren of Purity and those like them, for they are among their imams.[19] Much of their error has entered upon many Muslims and has circulated among them until it has come to be found in the books of groups of those adhering to knowledge and religion even though they do not agree with them on the principles of their unbelief.
>
> They call their accursed propaganda "The Greatest Attainment" (*Al-Balagh al-Akbar*),[20] and to it they add denial of the creator and mock-

ery of Him and whoever is close to Him, so that one of them might write the name of God on the bottom of his foot. In it there is a denial of His laws (*shara'i'*) and his religion (*din*) which the prophets brought.[21]

Ibn Taymiyya's criticism of other groups of Isma'ilis and *ghulat* Shi'a parallels that of his refutation of the Nusayris. Those who believe in the imamate and infallibility of the Fatimids are far worse than Twelver Shi'a, he states, for in the case of the Twelve Imams it is at least known that their exaggerated claims are made concerning holy men who are descendants of the prophet.[22] The whole Fatimid line, by contrast, were probably imposters in their claim of descent from Fatima, he claims, and many of them were not even upright Muslims, much less infallible imams. They failed in their responsibility to defend Islam by being unwilling and unable to defend Islamic territory from the Crusaders, and at times actually conspired with them against Muslims.[23]

Ibn Taymiyya's judgment is never more harsh than it is upon the Qarmatis. Because of their claim to a new revelation beyond that given through the prophets, and because of their rejection of the *shari'a*, he declares them to be the people the most unbelieving in God, and worse than the Ittihadiyyun—the followers of Ibn 'Arabi and his school of thought.[24] To the latter Ibn Taymiyya credits an ignorance of the true nature and the implications of *wahdat al-wujud*, but the Qarmatis, he claims, know that they are striving against God and His religion.

Just as Ibn Taymiyya's major polemical work against Christianity was occasioned by a previous polemic by a well-known Christian writer, so his great work on Twelver Shi'ism was written in response to a Shi'i apologetic work authored by one of the leading Shi'i thinkers of the day. This was the treatise *Minhaj al-Karama fi Ma'rifat al-Imama* by Al-'Allama Ala' al-Din ibn al-Mutahhar al-Hilli (d. 726/1325). Al-Hilli was a direct disciple of Nasir al-Din al-Tusi (d. 672/1273) and an exact contemporary of Ibn Taymiyya's.[25] His work, the *Minhaj al-Karama*, was only one of al-Hilli's voluminous writings on all aspects of *fiqh*, *tafsir*, and *kalam*, and it was commissioned by the Ilkhan Khudabanda, who had made Shi'ism the state religion. As might be expected in a work commissioned by the reigning sultan interested in using religious belief to legitimate his rule, political questions are central to al-Hilli's argument; this is naturally a factor which influenced Ibn Taymiyya's choice of argumentation in *Minhaj al-Sunna al-Nabawiyya*.

The essence of al-Hilli's argument is that the presence of an infallible imam is a necessary prerequisite for establishing and preserving the *shari'a*. The reasoning he offers in proof for this Laoust traces to Al-Farabi and the Ikhwan al-Safa'.[26] Man, because of his egoism and cupidity, seeks by his very nature to possess and dominate and is regularly eager to possess that owned by others and to gain control over the freedom of others. Rights are therefore constantly being violated, and it is inevitable that conflicting claims arise which demand a decision to determine whose rights are being violated. If this decision is to be made according to the judgments handed down by God, an authority which can affirm and apply the divine will with infallible certainty is necessary. This institution is the imamate; the legislator and interpreter of divine revelation and judgment is the infallible and impeccable imam.[27]

By contrast, claims al-Hilli, the various Sunni alternatives offer no certainty and thus no conviction that it is God's revelation which is expressed, and His will which is obeyed. *Ijma'* can provide no legal proof whatsoever, and there is no divine guarantee which prevents the community from agreeing on an error. It is only by consensus of the community that the prophetic hadith in which God promised that the community would not agree on an error is accepted as a source of divine information. What Sunnis offer, therefore, is merely a circular argument—if the hadith is correct, it proves that the community is correct in accepting its validity; if the hadith report is in error, it is merely an instance of how the community can agree on an error.

Without the objective measure of an infallible imam the other principles of Sunni law are worthless for any attempt to learn divine truth or to construct and impose a legal system. *Ra'y* (opinion) and *qiyas* (analogy) insert an element of subjectivity into the *shari'a* which would invalidate its nature as a divinely revealed religious law, were there not the guarantee of certainty which the infallible imamate offers. He claims that Sunnis introduced the four law schools, which did not exist in the time of Muhammad. What does exist from that time are the texts (*nusus*) of 'Ali and his companions, which they reject in favor of their own opinion.[28]

It is necessary for the preservation of Islam that there be an imam who not only is possessed of infallibility, but who is also impeccable. Sinfulness and wrongdoing are therefore clearly signs that an individual is not the imam. He enunciates the Shi'i principle of the election of the *fadil* (the preferable, better) over the *mafdul* (the less preferable). Al-Hilli uses this principle to give a Shi'i reading of the history of the califate, his point being that Sunnis have consistently followed the less preferable claimant to the califate, whose illegitimacy is manifested by his misdeeds.[29]

Al-Hilli continues his argument by attacking Sunni *kalam* and *fiqh*.

He attempts to demonstrate that Sunnism, by its internal contradictions and absurdities, is condemned in its theodicy, its eschatology, and its prophetology as well to a veritable self-destruction.[30]

He specifically attacks Ash'arites, whom he declares to be *mushrikun* for their hypostatization of the names of God, and condemns the inconsistency of Fakhr al-Din al-Razi's condemnation of Christian *shirk* for their belief in the existence of three hypostases while his own school of theology has increased the number to nine.[31] (Ibn Taymiyya, who with the Ash'arites accepts the hypostatization of the divine attributes, will endeavor in *Al-Jawab al-Sahih* to show the differences between the position accepted as orthodox in Sunni Islam and that proposed by Christians).[32]

Al-Hilli rejects strongly the Ash'arite teaching on *qadar* as reducing man to an automaton and destroying the value of religion.[33] Al-Hilli's criticism of the Ash'arite formulation on *qadar* is similar to that of Ibn Taymiyya; Al-Hilli, however, adopts a Mu'tazili position, which Ibn Taymiyya criticizes for its dualism and its incompatibility with the omnipotence of God.

In *Minhaj al-Sunna al-Nabawiyya* Ibn Taymiyya makes a careful point-by-point refutation of Al-Hilli's argument. Even the title is carefully chosen to counter that of Al-Hilli. Al-Hilli's *The Way of (God's) Favor in Knowledge of the Imamate* is answered by Ibn Taymiyya's *The Way of the Prophetic Sunna in Contradicting the Teaching of the Qadari Shi'a.* As he would do later in *Al-Jawab al-Sahih* Ibn Taymiyya cites the adversary's text *verbatim* and proceeds to refute it.

The focus of Ibn Taymiyya's attack is political, but it is a political critique which is based on his perception of Islam. The Shi'a argued that the imamate was a blessing of God for the benefit of the *umma*, and thus for mankind, but Ibn Taymiyya answers that their doctrine actually works against the community's general welfare (*al-maslaha*).[34] Their teaching on the infallible imamate has led them to exaggerate the role of the state and has been used to justify allegiance to unbelieving and oppressive rulers.[35]

According to Ibn Taymiyya, the purpose of the state is to fulfill a necessary but strictly limited function, that is, it is an instrument for attaining religious and moral ends. In his distrust of the state as a national entity, Ibn Taymiyya almost approaches a Khariji-type individualism, and his personal history of harassment and imprisonment at the hands of political authorities attests to his self-imposed role as spokesman for the *shari'a* against governmental departures from its proper function.

Ibn Taymiyya counters the Shi'i claim that the imamate gives them direct and certain access to infallible interpretation of the Qur'anic revelation by claiming that their institution of the imamate is an arbitrary and historically unjustified innovation not found in the earliest generations of Muslims and incompatible with the teaching of the Qur'an. The Shi'a claim that they can trace back the most minute details of their law and practice to infallible imams. Actually, holds Ibn Taymiyya, their reception of material from the Prophet can be no different from that of Sunni Muslims. Of their imams, only 'Ali can be said to have known the Prophet. (Hasan and Husayn were alive at the time of the Prophet's death, but were not of the age of reason and at any rate transmitted very little from Muhammad.)[36] Like the rest of the Companions, 'Ali was not preserved from sin and error.

The Companions, including 'Ali, were the most trustworthy of mankind, and thus one can confidently affirm that they would never intentionally lie or conspire on falsehood. Even the second generation of followers of the Prophet (*al-tabi'un*) were almost free from intentional error. Among all of these, however, unintentional error was quite possible, and it is only through careful study of the reports that a moral certainty can be reached on the correctness of what they have transmitted.[37]

When the Shi'a claim that their imams received their information from their ancestor Muhammad, they can mean only one of two things: either they received it directly through a kind of prophetic inspiration or that they learned it from others. The first is prophecy, which they do not claim, and the second is the method followed by the people of the prophetic sunna, i.e., Sunni Muslims.

On questions of what actually has been handed down from God through the prophet (*al-shar'iyyat*) they rely on false principles which prevent them from judging soundly. Instead of depending on those who have critically studied the hadith reports for their strengths and weaknesses, the Shi'a will accept even a weak *khabar al-wahid* from 'Ali and his companions according to the following principles:

1) On the basis that any one of these [Imams] is inerrant (*ma'sum*) similar to the inerrancy of the prophets, and

2) Whatever one of them says, he only says it as transmitted from the Prophet. It is known about them that they state: "Whatever we hold, we only hold it as transmitted from the Prophet," and they claim inerrancy in the transmitters, and

3) The consensus of the family [of the Prophet] is a proof. They claim that the family is the Twelve, and they claim that what is transmitted from one of them, upon that they all agree. These *usul al-shar'iyyat* among them are false principles . . . they do not depend on the Qur'an nor upon hadith reports, nor on consensus, except that an inerrant being is among them,[38] nor on analogy, even though it be clear and obvious.[39]

On controverted issues of rational theology (*al-nazar wal-'aqliyyat*), declares Ibn Taymiyya, the later Shi'a have adopted Mu'tazili formulations. Ibn Taymiyya carefully attempts to prove that this was a later development in Shi'ism, having occurred only about the year 300/913;[40] this was done, he holds, because of their disinclination to follow the accepted Sunni positions against the Mu'tazila.

Ibn Taymiyya's response to Al-Hilli on the controversial questions of theology was double. On some questions such as the future continuance in existence of the Garden and the Fire,[41] and the createdness of the Qur'an,[42] Ibn Taymiyya argues against the Mu'tazila and reaffirms a Sunni position which has been accepted as consensus since the time of the *salaf*.

On other questions, specifically those concerning the attributes of God and the problem of *qadar*, Ibn Taymiyya challenges Al-Hilli's formulation of the Sunni position. Al-Hilli describes certain anti-Mu'tazili *kalam* formulations as those followed by Sunni Muslims. Ibn Taymiyya denies that any of these formulations—whether Ash'arite, Karrami, Kullabi, or Hashwi—can be identified as "the Sunni view." The great failing of all these schools of thought, he states, is that they themselves try to identify their opinions with Islam, so that they pronounce *takfir* on those who reject their views.[43] In reality, Islam can be identified with none of these schools; Islamic belief is that upon which the *salaf* and the imams have agreed to be sound interpretation of the Book and the Sunna. There is no consensus to affirm that the speculation and the formulation of any later school, Ash'arite or other, is certain Sunni belief on any question.

It cannot be said, therefore, that Sunni Muslims hold that God can do evil, or that He acts in the universe without a purpose or without a wise design, or that He does not do what is best for mankind.[44] It would be true to say that some Sunni Muslims hold this, but since such statements can be shown to be opposed to the teaching of the *salaf* and their definitive interpretation of the *usul al-din*, it must be concluded that these statements of theirs are in error.

While one cannot identify, as does Al-Hilli, agreed-upon Sunni teaching with that of an individual school of thought, one can reject certain Mu'tazili formulations as being incompatible with the received sunna. Shi'a, in adopting these Mu'tazili theses, by denying the divine attributes[45] and by integrating extreme Mu'tazili free-will teaching[46] into their belief, have abandoned the message of the Qur'an and the sunna.

The most serious error of the Shi'a, and the one which caused their blasphemous slandering of the Companions and the Commanders of the Faithful like Abu Bakr, 'Umar, and 'Uthman, is their doctrine of the infallibility of the imams. Not only is it a view based on fraudulent hadith reports and opposed to the true teaching of the Qur'an and the sunna, but it is a serious assault upon the role of the prophet. Only a prophet is infallible in what he brings from God; to claim infallibility for others than prophets, as the Shi'a do for their imams, paves the way for multiple forms of *shirk*.

The Shi'a in their attitude towards the Imams resemble the Christians more closely than they do Muslims. Christians have taken their church leaders and holy men for lords by allowing them to dictate to them in matters of religion, to permit what the prophets have forbidden, and to forbid what they had permitted. This is the attitude of the Shi'a towards their Imams. On the basis of what they consider to be infallible teaching from the Imams, they have introduced practices and laws which were not ordained by God.

> They ignorantly intended to extol the prophets just as Christians intended in ignorance to extol Christ and their leaders and their monks. They committed *shirk* on them and they took them as lords beside God and ceased to follow them in what they commanded and what they forbade. Those who have gone to extremes in infallibility have thus turned away from obeying their command to imitate their deeds and turned to exaggeration and forms of *shirk* which they forbade. Thus they have taken them as lords beside God by praying to them in their absence and after their deaths and at their graves. They have entered into the idolatrous worship which God and His messenger prohibited which is similar to that of the Christians.[47]

As was seen in earlier chapters, Ibn Taymiyya was conscious of the idolatrous and superstitious nature of much in popular practices of Sunni Islam. The difference between this and the phenomenon in Shi'ism, as he saw it, was that in Shi'ism these practices were institutionalized and made acceptable religious expressions through the agency of the infallible Imams.

The Shi'a changed the religion of God by building shrines and by making centers of pilgrimage out of the graves of their Imams, although the practice is *shirk* and was expressly forbidden by the prophet.

> The mosques built upon the graves of holy persons among the people and of the People of the House are all forbidden novel inventions in the religion of Islam. God commanded only that He alone be intended in His worship, with no mosques or shrines participating in it.[48]

They challenge the necessity of the pillars of true Islam by their emphasis on their innovated practices. They make mosques irrelevant by eliminating Friday prayers. They make the *hajj* unimportant by the central place they give to pilgrimages to the tombs of the Imams. They diminish the importance of *salah* by their intercessory prayers to the Imams. Even worse than these things is their practice of pronouncing *takfir* upon those who refuse to engage in these innovated practices.[49]

From these innovated beliefs and idolatrous practices of worship it is but a short step to declaring the Imams to be the loci of God on earth, or that they are the manifestations of divine glory among mankind, that God himself dwells in them, or even that God has united Himself to them. All these formulations were adopted by the Shi'i extremists, and all of them constitute unbelief. For Ibn Taymiyya, the path which the Shi'a take towards unbelief and error parallels that taken by the Christians in the centuries between Jesus and Muhammad. He constantly alludes to Christian errors in elucidating those of the Shi'a, and in his criticism of Christianity in *Al-Jawab al-Sahih* it will be to errors of the Shi'a that he points far more than to those of any other Muslim group.

# CHAPTER 6

## IBN TAYMIYYA'S POLEMICAL WRITINGS AGAINST CHRISTIANITY

In addition to his controversialist activity in combatting what he saw to be deviations within the Islamic *umma*, Ibn Taymiyya's writings against the faith and practices of Christianity are extremely prolific. He far surpasses, both in the number of separate works which he wrote about various aspects of Christianity and in the volume of pages devoted to this subject, any other scholar before or since in the Islamic tradition.

Besides *Al-Jawab al-Sahih*—Ibn Taymiyya's magnum opus on Christianity—five other works by that author are listed in Brockelmann's *History* as "Polemik gegen die Dimmiya."[1] Fritsch adds another, Ibn Taymiyya's first important work *Al-Sarim al-Maslul 'ala Shatim al-Rasul*.[2] In addition, the early biographers of Ibn Taymiyya list other works, notably *Ihtijaj al-Jahmiyya wal-Nasara bil-Kalima*,[3] not mentioned in the modern lists.

In the case of several writings listed by the early biographers it is difficult to identify which work known at the present time to be among those of Ibn Taymiyya corresponds to titles listed in the early biographical studies. This is due to the fact that even Ibn Taymiyya frequently referred to his own works by various names, and this imprecision has been compounded by his students and those of succeeding generations.[4]

For example, Ibn Qayyim al-Jawziyya lists the treatise *Risala fi al-Nahy 'an A'yad al-Nasara*.[5] It is only by conjecture that this can be tentatively identified with either the *Su'al* of MF 10:320 or with *Tahrim Musharakat Ahl al-Kitab fi A'yadihim*, a short *risala* found in the collections of Ibn Taymiyya's legal judgments.

Even though this situation is disturbing in reference to such works, it becomes a crucial factor in the identification of works like *Takhjil Ahl al-Injil*. In the attempt to determine the historical nature of this work as a treatise distinct from *Al-Jawab al-Sahih*, the bibliographical lists of the 8th/14th-century biographers provide significant information. Although none of these lists record a work entitled *Takhjil Ahl al-Injil* (or any of its variants), there are works listed which do not refer to any work known at present; moreover the description of the contents of such works often coincide well with what we are led to expect in *Takhjil Ahl al-Injil* for other reasons. This will be discussed at length in the Appendix, but here it should be pointed out that although the knowledge which can be obtained from the early biographers regarding the identification of any works known at present is merely conjectural, nevertheless it cannot be dismissed as unimportant.

The purpose of this chapter is to study briefly the contents of these other controversialist works by Ibn Taymiyya against Christianity in order to build a context from which *Al-Jawab al-Sahih* can be more adequately viewed. Like most of Ibn Taymiyya's polemical works, *Al-Jawab al-Sahih* arose out of a specific situation—in this case as a response to a specific Christian polemical work. As such, it does not contain, nor does Ibn Taymiyya intend it to contain, the whole of his critique of Christianity. The other works treated in this chapter, for the most part occasioned by events or by questions addressed to Ibn Taymiyya in his role as *faqih*, form with *Al-Jawab al-Sahih* a consistent theological position regarding the Christian religion. In his individual treatises on Christianity, the circumstances which led him to compose the work cause him to develop this critique by means of diverse political, juridical, and theological methodology.

### *Al-Sarim al-Maslul*

The first major work by Ibn Taymiyya, entitled *Al-Sarim al-Maslul 'ala Shatim al-Rasul*, was occasioned by an incident in Damascus in 694/1293.[6] The affair involved a Christian cleric named 'Assaf al-Nasrani, who was accused of insulting the Prophet. He sought protection from one of the powerful families of Damascus, but Ibn Taymiyya and another Damascene *'alim* brought the case before the governor, and the Christian was found guilty. A crowd attempted to stone the Christian, and Ibn Taymiyya was arrested for the first time in his life and placed under house detention in the 'Adhrawiyya *madrasa*. At this point 'Assaf converted to Islam and proved to the satisfaction of the court that the charge of blasphemy had been the result of a plot perpetrated by his enemies; he was released. A short time later 'Assaf traveled to Mecca, where he was killed by his cousin.[7]

Ibn Taymiyya was released from prison and composed *Al-Sarim al-Maslul* to elucidate the legal questions of the case. Thus although this work was occasioned by the action of an individual Christian towards Islam, it could not be called polemical in the same sense as Ibn Taymiyya's later works. A close examination of this work shows, in fact, that Ibn Taymiyya's concern and motivation in writing this work was totally unconnected with *any* polemical intent.

The major questions treated in this work are four and show, even in this early work, an attitude typical of Ibn Taymiyya, by which he interprets Islam as a principle of social organization. The first matter which Ibn Taymiyya treats is to demonstrate that anyone defaming a prophet *must* be executed, whether he is a Muslim or not.[8] Secondly, this capital sentence is not to be conceived as a maximum sentence, so that on occasion lesser punishments, such as the enslavement of the offender or the payment of financial retribution, might be exacted; rather, it is an obligatory sentence, which must be passed by the governor.[9] This sentence is obligatory even if the offender is a *dhimmi* and thus exempt from some aspects of Islamic law.

The third matter treated by Ibn Taymiyya is whether the one who has insulted the prophet should be urged to repent or whether he should be put to death directly without that attempt.[10] The answer, which Ibn Taymiyya attempts to show from *hadith* and the opinions of the *salaf* and the early imams, is the latter. In detailing the law on this, Ibn Taymiyya states that even if the person who has insulted the prophet has repented, and if he had been a *dhimmi* and becomes a Muslim, it is still necessary that he be put to death.[11]

The final question that Ibn Taymiyya takes up is an important one in view of the seriousness of the offence and its punishment. What precisely constitutes such an insult? The legal decisions apply *a fortiori* to someone who has cursed or insulted God, but a number of questions still remain. Ibn Taymiyya concluded affirmatively that someone who has insulted not only Muhammad but any of the prophets must be killed, whether he be Muslim or unbeliever. However, one who has slandered the wives of the Prophet or the rightly guided caliphs or the Companions of the Prophet is an unbeliever, but not a *murtadd* worthy of death.[12] (The distinction between *ridda* [apostasy], which is worthy of death, and *kufr* [unbelief], which is not, which Ibn Taymiyya makes carefully here in his first major work and applies later in his judgments on Al-Hallaj and Ibn 'Arabi among others, has precise legal bases and implications. Neither term is one that he would ever use loosely or in mere invective.

Although *Al-Sarim al-Maslul* is usually listed among Ibn Taymiyya's polemical works against Christianity, the author conscientiously avoids involving himself in any polemical confrontation with Christians. The point which he makes time and again throughout this work is that it is irrelevant whether the defamer of the Prophet be Muslim or non-Muslim.

In his opinion, the crime is so serious that the case must be raised, and if guilty the offender must be executed. The fact that the offender in the particular case in Damascus was a Christian is no more an issue than is the fact that he subsequently repented and entered Islam.

Ibn Taymiyya's language in *Al-Sarim al-Maslul* is chosen to reinforce this position. The categories he uses are either believer and non-believer or Muslim and *dhimmi*. He purposefully limited himself to the precise legal terminology.

In this work Ibn Taymiyya can be seen reacting against the popular and emotional associations that surround religious issues. He had been arrested and imprisoned for the first time in his life for fomenting conflict between religious groups, and in doing so he gained an unwanted reputation as champion of Islam against its Christian detractors. In *Al-Sarim al-Maslul* he attempts to set his position straight; he is writing as he had previously acted—as a *faqih*. Has a law been broken, and if so what is the proper punishment? He rejects identification with popular partisanship of Damascene Muslims against Christians, just as he rejects a superficial and basically irrelevant solution—that of the Christian's repentance and conversion. Thus this work, although occasioned by Ibn Taymiyya's involvement in a religious confrontation between Christians and Muslims in Damascus, is his most consciously anti-polemical of those listed among his controversialist writings on Christianity.

## Wartime *fatwas* and *Al-Risala al-Qubrusiyya*

None of Ibn Taymiyya's later writings on Christianity can be dated so accurately, nor can their *Sitz im Leben* be so accurately pinpointed. However, a number of short *fatwas* and one major work, *Al-Risala al-Qubrusiyya*, can be said with some confidence to have arisen from the imperiled situation of Damascus of the years 699/1299-703/1303.

During these years the region of Damascus was invaded three times by the Mongols under the Ilkhan Ghazan.[13] Ghazan, along with many in his army, had accepted Islam a short time previously and, moreover, was supported by the Druze and 'Alawi Shi'a from the Jebel al-Druze and the Lebanon. They were also allied to an assortment of Christian peoples—Cypriots and Maltese, as well as those Christian elements described by Ibn Kathir as most hostile to Muslims—the Georgians and Armenians.[14] At times the Mamluk *amir* acquiesced to the realities of this powerful coalition, but Ibn Taymiyya consistently represented the opposition faction, even to the point of traveling to Cairo in 699/1300 to exhort the sultan Qalawun to *jihad*.[15]

Ibn Taymiyya also produced a number of *fatwas* in which he answered questions on whether or not Muslims could fight the Syrian Shi'a[16] and the Mongols.[17] It was not only lawful for Muslims to fight these peoples, he stated, but Islam demanded that these people be opposed. Because Shi'a do not follow the full prescriptions of the *shari'a* and because they befriend and give assistance to the enemies of Islam[18] they must be opposed by *jihad*. This judgment applies *a fortiori* to the Mongols; they are only Muslims in name, he states, pronouncing the *shahadatayn* and showing respect for Muhammad, but ignoring the demands of the *shari'a*.[19]

It is not by accident that these three groups—Shi'a, Mongols, and Christians—are allied, for their errors are theologically parallel. We have already seen Ibn Taymiyya's criticism of the Shi'a for their considering their imams to be infallible and allowing for divine *ittihad* and *hulul*. This same criticism is levied against the Mongols.

> The belief of these Tatars about Genghis Khan has been extreme. They believe that he is the son of God similar to what the Christian believes about Christ. They claim that the sun impregnated his mother. It descended through an aperture in her tent and entered her and thus she became pregnant. It is obvious to any religious person that this is a lie. It is merely an indication that he was a child of fornication.[20]

It is almost certainly out of this situation that Ibn Taymiyya wrote the *fatwa* mentioned by Ibn 'Abd al-Hadi concerning "fighting Christians and Maltese Christians allied to the Mongols."[21] Unfortunately this *fatwa* appears to be lost, and so one can only surmise at the precise reasons for the necessity of *jihad* against the Christian forces. From the prominent place the Christian analogies play in Ibn Taymiyya's *fatwas* against the Shi'a and the Mongols it can be assumed that the reasons would be parallel: failure to follow the *shari'a*, *ghuluw* in their attitude to Christ, and endangering Muslim lives and property.

In 699/1299 the Damascenes, who included Muslims and some Christians, defended themselves against the Mongol coalition and were severely defeated at Wadi Khazindar, their army put to rout, and many Damascenes taken prisoner. The Mongols occupied the city, but the following year Ghazan departed for Baghdad and left a governor in Damascus.

Ibn Taymiyya's activity at this time was bound up with obtaining proper treatment for the prisoners-of-war taken by the Mongols. He himself went to the camp of the Mongol general Bulay and negotiated for the release of the prisoners held there. Shortly after, in his letter to the king of Cyprus, Ibn Taymiyya described how the Mongol leader was willing to release the Muslim prisoners only.

> He said to me, "But the Christians we hold we have brought from Jerusalem and we will not release them." I said to him, "Whoever you have, whether Jew or Christian, are our protected peoples, and we do not agree to any prisoner-of-war—Muslim or *dhimmi*." By the will of God he released the Christians. This was our work and our uprightness and our reward is with God.[22]

The fate of other prisoners, however, was not so fortunate. In a letter to the Sultan al-Malik al-Nasir, Ibn Taymiyya describes how the Shi'a from Kasrawan and Jezzine sold their Muslim prisoners to the Cypriots.

> They informed the people of Cyprus and took possession of a portion of the coastline. And bearing the banner of the cross, they transported so many Muslim prisoners, weapons, and horses to Cyprus that only God knows the number. There they set up a market for twenty days where they sold Muslims, horses, and weapons to the people of Cyprus.[23] Thus they celebrated the coming of the Tatars—they and the rest of the people of this accursed *madhhab* (sect).

*Jihad* must be waged against these sectarians, Ibn Taymiyya told the sultan, and in fact, a successful campaign was waged against the people of Kasrawan in 699/1300 in which Ibn Taymiyya participated.

All this wartime activity set the stage for Ibn Taymiyya's first important work that can be properly called a polemic against the Christians. This was a letter written by the shaykh to Sirjwas the king of Cyprus requesting good treatment for the Muslim prisoners who were interned there. Most commonly referred to as *Al-Risala al-Qubrusiyya*, the letter is important for a number of reasons. It is the work which most closely resembles *Al-Jawab al-Sahih* in content, and, preceding the latter work as it does by over twenty years, it indicates how early Ibn Taymiyya's basic approaches to Christianity were formed. Viewed in retrospect from the standpoint of *Al-Jawab al-Sahih*, Ibn Taymiyya's attitude towards Christianity developed very little during his lifetime. The course of his life was not like Al-Ghazali's, with dramatic shifts of position and direction. He demonstrates, rather, a consistent theological synthesis, which he applied in all situations from early in his life as teacher in the Hanbali madrasa in Damascus until his final years when he was imprisoned in the citadel of the same city.

One is not surprised to find him using the same argumentation and making the case for Islam by the same logic and illustrations which he will later use in *Al-Jawab al-Sahih*. Where there is development, it is in scope and detail (the apology to Paul of Antioch is twenty-five times as long as *Al-Risala al-Qubrusiyya*), and thus the Qur'anic citations, the multiple refutations of Christian theology, and the numerous digressions which comprise a large portion of *Al-Jawab al-Sahih* are missing in this early work. The central thread of argumentation, however, is identical in the two works and may be easily traced in both.

The tone of *Al-Risala al-Qubrusiyya* is conciliatory and understated. The argumentation from the Qur'an is supportive, rather than expository. The letter is consciously modeled on the letters sent by Muhammad to his contemporary Christian monarchs, and the argument is designed to bring the unbelieving king to a recognition of the truth of Islam and its obligations. Ibn Taymiyya does not hesitate to call himself a representative of the truth to the Christian king, as he is confident that the message of the prophets is one, and in offering Sirjwas the truth of Islam, he is thereby delivering the teaching of Christ. He does not ask for the release of the prisoners-of-war, but merely good treatment of them. As people of the Abrahamic tradition (*umma hanifiyya*), Muslims deserve special consideration from Christians, much as the Islamic community singles them out for *dhimmi* status. At this point it might be beneficial to investigate more closely the theological method of *Al-Risala al-Qubrusiyya* in order to provide a basis for recognition of the same argumentation in *Al-Jawab al-Sahih*.

Ibn Taymiyya begins with the same salutation found in the letters of Muhammad to the Muqawqus of Egypt and to Heraclius, as preserved in the collections of the sound hadiths—"Peace be upon him who follows the Guidance."[24] By this choice of openings Ibn Taymiyya consciously identifies himself with a particular aspect of the prophetic role which Muhammad passes on to the community, that of inviting the unbelievers to Islam. This prophetic commission upon the community will play an important role in *Al-Jawab al-Sahih*.

Ibn Taymiyya's choice of phrases is determined by his desire to begin with what the Christian already believes and to lead him from there to Islam. Thus he praises Muhammad, the seal of the prophets:

> who was announced by Jesus, the son of Mary, the Messiah of true guidance, the servant of God, His spirit, and His word which He sent down upon Mary the daughter of Imran, the spotless virgin whom no man had ever sullied.[25]

God has made His will known by what He has commanded. The basis for true service of God is found in the knowledge and love of God, "the kind of love a young child has for its mother."[26] God's true believers permit no friend, mediator, angel, or prophet to share in their worship of Him, for all creation is to Him but a servant.

A salvation history is recounted, beginning with Adam and continuing through the early prophets to the time of Jesus. At that time there were two groups of people who formed the foundation of the two sects of the People of the Book. The first group rejected Christ and thereby disbelieved. The second exaggerated in accepting him and claimed that he was the son of God. Thus they described God, the Rock who is neither born nor gives birth nor has any equal, as being born and taking a son, as being humiliated, crucified, and killed.

This latter group (Christians) differ among themselves on all of their innovations and they mutually curse each other. They seize upon obscure passages in the Gospel which did not appear in any of the earlier sacred books, and, by inserting into their faith notions which go against the nature of God, they have corrupted the true prophetic religion. In this way the majority of their bishops and popes discarded the religion of Christ in favor of the ideas of the pagan philosophers against whom Abraham was sent. Their monks invented superstitions which deceived ignorant people, although those who were intelligent could tell that such things were frauds.

Thus, the first group, the Jews, belittled the prophets and even killed them, while the other—Christians—exaggerated their status until they worshiped them and worshiped even their statues. The first group claims that it is not permitted for God to change and abrogate by a later prophet what He previously commanded by a previous one; the other claims that their own leaders can permit what God forbade and can forbid what He permitted.

> The first group state "God has made many things *haram* for us." The others hold, "For us anything between a bedbug and an elephant is *halal*."[27]

The two religions divided up into conflicting parties, and the Christians into mutually contradictory sects of Jacobites, Nestorians, and Melkites. There were groups, however, both in early and later times who went out from these groups to God and His prophets, and discovered in the books of God indications of the coming Seal of the prophets, which they found in the unchanged places of the sacred books. At last God sent the one that Christ and the earlier prophets had announced and recalled the people to the community of Abraham and the prophets and to the true service of God.

Muhammad's call to the religion of the prophets is described, as is the response in faith and obedience of those who were seeking the truth. The universality of that call, since it is not under challenge at this point, does not receive the great emphasis which Ibn Taymiyya will give to it in *Al-Jawab al-Sahih*. The community formed by the divine message only permits what God permitted, only forbids what God has forbidden. Thus it is a community mediate between harshness and laxity, loving and being desirous of what is good for everyone.

This brings Ibn Taymiyya to the point of his letter. He has heard favorable reports about the king from Muslim travelers and, convinced of the king's desire for knowledge and goodness, he has begun this correspondence with him. It has even occurred to Ibn Taymiyya to go to Cyprus to meet with the king.[28] The problem at hand concerns the treatment of Muslim prisoners-of-war who are in the custody of Sirjwas.

Ibn Taymiyya relates the role he played in obtaining the release of the Christian prisoners held by the self-proclaimed Muslim Mongols. In spite of their profession of Islam, many actions and attitudes of the Mongols were corrupt and intolerable from an Islamic point of view. Ibn Taymiyya did not hesitate to inform them of their errors, and it is in the same spirit that he addresses the king. He is not a humble suppliant begging mercy, but writing from a position of strength—the strength of Islam, which arises from its divine support and protection. Islam was at the peak of its strength at the time he was writing, Ibn Taymiyya states, for it was the beginning of the new century (701-702/1301-1302), and God's promise of the *mujaddid* would be fulfilled.[29]

The errors of the Christians are briefly enumerated—their belief in the trinity, *tahrif* of Scripture, and innovation of practices. He does not distinguish, as he later will, between the differing Christian theologies of the trinity. He affirms textual *tahrif* more strongly and with less precision in *Al-Risala al-Qubrusiyya* than he does later in *Al-Jawab al-Sahih*:

> They distort (*yuharrif*) the texts of the Torah and the Gospel. In the four gospels there is contradiction and opposition between what God has commanded and what is obligated in them.[30]

In this *risala* he does not attack the conciliar system as the primary cause of the institutional *bid'a* in Christianity. However, he does state that many of their errors were inspired by the philosophers. This view, which Ibn Taymiyya will give a serious development in *Al-Jawab al-Sahih*, is a relatively new one in the history of the polemic and can be associated with Ibn Taymiyya's view of the philosophers as essentially anti-prophetic and thus anti-religious.

For all these reasons Muslims are commanded to wage *jihad* against Christians. However, Christ and the apostles never commanded their followers to wage *jihad*, especially against God-fearing monotheists.

> So how can you, O king, permit the shedding of blood, the capture of women, and the seizing of goods against the will of God and His prophets.[31]

Furthermore, many of his people have acted treacherously regarding the Muslim prisoners. How can the king permit this when such things are forbidden by all religions? Since the Islamic community is the most beloved to God, He will punish those who mistreat its followers, and He will reward those who treat them well.

The king must know also that among Muslims there are fedayeen who assassinate kings in their living quarters, even in their own beds. Among them also are good men whose prayers God does not ignore, whose requests He does not spurn, and whose anger arouses anger in God.

It is extraordinary that Christians should be taking prisoners in the first place. Christ said, "Whoever strikes you on the right cheek turn to him the left, and whoever takes your cloak give him also your shirt." He commanded mercy and goodness to all people—to enemies, and especially to the weak and the poor. A Christian might claim, "But they began the war against us." It is debatable who began the war, but the teaching of Christ and the apostles makes this question irrelevant.

In all of this Ibn Taymiyya is asking two responses from the king. Firstly, the king should sincerely seek knowledge and religion, work to discover truth, put an end to his involvement in disputes and warfare, and strive to serve God as He wills. Secondly, he should give the Muslim prisoners good treatment.

In conclusion, he states that this message is truly the message of Christ and the earlier prophets.

> Thus I am one of the representatives of Christ and the rest of the prophets in giving advice to the king and his companions and in desiring what is good for them.[32]

Christ will return again upon the white tower in Damascus to break the cross, to slaughter the pig, and to defeat the Dajjal, the anti-Christ. This imagery of the return of Christ which will precede the Judgment Day appears surprisingly often in Ibn Taymiyya's writing and is compiled from hadith reports.[33]

Thus ends Ibn Taymiyya's letter to the king of Cyprus. History has not reported the Cypriot reaction to the letter, or whether the treatment of Muslim prisoners was ameliorated. The letter did have an important effect, however, in establishing a correspondence between Ibn Taymiyya and the Cypriot court. It would be from here that the "Letter from Cyprus" would be sent to the shaykh upon his final return to Damascus. This in turn would prompt Ibn Taymiyya's *Al-Jawab al-Sahih*, completing the dialogue more than twenty years after it had begun.

## *Mas'alat al-Kana'is*

In the year 700/1301 administrative measures were taken against the People of the Book by the Mamluk sultanate. Jewish and Christian officeholders lost their posts, and some churches were closed. In Cairo, where the measures were carried out more strictly than elsewhere, the churches were closed for a year. Dress codes were instituted; Christians were made to wear blue turbans, Jews yellow, and Samaritans red ones.[34]

The reason for these measures is unclear, but Laoust poses the conjecture that it was a counteroffensive of the Mamluks against those elements in the population thought to be sympathetic to the Mongols. It may also have had to do with a crisis of unpopularity of the regime at the time, and hence an attempt by the sultanate to court popular favor.[35]

It is out of this situation of practical confrontation between the religious groups that a number of works on Christianity from Ibn Taymiyya's "middle period" come. This group includes the *Mas'alat al-Kana'is* and a number of shorter *fatwas* on related subjects.

It was again in his role as *faqih* that Ibn Taymiyya confronted these issues. Christians were claiming that the closure of churches was wrongfully done, because the agreement with 'Umar allowed them the right to keep them open. Since it was opposed to the policies of the rightly guided caliphs, the closure of churches could not be legally defended.

Ibn Taymiyya dismisses the Christian argument as a falsehood opposed to the consensus of Muslims. *'Ulama'* from all four schools, the early Imams, and even the Companions and the Followers:

> are all in agreement that were the ruler to destroy every church in *'unwa* land—such as the land of Egypt, the river valleys of Iraq, and the territory of Syria—he would be *mujtahid* in that and would be following those who considered that proper. There would not be any *zulm* [wrongdoing] in that on his part; rather, he would be owed obedience and assistance in that from him who thought that proper.[36]

He continues to elucidate Islamic law on the matter, stating that it is not permitted to build churches in new cities built by Muslims. Ancient churches may remain on *sulh* land,[37] but no new ones may be built. If no new ones could be built on *sulh* land, how could they be erected on new land, when Cairo was known to have been built 300 years after the time of 'Umar?

How did this unlawful situation arise in which churches had been built in the new city of Cairo? The blame must fall on the Fatimids, whom Ibn Taymiyya describes as having governed for 200 years outside the *shari'a* of Islam.

> They publicly claimed to be *Rafida* [Shi'a] but inwardly were Isma'ilis, Nusayris, and Batini Qaramita. As al-Ghazali said about them, "They manifest the view of Rafd; their hidden belief is pure *kufr*."[38]

He describes the cooperation between the descendents of the Fatimids—the Isma'ilis, Nusayris, and Druzes of Syria—who cooperated with Christians in assisting Mongols to fight Muslims. Throughout their history they have consistently made treaties and pacts with the enemies of Islam. It is well known in recent times how they transported Muslim prisoners and materiel to Cyprus; similarly it was the Shi'a who invited the Mongols to invade Iraq, destroy Baghdad, and kill the Khalifa.

In Egypt there had been long-standing cooperation between the Fatimids and the Crusaders. The Fatimids had Jews and Christians for wazirs; it was under a well-known Armenian Christian wazir that many churches were built and the status of Christians enhanced.[39] In short, "The Shi'a are the worst of all sects associated with the *qibla*."

It is not surprising that they were unsuccessful militarily against the Crusaders. By contrast, Salah al-Din and his family were victorious because they dispensed with assistance from the Christians and carried out God's commands concerning them; like earlier conscientious rulers such as 'Umar ibn 'Abd al-'Aziz and Harun al-Rashid they were supported by God and made victorious for establishing correct relations with the People of the Book. Other rulers who strayed from this path were defeated and overcome.

He continues with an argument that arises from the daily conflict of competing religious groups, rather than from revealed information.

> Every Muslim knows that they only do business in the lands of the Muslims for their own ends, not for the benefit of the Muslims. Were their rulers to forbid them this, their greed for wealth would prevent them from obeying.[40]

They are the people most desirous for wealth, he adds in a comment reminiscent of al-Jahiz, and they even gamble with each other in their churches.

Muslims are in no way in need of Christians and should try to make themselves independent of them. Their armies, for example, should consist only of believing Muslims. (One wonders whether Ibn Taymiyya had supported or opposed Christian assistance in the defense of Damascus against the Mongols in 699/1299-701/1301.) Finally, he concludes *Mas'alat al-Kana'is* with a warning against Muslims' establishing treaties with Christians and declares that it is better for Muslims to make use of a Muslim with fewer capabilities than a Christian with more.

Besides *Mas'alat al-Kana'is*, Ibn Taymiyya wrote a number of short *fatwas* similar to it in tone and subject matter. All dealt with the practical problems arising from the tension between the need for the Muslim community to exist in a pluralist society and yet to separate itself from any elements which may contaminate its pure monotheism. Thus, in all these *fatwas* Ibn Taymiyya is guided by a constant principle—that of attempting to isolate each *milla* in society from the other as the best means for preserving pure *tawhid* among Muslims.

This was the spirit behind the prescriptions of 'Umar,[41] and Ibn Taymiyya recommends that they be reinstituted in their entirety. Although Christians and Jews have always found these particularly insulting, their purpose, according to Ibn Taymiyya, is to structure a situation in which every detail of life is done in such a manner by Muslims whereby the original motivation is frozen and retained. "Anything new is *bid'a*, and every *bid'a* is an error."[42] Such an attempt to preserve and recreate a pristine religious inspiration must ultimately place greater strictures on Muslim life than on that of those outside it. Except for committed visionaries like Ibn Taymiyya, this ideal would hold little appeal, and it is not surprising that almost all of these *fatwas* remained dead letters.

The subject of Christian churches was raised frequently by Ibn Taymiyya in various legal judgments, and he concludes that churches unlawfully erected, such as all those in Cairo, should be razed. It should not be possible for worship services of unbelievers to be carried on in the same place which is used for the prayers of Muslims.[43] Thus the early practice, known in places like Damascus and Homs, of using separate portions of one and the same building for Islamic and Christian prayers is condemned by Ibn Taymiyya.

Churches which fall into disrepair must not be restored,[44] and no outward evidences of Christianity should appear in cities or villages in which Muslims live.[45] Several times Ibn Taymiyya blames the Fatimids for letting abuses develop, such as allocating state money for the maintenance of churches "where God and his prophet are subject to the worst calumny."[46]

Ibn Taymiyya upholds a special dress code for Christians, stating that they should not only wear different types and colors of clothes from Muslims but that their hair and beards should be cut differently from those of Muslims. He had been encouraging various Mamluk sultans to institute such a code; Ibn Qayyim writes that an unnamed sultan prescribed such regulations, but the Christians began complaining. They complied and changed their dress so that it differed from Muslims, they said, but when they went out into the street, their dress was a cause for their being severely mistreated by hooligans. They returned to their former dress and brought a case before the sultan upon which Ibn Taymiyya passed judgment. Three times he adjudged that they must return to the prescribed dress; when finally the case was taken to the sultan, his judgment was upheld.[47]

Ibn Taymiyya dismissed a popular but spurious hadith from the Prophet which said "Whoever harms a *dhimmi* harms me." This would amount to an absolute protection given to unbelievers; moreover it would make a travesty of justice, for, just as in the case of Muslims, there are times when they deserve punishment and physical harm.[48] Similarly a prophetic hadith which forbids the killing of monks came by custom to mean that monks need not pay the *jizya*. Ibn Taymiyya declares that the hadith includes no justification for this, and on the matter of the monks paying the *jizya* he distinguishes between anchorites living in seclusion and prayer, who need pay no *jizya*, and monks carrying on businesses or engaged in agriculture. *Jizya* should be collected from these people as from other persons of substance.[49]

Christians should not be appointed to posts of authority or as secretaries, and the Fatimid practice of this is severely criticized.[50] Under certain conditions the property of Christians may be confiscated.[51] On the other hand, Ibn Taymiyya affirms that it is permissible for Muslims to be treated by Christian and Jewish doctors.[52]

Although the exact date cannot be known for any of these writings, they seem to fall into the period 703/1303-705/1305, when tensions between Muslims and Christians developed in Cairo. As a respected *faqih* Ibn Taymiyya was in the midst of these disputes, and his uncompromising legal approach to these questions must have endeared him neither to *fuqaha'* of the more flexible legal traditions nor to the People of the Book against whom he most often decided.

In the years 709/1309-710/1310 Ibn Taymiyya again became particularly preoccupied with the Christian question,[53] and it is likely that his *risala*, *Tahrim Musharakat Ahl al-Kitab fi A'yadihim*, was written at this time. In this case the impetus came from an abuse within the Islamic community itself. This was the widespread participation in Christian feast-days and their festivals. Christian feasts like Epiphany, Christmas, the Thursday and Saturday before Easter, as well as the Persian *Nauruz*, were being celebrated by Muslims and Christians alike.[54] It was not so much a question of Muslim participation in primary acts of worship, which, apart from walking in popular processions on occasions of Christian feasts, does not seem to have occurred. The problem which Ibn Taymiyya addresses is Muslim participation in the secondary events which surround the feasts.

Many people were apparently of the opinion that activities like coloring Easter eggs, fixing a special meal, wearing new clothes, decorating houses, and lighting fires on the occasion of feasts was a matter of custom rather than any participation in disbelief. Ibn Taymiyya states, on the contrary, that Muslims not only may not themselves participate in these acts, but they may in no way support these feasts by selling Christians anything needed for the feast or giving them presents. Some *'ulama'* permit this, he states, and thereby fall into *kufr*. The reason is reflected in a prophetic hadith, "Whoever cultivates resemblance with a people is one of them." The same motivation produced the shaykh's stand on dress codes for Christians and the public manifestation of churches. Islam can only be kept pure by separating itself from contact with unbelief. Any of the acts surrounding the Christian feasts might be harmless in themselves, but by consciously imitating the actions of unbelievers, Muslims cease to maintain a condition of separateness. The role of the government is to establish the *shari'a*; in this case it means that the sultans must prohibit Muslims from giving or selling Christians anything which they might use in their feasts.[55]

A closely related problem, and one that Ibn Taymiyya sees as even more serious, is the imitation of Christian practices in the observance of festivals within the Islamic community. Muslims who prepare banners and form processions for the *mawlids* or who visit tombs to make intercessory prayer are merely imitating the *shirk* of Christians. As he says in *Iqtida' al-Sirat al-Mustaqim*, the great work in which Ibn Taymiyya deals throughout with this question, "He who wears someone's clothes begins to act like him."[56]

At this time the situation must have appeared to Ibn Taymiyya as a struggle between the ideal of the restoration of the pristine Islamic state and the People of the Book, who by the excess of power that they had obtained, were attempting to frustrate that goal. There still exists a letter from Ibn Taymiyya in Cairo to his relatives in Damascus dated A.H. 709, in which he requests that they send him his copy of *Mas'alat al-Kana'is* and several other works. He describes the situation in Cairo in terms of struggle where the forces of truth will be granted victory and mastery over those of falsehood, which will always be brought low. Thus conditions have been laid on the communities in error which will work for the victory of Islam and the defeat of their innovation and unbelief. This condition will bring about

> the glory of Islam and the subjection of the Jews and Christians after they had become arrogant and had obtained power.[57]

Ibn Taymiyya seems to have come to the conclusion that it was primarily through the attraction of their festivals that the *bid'a* into which Christians had fallen would enter and infect the Islamic community. He is convinced that there is something innately attractive in their *ghuluw* to man's natural aptitude for *shirk*. Thus, it is only in the Islamic community's separating itself from all manifestations of their religious attitude that the Muslim *umma* can maintain its integrity.

> More than any other sect Christians have exaggerated in their beliefs and religious practices. It follows necessarily that the more one avoids their guidance absolutely, the further will he be from falling into the destruction which has overtaken them.[58]

## *Iqtida' al-Sirat al-Mustaqim*

If in *Al-Risala al-Qubrusiyya* Ibn Taymiyya presented in outline form the line of argumentation which he would develop reflectively and in detail in *Al-Jawab al-Sahih*, a parallel case can be seen in the short *risala* described above and the major work *Iqtida' al-Sirat al-Mustaqim*. The latter work, usually dated about 721/1321,[59] adds no new approach to the subject matter of *Tahrim Musharakat Ahl al-Kitab fi A'yadihim*; rather, it elaborates in detail the argumentation implicit in the earlier short work.

In light of the recent (1977) publication of an excellent study on *Iqtida' al-Sirat al-Mustaqim* by M. 'Umar Memon,[60] it will not be necessary here to give a complete outline of the polemical argument in this work. Instead, I will summarize Memon's thesis and then mention several issues peripheral to Memon's theme, but which nevertheless pertain to Ibn Taymiyya's view of Christianity.

In Memon's view, Ibn Taymiyya's fight against popular devotions in order to reestablish the pure Islamic society of the Companions was doomed to failure. Aside from the fact that the community of the *salaf* might never have been so uncontaminated by non-Islamic influences as later tradition thus idealized it, history had moved on, and Islam had assimilated elements not explicitly expressed in the life of its earliest generations. This process was natural and inevitable because it responded to basic needs of human nature for a religious expression of subconscious and emotional movements of the human spirit.

> With all his resourcefulness and zeal, Ibn Taymiyya failed to recreate Muslim society in the image of its *salaf*. The innovations could not be wiped out and, as a final irony to his perilous enough career, soon after his death he became the cherished object of a veneration in discrediting which he had dedicated the best years of his life.
>
> His failure lay in denying any validity to the historical reality of Islam which had, away from its rigid orthodoxy, evolved in a series of brisk interactions with the traditions and faiths of diverse peoples, and in trying to comprehend the unconscious depths, the irrational side of the human mind through a medium of perception devised essentially for rational thought.[61]

Using prophetic hadith as his basis, Ibn Taymiyya develops the idea that the dissimilarity between believers and non-Muslims must be total. The prophet's injunction calls for a categorical difference, not merely a singularity expressed in secondary and marginal aspects of life. A major portion of *Iqtida' al-Sirat al-Mustaqim* is devoted to detailing this differentiation in every aspect of life—dress, language (Muslims should speak Arabic in preference to anything else),[62] personal appearance (much space is given to questions of cutting the hair and beard in a manner different from that of Jews and Christians), and, most of all, in acts of worship. For example, voluntary fasts by Muslims undertaken on days customary to Jews and Christians is seen as reprehensible imitation; similarly, Islamic feasts should be fixed by the sighting of the moon rather than by writing or computation, for the latter are techniques used by non-Muslims.[63]

The presence of the People of the Book in Islamic society is seen as a constant danger to the Islamic ideal. Although, as he mentioned in *Al-Risala al-Qubrusiyya*, Ibn Taymiyya recognizes a particular complex of bonds and responsibilities among the three religions deriving from their common Abrahamic origins and possession of the sacred books, nevertheless, the People of the Book are unbelievers whose presence must be carefully controlled so that it can be prevented from offering an occasion of *bid'a* and *kufr* to Muslims.

> In Ibn Taymiyya's vision of a true Islamic state there was, if at all, very little room for the religious minorities. The vision was particularly harsh to the Jews and Christians who must live in complete social isolation, Muslim contempt, and under the humiliating obligation of the *jizya*. This idea was very nearly realized by the early caliphs and was continued in varying degrees of stringency by others as well.[64]

Ibn Taymiyya's view, although it would always be considered extreme by the majority of Muslims, had a logical consistency. The religions of the Book, more especially Christianity because of a fertile history in which it outstripped all other peoples in innovating exaggerated forms of worship, appeared to Ibn Taymiyya as active agents of unbelief. From this point of view he sees the festivals of the People of the Book as even greater dangers to Islam than the remnants of pagan celebrations which still existed in fossilized form.

> The feasts and worship undertaken by the religions of the two Peoples of the Book are more strongly forbidden than a [pagan] feast undertaken for amusement and play. An act of worship which is displeasing and hateful to God is a greater evil than following one's desires in what He has forbidden. Thus, *shirk* is a greater sin than fornication, and *jihad* against the People of the Book is superior to *jihad* against the idolators.[65]

In *Iqtida'* Ibn Taymiyya developed a concept which provides an insight into his understanding of his own role and that of others like him in the context of Islamic history. He states that the Jahiliyya may be said to be continuing in existence in Islamic lands and in fact among a great many Muslims. The resistance to the implications of the Qur'anic message found among Jahiliyya Arabs and their compromising of pure *tawhid* by *shirk* are phenomena not entirely wiped out by the triumph of Islam.[66] There is a specific role of a small portion of the community to continue the *da'wa*, to proclaim to the Muslim community in every age the unadulterated *tawhid* brought by the prophets.

Ibn Taymiyya elsewhere refers to this small body of faithful whose mission it is to continually call Muslims back to the purity of Islamic faith, and it is with this group he identifies himself. It is from this understanding of his own mission that the uncompromising nature of his writing springs. He was not so benighted as to think that because of his preaching, legal decisions, and political pressures popular celebrations would be eliminated from Muslim life or that the prescriptions of 'Umar would be reimposed on the *Ahl al-Dhimma* in any permanent way. Rather, he felt that in every age uncompromised truth must be spoken by a small coterie of Muslims and that preaching contained its own value and reward with God. It was hoped that the great body of Muslims would comply with the message of truth, but in no way was it this compliance which lent value to the act of preaching.

> Even if it were supposed that not a single person would quit this hateful imitation, at least recognition and belief in its wickedness would be known. Even if it is not acted upon, the very belief and knowledge of what is hateful to God is worthwhile. The benefit arising from knowledge and belief is even greater than that which comes from a simple act to which no knowledge is joined.[67]

Although there is no way of knowing for certain, both Memon and Laoust place the date of *Iqtida' al-Sirat al-Mustaqim* at a time contemporaneous with the writing of *Al-Jawab al-Sahih* and with the religious tensions and hostilities mentioned by Al-Maqrizi.[68] More than any other work of Ibn Taymiyya's, the immediate occasion for writing *Iqtida'* approximates that of *Al-Jawab al-Sahih*.

# CHAPTER 7

## PAUL OF ANTIOCH'S CHALLENGE TO ISLAM

*Al-Jawab al-Sahih* was not composed as an isolated speculative study on the Christian religion, but in a truly polemical context. It is a response to a treatise written by a Christian to Muslims. The Christian work is the *Letter to a Muslim* by Paul of Antioch, the Bishop of Saida. It is the challenges to Islam raised by the bishop which form the structural framework of *Al-Jawab al-Sahih*. Ibn Taymiyya's critique of Christianity is strongly shaped by, although not limited to, the questions raised by Paul of Antioch. Hence a brief discussion of the Christian treatise does not seem out of place.

The outlines of Paul of Antioch's life are not well known. Although twenty-four distinct treatises in Arabic are in one way or another credited to him,[1] the collection of solid facts about his life presents a number of lacunae. Of the works credited to him, some are certainly incorrectly attributed, and the number of works whose authenticity is undisputed is five.

We must discard the early hypothesis that Paul of Antioch was a contemporary of Ibn Taymiyya's and that it was against him that several of the bishop's works were written.

> Perhaps it is Ibn Taymiyya himself, against whom Paul was exercising his energies in the last of the three treatises paraphrased here ["An Answer to a Shaykh"].[2]

Al-Qarafi's *Al-Ajwiba al-Fakhira* presupposes Paul of Antioch's *Letter to a Muslim*, and thus the bishop must certainly have written it before al-Qarafi's death in 683/1285. Other indications place the date much earlier than that, and there seems no compelling reason to dispute Khoury's hypothesis that Paul of Antioch lived between 534/1140 and 575/1180.[3]

Sayda' was at this time controlled by the Crusaders, and the Melkite bishop Paul seems to have had frequent dealings with Byzantine and European Christian leaders. His writings are primarily controversialist, although his polemical writings, like Ibn Taymiyya's, usually concerned disputes within his own religion. Thus he produced a study of Christian sects.[4] which is analogous to the *al-milal wal-nihal* literature common among Islamic writers. His writings include treatises against pagan disbelievers and the Jews, as well as an exposition of the Melkite position on controverted points of Christian trinitarian theology.

Paul's *Letter to a Muslim* (*Risala ila Ahad al-Muslimin*)[5] is allegedly written to a Muslim friend in Sayda and claims to treat questions about Islam directed at Paul by Christians during the course of his journeys. Both elements of this allegation are suspect of being literary devices created to give a structure of dialogue and topicality to this carefully composed defense of Christianity.[6]

The main theme is that there is nothing in Islam which can challenge, teach, or save Christians. This is not to say that Islam is a fraud as a revealed religion, that Muhammad was not a prophet, or that the Qur'an is not revealed scripture. Paul does not deny the legitimacy of the Qur'anic relevation through Muhammad and its embodiment in the Islamic *din* and *shari'a*; what he holds is that there is nothing in it which can challenge the nature of Christianity as an ultimate, self-contained instrument of salvation. The force of his argument, then, is not to accuse Islam of being false, but of being irrelevant and superfluous to Christianity.

His first point is to challenge the universality of Muhammad's prophetic nature. Muhammad may well have been sent with the Qur'an to the pagan Arabs of the *Jahiliyya*, but Christians in the time of Paul of Antioch can be confident that Muhammad was not sent to them. His argumentation here, as throughout the *risala*, is primarily from the Qur'an. He concludes:

> We know that he was not sent to us, but to the Arabs of the Jahiliyya of whom he said that there had come to them no warner before him. We know that he did not obligate us to follow him because there had come to us before him prophets who had preached and warned us in our own languages, and who handed on to us the Torah and the Gospel in our own languages.[7]

Paul next recounts Qur'anic praise for Jesus and Mary, mentioning the Qur'anic story of the annunciation of Jesus's birth, his miracles as recounted in the Qur'an, and his assumption into heaven. He points out Qur'anic praise for the Gospel and for Christian hermitages (Qur'an 22:40), and concludes:

> These and other things compel us to hold fast to our religion and prevent us from abandoning our faith and rejecting what we have. For we follow no one but the Lord Christ, the Word of God, and his apostles whom he sent to us to bring us warning.[8]

He mentions Qur'anic passages in which the disciples of Christ are extolled, and the number of these passages is increased by Paul's application of the Qur'anic term *rusul* to the apostles of Christ. In Christian Arabic usage *rasul* is the common term to identify the disciples of Jesus, and thus this transference of the Qur'anic usage is natural for Paul. It will prove to be totally unacceptable for Ibn Taymiyya, however, and it will prompt him to include a long discourse in *Al-Jawab al-Sahih* on the difference between *nabi*, *rasul*, and *hawari*.

Ibn Taymiyya realizes the full implications of the argument which is implied but not elaborated by Paul of Antioch. Christians never claim the Gospel to have been written by Christ, but by his disciples. By identifying the disciples of Christ with the messengers of God (*rusul Allah*), Paul would thus grant to these authors of the Gospel an inerrancy indisputable from an Islamic point of view. Thus, a question is here raised which will demand a detailed treatment in *Al-Jawab al-Sahih*—that of the prophetic or non-prophetic status of the apostles of Jesus.

Again using Qur'anic argumentation, Paul of Antioch makes a case for the accuracy of the scriptures as used by the Christians of his time. The question of *tahrif* was a central issue in all polemical debates between Christians and Muslims. The term indicates the Muslim contention that the original prophet-delivered books of the Bible had been subsequently changed, either inadvertently or by conscious distortion and corruption. Other terms, such as *tabdil* and *taghyir*, were used besides *tahrif*, with meanings sometimes synonymous and sometimes subtly distinguished from it by the individual Muslim author.

The term *tahrif* finds its origin in the Qur'an. In its verbal form it indicates an accusation hurled four times (4:46; 5:13; 5:41; 2:75) against Jewish leaders and carries the meaning that they quote their Scriptures wrongly out of context. On this basis a distinction was made early in the polemical tradition between *tahrif al-lafz* and *tahrif al-ma'na*, the first referring to actual textual distortion and corruption, the second referring to the false and distorted interpretation of basically sound texts.

The early Muslim polemicists, such as 'Ali al-Tabari, the Zaydi al-Qasim ibn Ibrahim, and Al-Hasan ibn Ayyub, applied the concept of *tahrif al-ma'na* to the Christian as well as Jewish scriptures. The later polemicists of the Ash'arite school, such as Al-Baqillani, Al-Ghazali, and Fakhr al-Din al-Razi, also approached the Bible as basically sound in its text but misinterpreted by Christians and Jews.

Ibn Hazm, in his *Al-Fisal fi al-Milal wal-Ahwa' wal-Nihal,*[9] carefully built a case for the verbal corruption of the biblical text. According to Ibn Hazm, the Bible is not a message of God which contains some erroneous passages and words, but is of the status of an anti-Scripture, "an accursed book," the product of satanic inspiration. His conclusion marked a departure from the prevailing opinion before his time and was followed by subsequent writers only with careful qualifications. Although the majority of later polemicists rejected Ibn Hazm's conclusions as extreme, by the strength of his argumentation he influenced all subsequent polemical literature. The question of *tahrif* of scripture was one that no polemicist—Christian, Muslim, or Jewish—could leave untreated.

Paul of Antioch's approach is to claim that the Qur'an itself (5:48; 10:94) denies any possibility that *tabdil* could have occurred in the Bible. Using other Qur'anic passages, Paul of Antioch distinguishes between the way Muslims should relate to Jews and Christians. Jews, who have worshiped idols, performed human sacrifice, and killed the prophets deserve to have *jihad* waged against them. He states that Christians have never done any of those things and thus have deserved the Qur'anic praise (5:82) of being the "People nearest those who believe [i.e., Muslims] in friendship."

He states that this passage also praises Christian monks and priests, but more importantly it absolves Christians from the accusation of *shirk* brought by Muslims. The Qur'anic story of the Table (5:112-115) is interpreted by Paul of Antioch as an affirmation and praise of the Christian Eucharist. The Qur'an guarantees the continuance and faithfulness of Christians until the Day of Judgment (4:159), he holds, and it is Christians whom Muslims are enjoined to imitate in the Fatiha, when they pray to be guided along the path of those upon whom God's favor rests. Finally, Paul of Antioch concludes this section:

> For we know that God is just, but it is not compatible with His justice that on the Day of Judgment He would demand a people to have followed a prophet who had not been sent to them, especially when they could not become acquainted with his scripture in their own tongue neither on his authority nor on that of some preacher before him. Thus we do not follow this messenger, nor do we turn away from what we already have.[10]

At this point Paul begins a completely new subject in his letter, which in many ways is the most important issue he raises. This is the matter of trinitarian theology, and the subject is such that it cannot be avoided in any Muslim-Christian controversy. Paul of Antioch's approach is to minimize the differences between Islamic and Christian belief; he affirms strongly the unity of God and interprets the trinity in the light of Muslim sensibilities. By refusing to employ the Christian term *'uqnum* (hypostasis), and preferring to it the native Arabic and theologically neutral term *ism* (name), he is apparently attempting to disassociate his explanation from the polemical tradition which preceded him and to present the doctrine in a manner acceptable to Muslims. In reality, however, his approach is merely a restatement of the Nicaean formulation, and the evidence of Al-Qarafi, Muhammad ibn Abi Talib, and Ibn Taymiyya shows that to Muslims Paul's interpretation of the trinity is nothing more than a subtly nuanced tritheism.

He begins by stating that were Muslims to understand the Christian belief in the trinity rightly, they would find nothing objectionable in it. By it the Christians are using three names to express that the one God is an existing being (*shay'*), living (*hayy*), and speaking (*natiq*). As credential for this nomenclature he offers a number of citations from Old and New Testaments and the Qur'an.

All the names and attributes of God stem from the three substantival attributes (*al-sifat al-jawhariyya*) of existence, speech, and life. It is the second of these that explains the incarnation of the Word and the sonship of Christ, and Paul uses the traditional Christian Arab analogies of the light of the sun on earth and the word given birth from the mind to picture non-physical generation. In this way, he claims, the Qur'anic disassociation from a belief that God could beget and be begotten does not refer to Christian belief.

Paul of Antioch approaches the incarnation of the divine word in Jesus from another perspective. Christ is the total revelation of the divine nature, which had been hidden from mankind throughout history. It was this revelation of the godhead to which the miracles performed by Jesus pointed. The question of whether Jesus's miracles were done through his human or divine nature leads Paul into a discussion of the hypostatic union in Christ. He is careful to elucidate the Melkite position of the dual nature in the unique person.

Paul gathers a number of citations from the Old Testament which speak of God as father, or speak of individuals such as David as sons of God, or which refer to the indwelling of the divine spirit in men. He states that just as there was no multiplicity implied in the use of these names, neither is there any fault in Christ or his followers referring to God by the same names. God has taught Christians these names, he states, and they have no indication that would make them stop using them. As final confirmation of the permissibility of these names Paul lists their Qur'anic usage. Thus he endeavors to place the Christian usage squarely within the prophetic tradition of the three divine religions. This is an argument tailored for the polemic against Muslims, based as it is on the Islamic belief that the religion of the prophets is one. The Muslim polemicists who answer Paul of Antioch will reverse the argument and portray Christian usage of fatherhood and sonship as anomalous within and ultimately contradictory to the prophetic tradition.

> If it is your belief that the creator is one, then what induces you to call Him three hypostases, one of which you call a Father, another a son, and third a spirit. Thus you make hearers imagine that you believe in a God composed of three parts, or three gods, or three parts, and that He has a son. One who does not know your belief would suppose that you mean a child of human intercourse and generation.[11]

The Christian polemicist presumes that the Christian position of divine unity has been convincingly established by his previous argument, and the question remains of the adequacy of Christian theological terminology to define this belief. The Islamic position, as presented by Paul of Antioch, is that Christian terminology is intrinsically inadequate and misleading and cannot help but give a distorted picture of Christian belief.

Paul of Antioch admits the inadequacy of Christian formulations to accurately describe the doctrine of the trinity, and his defense is to attack Islamic anthromorphic expressions as a parallel and similarly inevitable phenomenon of the inability of human language to depict divine reality. He phrases his argument in terms parallel to the Islamic case above. One who did not know Islamic belief might suppose from Qur'anic expressions that God had a hand, a foot, that he descended in the shadows of the clouds, that He moved spatially from place to place.

> If they compel us to conclude by holding *shirk* and *tashbih* because of our view that God is one substance and three hypostases—father, son, and holy spirit—because the obvious meaning of that demands multiplicity and anthropomorphism of God, then we can make them logically conclude by affirming materialization and anthropomorphization for saying that God has two eyes, a face, a leg, and a side, that He sits upon the throne after he had not been doing so, and other expressions whose obvious meaning demands *tajassum* and *tashbih*![12]

The bishop devotes a long passage at this point to the question of whether or not God can be called a substance (*jawhar*). The issue seems peripheral to the development of Paul's letter, but it indicates a point of conflict between Muslims and Christians in the

6th/12th century. The Muslim objection is that divine transcendence demands the inapplicability to God of philosophical categories predicated of creatures. Although Christian theologians previous to this time frequently brought objections similar to those of Muslim scholars, which would prohibit the proper application of such categories to God,[13] Paul of Antioch is firmly within the Christian Arabic tradition in his usage of the term *jawhar* to translate the Greek *ousia* (essence/substance). Elsewhere he will use *dhat* and does not hesitate in his *Letter to a Muslim* to refer to God as *shay'*.[14]

In the final section of his letter, Paul of Antioch's purpose is to show the superfluity of Islam in the divine plan of salvation. The revealed religions are two—Judaism, the religion of law, and Christianity, the religion of grace. As the religion of grace, Christianity reaches the limit of perfection, beyond which Islam can neither add nor offer anything. Thus Christians need to look to Islam for nothing, nor have they anything to learn from Muslims.

That Paul of Antioch's letter was widely circulated may be deduced from Ibn Taymiyya's remarks about it:

> A letter arrived from Cyprus in which there is an argument for the religion of Christians. In it the scholars of their religion as well as the eminent persons of their church, ancient and modern, plead their case with religious and intellectual arguments. . . . That which they state in this book is the basic support on which their scholars depend, both in our time and in previous ages, although some of them may elaborate further than others depending on the situations. We have found them making use of this treatise before now. Their scholars hand it down among themselves, and old copies of it still exist.[15]

Ibn Taymiyya's contention that Paul of Antioch's letter was widely circulated in Christian circles and known as well by Muslim authors is confirmed by the fact that in the mid-7th/13th century Shihab al-Din Ahmad ibn Idris al-Qarafi[16] wrote an independent refutation of the bishop's work. Al-Qarafi's treatise, *Al-Ajwiba al-Fakhira 'an al-As'ila al-Fajira*, is the most ambitious and comprehensive of all Islamic polemical writings on Christianity prior to the time of Ibn Taymiyya. Although *Al-Ajwiba al-Fakhira* has been neglected in modern scholarship, the work was unsurpassed until modern times in many of its observations and arguments.

Al-Qarafi never refers to the Christian bishop by name and it is possible that he did not know the identity of the author. He mentions only a letter in dialogue form disseminated by Christians "containing argumentation from the Qur'an for the truth of the religion of Christianity."

> I discovered that it was in confusion about what has been revealed and in darkness concerning the judgments of reason, for our beloved Book as well as their Books indicate the truth of our religion (*madhhab*) and the falsity of theirs.[17]

Moreover Al-Qarafi does not cite Paul of Antioch verbatim, but merely paraphrases the bishop's statements. Although this makes Al-Qarafi's work useless for any textual study of Paul of Antioch, there can be no doubt that it was the *Letter to a Muslim* which he was refuting. He follows the thought of the Christian work carefully, accurately epitomizing its argumentation, and scrupulously preserving (much more than Ibn Taymiyya did) its internal arrangement.

In addition to Al-Qarafi's *Al-Ajwiba al-Fakhira*, one more Islamic response to Paul of Antioch deserves mention. Muhammad ibn Abi Talib,[18] living at the same time as Ibn Taymiyya in the region of Damascus, received in 721/1321 a copy of the same *Letter from Cyprus* that was sent to Ibn Taymiyya and wrote a refutation entitled *Risala li-Ahl Jazirat Qubrus.*[19]

His work was narrower in scope that *Al-Jawab al-Sahih*, being limited to questions raised in the Christian letter. The author's style is that of a fiery popular preacher, in contrast to the studious nature of Ibn Taymiyya's work. Some of the argumentation is very similar to that found in *Al-Jawab al-Sahih*, indicating that not all of the basic arguments in Ibn Taymiyya's work were unique to him.[20] There was a body of Islamic polemical material concerning Christianity that was known to the *'ulama'* of the day, and Ibn Taymiyya's originality can be best appreciated in his selection of commonly known arguments which he reworked and integrated into a consistent, unified theological outlook.

Paul of Antioch's letter was not always handed down in the same form. The letter received by Ibn Taymiyya and Muhammad ibn Abi Talib was a considerably expanded recension of the original work by Paul of Antioch. This expanded version[21] was not the work of Paul of Antioch and was produced, long after his death, in clerical circles on Cyprus. This conclusion is based on the fact that Al-Qarafi responded to the shorter version, which the soundest manuscript tradition testifies to be the original work of Paul of Antioch.[22] It was the later redaction which was sent from Cyprus to Ibn Taymiyya and Muhammad ibn Abi Talib. The relationship between these two versions has not yet been studied in detail, although Fritsch has noted the general correspondence between the two versions of the work.

> The textual alterations [over against the original] manifest themselves only in a few adaptations and additions, in the acquaintance [of the later version] with Old Testament references, and in the editing of the context narratives.[23]

This is something of an understatement of the matter. A close examination of the two works gives evidence of considerable expansion of the thought of Paul of Antioch in four areas. Firstly, the section on *tahrif* is considerably expanded with the addition of new arguments.[24]

Secondly—and it is in this area that the "Letter from Cyprus" principally differs from that of Paul of Antioch—citations from the Old Testament abound in the "Letter from Cyprus." The anonymous author of this Letter was well acquainted with the Hebrew prophets and cites them frequently in his claim to show the logical development of Christianity from the prophetic tradition and its historical validity within that tradition. Thus, to supplement Paul of Antioch's statement that the Jews were those who had incurred God's anger, the "Letter from Cyprus" produces a series of condemnations from the Hebrew prophets of the behavior of the Jews.[25] To support the statement in Paul of Antioch's work that the Christian doctrine of the trinity was not an innovation within the line of prophetic revelation, the "Letter from Cyprus" offers extensive citations from the Pentateuch, the psalms, and the Old Testament prophets.[26]

The addition of biblical prophecies of the Messiah in the "Letter from Cyprus,"[27] while they are as numerous as in the "trinitarian" citations, are harder to explain. Their purpose seems to have been to show that Christ was announced beforehand by the Hebrew prophets. This is in keeping with a traditional Christian polemical argument against Muslims that contrasted a belief in the announcement of Christ with a claim that Muhammad was not so announced. This claim is not made here, and since the Islamic tradition never denied the announcement of Jesus as the "Messiah of guidance," one can conclude that these passages were included in order to confirm the belief of Christians in the prediction of Jesus by the Hebrew prophets. The supposition seems to be that the concept of *Messiah* implies divine status, and it is by rejecting any implication of divinity to the concept "Messiah" that Ibn Taymiyya will reply to this line of argumentation.

In two notable places,[28] the additional passages in the "Letter from Cyprus" elaborate the Qur'anic argumentation of Paul of Antioch and offer citations from the Qur'an not mentioned by the bishop of Sayda'. And finally, in the most dramatic reworking of Paul of Antioch's *risala*, the "Letter from Cyprus" offers a revision of the treatment of the incarnation of the word of God in Jesus and the hypostatic union which resulted from that.[29]

The author of the "Letter from Cyprus" showed himself more willing to use specifically Christian terminology, such as *'uqnum*, than Paul of Antioch had been. In some places his principal motivation was to clarify the argument found in Paul of Antioch (52:79). Elsewhere, his strong reliance on biblical and Qur'anic citations seems to have been meant to place Christian beliefs more forcefully within the line of prophetic tradition.

For a study of *Al-Jawab al-Sahih* it is the "Letter from Cyprus" which is the more relevant of the two *risalas*. It is this version of the letter against which Ibn Taymiyya responded, although he was under the same impression as Muhammad ibn Abi Talib that the treatise (*kitab*) they received from Cyprus was that of Paul of Antioch.

It remains briefly to mention and describe two works which play an important role in the structure and argumentation of *Al-Jawab al-Sahih*. These are Al-Hasan ibn Ayyub's *Risala ila 'Ali ibn Ayyub* and Sa'id ibn Bitriq's *Nazm al-Jawhar*.

The first of these is a polemical work written by a convert to Islam from Christianity, Al-Hasan ibn Ayyub. The original extent of this work is unknown because only the portion quoted by Ibn Taymiyya, consisting of forty-nine pages, has survived.[30] He introduces the author and his *risala* as follows:

> One of the people most knowledgeable about their [the Christians'] views had been one of their *'ulama'*, Al-Hasan ibn Ayyub. After his experience with their Books and opinions he conscientiously accepted Islam and wrote a *risala* to his brother, 'Ali ibn Ayyub, in which he mentions the reason for his becoming Muslim. He states the proofs for the falsity of the religion of the Christians and the truth of the religion of Islam.[31]

In the portion of his work quoted by Ibn Taymiyya, Al-Hasan ibn Ayyub shows himself to be exceptionally well versed in the gospels and in Christian trinitarian controversies. He is well acquainted with the scriptures of the Hebrew Bible and presents a lengthy treatment on how Jesus fulfilled—*as a prophet*—announcements from the Hebrew Bible of his coming.[32] He attempts to show from statements of Jesus in the gospels that Jesus himself never claimed to be more than a prophet and rejected attempts to identify him with God. The "theopathic utterances" of Jesus in the gospels he explains in a way that indicates that he is nothing but a prophet. For example:

> By his saying "I and the Father are one" he only means "Your accepting my command means that you accept the command of God." Similarly, by his saying "Whoever has seen me has seen the Father" he means "Whoever has seen these deeds which I have made manifest has seen the deeds of my Father."

That which shows most strongly the falsity of the belief of the Christians is that they themselves have not been able to agree on it. All Christian sects declare the others unbelievers.

> Each one declares his companion an unbeliever, and claims that he is in possession of the truth. But no one of them brings from the Book any clear proof which establishes his claim. Neither does he, by referring to his own experience, bring an interpretation according to what is known to be true by investigation. Rather, each one goes back in his religion and belief to what earlier interpreters have said in setting themselves in opposition to their Gospel and sacred books with their whims and stubbornness. Thus by their interpretation they commit *shirk* against God, who has no partner, and they allege that he has a child in respect to what they themselves have invented.[33]

Thus Al-Hasan ibn Ayyub accuses the Christians of *taqlid*—the blind following of what had been said before. In doing this they presumed the interpretations to be reliable. Al-Hasan never claims that the gospels are verbally corrupted; rather it is by prescinding from traditional interpretations and reading their scriptures anew that Christians can discover the errors into which they have fallen. At a much earlier date Al-Hasan ibn Ayyub had established this argument, which the author of *Al-Radd al-Jamil*—whether Al-Ghazali or its unknown author—has made prominent.

Ibn Taymiyya, who employs the work of earlier writers on most subjects which require a direct knowledge of Christian scripture, uses Al-Hasan's *risala* to establish the single human nature of Christ from the sacred books of the Christians and secondarily to delineate the differences in trinitarian theology among the three great Christian sects.

He chose Al-Hasan because he was "the person most knowledgeable about their views" on Scripture; for a similar reason Ibn Taymiyya chose another recognized expert, this time a Christian, to present Christian history and the background of the early trinitarian controversies. This was the Melkite bishop of Alexandria, Sa'id Ibn Bitriq (called Eutychius in the West), whose important ecclesiastical history, *Nazm al-Jawhar*, is cited (and answered) by Ibn Taymiyya for over 117 pages.

Sa'id ibn Bitriq (d. 329/941) is an unusual figure. Besides his ecclesiastical history quoted by Ibn Taymiyya, he wrote a companion piece, *Kitab al-Burhan*, in which he endeavored to show the falsity of Nestorian and especially Jacobite theologies of the trinity. Most remarkable about his writing, as W. Montgomery Watt has pointed out, is that he, perhaps more than any other Christian Arab writer, has incorporated Islamic theological ideas into his thought. Not only are early biblical personages such as Adam, Noah, and David treated as prophets by Ibn Bitriq, but he has adopted a great number of Islamic terms and uses them in a Christian sense.[34]

Ibn Taymiyya's use of Ibn Bitriq is limited, however, to the annals, *Nazm al-Jawhar*. In his first selection he quotes from Ibn Bitriq's treatment of early Christian history from Christ until Nestorius.[35] Ibn Taymiyya's interest in this section is to see when and how various innovations of belief and practice entered the religion of the Christians. Thus the story of Helena and the cross of Jesus, the anti-Jewish prescriptions of Constantine, the church of St. Michael in Alexandria, and the early heresiarchs such as Paul al-Shamshati (Samosata) and Maqdunius (Macedonius) all figure prominently in the narrative.

Sa'id Ibn Bitriq's principal interest lay with more specifically theological controversies, however, and his narrative gradually came to center on the controversies surrounding Arius, Nestorius, and the Councils of Chalcedon, Ephesus, and Nicaea. In the later passages quoted by Ibn Taymiyya from *Nazm al-Jawhar* Ibn Bitriq presents a defense of the Melkite position on trinitarian controversies, and a refutation of the Nestorian and Jacobite views.[36] Ibn Taymiyya is interested in this treatment, for he accepts Ibn Bitriq's argumentation against the other two theologies as valid and then attempts to show that the Melkite formulation, which the bishop offered as the mediate position, has none of the logical consistency of the other two and as a compromise view is the weakest of the three.

This use by a Muslim controversialist of a prominent Christian theologian to present Christian history in his own terms and refute positions he considers heretical is to my knowledge unprecedented in the history of Islamic polemic on Christianity. Ibn Taymiyya had a unique statement to make and was flexible in employing whatever means he deemed suitable. The following chapter investigates Ibn Taymiyya's view of Christianity, as he developed it in *Al-Jawab al-Sahih li-Man Baddal Din al-Masih*.

# CHAPTER 8

## IBN TAYMIYYA'S ARGUMENTATION AGAINST CHRISTIANITY IN *AL-JAWAB AL-SAHIH*

### Introductory

Most of the arguments used by Ibn Taymiyya against the religion of the Christians were already part of the common fund of knowledge of the educated Islamic community before his time. *Tahrif*, trinitarian and Christological argumentation, biblical announcements of Muhammad, the miracles of Jesus and Muhammad, all had been carefully and exhaustively treated before 700/1300. With Al-Qarafi's work, even a detailed response to Paul of Antioch's new challenges had been composed. It is not, then, in the area of producing startling new arguments against the Christian position that the originality and importance of *Al-Jawab al-Sahih* lay. Rather, it is that for the first time an Islamic author has taken these basic elements of polemics and incorporated them into a comprehensive view of mankind's response to revelation.

It is not surprising that so much space is given in *Al-Jawab al-Sahih* to *wahdat al-wujud* Sufism, Shi'i imamism, tomb veneration, and saint intercession, as these notions represent Islamic phenomena which, according to Ibn Taymiyya, parallel the errors of Christianity. The process which Ibn Taymiyya considers to have occurred in Christianity, whereby the early Christian church chose to follow the desires of those it took as masters and leaders rather than allowing the message that Christ brought from God be the criterion of judgment for the community, he saw taking place in Islam. The difference between the two historical processes, however, and that which would ultimately save Muslims from taking the path their Christian predecessors had taken, was that within the Islamic community there would remain at all times a kernel of devout, conscientious Muslims, who would continue to preserve and transmit the unadulterated sunna. This kernel, he states, had existed in Christianity, and at the time of Muhammad these true followers of Christ recognized Muhammad as the awaited prophet and became his followers.

It was the function of these God-fearing Muslims to act as the conscience of the *umma*, to subject the trends, ideas, and practices of the Islamic community to the scrutiny of the sunna, and to pronounce judgment on their conformity to or deviation from it. This role Ibn Taymiyya took upon himself in his life and in his writings, and it is from this standpoint that *Al-Jawab al-Sahih* was written.

It has been remarked that because of its exhaustive use of Qur'anic argumentation, which could have played no more than an ad hominem role against Christian polemicists, and because of its preoccupation with internal disputes within Islam, this work was written primarily for a Muslim audience. Cheikho suggested that its purpose was to strengthen the defense of Muslims against the Christian challenges,[1] while Fritsch conceived the work as a reflective theoretical study of the relations between the two religions.[2]

It does seem likely that *Al-Jawab al-Sahih* (in notable contrast, for example, to *Al-Risala al-Qubrusiyya*) was written primarily for the Muslim community; nevertheless, because the basic arguments against Christians predated Ibn Taymiyya the principal motive for his writing the work was not to buttress the faith of the Muslims by supplying them with polemical argumentation, but rather to let the Christian experience of *kufr* serve as a warning to tendencies within the Islamic *umma* that could lead Muslims to the same type of unbelief. In this way the work embodies his "philosophy of unbelief," delineating the process by which a people become unbelievers by substituting their manmade religion for the prophetic message. *Al-Jawab al-Sahih* is thus intended to play that role of conservation of the pure sunna which was an essential element in the life of the community.

On the other hand, *Al-Jawab al-Sahih* must not be construed as a theoretical essay on the errors of the Christian religion which was merely occasioned by the Letter from Cyprus. It is truly a response and was intended as a comprehensive refutation of the Christian apology. The mere fact that Ibn Taymiyya's response was over a thousand printed pages,[3] as compared to Paul of Antioch's twenty-four pages, indicates that the work was conceived as a definitive "answer" as well as an opportunity to explore more fully the nature of Christian unbelief and its relationship to religious phenomena within the Islamic community.

The presence of aberrations within the Islamic *umma* was not an embarrassment to Ibn Taymiyya; it had been expected and predicted by Muhammad himself; prophetic hadith show that the Prophet saw such deviations as inevitable.

> The Prophet disclosed that the occurrence of these things must befall some of this community, although he had disclosed that in his community there would remain a group established in the truth, whose enemies and deserters could never harm it even until the arrival of the Hour.[4]

Such people he never calls "Muslims" or "believers" (*mu'minun*), but consistently refers to them by the neutral terms "the people [who pray] in the direction [of Mecca]" (*ahl al-qibla*) or "those who consider themselves Muslims" (*al-muntasibun ila al-Islam*). Such people include hypocrites like Batinis and monist Sufis, renegades like the philosophers, and innovators and sectarians, who, although they follow some of the basic message of Islam both inwardly and outwardly, have strayed from the Straight Path in other fundamental matters.

> Our intention is to present the truth with which God sent His messengers and revealed His Books and to refute Christians and others who oppose that. We do not deny that among those who call themselves Muslims there are hypocrites, renegades, and crypto-Manichaeans; there are ignorant innovators, there are those who hold a view similar to that of Christians, and those who hold something worse than theirs. Our intention is to refute all these people. Infallibility (*al-'isma*) is established for the Book of God and the sunna of His messenger. That upon which His believing servants agree can only be true, but on matters about which Muslims dispute there can be found both truth and error.[5]

The errors of wayward Muslims in each case parallel ways in which Christians deviated from the prophetic religion handed on by Moses, Jesus, and other prophets, and in some respects their deviations are more serious than those of Christians.[6] The value in studying Christianity as a religion is that it sets in relief the inadmissible and heretical practices found occurring in Muslims and serves as a warning to them. In this, Ibn Taymiyya sees a parallel to the value for the Arabs at the time of Muhammad of studying the ancient destroyed civilizations in the teaching of the Qur'an; in seeing the end to which these civilizations came after refusing the summons to the prophetic religion, the pagan Arabs to whom Muhammad was preaching could gain insight into the threat hanging over them. Ibn Taymiyya applies Qur'anic statements (e.g., 24:44) expressing this warning for his purpose of examining the religion of the Christians: "He made all that befell them a lesson for those who can understand."[7]

The value of studying the nature of unbelief in Christianity is underlined by the Islamic belief that the religion (*al-din*) of the prophets is one, although the legal and ritual codes—the Laws (*al-shara'i'*)—are many. Thus it is one and the same religion of the prophets which is attacked in the innovative and substitutive programs of those who depart from the narrow path of the prophets.

> Similarly, heretics (*al-mulhidun*) who are changing the religion of Muhammad adopt a religion not legislated by God and His messenger; they designate a path to God and choose it in preference to the path which God and His messenger have ordained.[8]

Speaking in this passage of Muslims who adopt unorthodox Sufi practices such as musically accompanied prayer (*sama'*) and tomb visitation, Ibn Taymiyya describes them in terms parallel to and inclusive of his judgment upon Christians; he links the two attacks on prophetic religion and terms their proponents "the heretics who are changing the religion of the messengers—the religion of Christ or the religion of Muhammad" (*al-mulhidun al-mubaddilun li-din al-rusul din al-Masih aw din Muhammad*).[9]

In the earliest days of Christianity, states Ibn Taymiyya, Christians followed the one true religion announced to them by their prophet Jesus the son of Mary, much as the Jews had received that same prophetic message in an earlier age through Moses. He cites a hadith report which narrates a conversation between the Prophet and Qatada at the time of the visit by the Najrani delegation to Muhammad.

> Qatada said that when the Jews said, "The Christians follow nothing," he [Muhammad] said, "Yes, but the earliest Christians followed something; then they innovated and split into sects." When the Christians said that the Jews follow nothing, he said, "Yes, but the early Jews followed something; they innovated and split into sects."[10]

The path followed by both religions into unbelief was twofold. They began by changing the legal prescriptions and the scriptural teaching of their own sacred books and substituted for them teachings of their own, and secondly, when a new messenger was sent to them to warn them of their error, they rejected him. The new messenger (Christ in the case of the Jews, Muhammad in the case of Christians) abrogated some of the Law (*al-shari'a*) of the previous prophet and called on its followers to put faith in him. In their failure to do this the Jews and Christians became unbelievers and incurred God's wrath. Although God's wrath against the Jews was great for having first rejected Christ and the Gospel and later Muhammad and the Qur'an,[11] Christians were greater disbelievers in their rejection of Muhammad than were Jews simply by their rejection of Christ. He states that Christ basically reiterated the demands of the Law of the Torah, so that when the Jews rejected Jesus as a prophet, they were not substantially rejecting the Law; however, when the Christians refused to accept Muhammad as a prophet, they were rejecting with that a new, independent, and self-sustaining *shari'a*.[12] They were more unbelieving than the Jews, moreover, in that their innovated beliefs like the trinity and the hypostatic union in Christ departed more radically from the *tawhid* which was the central teaching in the message of the prophets.[13]

## Muhammad as messenger to all mankind

Ibn Taymiyya, although departing occasionally from the issues raised by Paul of Antioch, either to relate the question at hand to intramural controversies among Muslims or to incorporate extraneous material such as that from Al-Hasan ibn Ayyub or Sa'id ibn Bitriq, basically kept to the structure presented in the work of the Christian bishop. Like Muhammad ibn Abi Talib, but unlike Al-Qarafi, he followed the practice of citing Paul of Antioch's work (the *Letter from Cyprus*) verbatim and then offering his own refutation of the points raised in the cited passage.

In this way the first major subject treated by Ibn Taymiyya in *Al-Jawab al-Sahih*—prophecy—was a central one to his thought. He had written on the subject of prophecy in earlier works, but never from the perspective which he would apply in *Al-Jawab al-Sahih*. In *Kitab al-Nubuwwat* he treated the uniqueness and the characteristics of prophetic inspiration as understood through the Qur'an and the sound hadith reports in contradistinction to the theory of "natural inspiration" proposed by the peripatetic and monist philosophers. In *Takhjil Ahl al-Injil*, if it was, as it seems, an earlier and separate work from *Al-Jawab al-Sahih*, he treats the validity of various kinds of indications of prophethood (prediction, miracles, upright character, influence on mankind) in an attempt to prove that Muhammad fulfilled all these indications to an eminent degree.

In *Al-Jawab al-Sahih* Ibn Taymiyya is interested in the characteristics of prophethood. Paul of Antioch did not deny the prophethood of Muhammad, but he rejected its universal nature and held that in the Qur'an Muhammad himself affirmed the limited nature of the prophethood and the continuing validity of the Christian religion, and consequently the basic irrelevance of Islam to Christians. In response, Ibn Taymiyya built his case in careful steps.

Any claimant to prophethood, he states, is either truthful or lying. The questions facing anyone who intends to examine his teaching begin with two: is it possible to know what the claimant said, and secondly can it be ascertained whether or not he is lying?[14] Paul of Antioch did not challenge the Islamic position on the second question, but accepted the veracity of Muhammad. Because of this, the issue centers about the first question—that is, what did Muhammad actually say? It is obvious that the Muslim community claims that he declared himself a universal prophet sent to all mankind, abrogating all previous religious laws and summoning previous recipients of divine revelation as well as pagans to follow him: the question is whether in making this claim Muslims are faithful to the teachings of Muhammad himself.[15]

Ibn Taymiyya's first concern is to show that Muhammad himself did claim to have a universal prophetic mission. To this end he employs Qur'anic statements (e.g., 7:158, 34:28) in which it is stated that Muhammad is sent to all mankind,[16] and statements in which Jews and Christians are accused of unbelief.[17] In what are they unbelievers if not in the prophetic message which he has brought? If that message were not intended for them or if it were irrelevant to their religious status, they could not be called unbelievers for rejecting it.

He buttresses his Qur'anic argumentation by statements of Muhammad from the hadith reports which affirm his claim to a universal prophethood. For example, in one hadith it is reported that he said:

> I was given preference over the prophets in six things: I was given comprehensiveness in utterance; I was delivered from fear; I was permitted booty; for me the earth was made a pure mosque; I was sent to mankind in its entirety; with me the prophets were concluded.[18]

He holds that the life of Muhammad indicates that he believed in the universal nature of his mission, and specifically a mission to Jews and Christians. He relates the battles between Muhammad and his followers in Madina against the Jewish clans. These could be interpreted as purely political power struggles except that Muhammad saw them as religious battles; those Jews who accepted him were *mu'minun* and those who rejected him were disbelievers (such as in 59:2).[19] This presupposes that he saw himself as bearing a prophetic message to them.

With the Christians the situation is different in that they were never a military or political threat to Muhammad, and yet the declarations of unbelief against them in the Qur'an for their belief in the divinity of Christ and the trinitarian nature of God are clear.

He recounts the perception of some Najrani Christians that Muhammad was the awaited prophet spoken of by Jesus and implies that it was only Byzantine economic pressure that prevented more Najranis from accepting him.[20] The point is that in presenting himself to the Najranis as a prophet and accepting converts from their number, Muhammad is indicating his belief that his mission was not solely to the pagan Arabs.

> When two learned men [from Najran] addressed him, the Messenger of God said to them, "Surrender to God (*aslima!*)." They answered, "We have surrendered." He said, "You have lied. What prevents you from surrendering [or 'from Islam'] is your claiming a child for God, your worship of the cross, and your eating pork." They said, "Then who is his father, O Muhammad?" The Messenger of God was silent at this and did not answer them. At that time God revealed to him . . . verses of the Qur'an: "God, there is no God but He—the Living, the Everlasting" up to approximately verse eighty [i.e., 3:1-80].[21]

This view is strengthened by the letters sent by Muhammad to early Christian leaders—such as the Byzantine emperor Heraclius, the Muqawqus of Egypt, and the Negus of Ethiopia—in which he summoned them to Islam. The authenticity and even existence of these letters has been questioned in modern scholarship, but Islamic tradition is consistent in affirming that Muhammad did send letters to the Christian leaders of his time as well as to the Persian Khusraw in which he exhorted them to accept Islam. The texts of these letters are preserved in the collections of sound hadiths as well as in the biography of Muhammad by Ibn Hisham.[22] If the letters are indeed authentic, they provide strong evidence that Muhammad saw his mission as extending beyond the confines of pagan Arabia and including contemporary Christian peoples.

Finally, he gives evidence in the form of the summons to wage *jihad* against the Christians at Tabuk. He states that this must not be interpreted purely as a military operation, but rather in the context of Muhammad's rejection of the Christian religion as corrupted and abrogated and his understanding of his own mission as the reestablishment of the one prophetic religion.

> If Muhammad was a true prophet, then [it must be known that] he declared Christians unbelievers, commanded *jihad* against them, and declared himself quit of them and their religion [5:72-73; 9:30-31]. If he was false, nothing which he handed on from God can be accepted.[23]

In rejecting Paul of Antioch's interpretation of the verse in the Fatiha, "Guide us according to the path of those upon whom Your favor rests" (1:6), he states:

> No one with either general or specific knowledge about the religion of Muhammad and that of his community can dispute that what they received from him by way of declaring Christians unbeliving, ignorant, and wayward, in permitting *jihad* against them, in taking their women as prisoners and seizing their wealth—all this completely contradicts the possibility that Muhammad and his community could say in every prayer, "O God, guide us according to the path of the Christians."[24]

Ibn Taymiyya contends, therefore, that the statements handed down from him as well as his relationships with Jews and Christians during his lifetime—summoning them to Islam and declaring unbelievers those who rejected his summons—indicate that Muhammad himseif claimed to have a prophetic mission to Jews, Christians, and all other peoples. This contention cannot be challenged on the historical grounds that his community later fabricated statements and events, because the reports of such things have been communicated from the time of Muhammad in an unbroken line of critically attested transmission.

> He stated even that he was sent to all the children of Adam, to Arabs and to Byzantine, Persian, Turkish, Indian, Berber, and Ethiopian non-Arabs, and to all other nations. He even stated that he was sent to both the races—the human race and that of the jinn. All these are clear issues successively handed down from him, upon whose transmission from him his companions are agreed. This is despite their great number and their dispersal into various regions and situations—those who accompanied him were in the tens of thousands and their actual number cannot be counted and is known to God alone.[25]

This transmission, he holds, is far more widely attested than that of any other prophet, so that to challenge or reject the material known through it would be to deny any information received from any of the prophets.

> The transmission from Muhammad is over a short period of time, and those who transmitted [information] from him were many, many times more than those who transmitted the religion of Christ, and many, many times more than those who were in contact with the transmission of the religion of Moses. The community of Muhammad has never ceased to be numerous and spread from the eastern parts of the earth to the west, and there has never ceased to be among them one who is victorious in religion and supported by God over his enemies.[26]

Once he has established that Muhammad claimed to be God's messenger to all mankind, Ibn Taymiyya still has a number of other charges to answer. Paul of Antioch cited a number of Qur'anic verses in which it is said that Muhammad was sent "to his own people," and "with an Arabic Qur'an," and the Christians used such verses to argue for an exclusivity in Muhammad's mission. If indeed these verses did indicate a limited mission and other verses a universal one, would this not make the Qur'an self-contradictory on this point?

Ibn Taymiyya states that those passages which speak of Muhammad's being sent to the Arabs are not contradictory to those which claim a universal nature for his mission. Nowhere in the Qur'an is it stated that Muhammad was sent *only* to Arabs and not to others. Proceeding from the principles of Islamic jurisprudence, he states that a specifying or delimiting statement is not contradictory to a general or universal statement unless it expressly denies that statement. He cites a great number of Qur'anic passages as evidence of this[27] and then treats the verses mentioned by Paul of Antioch (2:151, 3:164, 9:128) with a view towards showing that none of them are intended to indicate an exclusive prophetic mission to the Arabs.[28]

He argues that if the teaching of the Qur'an were self-contradictory, it would not serve as an argument for Christians, for the internal contradiction would only indicate that the Qur'an was not a revealed book and that Muhammad was not a prophet. In such a case it would be useless for Christians to cite any statement from Muhammad or the Qur'an as evidence for anything.

> If they say that their intention is to point out that his teaching is internally contradictory with some of it contradicting the rest, they should be told that this would also require that he not be a prophet, and thus it would be improper for them to use any statement of his as an argument to the extent they do.[29]

Moreover the apparent contradictions in the Jewish and Christian scriptures are far more numerous than those in the Qur'an and closer to true contradictions, he holds,[30] and yet Muslims grant that there are no contradictions in the earlier scriptures. Were the Christians or anyone else to admit the possibility of a true contradiction in a sacred book, they would be rejecting one of the essential purposes of such revealed books, that is, to establish certain knowledge.

However, there are other alternatives in the argument as well. He pictures Muhammad's prophetic mission as roughly paralleling that of Christ, who began with delimiting statements like "I was not sent except to the sons of Israel,"[31] and concluded his preaching by his universal commission to the apostles to travel throughout the world baptizing all persons. This process, whereby God sends the prophet firstly to those nearest him in time, place, and relationship, and gradually leads the messenger to proclaim the message to a wider audience and eventually to all mankind, can be seen clearly in the life of Muhammad. He began preaching to his own relatives and neighbors, then to his clan, then to the Quraysh, then to other Arabs, and finally to the People of the Book and all mankind. Ibn Taymiyya details this developmental process in Muhammad's prophetic career in order to show that even if at one time in his life his mission had been, in accordance with the possibilities, to his clan, the Quraysh, or the pagan Arabs in general, this would not contradict a universal nature for his mission which was revealed only at a later time in his life.[32]

If his claims had been contradictory, the earlier specifying statements of the prophet would have been abrogated by his later universalist claims. Even though that was not the case with the Qur'anic citations mentioned by Paul of Antioch, the principle is one accepted by Christians and is thus a refutation of any charges of contradiction in the Qur'an.

> It is necessary that they believe one of two matters. Either the verses have meanings which are in agreement with what he used to say [elsewhere], or they are among those which have been abrogated. It is known, both generally and in particular, that Muhammad used to pray towards Jerusalem for about a year and a half after the Hijra. Then he commanded prayer towards the Ka'ba, the Sacred House. Christians agree that in the Laws of the prophets there are abrogating and abrogated [passages], although the verses mentioned [by Paul of Antioch] are not abrogated.[33]

If it can be established that Muhammad actually taught that he was sent as a prophet to all mankind, then his teaching must be accepted in its totality. There can be nothing false in it, nor can individual parts of his teaching be mutually contradictory. If this is the case, one must either accept the prophet and all that he teaches completely, or else reject him as a lying pseudo-prophet.[34]

With the prophet the situation is different from that of all other people who may be trustworthy in some matters and speak falsely in others. Ibn Taymiyya considers anyone who has made a claim to prophethood to be in another category. Either he is a true prophet, in which case everything he claims to have brought from God must be accepted as true, or else he is lying. In view of the enormity of the ruse he has perpetrated, the false prophet cannot be considered a misguided but well-meaning individual, but is less credible and far more suspect of lying than the ordinary person.[35]

Inerrancy in the messages which he claims to bring from God is the distinguishing characteristic of the prophet which sets him apart from the non-prophet.

> The prophets are inerrant in what they communicate, and it cannot be imagined that they speak about God anything but the truth, nor that there reside in their teaching anything but the truth, either intentionally or accidentally. With upright persons some one of them may err and make a mistake despite the manifestation of wonders at his hands. He would not thereby cease to be an upright individual. It would not be necessary that he be inerrant if he had not claimed inerrancy nor brought the signs which indicate that. If he claimed inerrancy and was not a prophet, then he would [simply] be lying and would undoubtedly manifest his falseness.[36]

An important criticism leveled by Ibn Taymiyya at both Jews and Christians is that they have failed to respect the prerogatives of the institution of prophecy.

> The Jews denigrated and cursed the prophets and mentioned faults beyond which God had elevated them. It would take too long to describe all the examples of this. Among them there was disbelief in the prophets of a kind which was vicious among their ancients.
>
> Christians, despite their exaggerated devotion to Christ and his followers, treated other prophets lightly. Sometimes they made the apostles equal or superior to Abraham and Moses. At other times they spoke like the Jews, declaring, for example, that Solomon was not a prophet but fell from the rank of prophet. Elsewhere they claimed that what God said about David and others was only intended to refer to Christ.[37]

Christians claim inerrancy for the apostles as well as the divine indwelling of the Holy Spirit in them, although they do not claim the rank of prophet for them.[38] This, according to Ibn Taymiyya, is contradictory, since for him inerrancy is indissolubly linked with the prophetic office. In this, Christians are deluded by the miracles and spiritual favors granted to the apostles and thus believe that they cannot be mistaken on any information which they transmit from the prophets.[39] He draws a parallel here to the followers of the Sufi masters or with the attitude of Shi'a toward the Imams. He argues strongly that wonderworking of itself is not an incontrovertible proof of prophethood (although truly miraculous deeds are among the "signs" or manifestations of the true prophet).[40] Frequently wondrous occurrences are merely evidence of demonic activity, he states; this is commonplace among those who engage in unlawful or innovated practices of worship, but even upright and holy people are sometimes deceived by demonic appearances.[41]

Ibn Taymiyya explains the Gospel account[42] which narrates the appearance to the apostles of "the one who was crucified and buried" as an example of this. Since Jesus was not crucified, nor did he die on the cross, it could not have been the resurrected Christ who appeared to the apostles, as is believed in the Christian tradition. Rather it was one of the jinn who personified Christ in order to mislead the apostles.

Demonic activity of this kind is extremely common in religious experience, and its purpose is twofold. The first goal of the demon is to lead people astray by delivering to them false information, as did the one who informed the apostles that he was Christ who was crucified. Secondly, the demons appear to people either in order to lead them into heterodox religious practices or to encourage them in such practices by appearing in the form of one besought for intercession.[43] He states categorically that whenever someone has a vision, while awake, of a prophet, an angel, or a holy person, that vision is fraudulent and produced by the demons.

> While he is awake, someone may see persons either riding or on foot who say this is such-and-such a prophet—whether Abraham, Christ, or Muhammad—or this is such-and-such a righteous person—whether Abu Bakr or one of the apostles. This may be some individual who is believed to be holy—whether St. George or others whom the Christians extol. It may be one of the Muslim shaykhs. In reality that is a demon claiming that he is a prophet, that shaykh, that righteous individual, or that saint.[44]

His purpose here is to debunk a widespread fascination with visions, miracles, and heavenly messages and an atmosphere in which believers from the various religions attempted to outdo one another in these matters. For Ibn Taymiyya the problem of satanic opposition and interference was endemic to the religion of the prophets, and he cites the Qur'an as evidence that it is of the same order as the opposition faced by their prophetic founders.

> We have never sent a messenger or a prophet before you except that when he recited Satan proposed [opposition] to his recitation. But God abolished that which Satan proposes (22:52).

The intention of the demons is to turn people away from the true *tawhid* preached by the prophets by insinuating false information and practices of *shirk* into that teaching. Ibn Taymiyya considers that the Christians have already succumbed to such "subtle whisperings," and their experience of this, he hopes, will serve as a warning to activities within the Islamic community which may lead errant Muslims in the same direction.

Ibn Taymiyya treats a final aspect of the question of the universal nature of Muhammad's prophethood. Could not Muhammad have been sincerely deluded into thinking of himself as a messenger from God to all mankind when in reality he was not? Thus, he might have been an upright individual, a conscientious political leader with a program of social reform, even a profoundly religious man, but mistaken in his belief that he was the seal of the prophets, sent to all with a new and definitive Law.

He concedes that such an interpretation might be possible for anyone other than a prophet, but that it is impossible for any claimant to messengership. The nature of prophecy demands that the prophet be preserved from even accidental or unintentional error in anything he claims to bring from God.[45] To hold that any claimant to prophecy spoke falsely in even one word of what he included in his message from God is tantamount to denying the person's prophethood. Moreover, God would not support with signs someone who falsely claimed prophethood, but would in some way make it evident that the claimant was an impostor.[46] The question of whether the person was sincerely deluded in considering himself a prophet or was an intentional impostor is ultimately irrelevant; anyone whose claims to be God's messenger are confirmed by the signs of prophecy cannot err even unintentionally in the words which he claims were communicated to him by God. Therefore for the Christians to admit that Muhammad was a prophet, but to hold that he was in error in his claim to be a messenger to all mankind is inconsistent.

Closely related to this position is an argument commonly raised by Christians, although Ibn Taymiyya admits that it is antithetical to the view of Paul of Antioch. This is the accusation that Muhammad was no prophet at all. Ibn Taymiyya responds by presenting the signs for Muhammad's prophethood—the nobility of the message of the Qur'an, his knowledge of unknown matters in both the past and the future, his miracles, the Qur'an, which is the greatest miracle, and the fine qualities of his community. The material is treated summarily here, and it epitomizes a more extensive elaboration of these signs in a previous work to which he frequently refers. As has been mentioned previously, the references in this section of *Al-Jawab al-Sahih*[47] are among the strongest evidence that the last 400 pages of the printed edition, in which Ibn Taymiyya built the case for Muhammad's messengership against Christians who had denied it, very probably existed as a separate work earlier than *Al-Jawab al Sahih*. Subsequently, because of the complementary nature of the subject matter, the works were usually joined together as one.

Christians had often asserted that Muhammad could not have been a true prophet because his coming had not been announced or predicted by any of the previous prophets. Ibn Taymiyya responds that the prediction of a prophet in earlier times is not a necessary sign of messengership. He mentions the sending of Moses to the Pharaoh without his having been announced beforehand, as well as the prophetic missions of Noah and Abraham to their people and those of the Arab prophets as examples of messengers whose coming had not been previously predicted.[48]

He states further that although the previous announcement of a prophet is not necessary, Muhammad was in fact announced in the sacred books of the Jews and Christians. He contends that this announcement was clearer and more frequent than that of any previous messenger. In failing to acknowledge these announcements, Christians have misinterpreted the teaching of Christ in their own books, just as did the Jews who consequently did not recognize Jesus as the awaited Messiah.[49]

Ibn Taymiyya asserts that "we know conclusively that Muhammad was mentioned in the Torah and the Gospel existing in his time."[50] This conclusion, derived from the Qur'an (7:157), is a clear indication for Ibn Taymiyya that at the time of Muhammad some, if not all, copies of the Bible clearly announced the future prophetic mission of Muhammad. The question of biblical alteration is hereby unavoidably joined between Muslims and the People of the Book.

## *Tahrif* of Scripture, *tabdil* of belief and practice

Paul of Antioch claimed[51] that Qur'anic confirmation of the earlier sacred books implied a denial of textual corruption of the biblical texts. Ibn Taymiyya countered that this confirmation applied only to the original revealed texts and neither affirms nor denies the presence and extent of alteration in the texts actually in use among Christians and Jews.

According to Ibn Taymiyya, two separate questions are involved in the question of *tahrif al-lafz*, and on both issues the views of Muslims are divided. The first concerns the question of whether or not the biblical books were textually altered before the time of Muhammad, while the second concerns the possibility of textual alteration after that time.

Ibn Taymiyya's response to these issues produced not only the most extensive medieval Muslim treatment of the issue of textual corruption of the Bible, but his was also the most carefully nuanced. He claims to be avoiding the two extreme views of the Muslims, both that which affirmed the textual accuracy of the earlier books and that of those like Ibn Hazm who denied any textual validity to the Bible.

> If by that they [Christians] mean that the Qur'an confirms the textual veracity (*alfaz*) of the scriptural books which they now possess—that is, the Torah and the Gospel—this is what some Muslims will grant them and what many Muslims will dispute. However, most Muslims will grant them most of that.[52]

Concerning the question of whether textual alteration occurred in the Bible before the time of Muhammad, Ibn Taymiyya's purpose is not to demonstrate that textual alteration occurred in the biblical books, still less to single out instances of its occurrence; rather his purpose is to define the limits of Islamic belief in the matter. Nowhere in the Qur'an or sunna, he holds, is it ever denied that *tahrif al-lafz* might or could have taken place. Anything beyond that is a matter on which different opinions among Muslims are permissible; the matter is ultimately unknowable and no one can presume to decide the question either way.

> When 'Umar ibn al-Khattab saw a copy of the Torah in the hand of Ka'b al-Ahbar, he said, "Ka'b, if you know that this is the Torah which God handed down by Moses ibn 'Imran, then read it." The issue is thus conditional on what we can in no way know; 'Umar did not decisively determine that the texts had been corrupted when he did not put confidence in everything that was in them.[53]

The second question was one raised by Paul of Antioch. His claim was that the Qur'an testified to the absence of change in the Christian scriptures. If that was the case, the Christians at the time of Muhammad possessed the correct text of the Bible; at such a late date, with Christians scattered all over the globe, how could any textual change subsequent to the time of Muhammad creep in?

Ibn Taymiyya responds by asserting that the Christian argument is based on a false presupposition—that the Qur'an attested the textual fidelity of the Bible in use among the Christians of Muhammad's time. Moreover, no Muslim ever made the claim that all the Christian scriptures were textually altered in a period subsequent to Muhammad.[54] Finally, clear differences in wording and translation indicate that all copies in use among the People of the Book are not textually identical.[55]

Conceding that "the corruption which occurred was only slight"[56] before the time of Muhammad, he holds, nevertheless, that no Muslim can positively affirm that no textual alteration occurred in the Bible. More significantly, Muslims must deny that Christians and Jews can point to an unbroken textual tradition which goes back to their prophets. Following earlier Muslim polemicists, he holds that the successive tradition of the Torah was broken at the time of the Babylonian exile. He agrees with Ibn Hazm and Al-Juwayni[57] that the scribe Ezra was the key figure in the reconstruction of the text, but whereas the two earlier writers rejected the prophethood of Ezra, Ibn Taymiyya holds it to be a matter upon which a conclusive judgment cannot be passed. Ezra may have been a prophet, in which case his dictation of the text of the Torah must have been inerrant; if he was not a prophet, errors could have crept in.[58]

In this way he holds that the Torah may have an unbroken textual attestation going back to Moses, but at the same time it must be noted that this unbroken tradition of textual fidelity is merely putative and cannot be proved.

> The Torah is the most correct of Books, and the most widely distributed among Jews and Christians. In spite of this, the text of the Samaritans is different from the text of the Jews and Christians, even to the very wording of the Ten Commandments. . . . This shows that *tabdil* has occurred in many copies of these books, for numerous copies exist among the Samaritans.[59]

The *tabdil* which occurred in the gospel is greater than that in the Torah.[60] Christians do not claim to possess a unitary gospel written by Christ. Their four gospels were written by four individuals for whom they claim inerrancy in spite of their not claiming prophethood for them after the death of the prophet Jesus; moreover two of the evangelists are said not to have known Christ personally.[61] Only that which a prophet hands on from God can be known to be revealed, therefore only those statements of Christ which can be attested by successive transmission of textual fidelity to contain the literal teaching of Jesus can be said to express the revealed gospel.

The gospels are therefore of the same status as the Muslim collections of hadith reports from Muhammad,[62] which, although they contain true statements and teaching of Muhammad, may differ verbally and may contain erroneous material. Even the Torah, although it is assumed to be textually sounder than the gospel, must be treated as *khabar* from the prophet Moses because it has no indisputable attestation of textual accuracy.

In viewing the Jewish and Christian scriptures as prophetic *khabar*, Ibn Taymiyya holds that the books cannot be treated as a whole, neither to rejected outright as fabrications and corruptions, nor to be accepted fully as the sacred books handed down from God through Moses, Christ, David, and the other prophets.

Rather, as *khabar*, each passage must be subjected to the same criteria which Muslims apply to *khabar* from Muhammad, that is, information contained in the hadith reports. Before being accepted as having been accurately handed down from the prophet, and thus ultimately from God, the individual passage must be tested for the soundness of its matter (*matn*) and the reliable and unbroken nature of its chain of transmission (*isnad*). Christians must fulfill another criterion, that is, to show that the translation of the prophetic report from its original language has been accurate.[63] Until Jews and Christians can adequately establish the veracity of any particular passage from their books, Muslims cannot give it full credence of faith.

Neither can anyone deny the possibility that an individual passage may contain the actual message of God handed down through a prophet. Muslims cannot dismiss the Jewish and Christian scriptures as a whole, for the likelihood is that most of what they contain is actually the divine prophetic message handed down in uncorrupted form. That which has been either accidentally changed or intentionally corrupted is relatively slight.[64]

In taking this position, Ibn Taymiyya is cautiously refusing to follow the position of Al-Ghazali and Al-Baqillani,[65] who treat the Jewish and Christian scriptures as sacred prophetic books, all of which repeat the same message of Islam. Nor does he follow the position of Ibn Hazm in his rejection of the sacred books as a collection of fabrications and inventions.

In treating the biblical passages cited in the Letter from Cyprus, Ibn Taymiyya's usual practice is to state the above-mentioned reservations about the necessity of establishing conclusively the authenticity of an individual passage, but then he frequently prefaces the divine statements in the prophecies with "God said"—the same formula used to introduce all verses cited from the Qur'an.[66] In this section his basic principle of interpretation is similar to that laid down by the author of *Al-Radd al-Jamil*. Since the message and religion of the prophets is one, the messages cannot contradict one another but must be mutually confirmatory.

All apparent contradictions, therefore, must be resolved, and any interpretation which is irreconcilable with consistent prophetic tradition must be rejected as incorrect.[67] Moreover any novel use of terminology or departure from the customary significations of terms and ideas in the sacred books must be considered suspect and probably invalid.

It is in this last matter that Ibn Taymiyya most often takes issue with the Christians. If *hulul* and *ittihad*, fatherhood and sonship, have a consistent tradition of meaning in the books of Moses and the later prophecies, how can their application of these terms to Christ in a radically different sense be justified? As a prophet offering the one consistent message from God, Christ could not be the source of these innovative interpretations, nor could the apostles—believers and upright persons—have introduced them.

The accusation is that, in the period subsequent to the apostles, the leading men among the Christians failed to see the revelation of Christ in the context of an ongoing prophetic tradition. Acting on their own authority, they applied literally and absolutely terms which consistently had carried a figurative or metaphorical significance in the earlier books, and applied specifically to Christ terms and concepts which had carried a general meaning among the prophets.

In refuting the passages quoted in the Letter from Cyprus, which, as has been mentioned, were not a part of the original treatise of Paul of Antioch, Ibn Taymiyya's efforts are directed towards showing that these passages could not possibly bear the meaning imposed upon them by the Christian adversary, and then secondly toward showing that the evident (*zahir*) significance of the terms as well as the context in which the terms are set demand a meaning not only consistent with prophetic statements elsewhere, but with the Qur'anic revelation later given through Muhammad. Several of the passages he takes a step further and argues that those prophecies more logically find their fulfillment in the revelation of the Qur'an and the establishment of Islam than in the birth and mission of Christ, as Christians had interpreted them.[68]

For Ibn Taymiyya the question of textual fidelity or corruption (*tahrif al-lafz*) in the Bible is, therefore, secondary to that of revised and singular interpretation of verses (*tahrif al-ma'na*). In fact, if it can be determined that the interpretations of the scriptural texts have undergone change, the question of textual corruption becomes much less relevant to Muslim charges of corruption of scripture against the People of the Book.

It is *tahrif al-ma'na* of which the Qur'an accuses the People of the Book, principally the Jews.[69] While Jews and Christians are never accused explicitly of *tahrif al-lafz* in the Qur'an, neither is it denied that such textual corruption could have occurred.[70] This is in contrast to the reinterpretation of the original meaning of the texts or the application of the wording of the texts in a context different from and opposed to its proper setting; such *tahrif al-ma'na*, he holds, is an accusation against the People of the Book which the Qur'an has expressly brought.

However, it is of no value for a people to possess the accurate wording of the scriptures if they have changed the interpretations, explanation, and legal prescriptions of their sacred books. Christians, for example, attest that the Jews possess the correct text of the Old Testament, and yet they deem them the most faithless of people.[71]

Moreover Christian tradition itself gives evidence that the interpretations of the Bible underwent change. Theological disputes among opposing sects of Christians necessitated constant reinterpretation and redefinition of scriptural passages.

> Any intelligent person knows that their exegesis of the Books which they now have, arising out of the opposition and dispute among sects of Christians and between Christians and Jews, is something that necessitates definitively that much of it is corrupted and distorted, just as the changing of the legal prescriptions of these books has occurred.[72]

A final issue involving the question of *tahrif* was raised by Paul of Antioch. He contended that when the Qur'an states "Let the People of the Gospel judge by what God has revealed therein" (5:47), it indicates that the gospels which were in use among Christians contained the Gospel revealed to Christ. How else could Christians fulfill the Qur'anic command to judge by it?

In response Ibn Taymiyya distinguishes between the passages in a sacred book which provide information about the deeds, sayings, and virtues of the prophet (*al-khabariyyat*) and those which contain commands and prohibitions (*al-amriyyat*); the latter are the basis for legislation. The command that Christians judge by what is contained in the Gospel indicates only that little or no textual alteration (*tahrif al-lafz*) was done on the *amriyyat* but only *tahrif al-ma'na*. Corruption of both text and interpretation may have occurred on the *khabariyyat*.

> They are commanded to be judged by them, since the judgments of God are in them. The generality of the judgments which they contain have not been textually changed, but only some of the texts of the *khabariyyat* and some of the interpretations of the *amriyyat*.[73]

An issue closely related to that of *tahrif* of scripture is the replacement (*tabdil*) of the practices and laws of the Gospel by new practices legislated by Christian church leaders. In permitting their leaders to abrogate legislation mentioned in the Bible and to introduce new practices in place of those delivered by the prophets, they have, in effect, "taken their great men and monks as lords" (9:31).[74] Ibn Taymiyya summarizes his objections to innovated Christian practices as follows:

> Christ did not ordain for you the Trinity, nor your thinking on the divine persons, nor your doctrine that he is Lord of the Universe. He did not prescribe for you that you make pork and other forbidden things permissible. He never commanded you to omit circumcision, or that you should pray to the east; nor that you should take your great men and monks as masters beside God. He did not tell you to commit *shirk* by using statues and the cross, or by praying to the absent or dead prophets and holy men and telling them your needs. He did not prescribe monasticism or the other reprehensible practices which you innovated. Christ never ordained such things for you, nor is that which you follow the Law which you received from the messengers of Christ.[75]

Following earlier Muslim polemical tradition, he places the beginning of most of the innovations of the Christian religion at the time of Constantine, but more than any polemicist who preceded him, he attempts to elaborate the rationale behind these substitutions of practice and law. Most of the innovations in practice which occurred in Christianity about the time of Constantine were, he contends, the result of anti-Jewish feelings in Christianity and the subsequent desire among Christians to distinguish themselves in any way possible from the Jews on matters of belief, religious practice, and legislation.[76] Thus, at the present time, states Ibn Taymiyya, Jews and Christians are lined up opposing one another from opposite extremes on religious matters, while Muslims occupy the centrist, moderate position.[77]

Christians accomplished this departure from prophetic religion by constructing a composite religion through assimilation of elements from the practices of the pagan philosophers.

> The Christians constructed a religion from two religions—from the religion of the monotheist prophets and from that of the idolators. In their religion, it developed that there was a portion containing that which was brought by the prophets and a portion which they innovated from the idolators by way of opinions and deeds. Thus, they innovated the terms of the hypostases, although these terms were not found anywhere in the message of the prophets. Similarly, they introduced printed idols in place of bodily idols [icons in place of statues], prayers to them in place of praying to the sun, moon, and stars, and fasting in the spring in order to combine revealed religion and the cycle of nature.[78]

The document composed by the early leaders who fashioned the composite religion to epitomize and solidify their teaching was the creed. According to Ibn Taymiyya, the creed opposes both the sense and the text of the Christian scriptures[79] and is a gratuitous departure from the teaching of the apostles. He holds that Christians have made the creed the unique principle of their religion (*asl dinihim*),[80] and the role played by the Qur'an and sunna in Islam is played by the creed in the religion of Christians. However, whereas the former is traceable directly back to the prophet, the creed, by admission of Christians, is something new, an innovation occurring over three centuries after the death of their prophet.

Those who produced it were neither inspired, inerrant prophets, nor even the followers of the prophet, but ordinary, fallible individuals who were not even unanimous in accepting the document. There is nothing, he states, in the creed which can be traced directly to divine origin or revelation through a prophet. In contrast to the gospels, which as *khabar* contain authentic revelation, the creed can in no way be considered inspired. A religion whose origin is human rather than divine can only be considered a corrupted, innovated human invention. Christians admit that the terminology of the creed is neither evangelical nor apostolic in origin. Ibn Taymiyya undertakes to show that the belief expressed by this terminology is similarly inconsistent with and even contradictory to the gospels and the apostolic community.

Christians reject the concept that only a teaching or a command which can be critically proved to be from a prophet can be the basis for a belief or a religious practice. Instead they rely on their leaders to dictate practices and beliefs for them, while they in turn have sought guidance from essentially unreliable and ambiguous personal experiences, such as Constantine's vision of the cross or Peter's dream (Acts of the Apostles 11:1-18).[81]

Christians are forced to rely on untrustworthy sources for faith and practice because they have no method for determining the actual teaching of Christ and the other prophets. They have no consensus either on matters of faith or in religious practices,[82] no critical apparatus for determining the correctness or falsity of prophetic *khabar*, and no successive transmission of their reports. Since they can make no conclusive statement about the authenticity of material reportedly received from the prophets, it is possible, and has actually happened, that they have transmitted false information about Christ.

An instance of this cited by Ibn Taymiyya is the Christian report of the crucifixion of Christ. He notes that the acceptance of this as a historical fact has not been unanimous among Christians.[83] In the Islamic tradition, also, there has not been unanimity on details of the crucifixion, and one must be careful not to state as certain what is only conjecture. It cannot be said, for example, whether the followers of Christ conspired to deceive on this matter or whether they themselves were in doubt about it. What is certain for Muslims is that the followers of Christ, who were not inerrant transmitters of prophetic information, were in error on the matter.[84]

It is essentially irrelevant to any judgment on the prophetic nature of Christ, which he sees as undeniably established irrespective of whether or not he was crucified. As such, the crucifixion of Jesus is a side issue for him and is of importance principally as evidence against the inerrancy of Christian apostolic transmission.

A word must be said about Ibn Taymiyya's treatment of the redemption. He sees it as an instance of the introduction into Christ's religion of a belief for which there is no philosophic warrant and whose presuppositions and conclusions are opposed to the teaching of the prophets. In the Qur'an, Adam repents and is pardoned; although this is not explicitly stated in the Bible, there is nothing which contradicts that. How, he asks, could God imprison in hell prophets like Abraham and Moses for the sin of Adam, when God forgave them their own sins and those of their parents?[85]

The Christian teaching is opposed to the justice of God and would allow Satan to imprison upright individuals for the sin of another. Moreover what is the connection in justice or logic between Christ's presumed death on the cross and the redemption of individuals from the power of Satan? If Satan was acting wrongly in this, God would not have needed a crucifixion to rectify their situation; if Satan was acting properly in imprisoning them, the crucifixion of Jesus would not make his action improper.[86]

Finally, their doctrine of the redemption has the effect of making God deficient in both knowledge and power. Ibn Taymiyya's technique in arguing against Christian teaching on the redemption is to elaborate conundrums into which he feels that their teaching leads. He does not try to discover the source of the teaching outside Christianity, as did Muhammad ibn Abi Talib in Persian dualism,[87] but limits his argumentation to pointing out the incompatibility between the doctrine and the consistent teaching of the prophets.

## Trinitarian questions

Ibn Taymiyya sees the doctrine of the trinity as the greatest innovation of belief among Christians. He finds nothing either in the explicit teaching of the prophets or in any valid interpretation of their statements which provides a basis for this Christian doctrine. They have built it, he declares, from ambiguous expressions in the Bible,[88] and have surrounded it with a rational argumentation that is unconvincing and internally contradictory.

Ibn Taymiyya's response is not to develop a logical and comprehensive refutation of the doctrine of the trinity in the tradition of 'Abd al-Jabbar in the *Mughni* and Al-Baqillani in his *Tamhid*.[89] Ibn Taymiyya was highly critical of earlier Muslim rationalist polemics against Christian trinitarian formulations,[90] and in *Al-Jawab al-Sahih* his goals in argumentation are limited to attempting to show that Paul of Antioch's proofs are invalid.

Of much more central concern to Ibn Taymiyya is his conviction that all aspects of the trinitarian doctrine among Christians are anomalous within the prophetic tradition and antithetical to it. He endeavors to show that all the terminology of the trinity—the hypostases, fatherhood, and sonship, the divine and human natures in Christ, the spirit—has been used by Christians to carry meanings that the words never could have borne in the teachings of Christ and the other prophets before him. Conversely, the meanings which the terms carry in the Qur'an bear witness that the message of the prophets is one by reiterating the constant teaching of the whole prophetic line.

Paul of Antioch claimed that the Christian formulation of the trinity was an attempt to describe the one God as a creating, living, communicating being,[91] but Ibn Taymiyya responds that the Christian teaching does not arise from observation of the universe.[92] They themselves claim to have learned the teaching from their sacred books, and it is therefore in the sphere of the teaching of the prophets rather than of natural philosophy or ontology where the question must be settled.

Rational argumentation has value for Ibn Taymiyya in that by the unreasonableness of Christian explanations of the trinity one can show that the Christian teaching could never have been taught by the prophets. The prophets, he states, teach things which go beyond what people could come to know simply through reason, but they can never teach that which the human intellect knows to be absurd or impossible.

On these grounds he attacks the analogies made by Paul of Antioch and common in Christian Arab literature that the divine hypostases are comparable to the sun whose rays and light are generated or proceed from it but are essentially different from it,[93] or the analogy to one individual with three descriptive attributes.[94] Whereas he considers the above analogies to be inapplicable to the trinity and to lead to absurd conclusions when brought to bear on the nature of divine hypostases, he finds other attempts by the Christians to erect a rational explanation for their doctrine even more inadequate and dangerous. He tries to show that the Christian explanation of the Word from the Father as an intellectual generation like speech from the mind is a theory more repugnant to reason than that Mary should be the spouse of God.[95]

Their final resort, when pressed with the rational absurdity of their teaching, he states, is to claim that their belief is beyond reason. In this they parallel those in Islam who have rejected rational and sense knowledge in favor of mystical intuition as the sole path to truth. He cites Al-Tilimsani in this regard, "Among us there is proven by [mystical] discovery (*al-kashf*) that which contradicts sound reason,"[96] and Ibn Taymiyya responds that such people are following not religious insight at all, but rather blind imitation of their teachers, just as do the Christians.

For Ibn Taymiyya, revelation must be in accord with what is reasonable, and so the primary question which must always be asked about any religious teaching is whether or not it is in agreement with what has been revealed through the prophets. He claims that Christians fail to be in agreement with the teaching of the prophets in various ways. Firstly, they adopt terminology and concepts (such as *uqnum*)[97] which are in themselves innovative and not mentioned by any prophet. Secondly, they adopt teachings whose conclusions are incompatible with what the prophets have taught, such as their explanation of intellectual generation, which demands potentiality and change in God[98]—conclusions which are incompatible with teachings handed down through the prophets.

Ibn Taymiyya sees a third way in which the Christian doctrine of the trinity is in opposition to that of prophetic instruction. This is their application of words and passages actually spoken by Christ or the other prophets in a sense which the prophet never could have meant and which the context of his speech could not bear. Ibn Taymiyya treats every biblical passage cited in the Letter from Cyprus in an effort to show that the critical words are cited out of context or that they are applied in a novel and unjustifiable sense.[99] He cites the Qur'an as evidence that it is for their departure from the teaching of the prophets for which Christians are condemned.[100]

Whenever the prophets spoke about God as "Father," their intent was always clearly to indicate the lordship of God over creatures. They mean that God was a creator and one who reared mankind by providing sustenance, support, and guidance. For this reason God was called "Father" by some of the prophets, but their purpose in this figurative usage was always to teach the one message about God delivered by all the prophets. There was nothing in this, he states, to imply any real generation in God or any unique relationship between God and Jesus.

When Jesus is called "son" in the Gospel, the situation is the same. The term means "he who is governed, reared"[101]—that is,

God's creature, His servant who is supported by Him. This teaching of the earlier prophets is restated in the Qur'an, and it is clear that no unique prerogatives to Christ are expressed by the term. Ibn Taymiyya cites the words of Jesus himself to indicate that he did not consider the term "son" as singularly applicable to himself. Christians, however, make the terms "father" and "son" equivocal and gratuitously apply them to Christ in a sense different from the sense in which they apply the term to others.

> When in their books the Christians are faced with their calling Christ a son and calling other prophets a son—as God's saying to Jacob "You are my firstborn son" and calling the apostles sons—they say that Christ is a son by nature and the others are sons by adoption. Thus they make the term "father" an equivocal term. They posit a nature for God and make Christ his son by expression of that nature. This is attested by the view of those among them who understand Christ to be God's son by the sonship known to creatures, and Mary as the spouse of God. In the same way they make "Holy Spirit" a term which carries both the meaning of the life of God and the Holy Spirit which descends upon the prophets and holy men.[102]

He contends that in the biblical books the Holy Spirit refers to one of two things—either the angel Jibril (Gabriel), who delivered the divine revelation from God to the prophets, or else it refers to the support and guidance which God implants in the hearts of prophets and upright persons whether or not that was done through the mediation of the angel. These two meanings are interconnected, for it is the angel which brings the revelation and guidance.

> This Spirit which God revealed, with which the angels descended upon whichever of God's servants He willed is different from the Faithful Spirit who descended with the Book. Both of these are called "spirit" and both are interdependent. Thus the spirit with which the angel descended as well as the Faithful Spirit who descended with it are each meant by the term "Holy Spirit." The exegetes explain the statement about Christ [2:87] by both of these views.[103]

Christians, he states, have admitted these two meanings for the Holy Spirit in the case of everyone other than Christ. They hold that the Holy Spirit descended upon the apostles and that it was the Spirit who inspired the prophets.[104] They hold that Jesus took flesh from Mary and the Holy Spirit, "and the meaning of this is that Jesus was created from the spirit which is Jibril the Holy Spirit."[105]

Ibn Taymiyya argues that the above-mentioned meanings were the only ones given to the terms "Father," "son," and "Holy Spirit" in the messages of the early prophets, Christ, and Muhammad. By identifying these with the divine hypostases—in particular, their identification of the son with the word of God and the Holy Spirit with the life of God—Christians have performed *tahrif al-ma'na* upon the texts of their own sacred books and on those of the Qur'an. If Christ actually said the passages they cite as bases for trinitarian beliefs, such as the baptismal formula in Matthew's gospel (Matthew 28:19), then his statement must have a sound meaning which is consistent with what had been taught by the prophets previous to him and that later was brought by Muhammad.

> The meaning of "Baptise people in the name of the Father and of the Son and of the Holy Spirit" is that they command people to believe in God and His prophet which God sent and in the angel by which God sent down the revelation which he brought. Thus, that would be a command for them to believe in God and His angels, books, and messengers.[106]

Paul of Antioch stated that the Christian teaching that the Word of God, eternally subsisting in Him, became incarnated in Jesus was not incompatible with the Islamic teaching that the Qur'an is the eternal and uncreated speech of God.[107] The reasoning is that the eternal divine message can manifest itself in time in a specific individual as well as it could in a sacred book.

Ibn Taymiyya responds that God has many "words," of which the Qur'an is but one; Muslims make no claim for the Qur'an they do not make for the Torah, the Gospel, and the many other utterances of God. However, Muslims never call any of these words creator, lord, or God.

He states that the Qur'an and the other words of God are but generically eternal (*qadim al-naw'*)—that is, that God "was always a speaker by will" or, "He always spoke whenever He willed."[108] The teaching that the Qur'an was eternal in its individual manifestation appeared only in the century after that of the *salaf* in an age of innovation. Ibn Taymiyya's purpose is not to defend every statement or doctrine mentioned by Muslims, but to elucidate the truth as it can be known from the Qur'an and the sunna.

> Our intention is to present the truth with which God sent His messengers and revealed His Books and to refute Christians and others who oppose that. We do not deny that among those affiliated with Islam there are hypocrites, renegades, and crypto-Manichaeans. There are ignorant innovators. There are those who hold a view similar to that of Christians and those who hold something worse than theirs. Our intention is to refute all these people. Infallibility is established for the Book of God and the sunna of His messenger, and His believing servants can only agree on that which is true.[109]

The fact that some views of Muslims may be compatible with, similar to, or more pernicious than those of Christians is no argument for them. The difference between Islam and Christianity in this matter is that in Islam whenever innovations have appeared God always raised up those who opposed the innovators and gave victory to those upholding the sunna, whereas in Christianity the innovators triumphed and those holding the religion of Christ became a scattered few.[110]

The words of God are not the same; the Qur'an is not the Torah in Arabic, and neither of those books is the Gospel. Moreover, when people recite the Qur'an, their sounds and movements are created, although the Qur'an which they read is the uncreated speech of God.

Ibn Taymiyya cites Ibn Hanbal to show that the Qur'anic verse (4:171) in which Jesus is called the Word of God indicates merely that by the creative word of God he was made.[111] Similarly his being called "a spirit from Him" does not indicate that anything of the essence of God united with the human nature of Jesus, neither an attribute of God like His speech nor the essence of God Himself.

The question of the hypostatic union in Christ, one that encompasses the concepts of union (*al-ittihad*) and divine indwelling (*al-hulul*) is complicated among Christians, holds Ibn Taymiyya, by the fact that Christians themselves are mutually opposed on their explanations of this doctrine. He cites earlier works by Muslims, namely, those of al-Juwayni, Abu al-Qasim al-Ansari, Abu al-Hasan ibn al-Zaghuni, Al-Baqillani, and Abu Ya'la ibn al-Farra'[112] to delineate the opposing formulations found among Christians to explain the hypostatic union.

His method of responding to the various Christian formulations follows the pattern which he created for answering Christians on other trinitarian questions. He tries to prove that the consistent teaching of the prophets has been to deny that any essential union could take place between God and a creature, to show that such a union is inconceivable and logically contradictory,[113] and that it would lead to conclusions which would destroy the nature of God as described by the prophets and which Christians themselves could not accept.[114]

The question of *hulul* is more complex because of the ambiguity of the term. Ibn Taymiyya admits that the prophets often spoke of God's dwelling on earth, or with His people, or in the hearts of believers, but he rejects the supposition that what is meant by that is any formulation of belief whereby the essence of God resides in a person or place. The consistent teaching of the prophets and the contexts of the individual passages show clearly that what is meant by such prophetic statements is that an intellective representation of the knowledge, power, guidance, and love of God is what resides in believers.

> By *hulul*, rather, is meant the presence of faith in God and knowledge of Him, love and remembrance of Him, worship of Him, His light, and His guidance. This may be expressed as an indwelling of the intellective representation (*al-mithal al-'ilmi*) as is mentioned in the Qur'an (6:3, 30:28). To God belong the highest representations in the hearts of the dwellers of the heavens and the dwellers of earth.[115]

Ibn Taymiyya cites a number of hadith reports from Muhammad to indicate both the extreme closeness between God and the believer through mutual love and at the same time the essential distinction and separation in essence which must be preserved between God and the creature.[116] It is the mind-disturbing power of a reciprocal love of the believer for God that has led some Muslims to err in thinking that God Himself has united with them or dwelt within them. They experience their overpowering love for the Beloved so strongly that they fail to perceive the distinction and distance in essence between God and themselves. It is out of such error that the ecstatic utterances of the Sufis arise.

The true union which exists between the prophets and upright believers and God is one of will and action. When this kind of unity exists, the believer only desires what God desires, only hates what He hates, only does what He commands, etc. Such an individual can in a metaphorical sense be said to be in union with God—that is, for one who would accept, listen to, or befriend that person it would be like accepting, listening to, or befriending God. It is in this sense that statements of Muhammad and the earlier prophets concerning God's indwelling among or within mankind should be taken.[117]

In this connection, also, Ibn Taymiyya draws a parallel between the Christian belief in divine *hulul* and *ittihad* in Jesus and popular beliefs among Muslims. It was often claimed that God dwelt in the persons of upright individuals, and while there is a correct sense in which this can be understood, it led to such people being granted honors and intercessory roles which constitute a form of *shirk*. The same process which occurred concerning Christ among Christians Ibn Taymiyya saw occurring among Muslims in reference to Sufi shaykhs and others known for their piety. Occasionally this led, as he claimed it had among Shi'a, to institutionalizing a kind of *shirk* in the form of pilgrimages to the tombs of such persons and prayers of intercession to them.

The theory among Muslims which strikes most directly at true

Islamic teaching—*wahdat al-wujud* —is seen by Ibn Taymiyya to be based on an error which seems to parallel that of Christians but is actually antithetical to their belief and surpasses it in *kufr*. Christian teaching, he states, demands partitioning, deficiency, and temporality in God, whereas that of *wahda* attacks God's very individuality and separate existence.

> They [Christians] hold that *hulul* and *ittihad* occur in time, and that the Eternal One has taken residence in or united with a temporal creature after the two had not been united. But these others declare an absolute unity. Those who assert it say that He is the existence of everything, not holding for the union of two existences, nor for the indwelling of one of them in the other. . . . They hold that if the essential manifestation has occurred for you, your worshiping idols and other things would not harm you, for they state clearly that He is at the heart of idols and rivals and that a person does not worship other than Him.[118]

The error in both Christians and proponents of the oneness of existence arises from a superficial reflection upon the facts of sense experience. Christians, reflecting upon good and holy qualities in Jesus, wrongly deduced that he must be divine; proponents of the oneness of being experience an undefined oneness within themselves through their mystical experiences and fail to perceive that this experience of oneness is limited to their own minds and cannot be predicated of external reality.[119] Christian believers in the hypostatic union in Christ are like the proponents of *wahda* in that both rely on another source of knowledge than reason and revelation for beliefs which contradict both.

## Epistemological questions

Ibn Taymiyya believed that with Christians as with proponents of wayward beliefs among Muslims the issues which separate them from the true teaching of Islam are ultimately based on questions of knowledge. What can be known by man about God, and what is the relationship and trustworthiness of the various sources of information about Him? How is intellectual knowledge (*'aql*) related to information obtained from revealed tradition (*naql*) and what is the relationship of sense knowledge (*hiss*) to both of these? How is what is known rationally related to information derived through mystical insight (*dhawq*), experience (*shuhud*), discovery (*kashf*), and ecstasy (*wajd*)?

The first form of knowledge about divine affairs which Ibn Taymiyya rejects as corrupt and useless is that derived from the speculations of the peripatetic school of philosophers. The Christians, he states, have repeatedly claimed that anyone acquainted with the writings of the philosophers would immediately find Christian teaching compatible with theirs. From this they infer that "whoever reads their [the philosophers'] books knows from them the truth of divine things not known by the rest of the followers of the religions."[120] To Ibn Taymiyya this indicates the bankruptcy of Christian theological speculation, for, in his opinion, the philosophers are the most ignorant of people in their knowledge of divine matters. Christians or Jews with even a slight amount of true information from the prophets are more knowledgeable about God than were the Greeks like Aristotle. The pseudo-philosophers among the followers of the three religions have only been able to approach the truth to the extent they reject the philosophical principles of the Greeks.

The endeavor of attempting to show the compatibility of the teaching of the prophets and that of the philosophers is misguided, he states, and doomed to lead either to the abandonment of the religion of the prophets—as the Christians had done and various groups within Islam were in the process of doing—or to a rejection of the philosophers' theses. He sees the theodicy and cosmology elaborated by the philosophers and the philosophical principles which they presuppose as being intrinsically incompatible with the message of the prophets, and thus one cannot look to the philosophers for information about God and remain a true follower of the prophets.

> Anyone who thinks that the message of the Messengers agrees with these Greeks indicates by this his ignorance of what the Messengers brought and of what these people [the philosophers] say. Something like this is only found in the teaching of the renegades of the three religions—the apostates among the Jews, Christians, Muslims, and others. I mean, for example, the writers of the Epistles of the Brethren of Purity, and those like them who associate themselves with the Shi'a or Sufism like Ibn 'Arabi, Ibn Sab'in and their kind. In the books held back from those outside his own circle and those similar to them, a portion of the teaching ascribed to Abu Hamid [al-Ghazali] is of this type.[121]

The Christians, when pressed that their doctrine is irrational, respond that their teaching is beyond what can be known by reason. In response Ibn Taymiyya distinguishes between what can be known by reason to be false and impossible and what, while it is in accord with the principles of sound reason, would not be known except through revelation. The latter, he claims, is the object of prophetic messages; the former can never be taught by the prophets, and yet it is this category to which Christian trinitarian doctrines belong.[122] Moreover, in their intramural theological disputes they reject the claim of their opponents that some proof is "beyond reason" as valid in argumentation against proofs of reason; what they disallow for others they cannot employ for themselves.

Rather, he holds, truth is unitary. Whatever has been truly revealed can never be contradicted by what is known through reason and sense perception, but can only be confirmed by such information. Similarly whatever is correctly known from intellectual knowledge or from accurate sense perception must be confirmed by revelation.

He criticizes two types of people for failing to adhere to the above principle.[123] Some, like Christians and the proponents of *wahdat al-wujud*, oppose doctrines which they claim to be reasonable to the sense and text of prophetic teachings as well as to what is known by sense perception. However, since truth is unitary, the demonstration that a teaching is opposed to that of the prophets indicates its falsity, and in every case it can be shown to be irrational as well. The second group of people criticized are the anti-rationalists, who oppose revealed information or sense perceptions to rational knowledge. Examples of the latter view would be those who believe manifestly impossible feats—such as bilocation—about holy persons.

Similar to the last group would be those who posit another critical faculty—that of immediate, mystical perception. It can be described as a form of intuitive knowledge (*dhawq*), a non-rational experience of reality (*shuhud*), or an ecstatic state of heightened perceptivity (*wajd*), but the common element in these phenomena is the positing of a non-rational form of knowledge independent of both reason and revelation. This immediate perception, according to its proponents, can contradict and transcend that which is known from the sacred books and from reason. Ibn Taymiyya cites the poetry of Al-Tilimsani to the effect that the ecstatic mystic must reject the religious teaching of the uninitiate as being opposed to the insight he has gained through his ecstatic experiences.

> My friend, you forbid me and you command me,
> But ecstasy is a more faithful prohibitor and commander.
> If I obey you and disobey ecstasy, I turn back in blindness
> From clear sight to imagined reports.
> The true nature of what you have called me to,
> If you examine it closely, neighbor, you'll find it forbidden.[124]

On the other hand, sense knowledge is extremely fallible and the validity of its perceptions must be judged by reason. Reason, on the other hand, can misjudge what has been correctly perceived by the senses, and a person can only be sure of judging in accordance with sound reason when his judgments are in agreement with what has been revealed through the prophets. In the same way mystical intuition can be followed only when it is clearly compatible with what has been taught by the prophets and therefore in agreement with sound reason as well.

A final source of information must be mentioned. Ibn Taymiyya considers it to be the weakest path to knowledge, and he accuses the Christians of basing much in their religion upon it. This is *taqlid*—the uncritical acceptance of what preceding generations have believed and done, which leads to a blind imitation of both their strengths and errors. In his evaluation of Ibn Bitriq's ecclesiastical history he charges that the Christians have adopted most of their religion by a subservient following of the errors taught by individual leaders in previous generations. The Christian teachers who were so slavishly imitated could themselves arrive at no consensus regarding which doctrines of the fathers were to be followed.[125]

Anyone who would make one of the fallible sources of knowledge primary—whether it be reason, sense perception, mystical intuition, or the teaching of previous generations—and interpret the prophetic message by what agrees with what they claim to know from one of the other sources can only conclude in error. The only way in which someone can be certain that what he has learned from one of the fallible sources of information is true is to examine critically the knowledge against what is infallibly known to be true from the prophets. Moreover, the contents of the prophetic message are a sufficient base from which to deduce rationally a judgment in any given issue.[126]

A related set of questions is raised by Paul of Antioch's fifth section. His argument was that human terminology is insufficient for defining the nature of God, and mankind is forced to settle for approximate descriptions of the divine reality. It is not surprising, therefore, that Christian formulations of the Trinity are necessarily inadequate in their attempts to state in human terms the true nature of God.[127] However, the Christian terminology is no more inaccurate than the anthropomorphic expressions found in the Qur'an and sunna.

Ibn Taymiyya's response to this challenge is that only by describing God as He has described Himself can one safely avoid erring in formulation. The prophetic message includes a detailed affirmation of every attribute of perfection in God as well as a denial that there is anything else which represents, shares in, or is similar to Him in such attributes.

> Whoever denies any of the attributes of God which He Himself has affirmed is a "transcendentalist" (*mu'attil*), while anyone who makes these attributes like those of creatures is a "representationist" (*mumaththil*). The former serves a god who is absent, the latter an idol.[128]

There is a consistency between the description of God found in the Qur'an and that found in the earlier sacred books. The anthropomorphic terminology found in the Qur'an is of the same order as that mentioned in the Old and New Testaments. By contrast, the trinitarian formulation appearing in the Nicene creed and elaborated by Christian theologians is an innovation both in terminology and in the description of God towards which it points.

> In the speech of the Prophets, either in that of Christ or of any of the others, there is no mention of the hypostases of God—either three or more—nor of an establishing of the three attributes, nor any calling of any one of the attributes God or son of God or Lord, or calling His life a Spirit, nor that God had a son who is true God from true God, from the essence of his father, and that he is creator just as God is creator. This is the case [as well] with other opinions comprising forms of disbelief—none of these was ever handed down by any prophet.[129]

Ibn Taymiyya thus attacks the analogy drawn by Paul of Antioch between the trinitarian formulation of the Nicene Creed and the anthropomorphic expressions in the Qur'an by holding that the latter is consistent with the prophetic teaching as a whole while the former is antithetic to it.

Once again he draws a parallel between Christians and "Muslim renegades who believe in the divinity of one of the People of the House or one of the shaykhs and who describe God with attributes not stated by the Book."[130] All of them, he states, invent a terminology to define views incompatible with prophetic teaching. Even if their intent were sound—that is, to represent the teaching of the prophets in a new vocabulary—their adopting a vocabulary which verbally contradicts the prophetic message would not be permissible. In the case of both Christians and wayward Muslims, however, their innovated terminology only serves to define erroneous teaching.

## The superiority and necessity of Islam

Paul of Antioch contended that religion is of two kinds: religion of law and religion of *fadl*—that is, of grace, preference, goodness. Judaism represented the religion of law and Christianity the religion of grace. Beyond this, nothing else was possible, and any new religious law or revelation must be necessarily superfluous.

In response Al-Qarafi rejected Paul of Antioch's dichotomy and presented the Torah as the law of Moses which contained many kinds of grace. The Gospel was basically a restatement of the law of Moses with the addition of exhortations derived from the upright personal qualities of Jesus; as a mere restatement, the Gospel did not deserve to be called "the religion of grace." When, however, the law of Moses and its restatement by Christ were abandoned during the period after the deaths of their messengers, Muhammad was sent with the true religion of grace, that is, Islam.[131]

Muhammad ibn Abi Talib responded to Paul of Antioch that there had been only one *din* which contained law and grace. The various legal and ritual systems (*shara'i'*) legislated by the various prophets were partial expressions of the one *din*, but only in Islam did the *shari'a* achieve the fullness of perfection in law and grace of the one prophetic religion.

Ibn Taymiyya's treatment of this question is far more extensive than that of either Al-Qarafi or Muhammad ibn Abi Talib. He presents twelve separate answers to Paul of Antioch's contention; he seems to have been the only one of the three Muslim polemicists who grasped that in his final point Paul of Antioch leveled his most serious attack against Islam. Where his letter earlier was apologetic, defending Christianity from Muslim accusations of corruption and unbelief, in his final section Paul takes the offensive and establishes an argument which presents Islam as an anomaly in the economy of salvation, totally superfluous to anything God had done through the prophets and therefore basically fraudulent.

Ibn Taymiyya's central position, around which he develops each of his responses, is that Paul of Antioch had misdrawn the relations among the religions. Properly speaking, there is a religion of law which is Judaism, a religion of grace which is Christianity, and a religion which combines perfectly both law and grace—that is, Islam.

His purpose is to show that in themselves both Judaism and Christianity are deficient. If God's purpose in religion is that He be affirmed by all mankind and that He be obeyed in His commands—it was necessary that the perfect religion combine the strengths of the two earlier religions of the Book and overcome their weaknesses. This, he states, has been accomplished in Islam, which perfects and completes the earlier religions.

In the matter of revelation, the Qur'an teaches much that was either unclear or not mentioned in the Torah and the Gospel. The Qur'an speaks of the afterlife and gives descriptions of the Garden and the Fire; it describes the various types of angels, the creation of mankind and jinn; it tells the stories of the Arab prophets and the controversies which took place between the prophets and their opponents. It mentions the names of God and gives information about other religions.[132] None of this was found in the Torah.

Regarding the Gospel his attitude is similar to that of Al-Qarafi. The Gospel does not bring much new revelation of the unseen, but is principally composed of moral lessons and exhortations to asceticism.

> As for the Gospel, there is no independent *shari'a* in it, nor any teaching about God's absolute oneness, nor the creation of the world, nor the stories of the prophets and their people. The Gospel refers people to the Torah for most of those matters. Christ, however, permitted for people some of what had been forbidden them, obligated them to goodness, to pardoning offenses, to bearing injuries, and to asceticism in this life. He [Christ] invented parables to teach these things.[133]

However, the moral traits taught by the Gospel and the asceticism encouraged by it are elaborated in the Qur'an more perfectly and with better balance. Ibn Taymiyya develops this position at great length and closes his response to Paul of Antioch with two arguments intended to show that such teachings of Jesus as "love your enemies, do good to those who wrong you" must lead inevitably to injustice towards the oppressed unless these statements be balanced by the severity of the Qur'anic judgments against wrongdoers.[134]

He turns Paul of Antioch's argument back on itself by declaring that the law of justice, since it requires special qualities of wisdom, courage, and fairness, is more worthy to be applied to God than is a more general exhortation to goodness which can be carried out by anyone.[135] Therefore, so long as commands to forgive one's oppressor are understood, according to the teaching of the Qur'an, as exhortations to supererogatory goodness but not as obligations in justice, the demands of both justice and goodness are served. In this way the teachings of the Torah and the Gospel are in need of the perfect legislation of the Qur'an to raise them to the fullness of justice and grace.

Even if the legal systems of the Torah and the Gospel were followed correctly by their adherents, the Qur'an and the sunna would be necessary to assert a perfect balance of justice and goodness. However, the laws handed down through Moses and Jesus were not followed by the vast majority of Jews and Christians.[136] He states, for example, that the Jews forbade many things which God had permitted, while the Christians permitted much of what God had forbidden. Even the specific exhortations of Christ to humility and moral uprightness have been abandoned by the rulers, scholars, and ordinary believers among the Christians.

> God sent Christ with pardon and tenderness, with forgiveness to the evildoer and bearing with his wrongs in order to moderate their morals and put an end to the pride and harshness in them. But Christians have gone to excess in laxity so that they have failed to command the good and prohibit what is forbidden. They have failed to do *jihad* in the way of God and to judge justly between people. Instead of establishing firm limits, their worshipers have become solitary monks. Conversely, the rulers of the Christians display pride and harshness and pass judgment in opposition to what was handed down by God. They have shed blood wrongfully in accordance with what their scholars and believers have told them as well as against what they have told them. In all that they have shared the Qur'anic accusations against the Jews.[137]

Holding that Islam is the perfect combination of justice and goodness does not mean that Jews or Christians who conscientiously tried to follow the teachings of the Torah and the Gospel were unbelievers.[138] Certainly before the sending of Muhammad, those Christians who followed the message of Jesus as best they knew it were Muslims and believers, just as were Jews before the time of Christ. Those who reject a new messenger when he is sent or the new book he brings, however, are unbelievers.

Even though they are unbelievers, Ibn Taymiyya is extremely careful not to pronounce eternal punishment on Jews and Christians either before or after the time of Muhammad. His position is surprising in view of his reputation for harshness and intolerance,[139] but he strongly affirms that any condemnation of such people—in contrast to those explicitly condemned in the Qur'an like the people of Pharaoh—is a matter known only to God.[140]

Moreover, those Jews and Christians who have not deliberately distorted either the text or the meaning of their sacred books and who strive independently for the truth from the materials available to them are of the same status as a Muslim *mujtahid*. Their very effort makes them worthy of a reward, and if their *ijtihad* leads them to true conclusions, they will deserve a double reward.[141]

Even if Jews and Christians had not distorted the religion of the prophets, he states, it would have been necessary that God send Muhammad with the new law of Islam in order that knowledge of His oneness and obedience to His command be brought throughout the earth. The political and military weakness of the Jews has made them unable to lead vast numbers of people according to the straight path of truth, whereas Christians themselves were weak and powerless until the time of Constantine, a time which coincided with their corruption and abandonment of the religion of Christ.[142]

Islam, by contrast, is a religion supported by God and granted victory by him. He points to the Muslim conquests in the first years after the death of Muhammad as evidence that the message of the prophets was brought to vast regions of the earth to which it had not extended previously. This conquering nature of Islam, coupled with the great material, cultural, and religious benefits it has brought to believers and non-believers alike,[143] are the conclusive argument, he states, against the claim of Paul of Antioch that Islam is superfluous to God's plan and irrelevant to the religious life of Jews and Christians. Moreover it completes and perfects the previous religions by correcting what their adherents had corrupted and by striking the necessary balance between harshness and laxity, between justice and goodness, between law and grace.

> They [Muslims] made the religion of the Lord conquer from the eastern parts of the world to the west by word and deed. Can any intelligent person having knowledge and fairness state that there is no benefit in God's sending Muhammad and that he is dispensed from his messengership because of what is held among the People of the Book?[144]

Ibn Taymiyya's rebuttal to the Letter from Cyprus, which had been based on Paul of Antioch's *Letter to a Muslim*, concluded with his refutation of the final argument presented in the Christian work. As has been mentioned above, in the printed editions of *Al-Jawab al-Sahih* the answer to Paul of Antioch is followed by another polemical work, directed not specifically against Christians, but against anyone who would reject the prophethood of Muhammad. The internal and external evidence is not sufficient to make a definitive statement on whether these two works were originally conceived as one long work or whether, as seems more likely, the final pages formed a self-contained work which was subsequently attached to the longer response to Paul of Antioch, either by Ibn Taymiyya himself or by an early disciple. The title of the shorter work, since it is not attested by any early biographer, does not seem to be original. In either case the final pages of the present-day *Al-Jawab al-Sahih* contain a carefully constructed defense of the prophethood of Muhammad. Although it is outside the scope of this study, Ibn Taymiyya's treatment of the prophetic nature of Muhammad's mission deserves a detailed treatment in modern scholarship.

# PART TWO
# A TRANSLATION OF
# *AL-JAWAB AL-SAHIH LI-MAN BADDAL DIN AL-MASIH*
# I. THE UNIVERSAL NATURE OF MUHAMMAD'S PROPHETHOOD

## A. FOREWORD.[1]

### THE PURPOSE OF WRITING *AL-JAWAB AL-SAHIH*

There is no god but God, and Muhammad is the messenger of God. Praise to God, the Lord of the universe, the merciful, the compassionate, the Master of the Day of Judgment. Praise to God who created the heavens and the earth and made the darkness light. Those who disbelieve in their Lord wander astray.

Praise to God who did not take a son, who has no partner in governance, nor has any associate from lower creation whom He has exalted in greatness. Praise to God who sent down upon His servant the Book, and did not permit any deviation in it, but established it in order to warn of a severe chastisement from Him, to make the believers who do good works rejoice so that for them there would be a fine reward, and to warn those who say that God has taken a son. They have no knowledge of that, nor did their forefathers; dreadful is the word that goes forth from their tongues. In any case, what they speak is but a lie (Qur'an 18:1-5).

As for what follows (*amma ba'd*): God—may He be blessed and exalted!—made Muhammad the Seal of the prophets, and perfected His religion for him and for his community. He sent him during an interval between the messengers, at a time when unbelief was manifest and the [correct] paths blotted out. Through him He gave life to the characteristics of faith which had been studied. By him He restrained the people of idolatry and unbelief and doubt from their service of idols and fires and crosses. By him He conquered the unbelievers of the People of the Book—the people of idolatry and doubt—and he erected the lighthouse of His religion which pleased Him.

Through him He celebrated the memory of His servants whom He chose. He elected him, and by him He manifested what the People of the Book had kept hidden. Through him He showed where they had gone astray from the correct path. By him He confirmed the trustworthiness of the Torah, the Psalms, and the Gospel. In him He disclosed what was not true in them by way of the falsity of corruption and replacement.

For that which God censured the Jews and Christians in His Book—like their rejecting that truth which is opposed to their whim; their being too proud to receive it; their envying and harming its people; their following the way of error, miserliness, cowardice, and hardness of heart; their describing Almighty God in terms similar to the faults and failings of creatures; their denial of that [Book] in which He described Himself by attributes of perfection particular to Himself in which no creature resembles him; their going to excess concerning the prophets and holy men, making such persons share in the worship due the Lord of the universe; their notion of divine indwelling (*hulul*) and divine union (*ittihad*) which makes a created servant become the Lord of the universe; their departing in works of religion from the legal traditions (*shara'i'*) of the prophets and messengers; their acting in religion simply from whim (*hawa*), intuition (*dhawq*), or ecstasy (*wajd*) in their hearts rather than following the knowledge which God handed down in His clear Book; their taking their great scholars and worshipers as lords whom they follow in the religion which they have introduced in opposition to that of the prophets (9:31); their opposing what is known by sound reason and correct tradition with what they think comes from divine revelations (*al-tanazzulat al-ilahiyya*) and holy inspirations (*al-futuhat al-qudsiyya*), although they actually stem from the whispering of the Accursed One[2] so that someone who accepts them is among those about whom God spoke (67:10; 7:129); and other kinds of innovations and errors for which God censured the people of the Two Books[3]—all that is what God warned his chosen community about. He made all that befell them a lesson for those who can understand.[4]

The prophet disclosed that the occurrence of these things must befall some of this [Islamic] community, although he had disclosed that in his community there would remain a group established in truth whose enemies and deserters could never harm even until the arrival of the Hour. He taught that his community would not agree upon an error, nor would those of other religious bodies outside it defeat this community; rather, it would remain manifest and triumphant, following its rightly guided, triumphant prophet. However, in its midst there must be those who follow the traditions (*sunan*) of the Jews, Christians, Byzantines, and Magians. It is reported in the collections of sound hadith reports[5] from Abu Hurayra that the Prophet said:

> "You will follow the traditions of those who came before you exactly, so that were they to enter a bear's den, then you would enter it." They said, "O Messenger of God, the Jews and the Christians?" He said, "Who else?"

It is also in the collections of reports from Abu Sa'id that the Prophet said:

> "My community will take up the way of acting of the peoples before them, inch by inch, foot by foot." They said, "O Prophet of God, Persians and Romans?" He said, "From what other people than them?"

Among those who outwardly profess Islam there are hypocrites, and those hypocrites are in the process of attaining the lowest portion of the Fire, below Jews and Christians. Thus, that for which God censured Jews and Christians may be found among the hypocrites associated with Islam. They are those who outwardly profess faith in all that the Messenger brought, but secretly are opposed to that—like the renegades (*malahida*) and the Batinis.[6] How much more will this be the case with those among them who openly manifest godlessness (*al-ilhad*).

Some of that is found among the innovators who, although they profess the generality of the message of the Prophet both inwardly and outwardly, are in confusion about the same things which are confused among the hypocrites. Thus they follow what is doubtful and depart from the solid path, like the Khajarites and other sectarians like them.

The Christians, on [the matter of] the attributes of God and His union with creatures, fall into an error in which many of these [innovators] share. Among the renegades [from Islam] there are those who are in greater error than the Christians. Divine indwelling (*al-hulul*) and union *al-ittihad*) is of two kinds; universal and particular. Universal *hulul* and *ittihad* is like those who say, "God in His essence has taken residence in every place," or "His existence is the very existence of creatures."

The particularized form is like [the belief of] those who claim divine indwelling and union for a member of the family of the

Prophet—like 'Ali and others—such as the Nusayriyya and people like that. Or it is like those who attach themselves to the descendants of the Prophet such as al-Hakim—as do Druzes and people like them, or like someone who believes these things about one of the Sufi masters—the followers of Al-Hallaj and people like them.

Whoever says that God has taken residence in or united with some one of the Companions or relatives [of the Prophet] or one of the shaykhs is in this respect more unbelieving than Christians, who hold for divine union and indwelling in Christ, for Christ is superior to all these others. Whoever holds for a universal indwelling and union has fallen into an error more universal than that of the Christians. This is the case also for someone who holds for the eternity of the souls of human beings, or their deeds, their speech, their sounds, the materials of their writings, or anything like that. In his holding this, someone has a portion of the view of Christians.

Through an understanding of the real nature of the religion of the Christians and its falsity one can also know the falsity of those views which resemble theirs—that is, the views of the perpetrators of apostasy and innovation. When the light of faith and the Qur'an arrives, God destroys that which opposes Him. He said, "Truth has come and falsehood has vanished away. Falsehood is ever bound to vanish" (17:81). God has made clear the good and superior qualities of truth, for which reason He established it as true.

One of the reasons we treat this religion and its appearance is that a letter arrived from Cyprus in which there is an argument for the religion of the Christians. In it the scholars (*'ulama'*) of their religion as well as the eminent persons (*fudala'*) of their church, ancient and modern, plead their case with religious and intellectual arguments; thus it demands that we mention by way of answer the final conclusions to which [their arguments] lead, and that we make clear their straying from what is correct, in order that thinking people may benefit thereby, and that the Balance (*al-Mizan*)[7] and the Book with which God sent His messengers may prevail.

I will include the exact wording of what they have stated, chapter by chapter, and following each chapter I will mention in response the primary and secondary arguments which pertain to it, both joining argument and settling it. That which they state in this book is the basic support upon which their scholars depend, both in our time and in previous ages, although some of them may elaborate further than others depending upon the situations. We have found them making use of this treatise before now; their scholars hand it down among themselves, and old copies of it still exist.

It is attributed to Paul of Antioch, the monk, bishop of Sidon.[8] He wrote it to one of his friends, and had previously written works about the supremacy of Christianity.[9] He stated that when he traveled to the land of Byzantium and Constantinople, to the country of Amalfi, and to some of the districts of northern Europe and Rome,[10] he met with the leaders of the people of that region and conferred with their finest scholars.[11] They thought highly of this letter which he called *The Eloquent and Renowned Treatise Proving the True Belief and the Upright Opinion.*

The contents of this letter are in six chapters.

1) Their claim that Muhammad was not sent to them, but rather to the Arabs of the Jahiliyya, and that this is indicated by what is in the Qur'an and also proven by reason.

2) Their claim that Muhammad in the Qur'an extolled the religion they followed, and his praise for it is something which obligates them to adhere to it.

3) Their claim that the messages of the preceding prophets, like the Torah, the Psalms, and the Gospel, and other messages than these, bear witness to their religion in that what they hold concerning the divine hypostases, the trinity, divine unions and other matters is true and correct. They must firmly adhere to it. Since divine religion (*shar'*) extols rather than opposes it [their belief] and reason does not object to it, it is not permissible for them to renounce it.

4) [Their claim] that their professing that [religion] is reasonable, that what they hold concerning the trinity is demonstrable by rational argumentation, and that revealed religion is in agreement with its principles (*al-usul*).

5) Their claim that they are monotheists, excusing what they say in such expressions as those of the divine hypostases which manifest a multiplicity of gods by holding that those are of the same type as the texts among Muslims in which anthropomorphism (*al-tashbih*) and corporality (*al-tajsim*) are evident.

6) [Their claim] that Christ came after Moses bringing the final limit of perfection; there is no need, after the end point has been reached, for an additional divine law beyond the [ultimate] goal. Rather, what comes after that is unacceptable as a religion.

We will show—to God be praise and strength—that all which they adduce as religious argument, whether from the Qur'an or from the books preceding the Qur'an, as well as reason itself is an argument, not for them, but against them. The generality of what they produce as arguments from the prophetic texts and from what is reasonable is in itself a proof against them and manifests the corrupt nature of their teaching, as do other prophetic texts and the criteria formed by rational standards of proof.

This is the case with most of what the innovators (*ahl al-bida'*) call upon as proof in the books of God. In those texts there is that which clearly shows that no argument for them can be found in the books; rather, the texts themselves are a proof against them. Such matters have been stated in the refutation of the innovators, the sectarians, and others affiliated with Islam (*ahl al-qibla*). Generally they only deal in obscure expressions to which they cling obstinately and in which they suppose there is proof. To these things they add whatever is connected with their whims while they avoid clear-cut, direct, and unambiguous expressions.

This is the state of all people of falsehood, as God said: "They follow but a guess and that which they themselves desire. And now the guidance from their Lord has come to them" (52:23). They are in ignorance and wrongdoing (33:72-73), but believers are those whom God has absolved from ignorance and wrongdoing. They are the followers of the prophets, for the prophets were sent with knowledge and justice (53:1-4). God has disclosed that he [the Prophet] was not erring and ignorant, nor straying and following whims. He did not speak from whim, but only spoke the revelation handed down to him by God (48:28).

Guidance contains beneficial language, and the religion of truth includes right action and is based on justice (57:25). The basis of uprightness (*al-'adl*) in the truth about God is the worship of God alone, allowing no one else to share in that worship. As Luqman told his son, "*Shirk* is great wrongdoing" (31:13).

In the collections of sound hadith it is reported from 'Abd Allah ibn Mas'ud that when the verse "Those who believe and have not obscured their faith by wrongdoing" (6:82) was revealed, it bothered some of the companions of the Messenger, and they asked, "Which of us has not ourselves done wrong?" The Messenger answered, "It is not as you think; it [the wrongdoing] only means *shirk*. Have you not heard the saying of the upright servant, '*Shirk* is great wrongdoing'?"

Whenever the followers of the prophets—who are the people of knowledge and justice—have been in discussion with unbelievers and innovators, the statements of the people of Islam and the sunna have always proceeded from knowledge and justice, not from guesswork and what their own minds imagine. The Prophet has said about this:

> The judges are three—two judges in the Fire and one judge in the Garden. The man with the knowledge of the truth who has judged in

opposition to it is in the Fire, as is he who judged people through ignorance.

Abu Dawud and others have related this report.

If he who is judged among people in matters of property, homicide, and honor without being knowledgeable and impartial is consigned to the Fire, how much more so will he be who passes judgment on sects and religions, on the principles of faith, on divine affairs and universal questions, with neither knowledge nor fairness? Yet this is the situation of the innovators and sectarians who cling tightly to doubtful obscurities while they claim clear and accurate judgments from the texts of the prophets. They cling to the common factor which is apparently the same in analogies and opinions, but they do not pay attention to the differences [among them] which prevent their being connected together and regarded as the same. This is like the situation of the unbelievers and the rest of the innovators and sectarians who make the creature resemble the creator, and the creator the creature. They have coined an evil similitude about God and a contemptible opinion.

The false religion of Christians is nothing but an innovated religion which they invented after the time of Christ and by which they changed the religion of Christ. Not only that, they strayed away from the law (*shari'a*) of Christ to what they innovated. Then, when God sent Muhammad, they rejected him. Thus their unbelief and error came to be of two aspects—that of changing the religion of the first messenger and of rejecting the second messenger. It is like the unbelief of the Jews who changed the legal prescriptions of the Torah before God's sending Christ, and then they rejected Christ.

We will show, God willing, that what the Christians hold by way of the trinity and [divine] union has not been indicated by anything in the books of God—neither by the Gospel nor by any other. Rather, they all indicated what is contradictory to that. Neither has reason indicated that; rather, sound reason—as well as the texts of the prophets—have indicated the contrary of that. Similarly, [we will show] that the generality of the laws of their religion were invented and innovated, and were not legislated by Christ.

Their rejection of Muhammad is their form of unbelief which is evident to every Muslim, like the Jews' rejection of Christ. The Christians' unbelief is more profound that that of the Jews, although they have gone to great lengths to pronounce the Jews unbelievers. They are far more deserving of being declared unbelievers than are the Jews. The Jews claimed that Christ was a lying magician, and even said that he was the child of fornication (4:56). The Christians claim that he is God who created the first and the last, and that he is judge of the Day of Judgment. The two peoples have thus gone to the limits of contradiction and mutual opposition and antithesis. Each group condemns the other on matters for which [the condemnation] is usually deserved (2:113).

Muhammad ibn Ishaq stated from Muhammad ibn Abi Muhammad, the mawla of Zayd ibn Thabit, from 'Ikrima or Sa'id ibn Jubayr, from Ibn 'Abbas that when the delegation of Christians from Najran came to the Messenger some Jewish rabbis approached them and they all argued in the presence of the Messenger. Rabi' ibn Harmala said "You don't have anything [of truth]," and he disbelieved in both Jesus and the Gospel. One of the Christians from Najran said to the Jews, "You don't have anything [of truth]," and he rejected the prophethood of Moses and disbelieved in the Torah. Then God sent down the verse in which He says about the two peoples, "The Jews say that the Christians follow nothing [true], and the Christians say that the Jews follow nothing, yet both are readers of the scripture" (2:113). He [Muhammad] said, "Each reads in his book the confirmation of that whereby he disbelieves." That is, the Jews reject Jesus, although they have the Torah in which there is the confirmation of Jesus which God placed on the tongue of Moses. In the Gospel there is the answer of Jesus confirming Moses and that which he brought in the Torah. Each group rejects what its opponent holds.

Qatada said that when the Jews said "The Christians follow nothing," he [Muhammad] said, "Yes, the earliest Christians followed something but then they innovated and split into sects." When the Christians said that the Jews follow nothing, he said "Yes the early Jews followed something but they innovated and split into sects." Thus the Jews reject the religion of the Christians and say "They follow nothing," while the Christians reject all of that by which the Jews are distinguished from them, even the things legislated in the Torah which Christ did not abrogate but commanded them to perform. The Jews reject most of that by which the Christians are distinguished from them, so that they even rejected the truth which Jesus brought.

Although the Christians went to excess in pronouncing *takfir* upon the Jews and transgressed beyond the proper limits by the excess and error which they innovated, nevertheless, there is no doubt that the Jews became unbelievers when they rejected Christ (3:55; 61:14). The unbelief of Christians in rejecting Muhammad and in opposing Muslims is greater than the unbelief of the Jews in simply rejecting Christ. Christ only abrogated a little of the legislation of the Torah, and the rest of his law referred back to it. The greater part of the religion of Christians, however, they invented after [the time of] Christ. Thus in the Jews' simple rejection of Christ there was no opposition to the law, as there *was* when the Christians rejected Muhammad who brought an independent Book from God, none of whose legislation was a mere reiteration of another law (29:51).

The Qur'an, although it is greater than the Torah, is of similar origin, and for this reason learned men among the Christians used to consider Moses and Muhammad together. The king of the Christians, the Negus, said upon hearing the Qur'an, "The spirit which visited Moses has come upon you."[12] Similarly, Waraqa ibn Nawfal, who was one of the educated Christian Arabs, said upon hearing the teaching of the Prophet, "This and that which Moses brought were taken from the niche."[13]

Similarly, God Himself has linked the Torah and the Qur'an:

> But when there came to them the Truth from our presence, they said: Why is he not given the like of what was given to Moses? Did they not disbelieve in that which was given to Moses of old? They say: Two magics that support each other (28:48).

"Two magics," that is, the Torah and the Qur'an, and in another reading, "They say, 'Two magicians,'" that is, Moses and Muhammad.

> And they say, "In both we are disbelievers." Say: Then bring a Scripture from the presence of God that gives clearer guidance than these two [that] I may follow it, if you are truthful (28:48-49).

But there has never been a book sent down from God more rightly guided than the Qur'an (28:50). And these [disbelievers in the two books] are the Christians.

In his treatise the author of the Christians' Letter stated that he [his Muslim friend][14] asked him to make a careful investigation of what various Christians—the followers of Christ[15]—people of various languages, dispersed to the four corners of the world, from east to west and from north to south, residing on the islands of the Sea,[16] dwelling on the continent which stretches to the setting of the sun—believe concerning him [Muhammad]. The bishop, a religious leader of the Roman [Byzantine] empire, met with members of their intelligentsia and their rulers. He conferred with their scholars and their finest people on what he knew about the opinion of people whom he had met on islands of the Sea before his arrival at Cyprus. To them he had preached about their religion, and discussed what they believed about him [Muhammad], and what they themselves had debated about him.

## B. THE NATURE OF PROPHETHOOD

Said the scribe in the bishop's words:

> They said, "We heard that a man appeared from among the Arabs named Muhammad who said that he was the Messenger of God and that he was bringing a Book which he said was handed down from God." I said to them, "If you have heard of this Book and this person, and have gone to the trouble of obtaining among yourselves this Book which he brought, then why do you not follow him, especially as it says in this Book 'If anyone seeks something other than Islam as a religion, it will not be accepted from him, and he will be a loser in the Hereafter?' " (3:85). They answered, "For various reasons, among which is that the Book is in Arabic, which is not our language. But it says in the Book, "We have sent down an Arabic Qur'an that perhaps you may understand" (12:2; 26:195; 2:151; 3:164; 28:48; 36:6). When we saw these verses we knew that he was not sent to us, but to the Arabs of the Jahiliyya of whom they say "There was not sent any messenger or warner before him." He did not obligate us to follow him, because there were sent messengers to us before him who preached to us and warned us in our own languages through our religion to which we hold fast until today. They handed on to us the Torah and the Gospel in our language, as this Book which this Messenger brought bears witness (14:4; 16:36; 30:47). This Book also makes clear that he was only sent to the Arabs of the Jahiliyya (3:85).[1]

This passage is taken verbatim from the first chapter. This chapter does not oppose him [Muhammad], neither confirming him nor rejecting him. Rather, they claim that in this Book [the Qur'an] itself he did not say that he was sent to them, but rather to the Arabs of the Jahiliyya, and they hold that reason also prevents his having been sent to them.

In answer, we will begin by pointing out that God disclosed that he was sent to them, and to all mankind and jinn. We will show that he never said that he was not sent to them, and that there is nothing in this Book to indicate that. We will show that they have argued from verses whose meaning they have misunderstood. They have omitted many unambiguous texts in his Book which show clearly that he was sent to them. This is similar to what they have done to the Torah, the Gospel, the Psalms, and the teaching of the prophets—they have omitted many clear texts, and have clung to a few obscure ones whose meaning they do not know.

It is obvious that the discussion of the veracity or falsity of a claimant to prophethood must be antecedent to the discussion of the general and specific elements of his prophethood, even though it may occur that one of the two be known before the other.[2] But these people claim [to know] specific characteristics of his prophethood and state that the Qur'an indicates such things. We will answer their claims in order, chapter by chapter.

The discussion concerning anyone who taught mankind that he was a messenger of God to them—as did Muhammad and others who said they were messengers of God like Abraham, Moses, and prophets like them, and as did the lying, would-be prophets like Musaylima al-Kadhdhab[3] and Al-Aswad al-'Ansi[4]—ought to be based on two principles:

1) That what he said in his message and his command is known, and that what he disclosed and what he commanded is known. That is, did he say that he was the messenger of God to all people or that he was only sent to a specific group, and not to others?

2) That we know whether he is truthful or lying.

On these two principles a detailed faith is achieved, i.e., knowledge of the truthfulness of the prophet and knowledge of what he brought. A summary faith is achieved by the first of these principles—that is, a prophet's trustworthiness in what he brought—like our faith in the previous messengers. The truthfulness or falsity of a prophet may be known before one knows what a prophet said. Conversely, what he uttered may be known before it is learned whether he was trustworthy or false. In this book of theirs these people have built their argument on what the Messenger stated; they claim it as a proof that they have no obligation to follow him, and that it commends the religion which they follow at present, even after its abrogation and corruption. After that they mention independent arguments for the correctness of their religion, and then they state what they reject as objectionable about him [Muhammad] and his religion. Thus we begin by presenting an answer to what they have argued from the Qur'an, just as they have presented it in their treatise.[5]

———

These people have claimed that Muhammad was not sent to them but to the Arabs of the Jahiliyya. This claim has two alternatives: either they hold that he himself did not claim that he was sent to them and that only his community has made that claim, or they hold that he claimed that he was sent to them, and that he was lying in this claim. Their claim in the beginning of this book demands the first alternative.

About other works it may be said that they have suggested the other alternative [that he was lying]. Here they do not really deny his messengership to the Arabs, but only reject his having been sent to them. As for his mission to the Arabs, they make no firm statement about confirming or rejecting it, although it is evident that their formulation demands a confirmation of his messengership to the Arabs. Actually they confirm what agrees with their view while rejecting that which opposes it.

We will show that their argumentation is not correct in anything of that which the Prophet brought. Subsequently we will address two questions. We will show that in the Qur'an there is no proof for them, nor does it contradict itself or any of the previous books of the prophets. That from which they argue is an argument against them, and even if Muhammad had not been sent, it would not have been in any respect an argument for them. How could it have been an argument for them when the Book which Muhammad brought is in agreement with the rest of the teaching of the prophets, as well as with sound reason, in showing the falsity of their religion—their view of the trinity, divine union, and other things.

This is in contrast to Muslims, for their argumentation against the People of the Book—the Jews and Christians—is consistent with what was brought by the prophets before Muhammad. But the argumentation of the People of the Book is not acceptable if they argue from what Muhammad brought. The reason is because Muslims admit the prophethood of Moses, Jesus, David, Solomon, and the other prophets, and according to them they must put faith in every book which God revealed and in every prophet whom God sent. This is the basis of the religion of the Muslims. Whoever disbelieves in one prophet or in one book is, according to them, a disbeliever. Among them whoever even insults any of the prophets is a disbeliever worthy of death[6] (2:136-37; 2:285; 2:177).

"The Book" is a generic term for every book revealed by God, and includes the Torah and the Gospel, just as it includes the Qur'an (42:15; 2:285;[7] 2:1-5). In these passages God has stated that this Book which He has revealed is a guidance for the god-fearing who believe in the unseen, who undertake the prayer (*al-salah*), who pay the poor tax, who believe in what God has revealed to him [Muhammad] and in what He has revealed to those before him, and who are certain of the afterlife. God then disclosed that it is these people who will prosper.[8] He has encompassed these people with prosperity, and no one will be among the prosperous unless he be from those whom God called "those who believe in what was revealed to you [Muhammad] and what was revealed to those before you" (2:4).

It is not permitted for any Muslim to reject a single thing of what was handed down to those who preceded Muhammad, but any argumentation from that demands that three prerequisites [be fulfilled].

1) Its being established as [having come] from the prophets.

2) The correctness of its translation into Arabic or into the language in which it appears—e.g., Greek or Syriac. The language of Moses, David, Jesus, etc., of the Israelite prophets was Hebrew, and whoever says the language of Jesus was Syriac or Greek is in error.[9]

3) Exegesis of the passage and knowledge of its meaning. Muslims have not rejected a single one of their arguments by denying what any one of the prophets said. They may, however, reject the transmitter [of prophetic statements] or they may misinterpret what has been handed down from the prophets by some other meaning which they desire. Even though Muslims may err in rejecting some transmitted information or in their interpretation of something handed down from the prophets, it is like someone among them or among the people of the other religions who errs in respect to something of what was handed down from him whose prophecy he accepts or in interpreting that which was handed down from him.

This is different from rejecting the prophet himself; blatant (*sarih*) disbelief is not the same as that of the People of the Book. Their intention is only achieved by rejecting some of what God has revealed. When someone rejects one word of what a person who declares himself to be a messenger of God has disclosed, that person's argumentation from the rest of his teaching is invalid, and their argument for what they are trying to prove is untenable. The reason is that someone who says he is the messenger of God either is truthful in his calling himself messenger of God and in everything else which he discloses from God, or he is false if he lied in even one word from God.

If he is truthful in that manner [in his claiming to be the messenger of God], he is prevented from lying concerning God in a single thing which reached him from God. Whoever lies about God, even in one word, is someone perpetrating falsehood against God and is no messenger of God. It is clear that whoever perpetrates a lie against God is a lying pseudo-prophet, and it is not permissible to make an argument from the information he has disclosed from God. It can be known that God did not send that person. If he said that something was merely a statement [of his own] and it was correct, it could be accepted, not because he received it from God nor because he was a messenger from God, but rather just as something true is acceptable from idolators and other unbelievers. If idol worshipers speak what is true concerning God, like the affirmation of the idolatrous Arabs that God created the heavens and the earth, we do not accuse them of lying on such a matter, even though they are unbelievers. Thus if an unbeliever holds that God is living, omnipotent, a creator, we do not reject him for [holding] this opinion.

However, anyone who has lied about God in even one word and said that God revealed it to him—when God did not reveal it to him—that person is one of the liars nothing of whose statements which they claim to have received from God may be used as argumentation. They are like other people in whatever they say other than that, and even like other liars similar to them. If the truth of their statement is known from a source other than them, this is acceptable for establishing an indication of its correctness, rather than for their having said it. But if its correctness is not known from a source other than them, there is no proof for it in their saying it after it is established that they have lied about God.

Therefore, if these people affirm the messengership of Muhammad and hold that he was trustworthy in the Book and the Wisdom which he received from God, they must place faith in everything in the Book and the Wisdom which is proven to be from him, just as faith must be placed in everything which the [other] messengers brought.

If they reject him in even one word or if they doubt his truthfulness in it, they are prevented by that from affirming that he is a messenger of God. If they do not affirm that he is messenger of God, then their argumentation from what he said is like their arguing from the statements of the rest of those who are not prophets or even of those who are liars or whose truthfulness is doubtful.

Obviously a person who is known to have spoken lies about God in what he claims to have received from Him or whose veracity is doubtful is not known to be the Messenger of God or that he is truthful in all of what he says and [claims] to have received from God. If that is not known about him, it is not known that God revealed a thing to him. On the other hand, if his falsity is known, it is known that God did not reveal a thing to him, nor did He send him. In this way the falsity of Musaylima al-Kadhdhab, Al-Aswad al-ʿAnsi, and Tulayha al-Asadi[10] is known, just as is known the falsity of Mani and similar lying false prophets.

If his truthfulness is doubted in even one word—if it is possible that a single word be incorrect either intentionally or inadvertently—then it is not possible at the same time to confirm him in the rest of what reached him from God. Confirmation in what someone discloses from God is only [possible] if he is a faithful messenger who lies neither intentionally nor inadvertently. Everyone whom God sent must be truthful in every thing which he receives from God and lie neither intentionally nor accidentally.

This is a matter on which all people—Muslims, Jews, Christians, and others—agree. They agree that the messenger must be truthful and that he lie neither intentionally nor accidentally. Without that [infallibility] the goal of prophethood is not attained (7:104-05; 69:44-47; 16:101-02; 10:15). This is elaborated elsewhere.

The point here is that their arguing from even one word of what Muhammad brought is inadmissible in any respect. If he was a truthful messenger in everything which he disclosed from God (and everyone knows that what he brought is opposed to the religion of the Christians), it is necessary that the religion of the Christians be false. If they hold that one word of what he brought is false, it is necessary that he [cannot be][11] for them a truthful prophet receiving information from God.

Whether they say that he is a just ruler, a scholar, an upright man, or whether they make him a great saint among the very greatest saints, however much they extol him or praise him when they see his dazzling virtues, his obvious favors, and his spotless Law, when they reject or doubt him in one word which he brought, they have rejected his claiming to be messenger of God and [his claim] to have received this Qur'an from God. Someone who was false in his claiming to be the messenger of God is not one of the prophets or messengers. The statement of anyone who is not one of them[12] is no proof at all, but his situation is the same as other people like himself. If the truth of what he says is known by detailed argument, his statement is accepted because his truthfulness is known from a source other than himself, not because he said it. If the truth of the statement is not known [from external reasons], it is not acceptable. Thus it is clear that someone who does not profess about a person who has stated that he is the messenger of God and infallibly preserved from establishing intentional or inadvertent error cannot properly use any statement of that individual as an argument.

This principle disproves the view of the insightful among the People of the Book, and against the ignorant among them it is even more confounding. Many or most intelligent People of the Book extol Muhammad for his calling on people to [affirm] the oneness of God, for his prohibition against the worship of idols, for his confirmation of the Torah, the Gospel, and those sent as messengers before him, for his manifesting the wonder of the Qur'an which he brought, for the good qualities of the Law which he brought, for the superior characteristics of the community which believed in him, for the signs, proofs, miracles, and favors which were manifested at his and their hands.[13]

Nevertheless, in spite of this they hold that "he was sent to others than us," or else that he was [merely] a just ruler with a just government, and that he attained kinds of knowledge like those of the People of the Book and others, and that through his knowledge and his rituals he laid down and systematized for them a Law just as their own leaders had imposed on them the canons and laws which they possessed. Whenever they say this, they do not thereby become believers in him, and simply from their saying that it is not permissible for them to use a thing of what he said as an argument. It is known by overwhelming transmission[14] that which all groups of people from all religious traditions admit as true, that is, that he said that he was messenger of God to all people, and that God sent down upon him the Qur'an. If he was truthful in that, anyone who rejects him in a single word has rejected the messenger of God, and whoever rejects the messenger of God is an unbeliever. But if he was not truthful in that, then he was not God's messenger, but rather a liar. It is not possible to use as an argument anything in the statements of someone who lies concerning God by saying "God sent me with this [message]" when God did not send him.

———

If they say that their intent is to point out that his teaching is internally contradictory, some of it contradicting the rest, they should be told that this would require that he not be a true prophet, and thus it would be improper for them to use any statement of his as an argument to the extent they do. If we show that the elements of his teaching are mutually confirmatory and similarly that his teaching confirms that of the prophets before him and that the teaching of all the prophets agrees with sound reason, then [it should be granted that] nothing of known truth is contradictory to revealed religion or to reason. If this is accepted, we then say to someone who holds that he was a messenger sent to the Jahiliyya Arabs but not to the People of the Book that it is necessarily obvious to everyone who is acquainted with his affairs—which are known by a successive transmission which is more strongly consecutive than what is transmitted from Moses, Jesus, and others, through the Qur'an which is transmitted from him and his sunna which has been successively handed down from him, and the sunna of the rightly guided *khalifas*—that he stated that he was sent to the People of the Book, Jews and Christians, just as he said that he was sent as a messenger to those without a Book. He stated even that he was sent to all the children of Adam, to Arabs and to

Byzantine, Persian, Turkish, Indian, Berber, and Ethiopian non-Arabs, and to all other nations. He even stated that he was sent to both the two races—the human race and that of the jinn.

All these are clear issues successively handed down from him, upon whose transmission from him his Companions are agreed. This is despite their great number and their dispersal into various regions and situations—those who accompanied him were in the tens of thousands. Their actual number cannot be counted and is known to God alone.

The Followers (*al-tabi'un*),[15] whose number was many times that of the Companions, handed that down from them. After that it was transmitted century after century until our own time with its great number of Muslims and their dispersal into the eastern and western regions of the earth. This occurred as he had foretold beforehand in a sound hadith: "I knit my brows towards earth and I saw its eastern and western regions; the possession of my community will include that which I see when I squint."

He was disclosing that the possessions of his community would extend to either limit of the civilized world to the east and west, and that his summons would spread forth through the center of the earth—the third, fourth, and fifth climes[16]—because the people of those regions are the most perfect in intelligence and moral qualities, and have the most balanced humors. This is in contrast to the southern and northern extremes, for the people of those regions are deficient in their minds and morals and unbalanced in their humors. In the southern extremes people's humors have burned, due to the severity of the heat; their complexions have become black and their hair kinky. On the other hand, due to the severity of the cold, the humors of the people of the extreme north have not matured, but have remained unripe. Thus they have gone to excess in the lankiness of their hair and a cold whiteness, which is not considered attractive.

For this reason, when Islam conquered, its people overcame the central part of the civilized world. Its people are the most balanced and most perfect of the children of Adam. Christians who have been reared under the protection of Muslims (*taht dhimmat al-Muslimin*) are more perfect in their minds and morals than other Christians. However, Christians of the north and south who live outside *dhimmi* status and wage war against Muslims are deficient in mind and morals. When there is an intellectual and moral deficiency among people, Christianity without Islam is victorious over them.

The point is that Muhammad himself called the People of the

Book—Jews and Christians—to faith in him and in what he brought, just as he called the Arabs and other nations who had no book. It was he who disclosed from God that whoever of the People of the Book and others did not believe in him was an unbeliever who would land in hell and receive an evil fate. It was he who commanded *jihad* against them, and he himself and his representatives who summoned them [to Islam].

Therefore their saying in this book, "He did not come to us but to the Arabs of the Jahiliyya" cannot be sustained—whether by that they meant that God sent him to the Arabs and not to them, or whether by it they meant that he claimed that he was sent to the Arabs and not to them. All religious groups have known that Muhammad summoned Jews and Christians to faith in him, and declared that God sent him to them. He commanded *jihad* against whoever of them did not believe in him. In spite of all this, if it is said that "He was not sent to us but to the Arabs," this is an evident lie no matter whether the person believes or rejects him [Muhammad]. The point here is that he himself summoned all the people of the earth to place faith in him, and called the People of the Book, just as he called those without a book.

The Jews were his neighbors in the Hijaz, in Madina and its environs, and at Khaybar. The Muhajirun and the Ansar[17] all believed in him without sword or fighting; when he manifested to them proofs of his prophethood and indications of his truthfulness, they believed in him, although insults for the sake of God befell those who believed in him. This is well known from the biography of the Prophet.[18]

Many Jews and Christians—some in Mecca and some in Madina and many from elsewhere than Mecca and Madina—believed in him. When he came to Madina, he made a pact with those Jews who did not believe in him. Then when they broke the pact, and he exiled some of them and killed others for making war upon God and his messenger. He fought against them time after time. When he fought the Banu Nadir, God revealed the Surat al-Hashr about them.[19] He fought the Qurayza the year of the clans and God mentioned them in the Surat al-Ahzab.[20] Before that he fought the Banu Qaynuqa'. After this he and the people of the Bay'at al-Ridwan—who pledged allegiance to him under the tree[21]—raided Khaybar. They were 1,400 people. God conquered Khaybar for them, where the Jews had been residing as farmers. God revealed the Surat al-Fath[22] in which he mentioned this incident. When this was the situation of the Jews with him, how can it be said that he was sent only to the idolatrous Arabs?[23]

———

Muslim has extracted a hadith report from Anas that the Messenger of God wrote to Khusraw, Caesar, the Negus, and to every important leader, summoning them to God.[24] (This was not the Negus for whom he [Muhammad] mourned to his companions on the day he died. He went out with them to the prayer room and lined up and did *salah* for him.) Rather, it was another Negus who reigned after him.[25]

Muslim extracted from Abu Haritha a report in which the Messenger of God said:

> I was given preference over the prophets in six things: I was given comprehensiveness in utterance; I was delivered from fear; I was permitted booty; for me the earth was made a pure mosque; I was sent to mankind in its entirety; with me the prophets were concluded [sealed].

The Prophet said, "The prophet is sent to his people specifically and I was sent to people in general." God said:

> Say: O mankind! Lo! I am the messenger of God to you all—the messenger of Him unto whom belongs the Sovereignty of the heavens and the earth (7:158).

and

> We have not sent you [O Muhammad] save as a bringer of good tidings and a warner to all mankind (34:28).

In the Qur'an, in very many places there is mention of his summoning the People of the Book to faith in him. In it God even states the disbelief (*kufr*) of those of the Jews and Christians who disbelieved, and in it He commanded that they [the Muslims] should fight them (5:17; 5:72-77; 4:171-73; 9:29; 9:30-32).

———

These indications and others many times as many are among that which make it clear that he himself reported that he was Messenger of God to Christians and other People of the Book. He summoned them [to Islam] and waged *jihad* against them, and commanded others to summon them and wage *jihad* against them.

This is not an innovation which his community invented after him, as Christians did after Christ. Muslims do not permit a single person after Muhammad to change a thing of his Law—to permit what he forbade, to forbid what he permitted, to necessitate what he eliminated, to eliminate what he necessitated. Rather, what is permissible (*al-halal*) among them is what God and His messenger permitted, and what is forbidden (*al-haram*) is what God and His messenger forbade. Religion is what God and His messenger legislated, as opposed to the Christians, who introduced after Christ innovations which were not legislated by Christ nor were mentioned in any passage from the gospels or the earlier books of the prophets. They claim that what their great leaders legislated for them by way of religion was passed on to them by Christ. This is an area over which the three communities—Muslims, Jews, and Christians—have disputed, just as they have disputed about Christ and other things.

Jews do not permit God to abrogate anything of His legislation. Christians permit their leaders to abrogate God's legislation by their opinions. Muslims, however, believe that to God belongs creation and command. There is no legislation but that which God legislated by the tongues of His messengers. To Him [belongs the right] to abrogate whatever He wills, as He abrogated through Christ what He had legislated to the prophets before him. Among the Christians, however, their great men imposed their beliefs and legal prescriptions upon them after [the time of] Christ, as the 380 men who lived in the time of Constantine imposed the creed upon which they had agreed. They cursed the Arians and others who opposed them. In this creed there are matters which God has not revealed in any book; rather it opposes the books which God revealed and it opposes sound reason as well.[26]

They have prescribed for them laws and rules which were not found in the books of the prophets nor indicated by them. Some of it is found in the books of the prophets, but their religious leaders added things of their own which were not found in the books of the prophets. They changed much of what the prophets had legislated. The laws and regulations of the Christians, which are the legal prescriptions of their religion, are in part handed down from the prophets, partly from the apostles, while many come from the innovation of their great men in spite of their opposition to the legislation of the prophets.

Their religion is the same type as that of the Jews. They [the Jews] had clothed what was true with falsehood, and Christ was sent with the [same] religion of God as the prophets before him. It is the service of God alone allowing nothing to participate in that worship; it is prohibition from worship of everything except Him. He [Christ] permitted to them some of what God had forbidden in the Torah, and he abrogated some of the law of the

Torah. The Romans, Greeks, and others were pagans who were worshiping celestial temples and terrestrial idols. Christ sent his messengers to summon them to the religion of God. He sent some of them during his lifetime on earth, and others after his assumption into heaven. He called them to the religion of God, and there were some who entered into God's religion. They held to that [religion] for a while, and then Satan tempted some of them to change the religion of Christ. They innovated a religion combining the religion of God and His messengers—i.e., the religion of Christ—and the religion of pagans.

The pagans used to worship bodily images which cast shadows, for this was the religion of the Romans and Greeks. It was the religion of the philosophers among the people of Macedon and Ephesus,[27] such as Aristotle and the peripatetic philosophers like him and others. Aristotle lived 300 years before Christ, and was the minister of the Greek Macedonian, Alexander, the son of Philip, whose exploits were recorded in the Roman history of Jews and Christians. He was a pagan who with his people worshiped idols.

He was not named Dhu al-Qarnayn, nor was he the Dhu al-Qarnayn mentioned in the Qur'an.[28] This Macedonian did not reach the land of the Turks nor the sons of the dam.[29] He only reached the land of the Persians. Whoever supposes that Aristotle was the minister of Dhu al-Qarnayn mentioned in the Qur'an has erred, and his mistake shows that he is not knowledgeable about the religions of these people and their times. When the religion of Christ appeared 300 years after Aristotle in the land of the Romans and the Greeks, people followed *tawhid* up to the appearance of innovations among them. Then they fashioned images drawn on the wall and made these images a substitute for those other images. Others used to worship the sun, moon, and stars, and so these began to prostrate themselves before them towards the direction of the sunrise from which sun, moon, and stars appeared. They made their prostration towards it [the east] a substitute for their prostration before them [the heavenly bodies].[30]

For this reason came the Seal of the Messengers, with whom God concluded messengership. Through him He made manifest the fullness of *tawhid*, which He had not manifested before him. He commanded that each person take care not to do *salah* during the rising of the sun or its setting because pagans prostrate themselves before it at that time. If those professing the oneness of God pray at that hour, that would be a type of imitation of them, and it could be taken as a pretext for making prostration before it [the sun].

One of the greatest causes of idol worship has been the fashioning of images and the glorification of tombs. In Muslim's collection of sound hadiths and elsewhere he said from Abu al-Hayaj:

> 'Ali ibn Abi Talib said to me: "Didn't I send you with what the Messenger of God sent me?" He commanded me that I omit no honored tomb but to level it, no statue but to efface it.

It is in the Collections that the Messenger said during his fatal sickness:

> May God curse the Jews and Christians who have taken the tombs of the prophets as mosques.

Thus he warned against doing what they did. It is in the Collections that five nights before his death he said:

> Those who were before you used to take tombs as mosques. Do not do that. Do not take tombs as mosques, for I have forbidden you that.

When they mentioned to him the church in the land of Ethiopia and related to him the beautiful things and pictures in it, he said:

> Those people, when some upright man among them dies, they build a mosque on his tomb and they fashion those pictures. Those people are the worst of creation before God on the Resurrection Day.

He forbade a man to face a grave in prayer so that he would not resemble the pagans who prostrated themselves before graves.[31] It is in the Collections that he said, "Do not sit at graves and do not pray towards them."

Hadith reports similar to that could be mentioned in which there is a stripping of *tawhid* to God, the Lord of the Universe. This is what God has revealed in His books; it is with this He has sent His messengers. What relationship is there in this to someone who fashions pictures of created things in churches, who extols them and seeks intercession from him whose picture he has fashioned? Hasn't this been the basis for idol worship among mankind from the time of Noah until now? Prayer towards the sun, moon, and stars and prostration in their direction is a pretext for prostrating before them. Not one of the prophets ever commanded the use of pictures or seeking intercession from their patrons or making prostration towards the sun, moon, and stars. Although it was mentioned about one of the prophets that he fashioned an image for the sake of general welfare,[32] this is one of the matters on which the laws may vary; by contrast, prostration before them and seeking intercession from those represented was never legislated by a single prophet. No one of the prophets ever commanded anyone to pray to someone other than God, neither at his grave nor in his absence, nor to seek intercession in his absence after his death. By contrast, seeking intercession from the Prophet during his lifetime and on the Resurrection Day, and mediating one's prayers through him and one's faith in him, is something commanded by the prophets, as God has said (43: 45; 21: 25; 16: 36; 10: 18; 39: 1-4).

Among the pagans of all peoples there has not been anyone who said, "For created things there are two separate creators, mutually resembling each other in attributes." No known group of people has ever held this. Dualists among the Magians and others hold that the universe has issued forth from two principles—light and darkness. According to them light is the praiseworthy god of goodness and darkness is the accursed god of evil. Some of them hold that darkness is Satan, and this is to make the evil in the world to issue from darkness. Some of them hold that darkness is pre-eternal and everlasting. As well as its being accursed it is not, according to them, similar to light. Some of them hold, rather, that it has come into being in time, that light had a wicked thought and that darkness came into being from that wicked thought.

The people of *tawhid* say to them: "In spite of your claim that you hate to ascribe to the Lord the creation of evil that is in the universe, you have made Him a creator of the principle of evil." These people, despite their affirming two [ultimate principles] and their being called Dualists by people, do not hold that evil is similar to good.

Similarly, the Materialists (*al-Dahriyya*)—the materialist philosophers and others—some of them deny a Maker for the world, like the view manifested by Pharaoh—may God curse him! Others among them, like Aristotle and his followers, hold for a Cause of the movement of the celestial spheres which [movement] is attendant upon It. Still others among them, like Ibn Sina and Al-Suhrawardi—the one killed in Aleppo—and the would-be philosophers of the [three] religions like them, hold for the necessity of the essence prerequisite for the heavenly spheres.

The pagan Arabs and those similar to them used to confess a Maker who created the heavens and the earth. The belief of the pagan Arabs was better than the belief of these materialist philosophers, since they believed that the heavens were created by God and came into being after they had not been. This is the belief of the masses of the people of the earth among the adherents to the three religions—Muslims, Jews, and Christians—as well as Magians and pagans. But these materialists among the philosophers and others claim that the heavens were pre-eternal, that they had never ceased to be.

The pagan Arabs used to hold that God was able to act according to His will and to answer the prayer of one who prayed to Him, but according to these materialist philosophers God does not do a thing by His will, nor does He answer the prayer of one who prays. Rather, He does not know particulars, nor does he distinguish this suppliant from that. He does not know Abraham from Moses from Muhammad from others of His greatest messengers. There are even those among them like Aristotle and his followers who deny His knowledge absolutely, while others like Ibn Sina and those like him state that He only knows universals.[33]

It is obvious that everything existent in external reality is a specific particular. If, therefore, He does not know anything but universals, He does not know a thing of specific existent beings—neither celestial spheres, nor sovereigns, nor anything else of existing beings in their real natures. Among them prayer is the manipulation on the part of a powerful Soul upon the matter of the universe, as say Ibn Sina and those like him.[34] They claim that the Inscribed Tablet (*al-Lawh al-Mahfuz*) is the celestial Soul, and that all the things coming into being in time on earth occur only from the movement of the spheres, as has been elaborated in the refutation of them elsewhere.

The point here is that the pagans do not establish alongside God another god equal to Him in deeds and attributes. They did not even hold that the stars, sun, and moon created the earth, nor that idols created a single thing of the earth. Whoever supposes that the people of Abraham al-Khalil used to believe that the stars or the sun or the moon was the Lord of the Universe or that al-Khalil when he said "This is my lord" meant by that the Lord of the Universe is clearly mistaken. The people of Abraham, rather, used to admit a Maker, but used to commit *shirk* in worshiping him like other idolaters.

God disclosed about Abraham (26:69-101) that he was an enemy to all that they were worshiping except the Lord of the Universe. He disclosed about them that on the Resurrection Day they will say: "By God, we were truly in manifest error when we made you equal to the Lord of the Universe" (26:97-98). They were not acting worthily towards the Maker, but they strayed from Him and made partners to Him in worship, love, and prayer, as God has said elsewhere (43:26-27).

He [Abraham] said, "I have turned my face to Him who created the heavens and the earth as a *hanif*, a Muslim, and I am not one of those who commit *shirk*." He did not say "One of those who raise God to irrelevance (*mu'attilin*)." His people were committing *shirk*, and were not making God distantly transcendent like the accursed Pharaoh. However, they were not acting worthily towards the Maker, but they strayed from Him and made partners to Him in worship, love, and prayer, as God said (6:1; 2:165; 25:68; 26:213; 17:22). In what He related about the people of Noah, He said:

> And they have said: Forsake not your gods. Forsake not Wudd, nor Suwa' nor Yaghuth and Ya'uq and Nasr. And they have led many astray (7:23-24).

Ibn 'Abbas and other scholars have said that these ["gods"] were upright individuals among the people of Noah who when they died, people devoted themselves to their tombs, and then fashioned statues of them and worshiped them. Thus it is among the Christians about Christ in the book, *The Secret of Peter*—who is called Simeon (*Sham'un*), Simon (*Sam'an*), Cephas (*al-Sufa*), and Peter (*Butrus*). The four names represent one person among them. From him there is a book about Christ in which are the secrets of [divine] sciences.[35] According to them all of this comes from Christ. That which Christians do forms the basis for idol worship. Thus said their great scholar who they call "the Golden Mouth" [John Chrysostom]—and he is one of their greatest scholars—when he mentioned the birth of great sins from the small. He said, "In this way idol worship invades upon that which preceded it—when people honor individuals and extol one another, the living and the dead, beyond the level they should." God said:

> Say: Pray to those whom you assume beside Him, yet they have no power to rid you of misfortune nor to change. Those unto whom they cry seek the way of approach to their Lord, which of them shall be the nearest; they hope for His mercy and they fear His doom. Lo! the doom of your Lord is to be shunned (17:56-57).

A group of scholars has said that the peoples were praying to angels and prophets like Elijah, Christ, and others. God has made it clear that these are His servants just as you are His servants, they hope in His mercy just as you hope in His mercy, they fear His punishment just as you fear His punishment, they draw near to Him just as you draw near to Him (3:79-80).

God has announced that whoever takes the angels and prophets as lords is an unbeliever even though he believes they are created. No one ever held that all the angels and prophets shared with God in the creation of the earth, but God said: "And most of them believe not in God except that they attribute partners [to Him]" (12:106). Ibn 'Abbas, Mujahid, and others have said: "Ask them who created the heavens and the earth and they will say 'God' But they worship other than Him." This is similar to God's statement (31:25). Elsewhere God has disclosed about the idolaters that they hold that the creator of the world is one despite their taking gods beside Him whom they worship and their taking intercessors before Him or their drawing near to Him through them.

———

In this way their exaltation of the cross, their permitting pork, their honoring monasticism, their abandonment of circumcision, their omission of purification from ritual uncleanness (*al-hadath*) and impurity (*al-khubth*), their not necessitating the complete washing (*al-ghusl*) after sexual intercourse, nor the simple ablution—they do not oblige one to avoid a single ritually contaminating thing in prayer, neither excrement, urination, nor any other contaminating thing—all these laws of theirs they have invented and innovated after Christ. Their priests and their people obeyed these [laws] and cursed whoever opposed them, so that anyone among them who held firmly to the pure religion of Christ came to be defeated and persecuted before God sent Muhammad. Most of the laws and the religion which they hold are not found to be stipulated by Christ.

Among Muslims, however, everything upon which they have attained evident consensus is known both generally and specifically to have been handed down from their prophet, and it is known that no one after him introduced it either by his own creative application (*ijtihad*) or in any other way. What they declare firmly by consensus of the community of Muhammad is found to be taken from their prophet.[36]

That on which their consensus is supposed but is not firmly stated contains some things upon which that supposition may be in error, and there may be dispute among them about it. Furthermore, there may be a text of the Messenger to support this saying, and it may be in accordance with this saying. On some things of this kind the supposition of consensus is correct, and it may include something whose proof that it is a true tradition from the prophet is hidden or knowledge of it is [only] among some people. That is because God has perfected religion in Muhammad as the seal of the prophets. He has made it manifest and communicated it as the clear pronouncement. His community thus has no need for anyone after him to change a thing of his religion. Only that which he brought is needed for knowledge of his religion. His community does not agree on an error; moreover, there will not cease to be in his community a group grounded on the truth until the Hour arrives. God sent him with guidance and the religion of truth to make it conquer over all religion. He has made it conquer with proof and clear argument, and He has made it conquer by power and spear. Until the arrival of the Hour, there will never cease to be in his community a group manifesting [the truth].

The point here is that whatever the community agrees upon in evident consensus it knows in general and in specifics that it is handed down from their prophet. We do not bear witness to infallibility except for the sum of the community. Among the many sects of the community, however, there are innovations opposed to the Messenger, some of which are of the type of innovation of the Jews and Christians. There is rebelliousness and disobedience in them, but the Messenger of God is innocent of that, as God has said (26:216; 6:159).

The Messenger said, "Whoever prefers something other than my sunna is not of me." This is similar to the consensus [of Muslims] that Muhammad was sent to all people—People of the Book and others. If they have received this from their prophet, and it is something handed down among them by successive transmission, they know it by necessity. It is similar to their consensus on facing the Ka'ba, the Sacred House, in their *salah*. This consensus of theirs for [the direction of prayer] is based upon successive transmission from their prophet, and is mentioned in their book. Similarly, the consensus upon the necessity for the five prayers, the fast during the month of Ramadan, the pilgrimage to the Ancient House [the Ka'ba] which Abraham the Friend of the Compassionate One built and called his people to pilgrimage, the pilgrimage of the prophets and even the pilgrimage of Moses ibn 'Imran and Yunus ibn Matta and others, their consensus on the necessity of ablution from ritual impurity and the prohibition of disgusting things, the obligation of purity for prayer—all this is among what they have received from their prophet, and it is handed down from him by successive transmission and is mentioned in the Qur'an.

Among Christians, however, the prayers which they say are not handed down from Christ, nor is the fast which they make handed down from him. Rather, they first made the fast forty days, then they increased it by ten days and moved it to spring, but this has not been handed down among them from Christ. Similarly, nothing in their pilgrimage to his sepulchre and Bethlehem and the church of Saydnaya[37] was handed down from Christ. Similarly, even the generality of their feasts like the feasts of the Qalandas,[38] Christmas, the Epiphany—and it is the most sacred[39]—the Feast of Thursday,[40] the Feast of the Cross which they began at the time of the appearance of the cross when Helena the Harranian innkeeper, mother of Constantine, made it known two hundred years after Christ, the feasts of Thursday, Friday, and Saturday at the end of their fast, other feasts which they derive from the affairs of Christ, and the feasts which they have innovated for their great persons—all of these are innovations of theirs which they have invented without the sanction of a revealed book. They have even built churches in the name of someone they extol, as in the Collections from the prophet:

> If some upright man among them dies they build a mosque on his grave on which they draw those pictures. On the Day of Resurrection they will be the worst of mankind before God. As God has said (72:18; 24:36; 7:29; 9:18).

## C. QUR'ANIC TESTIMONY FOR THE UNIVERSALITY OF THE PROPHETHOOD OF MUHAMMAD

Our intention here is to show that what Muslims profess is that Muhammad was sent as a messenger to the two races—human and jinn—to the People of the Book and others. They profess further that whoever does not believe in him is an unbeliever deserving of God's punishment and deserving of *jihad*. This is a matter on which the people of faith in God and His messenger agree, because the messenger is the one who brought that and God stated it in His Book. Moreover the messenger made it clear in the Wisdom handed down outside the Book.

God handed down upon him the Book and the Wisdom. Muslims have not innovated a single thing of that of their own accord, unlike Christians who have innovated much if not most of their religion. They replaced the religion of Christ and changed it. For this reason the unbelief of the Christians when Muhammad was sent was like the unbelief of the Jews when Christ was sent. Before the coming of Christ the Jews had replaced the law of the Torah and thereby disbelieved. When Christ was sent to them they rejected him and became unbelievers by changing the interpretations of the first book and its legal judgments and by rejecting the second book.

Before Muhammad was sent Christians had already changed the religion of Christ, for they innovated the trinity and divine union [in Christ] and changed the legal prescriptions of the Gospel. These are things not brought by Christ; rather, they are opposed to what he brought. Over these matters they split into numerous sects, with each sect declaring the others unbelievers. When Muhammad was sent they rejected him, and so became unbelievers by changing the interpretations of the first book and its laws and by rejecting the second book. The Muslim scholars say that their religion is corrupted and abrogated, although at the sending of Muhammad there were a few Christians who were holding fast to the religion of Christ.

However, those who did not change the religion of Christ were all following the truth. This is like someone who at the sending of Christ had been following the law of the Torah would have been holding fast to the truth like the rest of those who followed Moses. When Christ was sent, all those who did not believe in him became unbelievers, and similarly when Muhammad was sent, whoever did not believe in him became an unbeliever.

The point here is to clarify what Muhammad brought by way of the universality of his message, that it was he himself who disclosed that God had sent him to the People of the Book and others and that he himself summoned the People of the Book, waged *jihad* against them, and commanded *jihad* against them. After this, whoever of the People of the Book—Jews and Christians—says "He was not sent to us" in the sense that he did not say that he was sent to us is an arrogant denier of what is known by necessity, a perpetrator against the messenger of an evident lie which is known [to be false] generally and in specifics.

For someone to reject this about him would be just as if he were to disavow that he [Muhammad] brought the Qur'an or legislated the five prayers, the fast of Ramadan, and the pilgrimage to the Sacred House. The rejection of Muhammad and what is successively handed down from him is greater than if the followers of Christ's apostles should deny his sending them to the nations and his bringing the Gospel, or the denial that Moses brought the Torah and rested on the Sabbath.

The transmission from Muhammad is over a short period of time, and those who transmitted [information] from him were many, many times more than those who transmitted the religion of Christ from him, and many, many more times more than those who were in contact with the transmission of the religion of Moses. The community of Muhammad has never ceased to be numerous and spread from the eastern parts of the earth to the west, and there has never ceased to be among them one who is victorious in religion and supported by God over His enemies.[1] Conversely, the rule of the sons of Israel came to an end during the period when Jerusalem was destroyed the first time after David, and the number of those who transmitted their religion diminished until it was said that there did not remain any but one who knew the Torah by memory.

Only a small number transmitted the religion of Christ from him, but Christians claim that they were inerrant messengers of God like Abraham and Moses. This subject will be discussed, God willing, if we get that far, but the point here is to show clearly that if anyone claims that Muhammad used to say that he was not sent to any but the pagan Arabs, that person is in the depths of ignorance and error or else at the limits of pride and stubbornness. This is greater ignorance and stubbornness than one who denies that he used to commit [ritual] purification, ablution from impurities, prohibition of wine and pork, and greater ignorance and stubbornness than someone who denies what has been successively handed down of the affairs of Christ and Moses. Thus may be known the falsity of their statement: "We have known that he was not sent to us but rather to the Arabs of the Jahiliyya."

———

If this is known, then the argumentation of these people from [Qur'anic] verses which they suppose to be indications of his exclusive prophetic mission to Arabs shows that they are not people for whom it is possible to base an argument on the statement of someone according to that person's intention and purpose. They are among those about whom God said:

> What is wrong with these people that they do not come close to understanding an event? (4:78)

They are not a people who argue from the Torah, the Gospel, and the Psalms according to the intention of the prophets, for the rest of the teaching handed down from the prophets is according to the intent of the prophets. They do not even argue from the teaching of the doctors, the philosophers, the grammarians, the mathematicians, or the astronomers according to their intents, for all people agree that the language of the Arabs is one of the most sincere and correct languages of mankind. They are agreed that the Qur'an exhibits the highest degree of clarity, eloquence, and fine composition, and that in the Qur'an are innumerable indications according to the intent of the Messenger in which he states that God sent him to the People of the Book and others.

Besides that, there is the information successively transmitted from his lifetime concerning his summoning the People of the Book and commanding them to place faith in him, and his waging *jihad* against them when they disbelieved in him. None of this can be concealed from anyone who has the slightest knowledge of his life. This is a matter with which the world is full, which has been heard by both judge and miscreant. People—those who believe in him and those who do not—know that he said that he was the messenger of God to the People of the Book and others. The evident intention of that is something which can be known with certainty both specifically and generally. When they begin supposing that he was saying that he was sent only to the Arabs and that he continued holding that until his death, this is an indication either of the corruption of their viewpoint and their minds or of their stubbornness and pride.

If they have no knowledge of the meaning of those [Qur'anic] verses which they employ as arguments for the specifics of his messengership, it is necessary that they believe one of two matters. Either the verses have meanings which are in agreement with what he used to say [elsewhere], or else they are among those which have been abrogated. It is known, both generally and in particulars, that Muhammad used to pray towards Jerusalem for about a year and a half after the Hijra. Then he commanded prayer towards the Ka'ba, the Sacred House. Christians agree that in the Laws of the prophets there are abrogating and abrogated [passages], although the verses which they mention are not abrogated.

The point here is that knowledge of the universality of his call to all creation—the People of the Book as well as others—is handed down successively and necessarily certain, as is knowledge of his sending itself, his summoning all creation to believe in him and to obey him, the knowledge of his migration from Mecca to Madina, his bringing the Qur'an, the five prayers, the fast of the month of Ramadan, the pilgrimage to the Ancient House [the Ka'ba], his obligating people to truthfulness and justice, his prohibition of wrongdoing and shameful acts, and other things which Muhammad brought.

Someone may say, "But in the Qur'an there is found that which demands that his messengership be limited, and there is in it what demands that his messengership be universal. This is contradictory." In answer it must be said that one knows the falsity of this before one has knowledge of his prophethood. It is evident both to someone who believes in him and to one who rejects him that he was one of the greatest people in intelligence, politics, and experience. His intention was to summon all creation to obey him and to follow him. He used to read the Qur'an to all people, and commanded them to communicate it to all nations and to whomever he sought to believe in him, so that he recited the Qur'an before unbelievers and they had to accede to it. If it was like this with a pagan, what must it have been like with a scriptuary! As God said:

> And if anyone of the idolators seek your protection, then protect him so that he may hear the word of God, and afterward convey him to his place of safety. That is because they are a folk who know not (9:6).

He had made it clear that he was sent to the People of the Book and the rest of creation, and that he was the messenger of God to the two races, of mankind and jinn. It was impossible that in addition to this he announced something which would indicate that he was not sent to them. Even the person of lowest intelligence would not do something so contradictory to his desired goal, so how could it be done by him upon whom intelligent people of all the religions agree that he was the most intelligent of people and the finest in diplomacy and law?

Furthermore, even if it were possible that in the Qur'an there were [verses] which indicated that he was sent only to the Arabs and also those which indicated that he was sent to the rest of mankind, this would merely be an indication that he was sent to other people than [the Arabs] after he had been sent only to them, and that God made his summons universal after it had been specific. There is no contradiction between the two. So how could there be [a contradiction] when there is not a single verse in the Qur'an which indicates the exclusive nature of his messengership to the Arabs? In it there is only the proof of his messengership to them, just as there is the proof of his messengership to the Quraysh. There is no contradiction between these two.

In it there is proof of his messengership to the People of the Book when he said, "O People of the Book, believe in that which we have handed down,"[2] just as there is proof of his messengership to the sons of Israel when God said, "O sons of Israel." This specifying of the Jews is not inconsistent with [His] making it universal. In his mission of preaching sometimes to the Jews and sometimes to the Christians, his preaching to one of the two groups and his summoning them is not contradictory to his preaching to the other and summoning them [to Islam]. In his Book there is nothing in his preaching to those of his community who believe and in summoning them to the legal prescriptions of his religion which is contradictory to his preaching to the People of the Book and summoning them. In his Book he commanded them to fight the People of the Book—the Christians—until they should pay the *jizya* readily when they are overcome.[3] This does not prevent his having commanded them to fight others like Jews and Magians until they readily pay the *jizya* once they are overcome; rather, this judgment is established concerning the Magians by his sunna and the agreement of his community.

If it is said that they [the Christians] are not the People of the Book, we say that all of this is among what is known by necessity from his religion before knowledge of his prophethood. So how can this be the case when we are speaking on the supposition of his prophethood, and the prophet does not contradict his own statement? If the knowledge of the universal nature of his call and his message is evident by necessity both before and after knowledge of his prophethood, then this necessary, certain knowledge is not contradicted by anything. This, however, is the concern of those people of innovation—Christians and others—in whose hearts there is a doubt; they follow vagueness while they claim precision.

Because of the disputation of Christians with the Prophet by means of obscure [passages] and their straying from the unambiguous, God revealed this about them:

> He it is who has revealed to you [Muhammad] the Book in which are clear revelations. They are the substance of the Book and others obscure. But those in whose hearts is doubt pursue that which is obscure seeking [to cause] dissension by seeking to explain it. None knows its explanation but God. And those who are of sound instruction say: We believe in it, the whole is from our Lord. But only men of understanding really heed (3:7).

By *ta'wil* is meant the explanation of the Qur'an, the knowledge of its meanings. This is known by those who are of sound instruction. By it is also meant what is the exclusive property of the Lord, who in His knowledge understands to the utmost degree what He promised—the time of the Hour [of Judgment] and similar matters which are not known except by God.

The wayward state verses the knowledge of whose interpretations is obscure for them, and then they follow their interpretation of them "seeking to cause dissension by seeking to explain it."[4] They are not people properly instructed in knowledge who know the interpretation of these [verses], even though the verses which they cite are among the clearest. This procedure which they follow with the Qur'an is similar to what they follow in the earlier books and the teaching of the prophets in the Torah, the Gospel, and Psalms, and other books. In those books there are so many clear passages on the oneness (*tawhid*) of God and the servanthood of Christ that they can only be counted with difficulty. In them there are a few phrases which contain ambiguity; they seize upon the few, hidden, complex ambiguities of the earlier books, and omit the many clear, definite, unambiguous passages. They have followed in the Qur'an the same procedure they followed in the earlier books. Those books, however, confess the prophethood of their authors and of Muhammad. In this they are confounded and contradictory. Thus the falsity of any statements which they make about [the Qur'an] and their lying about it is manifest if they do not put faith in all that He revealed to him.

If they say, "Its teaching is contradictory, and so we argue for what agrees with our view, since our intention is to clarify the contradiction," they are answered from various aspects.

1) In the earlier books those things which are supposedly mutually contradictory are many times what is in the Qur'an, and closer to true contradictions. But it is agreed that there is no real contradiction in those books, only what appears to be so due to ignorance of the true meanings and the intentions of the prophets. It is as it is said:

> How many are they who disfigure a sound statement
> And damage it by a faulty understanding!

How much more will this be the case with the Qur'an, which is the finest of books!

2) They are seizing upon ambiguities in those books and opposing the unambiguous meaning in them, as they have done with the Qur'an, but more seriously.

3) If what he brought was internally contradictory, then he was not the messenger of God, for that which he brought from God could not be diverse and contradictory (4:82). There must be contradiction in every book which is not from God. Therefore, it is not permitted for them to use anything as argument from any book in which there is contradiction, for such a book is not from God. But if there is no contradiction, this proves that there is nothing contradictory in the universal nature of his messengership and that he is messenger to them. Whatever comes from God is not contradictory.

4) We will show that what is stated in it [the Qur'an] of the universal nature of his messengership is not incompatible with his being sent to the Arabs, just as what is mentioned about his warning the clan of his relatives and his commanding the Quraysh is not incompatible with his summoning the rest of the Arabs. The specifying of part of the whole by name, when there is a reason for it which demands that specification, does not indicate that what

is outside the thing mentioned is excluded from it. It is this which is called "what is understood to be excluded" (*mafhum al-mukhalafa*) and "what the address implies" (*dalil al-khitab*);[5] people are all agreed that specification by name when there is a reason for it demands a non-specifying mention in a judgment which was not understood to be for the individual noun nor even for the description of it.[6] God said:

> Slay not your children, fearing a fall to poverty (17:31).

He forbade them to do that because that is what they were actually doing at the time. He had forbidden them in other places to kill anyone wrongly, whether it was a child or not. In that there was nothing contradictory to his specifically mentioning "children."

5) In this Muhammad would be following the pattern of Christ, for Christ first specified his call, and then universalized it. As he said in the Gospel, "I was not commissioned and sent except to the sons of Israel." In the Gospel he also said, "I was not sent except to this rotten branch." Then he made it universal, and when he sent his disciples he said to them, "As my Father sent me, so do I send you; so whoever receives you receives me." And he said, "As I have done for you, so do you for the servants of God; travel in the land, and baptize people in the name of the Father, and the son, and the holy spirit. Let no one of you have two cloaks; carry with you neither silver nor gold, neither staff nor spear." There are other verses like that in the gospels which they use today which particularize his call and then universalize it, and he is truthful in all that. How can they possibly deny what is in the Gospel about Christ of someone like him?

To clarify the matter one can say that God sent Muhammad just as He sent Christ and others—although his [Muhammad's] messengership was the most perfect and complete, as will be mentioned in its place—and He commanded him to extend his message in accordance with the possibilities to group after group. He commanded him to extend it to his neighbors in place and descent, and then to group after group until his warning reached all people of the earth. As God said:

> This Qur'an has been inspired in me, that I may warn with it you and whomsoever it may reach (6:19).

—that is, whomsoever the Qur'an reach. Everyone who was reached by the Qur'an had been thereby warned by Muhammad. It is clear that this warning was not limited to those he was addressing in his preaching; rather, he warned them by it, and he warned whomever the Qur'an would reach. God commanded him first to warn his own tribe, and that was the Quraysh, when He said, "Warn your tribe of near kindred" (26:214).

He summoned the Quraysh to God and commanded them to worship God alone, allowing no one to share [in that worship] (106:1-3). Elsewhere God revealed the command to all creation to worship Him (2:21; 51:56; 61:66).

The majority of the sons of Israel—and they were the people of Christ—rejected him [Muhammad] at first. Then God commanded him to summon the rest of the Arabs. He himself used to go out with Abu Bakr to the tribes of Arabs, tribe by tribe. The Arabs had never ceased to make the pilgrimage to the House since the time of Abraham. He [Muhammad] came to them in the places where they lived in Mina, 'Ukaz, Majanna, and Dhu al-Majaz, and never found anyone but that he summoned him to God. He said:

> O people, I am the Messenger of God to you, commanding you to worship God and not to associate anything with Him, to give up whatever of these rivals is worshiped beside Him, to put faith in me, to trust me, and to defend me so that I can disclose that which I bring from God. O people, the Quraysh prevented me from announcing the teaching of my Lord. The one who defends me so that I can announce the teaching of my Lord is only he who conducts me to his people, for the Quraysh have prevented me from announcing the teaching of my Lord. O people, say "There is no god but God." By this statement you will prosper. By it you will govern the Arabs. By it will the non-Arabs be brought low before you.

They were saying, "O Muhammad, do you want to make the gods into One God? This command of yours is amazing."

The Messenger of God did not cease to announce his call and to manifest his message and to summon all mankind to him. They used to persecute him, debate with him, and when they spoke with him they used to reply to him with most insulting responses. But he was patient with their insults.

When Muhammad returned to Mecca,[7] and it came time for the season of the Hajj, some individuals from Madina made the pilgrimage and Muhammad came to the knowledge of a group of them. He read the Qur'an to them, summoned them to God, and disclosed to them that with which God had sent him. They became convinced and their hearts became assured of his call. They knew what they had been hearing from the People of the Book in respect to their mentioning him by their description of him and that to which they were calling them. They believed in him and put faith in him.

One of the causes of the goodness to which God was guiding the Ansar was the information describing him which they used to hear. When they returned to their people, they began to call them secretly and to inform them of the sayings of the Messenger of God and the light, guidance, and the Qur'an with which God had sent him. They accepted Islam so that the homes in which the people did not accept Islam remained very few indeed. God mentioned that in the Qur'an and disclosed that the People of the Book were informing the [pagan] Arabs about him and seeking victory over them through him. The People of the Book were professing, disclosing, and predicting his prophethood before he was sent. This is what God said in His teaching about the People of the Book (2:87-91).

God disclosed that the People of the Book were asking God for victory over the Arabs by Muhammad before he was sent—that is, that they would be granted victory through him. They and the Arabs had been fighting and the Arabs were defeating them. They used to say, "The prophet unlearned [in the books] will be sent from the children of Isma'il. We will follow him and we will defeat you severely by him." They used to characterize him by his own description and the reports of their doing that are numerous and successively handed down (2:89).

He disclosed that whenever a messenger brought the Jews what they themselves did not desire they would reject some and kill the others. He disclosed that they incurred "anger upon anger" (2:90), for they did not cease to do those things for which God was angry with them. The doubling ["anger upon anger"] may mean to emphasize the anger of God against them or possibly what is meant is "two times"—the first anger being their rejection of Christ and the Gospel and the second [their rejection of] Muhammad and the Qur'an.

## D. SIGNS OF THE PROPHETHOOD OF MUHAMMAD

God sent them [the People of the Book] signs which indicated the prophethood of Muhammad. His miracles were in excess of a thousand—such as the splitting of the moon and other signs like the miraculous Qur'an, the foretelling of him by the People of the Book and his prediction by the prophets, the sorcerers and invisible voices making him known, the story of the elephant which God made occur as a sign in the year of his birth, and the other amazing events which happened in the year of his birth to indicate his prophethood, like the heavens filling up and the hurling of the shooting stars in which the devils had taken refuge.[1] All this is in contrast to what was customary for him both before and after his sending, such as his giving information about the unseen which God had not given anyone to know or of which no human was given knowledge. He disclosed the past, like the stories of Adam, Noah, Abraham, Moses, Christ, Hud, Shu'ayb, Salih, and others. There was no scholar in Mecca from whom he learned; he did not even confer with anyone among them who knew the Arabic language, and he himself was not conversant in a language other than Arabic. He was not accustomed to correspond nor to read any written book.

He did not travel before his prophethood except for two journeys. His first journey was when he was small and traveled with his uncle Abu Talib, but he did not leave his company nor meet anyone of the People of the Book or others. His second journey was as an adult when he rode with the Quraysh, but again he did not leave their company nor did he meet with anyone from the People of the Book. Those who were with him have reported the announcement by the People of the Book of his prophethood, like the monk Bahira[2] announcing his prophethood, and those evident qualities in him which indicated his prophethood to them. Thus Khadija bint Khuwaylid married him when she was informed of his upright qualities. All these matters are elaborated elsewhere.

The point here is to show that Muhammad performed many miracles, like the water which sprang forth from between his fingers more than once, like the multiplication of a little food so that a great number ate from it, the multiplication of a little water so that a great number drank from it.[3] There occurred for him and for his community more than once signs whose description would go on at length. Thus for one of his followers God raised the dead of mankind and animals to life and another walked with a great army across a sea so that they crossed to the other side. There are many examples like these.

Some of the matters from the past of which he informed them in the Qur'an with detailed information were not known by anyone but someone who is a prophet or who was informed of it by a prophet. The people of his time knew that no human being informed him of that [material], and it was on this that the case against them was based. Despite the strength of their emnity against him and their eagerness for something on which to challenge him, they were not able to make an acceptable challenge. The other religious communities knew that his people were inimical to him and energetic in challenging him. That they were [not] able to say that some human person taught him these unseen matters makes it necessary for all mankind to know that these things were not taught him by another person (11:49). God thus disclosed that neither he nor his people knew such [matters]. His people admitted that he did not learn from anyone other than his own people, and so when some of them claimed that he learned from a man, the lie was evident to everyone (16:98-103).

In Mecca there was a non-Arab man,[4] a slave to one of the Quraysh. Some people claimed that Muhammad used to learn from the foreigner. God made it clear that this was an evident lie, for that foreigner was not able to speak a word of this Arabic Qur'an, and Muhammad, an Arab, did not know a thing of the languages of foreigners. Thus he did not understand the speech of anyone who spoke something other than Arabic. That man was not proficient at speaking Arabic, nor could Muhammad speak anything other than Arabic. Therefore God said "the speech of him at whom they falsely hint" (16:103). In a similar vein some people said about the Qur'an:

> This is nothing but a lie that he has invented, and other people have helped him with it, so that they have produced a slander and a lie. And they say: Fables of men of old which he has written down so that they are dictated to him morning and evening. Say: He who knows the secret of the heavens and the earth has revealed it. He is forever forgiving, merciful (25:4-6).

God made it clear that such a statement was a clear lie which was evident to his enemies much less to his friends. They knew that he had no one to help him with that, for there was no one, either among his people or in his town who could properly assist him. Thus God said, "They have produced a slander and a lie." All the inhabitants of his town, as well as the people who were inimical to him, knew that this was a slander against him and a lie, and so this was not said by any one of the knowledgeable and intelligent among them. Similarly, against their saying [that these were] legends of the men of old which he had written down so that they were dictated to him morning and evening, his people who were inimical to him knew that he did not have anyone to dictate any writing to him. God has made clear that which shows their falsity. "He who knows the secret of the heavens and the earth has revealed it."

In the Qur'an there are secrets which no man knows except he who is given knowledge of them by God, for God knows the secret of the heavens and the earth. Subsequently, when He had shown the falsity of their saying this, He mentioned what it was they rejected in his prophethood.

> And they say: What ails this messenger that he eats food and walks in the markets? Why is not an angel sent down to him, to be a warner

> with him? Or a treasure thrown down to him, or why has he not a paradise from which to eat? (25:7-8)

This was the speech of those opposing him who rejected his eating and walking in the markets in which was sold that which is eaten and worn. They said, "Why hasn't God sent down an angel for him to be a warner with him, or instead of that a treasure from which he could derive benefit or a garden from which he could eat." "And the evildoers say: You are only following a man bewitched" (25:8). Then God said:

> See how they coin similitudes for you, so that they are all astray and cannot find a road! (25:9)

He is saying, "They have made you resemble a liar, someone bewitched, or a reporter from someone else, but the falsity of whoever said these things is evident to anyone who knows you." Thus God said, "They are astray and cannot find a road." The wayward, the ignorant, the one who has strayed from the path is unable [to find] the road which leads to his goal; rather, their powerlessness and incoherence in debate is evident. God said:

> And they say: If only he would bring us a miracle from his Lord! Has there not come to them the proof of what is in the former Scriptures? (20:133)

He brought them a plain fact of what was in the earlier books like the Torah and the Gospel along with their knowledge that he did not take a thing from the People of the Book. If, therefore, he reported to them matters unseen and unknown to anyone but a prophet or one who has received information from a prophet, when they knew that he did not learn that from the report of any of the prophets, it became clear to them that he was a prophet. That has also become clear to all other peoples, since his people, those who were inimical to him as well as those not inimical, admitted that he did not meet anyone who taught him such things. This has been handed down by successive transmission. Among those who admitted this were his opponents, in spite of their eagerness to challenge him—were that possible. The proof against his people and against everyone to whom report of that information reached is based on these reports of the unseen events of the past.

He reported the unseen events of the future, and on these [reports] is based the proof against anyone who knows the confirmation of that information (30:2-5).[5] God disclosed (2:23-24; 17:88) that until the Day of Resurrection mankind and jinn would not be able to bring the like of this Qur'an. More than 700 years have passed since this was reported, and no one, man or jinn, has been able to bring the like of the Qur'an.

He said about the unbelievers when he was still in Mecca, "The hosts will be routed and will turn and flee" (54:45). He said:

> God has promised such of you as believe and do good works that He will surely make them to succeed on earth even as He caused those who were before them to succeed; and that He will surely establish for them their religion which He has approved for them, and will give them in exchange safety after their fear. They serve Me. They ascribe no thing as partner to Me (24:55).

The matter happened just as He promised, and the confirmation of that became evident many years later. As He said (48:28), God made manifest what He sent by signs and proofs, by power and spear.

God said, "Say to those who disbelieve: You shall be overcome and gathered into Hell, an evil resting place" (3:12). It occurred just as He had informed them. They were overcome in [this] world, to which people have borne witness, and this confirms the latter information that they will be gathered into Hell and that it is an evil resting place.

God supported him greatly with the support He gave only to prophets. He did not support any one of the prophets as He supported him, just as it was he who brought the finest of books to the finest of communities with the finest of laws. God made him master (*sayyid*) of the children of Adam. No one has ever been known who falsely claimed prophethood but that God rooted him out, brought him low, and made his falseness and rebelliousness manifest. Everyone of those who claim prophethood who is supported by God can only be true, as God supported Noah, Abraham, Moses, Jesus, David, and Solomon, and just as He supported Shu'ayb, Hud, and Salih. God's customary pattern of behavior (*sunnat Allah*) is to grant victory to His messengers and to those who believe both in this world and on the Day of Witnesses, and this is the case.

If anyone holds that what God does is not known except by His habitual activity (*al-'ada*), then this is God's habitual activity and customary pattern which is known by what He does. If someone holds that it is known by the demands of His wisdom, then it is known that He does not support someone who claimed prophethood and thus perpetrated a lie against Him. It is not possible for anyone to oppose Him, and so the prophets before him reported that God does not bring the affairs of a liar to completion, nor does He grant him victory or support him. Seen from this viewpoint, the matter becomes evident. God has commanded that we be attentive to what He has done among former peoples by way of granting reward to the prophets and their followers and His vengeance against the liars and disobedient among them (40:51; 37:171-73; 40:5; 22:40-46; 30:9-10; 40:4-5; 40:21-22; 40:82-85; 38:12-14; 26:5-6). He disclosed that there would in the future come to those who were rejecting him messages of the Qur'an at which they had scoffed. He made clear that what he had reported to them was true because the event occurred in conformity with his report of it (41:53).

He disclosed that he would show within themselves and on the horizons that which would make clear that the Qur'an is true and that they would see what He disclosed [occur] as He had foretold it. Then He said, "Does not your Lord suffice, since He is witness over all things?" He would bear witness to the Qur'an that it was true by signs, evidence, and proofs which would indicate its truthfulness, the veracity of which was [already] clear from the witness of the Lord. There is no need to wait for future signs in addition to the witness of the present.

He disclosed (54:1-5) the drawing near of the Hour and the splitting of the moon. They saw and witnessed with their own eyes the splitting of the moon, and information on that has been successively transmitted. The Prophet used to read this sura in the great congregations, like Friday and feasts, so that people would hear the signs, indications, and warning of his prophethood which was in it, so that all people would confess that and not deny it. It is obvious that the splitting of the moon must have been evident among the generality of people.

Then he mentioned (54:9-15) the situation of the prophets and those who rejected them. He disclosed that He caused the ark [of Noah] to remain as a sign of His power and of what happened to Noah and to his people. Then He said, "How [dreadful] was my punishment to him who rejected My warnings" (54:16).

Similarly He mentioned the stories of 'Ad and Thamud and Lot and others, saying at the end of each story "How great was My punishment and warnings." His warning is that which was related from Him through His messengers' announcement of warning; their giving warning is the announcement of doom. Thus becomes clear the truthfulness of what the messengers have reported by way of giving warning of the severity of punishment for those who have rejected His messengers. God mentioned this in the story of Pharaoh (54:41-45).

He mentioned in the story of Muhammad and his people various kinds of [warning] (3:13; 59:2-4). Like these, there are many places in the Qur'an which mention the indications of his prophethood and the signs of his messengership. This has been elaborated elsewhere, and my only purpose here is to point out that type [of passage].

What some People of the Book and others mention, that He granted victory to Pharaoh, Nimrod, Sennacherib, Genghis Khan, and other unbelieving rulers, has an obvious answer. None of these people ever claimed prophethood or that God commanded him to call [people] to service and obedience to Him, that whoever obeyed him would enter the Garden and whoever disobeyed him would enter the Fire. By contrast, whoever claims that God sent him with that [message] must either be a truthful messenger for whom God would grant victory and a reward, or else he would have to be a liar against whom God would take vengeance and thoroughly uproot.

It is clear that what he brought was not signs and proofs which could admit opposition, nor was it similar to wonders [wrought by] magicians, sorcerers, and tricksters, which could admit opposition. One of the special characteristics of the miracles of the prophets is that no one is able to oppose them or, in contrast to other wonders, perform the like of them.

The Anti-Christ al-Dajjal will claim divinity and will work wonders, but his very claim to divinity is a claim impossible in itself. God will send Christ the son of Mary to kill him and expose his falsity, and will send with [Christ] that which will indicate [Al-Dajjal's] falsity in various ways.[6] "*Kafir*" (*unbeliever*) will be written between his eyes. He will be one-eyed, and God is not one-eyed. No one will see his Lord before he dies. He [Al-Dajjal] would want to kill him who would be wanting to kill him first, and will be unable to kill him. Thus he will have with him indications pointing to his falseness which show clearly that [the wonders] he has are not a sign of his truthfulness.

Conversely the miracles of the prophets cannot be duplicated by either man or jinn nor can they be proven false, like Moses' changing his staff into a snake, the she-camel of Salih springing out of the ground, Christ raising the dead to life, the splitting of the moon, the revelation of the Qur'an, and other wonders of Muhammad. When the idolators brashly demanded a sign from Muhammad, the splitting of the moon occurred and he showed them that. (54:1-8).

He disclosed that all mankind and jinn, even if they gathered together, would not be able to oppose the Qur'an with another like it. Its expression, its meaning, its forms of knowledge and sciences are the most perfect miracle and the greatest in importance.

It has been the case that no one of the Arabs or others, despite the strength of their enmity for him and their eagerness to prove him false by any means and their proficiency with various kinds of speech, have been able to bring forth something like the Qur'an.

God at that time revealed verses in which He made it clear that [Muhammad] was a messenger of God to them, and He did not mention in them that he was not sent to others than [the Arabs]. In three passages (28:43-47; 32:3; 36:1-6) God stated His favor to these people and His argument against them by sending him. In sending him [to the Arabs] He mentioned some of His wisdom, but that does not demand that he was only sent to these people. Many examples like this are well known in the Arabic language and in that of others.[7]

———

They use as proof God's saying:

> Even as We have sent to you a messenger from among you, who recites to you Our verses (2:151).

> God has truly shown grace to the believers by sending to them a messenger of their own who recites to them His verses (3:164).

> There has come to you a messenger from yourselves, to whom anything in which you are overburdened is grevious, full of concern for you, for the believers full of pity and merciful (9:128).

There is a dispute among scholars about this. Some hold that this was a preaching to all people, and its intent is "I was sent to you as a messenger from among mankind since you could not bear to take [the message] from one of the angels, so it is a favor from God upon you that He sent you a human messenger" (6:8-9). Others hold that it is preached to the Arabs. Whichever the case, it contains mention of His granting favor upon those receiving the preaching by His sending him as a messenger from their own kind.

In this there is nothing which prevents his being sent [as well] to others than them. If it is interpreted as a preaching to all mankind, what is meant is that [it must be remembered that Muhammad] was also sent to the jinn, and he was not of their kind. If what is meant is that it was preached as a lesson to the Arabs in that He bestowed him as a blessing upon them, how does this deny that God could have thereby blessed others as well? Non-Arabic speakers are closer to Arabs than are the jinn to mankind, and yet in the beloved Book He disclosed that when the jinn heard the

Qur'an they believed in it (46:29-32; 72:1-28). Similar to this is his saying:

> It is a reminder for you and your people; and you will be questioned (43:44).

His people were the Quraysh, but that did not prevent [the Qur'an] from being a reminder for the rest of the Arabs and even for the rest of mankind. As God said:

> Those who disbelieve would like to disconcert you with their eyes when they hear the reminder, and they say: He is mad indeed; when it is nothing else than a reminder to creation (68:51-52).

God indicated that He himself claimed that [Muhammad] was sent to bring warning and reminder to all creation (25:1; 38:86-89; 81:19-29; 4:79; 6:66; 6:9; 12:104).

———

In more than one place in [the Qur'an] he called out to the People of the Book with his summons to them and with his summoning the jinn. If they admit that he stated that, but they reject him as lying about that, then they either accept his messengership to the Arabs or not. But if they admit that he was a messenger sent by God, they would not along with that reject him in what he had previously stated. Rather it is necessary to admit his messengership to all creation, just as he disclosed.

## E. IMPLICATIONS OF DENYING MUHAMMAD'S PROPHETIC CALL

The other alternative for them is not to admit his messengership to the Arabs or to anyone else, but rather say about him what the pagan Arabs used to say—that he was a poet, a magician, a lying slanderer, or suchlike. Against this supposition they should be told: "Your proof is also false." It is not possible to use such a thing from the teaching of the prophets before him as an argument for your proposition to reject Muhammad. Whether you believe Muhammad in all of what he says, in some of it, or whether you reject him, your proof is false and it necessitates the falsity of your religion by any estimation. By whatever criterion it is shown to be false [your religion] is false in the same matter. It can be clearly proved that it is false in the same way.

If you reject Muhammad, there does not remain any way by which you can know the truthfulness of other prophets than him. It is impossible to reject him and to hold for the truthfulness of others than him. Anyone who believes his falseness and believes other [prophets] than him has no knowledge about the truthfulness of others. He is even believing them without knowledge, and if he is not knowledgeable about their truthfulness, it is not possible for him to use their statements as argumentation. He is offering a view without knowledge and debating about that of which he has no knowledge.

The indications which point towards the truth of Muhammad are greater and more numerous than the indications which point to the truthfulness of Moses and Jesus. His miracles are greater than those of others. The Book with which he was sent is more noble than the book with which the others were sent. The Law which he brought is more perfect than the law of Moses and Jesus. His community is more perfect in all virtues than that of either of these [two earlier prophets].

There is not found in the Torah or in the Gospel any beneficial knowledge or righteous work of which the like or what is more perfect is not found in the Qur'an. However, in the Qur'an there is found beneficial knowledge and righteous action of which the like is not found in the Torah and the Gospel. Thus whatever challenge the enemies of the prophets may hurl against Muhammad, it is all the more possible to direct that challenge and greater against Moses and Jesus. But all this is elaborated elsewhere, and we will not go into it here.

There is no need for that to rebut their teaching. It is impossible to affirm the prophethoods of Moses and Jesus and at the same time to reject the prophethood of Muhammad. No one could do that but someone who is the most ignorant and wayward among people or one of the greatest among them in stubbornness and in pursuing his own whims. That is because these people argue from that which they have transmitted from the prophets, but they have not mentioned the indications which point towards their truthfulness. They have accepted all that without contesting it, and then they have sought to argue from what they have transmitted from the prophets before him and from what they have transmitted from him for the soundness of their religion.

This, however, is an argument which refutes them whether they believe in him or reject him, for if they believe him, their religion is false, and if they reject him, their religion is false. If they believe him, it is known that he summoned them and all people of the earth to place faith and obedience in him, just as Christ, Moses, and other messengers had done. It is known that he showed the falsity of what they were holding by way of [divine] union and other things, and that he called them unbelievers in more than one place. Thus in simply affirming that Muhammad was messenger of God, even solely to the Arabs, the falsity of the religion of Christians and Jews and every religion opposed to his religion follows necessarily. Whoever is a messenger for God does not speak falsely about God, and Muhammad is the messenger of God. It is known from him that he summoned Christians and Jews to put faith and obedience in him as had others before him, and that he called disbelievers whoever did not believe in him and promised them the Fire. This is handed down from him by overwhelming transmission and known both by the general public and by individual persons. In the Qur'an there is frequent mention of that (98:1-8; 3:18-20). He stated the unbelief of Jews and Christians in various places, such as His statement about the Christians (5:17; 5:72-77; 4:171-75; 9:30-31; 5:116-17). He said in two places, "They have disbelieved who say that God is Christ the son of Mary" (5:17, 72).

God said, "They have disbelieved who say that God is the third of three" (5:73). God said, "Do not say 'three'; cease! it is better for you" (4:171). God said, "The Christians say: 'Christ is the son of God'" (9:30).

God mentioned these three views among them, and Christians have held these three views. Some people suppose that each view corresponds to a group among them. The view that [God is] the third of three is that of the Nestorians. The saying that he is the son of God is that of the Melkites. Some people hold that the opinion that God is Christ the son of Mary is the view of the Jacobites in their holding for the son and the Holy Spirit.

Ibn Jarir al-Tabari supposed that these groups were antecedent to the Jacobites, Nestorians, and Melkites, as a group of exegetes like Ibn Jarir al-Tabari, Al-Tha'labi, and others have mentioned. Sometimes they relate about the Jacobites that [they hold] that Jesus is God, about the Nestorians that he is the son of God, and about the Maryusiyya [Marcionites?] that he is the third of three. Sometimes they relate that the Nestorians hold that he is the third of three, about the Melkites that he is God, and they explain their view "the third of three" by the Father, the son, and the Holy Spirit.

What is correct is that all these statements are the view of the well-known Christian groups—Melkite, Jacobite, and Nestorian. All these groups speak of the three hypostases—the Father, the son, and the Holy Spirit. They say "God is third of three." They say about Christ that he is God, and they say that he is the son of God. They are agreed on the union of divine and human natures and that what unites is the Word. They are agreed on the creed of their faith which includes that when they say:

> We believe in one God, the Father, the Governor of all, the Creator of the heavens and the earth, everything that is seen and all that is unseen, and in one Lord Jesus Christ the only son of God, begotten from the Father from before all ages, light from light, true God from true God, born not created.

But God has said, "Do not say 'three'" and "They have disbelieved who say that God is the third of three." They [the exegetes] have explained it by the trinity which is well known about them and mentioned in their creed. There are people who say that "God is Christ the son of Mary" is the view of Christians who hold the Father and the son. Such people in the creed have made God a third out of three, and have explained it by making Jesus and his mother into two gods to be worshiped apart from God. Al-Suddi said about God's statement, "They have disbelieved etc." that "Christians say that God is Christ and his mother." Thus God said, "Did you say to people 'Take me and my mother for two gods besides God?'" (5:116).

A third view, stranger than that, was mentioned by Abu Sakhr.[1] He said that "They have disbelieved who say that God is third of three" refers to the view of the Jews that Ezra ['Uzayr] is the son of God and that of the Christians that Christ is son of God, and thus they have made God the third of three. This is weak. Sa'id ibn Bitriq[2] has mentioned in his history of Christianity that there is a group of them called the Marsiyya who hold that Mary is a god and Jesus is a god. It may be said that this is the view [only] of these people, just as the statement that Ezra is the son of God is the view of a sect of Jews.

The first can be given an intelligible meaning about Christians who are agreed on the creed; they all say "God is third of three." God has forbidden them to say that, and He said:

> O People of the Book! Do not exaggerate in your religion nor utter anything concerning God except the truth. Christ—Jesus, the son of Mary—was only a messenger of God, and His word which He conveyed to Mary, and a spirit from Him. So believe in God and His messengers, and do not say "three"—cease! it is better for you (4:171).

In this verse God mentioned the trinity and divine union and forbade them both. He made it clear that Christ is only the messenger of God and His word which he sent down upon Mary and a spirit from Him. He said "Believe in God and His messengers." Then He said "Do not say 'three'—cease! it is better for you," and He did not mention here his mother. About God's saying "His word which He conveyed to Mary" is His saying "Be!" and he [Jesus] was. Thus Qatada said: "It is not that the word became Jesus, but it is *by* the word that Jesus came to be."

The Imam Ahmad ibn Hanbal spoke similarly in his work which he composed as a refutation of the Jahmites (*Al-Radd 'ala al-Jahmiyya*).[3] Moreover, Khallal[4] and Abu Ya'la have mentioned it from him. Ahmad said:

> Then Jahm laid claim to another matter and said: "We have found in the Book of God a verse which indicates that the Qur'an is created." We said, "What verse?" He said, "God's saying, 'Christ the son of Mary is only the messenger of God and His word which He conveyed to Mary, and a spirit from Him.' But Jesus is created." We said: "God has prevented you from understanding the Qur'an. Jesus is customarily predicated by expressions which are not predicable of the Qur'an. Jesus is described as a living creature, born, a child, a boy, a young man, as eating and drinking and teaching the command and the prohibition as well as the promise and the threat, and as being of the descendants of Noah and Abraham. But it is not permissible for us to state about the Qur'an what we say about Jesus.
>
> Have you heard God say in the Qur'an what He said about Jesus? But the meaning of His saying "Jesus, the son of Mary, was only a messenger of God, and His word which He conveyed to Mary, and a spirit from Him," is that the word which He conveyed to Mary is when He said for him "Be!" and Jesus was by the "Be!" It is not that Jesus was the "Be!" but by the "Be!" he was. The "Be!" is from God, His speech, and the "Be!" is not created. Thus both the Christians and the Jahmites have spoken falsely about God in the matter of Jesus, for the Jahmites say "Jesus is the spirit of God and His word because He is the created Word." Christians say that the spirit of God is of the essence of God, and the word of God is of the essence of God, as it can be said that this piece of cloth is from this garment. But we say that by the word Jesus was, not that Jesus was the word.
>
> As for God's saying "a spirit from Him," He says that by His command the spirit was in Him, like His saying "He has made of service to you whatever is in the heavens and whatever is on earth; it is all from Him" (45:13). He means from His command, and the explanation of the Spirit of God only carries the meaning that it is a spirit which by the word of God He created.

Al-Sha'bi[5] said about God's saying "His word which He conveyed to Mary" the word was when He said for him "Be!" Jesus was by the "Be!"; Jesus was not himself the "Be!" but by the "Be!" he was.

Al-Layth[6] said from Mujahid: "A spirit from Him" means "A messenger from Him," like God's saying:

> Then We sent to her Our spirit and it assumed for her the likeness of a perfect man. She said: I seek refuge in the Beneficient one from you, if you are God-fearing. He said: I am only a messenger of your Lord, that I may bestow on you a faultless son (19:17-19).

The meaning is that Jesus was created from this spirit, which is Jibril the Holy Spirit; he is called a spirit as he is called a word, because he is created by the Word. Christians say in their creed, "He took flesh from Mary and from the Holy Spirit," because it appeared like that in earlier books. But they supposed the Holy Spirit to be an attribute of God. They made it His life and His power and [they made] it Lord.

This is an error of theirs, for no one of the prophets ever called the life of God or His power or anything of His attributes the Holy Spirit. Elsewhere in the teaching of the prophets, by the Holy Spirit is meant that which God sends down upon the hearts of the prophets, like revelation, guidance, and support. Also by it is meant the angel. Thus, in the *tafsir* of Ibn Sa'ib from Abu Salih from Ibn 'Abbas [it is related] that Jesus the son of Mary met a group of Jews. When they saw him, they said, "Here comes the sorcerer, son of the sorceress, the inventor son of the inventress." Thus they slandered him and his mother. When Jesus heard that, he said, "O God, you are my Lord. I am from Your spirit which has gone forth and by Your Word You have created me. I did not come to them of my own accord." He recounted the complete hadith. God mentioned this as well in other places (21:91; 66:12; 19:17-18).

The point here is that whether they have believed Muhammad or rejected him, in either case the falsity of their religion necessarily follows. If he was a truthful prophet, then in this book he reported from God the unbelief of Christians in more than one place; he summoned them to put faith in him; he commanded *jihad* against them. Whoever knows, therefore, that he is a prophet, even to a specific group of people, must believe in all that he reported, and he reported the unbelief and the waywardness of Christians. If this is established, then there is no need for them to try to prove a thing from the [sacred] books or from reason. It is known that all of that from which they draw for argumentation for the soundness of their religion is false, even though the falsity of their arguments may not be clear in detail. This is because the prophets only speak the truth, just as when Christ passed the judgment of unbelief on those Jews who rejected him. All that which the Jews argued in opposition to him was false, for whatever opposes the statement of an inerrant prophet is false. But if they have rejected Muhammad with an absolute, universal refusal and said, "He is not a prophet at all; he was not sent to anyone, neither to the Arabs nor to anyone else, but he is one of the liars," they cannot at the same time believe in the prophecy of others. By the same way in which the prophethood of Moses and Jesus is known, one can know *a fortiori* the prophethood of Muhammad. If they say they know the prophethood of Moses and Christ by miracles, and the miracles are known by successive transmission back to them, it should be said to them that the miracles of Muhammad are greater, their transmission more complete and richer, the book which Muhammad brought more perfect, his community finer, and the laws of his religion better. Moses brought justice, and Jesus brought its completion in grace (*al-fadl*), but [Muhammad] in his religion combined justice and grace.[7] If it is still possible for someone to say in spite of this that he is a lying schemer, one could *a fortiori* make that estimation of the other [prophets]. Their rejection of Muhammad would declare the falsity of whatever they had by way of prophethoods. If someone passes judgment on one of two things, he passes judgment on the thing like it; how much more will he when the one is superior to the other?

If someone should say that Aaron, Joshua, David, and Solomon were prophets, but Moses was not a prophet, or that David, Solomon, Joshua, and John were prophets, but Jesus was not a prophet, or say as do the Samaritans that Joshua was a prophet, but those after him like David, Solomon, and Christ were not prophets, or say as do the Jews that David, Solomon, Isaiah, Habakkuk, Malakhi, Amos, and Daniel were prophets, but Christ the son of Mary was not a prophet, this would be a statement whose falsity would be evident. Those whose prophethood they denied were truer and more complete in prophethood than those whose prophethood they affirmed. Since the indications of their prophethood are more complete and finer, how is it possible to affirm the prophethood of a less excellent prophet without that of the more excellent? This is like someone saying that Zufar and Ibn al-Qasim and Al-Muzani and Al-Athram[8] were legal scholars, while Abu Hanifa, Malik, Al-Shafi'i, and Ahmad [ibn Hanbal] were not. Or it is like saying that Al-Akhfash and Ibn al-Anbari and Al-Mubarrad[9] were grammarians, but Al-Khalil and Sibawayh and Al-Farra' were not. It would be like saying that the authors Al-Maliki and Al-Masihi[10] and people like them who wrote medical texts were physicians, while Hippocrates and Galen and people like them were not. It would be like saying that Kushyar and Al-Khiraqi[11] and people like them used to elucidate the science of astronomy, but Ptolemy and others like him did not.

The contradictory nature of someone's saying that David, Solomon, Malakhi, Amos, and Daniel were prophets but that Muhammad ibn 'Abd Allah was not a prophet is more obvious, and the falseness of his statement is more evident than all these. Similarly, even saying that Moses and Jesus were two messengers and the Torah and the Gospel two books revealed by God is false to the limits of obviousness and clarity to anyone who reflects upon what Muhammad brought and what was brought by those before him, who contemplates his Book and the books which were before him, the signs of his prophethood with those of these others, the laws of his religion with the laws of the religion of these [earlier prophets].

All this has been exposed and detailed elsewhere,[12] but my purpose here is to point out the underlying bases of their responses. These people have not brought a single proof which indicates the truthfulness of what they have used as proof from the prophets. If the pagans and the atheists who reject all these prophets debated with them they would have no argument in what they have stated, and they have no argument either against Muslims who admit the prophethood of these people. The majority of Muslims only know the truthfulness of these prophets, because of Muhammad's disclosure that they are prophets. It is impossible, therefore, that they believe in the branch while rejecting the root whose trustworthiness they know. Moreover, in the way by which the prophethood of these [earlier prophets] is known through what is proven concerning their miracles and their information, there is known the prophethood of him whose miracles and information can be established *a fortiori*. It is thus impossible for any Muslim to believe in the prophethood of one of these people while rejecting even one word of what Muhammad has brought.

———

It ought to be known that many Christians only use the prophecies as bases for predictions by the prophets of what comes after them. They say that Christ was predicted by the prophets before him, in contrast to Muhammad who was not announced by any prophet. The answer to these people is in two ways.

Firstly, they should be told that, on the contrary, the prediction of Muhammad in the previous books is greater than the prediction of Christ. They are like the Jews who were interpreting the prediction of Christ in such a way that it was not Jesus the son of Mary but another for whom they are waiting. In reality they were only waiting for the Antichrist, al-Dajjal. It is he whom the Jews were following when 70,000 shawl-wearing Jews of Isfahan[13] went out [in revolt] with him. Muslims killed them until the trees and rocks were saying, "O Muslim, here is a Jew behind me. Come, kill him." That is in a sound hadith from the prophet when he said:

> Jesus the son of Mary will descend from heaven upon a white minaret to the east of Damascus. He will break the cross, kill the pig, and impose the *jizya*. The Messiah of Guidance—Jesus the son of Mary—will kill the Messiah of Error, the one-eyed Dajjal, a dozen steps or so from the gate of Ludd.[14] Thus it will be clear to all people that man is not a god. He [Jesus] will kill the one who claimed that he was God; he is innocent of that which others have claimed about him.

Thus some of the predictions of Muhammad in the preceding books were interpreted wrongly by some People of the Book, as has been elaborated elsewhere, and the question of the mention of Muhammad in the books which the People of the Book possess is discussed at length elsewhere.

Secondly, they should be told that it is not required that a prophet be announced beforehand. For example, Moses was a messenger to Pharaoh, but no prediction about him had preceded him before Pharaoh. Also, God's Friend [Abraham] was sent to Nimrod, and there had not previously been any announcement of a prophet to him.[15] Similarly, Noah, Hud, Salih, Shu'ayb, and Lot were none of them preceded by a prediction concerning them to their people despite their being true prophets.

The indications of a prophet are not limited to reports beforehand. The indications of prophethood include miracles and other things than miracles, as has been elaborated elsewhere. These Christians, however, rely for the doctrine of the trinity and divine union and other things on revealed tradition (*al-sam'*), and it is their claim that the divine books have brought all that. Their reliance is not upon reason. Therefore, if it is clear that in their rejecting Muhammad it becomes impossible for them to establish the prophethood of anyone other than him, it thereby is impossible for them to draw any conclusions from revealed traditions. As for rational arguments, in spite of their insisting on certain ones, nevertheless they must admit that their arguments from them are weak, and that [such arguments] are actually more indicative of the opposite of their belief than they are of their belief itself. We will show, God willing, that they have no argument either from revealed teaching or from reason but that it is wholly an argument against them.

In the case of someone who stated that he was messenger of God, it is not possible to hold that he was messenger of God in some of what he prophecied from God but not in other things, nor is it possible to follow some of his Book which he stated to have been revealed from God without [following] the rest. If he was truthful in his claiming that he was messenger of God, he would be inerrant in all of what he reported from God. It would not be possible for him to speak falsely about anything in it, either intentionally or accidentally. It would be necessary to follow the Book which he brought from God, and it would not be possible to refute a thing of what he said he brought from God. If he was lying in even a single word of what he reported from God, he would be a lying impostor, and it would not be possible to argue for a thing of their religion nor the religion of anyone else simply by his report from God. It would not be possible to argue from it even as his own report and opinion if he had not said that he reported it from God, just as that would be impossible with the rest of those who are known to be lying in their saying "I am the messenger of God," like Musaylima al-Hanafi, Al-Aswad al-'Ansi, Tulayha al-Asadi, Al-Harith al-Dimashqi,[16] the Pope of Rome,[17] and other liars.

Although God does not blame any given Muslim for forgetfulness or error, nor does He blame the messenger for forgetfulness and error in anything other than that which he has communicated from God—according to the early generations, the imams, and the majority of Muslims—nevertheless it is not possible for error to reside in that which he communicates from God.[18] If it were possible for him to communicate from God what God did not say and that would remain permanently so that people would believe God said a particular thing when He had not, this would be contradictory to the purpose of messengership. In that case he would not be a prophet of God, but would be lying in that, even though he did not intend it.

If someone communicated from God what He did not say but acted honestly in that, then it would be a case of a person's having spoken sincerely when he spoke wrongly about God in making Him say what He did not, although he was not doing so intentionally. It would be impossible in such a case that God would confirm that person in everything which he reported from Him or that He would establish for him signs and proofs which point to his truthfulness in everything which he reported from Him when that was not the case. Anyone whose trustworthiness in what he communicates from God is attested by proofs and signs is sound in everything which he reports from God. It is not possible for there to be in his information from God any falsehood, whether intentional or unintentional. This is something on which all people—Muslims, Jews, Christians, and others—agree; they do not dispute that it is impossible for an error to remain in his information from God.

They only dispute whether it is possible for error to occur in what he emends or clarifies. They do not deny the purpose of messengership, as it is transmitted from him who stated, "Those cranes are high-flying so that you may hope for their intercession."[19] On this, people hold two views. There are some who deny that and challenge its occurrence.Others hold that they have heard what he did not say. Thus the error was in their hearing, for Satan had put that into their hearing. Some would allow the possibility of that and say that if a clear sign occurred and abrogated what Satan had cast upon them there would not be any object of caution in that. [The incident] is an indication of his trustworthiness, his reliability, and his religion, a sign he was not following his whim nor wrongly accepting fate as a seeker of leadership would have done in his error.

According to every view, people are agreed that someone sent by God whose trustworthiness in what he communicates from God is established by signs can only communicate the truth from Him. Otherwise the signs indicating his truthfulness would be indicating the truthfulness of one who was not truthful. The falsity of what is indicated prevents there being indisputable evidence for its correctness.

The truthfulness which is indicated by the signs and the proofs of the prophets is that their information from God corresponds to its Discloser and is not opposed to Him either intentionally or accidentally. Should someone say "I do not call an error a lie" or "There is no offense accruing to him who errs in his speech," he should be told that this is irrelevant here. Signs (*al-ayat*) indicate that God sent someone to communicate His message from Him. God does not send someone about whom it is known that he reports from Him something different than what He said to him, just as it is not possible that He send someone who intentionally speaks falsely about Him. Even an ordinary person does not send one about whom it is known that he communicates something different from that with which he was sent. Were it known that such a person tells what was not said to him, and someone sends him in spite of that, he would be ignorant and foolish and not intelligent or wise. So how would it be possible for the Most Knowing of those who know, the Wisest of wise [to do that]?

Moreover, the signs and proofs indicate his truthfulness in everything which he communicates from God and [indicate as well] that God confirms him in everything which he communicated from Him. It is impossible for him to be untrustworthy in a single part of that, just as it is impossible that God confirm someone in everything who does not speak correctly in all of it. The confirmation of him who does not speak truly is a lie, and a lie is impossible with God.

With anyone who says that he is the messenger of God, it is not possible to believe in some of what he reported from God and to reject the rest. If he was lying in even a single word, then he was not one of God's messengers, and one cannot use his statements as arguments. If it was possible that the teaching was in itself trustworthy but his relationship to God was that God did not send him with it and reveal it,[20] he would not be trustworthy in it if he lied in even one word, because God did not send a liar.

If he was not lying in a single word, then it is necessary to believe him in everything which he reported from God without the rest, in contrast to someone who [merely] attests and witnesses [to the prophet]. If their intention is to show a contradiction [in his teaching], then this would be an argument that he is not a messenger, and such an argument would not benefit them. Nevertheless it is clear that he was not self-contradictory. If their intention is to obligate Muslims by [his teaching] to accept that he was not sent to Christians, then we have shown clearly that his argument fails to do so from numerous aspects. This is a proof that it is not possible for them to argue from a thing of the teaching of Muhammad whether they believe in him or reject him.

## F. GOD'S TREATMENT OF THOSE IN ERROR

The sacred texts indicate that God only punishes those to whom He has sent a messenger to establish an argument against them; this is a principle which must be accepted as proven by many sayings of God (17:13-15; 4:165; 67:8-9; 39:71; 6:131; 28:59; 28:47-48; 5:19).

If this is the situation, it is obvious that the Qur'an only establishes a case against someone that it [actually] reaches. As God said, "That by it I might warn you and whomever it may reach" (6:19). When someone is in contact with some of the Qur'an without the rest, the case is established against him by that with which he is in contact without that which has not reached him.

If the meaning of some of the verses is obscure, people may dispute in interpreting the verse, but it is necessary to return to God and His messenger [for judgment] on the dispute. If people have independently striven to understand what the messengers have meant, then he who is successful will receive a double reward and he who is in error will receive one reward. Nothing prevents that being said about the People of the Book before us. Whoever before us was not in contact with all the texts of the prophets will not find a case established against him in something the meaning of which was unclear to him. If he strives independently to understand it and is successful, he will receive a double reward, if he errs, he will still receive a reward and his error will be taken away from him. However, the person who intentionally corrupts the Book in its text or meaning and and knows what the messenger has brought but stubbornly opposes him is deserving of punishment, as is anyone who is remiss in seeking truth and following it, but rather pursues his own whims and is distracted [from the truth] by his preoccupation with his daily life.

For this reason, if some People of the Book have distorted some of the Book, and others among them did not know that and were independently striving to follow what the prophet brought, it is not necessary to make these people answerable to the threat [of punishment]. Since it is possible that there be among the People of the Book someone who does not know everything which Christ brought, but some of what he brought or some of its meanings are hidden from him so that he does *ijtihad*, he will not be punished for what did not reach him.

In this connection the reports may be related about those Jews who were waiting with Tubba' and those from among the people of Madina like Ibn Hityan and others who were waiting to place faith in Muhammad.[1] They were not rejecting Christ as were other Jews, and people may dispute whether, despite someone's independent searching and striving his utmost, that which indicates the truthfulness of the prophet would not become clear to the one waiting.

If it is not clear to him, is he deserving of punishment in the hereafter or not? Some people have disputed about what is handed down from them, and the discussion is about two matters. The first concerns the waywardness of the person who opposes truth. This is something that is known in numerous rational and revealed ways. There are many kinds of indications which give evidence of the error found in many views of the people of the *qibla* who are opposed to truth, and others than the people of the *qibla*. The second question concerns their unbelief and their deserving punishment in the afterlife.

In this three views are held by those who are the followers of the well-known imams—Malik, Al-Shafi'i, and Ahmad [ibn Hanbal]. The three views are as follows:

1) He punishes in the Fire whoever has not believed, even if no messenger was sent to him to establish a case against them by reason. This is the view of many among the people of *kalam* theology and *fiqh*, the followers of Abu Hanifa and others who hold for the rational judgment. It is the choice of Abu al-Khattab.[2]

2) There is no argument for him from reason; it is even permissible[3] for Him to punish someone against whom a case has not been established either by revelation or by reason. This is the view of those who permit the punishment of the children and the insane of unbelievers, and it is held by many of those who practice *kalam*, like Jahm [ibn Safwan], Abu al-Hasan al-Ash'ari and his followers, the Qadi Abu Ya'la [ibn al-Farra'], Ibn 'Aqil, and others.

3) The view of the *salaf* and the Imams is that He only punishes those whom His message has reached, and He punishes only those who are opposed to the messengers. This is what is indicated by the Book and the sunna. God said to Iblis: "I shall fill hell with you together with such of those who follow you" (38:86).

If the situation is like this, it is similar to what is discussed about both the early and recent People of the Book. Sometimes they speak about the first matter, which is a clarification of their opposition to the truth, their ignorance, and their waywardness. This is indicated by all proofs from revelation and reason. They clearly show their unbelief for which they deserve punishment in this world and the next. But this is a matter for God, and his prophet has not spoken about it except in what the messengers have disclosed. Just as we do not bear witness to the faith and [their reward in] the Garden except for those whom the messengers bore witness, so [we do not bear witness against] those against whom no argument is established by the [divine] message, like children, the insane, and the people of the intervals [between prophets]. About this last group, the most evident opinion is that there are traditions brought by the prophets that on the Day of Resurrection they will be examined. There will be sent to them one who will command them to obey him. If they obey him, they will be deserving of the reward, but if they disobey, they will deserve judgment.

If this is the case, we bear witness in favor of anyone who was a believer in Moses and a follower of his that he is a believer, a Muslim deserving of the reward, and similarly, whoever was a believer in Christ who followed him. We bear witness about anyone against whom Moses established a case, like the people of Pharaoh, that such people were not followers of his and that they are among the people of the Fire. Similarly, [that will be the situation of] anyone against whom Christ established a case, like those about whom he spoke (5:115; 3:55-57).

As for those after the time of Christ who were in contact with some but not all of his information, or those after Moses' time who were in contact with some of his information, the case against these people is established on the information with which they were not in contact. If they differed in interpreting some of the Torah and the Gospel, it would not be necessary that someone who desired the truth and strove independently to seek it would have to be punished, even though he be erring in the truth, ignorant of it, and wayward from it, just like the independent striver in search of the truth within the community of Muhammad.[4]

Accordingly, it may be said that the apostles, or at least some of them, or many or even most of the People of the Book used to believe that Christ himself was crucified. They were erring in this, but this error was not something which detracted from their putting faith in Christ.[5] If they believed in what he brought, it would not be necessary for them [to be sentenced to] the Fire, for the gospels which the People of the Book possessed contained mention of the crucifixion of Christ. They hold that these were received from four men—Mark, Luke, John, and Matthew. No one among these four witnessed the crucifixion of Christ, nor any of the apostles, nor did even any of his followers witness the crucifixion. The only ones who witnessed it were a small group of Jews. There are those people who say that the crucified man was not him, but that they[6] intentionally lied [in saying] that they crucified him. Thus his crucifixion appeared so to those to whom it was reported. This is the view of a group of those who do *kalam*, Mu'tazila and others. It is the view of Ibn Hazm and others.

Others say that it was doubtful for those who crucified him. This is the view of most people. The first group hold that God's saying:

> They did not kill him, nor did they crucify him, but it was made to appear so to them (4:157)

means that it was meant to appear so to those to whom others had reported his crucifixion. The majority of people hold that it was made to appear so to those who were saying that they crucified him, as the story has been mentioned in more than one place. The point here is that on this question people hold two extreme views and a moderate one. The first is that of the extremists (*al-ghulat*) among the Christians who claim that the apostles were inerrant in what they said, reported, and saw. Thus they hold the Christian scholars to be correct in whatever they have said in interpreting the Gospel. The other extreme holds that whoever has been mistaken and erred in anything of that is deserving of the threat and is even an unbeliever.

The third and moderate position is that they are neither inerrant nor blameworthy, rather they may commit an error which is pardonable for them if they were independently striving for knowledge of the truth and followers of it in accordance with their scope and ability. For this reason sound proofs certify and the books of God indicate God's censure of the wayward and the denier and His hatred for them. This is indicated by the books of God. Nevertheless He does not punish anyone except after he has been warned.

It is established in a sound hadith report from the Prophet that he said:

> God looked at the people of the earth and despised them, Arabs and foreigners, except for a few People of the Book.

He disclosed that He despised them except for these remnants. His detestation is even the strongest kind of hatred, and yet He has disclosed in the Qur'an that He would not punish them until He sent them a messenger (20:134; 28:47). These verses point out that the demand for their punishment is present, but the conditions for punishment are only after the arrival of the message. For this reason God said:

> So that people would not have an argument against God after the messengers (4:165).

In the collections of sound hadiths from the Prophet it is reported that he said:

> There is no one to whom pardon is more beloved than it is to God. For the sake of that He sent messengers and revealed the Books.

In another report:

> For the sake of that He sent messengers announcing good news and warning. No one is more loving of praise than is God, and for the sake of that He praises Himself. No one is more jealous than God, and for the sake of this He forbade disgusting things, both those which are manifest and those which are hidden.

People have argued about the relative merits of opinions on questions such as the goodness of justice, *tawhid*, and veracity, and the evil of injustice, *shirk*, and falsehood. Are these things known by reason or only by revealed truth? If they are known by reason, does He punish those who act wrongly before a messenger is sent to them?

Three views are held by followers of the four law schools and others, and these three opinions are held by the followers of Ahmad [ibn Hanbal] and others.

One group says that those things are not known by reason but only by revelation. This is the view of prominent compulsorists like Jahm ibn Safwan and those like him; it is the view of Abu al-Hasan al-Ash'ari and his followers in the four legal traditions like the Qadi Abu Bakr ibn al-Tayyib [al-Baqillani], Abu 'Abd Allah ibn Hamid,[7] the Qadi Abu Ya'la, Abu al-Ma'ali,[8] Abu al-Wafa' ibn 'Aqil, and others.

Others hold, rather, that the goodness and evil of acts may be known by reason. Abu al-Khattab Mahfuz ibn Ahmad[9] held this, and this is the view of most of the jurists and theologians. This is handed down from Abu Hanifa himself and is held by the generality of his followers and by most of the followers of Malik, Al-Shafi'i, and Ahmad, and by the *hadith* scholars like Abu al-Hasan al-Nu'aymi[10] and Abu al-Khattab and Abu Bakr al-Qaffal[11] and Abu Nasr al-Sijzi[12] and Abu al-Qasim Sa'd ibn 'Ali al-Zanjani.[13] It is the view of the Karramiyya and other prominent arguers for *qadar*. It is the view of the Mu'tazila and other prominent Qadaris. These people are divided into two opinions.

Some of them hold that they are deserving of punishment in the afterlife simply because of their opposition to reason, as the Mu'tazila, the Hanafis, and Abu al-Khattab say. This view is opposed to the Book and the sunna. Others hold that they are not punished until a messenger is sent to them, as the Book and the sunna indicate; nevertheless their deeds are blameworthy and hateful. God hates and censures their acts; they are described by unbelief which is hated and censured by God, even though they would not be punished until a messenger be sent to them. It is like the Prophet said in the aforementioned sound hadith report:

> God looked at the people of the earth and despised them, Arabs and foreigners, except for a few People of the Book. My Lord said to me: Stand up among the Quraysh and warn them. I said: And if they break my head until they could call it a piece of bread? He said, I am testing you and through you I am testing [others]. I am revealing to you a Book which cannot be washed with water. Recite it sleeping and waking. Raise up an army; I will send you twice like them. With those who obey you fight those who disobey you. I will provide for whatever is the greatest need among you. He said: I have created My servants as monotheists (*hunafa'*), but the demons have caused them to wander; they have forbidden them that which I permitted to them, and have commanded them to commit *shirk* against Me for which no authority was given.

The Prophet said in another hadith:

> Everyone is born according to the law of nature,[14] and then his parents turn him into a Jew, a Christian, or a Magian; just as the animal gives birth to a sound offspring, do you consider proper those which are mutilated?

Abu Hurayra says about him:

> Recite if you will! The natural characteristic of God according to which He created people. It was said: O messenger of God! Have you seen someone die while he was young? He answered: God is more knowing of what they were doing.

Although God despised them, He disclosed that He would not punish until He sent them a messenger. This indicates the falsity of the view of those who say that they were not acting wrongly or perpetrating wickedness until revelation came to them. However, anyone who says that they were punished without revelation either is establishing an argument for reason as some Qadaris hold, or for pure will, as the compulsorists say. Nevertheless it is clear from what God has said (28:59; 28:47; 20:134) that He would not punish unbelievers until there was sent a messenger to them. He made it clear that before the messenger they had acquired acts which necessitate hatred and censure and are reason for punishment, but the condition for punishment is the establishment of a case against them by prophecy.

## G. CAUSES OF ERROR AMONG CHRISTIANS AND THOSE LIKE THEM

It should be known that the cause of error among Christians and similar extremists—like the extremism of pious Muslims and Shi'a—are basically three:

1) Complex, general, ambiguous expressions handed down from the prophets. They hold fast to these and forego straightforward univocal expressions. Whatever passage they hear which has in it some obscure meaning for them they hold firmly to it and bring it to bear upon their belief, even if there is no indication for that. The clear-cut expressions opposed to that they either ignore or they interpret as do those in error. They follow ambiguity in rational and revealed proofs and stray from what is straightforward and unambiguous in both.

2) Extraordinary wonders. They suppose them to be signs when

they are demonic affairs. It is through these things that many wayward idolaters and others have gone astray. For example, the demons enter into the idols and speak to people; demons also disclose to sorcerers unseen matters, and there is no doubt that they report falsehood to them as well. Like that also are various kinds of behavior which occur from the demons.

3) Information handed down to them which they suppose to be truthful, but which is false. Aside from these things, Christians and other people in error have no sound rational argumentation or correct revealed information for their false beliefs or any sign from the prophets. If they speak from rational argument, they use general ambiguous passages. Were they to seek an explanation of the meanings of those passages and the distinction between what is true and false in them, the deception and ambiguity which is in them would become clear. If they speak from what is handed down as revealed, either their information would be correct but not a proof for their erroneous beliefs, or else it would not be established [as sound] but rather forged.

Similarly, the supernatural wonders which they mention either are correct and were manifested at the hand of a prophet, like the miracles of Christ and other prophets before him like Elijah and Elisha and the miracles of Moses—all these are true—or they would have been manifested at the hand of upright persons like the apostles. This would not make it necessary that these latter be inerrant like the prophets. The prophets are inerrant in what they communicate, and it cannot be imagined that they speak about God anything but the truth, or that there resides in their teaching anything but the truth, either intentionally or accidentally. But with upright persons, some one of them may err and make a mistake despite the manifestation of wonders at his hands. He would not thereby cease to be an upright individual. It would not be necessary that he be inerrant if he had not claimed inerrancy or brought the signs which indicate that. If he claimed inerrancy and was not a prophet, then he would be lying and would undoubtedly manifest his falseness. The demons would associate themselves with him and lead him astray so that God's statement would apply to him:

> Shall I inform you upon whom the devils descend? They descend upon every sinful, false one (26:221-22).

Among the Christians it is handed down in the gospels that the one who was crucified and buried in the grave was seen by some of the apostles and others after he was buried. He rose from his grave two or three times. He showed them the place of the nails and said, "Do not suppose that I am a demon." If this [report] is sound, then that was a demon who claimed he was Christ and thereby deceived them. Things like that have happened to many people in our time and in earlier times. For example, there were people in Palmyra who saw a huge person flying in the air who appeared to them several times in various kinds of dress. He said to them "I am Christ the son of Mary" and gave them commands which it would have been impossible for Christ to have commanded for them. He arrived among the people and they saw clearly that he was a demon intending to lead them astray.

Among other people also, someone comes to the grave of someone he extols and considers to be among the upright or others, and sometimes he sees the grave open and a person in the likeness of that individual emerge from it, and at other times he sees that individual enter the grave. Sometimes he sees him either riding or walking, entering the place of that dead person, like the dome built over the grave. Sometimes he sees him emerging from that place and supposes that that is the upright man or he may suppose that this is a person to whom he can appeal for help, and so he goes to him. But that is a demon imitating his likeness.

This has occurred to more than one person I know. Sometimes people seek help from a person either dead or absent whom they suppose to be good. When he comes, they see him with their own eyes. He may speak to them and he may fulfill some of their needs. They suppose him to be the dead person, but it is only a demon who claimed that he was that person. However, it is not the person.

There are many stories of people to whom someone comes after death in the likeness of the dead person, who speaks to them, fulfills their debts, and returns back those things entrusted to his custody and informs them about the dead. They suppose that he is the dead person himself who has come to them, but it is only a demon impersonating his likeness.

This is extremely common, especially in idolatrous countries like India. Among these people you may see someone [who has died] under his bed taking the hand of his son at the funeral. One of them might say, "When I die do not summon anyone to wash me, for I am coming from this direction to wash myself." After his death someone comes in the air in his likeness. The one to whom he entrusted his final command thinks that he has come, but it is only a demon impersonating his likeness.

Sometimes one of them sees a person flying in the air or of great size or someone who discloses to affairs of the unseen and things like that. He may say to him "I am al-Khidr" but that is a demon lying to that person. The one who sees him may be a person of religion, asceticism, and worship. This has happened to more than one.

Sometimes it is seen at the grave of a prophet or others that the dead person comes forth either from his chamber or from his grave and embraces the visitor and greets him. That is a demon impersonating his likeness.

Sometimes someone will come to the grave of some person and ask his permission about things. He asks him about [various] matters, and a person responds to him. He may see him or hear a voice or see a person, but that would be a demon to lead him astray.

While he is awake, someone may see persons either riding or on foot who say this is such-and-such a prophet—whether Abraham, Christ, or Muhammad—or this is such-and-such a righteous person—whether Abu Bakr or one of the apostles. This may be some individual who is believed to be upright—either St. George or others whom the Christians extol. It may be one of the Muslim shaykhs. In reality that is a demon claiming that he is a prophet, that shaykh, that righteous individual, or that saint.

Things like this occur very often to many idolaters and Christians and to many Muslims. One of them sees a shaykh whom he supposes to be good who says to him "I am Shaykh So-and-so." It is only a demon. I know a great many things of this kind. I know more than one person who sought help from one of the dead or absent shaykhs, who saw someone who came to him while waking and helped him.

Something like this has happened to me and to someone I know. More than one person has mentioned that he sought my help from a distant country and that he saw me when I came to him. Some of them say, "I saw you riding in your own clothes and in your likeness." Some say, "I saw you on a mountain." Some say other things than that. I told them that I did not help them, and that that was only a demon impersonating my likeness to lead them astray since they were making a partner to God and praying to other than God.

Similarly, more than one person I know among our friends was appealed to for help from someone who supposed him to be good. Then that person saw him come to him and he fulfilled his request. My friend said, "And I don't know anything about that."

One of these shaykhs relates that he heard the voice of the person who was appealing to him for help and he answered him. Actually, the demons were making him hear a voice resembling that of the person who was calling upon him for assistance. The shaykh answered him back in his normal voice, and the demons made the one seeking help hear a voice which resembled that of the shaykh, so that the other thought that it was actually the voice of the shaykh.

This has occurred to someone I know who told me about it himself. He said, "The *jinni* who was addressing me went on addressing me with the voice of those who were imploring me for help, and he was addressing them in a voice like mine. He was appearing to me in something white the likes of what I would be asking about. He informed people that I had seen him and that he would come. But I did not see him [at all]; I only saw his likeness." The jinn do many things like this to those who invite them and swear by them.

Similarly the cross which Constantine saw among the stars and the cross which he saw another time are what the demons fashion and show to lead people astray. Demons have done what is even greater than that for the worshipers of idols.

In the same way whoever has stated that Christ came to him while he was awake and said that he was Christ [actually saw] one of the demons. Similar things have happened to more than one person. Satan only leads people astray and causes them to err by that in which he supposes they obey him. He speaks to Christians in what agrees with their religion. He addresses whatever wayward Muslim he confronts by that which agrees with his belief, and he hands on to him whatever he deems necessary for them in accordance with their belief.

For this reason he represents himself in the likeness of St. George to whomever among the Christians seeks help from St. George or in the likeness of whichever of the great men of their religion Christians seek for assistance—one of their patriarchs, bishops, or monks. To wayward Muslims seeking help from one of the shaykhs he represents himself in the likeness of that shaykh, as he showed himself to a group of people I know in my likeness and in the likeness of a group of shaykhs who mentioned it. He appears often in the guise of one of the dead. Sometimes he says "I am Shaykh 'Abd al-Qadir [al-Jiliani]," sometimes "I am Shaykh Abu al-Hajjaj al-Uqsuri,"[1] sometimes "I am Shaykh 'Adi,"[2] sometimes "I am Shaykh Ahmad al-Rifa'i,"[3] sometimes "I am Abu Maydan al-Maghribi."[4] If he used to say "I am Christ" or Abraham or Muhammad, he could do so about others *a fortiori*.

The prophet said:

> Whoever has seen me in sleep has truly seen me; for Satan cannot imitate my likeness.

In another account he said "in the likeness of the prophets." Thus the vision of the prophets in sleep is true, but the vision of the dead while awake is a *jinni* impersonating his likeness.

Some people call this the "spiritual nature" of the shaykh, while others call it his comrade. There are many demons who take someone's place or they may leave that person's likeness in some other place. Often the person [himself] and the demon appearing in his image are seen in two places [at once], or they may be seen standing on Mt. 'Arafat while they are in their own land and have never left it.

People who do not know become confused, but sound reason knows that one body cannot be at one time in two places. Trustworthy people have seen that with their own eyes and do not doubt it. Thus a dispute may often arise between one group of people and the next, as has occurred more than once. One person believes what he has seen and witnessed, the next person believes in what sound [reason] shows him.

What is seen is a *jinni* impersonating the likeness of a human. Sense perception, if it is not accompanied by rational proofs which uncover the real natures of things, will only fall into much error. This kind of thing which is witnessed in external reality is different from what a person imagines within himself. This is something everyone knows, and all intelligent people know that they imagine things within themselves just as a sleeper fantasizes in his dream but knows that the picture existing in his imagination is not found in external reality.

The philosophers and many intelligent people know this, but many philosophers suppose the angels which the prophets saw and the speech which they heard to be of this kind. They suppose that the jinn which are seen are of this nature. They are ignorant and erring in this matter, just as those people were ignorant and erring who supposed that the cause of supernatural wonders was natural, psychological, or astrological powers, and that the difference between the prophet and the magician is only the good intention of the former and the presumed false intention of the latter. Except in that, the cause of the wonders of both of them are psychological or astrological powers. This rejection [of true prophethood] is false, as we have discussed at length elsewhere and have pointed out the ignorance and error of these people in other matters.

The existence of [true revelations] in external reality is established among those who have witnessed that outside the mind by trustworthy reports successively handed down. They know that these others are ignorant, erring people. They know that angels have appeared in the form of men, as they appeared to Abraham, Lot, and Mary in human form. Jibril used to appear to the prophet, sometimes in the form of Dahya al-Kalbi[5] and at other times in the form of a bedouin. Many people saw him with their own eyes, whereas whatever is in the imagination of someone is not seen by others than him. Similarly Satan appeared to the idolaters in the form of Al-Shaykh al-Najdi and others, and he appeared to them on the day of Badr in the likeness of Suraqa ibn Malik ibn Ja'tham. When he saw the angels, he fled (8:48). It is related from Ibn 'Abbas and others that he said:

> Iblis appeared among the army of demons. He had with him a banner in the likeness of that of the men from Mudallaj. Satan was in the likeness of Suraqa ibn Malik ibn Ju'shum. He said: There will be no victor from among mankind over you today, for I am a neighbor to you. Jibril drew near to Iblis, and when he saw him, his hand was in the hand of one of the idolaters' men, and Iblis withdrew his hand and headed for the rear—he and his people. The man said: Hey Suraqa! Didn't you say you were a neighbor to us? He said: I see what you do not see; I fear God, for God is severe in punishment.

Ibn 'Abbas said, "That was when he saw the angels." Al-Dahhak said:

> Satan traveled with them with his banner and his army. He cast into the hearts of the idolaters that "No one will overcome you while you are fighting for your religion and the religion of your fathers."

Many people have been carried off by the jinn to a distant place. They have borne away many people to 'Arafat and to other places than 'Arafat. Should someone see one of these people in a land other than their own that would be someone [who was] carried off; sometimes it was a case of the jinn having carried him off and at other times of their having impersonated his likeness. This person would not be one of the God-fearing friends of God to whom were granted special favors (*karamat*), but he could be even an unbeliever or a dissolute person. I know many stories about that, but I will not go into the details here.

Among the idolaters and the Christians there are many things like that which they suppose to be in the nature of signs which belong to the prophets, but they are rather of the nature of what pertains to magicians and sorcerers. Whoever does not distinguish between the friends of the Merciful One and the friends of Satan and distinguish between the miracles of the prophets and the special favors of the upright on one hand, and the wonders of magicians and sorcerers on the other, whoever lumps them all together is in likelihood that the demons will make him confuse truth and falsehood. He will either reject the truth brought by the trustworthy prophets or will believe the falsehood spoken by unbelievers and mistaken individuals.

These matters are elaborated elsewhere. The point here is to elucidate this principle. Christian scholars accept this, and on this matter they have many reports of stories of the friends of Satan who opposed the friends of the Merciful One. These latter have proven false the affairs of the former. Moses proved false the magicians who opposed him with wonders, as is stated in the Torah. They [Christians] relate it about one individual or another, like the story of Simon Magus and the apostles.

If they accept this, they should admit that what they mention is of this kind. If it is opposed to what is established from the prophets, it is from Satan. It is not permissible to argue from anything which opposes the Laws of the prophets which have been established on them; rather, such people are of the same nature as the great Dajjal, against whom all the prophets warned. Even Noah warned his people [against him]. The Seal of the prophets [Muhammad] said:

> There has never been a prophet but he has warned his community, so that even Noah warned his community. But I will tell you a statement about him which no prophet said to his community. He is one-eyed, but your Lord is not one-eyed. There is written between his eyes "unbeliever" (*k-f-r*) which every believer, literate or not, can read. He said: know that no one of you will see his Lord until he die.[6]

All of this is established in the sound hadiths from the prophet. He has commanded his community to seek refuge in God from his [al-Dajjal's] machinations. He said:

> If one of you is seated speaking the *shahada* during prayer, let him take refuge in God from four things: from the punishment of hell, from the punishment of the grave, from the machinations of life and death, and from the machination of the Anti-Christ al-Dajjal.

All the prophets warned against the liars who imitate the prophets. There are people who intend falsehood. Many people, however, do not intend it, but are deceived and err, reporting what they suppose to be the truth when it is not. They may see in a waking state what they suppose to be such-and-such a friend of God or a prophet, or Al-Khidr, when it is not.

Error is possible for everyone except the prophets, for they are inerrant. Therefore if anyone does not weigh his learning, his acts, his views, and his deeds by what is known from the prophets, he will go astray. We ask the great God that He guide us along the straight Path, the path of those on whom His blessing rests—prophets, the righteous, martyrs, doers of good works. May their goodness be a companion.

The supernatural occurrences by which the demons have led the sons of Adam astray, such as Satan appearing in the form of some dead or absent person, through which occurrences many people adhering to Islam as well as the People of the Book and others have fallen into error—these events are all based on two premises.

1) Those at whose hands such events occur are friends of God, or as Christians would say, "a great saint."

2) Those who perform such actions are inerrant, and everything they teach is true and everything they command is just.

It may be that what occur are not supernatural events at all, neither divine nor satanic, but it is possible that their perpetrator has performed some trick of the kind done by liars and charlatans. These liars and charlatans have deceived a great number of people who think that their tricks are a type of supernatural miracle. But they are not like that, just as the tricks related about the monks are not.

Someone has written a book about the tricks of the monks.[7] There is the trick related about one of them who made water into oil. The oil was in a hidden cavity of a tower, so that if it ran low, he would pour water on it, and the oil would float to the top of the water, and those present would think that the water itself had changed into oil.

Similarly there is the trick told about them of the rising of the palm tree. Someone passed by a monk's hermitage, and below him there was a palm tree. Then the monk showed him the palm tree rise up until it towered over the monastery. He took the dates from it and then it descended until it was back in its customary position. Finally the man discovered the trick. He found the palm tree was on a boat in a low-lying place. If the monk released water on it, it would fill and the boat would rise; if he diverted the water to another place, the boat would go down.

Another trick related about them is that of putting *kohl* on the Virgin's eyes for tears. They put *kohl* in water moving with a very slight movement, which then flowed slowly so that it ran down the picture of the Virgin and came out her eyes. People thought that it was tears.

There is also the trick which they have performed with the picture which they call the icon in Saydnaya.[8] It is their greatest place of pilgrimage after Calvary, where Christ's tomb is found, and Bethlehem, where he was born. The basis of the trick is palm branches dipped in fats so that they become greasy and fat begins to exude from the picture. It is produced naturally, but people think that it is a *baraka* [miraculous property] of the picture.

Another of their many tricks is the fire which crowds believe to be descending from heaven during their feast at Calvary. It is a ruse which more than one Muslim and Christian have witnessed, and have seen with their own eyes that the fire is naturally produced while the praying crowds believe that it has descended from heaven and blessed them.[9] Actually it is merely an invention and deception performed by those in charge of the place.

There are many other tricks of the Christians like these; in all the extraordinary events which the Christians follow they are changing the religion of Christ. These things are either demonic wonders or clever absurdities in which there is nothing of the *karamat*—the miraculous favors granted to upright persons.

Similarly the heretics who are changing the religion of the messengers—the religion of Christ and the religion of Muhammad—adopt a religion not legislated by God and His messenger; they designate a path to God and may choose it in preference to the path which God and His Messenger have ordained. For example, they may prefer hearing[10] tambourines and flutes to hearing the Book of God. There may occur to one of these people a satanic emotion and passion by which the demon deceives them until he speaks by the tongue of one of them a message which that person on regaining consciousness is unaware that he uttered. It is just like one of the *jinn* might speak through the voice of a madman. He may inform one of those present of something that person knows, but this is actually from Satan. When the demon departs from that person, he will not be aware of what he said.

There are those whom the devil will carry in the air and raise up before people. There are those who point at someone present and that person dies, becomes sick or stiff like a board. Others point at one of those present so that the demon deceives him and his mind ceases operation and becomes absent for a long time against his will. Still others either enter a fire or eat it and their bodies and hair are engulfed in flames. Some people are presented with food, drugs, liquor, saffron, or rosewater by the demons, while others are brought money which the devils have stolen elsewhere. Then if the money is parceled out by these people among those present, the money disappears, so that it is not possible to spend it.

There are other matters which would take too long to describe, as well as other people who have no one among the demons helping them with these things, and so they perform extraordinary ruses.

Thus act the heretics who are changing the religion of the prophets—the religion of Christ or that of Muhammad—and those like them among the renegades, the wayward, the idolatrous apostates, and others like Musaylima the Liar, Al-Aswad al-'Ansi, Al-Harith al-Dimashqi, the Pope of Rome, and others who perform satanic preternatural deeds.

Charlatans—and there are many of them—are not friends of God. Even if their wonders are of the demonic order like those of the sorcerers and magicians, they possess no satanic state (*hal*) but [perform] pointless deceptions. They depend on falsehood and deception, in contrast to those who associate with demons. There are those among them who can deceive one so that he thinks these wonders are of the type of supernatural gifts granted to the holy men, just as others among them know such things to be from the demons and yet perform them to accomplish their own goals. The point is that many wonders, whether those which are from demons or those which are clever tricks and ingenious feats, are often thought to be extraordinary gifts (*karamat*) of upright persons.

Those feats whose purpose is *shirk* and rebelliousness come only from the demons. For example, when someone engages in idolatrous worship of God, claiming a share in divine worship for the stars or some created person, dead or absent, or making decisions and swearing by unknown names whose meaning he does not know or which he knows to be names of demons, or having recourse to things of darkness and obscenity, whatever miraculous events occur from these practices are from Satan. This we have elaborated at length more than once.

The holy men, such as the holy men of this community and the apostles and others who followed the religion of Christ, have wondrous gifts, but the existence of wonders performed at the hands of holy men does not necessitate that these men be inerrant like the prophets. Rather, he is simply a holy man, a friend of God who has these wondrous gifts. Nevertheless, he may err or make an error in what he thinks, or in what he hears, relates, and sees, or in what he understands of the Books. This is the case for everyone except the prophets. There must be extracted from their opinion what is contrary to the prophets, and it must be renounced. It is necessary for people to put faith in everything the prophets disclosed concerning the unknown and to obey them in all they have commanded. God has obligated men to faith in everything which they brought, but did not obligate them to faith in all that others than they have brought (2:136; 2:177).

Therefore Muslims are in agreement that whoever rejects a prophet whose prophethood is known is an apostate unbeliever.

It is necessary that anyone who curses a prophet be killed. It is even necessary to put faith in everything all the prophets have brought, and not to distinguish between them by believing in some and rejecting others (4:150-51). However, this is not the case with anyone other than the prophets, even though these others be messengers of the prophets and among the early great friends of God.

The error of the wayward among these people is based on two premises.

1) This person does wondrous deeds, therefore he is a friend of God.

2) It is not possible that a friend of God err, but it is necessary to put faith in all that he teaches and to obey all he commands.

Actually there is no human who should be believed in all that he teaches or obeyed in all that he commands, unless that person be a prophet. Of these two premises which we have mentioned, it may be that one of them is false, and it may be that both of them are false. A certain man may not be one of the friends of God, but his miraculous deeds might be from the demons. Conversely, he may be one of the friends of God, but as he is not inerrant, it would be possible that he make a mistake. Again he may not be one of the friends of God, or even be performing miraculous acts, but might be a master of tricks and deception.

Muslims and People of the Book agree on confessing two Christs—the Messiah of True Guidance of the line of David, and the False Messiah whom the People of the Book say to be of the line of Joseph. Muslims and Christians say that the Messiah of True Guidance is Jesus the son of Mary, whom God has already sent and will send again. Muslims say he will descend before the Resurrection Day and kill the False Messiah, break the cross, and kill the pig. Then there will not remain any religion but that of Islam, in which the People of the Book, Jews and Christians, will believe (4:159). The correct opinion on which the majority agree is [that this will occur] before the death of Christ (43:61).

Christians, however, think that Christ is God and that he will come on the Resurrection Day to reckon up the good deeds and the bad. This is one of the cases in which they are in error.

The Jews also confess the coming of the Messiah of True Guidance. He is coming, they say. But they claim that Jesus was not this Messiah because of their claim that he brought the corrupted religion of the Christians, and whoever brought that is false. Thus they await the two Messiahs.

# II. *TAHRIF*: THE CORRUPTION OF SCRIPTURE

## A. CORRUPTION OF SCRIPTURE BEFORE THE TIME OF MUHAMMAD

They say: [The Qur'an] proves that what we have is a blessing, and it denies the accusation that there is *tabdil* in our Gospel and in the books we possess, and by its confirming them it denies any alteration (*taghyir*) of what is in them.[1]

One should say to them: Your view which you argue here and elsewhere is either pure falsehood or is an instance of where you have clothed the truth with falsehood. If by your statement of the Qur'an's confirming those books you mean that it confirms the Torah, the Gospel, and the Psalms which God revealed to His prophets, this is undoubtedly so. It is mentioned more than once in the Qur'an that He obliged His servants to put faith in every book which He revealed and every one of the prophets, just as He stated that He revealed these books before the Qur'an, and that He revealed the Qur'an as a confirmation of the previously existing scripture and a guardian over it (3:14; 5:48; 35:31; 2:101; 4:47). He made it necessary for His servants to put faith in all the Books and prophets, and judged it as unbelief for anyone who would put faith in some and disbelief in others (2:136-37; 2:285; 4:150-52). He censured him who discriminated among them or who indicated that he preferred some of them over others (2:253; 17:55).

Muslims have agreed that what is known with certainty in the religion of Islam is that faith in all the prophets and messengers and all the books God has revealed is obligatory, and that whoever disbelieves in one prophet whose prophethood is known—such as Abraham, Lot, Moses, David, Solomon, Jonah, and Jesus—is an unbeliever, and among all Muslims he receives the judgment pronounced upon unbelievers. If he is an apostate [to this belief], he must be called to repent, and unless he repent, he must be killed.

Whoever insults any one of the prophets must likewise be killed, according to the agreement of Muslims. Whatever they know to have been related by any one of the prophets must be accepted by them, just as they accept whatever Muhammad related to them. They know that the messages of the prophets cannot be contradicted nor opposed. That which they do not know whether or not it was declared by a prophet is similar to that which they do not know whether or not it was stated by Muhammad. They reject only what they know to be false. It is permissible for them to believe only what they know to be the truth, so that something whose truth or falsity is unknown they neither believe nor reject. That is what their prophet Muhammad taught them. Similarly, Christ commanded them:

> There are three kinds of matters. Those whose right guidance is clear, follow them. Those whose error is clear, avoid them. Those whose value is questionable, entrust them to Him who knows their truth.

———

In stating that the Qur'an has confirmed their books, they hold that it confirmed those beliefs and laws which they innovated without the permission of God and which they oppose to the laws of Muslims which have superseded them. Or else they claim that it confirms that which they have set in opposition to the religion (*shar'*) sent from God—like their doctrines of the trinity and divine persons, divine indwelling, the hypostatic union of divine and human natures, their belief that Christ is God and the son of God, their denial of what faith in God and the Last Day demands, and their permitting what God and his prophets have forbidden, such as the eating of pork. It is clear that they do not profess the religion of truth which he revealed through His Book, with which He sent His Prophet. Rather, it is a heretical religion which their leaders innovated for them (9:31). Muhammad made this clear to the Christian 'Adi ibn Hatim when the latter came to the Prophet and professed faith in him. ('Adi subsequently believed in the Prophet and was one of the finest of the Companions.) He heard the Prophet recite this verse:

> They have taken as lords beside God their rabbis and their monks and the Messiah son of Mary, when they were bidden to worship only one God. There is no God save Him. Be He glorified from all that they ascribe as partner [to Him] (9:31).

Said 'Adi, "I said, 'O prophet of God, they don't worship them.' He said, 'They make *halal* for them what is *haram*, and make *haram* what is *halal*.'" In that consisted their worship of their leaders.

Therefore if they meant its confirmation of them in these matters, or that Muhammad confirmed anything in their religion which had not been brought by the prophets from God, they have perpetrated against Muhammad an evident lie, known with certainty from his religion. He confirmed only what the prophets before him had brought.

That which they created and innovated was not confirmed by the Qur'an, nor did it command them to continue following what they held from the first Law, even if it had not been corrupted; rather it called on every man and jinn to put their faith in him and what he brought, to follow the Book and Wisdom he handed on, and to judge it as unbelief whenever anyone did not follow the Book which was handed down by him. He imposed the punishment of the Last Day for their remaining in unbelief, and necessitated *jihad* against them in this life until all religion should be God's and the Word of God should be uppermost.

He summoned Jews and Christians generally as People of the Book, and then each of the peoples specifically more than once, just as he called all people—People of the Book and others (7:156-58; 4:171-73; 5:72; 5:14). God the Exalted declared that the Christians abandoned part of what He had prescribed for them. Because of that, He incited enmity and hatred among them which will last until the Day of Resurrection. Thus it is known that God the Exalted has made it clear that they abandoned some of what Christ and the prophets before him had brought, and so deserved the perpetual enmity and hatred stirred up in their midst (5:77).

God forbade them to exceed the proper bounds in their religion, or to follow the whims of those who innovated the heresies with which they changed the Law of Christ. These early innovators first went astray, and then led astray many others, including these followers of theirs. They went astray from that path which is the mean between [the extremes of] error. After having made this innovated error absolute and universal, they laid it down as law.

> Fight against such of those who have been given the Scripture as believe not in God nor the Last Day, and forbid not that which God has forbidden by His messenger, and follow not the religion of the truth, until they pay the tribute readily, being brought low (9:29).

The prophet himself went out to fight them the year of Tabuk, and called upon all believers to join in fighting them. He permitted no one able to engage in the campaign to remain behind. Whoever held back through slothfulness and did not see fighting them as obligatory was an unbeliever. Even though he may have manifested Islam externally, he was actually an accursed hypocrite. God declared this to be unpardonable, and the prophet forbade Muslims to pray for them. He revealed most of Surat al-Bara'a[2] about that in order to make clear the unbelief of those who sought to abandon their duty to join the prophet in battling the Christians (9:38-48).[3]

———

It is clear that if by this statement of theirs [*PA*, par.14] they mean that the Qur'an gives evidence for what the prophets before Muhammad brought from God, then it is true. If they mean by it that the Qur'an approves of what they hold as a religion which is opposed to Muhammad's religion after he had been sent, or that it gives evidence for what they have innovated apart from what the earlier prophets have brought, then their statement is false.

If by it they mean that the Qur'an confirms the textual veracity (*alfaz*) of the scriptural books which they now possess—that is, the Torah and the Gospel—this is something which some Muslims will grant them and what many Muslims will dispute. However, most Muslims will grant them most of that.

Concerning the corruption of the meaning of the sacred books by their explanation and interpretation and their replacing its legal judgments with their own, all Muslims, Jews, and Christians witness to this corruption and substitution of theirs. Similarly, Muslims bear witness against the Jews regarding their corruption of many of the significations of the Torah, and of their substituting for its legal decisions. Nevertheless, Jews claim that the Torah has not undergone any textual corruption.

However, their preservation of the correct wording of the sacred books cannot benefit the Christians at the present time, since its meaning has been corrupted, any more than Jews are able to reap benefit from the preservation of the correct wording of the Torah and the prophets because of the corruption of their meanings. In spite of all the prophecies which they admit that the Jews possess—and they with the Jews deny any accusation of textual corruption in them—according to the Christians Jews are the greatest unbelievers of mankind, deserving of God's punishment in this world and the next. And they, according to Christians, are the ones who call Muslims unbelievers more than do the Christians, and worse than do the Christians. Christians agree that Muslims are better than Jews; similarly, Jews agree that Muslims are better than Christians. Actually, all peoples other than the Muslims bear witness that Muslims are better than the rest of the religious communities except themselves. Their witness to themselves carries no weight, however, so that there has come to be an agreement of the people of the earth upon the superiority of the religion of Islam.

It is obvious that preserving the wording of the Book while refusing to follow its meanings and corrupting them does not mean that a person has faith nor prevent his unbelief.

When Muhammad and his community bore witness to Christ and the Gospel which God had handed down through him, he was in no way confirming what the Christians at that time were holding, any more than did Christ's, the apostles', and the rest of his followers' bearing witness to Moses and the Torah revealed by God through him mean their confirmation of what the Jews of their day were following. Christ commanded his followers to keep the Torah, except a slight bit of it which he abrogated.

Muhammad, however, was sent with an independent book and a perfect, complete, and self-sufficient law which needed no previous law for his community to learn from others, nor any subsequent one to complete its legislation. In a sound hadith report the Prophet said:

> In the peoples before you there were those who received inspired messages (*muhaddathun*); if there were one in my community it would be 'Umar.

He affirmed that those who went before him had individuals who received inspired messages, but then he made the matter conditional in his community. It needs no other prophet after him nor has any need, from start to finish, for anyone aside from him to receive inspired messages.

Those who went before Muhammad were in need of prophet after prophet, and their need thus made possible these inspired successors [*al-Muhaddithin al-Mulhamin*]. When God sent Christ among his people, he only judged them according to the law of Moses.[4] As this was the case, Christ, the apostles, and all those who believed in Christ were bearing witness to the truth of the Torah and that Moses was a true messenger of God. This did not prevent the Jews from being unbelievers or prevent the fact of their having changed the law of the Torah and their rejecting Christ and the Gospel. Therefore, how could the witness borne by Muhammad and his community that the Gospel was revealed by God and that Christ was the messenger of God be an argument against the unbelief of the Christians for their corrupting the law of the Gospel and rejecting Muhammad and the law of the Qur'an?

There is equally nothing to prevent one from considering as an unbeliever someone who places faith in Muhammad only as messenger of God to the Arabs, or who believes only in a great part of the message of the Qur'an. Similarly, there is nothing that prevents their being unbelievers if they reject some of what he brought. Rather, whoever rejects a single thing of that which the prophets have brought from God is an unbeliever, even though he believes in most of it (4:150; 2:85). The Christians were clearly described as being in unbelief in more than one place, and God commanded *jihad* against them and to fight them, and to judge as unbelievers those who did not deem this *jihad* and fighting against them as necessary.

He in no way considered this inaction as service and obedience to him, as has been pointed out before. Thus, if someone who did not consider waging *jihad* against them as worship of God was considered by Muhammad as an unbeliever, what about the state of those people themselves in the mind of Muhammad?

———

The majority of Muslims deny both [the proposition] that none of the wording found in the previous sacred books of Christians and Jews has ever undergone textual substitution and that all of its wording was handed down from God. They hold either that *tabdil* has occurred in some of its formulations, or that it cannot be said with certainty that its expressions were revealed by God. It is not possible to make an argument of the expressions in these books in opposition to what has been already established. Muslims claim that the Torah and the Gospel which the People of the Book today possess are not the products of successive transmission from Moses and Jesus [*lam tatawatar 'an Musa wa-'Isa*].

The chain of transmission of the Torah was broken first at the time of the destruction of Jerusalem and the expulsion of the Israelites from the city. They state that the one who dictated the Torah to them at a later date was a certain person called Ezra, whom they claim to be a prophet. Some people say that he was not a prophet, but that he only discovered a copy which they found to be ancient. It is also said that he produced a text which had been in the Maghrib. None of this necessitates the successive transmission of every expression nor prevents the occurrence of error in some cases. A similar situation occurs with those books whose copying and collation follows closely upon them, but which are memorized by only a few, perhaps two or three persons.

Christians admit that the Gospel which they possess was not written down by Christ nor dictated by him to those who wrote it down. Matthew and John, companions of Christ, dictated it only after the ascension of Christ; moreover, it had not been memorized by the great number of people necessary according to the principles of successive transmission. Neither Mark nor Luke ever saw Christ. All these men stated that they mentioned some of what Christ said and some of his messages, and that they did not have room to mention other words and deeds.

Error is possible in the transmission by two, three, or four, especially when they erred concerning Christ himself, so that it even seemed to them that he was crucified. But Christians claim that the apostles were messengers of God like Jesus the son of Mary or Moses.[5] They claim that the apostles were infallible, that they handed on to them the Torah and the Gospel, and that they performed miracles. The apostles, they say, taught them the Torah and the Gospel, and yet in spite of all this they do not claim that they were prophets. However, if they were not prophets, then they were not infallible, for even one of the greatest friends of God, were he to perform extraordinary miraculous feats, unless he be a prophet he would not be preserved from error.

Abu Bakr, 'Umar, 'Uthman, 'Ali, and other Muslims among the finest of the Companions were better than the apostles, yet Muslims do not claim them to be inerrant, but claim such only of one who is a prophet. Their claim that the apostles are messengers of God while they do not claim them to be prophets is contradictory. The claim that the apostles are messengers of God is only based on Christ's being God, for they are messengers of Christ.

This basis is false, but in the context of the discussion—"disputing with them in the best possible way"—we deny them this position and demand that they offer a proof that the apostles are prophets of God. They have no proof for this, for they cannot prove them to be messengers of God unless they prove that Christ is God. But their proof that Christ is God is either rational or theological. Reason cannot prove that but considers it impossible; they themselves do not claim to prove it by reason.

Thus it must be said to them concerning this position, "You are not able to prove Christ's being God except by these books. You are not able to show the correctness of these books except by proving that the apostles are inerrant messengers of God. You are not able to prove that they are messengers of God except by proving that Christ is God." Their position has thus become a vicious circle.

That is, the divinity of Christ is only known by establishing these books. These books are only established by establishing that the apostles are messengers of God, which in turn is only established by proving that Christ is God. The proof of his divinity has thereby become dependent upon their being messengers of God, and thus the vicious circle.

They claim inerrancy for the apostles, and inerrancy for the men of the Councils after the apostles, like the representatives of the First Council held in the presence of Constantine attended by 380 men. They drew up for Christians the creed which is their formula of faith. It is only after professing this creed that attendance at the Eucharist is lawful for them.

They claim further that miracles occurred at the hands of the apostles and these men. They might claim that raising the dead to life occurred at the hands of some of them, but even if it were true, unless the one who performed these deeds claimed that he was a prophet, this would not indicate that he was inerrant. The friends of God among the Companions and those who followed them in goodness, and the rest of the friends of God in this community as well as in the others—all of these have to their credit too many miraculous feats to describe, and yet not one of them is inerrant. It is necessary to accept what each of them says, but error is possible for any one of them. In the teaching of each, except for the prophets, some things are accepted and other things rejected.

God has necessitated faith in everything which the prophets have brought, but He has not made it obligatory to put faith in everything which any friend of God has said (2:136; 2:177). He has, however, demanded faith in all the prophets and what they have brought.

Anyone who rejects even one prophet whose prophethood is known is an unbeliever by agreement of Muslims. Similarly, whoever insults one of them must be killed. By contrast, a person who opposes someone other than a prophet is not an unbeliever, nor need he be killed for simply insulting him unless there be something connected with the insult which warrants death.

This is what the *salaf* of the community have held, like the Companions and their right-acting followers, the great imams of the religion, and the masses of Muslims—that the finest man in this community after the Prophet is Abu Bakr and then 'Umar. Subsequent to the prophets there has been no one finer than they, and this community is the finest community. This has been shown in the sound hadith reports from the Prophet, where he said:

> In the peoples before you there were those who received inspired messages (*muhaddathun*); if there were one in my community it would be 'Umar.

A *muhaddath* is one who receives an inspired message.

God had placed His truth in the heart of 'Umar and on his tongue. He never said "I hold such-and-such an opinion" unless the situation was actually as he had said it. The presence of God spoke by his tongue. Nevertheless, neither 'Umar nor anyone else other than the prophets has ever been immune from error. No Muslim ought to accept what he says unless the Book and the sunna indicate it, nor has it been possible for a Muslim to put into practice what has occurred in his heart unless he has tested it by the Book and the sunna to see whether it agrees with or opposes that which went before him.

Muslims do not hold the followers of Christ to be like Abu Bakr and 'Umar. So if they say that the apostles are not inerrant, it is because they say that about those who in their belief are greater than the apostles. Similarly, when they claim that Christ is not God but rather His created servant, that is because they claim the same thing for those whom they hold to be greater than Christ, for example, Muhammad and Abraham.

Among the renegades who attach themselves to Islam there are those who have extremist innovations which resemble those of the Christians. They desire some sort of divinity for the descendants of Isma'il like the line of 'Ubayd al-Qaddah or Al-Hakim or others. They may claim divinity for 'Ali ibn Abi Talib or for someone else like the claims of the Nusayris.[6] However, all these are considered unbelievers by Muslims. Similarly, there are those who claim divinity for one of the shaykhs, like the extremists among the 'Adawiyya, the Hallajiyya, or the Yunusiyya.[7]

There are those who claim infallibility for the Fatimids, the Twelve Imams, or for one of the shaykhs. While the Christians claim infallibility for one of the twelve apostles, these latter claim infallibility for the twelve imams. The Christians trace the origins of their religion to the belief of the apostles which they consider infallible. They hold them inerrant in what they have transmitted from Christ and in their legal judgments, even if what they state is opposed to what the Prophet has stated. But this is more fully discussed elsewhere.

The point here is that the Christians have no successive transmission from Christ concerning the texts of these Gospels, and neither successive transmission nor fragmentary units[8] for most of their laws. Moreover, the Jews have no successive transmission for the texts of the Torah and the prophecies of the prophets. Muslims, on the other hand, have for the Qur'an and their laws a successive transmission which is evident and well known as to their general and particular applications. The creed, which is the basis of their faith (*asl dinihim*), their praying to the east, their permission of pork and omission of circumcision, their glorification of the cross and use of pictures in their churches, and other practices than these—none of these are transmitted from Christ, nor is there a mention of them in the Gospels which they hand on concerning him. They agree that the creed which they have made the source of their religion and the basis of their faith has phraseology not found in the gospels nor handed down from the apostles. They agree further that those who drew up the creed were the 380 individuals who formed the First council held in the presence of Constantine. However 'Abd Allah ibn Arius, who held Christ to be the servant of God as do the Muslims, opposed them. Thus they drew up their creed.

This council took place over three hundred years after the time of Christ, as is discussed elsewhere. My purpose here is to respond to their claim that Muhammad confirmed what they hold and that he denied, by his endorsement of the books then in use by Christians, that any verbal substitution or change had occurred in their Gospel.

It is evident that Muhammad did not endorse a single element of their corrupted and abrogated religion. He confirmed, rather, the prophets before him and what they brought from God. He praised those who followed them, but not those who opposed them, nor those who rejected some one of the prophets. The unbelief of the Christians is like that of the Jews. The Jews corrupted the meanings of the first book and rejected the second [the Gospel]. Similarly, the Christians corrupted the meanings of the first book [the Bible], and then rejected the second book [the Qur'an]. Then they claim that Muhammad confirmed all the expressions of the books in their possession.

The majority of Muslims, however, deny this. They hold that some of the texts have undergone change as have many of the meanings. Some Muslims say that *tabdil* occurred not in the texts but only in their interpretations; this opinion approaches what the generality of Jews and Christians hold.

Against these two opinions they can offer no proof that Muhammad confirmed anything of what they hold in their corrupted religion. For the divine books in their present state offer no evidence for those things for which Muhammad and his community have declared them disbelievers. Trinity, divine union, divine indwelling, changing the law of Christ, rejecting Muhammad—there is nothing in their books, neither in the text nor in its evident meaning, which suggests their creed which is the basis of religion for them, and what it contains by way of trinity, divine union, and indwelling. Moreover their books do not give evidence for most of their practices, such as praying to the east or permission of forbidden things like eating of pork or dead animals. This has been explained at length elsewhere.

It must be said to them: "Where have you found in the material you have concerning Muhammad anything which indicates that the texts of the books which you today possess have not undergone any change?" It is evident that when Muslims and others differ, the view of one party is not a proof against the other party. If Muslims differ concerning the *tabdil* of some of the expressions of the preceding divine books, the view of one group will not be a proof against the other; nor is it possible for a Muslim or anyone else to attribute any view to the prophet except by a proof.

Where in the Qur'an or in the established sunna from the prophet does it say that no expression in the books now in use among the People of the Book—the Torah, the Gospel, Psalms, or prophetic books—has ever undergone change? Yet they claim that Muhammad denied that to have occurred in their books. These people have erected their argument on the supposition that the expressions of their books indicate the truth of their religion which they have followed after the sending of Muhammad and after their rejection of him, and that no change has occurred in these expressions.

This has been shown to be false from numerous aspects. Next they claim that Muslims hold that the expressions of these books have all undergone verbal change in their languages after the sending of Muhammad. No Muslim has ever held this view, so far as I know. Finally, they think that by answering this view they have answered Muslims.

## B. CORRUPTION OF SCRIPTURE AFTER THE TIME OF MUHAMMAD

Their spokesman writes:

> I said to them, "If someone should claim that *tabdil* and *taghyir* might have occurred after this opinion [of Muhammad that the scriptural texts are sound], then we reply that we are astonished at these people, with their learning, their intelligence, their knowledge, that they would make a claim like this. I would be no less amazed at myself were we to bring this type of argument against them and say that the Book which they now use in our day has undergone change and substitution and they have written in it what they wanted and desired. Would they allow this statement of ours as possible?" Thus writes their spokesman.

But I said to them, "This statement is not able to be made by anyone. It is not possible that it be changed from Muhammad until the Last Day."[1]

My answer to this is that the Christian disputant has attributed to Muslims a position they have not held, and to Christian scholars its response. But he and they have built their argument on two false bases.

Firstly, they suppose that the prophet confirmed what they followed at that time, and denied any accusations of *tabdil* or *taghyir* against their books. Their intent by this argumentation is only complete if Muhammad denied any *tabdil* both of the wording and the meaning of their books. Any intelligent person knows that the prophet never denied this of their books, and in fact the successive transmission (*al-naql al-mutawatir an-hu*) from him contradicts that.

They themselves also contradict that argument. Any intelligent person knows that their explanation of the books which they now have, arising out of the opposition and dispute among sects of Christians and between Christians and Jews, is something that necessitates definitively that much of it is corrupted and distorted, just as the changing of the legal prescriptions of these books has occurred. The books include two principles: message and command. Faith in the books is only complete by believing in the revealed message and by obliging obedience to what has been commanded. However, the People of the Book reject much of what was revealed to them, and do not necessitate obedience to what was commanded and made necessary for them. Each sect among them witnesses something similar against the others.

Christians have had seven well-known councils. In each council they have censured a large group of people, have excommunicated them, and said about them that they did not command obedience to some of what was ordered. That sect in its turn has borne witness against the others that they have rejected some of what was revealed. Of their three great divisions—the Nestorians, the Melkites, and the Jacobites—each sect excommunicates the others, curses them, and bears witness against them that they reject part of what was revealed in the prophetic books or that they do not oblige obedience to part of what is in them. Their dispute is even about *tawhid* and prophecy itself.

Each one of their sects claims that Christ brought what they believe. But Christ and all the prophets are innocent of that by which they have divided their religion and become sects. They are innocent of what they have declared about God other than the truth, or what they have claimed about God from lack of knowledge. The prophets are preserved from holding any false view concerning God, even that one of them should mistakenly speak falsely without intending it; but in the doctrines of Christians there are too many of these kinds of errors to describe.Thus, if it is known that all groups of Muslims, Jews, and Christians witnessed to there having occurred *tahrif* and *tabdil* in these books in their meanings, exegesis, and legal prescriptions, this is sufficient. Moreover, after the time of the sending of Muhammad, whoever did not believe in him is an unbeliever. This is in contrast to the situation before the sending of Muhammad, for there were true followers of the religion of Christ among them. Although some Muslims have distorted and corrupted their religion, the majority has opposed these people. There will never cease to be among them a group clearly knowing the truth, whose opponents cannot harm, and who will remain until the Final Hour. By contrast, the Christians have all disbelieved, just as all Jews disbelieved by rejecting Christ.

Muslims can prove by many arguments that they have corrupted the meanings of the Torah, the Gospel, the Psalms, and the prophetic books. They have innovated a religion brought neither by Christ nor by any other prophet. No intelligent person could hold it, like their claim that every descendant of Adam—prophet, messenger, or otherwise—was in hell in the bonds of Satan because their father Adam ate from the Tree, and that mankind was not saved from that until Christ was crucified.

Had some transmitter reported this statement from one of the prophets, we would have categorically denied it of them. So how [can we accept it] when this statement has not been transmitted among them from any of the prophets? They only hand it on from someone whose opinion is no obligating proof. Much of their religion has been derived from their leaders who were not prophets. If we categorically reject someone who transmits this from the prophets, what about when they do not transmit it from them? The prophets inform people of what their minds fall short of knowing, not of what they know to be false and impossible. They reveal to people the marvels of the intellect, not its absurdities.

Although Adam ate from the tree, God pardoned him, chose him, and guided him (20:121-22; 2:37). There is nothing in the books of the Jews and Christians which denies that God pardoned him. One of them might say, "We don't know that God pardoned him," or "We have no knowledge of God's pardoning him." But the lack of knowledge of a thing is not knowledge of its lack. The absence of something in one of the books of God does not prevent its being in another book. There is found in the Torah what is not found in the Gospel, and in both what is not in the Psalms, or in the Gospel and the Psalms what is not in the Torah. There is in the other prophetic books what is not found in these books. Were the Qur'an inferior to the Torah, the Gospel, the Psalms, and the Prophets or were it similar to them, it would be possible for there to be in it what was not in them. How much more so, then, since it is finer and more noble and there is found in it greater knowledge than what was in the Torah and the Gospel. God has revealed its superiority to the two earlier books in more than one place (39:23; 12:3; 5:48).

Whether God pardoned Adam or not, how is it possible that the messengers of God who were finer than him were imprisoned in the bonds of Satan in Hell for his sin? The father of Abraham was an unbeliever but God did not punish Abraham for his father's sin, so how could He cast him into hell in the bonds of Satan because of the sin of his more distant father, Adam, despite [the fact] that he was a prophet? Noah lived among his people 995 years and called them to the worship of God alone. God drowned the people of the earth at his plea,[2] and made his descendants the survivors. How could he have been in Hell in the bonds of Satan because of the sin of Adam?

Moses was the mouthpiece of God. God performed at his hands signs and wonders which He did not make evident at the hands of Christ. He killed a man against God's commandment, and God pardoned him that. He held a status and nobility with God which is not possible to be measured; how could he have been in Hell in the bonds of Satan?

Furthermore, what is the correlation between the crucifixion which is one of the greatest of crimes—whether Christ was actually crucified or whether it only appeared so—and between the salvation of these men from Satan? Had Satan done such a thing to these descendants of Adam, then he would have been acting wrongfully and outrageously. At the same time God was able to prevent him from treating mankind unjustly, and even to punish him if he did not cease from such wrongdoing against them.

Why would God delay preventing Satan from oppressing men until the time of Christ? He is the Exalted, the friend of believers, the one who grants them victory, and their support. They are His messengers whom He grants victory over those who oppose them, whose enemies—the soldiers of Satan—He destroys. How could He not have prevented Satan from oppressing these men after their deaths and taking their spirits to Hell? Even if it were supposed that Satan had been able to accomplish this, how could it have been possible for him to overturn what God had ordained for his prophets and friends after their death—their deserving His favor and beneficience and the reward of His Garden according to His judgment and promise and the demands of His wisdom? How could Satan gain dominion over them by imprisoning them in Hell?

They may claim that although God knew that Satan was unjustly mistreating these holy men after their deaths, He was only able to save them from him by resorting to the stratagem of concealing Himself so that He could thus gain power over him. This is what they claim, but there is great blasphemy in this. They make the exalted Lord powerless, just as they at first had made Him unjust.

There is a contradiction in this which demands tremendous ignorance in them, for by this they have made the Lord ignorant. They say: God deceived Satan into taking him justly, just as Satan had deceived Adam by the snake; for God concealed Himself from Satan so that he did not know He was the human nature of the Godhead which had never, in contrast to all others, committed a sin.

When Satan wanted to seize his spirit to imprison him in Hell like those who had preceded him, Satan did not realize his error. Thus Satan deserved that the Lord should seize him, and set free the descendants of Adam from their captivity.

If, as they say, God gave power over mankind to Satan, this amounts to their declaring ignorance in God by what they claim, as well as claiming powerlessness and wrongdoing in Him. There is no difference between the human nature of Christ and that of others, since all are children of Adam.

Moreover, if it were supposed that the human nature defended itself rightfully from Satan—for they say "He entered Hell and released from it the descendants of Adam"—it should be said that if Satan had rightfully been given power to imprison them in Hell because of their sins and the sin of their father, then it would not have been possible to release them because of the freedom of the human nature of Christ from sin. On the other hand, if they were wrongly imprisoned by Satan, then they should have been set free before the crucifixion of Christ's humanity. It was not possible that [this redemption] be delayed, for it was not simply the sinlessness of Christ which necessitated the safety of others. If they say that Christ without overcoming his cross was unable to defend himself [from Satan], then by Satan's gaining dominion over his crucifixion, he was even more unable.

The second false principle on which they built their question which they directed to Muslims—and their answer to it—is equally ineffectual. They think that Muslims hold that the wording of all the existing copies of the Books of the Christians since the mission of Muhammad have undergone corruption.Muslims do not claim this. However some of them may claim that the wording of some of the copies has undergone change since the sending of Muhammad. Of the majority who claim that some of the wordings in the books have undergone change, some claim that it was subsequent to [the time of Muhammad], while others try to prove both cases, or make both possible. They do not say, however, as this spokesman of theirs relates, that the expressions of all the copies existing from east to west on earth have undergone corruption. However, Muslim scholars and those of the People of the Book agree on the occurrence of *tahrif* on the meaning of the text and its explanation. Each group of them has claimed that the others have corrupted the meanings of the books.

Regarding the texts of the books, a group of Muslim scholars has followed the view that the texts themselves have not been changed, just as some People of the Book say. However, many Muslim scholars and People of the Book have held that some of their texts have undergone change. This is well known among many Muslim scholars, and many scholars among the People of the Book hold it also. Even on the matter of the crucifixion of Christ, a group of Christians has held that only someone who appeared to be Christ was crucified, as is reported in the Qur'an. Those who reported his crucifixion were only reporting the ostensible situation. For when the man who resembled him hung on the cross, they thought that it was really Christ, or else they intentionally lied. Still others among these people say that the texts of the books have been changed.

Some consider much in the Torah and the Gospel to have undergone change. Possibly some people consider a majority of the two books to be corrupted; this is especially the case with the Gospel. For the discredit against it is greater than that against the Torah. Some of these people go to extremes so that they even say that there is no sacredness in anything in either book, and it is possible to dispense with both.

Some state that the texts of the two books which have undergone change are but a few, and this is the more likely view. The textual corruption in the Gospel is more evident, so that many people even claim that there is only a little of the word of God in the gospels. The Gospel which is the word of God is not these four gospels.[3]

What is true is that in the Torah and the Gospel which the People of the Book possess today there is contained the judgment of God, although some of their texts have undergone corruption and change (5:41-43). It is known that the Torah existing after the destruction of Jerusalem and the coming of Nebuchadnezzar and the missions of Christ and Muhammad contained God's judgment, as did the Torah which was used by the Jews of Madina at the time of the prophet.

Even should someone claim that some of its texts underwent change after the sending of Muhammad, still we cannot bear witness that every copy in the world is like that. This is something unknown among us; it is also impossible. But it is possible to claim the corruption of many of the texts, and the dissemination of those among their followers, so that there is found among many people what has undergone change after his time.

Nevertheless, many copies of the Torah and the Gospel agree for the most part, differing only in insignificant expression. The corruption of insignificant texts in copies after the mission of the Messenger is possible, which no one is able to deny with certainty. None of the Jews or Christians can bear witness that all copies of the two books in the world are in textual agreement, since there is no way of anyone's knowing this. Moreover the insignificant differences found in the texts of these books are present in many of its copies, just as the copies of some of the books of hadith differ and some of the texts of some of the books have undergone change. This is in contrast to the glorious Qur'an whose wording was memorized in the hearts of men and handed down by successive transmission, so that there is no need that it be preserved in a Book (15:9).

It was the case before the time of the Prophet, during his time, and after it that the Jews were spread abroad from east to west on the earth, and they possessed many copies of the Torah. Similarly Christians had many copies of the Torah, and no one was able to collect these copies and change them. Even if this had been possible, that would have been one of the great occurrences which their propagandists would have related about its transmission.

The case with the Gospel is similar (5:47). It is known that in this Gospel there is a judgment handed down from God, but this judgment is in the matter of commands and prohibitions. But this does not prevent alteration occurring in the area of information (*ikhbar*), and it is in this where *tabdil* occurred as regards the text. Regarding the legal judgments found in the Torah, almost no one claims *tabdil* in their wording.

A group of scholars state that God's saying: "Let the people of the Gospel judge by that which God has revealed in it" is addressed to those who were following the religion of Christ before its abrogation and corruption, not to those living after the sending of Muhammad.

This view is consistent with the obvious meaning of the text of those who read, as does Hamza, "*wa-li-yahkum ahlu al-kitab*" with a *kasra* on the *lam*. This *lam* means "in order to," so that in God's statement (5:46-47) "*wa-li-yahkum*" has the meaning "We bestowed on him the Gospel, etc. . . . *in order that* the people of the Gospel judge by what God has revealed in it." This obliges them to judge by what God had revealed in the true Gospel, but it does not indicate that the Gospel found in the time of the Messenger is that Gospel.

According to the more common reading, the verb is an imperative: "and *let* the People of the Gospel" etc. Some scholars say that it is a command to those among whom the true Gospel was present that they judge by what God revealed in it, and thus God's saying "*wal-yahkum*" is a command to them before the sending of Muhammad.

Others hold that there is no need for such contorsions, for the statement about the Gospel is like the statement about the Torah (5:41-46). Here it is stated clearly that those Jews who came to the Prophet for judgment had the Torah, in which was contained the judgment of God, but they had turned away from God's judgment. He continues, saying, "And let the People of the Gospel judge by what God has revealed in it." This is the *lam* of command, and it is a command of God which He sent down by the tongue of Muhammad.

God's commanding those who died before this statement is impossible. This command could only be a command for those who put faith in Him after God's addressing His servants by command. It can be seen, therefore, that God commanded those who were present at that time that they judge by what God had handed down in the Gospel. God handed down in the Gospel the command to follow Muhammad, just as He commanded it in the Torah. They should judge by what God handed down in the Gospel of what Muhammad had not abrogated, just as He commanded the People of the Torah that they judge according to what He handed down which Christ had not abrogated. He did not abrogate it, but they were commanded in it to follow Christ, and in the Gospel they were commanded to follow Muhammad. After the sending of Muhammad, any one of the People of the Book who judged according to what God revealed in the Torah and the Gospel would not be judging contrary to the judgment of Muhammad, since they were commanded in the Torah and the Gospel to follow Muhammad

(7:157; 5:48). God thereby made the Qur'an a watcher, and this watcher was their witness, their judge, and their trustee. It judges according to that in the previous books which God had not abrogated, and it bears witness by confirming that in them which was not corrupted (5:48).

It is not possible that someone should say that God abrogated in the second book all that He commanded in the first book; what is abrogated is only a little by comparison with that on which the books and laws agree. Moreover, there are indications in the Torah and the Gospel which point to the prophethood of Muhammad. Therefore, whenever the People of the Torah or the Gospel judge according to what God has revealed in them, they judge according to what necessitates their following Muhammad. This shows that the Torah and the Gospel contain what they know to have been revealed by God, since they would not be commanded to judge according to what God has handed down, if they did not know what it was He revealed. The judgment is only concerning commands and prohibitions. The knowledge of the sense of some of the passages in the books does not prevent the lack of knowledge of some others.

Concerning the sense there is agreement. Muslims, Christians, and Jews all agree that in the divine books there is the command to serve God alone allowing no rivals beside Him, that He sent mankind human messengers, that He ordained justice and forbade wrongdoing, obscenities, and idolatry, and similar universal laws. Within these laws He promised reward and threatened punishment. They all even agree on faith in the Last Day. They may, on the other hand, differ on some of the meanings of the books, and they have differed in explaining them. Jews and Christians, for example, have differed concerning the Messiah predicted in the prophecies, whether this was Christ the son of Mary or another awaited Messiah. Muslims know the Christians to be correct in this, but they do not agree with them in what they have innovated by way of lies and idolatry.

Therefore it is said that since a few of the informational texts in the books underwent alteration, this does not prevent most of the texts from not having suffered change, especially since there is in the same book that which indicates what has been changed. It may be also said about the wording in the Torah and the Gospel that was changed that there is in the same Torah and Gospel that which points out its alteration.

A reply is found to the specious argument of those who say that none of their wording was changed. They claim that if the *tabdil* has occurred in the wording of the Torah and the Gospel before the mission of Muhammad, one would not be able to know truth from falsehood. Using these books as an argument against the People of the Book for their acting according to their books would fail. They were not censured at that time for failing to follow their books, but the Qur'an did censure them for neglecting the judgment which their books contained. At times it calls the earlier books to bear witness.

The answer to this is that the corruption which occurred was only slight, and the greater part of the earlier books was not corrupted.

In the earlier books, that which was not corrupted contained correct wording whose intent was clear. It delineated the error of what opposed it, and offered numerous proofs and correspondences for it. The various passages confirmed one another. In contrast to this, what was corrupted was only a few expressions, and the rest of the texts of the Book contradict them.

These books are thus of the same status as the books of hadith transmitted from the prophet.[4] When there occur some few weak hadith reports in the Sunan of Abu Dawud, Al-Tirmidhi, and others, there are also found true hadiths, established as being from the Prophet which clarify the weakness of the former. This is even the case with the *Sahih* of Muslim. In it there are a few incorrect texts, but in the same book there are found correct hadith reports which, with the Qur'an, show the error [of the incorrect passages].

Therefore it can be said that while *tabdil* occurred in some of the wording of the previous books, the books also contained that which pointed out the error. What we have presented shows that Muslims do not claim that every copy in the world of the Torah, Gospel, and Psalms in every language since the time of Muhammad has undergone verbal change. I do not know even one of the *salaf* who claimed that. There may be some of the later Muslims who have made that claim, just as some later Muslim writers may allow someone to wipe himself with all the copies in the world of the Torah and the Gospel. However, these and similar opinions are not those of the *salaf* and the *umma* and its imams.

When 'Umar ibn al-Khattab saw a copy of the Torah in the hand of Ka'b al-Ahbar, he said, "Ka'b, if you know that this is the Torah which God handed down by Moses ibn 'Imran, then read it." The issue is thus conditional on what we can in no way know; 'Umar did not decisively determine that the texts had been corrupted when he did not put confidence in everything that was in them.

The Qur'an and the transmitted sunna both attest that the Torah and the Gospel which existed in the time of the Prophet contained what God had revealed. A definitive decision on the matter of their *tabdil* in every copy of the world is unfeasible, and there is no need for us to mention it. Nor do we have any knowledge about that. Neither is it possible for anyone of the People of the Book to claim that all the texts in the world in all their languages agree on one wording. This is something that nobody can know, either spontaneously or by investigation. Something like this can only be known by revelation, and except through revelation it is impossible. It is not possible for any human to compare every copy of the twenty-four books[5] existing in the world in every one of their languages.

Moreover, we have seen clear differences in wording. The Torah is the most correct of the books, and most widely distributed among Jews and Christians. In spite of this the text of the Samaritans is different from the text of the Jews and Christians, even to the very wording of the Ten Commandments. There is mention in the Samaritans' text on the matter of the reception of the commandment on Sinai of what is not found in the text of the Jews and Christians. This shows that *tabdil* has occurred in many copies of these books, for numerous copies exist among the Samaritans.

Similarly we have seen numerous copies of the Psalms differing one from the other with many variations in both wording and meaning, so that one who has seen them can assert that many of these copies actually mislead one from the Psalms of David. As for the gospels, the *tabdil* in them is greater than that in the Torah.

It may be asked why God censured the People of the Book for neglecting the judgment which God revealed in their books, if it was the case that these books were abrogated. The answer is that the abrogation occurred only in a few laws; the information about God, the Last Day, and other things was not abrogated.

Thus there was no abrogation of the universal religion and its universal laws. God censured the People of the Book for failing to follow the first book. Therefore, the People of the Book disbelieved in two ways: firstly for the *tabdil* they worked on the first book and their failure to believe in and act according to some of it; secondly, for rejecting the second book, that is, the Qur'an (2:91).

It is clear that before the sending of Muhammad they disbelieved in what he revealed through the prophets whom they killed. In the same way they disbelieved when Muhammad was sent to them with what he revealed through him (3:183-84; 28:48-49).

If this is the case, God censured them for failing to follow what He revealed in the Torah and the Gospel, and for failing to follow what he revealed in the Qur'an. He thereby clearly shows their disbelief in both the first and second books. There is nothing in any of this that commands them to judge by what was abrogated by the second book.[6]

## C. THE EXTENT OF CORRUPTION IN THE BIBLE

Next they state: We are amazed at these people, that with all their knowledge, intelligence, and learning, they can make a claim like this against us. It is just as if we were to bring a similar charge against them: "They have changed and corrupted the Book which they possess at this time, and have written in it whatever they wanted and felt like." Would they approve of our saying this?

But I say: This is something that is not possible for anyone to claim—the changing or substitution of even one word is impossible.

Praise to the great God! If it is impossible for their Book which is in one language to have undergone the change or substitution of even a word, then how could the alteration of our books which are written in 72 languages have occurred? In each of those languages there are so many thousands of copies. Our books lasted over 700 years before the coming of Muhammad, and came to be used by peoples who read them in different languages in far distant countries. Who has ever spoken 72 languages or governed the whole world, with its kings, priests, and scholars so that he gained control over all copies of our Books in all areas of the earth, collected them from the world's four corners so that he could change them?

It would not even have been possible for him to have changed some copies and omitted others, because all copies of our Books have one wording, one expression in all languages. Thus no one can ever make such a charge as theirs.[1]

2) The analogy of their books to the Qur'an—that just as no claim of *tabdil* is heard concerning it, so should it be with their books—is a false analogy in its meaning and expression. As for the the meaning: everything in their religion on which Muslims agree by a well-known, openly manifested consensus is transmitted from the Messenger by successive transmission, and even known by necessity to be from his religion. The five prayers, the poor tax, the fasting during the month of Ramadan, the pilgrimage to the Ka'ba, the necessity of justice and honesty, the prohibition of *shirk*, impurities, and wrongdoing, even the prohibition of wine, gambling, and interest-taking, and still other things—all these are successively transmitted from the Prophet, just like the transmission of the texts of the Qur'an which indicate them.

In this category is the universality of the prophetic mission of Muhammad, and his being sent to all men—People of the Book as well as others, even to all mankind and jinn. It is similarly known that he accused those Jews and Christians who did not follow what God revealed through him of unbelief, just as he accused others than them of unbelief who refused to believe the message; he waged *jihad* against them and commanded his followers to also wage *jihad* against them.

Muslims know three matters as handed down by successive transmission from their prophet: the text of the Qur'an, its interpretations on which Muslims find consensus, and the successively transmitted sunna, which is the "Wisdom" (*hikma*) which God handed down outside the Qur'an (2:151; 4:113; 2:231; 33:34). Moreover the Muslims preserve the Qur'an by memory in their hearts, thus dispensing with the printed text. This is proven by the sound *hadith* from the prophet reported by Muslim:

> The Lord said to me, "I am handing down to you a Book which is not washed by water, which you can read waking and sleeping."

What He is saying is that even if the text were washed off the printed copies by water, it would not be washed off men's hearts. By contrast, the preceding Books, if their printed copies were lacking, there would not be found anyone who could transmit them successively by preserving them in their hearts.

The Qur'an is still preserved in men's hearts by successive transmission, so that if someone should want to change a thing in a printed copy, and that were presented for inspection to Muslim youths, they would know that he had changed a copy because of their memorization of the Qur'an. Rather than accepting the printed copy, they would reject it.

Among the People of the Book, however, some one of them could transcribe many copies of the Torah and the Gospel and change some of them and present them to their scholars, who would not know what he had changed if they did not have their own copies at hand. Thus, were those copies which had been changed to circulate among groups of Christians, they would not have been aware of the alteration.

Moreover, Muslims have chains of reliable, trustworthy authorities connected to one another on the authority of reliable men whom one can trust in the minutiae of religion just like the generality of Muslims have transmitted its main tenets. The People of the Book have nothing like this.

It is not possible for anyone to alter the Qur'an, since it is preserved in the hearts of men and handed down by consecutive transmission. We do not bear witness, nevertheless, that every one of the copies are in agreement. An error may occur in one of the handwritten copies which will be recognized by those who have memorized the Qur'an; they have no need to refer to another copy.

Their books are not memorized, nor is there a group of transmittors who can act as a reference for their copies. In the time when the prophets were present among men, they acted as the competent authority for people, on whom others could depend if some among them had changed something in the books. But when prophecy was interrupted, some people were quick to make changes in the books.

Many Christians replaced much in the religion of Christ only a short time after the ascension of Christ. They began replacing one thing after another, although there remained a group among them who held fast to the true religion until God sent Muhammad.

The religion on which Muslims have agreed by a clear and well-known agreement has been handed down from their prophet by successive transmission. They transmitted the Qur'an as well as the sunna, which explains and clarifies the Qur'an (16:44). The wording and the meaning of what God revealed is clear. The meanings of the Qur'an which Muslims have agreed upon by evident consensus are among what the community has inherited from their prophet, just as they have inherited from him the texts of the Qur'an. And since, thank God, the community has never agreed on any altered or corrupted interpretation, how could it have done so for the texts of those meanings?

The transmission of the texts and the consensus upon them was even clearer in the case of the wording than it was on the interpretations. Thus the religion manifested among Muslims is that upon which they have agreed, whose text and interpretation is among what they have transmitted from their prophet. There was no *tahrif* or *tabdil* in it, neither in wording nor in meaning.

In contrast to this, in the Torah and the Gospel are found texts on whose meaning (*ma'na*) and legal judgments (*ahkam*) Jews, Christians, or both have done evident substitution. This is well known among the generality of their people. For example, the Jews changed what was found in the earlier books by way of prophecies of Christ and Muhammad, laws in the Torah, and His command in some of its information. Christians similarly replaced much in the reports and laws in the Torah and the prophetic books which Christ had not changed. However, Christ must be followed in what God abrogated of the Torah through his preaching.

As for what they replaced after Christ, like permitting the eating of pork, and their changing what God had forbidden and Christ had not permitted, like the omission of circumcision, prayer to the east, the lengthened period of fasting and changing it from one time to another, the use of pictures in churches, glorifying the cross, establishing monasticism—none of these practices were legislated by Christ or any other prophet. By these things they followed what God had not commanded through the preaching of any prophet in opposition to what God had commanded and sent through His prophets.

The Qur'an has been established by successive transmission, and it is known by necessity to those who agree with or oppose Muhammad that he claimed the Qur'an to be the speech of God—not his own speech—and that it reached him from God. He used to distinguish between the Qur'an and what he spoke from the sunna, even though the latter was among that which had to be followed by acceptance and deed.

God handed down the Book and the Wisdom, and taught the Book and the Wisdom to his community, as He himself has said (3:164; 2:231; 4:113; 33:34). God spoke thusly about Abraham and his son Isma'il (2:128-29). The Prophet said: "I was given the Book, and along with it what is similar to it." He was teaching his community the Book which is the beloved Qur'an, and he informed them that it is the speech of God, not his own speech. The Qur'an is that about the excellence of which God spoke (17:88).

It is that which he commanded his community to recite in their prayer, so that the prayer is not correct without it. In addition to this Book he also taught them the Wisdom which God handed down; he distinguished between it and the Qur'an in various ways:

1) The Qur'an is miraculous.

2) The Qur'an is that which is read at prayer without the sunna.

3) The Arabic text of the Qur'an has been handed down according to the exact wording of its verses, and no one may change them in the Arabic language by the agreement of Muslims. It is possible, however, to explain them in Arabic or to translate them in other languages than Arabic. Their formal recitation in Arabic with other than their proper wording is not permissible by the agreement of Muslims. This is in contrast to the Wisdom he taught them, for there is no judgment made on its wording as there is on the wording of the Qur'an.

4) The Qur'an is that which "None touches but the purified" (56:79). One in a state of ritual impurity may not read it, as his sunna has indicated according to the majority of the community. This is in contrast to anything else than the Qur'an.

The community received the Qur'an from him by memory during his lifetime; more than one of the Companions memorized the whole Qur'an during his lifetime, and all of the Companions memorized some of it. Some of them memorized what others had not memorized. Thus all of it is handed down from him by hearing in successive transmission, and he claimed that it reached him from

God, that it was the speech of God, not his own speech.

In the Qur'an there are many texts which show it to be the speech of God. Those who saw Muhammad and transmitted his miracles, his deeds, and his Law, which they saw with their own eyes, and the Qur'an and hadith which they heard, were thousands taken from more than a hundred thousand who saw and believed in him.

But the Gospels which the Christians possess are four—that of Matthew, Mark, Luke, and John. Christians agree that Luke and Mark had never seen Christ, but only Matthew and John saw him. These four writings which they call the Gospel, and they may call each one of them a gospel, were only written after the assumption of Jesus. It is not stated in them that they are the speech of God, nor that Christ received them from God; rather they transmit some things from the speech of Christ and some things from his deeds and miracles. They state that they have not handed on all that they saw and heard from him. They are therefore of the same nature as the sayings and deeds of the Prophet related about him by the hadith-collectors, the biographers, and the narrators of his campaigns. But these latter are not a Qur'an.

The gospels which they possess are similar to the biography, the books of hadith, and books like these. If most of it is true and what Christ actually said, it has come to him from God and one should confirm its message and obey its command, just as the Messenger said about the sunna. It resembles what the Messenger said about the sunna, for there is found in it what the Messenger states to be the word of God, as when he says God says:

> Whoever treats a friend of Mine as an enemy, I permit [My friend] to war against him.

In the sunna there is also that which he [Muhammad] says, but this also is among that God revealed to him. Whoever obeys the Messenger has obeyed God. So it is with what is handed down in the Gospel, for it is of this type. If it is a command from Christ, then the command of Christ is the command of God. Whoever obeys Christ has obeyed God. Whatever Christ reported about the unknown, God has informed him of it, for he is preserved from error in the message he brings.

If the Gospel is similar to the transmitted sunna, error mars it in some of its expressions, just as occurs in the biography, or the books of sound hadiths by Abu Dawud, Al-Tirmidhi, and Ibn Maja. These books have been spread and circulated widely among Muslims; consequently it is not possible for anyone, after their dissemination and the proliferation of their copies, to change all of them.

Nevertheless in some of their expressions error occurred before they were widely disseminated. The narrator, although he was honest, may have erred. However, the information which Muslims have accepted by assent, confirmation, and action is firmly claimed by Muslims to be truly from their prophet.

The books handed down through the prophets were of the same type as the book handed down through Muhammad, but there was no successive transmission of them, nor was there the confirmation of the fallible as a proof, nor was there among them means for distinguishing between what is truthful and what is false as there is among Muslims. For this reason the gospels which the Christians possess are of this type; they contain many of the sayings, deeds, and miracles of Christ, but also contain what is undoubtedly in error against him and against that which he wrote in them in the beginning.[2] Even if there is no one who has accused them of intentionally lying, still one, two, three, or four persons do not prevent the occurrence of error or omission in the books.

There is especially much error in what someone has heard or seen and then reports many years later. Moreover there was no inerrant community at the time to receive those reports by giving assent and confirmation which would necessitate knowledge in these matters, for the inerrant community could not agree on an error. But the apostles were only twelve men.

The story of the crucifixion is a case in which doubtfulness occurred, and an argument has been established to show that the one crucified was not Christ, "but it was made to appear so." They thought that it was Christ, although not one of the apostles had seen Christ crucified, but it was only reported to them by some Jews who had witnessed it.

Some people hold that they intentionally lied, but the majority hold that they were uncertain about the matter. The majority of Muslims have held that the words in God's saying "But it was made to appear so to them" refer to the hearers of their report. It is possible that they erred in this report, and they were not inerrant in transmitting it. Therefore it is possible that they erred in some of what they reported about Christ. This is not anything that maligns the messengership of Christ, nor is it included in what religious tradition has successively transmitted about him which says that he is messenger of God and must be followed whether he was crucified or not. What is successively transmitted about him demands faith in him whether or not he was crucified.

The apostles believed what they were handing on about Christ, and are not charged with intentionally lying about him, but there is nothing to prevent some of them from having erred in what they reported about him; that is, we do not know otherwise, especially when the error of that on which they were mistaken is clearly shown in other places.

Christians themselves have differed concerning the generality of that in which error occurred, even to the matter of the crucifixion. Some of them hold that the one crucified was not Christ, but someone similar, as Muslims say. Some Christians hold for his being the servant of God, and deny any indwelling or union, like the Arians. Others, like the Nestorians, deny the union but profess the divine indwelling.

As for their religious practices, their scholars know that most of them are not from Christ. Christ never commanded them to pray to the east or to keep a fifty-day fast, or to fix it in the spring, or the feasts of Christmas, Epiphany, the Holy Cross, or other feasts. Most of those things, rather, were what they innovated after the time of the apostles.

The feast of the Holy Cross, for example, is something innovated by Helena al-Harraniyya, the mother of Constantine. In the time of Constantine many beliefs and practices of the religion of Christ were changed. They innovated the creed which is the basis of belief of their faith. This creed was not enunciated in anything found in the prophetic books which they possess, nor is it transmitted from any of the prophets or any of the apostles who accompanied Christ. Rather it was invented by a group of 380 of their leaders.

In that they relied on ambiguous expressions in their books, although in the same books there were univocal expressions which contradicted what they stated, as we have elaborated elsewhere. Similarly the generality of their laws which they have laid down in the book of "The Canon"[3] are handed down from the prophets, some from the apostles, while many of them are what they innovated without their having been handed down from any one of the prophets or the apostles. They permitted their leaders, the people of learning and religion, to change whatever laws they found and to impose a new law. Most of their religion has been innovated; it was not handed down in any book nor legislated by any prophet.

———

If Christians claim that Christ confirmed the texts of the Torah, then it is answered that if Christ was unable to impose on the people the faith in God and obedience to Him to which God had obliged them, how would it have been possible for him to correct the texts of the Torah which they possessed in multiplicity? They were seeking to crucify and kill him, due to his weakness and powerlessness, and they crucified someone who resembled him, as Muslims say, or actually crucified Christ himself as the Christians claim—how could it have been possible for Christ to have corrected what had been changed in the Torah?

No one after Christ was inerrant. Christ changed some of the legal judgments of the Torah but confirmed most of them. Muslims claim that Christians abrogated these legal judgments and replaced them by the creed, instead of deeming them necessary and acting according to them. It is not necessary to claim that their texts have been replaced.

They replaced the law of stoning by another, although it is written in the law of Moses. By contrast, most Muslims hold that actual textual alteration has occurred in some of the informational passages.

As for the prophecies handed down from twenty-two prophets, there is not one of these whose entire text has been successively transmitted. The most that can be said for them is that they are of the same status as the Gospel, that is, the status of works handed on concerning the sayings and lives of the prophets, like Ibn Ishaq's biography or some of our books of *musnad* and sunna, in which the transmitters hand on material concerning the sayings and deeds of Muhammad. Most of it is trustworthy, but some of it is in error.

God has protected for this community what he has revealed to it (15:9). Whenever there is error in the *tafsir* of the Qur'an, or in the transmission or incorrect interpretation of a hadith, God has always raised up someone from the community who clarified it, shown proof for the error of the one who made it, and the falsity of the liar. This community will never agree on an error; there will remain in it a group of people manifesting the truth until the Day of Judgment. This is because theirs is the last of the religions—there is no prophet after their Prophet, no book after their Book.

Whenever the previous communities replaced and corrupted His message, God sent them a prophet to make this clear to them and to command and forbid them. But there was no prophet after Muhammad. Therefore God guaranteed that He would be the one to preserve the divine admonition which He had handed down, and that this community would never agree on an error. God has therefore raised up in every age people of knowledge and the Qur'an who guard His religion and keep it safe from the *tahrif* of the extremists, the syncretism of the wayward, and the groundless interpretation of the ignorant.

———

The answer is clear to their saying:

> Therefore, who has ever spoken 72 languages or governed the whole world with its kings, priests, and scholars so that he gained control over all copies of our books in all areas of the earth, collected them from the world's four corners so that he could change them? Even if it were possible to collect all or some of them, this alteration would not be possible since all of the copies contain one wording, one text, one belief.[4]

The answer to this is clear from various aspects.

1) We have not claimed that the textual alteration took place after the books came to be in all these languages, nor after their circulation in many copies. We do not even claim textual alteration after the distribution of copies in books other than those of the prophets, such as books of grammar, medicine, mathematics, hadith reports, and traditions handed down from the prophets. The transmission of these works was originally in individual units, and afterwards their copies became numerous and widespread. No one claims that after the copies of a book had spread from the eastern regions of the earth to the west that someone gained control over the whole civilized world and gathered the copies and changed them.

Neither does anyone claim anything like that concerning the Torah and the Gospel. Such a thing is only claimed about them when their copies were still a small number—one, two, or four, or the alteration of some of the texts of the copies is claimed, for some copies may have undergone change. There are differences in some of the copies of the Torah, the Gospel, and the Psalms existing today, but the difference is slight, while generally they agree.

2) This clarifies the second point, that in their stating that all of the copies have one statement, one text, and one belief, the reality is not as they claim. The copies of the Torah differ in places.

Between the Torah of the Jews and Christians, and that of the Samaritans there are differences,[5] and among the copies of the Psalms there are even more differences. This is the case with the gospels, and how much more so with the texts of the prophecies.

I have seen copies of the Psalms in which the prophethood of Muhammad is confirmed by name, while I have seen other copies of the Psalms in which I did not find that. There was nothing to prevent some of the copies from containing the characteristics of the prophet, while others did not.

3) *Tabdil* in exegesis is a matter about which there is no doubt. In this matter our purpose is achieved, for we know conclusively

that Muhammad was mentioned in the Torah and the Gospel existing in his time[6] (7:157). There is no doubt that the copies of the Torah and Gospel in his time were numerous and widely distributed from the east to the west on earth. Thus one of two judgments must apply:

a) either the text must have been changed in some copies, and the altered copies circulated,

b) or mention of him would have been found in all the copies, as it was extracted by many of the scholars who had been Jewish or Christian. Those who had not been their scholars also discovered his mention and prediction in a great number of places in the Torah, the Gospel, and the books of the prophets, as we have elaborated elsewhere. Some say that mention of him was found in these books even more often and more clearly than this in some of the texts.

It is not possible for these people to defend their saying "We have been acquainted with every text of the Torah and the Gospel in the world, and have found them to be of one wording." This could only be claimed by a liar, for it is not humanly possible for someone to be acquainted with every copy in the entire world. Even if the actual difference in the various copies were not known, it would not be possible to state conclusively their verbal agreement. So how can this be said when people have expressly mentioned that they can point out differences in wording. All this makes it clear that he speaks falsely who claims a verbal consistency in the texts.

## D. CLAIMS OF QUR'ANIC APPROVAL FOR CHRISTIANITY

> They say: We Christians have not committed any of the evil deeds of the Jews.[1]

It is said to them that unbelief, iniquity, and disobedience are not confined to the sins of the Jews. Although you have not done acts like theirs, you possess views and deeds some of which are more shocking than the unbelief of the Jews. While you are more tractable than the Jews and nearer to us in friendship, nevertheless you are at the same time more ignorant and erring than the Jews. God has frequently chastised the Christians in the Qur'an (19:88-95; 18:1-5; 9:29; 9:30-31; 9:32-34; 5:14; 19:34-38; 5:77).

Whoever reflects on the situation of the Jews and Christians along with that of Muslims will find that Jews and Christians are confronting each other from the opposite extremes of error. While these two peoples are situated at extremes, Muslims are in the center. This is the case concerning their view on God, the prophets, laws, what is permitted and forbidden, morals, and other things.

*On God*: Jews make the creator resemble what is created by attributing to Him qualities of deficiency particular to a creature far above which God ought to be deemed. For example, some of them have said that He is poor, miserly, and became tired when He created the heavens and earth.

Christians, on the other hand, make the creature resemble the creator by attributing to him attributes of perfection specific to the Creator but which are not found in any creature. They say, for example, that Christ is God, and the son of God, and each of these two views demands the other. Christians, moreover, describe the divine nature with attributes of deficiency beyond which the Lord must be declared to be. They abuse God with an insult such as no human has ever insulted him. Mu'adh ibn Jabal said, "Do not have compassion for them for they have abused God with a blasphemy with which no human has ever before insulted Him."

*On religious practices*: Jews claim that God is prevented from abrogating what he has commanded, as He is prevented from [doing] what does not enter into His omnipotence or from [knowing] what is against knowledge and wisdom.

Christians, on the other hand, make it possible for their own leaders to abrogate the command of God which He sent with His prophets. Thus they make what is *haram* permissible, as they have permitted pork and other despicable things; they have not made a single thing of that sort *haram*. Conversely, they have prohibited what is permissible, as they have done in their monasticism which they invented. In doing so they have forbidden good things which God has permitted. They have abolished that to which people had been obligated, as they have abolished—among other things—circumcision, kinds of ritual purificatory ablutions, and have eliminated ritual impurity. They obligate people to matters which were abolished, just as they oblige men by laws which God and His prophets never imposed.

Muslims, however, have described the Lord by the attributes of perfection of which He is worthy, and declare Him far above any imperfection and that there is nothing like Him. They have thereby described Him as He has described Himself and as His prophets have described Him—that is, without textual corruption, without making Him ineffectively transcendent, without trying to explain or represent His divine nature, always with the knowledge that there is nothing like Him, either in His essence, in His attributes, or in His deeds.

They say: "His truly is all creation and commandment" (7:54). Therefore there is no creator but He and no commander but He. All of religion is for Him. He is the worshipped one, the one who is obeyed. There is no one but He who deserves worship or obedience. He has abrogated what He willed of the Law, and it is not in the power of any other than Him to abrogate His law.

Jews have exaggerated in avoiding ritual impurity, and have forbidden good things. Christians have made disgusting things licit, and allowed contact with [ritually] impure things. God made good things lawful for Muslims in contrast to the Jews, and forbade the disgusting in contrast to Christians. Jews exaggerate in the purity of their bodies despite the wickedness of their hearts, while Christians claim that their hearts are pure despite the uncleanness of their bodies. Muslims are pure in both bodies and hearts.

Christians have practices of worship and morals without learning, knowledge, or intelligence. Jews have knowledge and learning without practices or worship or good moral qualities. Muslims combine wholesome learning and upright activity—integrity and intelligence.[2]

God sent his messengers with guidance and the religion of truth. This guidance includes salutary knowledge, and the religion of truth encompasses upright activity "that He might make it conquer over all religion."[3] This conquest is by knowledge and argumentation to show that it is truth and guidance and by strength and sword [to show that] it is supported and made victorious [by God]. God has given this religion victory for they are "the people of the straight path, the path of those God has favored" with prophets and martyrs, as well as good, upright, and righteous persons. Like a comrade He treats them well.

"Not of those who earn His anger"[4]—this refers to those like the Jews, who know the truth but do not act according to it; "nor of those who go astray"—this means people like the Christians, who act properly, worship, and lead ascetical lives without knowledge. The Jews killed the prophets and those who commanded them to act justly among people. Christians took their priests and monks as masters aside from God, as they did with Jesus the son of Mary.

Muslims remained moderate and believed in God, His angels, His books, and His messengers. They did not reject the prophets and curse them, nor did they exaggerate them beyond proper bounds. Jews get angry and take revenge for their own sake; Christians neither get angry nor take vengeance for the sake of their Lord.

God has described the community of Muhammad as being the

most beneficial of all communities for creation (3:110). In the community of Muhammad there is the commanding of what is right and the prohibition of what is forbidden. In this there is godliness in this life and the next, the like of which is not found in the other two communities.

———

The Christians state: We have also found in their Book that it says:

> "You will find the most vehement of mankind in hostility to those who believe [to be] the Jews and the idolaters. You will find the nearest of them in affection to those who believe [to be] those who say: Lo! We are Christians. That is because there are among them priests and monks, and because they are not proud" (5:82).
>
> It mentions priests and monks, so that it cannot be said that any other group than us is meant. This verse indicates our acts and the goodness of our intentions. It rejects the application of the term *shirk* to us when it says: "The Jews and those who commit *shirk* are the most vehement of mankind in hostility to those who believe, and those who say 'We are Christians' are the closest of them in friendship."[5]

In answer to them the completion of this passage should be pointed out.

> When they listen to that which has been revealed to the messenger, you see their eyes overflow with tears because of their recognition of the Truth. They say: Our Lord, we believe. Inscribe us among the Witnesses (5:83-85).

Thus God only returns a reward in the afterlife to those who believe in Muhammad. It is about them these verses were spoken. The Witnesses are those who have borne witness to Muhammad of his messengership. They have witnessed that there is no God but God, and Muhammad is the prophet of God. They are the witnesses about whom God spoke (2:143). Ibn 'Abbas and others said that the verse "Enroll us among the Witnesses" (5:85; 3:53) means "with Muhammad and his community."

Everyone who witnesses to the Messengers by placing faith in them is among the witnesses. As the apostles [of Jesus] said:

> Our Lord! We believe in that which you have revealed and we follow him whom You have sent. Enroll us among the witnesses (3:53).

God spoke [similarly about the earlier believers] (22:77-78).

As for God's saying in the verse (5:82), it is like God disclosing that the enmity of the Jews and idolaters to the believers is greater than that of the Christians, and the Christians are nearer to them in friendship. This is obvious from the natural dispositions of the Jews, for in the Jews there is hatred, envy, and enmity which is not found in the Christians. In the Christians there is mercy and friendliness which are not found in the Jews. The origin of enmity is hatred. The Jews used to hate the prophets, why would they not hate the believers? On the other hand, there is nothing in the religion of Christians which obliges them to have enmity or hatred for the enemies of God who wage war against Him and His prophet and spread corruption on earth, so how would they have enmity and hatred for the moderate believers,[6] the people of the community of Abraham, the believers in all the books and messengers?

Nothing in this praises Christians for having faith in God or promises them salvation from punishment or that they are deserving of a reward. It only says they are nearer in friendship. In God's saying "That is because there are among them priests and monks, and because they are not proud," He is saying that because of these people and because they have forsworn pride He has made a friendliness in them which has thereby made them better than the idolaters, and closer [to Muslims] in friendliness than the Jews and idolaters.

Then God said:

> When they listen to that which has been revealed to the messenger, you see their eyes overflow with tears because of their recognition of the Truth (5:83).

These are those whose faith God praises and who are promised the reward of the afterlife. The pronoun refers back to earlier people, and so what is meant by it is a certain type of earlier people, not each one of them.

Similar to this is God's saying "The Jews have said 'Ezra is the son of God'" (9:30). It means that a certain kind of Jew said that, not every Jew held that. From this it follows that there is in Christians a certain softheartedness which demands in them faith which is not in the Jews. This is true. As for their stating "It rejects the application of the term *shirk* to us," there is no doubt that God distinguished between the idolaters and the People of the Book in a number of places, and described in various places who was the most idolatrous of them. Elsewhere He even distinguished between Sabaeans, Magians, and the idolaters.

Thus both matters are true (i.e., People of the Book are distinguished from idolaters and are elsewhere identified with them). They are distinguished from those who commit *shirk* in such verses as 98:1; 22:17; and in the verse in question 5:82. But they are included with the idolaters in 9:31, for example, where God declares Himself exalted beyond their *shirk*.

The reason for this situation is that in the origin of their religion there is no *shirk*, for God only sent His messengers with the pure *tawhid* and a prohibition of *shirk*[7] (43:45; 16:36; 21:25). Christ and the messengers who went before him only called people to the worship of God alone, allowing no partner to Him. In the Torah the same message is greatly described, and not a single one of the prophets ever commanded the worship of an angel, prophet, heavenly body, or idol, nor did they ever command people to seek intercession with God from someone dead or absent, angel, or prophet. No one of the messengers ever related that the angels claimed to say "Seek intercession with us before God," nor that the dead or absent prophets and holy men ever claimed to say "Seek intercession with us before God," nor to fashion statues of them—either bodily ones casting a shadow, nor those painted on walls. They never demanded prayer to their statues or that people extol [the images] by devotion and obedience to them, whether people intended prayer to the ones represented by the statues, extolling and seeking intercession from them, asking them to speak to God for them—thus making the statues a reminder of those pictured on them—or whether they intended prayer to the statues themselves, not conscious that the ones intended by their prayer were the persons represented by them [the images]. This is similar to the acts of the ignorant idolaters, although in all this they are only worshiping Satan, even though they were not intending to worship him.

Sometimes it may seem to them that a picture which they think to be that of the person they are extolling will speak to them and say, "I am al-Khidr," "I am Christ," "I am St. George," or "I am Shaykh So-and-So." Something like this has occurred to more than one person of those considering themselves Muslims or Christians. Satan may enter into some of the statues and speak to them; he may fulfill some of their needs. In this and similar ways *shirk* has appeared in ancient and modern times, and thus have Christians and those who resemble them performed their *shirk*.

The prophets and the messengers forbade all this. At no time did they ever command anything of that nature. The Christians do not command the glorification of bodily idols, but rather the extolling of carved statues. They do not follow pure *tawhid*, but neither are they like the idolaters who worshiped idols and rejected the messengers. God has therefore sometimes categorized them separately from the idolaters, and elsewhere cursed them for the *shirk* which they innovated.

———

The Christians state, "It says in Surat al-Baqara:

> Lo! Those who believe, and those who are Jews and Christians and Sabaeans—whoever believes in God and the Last Day and does right—surely their reward is with their Lord, and no fear shall come upon them neither shall they grieve (2:62).

> "By this statement the Qur'an makes all people—Jews, Muslims, and others—equal."

In answer it should be said to them, first of all, that there is no argument in this verse for what they are trying to prove, for it makes an equality between them and the Jews and the Sabaeans. They agree with Muslims that the Jews are unbelievers after God's sending Christ to them, for they rejected him. Similarly, the Sabaeans are unbelievers in respect to the prophet who was sent to them whom they rejected. Thus if there is praise in this verse for the religion which the Christians possess after the sending of Muhammad, there is praise in it as well for the religion of the Jews, and this is false according to them as well as to Muslims. Conversely, if there is no praise in it for the Jews after the abrogation and corruption of their religion, in the same way there is no praise in it for Christians after the corruption and abrogation of theirs.

The same is said to the Jews if they use this verse as an argument for the correctness of their religion. Moreover, the Christians declare the Jews unbelievers, and if their religion is true, there necessarily follows the unbelief of the Jews. Even if it is false, there follows the falsity of their religion, for one of their two religions must be false. It is impossible that this verse be praising both or that it has made an equality between them.

However, this verse does not praise either of them after their abrogation and corruption, but the meaning of the verse refers only to those who believe in Muhammad, those Jews who followed Moses, that is, those who followed his Law before its abrogation and corruption, and the Christians who followed Christ, that is, those who followed his religion before its abrogation and corruption.

"The Sabaeans" refers to the Sabaean *hunafa'*,[8] such as those

Arabs and others who followed the religion of Abraham, Isma'il, and Ishaq before its corruption and abrogation. The Arabs who were descendants of Isma'il and others who lived near the Ka'ba which Abraham and Isma'il built were monotheists of the community of Abraham until some of the leaders of the Khuza'a changed his religion. 'Amr ibn Luhayy[9] was the first to change the religion of Abraham by ***shirk*** and by permitting what God had forbidden. Muhammad said, "I saw 'Amr ibn Luhayy dragging along his intestines in Hell." He was the first to navigate the lake and cause lax practices and change the religion of Abraham.

Similarly, those of the line of Ishaq who lived before the prophetic sending of Moses who were holding fast to the religion of Abraham were among the happy and praised. Therefore it is those who followed the religion of Moses, Christ, and Abraham, and those like them, whom God praised in this verse.

But the People of the Book after the abrogation and corruption of their religion were not among those who put faith in God, the Last Day, and good works—as God has said (9:29). As we have stated previously, God declared in more than one place that those who changed the religion of Moses and Christ and rejected Christ or Muhammad were unbelievers. Those verses are clear, the texts are many, and this is successively transmitted, and known by necessity from the religion of Muhammad.

These Christians follow the Qur'an like they follow the Torah and the Gospel. They ignore clear, evident, straightforward, unambiguous texts for which there is no possibility of more than one meaning, and they cling to the uncertain ambiguous ones, even though there be in them that what shows itself contrary to their intent. This God has spoken about them and those like them (3:7).

———

> They say: Why do you bring this opinion which is unworthy of any intelligent person that we neglect the Holy Spirit and the Word of God who are witnessed to in this Book [the Qur'an] with glorious praises? It says concerning the Word of God: "There is not one of the People of the Book but will believe in him before his death, and on the Day of Resurrection he will be a witness against them."[10]

The answer: God did not send Muhammad to disregard what Christ had truly prescribed. Rather, He commanded him to put faith in what Christ brought, just as He commanded faith in Moses and what he brought. Muhammad commanded the disregard of what had been innovated in religion which was not commanded by God by way of the teaching of Christ, as well as what God abrogated of the Law by the speech of Muhammad. He disregarded what was corrupted and that which was abrogated. In the same way God commanded Christ to disregard what the Jews had innovated in religion which He had not commanded, and what He abrogated of the Law of Moses.

Similarly, He commanded Christ to disregard what was corrupted and abrogated in the Torah which Moses brought, but in that there was no disregard for what was truly enjoined by the Torah and Moses. So also when Muhammad disregarded what was corrupted and abrogated from the religion of the people of the Gospel, there was not in that any disregard for what was truly enjoined by the Gospel and Christ. What Muhammad brought included faith in all the books and prophets, rather, and we do not distinguish between any of them, and we are submitting to Him (2:136).

Christians are like Jews in accepting some while rejecting others. Which is more suitable for intelligent people—that we place faith in all the books and prophets of God, or that we believe only in some and reject others? Which is more worthy of those who have understanding—that we worship God alone, allowing nothing as a partner to Him, and serving Him as He commanded by the message of His prophets, or that we invent idolatrous and innovated forms of worship which were not revealed by God in any book nor brought by any prophet? We would thereby resemble the idolaters who are worshipers of graven images (9:30; 3:64).

Muslims have not ignored the Holy Spirit and the word of God. Concerning the latter, God has said:

> There is not one of the People of the Book but will believe in him before his death (4:159).

This refers to those who followed Christ's faith and that of the messengers before him. The faith of all prophets is one, as is shown in a statement of the prophet preserved among the sound hadith reports: "O assembly of prophets, our faith is one." God also informed us of this in the Qur'an (42:13).

The faith (*din*)[11] of all the messengers is the same faith, but their legal system and their methods vary, just as the law of the one messenger may vary.[12] The faith of Christ is the faith of Moses, which is the faith of Abraham before them and the faith of Muhammad after them, even though Christ had followed the Law of the Torah. God abrogated some of it through the teaching of Christ. Nevertheless both before and after the abrogation [of the *shari'a* of Moses], Christ's faith was that of Moses, and Christ did not disregard the faith of Moses.

Similarly, Muslims are those who follow the religion of Christ, Moses, Abraham, and the rest of the messengers; they are those who follow Christ, and so God has placed them above the Christians until the Day of Resurrection. Christians are those who changed the religion of Christ and rejected Muhammad. In doing so they are quit of the faith of Christ. Christ is innocent of what they do, just as Moses is innocent of those who changed and corrupted his religion and rejected Christ.

Muslims glorify Christ better and follow him more truly than those Christians who corrupted and opposed his religion. Muslims confirm him in all which he himself brought. They have not altered what he said out of context, nor have they explained his teaching and that of the other prophets contrary to his intent, as Christians have done.

———

> They state: Muhammad was commanded in the Fatiha to seek guidance towards the Straight Path, the path of those on whom God's favor rests, not that of those who have incurred His anger, nor that of the wayward. He meant by that the three communities which existed in his time: those whom God favored, those who incurred His wrath, and those who were astray. This must be the Christians, the Jews, and the idolaters, for there were no other groups in his time.
>
> Those whom God favored are the Christians; those who incurred His wrath are undoubtedly the Jews, for God's wrath was enkindled against them in the Torah, the Prophets, and in this Book [the Qur'an]; the wayward are the idol worshipers who went astray from God. This matter is clear and its proof obvious to all men, especially those with intelligence and knowledge. "*Al-Sirat*" means the way, the road. This is a Latin word, for the word for "road" in Latin is *istrat.*[13]

The answer: Their saying that the Christians are those on whom God's favor rests is remarkable for showing the extent of the ignorance of their spokesman. What is even more amazing is their statement that this is something clearly proven among all people, especially those possessing intelligence and learning. God be praised! No one with either general or specific knowledge about the religion of Muhammad and that of his community can dispute what they received from him by way of declaring Christians unbelieving, ignorant, and wayward, permitting *jihad* against them, taking their women prisoners, and seizing their wealth. All this completely contradicts the possibility that Muhammad and his community could say in every prayer "O God, guide us along the path of the Christians." Could Muhammad and his community refer to them in every prayer to ask God to guide them along the path of the Christians without his being the greatest of liars and the most deceitful, impudent, ignorant, and wayward of men? If they were asking God to guide them along the path of Christians, they would have entered the Christians' religion, and not have declared them unbelievers and fought against them, and imposed the *jizya* which they levied upon them after they had been brought low. They bore witness that they were among the people of the Fire. Muhammad's community received all of this from him by successive transmission. They [Christians] agree that they have not innovated this, as the Christians have innovated so many beliefs and practices which God had not permitted them. Muslims have not been half-hearted in their following the clear proofs and guidance which their messenger brought them.

If Muhammad was a true prophet, [it is clear that] he declared himself quit of them and their religion (5:72-73; 9:30-31). If he was false, then nothing which he handed on from God can be accepted.

If some Christian should claim despite these statements: "Did not God command Muslims to say in every prayer, 'Guide us along their path'?" they should be challenged to show what in the verse indicates that by God's saying "the path of those on whom His favor rests" He refers to Christians. Rather those whom He has favored are those about whom God stated:

> Whoever obeys God and the Messenger, they are with those to whom God has shown favor, of the Prophets and the saints and the martyrs and the righteous. The best of company are they! (4:69).

These are those from whom God commanded His servants to seek guidance along their path.

The Christians who followed the religion of Christ before its abrogation and replacement are among those whom God has favored, just as were the Jews who followed the religion of Moses before its abrogation and replacement are among the wayward before God and his prophet, not those on whom His favor rests (5:77; 19:38).

The idol worshipers are among the wayward who have incurred God's wrath. The prophet has said:

> The Jews are those who have incurred His wrath, and the Christians are wayward,

as is related by Ibn Hanbal and Al-Tirmidhi from 'Adi ibn Hatim from the prophet.

Al-Tirmidhi said that this is a sound hadith, and the reason for the prophet's saying it is that the Jews knew the truth but did not act according to it, while the Christians were worshiping without knowledge. God described the Jews by some of their acts and Christians by others. He described the Jews as proud, stingy, cowardly, hard-hearted, suppressors of knowledge, and spreaders of error. They follow the path of enmity and their own desires. About the Christians he mentions their exaggeration and innovation in worship, their *shirk*, error, and permission of what He has forbidden (4:171-73).

> But monasticism they invented—We ordained it not for them—only seeking God's pleasure, and they observed it not with right observance (57:27).

That is, "We have ordained that they seek God's pleasure," not "We have ordained monasticism for them." Rather "they innovated it; and along with their inventing it they did not observe it properly." All innovation is error. They are censured for innovating monasticism and for not observing it properly.

As for what God prescribed for them about seeking His pleasure, that is achieved by acting according to what God has commanded them as necessary and commendable. If an act is such, God is pleased with it. Whoever does that which pleases God has performed what was ordained for him. The pleasure of God is also achieved simply by performing obligations, and this is what was ordained for God's servants. If they are only commanded to seek the pleasure of God, then seeking God's pleasure is a necessity. Thus, whatever is not obligatory cannot be a condition for achieving what was ordained for people.

Ibn Hanbal and others often mentioned a hadith saying:

> At the first moment is the pleasure of God, at the last His pardon.

Whoever prays by the end of the prescribed prayer time has fulfilled his obligation and God is pleased with him. He who performs what is commendable and has sought to be first in obedience is more deserving of God's pleasure, and thereby achieves God's love and pleasure beyond what was obtained by simply performing obligations.

Moses said, "I have hurried to you, Lord, that you may be pleased with me." In a sound hadith related by Al-Bukhari and others from Abu Hurayra from the Prophet, he says:

> God says: Whoever treats My friend as an enemy has engaged Me in battle; for whenever one of My servants has drawn near Me by performing what was incumbent upon him, and then approaches still nearer by works of supererogation, I love him. When I love him I will be his hearing with which he hears, his sight with which he sees, his hand with which he hits, and his leg with which he walks. In Me he sees, in Me he strikes, in Me he walks. When he asks I will give. When he takes refuge in Me I will shelter him. I have not hesitated to do anything I might do, like my hesitation to take the spirit of My believing servant. He dislikes death, and I dislike hurting him, but there is no escape for him.

By God's saying "so that I love him" is meant absolute, complete love. As for the origin of that love, it is achieved by the accomplishment of obligations, for God loves those who fear Him and act justly.

God informed the Christians (9:30-31; 5:77) that they depended in their religion on what their leaders say; it is these who laid down for them their practices and laws. They made it possible for their leaders who became great in religion to construct a new Law for them, and to abrogate some of what they held before that. They do not refer back to God and His messengers for an answer to their disputes, for God's messengers do not allow anyone to depart from the revealed Books of God like the Torah and the Gospel, or from following what Christ and the prophets before him brought. God said:

> Say: O People of the Book! You have nothing [of guidance] until you observe the Torah and the Gospel and that which was revealed to you from your Lord (5:68).

Some of the religious practices and the sacred laws which their leaders laid down for them are transmitted from the prophets, some from the apostles, while many are not the result of transmission at all, neither from prophets nor apostles, but from the invention and prescription of their leaders. They invented for them the creed which is the basis of their faith, prayer to the east, and the permissibility of pork and other forbidden things. They innovated the season of fasting in spring and made it fifty days. They invented for them their feasts, such as that of the Holy Cross.

When 'Adi ibn Hatim heard the Prophet reciting the verse "They have taken as lords besides God their rabbis and their monks" (9:30) he said "They don't worship them." The Prophet answered him: "They make what is permitted *haram* for them, and what is forbidden *halal*. Thus is their worship of them."

The Christians follow the whims of their great men who went before them. These latter were astray and led those who followed them off the path (5:77). There are many, but they strayed from the path which is the central path, the *sirat al-mustaqim*. If Christians had been following those who strayed from the Straight Path, how could God have commanded His servants to be guided along that Straight Path if it is the path of those who are errant followers of false guides, wayward from the path which is *al-sirat al-mustaqim*?

God said: "Do not follow their whims" (5:77). The source of their innovation of this heresy came from their own eagerness for an opinion that was false (53:23). God said:

> And who goes farther astray than he who follows his own lust without guidance from God? (28:50)

Because of that, after Christ ascended to heaven, when the Jews acted in great enmity towards him and his followers, by going to excess in injuring and degrading them and seeking to hinder and kill them, there grew in their hearts a hatred for the Jews and an indescribable desire to avenge themselves on them. When the state and authority fell to them as it did in the time of Constantine, they began to want to oppose the Jews. This is similar to the enmity which occurs in any opposing groups struggling for power or disputing over innovation—like the Khawarij and the Shi'a, the Compulsorists against the proponents of free will, the transcendentalists against the representationists, or like two states competing for power or various goals at the level of prosperity, fairness, and the like.

If one group overcomes the other after the first have oppressed it, it feels vindictive towards the first group and wants to take its vengeance upon them. It does not stop at the limits of justice, but oversteps its bounds as the other group has done against it. In the same way, the Christians began to want to contradict the Jews, and so they permitted what the Jews had forbidden, such as pork. They began to test those who entered their religion by eating pork; if and only if one ate it was he a Christian.

They omitted circumcision and claimed that baptism substituted it. They prayed in a direction different from that of the Jews. Because the Jews had slandered Christ and claimed that he was the child of fornication and a lying magician, the Christians went to extremes to extol him and claimed that he was the son of God and suchlike. When a large number of their theologians and believers wanted to express a moderate view about Christ, they all gathered in a council in which the moderates were cursed by the extremist party—the followers of their own desires, those who go to extremes about the one they extol.

In this we see a case similar to those people who follow their own whims among the extremist followers of one of the holy men, a member of the family of the prophet, some scholar, one of the kings, tribes, *madhhabs*, or Sufi *tariqas*. The basis of the error of these people is nothing but their own whims. It is for this that God criticized the Christians living in the time of the prophet (5:77).

They say that *al-sirat* means "The Path," that is "the road," and that this is a "Roman" word because the word in Roman is *istrat.*[14] It should be said to them that in Arabic *al-sirat* means "the Path." It is "the clear Path." It is the path bounded on two sides from which one does not depart, and outside it is the path leading to Hell. It is the bridge on which the believers cross to the Garden, and if unbelievers cross over it, they fall off into Hell. It carries the meaning of levelness and straightness which is necessary for fast travel on it.

*Al-sirat* means the straight fixed path which conducts the traveller speedily to what he desires. God has mentioned the word *al-sirat* in more than one place in His Book. He did not call the paths of Satan *al-sirat* but called them *subul* "paths." He specified His way by the term *al-sirat*, as in His saying:

> This is My straight Path (*al-sirat*), so follow it. Follow not other ways (*subul*), lest you be parted from His way (*sabilihi*) (6:153).

In the *Sunan* from 'Abd Allah ibn Mas'ud he said:

> The Messenger of God drew a line for us on the ground, and drew other lines to the right and left of it. Then he said: This is the path of God and all these others are paths to which Satan invites [people]. Whoever responds he casts into the Fire. Then he recited this verse (6:153).

God called His way *al-sirat*, but He called those others *subul*. He did not call them *sirat* as He called them *sabil*, but His own way he called *sabil*, just as He called it *sirat* (37:117-18; 48:1-2; 17:9).

# III. TRINITARIAN QUESTIONS

## A. PHILOSOPHICAL EXPLANATION OF TRINITY

Paul of Antioch: They reject our belief in the Father, the son, and the Holy Spirit, as well as our view that they are the three hypostases, and that Christ is the Lord, God, and Creator. They ask us to clarify "incarnation"—the creative Word of God taking flesh in a created man. If they really understood that by this belief of ours we mean that God is some thing living and speaking, then they would not reject our holding it.

We, O Christians, when we see things coming into being in time, know that something not created in time has brought them into being, since their temporal creation from their own essences involves a contradiction. We see that created things are divided into two groups: living and non-living things. In reference to these two classes we describe Him as a living thing in order to deny any death to Him. We see living things divided into two groups: speaking and non-speaking living things. We describe Him by the higher of the two categories, and say that He is a thing living and speaking in order to deny any ignorance in Him. The three names thus signify that the one God who is called one Lord and one Creator is a living, speaking thing—that is, essence, speech, and life. The essence we hold to be the Father who is the source of the other two. The speech is the Son who is born from the Father in the manner of the birth of speech from the intellect. The life is the Holy Spirit. These names we have not invented on our own part.[1]

We will answer this in several ways.

1) They claim, "If the Muslims knew that by our saying Father, Son, and Holy Spirit we only mean by this to affirm the view that God is living and speaking, they would not reject our belief." But the matter is not as they have claimed, for Christians hold that they have received this belief from the Gospel, and that in the Gospel Christ said "Baptise in the name of the Father and the Son and the Holy Spirit." The origin of their belief is what they claim to have been received from revealed religion, not that they have proved the life and speech of God which they then assert by these expressions. But this is what they have claimed in their argumentation.

Even were the matter as they have said, they would not have needed to use these expressions, nor would they have had to make the hypostases three. It is well known among them, as among people of other religions, that God is existing, living, knowing, acting, speaking. Three attributes of His are not singled out,[2] nor are three of His attributes ever referred to by an expression which [does not] indicate that. In the expression "the Father, the Son, and the Holy Spirit" these terms do not indicate what they describe by them in the language of a follower of any of the religions, nor is it found in the message of any one of the prophets that he asserted by these terms what they have claimed to be their meanings, by use of which they have even tried to prove what they have claimed concerning the trinity and its formulation. This expression is something which they have invented for which there is no proof, neither religious nor rational.

They claim that they only arrived at belief in the trinity, the divine indwelling, and hypostatic union from the viewpoint of religion—the texts of the prophets and the revealed books and not on the authority of reason. Then they affect a rational method for what they think is indicated by the books, and bring it to bear on what they think to be a possible explanation in reason. Thus we find the Christians only have recourse to religion and the books for their views on the trinity and divine union, and divine indwelling. The natural disposition according to which God created people, and the intellectual knowledge placed in the hearts of men which may be called a natural intellectual spirit opposes such ideas; it denies them and is adverse to them. But they claim that the divine Books have revealed these views and that they constitute a matter beyond reason. They hold this belief to be of a degree beyond that of the intellect.

They report that the sacred books, according to their thinking, have delivered these views, not that rational argumentation has indicated them. This is in spite of the fact that there is nothing in the divine Books which indicates such things; rather they contain what proves their contrary, as we will show, God willing. They do not distinguish between what the mind imagines and proves false and knows to be impossible and that which the mind is unable to conceive since it knows nothing about it, and has no information on it either by affirmation or denial. The prophets have informed mankind about the second of these. It is not possible for the first type of information to have been reported. The Christians do not differentiate between the absurdities of reason and its pearls. In this they resemble the idolaters who preceded them who made a child and helpmate for God (9:30).

The innovators and the wayward among those who associate themselves with Islam resemble the Christians in this matter and can be likened to them. These are people who hold a view like that of the Christians which exaggerates concerning the prophets, people of the family of the Prophet, shaykhs, and others.[3] Whoever claims pantheism and divine indwelling, or a specified particular divine union like that held by the Christians is in this category—thus the view of Shi'i extremists on 'Ali and that of a sect concerning the family of the Prophet like the Nusayris and those like them who claim divinity for 'Ali, like the claim of some Isma'ilis of divinity for Al-Hakim or another of the Fatimids who affiliate themselves with Muhammad ibn Isma'il ibn Ja'far.

The belief of many people is like that for some of the shaykhs, who are either well known for goodness or thought to possess goodness but actually do not. The views of all these people are of the same kind as those of the Christians, and some of them are worse than those of Christians.

Most of these people when presented with an argument showing the falseness of their opinion say something like the statement of the Christians, that this is a matter beyond reason. Some of them say what Al-Tilimsani, the shaykh of the people of pantheism (*al-wahda*) used to say: "Among us there is proven by insight (*al-kashf*) what contradicts sound reason." They say to those who want to follow their path: "Leave behind reason and revelation." Or "Depart from reason and revelation." It is they about whom it is written:

> They are mad, but the secret of their madness
> Is dear to his feet whose mind has bowed.
> They are those who have untied their system and deflected the shield,
> No obligation in their faith nor true tradition.

These people are merely imitating their *shaykhs*, following them in that by which they have departed from the religion of the prophet and in what they have innovated without God's permission by undertaking the innovation of religious practices and the permission of what is forbidden, just as some Christians blindly imitate their teachers. If anyone opposes them on any of these practices they say, "The shaykh accepts it," and they do not oppose him, just as the Christians say about their teachers. Some of these people say, "We are the children of God," and that the shaykh is the son of God. They use the term "desire" (*al-shahwa*) and say that they are the children of God's desire, and say that God is the husband of Mary, as some Christians hold.[4]

The extent of their evidence is what they tell about their shaykhs concerning a kind of miraculous event which may be false or may be true. If it is true, it may be of the type of act performed by the friends of Satan like magicians and sorcerers. It may be of the type of deed done by the friends of God. Even then there is nothing in that which necessitates the blind imitation of this friend to be inerrant, there is no need to follow him in everything he says.

It is one of the special characteristics of the prophets that we must put faith in all that they say, that we must believe in all that they report of the unseen, and that we must obey [the commands] they have made obligatory upon the communities. Whoever disbelieves in a thing of what they reported is a disbeliever. Whoever defames a single prophet must be killed. None of these characteristics apply to the holy men who are not prophets.

These extremist idolatrous innovators who hold for a kind of divine indwelling resemble the Christians in that by which they have opposed the religion of Islam. Some of them may be more in agreement with the religion of Islam, while the extremists among them are more in agreement with the Christians. Some of them are more unbelieving than the Christians.

The cause of the Christians' error was in what they had handed down, whether from the prophets or from others who obliged them to follow them. When they would bring before their scholars something which needed to be prohibited, their scholars told them that such a thing was in the book, that the books spoke about this, and that these books were brought by the apostles (*al-rusul*)—they meant those supported by miracles. By *al-rusul* they meant the apostles (*al-hawariyyin*), for their attribution of inerrancy to them was only according to what they supposed was mentioned in the divine books, even though they could see that it was opposed to sound reason.

They prevented the majority of their people from investigating and discussing those matters because of their knowledge that sound reason when it viewed their religion would know that it was false. Thus the claim of someone who says, "We only speak of Father, Son, and Holy Spirit to certify that God is living and speaking" is an evident falsehood. They know that he is lying, and that to assert the belief that God is living and speaking one does not need to seize upon this expression, but it is possible to assert that by religious and rational proofs and express it with clear formulations as do Muslims and others without saying "Father, Son, and Holy Spirit."

2) The Christians who claim that this formulation in the Gospel was taken from Christ differ in explaining this statement. Many of them hold the Father to be existence, the son the Word, and the Holy Spirit life. Others say, rather, that the Father is existence, the son the Word, and the Holy Spirit is power. Still others speak of divine Goodness, the Judge, and the all-Powerful. They identify the Father with Goodness, the Son is the Judge, and the Holy Spirit is

the all-Powerful. They allege all the attributes of God to be included under these three. They state: "We have drawn our conclusions regarding His existence from His bringing things out of nothingness into existence; this occurred from His generosity."

I have seen each of these positions expressed in the books of the Christians.[5] Some of them designate the Word as knowledge. They hold for the Existing, the Living, the Knowing, or the Existing, the Knowing, the Powerful. Similarly some of them hold for the Speaker. Others affirm the Existing, the Living, the Judge, while still others the Self-subsisting, the Living, the Judge.

They agree that what united with Christ and dwelled in him was the hypostasis of the Word; it is what they call the son without the Father. There are those among them who deny divine indwelling and the hypostatic union, such as the Arians. Arius said that Christ was a servant of God sent by Him, like the rest of the messengers. In agreeing with the others on the expression "the Father, the son, and the Holy Spirit" he did not explain it according to what the controversialists held about *hulul* and *ittihad*. Similarly the Nestorians agree with them on this formulation, and dispute with the Jacobites and Melkites on the belief in the hypostatic union held by the latter groups. Since Christians have been agreeing on the term (*al-lafz*) while disputing about its meaning, one knows that they first confirmed the term because of their belief that it was brought through revelation, after which they disputed about its explanation.

In a similar way, they and the rest of the people of the [three] religions differ on the explanation of some of the message which they believe to have been handed down by the prophets. From this it is known that the origin of their holding "the Father, the Son, and the Holy Spirit" was not to assert the position that God was existing, living, and speaking which they had already known by reason.

3) They state, "When we see the creation of things in time we know that something other than them has brought them into being." If their spokesman is representing a specific group of Christians, it should be said to them that the belief in the Father, the son, and the Holy Spirit existed among Christians before that particular group existed and before their observing this phenomenon or drawing conclusions from it. It can therefore not be possible that their observation of this is what determines the position of Christians on this matter. If what is meant by this statement is that all Christians from the time when they affirmed this expression observed this and deduced from it that they should hold this, it is an evident falsehood. Christians allege that they received it from the Gospel

when Christ said "Baptize in the name of the Father, and the son, and the Holy Spirit."

Christ and the apostles never commanded them this observation by which [they claim] their view is determined, nor did Christ make this expression among them dependent upon this investigation. It is clear that their making this expression stem from this investigation is a false statement and they know it to be false.

4) This statement, unless it was made by Christ, cannot be held. Moreover even if some individual intended a true meaning by it, nevertheless this expression is only understood by the application of false meanings. Many of the masses of Christians believe that Christ is the son of God according to the sonship known among creatures. They say that Mary is the wife of God. Even if they do not state this, it is a consequent for the generality of Christians, for he who gives birth must have a spouse (6:102).

Making the Lord give birth to something is more repugnant to reason than claiming a spouse for Him, whether that begetting is explained as the well-known begetting or as an intellectual production like Christian scholars hold. It is possible for those who claim a spouse for God to interpret it as those others interpret begetting. They claim that from the Father was born the Word, and from Mary was born the human nature. The human nature united with the divine nature. Just as the Father is the father of the divine nature but not the human and Mary the mother of the human nature but not the divine, she becomes the spouse of the Father by Christ's human nature. Similarly, God would be the husband of Mary by Christ's divine nature as He is the Father of Christ by the same divine nature.

If the divine nature united with the human nature of Christ for a long time, what should prevent Him from having united with the human nature of Mary for a brief period? If the human nature to which Mary gave birth is made a son of the Divinity, for what reason is she not considered a spouse and wife of the Divinity? According to them Christ is the name for the conjunction of the divine and human natures. Among them he is fully God and fully man. His divine nature is from God and his human nature is from Mary. He is thus two principles—divine and human. Therefore if one of these two principles is his father and the other is his mother, why does his mother not become the wife of his father according to this formulation, in addition to the fact that this conjugality would have preceded his prophethood? How can the necessary conclusion be proven without the necessitating principle?

There is nothing in this which is absurd according to their starting point except their trying to base it on the prophetic message of Christ. It is even less impossible [than the latter.] We know that

Christ and the other prophets were inerrant and never said anything but the Truth. Therefore if Christ actually made that statement, there is no doubt that it must have a correct meaning.

It is impossible that the prophets in their teaching intended a statement whose falsity is clear by revelation and reason. Therefore, since the prophetic teachings were reasonable and the texts of the earlier sacred books as well as the Qur'an contradict what the Christians innovated about Christ, it can be known that Christ never intended a false meaning contrary to sound reason and truly revealed teaching.

5) If it is true that this expression truly comes from Christ who is inerrant, what he meant by it must correspond to the rest of his teaching. It is found in their books that he called the Lord a father and that he called His servants sons. Similarly, they state that God said in the Torah to Jacob Israel "You are my first-born son." In the Psalms God said to David "You are my son and My beloved." In the Gospel in more than one place Christ says "My Father and your Father," as when he says "I am going to My Father and your Father, to my God and your God."

He calls God a father to them just as he calls them sons of God. If this is correct, then what he meant is that God is the merciful sustainer. God is more merciful to His servants than a mother to her child. The son is the one reared, the subject of mercy, for God's rearing His servant is more perfect than a mother's rearing of her child. Thus what is meant by "father" is the Lord, and what is meant by "son" in Christ's teaching is Christ whom God rears.

As for the Holy Spirit, this expression is found in more than one place in the books which they possess, and by their own agreement it never means the life of God. Rather, among them the Holy Spirit takes up residence in Abraham, Moses, David, and others of the prophets and holy persons. The Qur'an has borne witness that God supported Christ with the Holy Spirit (2:87; 2:253; 5:110). The Prophet spoke similarly to Hassan ibn Thabit, "The Holy Spirit is with you as long as you defend his prophet." He also said, "God has supported him with the Holy Spirit." All of this has been previously elaborated.

By the Holy Spirit may be meant the holy angel such as Jibril, or it may mean the revelation, guidance, and support which God sends down either by mediation of the angel or without it. The two notions may be mutually connected, for the angel sends down the revelation, and with the revelation descends the angel. God supports His messengers with angels and with guidance, as God stated concerning His prophet Muhammad (9:26,40; 33:9; 8:12; 58:22; 16:2; 40:15; 42:52).

Therefore, if it is known from the teaching of the earlier and later prophets that God caused the Holy Spirit to descend upon His prophets and the holy ones of His people, whether it was the angels descending with revelation and victory, or revelation and support with or without the angel, then what is *not* meant by the Holy Spirit is that it is the life of God subsisting in Him. The meaning of "Baptize people in the name of the Father, the son, and the Holy Spirit" is that they command people to believe in God and His prophet which God sent and in the angel by which God sent down the revelation which he brought. That would be a command for them to believe in God and His angels, books, and messengers. This is the truth to which sound reason and correct religion give evidence.

This explanation of the inerrant speech is the explanation which agrees with the rest of the passages of the books which they have, and agrees with the Qur'an and with reason; it is superior to that exegesis which opposes sound reason and true religion. This explanation is the evident one. It is not a strained application, nor is there in it any *ta'wil*—allegorical interpretation—which turns the message away from its evident meaning to one which opposes that evident meaning. It is instead an explanation whose evident meaning is indicated by the commonly accepted language and the usual expression in the speech of Christ and the rest of the prophets.

The Christian exegesis that the son is eternally begotten of God and the knowledge or the word of God is an explanation in terminology which is not used in the teaching of any one of the prophets nor in the wording of a single prophet. Their explanation of the Holy Spirit as the life of God is like this also, for what the Christians interpret as the obvious teaching of Christ is an explanation not indicated by the language of Christ and his custom in speaking, nor by the language of any one of the rest of the prophets. Rather, what is known from his language and speech and that of the rest of the prophets is the exegesis which we have given and that made by the great scholars of the Christians. The error of the Christians who have corrupted the true meanings of the Books of God is that they have interpreted them according to what opposes their evident meaning and through what is rejected by reason and religion.

6) When in their books the Christians are faced with their calling Christ a son and calling other prophets a son—as God's saying to Jacob "You are my first-born son" and calling the apostles sons—they say that Christ is a son by nature and others are sons by adoption. They make the word "father" an equivocal term. They posit a nature for God and make Christ His son by expression of that nature. This is attested by the view of those among them who

understand Christ to be God's son by the sonship known to creatures and Mary as the spouse of God. In the same way they make the Holy Spirit a term which carries both the meaning of the life of God and the Holy Spirit which descends upon the prophets and holy persons.

It is well known that equivocation is contrary to the root meaning of a word, so that when a word is used in various places, someone who makes its true meaning consistent by carrying the same value each place is preferable to one who makes it verbally the same while its real meaning specifies one thing in one place and another thing in another place, or makes a metaphor of it in one of the places. Both metaphor and equivocation are contrary to the root meaning. How can it be considered, as the Christians claim, that the terms "son" and "Holy Spirit" are used to refer to the speech and life of God when it is never found in the teaching of the prophets that they used these expressions to mean any of the attributes of God—whether His speech, His life, knowledge or any other? On the contrary, the use of the term "son" in the message of the prophets is never applied except to something created. Similarly the use of the "Holy Spirit" is never found applied to an attribute of God subsisting in Him.

We have interpreted "the Father" and "the son" as the sonship of rearing, and the Holy Spirit as that which descends upon the prophets. In this we have applied these terms univocally, while they are forced to make the expression either equivocal or metaphorical in one of its meanings. Thus, their exegesis is opposed to the evident meaning of the language which they speak on one hand, and to the evident meaning of the books which they possess on the other, whereas ours is in agreement with the evident meaning of their language and the books they possess. This makes it clear that they have no argument, religious or rational, for the trinity; rather it is false on both counts.

7) In their creed they have affirmed meanings, the expressions of the divine persons, and other things, which are in no way indicated by the books which they possess. They have understood a false meaning from these books, and then have added to it other false meanings on their own part. In this they have actually corrupted the books of God and perpetrated a lie against Him. This is elaborated elsewhere.

8) The hypostases (*aqanim*) which they profess—besides the falsity of this notion from reason and revelation—are never mentioned in any sacred book among them, nor is this expression found in a single one of the books of the prophets which they possess, nor in the teaching of the apostles. Rather this is a term which

they have invented, and it is said to be "Roman."[6] It has been said that the meaning of *uqnum* in their language is original, and thus they are compelled to explain the *aqanim* sometimes as persons, sometimes specifications, attributes, or essences. At other times they make the *uqnum* a name for the essence and the attribute together, and this is the position of their most intelligent scholars.

9) Their view of Christ as creator is a view which besides being false by revelation and reason is never mentioned in any of the prophecies which they possess. They try to prove it by producing arguments which do not indicate it at all, as we will show, God willing.

10) Their view of the incarnation of the divinity is also a position whose falsity is apparent from reason and revelation and not indicated by anything in the teaching of a single inerrant prophet or messenger.

11) I hold that there is no doubt that God is living, knowing, powerful, and speaking. For that Muslims have rational proofs indicated by the Messenger. He guided them to these proofs, and thus there became known by reason what was indicated by revelation. This is elaborated elsewhere. But you Christians, although you claim that by reason, you do not mention a single rational proof for it.

You state: "When we see things coming into existence, we know that something other than them has brought them into existence, since it is not possible that they come into existence from themselves, for there is contradiction and fluctuation in them." This is a weak position from various aspects:

a) You have not seen the coming into existence of all created things, but you have only seen those things whose creation in time may be mentioned, such as clouds, rain, animals, plants, and the like. Where is your proof for the rest of things?[7]

b) You should have said, "when the coming into existence of temporal things is known, or the creation in time of created things, or the creation in time of all that is other than God" or something like that which makes it clear that what comes into being in time is everything other than God. To affirm absolutely the coming into existence in time of *all* things is false, for according to you and the majority of Muslims, God is called a thing. This is in contrast to God's saying "God is the creator of every thing" (13:16). This construction makes it clear that the creator is other than the creature, in contrast to the view of one who speaks of the creation of all things in time.

c) Knowledge about something created in time demands knowledge of One who brings into being, that is, knowledge of a necessary creator. God said in the Qur'an "Or were they created out of nought? Or are they the creators?" (52:35).

The creation by which God created His servants is known by sound reason, that is, that whatever comes into being only does so by one who brings it into being. The falsity of some creature's coming into being without a creator bringing it into being is evident from the necessity of reason. This is a matter firmly embedded in every person, even in children. If a child is hit, he asks, "Who hit me?" If it is said, "No one hit you," his mind does not believe that a blow could not occur without an agent.

Thus, if someone were to declare it possible that writing, weaving, planting, and the like could occur without someone performing those acts, among intelligent people he would be considered either crazy or a sophist like those who deny necessary forms of science and knowledge. It is certain that no one brings himself into existence, for if he were non-existent before his coming into existence, he was nothing, and thus it would be impossible that he bring anything else into existence much less that he bring himself to exist.

The Christian's explanation that the coming into being of things in time could not be from themselves, since there is contradiction and fluctuation in them, is a false explanation. We know that their creation in time is not from themselves, not because there is contradiction and fluctuation in them, but whether they are identical, different, or contradictory, we know by sound reason that what comes into being in time does not do this by itself. This is one of the most evident propositions known and the clearest to reason, just as it is known that what is non-existent does not create what exists, and that the bringer into existence of created things cannot be non-existent.

d) You have stated a proof, although it is a weak one, for things not bringing themselves into existence, but you have not presented an argument against their coming into existence without any creator, either themselves or something else. If the impossibility of their being brought into existence by themselves demands a proof, in the same way does the impossibility of their coming into existence with no creator. As the first of these is known by the immediate perception of the mind and is one of the things known by necessity, the second is known the same way. Mentioning the first of these propositions without the second would have been an error had you been stating a correct proof, so what is it when your argument is false? Is this the extent of their knowledge of intellectual argumentation by which they try to establish knowledge of the Maker and His attributes? In spite of this they want to demonstrate rational meanings, and claim that they are in agreement with their false understanding of the divine books. They are those about whom God spoke in the Qur'an (24:39-40).

12) They state, "We have said that God is a thing not like created things, since He is creator of everything, in order to deny any lack in Him." It must be said to them that God is as He described Himself in the Qur'an (42:11; 19:65; 112). Reason itself has indicated that [there is nothing comparable to Him], for in the case of two similar things whatever is correct for one is correct for the other. What is necessary for one is necessary for the other, what is forbidden for one is forbidden for the other, what is possible for one is possible for the other. Were there something similar to the creator, it would necessarily follow that they would share in what was necessary, possible, and forbidden.

It is necessary for the creator that He have existence and eternity, and it is forbidden that there be any lack in Him. Thus it would be necessary for the creature [which is like God] to be necessarily existing, eternally without any beginning whatsoever. His being created and coming into being in time necessitates that he had been non-existent, and thus it follows that he be existent and non-existent, eternal and coming into being in time, and this is a joining together of what is mutually incompatible, and forbidden by the first operations of the intelligence.

Moreover his being a creature forbids his being eternal and necessitates that he previously be non-existent. If what is necessary for him were necessary for the eternal creator, it would be necessary for the necessarily eternal to be also necessarily coming into existence in time by the lack of his non-existence, and this is a joining of contradictories. Sound reason categorically demands that there is nothing like God. The elaboration of this is found elsewhere, but the point is that you have not mentioned this argument for His being creator of everything, since you depend on those things whose temporal creation you witnessed, and that is not each thing that exists. Besides His being creator of all things you have not mentioned the proof that there is nothing like him. Even if your proof for our knowledge of the Maker were sound it would only prove that He is a Creator, so what is it worth when it proves not even that?

## B. THE DIVINE HYPOSTASES

The Christians state: The three names are one God, one Lord, one creator, called one from eternity to eternity, one living speaking thing—that is, essence, word, life. We hold the essence to be the Father, who is the origin of the other two. The word is the son who is born from Him as the birth of speech from the mind. The life is the Holy Spirit.

The answer to this is from various aspects.

1) The names of God are extremely numerous, as God tells us in the Qur'an (59:22-24; 7:180; 17:110; 20-1-8). In one of the sound hadith reports from the Prophet, he says:

> God has 99 names; whoever counts them will enter the Garden.

The meaning of this according to the more widespread and correct view of the scholars is that of God's names there are ninety-nine; that person and only that person who counts them will enter the Garden.

However, God's names are more than that, as the prophet said in another report recounted by Ibn Hanbal in his *Musnad* and Abu Hatim in his sound hadith from Ibn Mas'ud from the Prophet.

> No care or sadness ever befell a servant who says: "O God, I am Your servant, the son of Your servant, the child of Your community. My forelock is in Your hand, the past in Your wisdom, justice in Your judgment. I have called upon You by every name by which You have called Yourself, or You have revealed in Your book, or You have taught to one of Your people, or You have taken to Yourself in Your knowledge of the unseen, so that You make the Qur'an the springtime of my heart, the light of my breast, the banishment of my sorrow, the passing away of my worry and care," so that God makes his worry and care depart and replaces it with joy. They said, "O messenger of God, should we not learn them" [the names]? He said, "Certainly, the one who hears them should learn them."

Since the names of God are many, such as the Loving, the Powerful, and others, to limit them to three without the others is wrong, as we have explained elsewhere.

2) Their calling the Father the one who is the origin of the other two, and the son the Word which is born from Him as the birth of speech from the mind is a false statement. The attributes of perfection necessarily follow upon the essence of the Lord from the beginning to the end. From eternity to eternity He is living, knowing, acting. He did not become living after He had not been, nor knowing after He had been unknowing. If they say that the Father who is the essence is the origin of life and speech, that demands that the Father exist before life and speech, for that which is the origin of something other than it is precedent to it or its maker. This is false in the case of God.

In the same way, their statement that the Logos (*al-Nutq*) is born from the Father like the birth of speech from the mind is false. Something born from something else takes its existence from it, and thus comes into being in time after it was not, and so the Logos would come into existence gradually, whether by "Logos" were meant knowledge or expression. Neither of these follow necessarily from a soul endowed with speech, but comes into existence in it, and the soul is described by them after it was not, although it had been receptive for the power of speech—in potency for it. Therefore if they represent their spokesman's view that the Word is from the Lord like the production of speech from the mind, it necessarily follows that the Lord was potentially capable of speech, and then became speaking in act. It meant that He became cognizant after He was unknowing. This is one of the greatest forms of unbelief, and the most impossible. It is nothing other than making God be described by attributes of perfection after He had not been described by them. Since everything other than God was created by Him, and finds its perfection in Him, it is impossible for anything to be that which makes the Lord complete.

This is a vicious circle against sound reason. It is a case of a thing not making another thing described by attributes of perfection until it itself is so described by the other. If it is not described by these attributes until it makes something else described by them, a vicious circle follows similar to that of each of two things being an actor upon the other, its cause, or [the cause] of some of its attributes which are conditional on its act. It is clear that the view of His speech being born from Him like the birth of speech from the mind is false, just as it is false that there be for His necessary attributes a basis precedent to them or previous to His actualizing them.

3) They say about the son that he is born from God. If they mean by that that he is a necessary attribute of God, the Holy Spirit would be a second son, since life is also God's necessary attribute. If they mean that he resulted from God after he had not existed, it would necessarily follow that God be knowing after He had not been. This view, prescinding from its falsity and blasphemy, also necessitates a parallel view of God's life, that is, that He became living after He had not been living.

4) Calling the life of God the Holy Spirit is a matter which is not mentioned in a single one of the revealed books of God. Their application of the notion of the Holy Spirit to the life of God is an instance of their alteration and corruption of the books.

5) They claim that it is the Word of God—His knowledge—which has united with Christ. If by this is meant the knowing,

speaking, divine essence itself, Christ is the Father. Christ is Himself the Father, the son, and the Holy Spirit; according to them and to all people this is false and blasphemous. If, however, they state that what is united with Christ is the knowledge of God, it must be answered that knowledge is an attribute not separable from the knower, nor from the other attribute which is life. It is impossible that the knowledge of God could be united with Christ without His essence or without His life.

6) Knowledge is also an attribute, and an attribute does not create or give sustenance. By agreement of their scholars, Christ is himself not an attribute subsisting in another, and yet according to them He is held to be creator of the heavens and the earth. Thus it is impossible that what is united with Him be an attribute, for the God who is worshiped is the living, knowing, acting God. He is not Himself life, nor is He Himself knowledge or speech.

Were someone to say "O life of God" or "O knowledge of God," or "O speech of God, pardon me, have mercy upon me, guide me," this would be considered contrary to sound reason. It is not permissible for a member of any of the religions to say to the Torah, the Gospel, or some other expression of the Speech of God "Pardon me!" or "Have mercy on me!" These supplications are only made to the God who speaks through this speech.

According to Christians, Christ is God, the creator to whom is said, "Pardon us, have mercy on us!" Even if Christ were himself the knowledge of God and His speech, it would not be permissible that he be the worshiped divinity. So how can it be possible when he himself is not the knowledge and speech of God, but rather is created by God's speech when He said to him "Be!" and he was?

It is clear from this that the words of God are many—infinite. In the divine books such as the Torah it is said that God created things by His speech. In the very beginning of the Torah it is written that God said "Let there be such-and-such, let there be such-and-such." It is obvious that Christ is not many words; rather, the intent of the Qur'an is that he is one word since he was created by one of the words of God.

7) The creed which the Christian's leaders drew up in the presence of Constantine, the formulation of their faith which they laid down as the basis of their religion, contradicts their claim that God is one. Evidently, what they say to their adversaries is contrary to what they actually believe.

These are matters well known in their religion—their internal contradiction and their displaying in disputation what is opposed to that which they hold as the basis of their faith. According to the agreement of all groups of Christians, their creed which they have made the basis of their religion[1] states faith in three things.

a) One God, creator of the heavens and the earth, creator of what is visible and what is invisible. This is the Lord of the Universe beside whom there is none, no Lord other than He. This is the God of Abraham, Isaac, Jacob, and the rest of the prophets and messengers. He is the One whom all the messengers called men to worship alone allowing no partner to Him, and to cease worshiping any other (21:25; 43:45).

b) Then they say: "And in one Lord Jesus Christ, the only son of God, born of the Father before all ages, light from light, true God from true God, from the substance of his Father, born not created, equal to the Father in substance." Alongside their faith in the creator of the heavens and the earth they clearly state faith in one created Lord, the unique son of God equal to the Father. They state, "He is true God from true God, from the substance of his Father."

This is a clear statement of faith in two gods, one of which is from the other—God's knowledge subsisting in Him which they call a son. No one of the messengers ever called an attribute of God a "son." He is not a "true God from true God," but rather there is one God, and this is an attribute of God; however, an attribute of God is not a God, just as God's power, hearing, sight, and the other attributes are not gods. There is one God, but His attributes are many. God is the essence which is described by attributes subsisting in Him, while an attribute subsists in that which is described. Because they call God an essence, they say He subsists in Himself.

An attribute is not a self-subsisting substance, but in this creed they have made God a begetter and this is the Father, and the one begotten and this is the son. They have made him equal to the Father in substance. Nevertheless, God declared Himself transcendent to all three kinds[2].

They say, "born not created, equal to the Father in substance." They clearly state that he is equal to Him in substance; but what is equal is not identified with that to which it is made equal. Nothing is equal to the Father in substance except a substance, and therefore it is necessary that the son[3] be a second substance. The Holy Spirit will need to be a third substance, as we shall show.

This is a clear statement establishing three substances, and three gods, and yet they say, "We hold for one substance and one God." This is a joining together of contradictories. It is a fact that their view combines making God one and proving three gods, holding for one substance and proving three gods, holding for one substance and proving three substances. God has declared Himself beyond giving birth, as when they say that He is the Father, or that He is begotten as when they say He is the son, or that there is anything like him (112).

They say that there is something equal to him in substance. If they state, "We say, 'One in essence, three in attributes,'" they should be answered that they have already clearly expressed "true God from true God," and that he is equal to the Father in substance. This is a clear statement showing a second substance, not an attribute. They have thus combined two views, proving three substances despite their claim they they are proving one substance. There is no defense for your saying, as do Yahya ibn 'Adi and others like him, that this is the same as saying "Zayd the doctor, the accountant, the writer" and then saying "Zayd the doctor," and "Zayd the accountant," and "Zayd the writer."

He holds that each of these attributes gives a definition different from that of the others, and that they may describe the hypostases in this way. The hypostasis is the essence with the attribute, and so the essence with each attribute is a hypostasis. The hypostases thereby become three, but this example does not correspond to their teaching. Zayd here is one substance having three attributes of medicine, accounting, and writing. These are not three substances here, but each attribute offers a definition which the other does not.

No intelligent person says that the attribute is equal to that which is described in the substance, nor that the essence with this attribute is equal to the essence with the other attribute in substance. The essence is one, while something equal to another is not that to which it is equal. Since the essence with its attribute is the Father, if it was this which united with Christ, then that which united with him was the Father. Therefore what they state about this in their creed demands that there be a true God equal to the Father in substance who was crucified and who suffered. Therefore the divine nature is crucified and suffering; some of their sects have approached this position while others have denied it, but what their creed demands is to accept it.

Moreover, if he was born of the Holy Spirit and of Mary, and if the Holy Spirit is the life of God as they claim, Christ would be the word of God and His life. His divine nature is thereby two of the three hypostases, while they hold that he is only the hypostasis of the Word. If the Holy Spirit is not the life of God in this instance, their explanation of him as the life of God is false.

It should be said to them that the Holy Spirit ought not to be considered either an attribute of God or a hypostasis. But you have stated in your creed that you believe in the "Holy Spirit, the Giver of life." Thus you prove a third lord. You state, "Who proceeds from the Father." Processing here means an overflowing, a pouring forth, an emanation from something. It is said, "The stream *gushed forth* from such-and-such a place." Or: He *broke* it *open* [so that its contents would pour out]. It indicates a cracking or splitting of something in the first form [of the Arabic verb], and the seventh form means a pouring forth, a springing from, or an emanating from. The term demands, therefore, that this Lord Giver of Life sprang from the Father or emanated from Him.

Then they say: "With the Father he is adored and glorified, and speaks through the prophets." They place him with the Father as worthy of worship, and thereby establish a third god who is to be worshiped. It is obvious that the life of God is an attribute of His which does not emanate from Him, but rather subsists in Him. It does not proceed out from Him in any way. It is one of God's necessary attributes, not dependent upon anything other than God. Knowledge is dependent upon knowables, power upon things which can be acted upon, and addressing (*taklim*) upon those which can be spoken to. This is in contrast to speech (*takallum*) which is a necessary attribute. One says that God knew such a thing, that God was powerful over all things, or that God addressed Moses.

The expression indicating the life of God is by necessity not dependent upon anyone other than Him who is living. People say, "May He who grants life, preserve [yours]!" They do not say "May He live you" or "live by you."[4] One can only say, "He *gives* life to such-and-such a thing." Giving life is an act different from being alive, just as imparting knowledge is not the same as knowing, empowering is not equivalent to having power to act, nor is making someone speak speaking.

They identify this Holy Spirit who speaks in the prophets with the life of God, an attribute of His which subsists in Him and has no place outside Him. However, the Holy Spirit who is in the prophets and holy persons is not the life of God subsisting in Him. If the Holy Spirit who is in the prophets were one of the three divine hypostases, every one of the prophets would be a god to be worshiped, for his humanity would have united with the divinity as they claim about Christ. According to them, when one of the divine persons united with him, he became humanity and divinity. Therefore, if the Holy Spirit who is one of the three divine persons spoke in the prophets, each one of them would have divinity and humanity like Christ. However, they claim divine indwelling and union for Christ alone, in spite of their proving for others what they prove for him.

Sometimes they liken the two hypostases—knowledge and life,

which they call the Word and the Holy Spirit—to the light and heat which belong to the sun and are with it. They liken this to life and speech which belong to the soul and are with it. This comparison is false. If they mean by light and heat what subsists in the essence itself, there are attributes of the sun subsisting in it which do not have a place outside it or unite with anything other than it. The attributes of the sun are like that. It can be said that heat subsists in the sun. Any other meaning than this is impossible.

The point here is that their explanation is false, both in what they claim and in their analogy. If they mean about the sun what is obviously subsisting in something other than it, like its rays which subsist in the air or on the earth, or its heat which is similarly subsistent outside it, this analogy can be shown false in various ways.

a) There are accidents obviously separated from the sun subsisting in other things, not in it. Similar to this is the knowledge, wisdom, and revelation which subsisted in the hearts of the prophets, by which and according to which power they gave warning. There was not in their humanity anything of divinity, but they possessed only the effects of God's wisdom and power.

b) The heat and light which subsist in the air and on walls are accidents subsisting in something other than the sun, whereas the Word and the Holy Spirit according to them are two substances (*jawharan*).

c) These things are not the sun, nor any of the attributes of the sun, but only effects resulting from the sun on other things. It is not denied that something like this subsisted in the prophets and upright persons, but there is no uniqueness to Christ in this. What took up residence in Christ took its place in other messengers than him; nothing that did not inhabit others indwelt in him. There is no unique characteristic in this matter which demands that he be a god in contradistinction to the other messengers. There is here no union of humanity and divinity, just as neither the sun nor any attribute subsisting in it united with the air and earth which received the results of its rays and heat.

———

Paul of Antioch states: We have not invented these names for God of ourselves, O Christians, but God has called His divine nature by them. God spoke in the Torah: [Deut. 32:6; Gen. 1:2; Ps. 51:13; Is. 40:7-8; Job 33:4]. Our master Christ spoke thus in the Gospel [Matt. 38:19-20]. In the Qur'an it speaks of the Holy Spirit [37:171; 5:110; 66:12].

> Muslims say that the Book is the speech of God. There is no speech except to one who is living, speaking. These are essential attributes which flow in the current of things, each one different from the others, and thus God is one, not partitioned or divided.[5]

There are several responses to this.

1) We say firstly that the teaching of the prophets contains nothing but trust and trustworthiness. There is nothing in it which is known to be false by sound reason, although it does contain that which the mind would be unable to know had not the prophets informed us of it. There is nothing in the message of the prophet which he brings us which contradicts his message elsewhere or that of any of the other prophets. Everything which the prophets announce, rather, is true and trustworthy, and all its parts confirm each other.

God has enjoined us to put faith in all which they have brought, and has declared a person an unbeliever who believes in some of the message and disbelieves in some. Some of the divine legislation and method, however, may differ in what is commanded and forbidden.

On what they teach concerning God, His angels, His Books, His messengers, the Last Day, and other things, it is not possible for [the prophets] to contradict one another. Therefore if such passages are among what they have handed down from the prophets, their proof for this is only complete if the soundness of the text and its chain of transmission is known, so that it is known to be correctly handed down from the prophets. We must know, moreover, that the translation from the Hebrew to another language like Greek, Arabic, or Syriac is correct, and after that we must know that the prophets intended that meaning by these texts. The Christians have no proof from the prophets in which these three prerequisites are established. On these matters it suffices to deny their view and demand that they fulfill these prerequisites, for they claim to have taken their idea of the trinity from the prophets. We demand, therefore, that they fulfill these preconditions.

2) We will state the exegesis of the passages which they have mentioned. In the passage from Deuteronomy Moses says to the Israelites, "Is this not the Father who made you, sharpened you, and purchased you?" In this passage God is being called a father to someone other than Christ, and this is similar to God's saying to Israel, "You are my son, my first-born," and to David, "My son and my beloved," or Christ's saying, "My Father and your Father." They accept that what is meant by this in the case of others than Christ is in the sense of lordship, not in the sense of begetting which [they claim] is unique to Christ.

3) This is actually an argument against them, for if in the earlier books God is called a Father to others than Christ, and only lordship is meant, one can know from this that in the language of the Sacred Books this term only means "the Lord." This meaning must be borne over into the case of Christ, because the root meaning is unequivocal in speech.

4) The use of the term "Father" in the meaning which Christians make particular to Christ is only established if it is already known that by it was intended the meaning which they claim about Christ. If that meaning were proved merely by the application of the term "father," a circular argument would necessarily follow. It would be obvious that that meaning was intended by it insofar as it was established that this meaning was intended by it in the case of God, but this latter is not demonstrated until it is known that the meaning was intended for the term in the case of Christ. If the knowledge of each of these two depends upon the other, neither of them is known. From this it is clear that they have no knowledge that what is meant in the case of Christ by the expression "father" is what they have particularized to him in their absurd argumentation.

5) There is never found in the books of the prophets or their message the application of the term "father" with the meaning of the father of the divine nature, nor [is it found that] by their application of the term son is meant anything divine, either the Word or the Life. Rather the expression "son" is only found to signify a creature, and the term "son" is only applied to a created son.

Consequently it follows from this that calling Christ "son" refers to his humanity. This shows the falsity of their view that the son and the Holy Spirit are two attributes of God, and that Christ is the name of the divine and human natures. It is clear that the texts of the Books of the prophets disprove the belief of Christians and contradict their creed. They are thereby caught between two choices: either they put faith in the message of the prophets and show their religion to be false, or else they affirm their religion and disprove the prophets. This latter is what they have sought to do.

———

> Paul of Antioch states: In the holy Gospel the Lord Jesus Christ said to his saintly disciples: "Go to the whole world and baptize them in the name of the Father and the Son and the Holy Spirit—one God, and teach them to observe all that which I have commanded you."[6]

It should be said to them that this passage which they cite in support for what they claim about the three divine persons actually contains nothing, neither in the text itself nor in its evident meaning, which indicates such a thing. The term "son" is never used in the divine Books with the meaning of any attribute of God. Not one of the prophets ever called the knowledge of God His son. It is clear in your own tradition that the prophets called God's servant or servants His son or sons. If this is so, then your claim that by "son" Christ meant the knowledge and word of God goes to the extent of perpetrating a lie against Christ. It is making the term carry a meaning in which it was never used either actually or metaphorically by either Christ or any other prophet. What lie or corruption of the message of the prophets could be greater than this?

If the term "son" was used for an attribute of God, His life or His omnipotence could be called a son. Specifying knowledge by the term "son" without life is a second error. If this is not done, how can the term "son" be used to mean an attribute of God?

Similarly, they did not use the term "Holy Spirit" to mean the life of God, nor did they mean by this term the life of God which is His attribute. By it they only meant that which descends upon the holy men and prophets by which God supports them. As David said, "Your Holy Spirit do not take away from me." In your own tradition you hold that the Holy Spirit descended upon the apostles. We have already established that what is meant by the Holy Spirit is the angel and God's guidance and power which He places in men's hearts. This is what is found in God's message in some of the prophecies: "In those days I will pour out My spirit on every holy person." In the Psalms of David, "Your Holy Spirit guides me straight upon the earth."

This is made clear by what they say in their creed: "Who for us men and for our salvation came down from heaven, took flesh from the Holy Spirit and from the Virgin Mary. . . ." They state that this is in the sacred books and that what is in the sacred books is true. There is no doubt that this contains what is similar to the Qur'an. In the Qur'an it is stated that God sent His spirit to Mary and breathed upon her and she conceived Christ (19:17-22; 21:91; 66:12). This spirit is God's messenger as it says in the Qur'an, "I am only a messenger of thy Lord, that I may bestow on you a faultless son" (19:19).

God breathed this spirit upon Mary and Christ was created from this spirit and from his mother Mary, just as it says in their creed, "He took flesh from Mary and from the Holy Spirit." However, they believe that this Holy Spirit from which Christ was created as well as from Mary is the life of God. There is nothing in the sacred books which indicates this; the books, rather, are decisive in their contradicting this, just as they contradict the Christian view that what united with Christ was the hypostasis of the Word, which is God's knowledge. If he took flesh from Mary and the hypostasis of the Word, then he was not incarnate from the Holy Spirit; if he took flesh from Mary and from the Holy Spirit, then it was not from the Word. If it was from both hypostases together, then Christ was two divine persons—the person of the Word and that of the spirit.

All three sects of Christians state that what united with Christ was only the hypostasis of the Word, not that of Life. In this the mutual contradictions in their creed are obvious, as well as their error in how they interpret the message of the prophets.

It is clear that what is established from the prophets is true and in agreement with what was handed on by Muhammad the Seal of the prophets. His teaching does not contradict a thing of the message of the prophets, just as nothing in their message contradicts sound reason. It is also clear that they make the message of the prophets about the "son" and the "Holy Spirit" and other things bear a meaning whose use is never found in their texts, and they refuse to apply to these terms the meaning found in the prophets' speech. How is it possible for the term "Holy Spirit" to bear a meaning neither used nor intended by the prophets, and for it to depart from the well-known sense in which they always used it?

Is this anything but the act of corrupting the speech of the prophets and perpetrating a lie against them? The evident meaning of this speech is that by the word "father" the prophets intended in their language "Lord"; by "son" in their language is meant "him who is governed, reared," that is, Christ; by "Holy Spirit" is meant the angel, the revelation, etc., by which God supported Christ. Thus do their leading scholars who interpret this passage explain it.

This passage which they state from their book is an argument against the belief in the three divine hypostases of those who say "Calling God Father, Son, and Holy Spirit are names which we Christians have not made up ourselves, but God has called His divinity by them." It is clear that there is nothing in what they have stated from the prophets which indicates, either in its text or evident meaning, that any one of the prophets ever called God or any attribute of His either "son" or "Holy Spirit."

It is clear, furthermore, that their calling the knowledge and Word of God "son," and their calling His life "Holy Spirit" are names which they have innovated and were not revealed by God on His authority. They have absolutely no argument, either from revelation or from reason, for what they claim concerning divine persons. Moreover, they have no religious authority for their view of the trinity and their restricting the attributes of God to three.

Similarly, it is clear that neither do they have any rational basis for these things. They are people about whom the Qur'an speaks: "Had we been wont to *listen* or *have sense* we would not be among the dwellers in the flames" (67:10). "Or do you think that most of them *hear* or *understand*? They are but as the cattle—nay, they are farther astray" (25:44).[7]

———

Paul of Antioch states: It is said in the Qur'an "O Jesus son of Mary, remember My favor to you and to your mother, how I strengthened you with the Holy Spirit" (5:110).

It should be said to them that this passage is without doubt an argument against the Christians, not for them. God strengthened Christ with the Holy Spirit, just as the Qur'an says in other verses (2:87; 2:253). In this there is nothing peculiar to Christ; rather, God similarly strengthened others than him. They have stated that God said to David, "Your Holy Spirit do not take from me." Our prophet said to Hassan ibn Thabit, "God strengthened him with the Holy Spirit," and "The Holy Spirit is with you as long as you defend His prophet." Both these statements are in the sound hadith reports.

The Christians hold that the Holy Spirit descended upon the apostles, and also that the Holy Spirit descended upon all of the prophets. The same is also often mentioned in the Qur'an (16:98-102; 26:194; 2:97). It is clear that the Holy Spirit here refers to Jibril (58:22; 42:52; 16:2; 40:15).

This Spirit which God revealed, with which angels descended upon whichever of God's servants He willed, is different from the Faithful Spirit who descended with the Book. Both of these are called a "spirit" and both are interdependent. Thus the spirit with which the angel descended as well as the Faithful Spirit who descended with it are each meant by the term "Holy Spirit." The exegetes explain the statement about Christ (2:87) by both of these views.

No one, however, has ever said that what is meant by that is the life of God. The word itself does not indicate that, nor does its usage in [this context]. They must accept one of two things. Either in the case of others than Christ the term "Holy Spirit" does not mean the life of God, thus establishing that the term has a meaning other than the life of God, so that even if it were sometimes used to mean the life of God, it would not at the same time necessarily follow that this is what was meant by it in the case of Christ. (How could it mean that when it is not used for the life of God in the case of Christ?) Or they must claim that by this term is meant the life of God in the case of the prophets and apostles. If they hold for this latter, it is necessary that they hold that the divinity descended upon all the prophets and apostles, and thus there is no difference between them and Christ.

Moreover it necessarily follows for them that there be in Christ two divine natures, that of the Word and that of the Spirit, for two hypostases would have united with him. Furthermore it is impossible that by God's saying, "We have supported him with the Holy Spirit" He meant the life of God, for the life of God is an attribute subsisting in God's essence, not in anything else, nor particularized in some one of created things outside of Him. As for their saying that Christ is God the creator, how could he be supported by what is other than he? Finally, what united with Christ is said to be the Word without the Life, and thus it is not correct to say that he was supported by it. Therefore, it is clear that they mean to corrupt the Qur'an just as they have corrupted the Sacred Books which preceded it, and that their manner of interpreting the ambiguous passages in the divine books is of one sort.

## C. THE INCARNATION OF THE DIVINE WORD IN CHRIST

> They say: Muslims say that the Qur'an is the speech of God. But there is no speech unless there is someone living and speaking. These are essential attributes flowing in [an infinite] succession of names. Each attribute is different from the other, but God is one, one creator, one Lord, undivided.[1]

It should be said to them that it is true that the Qur'an is the speech of God, and that speech is not without a speaker. Muslims say that God is living and speaking, and that He spoke the Torah, the Gospel, the Qur'an, and other speech than these. The Qur'an has informed us of the speech of God in many places. Is He thus called a speaker and His speech an utterance?

This is a matter of dispute, and some Muslims declare this possible while others reject it on the grounds that revelation never meant this. They say that in the Torah, Gospel, and Psalms God is not called a speaker, in contrast to the expressions "saying" and "speech."

After the appearance of innovation among Muslims they have disputed about this, just as the People of the Book have disputed about the speech of God—is it subsisting in Him or created and separated from Him? What the *salaf* of the community, its imams and its majority, have agreed on is that the speech of God is subsisting in Him, and similarly the rest of what is described about God—His life, power, etc.

After the passing of the age of the Companions and the great followers, more than a hundred years after the death of the Prophet, a group of Muslims introduced the notion that the speech of God was a creature which God created outside Himself. Many Jews and Christians participated in this heresy.

This opinion appeared in the second century, and a group of rulers and others sided with it. Then God snuffed it out through those imams of Islam and the sunna whom He raised up, who demonstrated its falseness.

They showed that what the *salaf* had agreed upon was that the speech of God was handed down from him uncreated. It originated from Him, not from anything created. Nevertheless no Muslim ever said that the speech of God is a god or a lord. Similarly no Muslim ever declared that God's life is a god or a lord, nor that it is equal to the Lord in essence.

———

Paul of Antioch says that "Each one of God's attributes is different from the other." If by this they mean that God's attributes are differentiated and separated from Him—and this is in reality what they claim—and yet claim at the same time that they are connected with Him, this is a mixing of contradictory statements. Their representing this by the example of the rays of the sun is a false image, and is an argument against them.

The rays subsisting in the air, on earth, on mountains, trees, and walls are not subsisting in the sun itself. What is subsisting in the sun itself is not subsisting in the air and on earth.

If they say that the knowledge which subsists in God overflows from Him upon the hearts of the prophets as forms of knowledge, just as rays emanate from the sun, they should be answered that there is nothing special to Christ in this. This is rather a phenomenon shared by Christ and the other prophets. Moreover there is no indwelling of the Lord Himself in this, nor is it a matter of an attribute of God subsisting in Him existing in some creature. Neither is it a case of God's servant in whom dwells knowledge and faith becoming a god to be worshiped.

If by Paul of Antioch's statement they mean that the attributes are subsisting in God, it is a matter of each one being *called* different from the other. However, it is merely a semantic argument whether or not they are to be called different. There are people who say that every attribute of the Lord is different from the other. What is different about them is what makes the existence of one of them possible with the absence of the other, or what makes the knowledge of one of them possible with ignorance of the other. Others say that one attribute is neither different from the others nor identical to it, for they are two dissimilar things, the existence of one of which is not possible with the non-existence of the other, nor is it possible to separate one from the other, neither in time, place, nor existence.

The *salaf* and the imams of the community, if they were asked whether the knowledge and speech of God were different from Him or not, would not answer definitively either by affirming or denying it. If they were said to be other than Him, it would seem that God was dissimilar to them. If they were said to be not different from Him, it would seem that they were to be identified with Him.

The questioner should be made to be more precise, whether by saying "other than Him" meant that the attribute is dissimilar to God and separated from Him, or whether by "other" he meant that the attribute is not to be identified with the Godhead. In the first case, even in a creature the attributes of something described are not dissimilar to it and separated from it, so how could this be the case with the creator? In the latter case, the attribute is not what is described, and in this sense is other than it. The term "Lord," when applied absolutely, embraces the sacred essence with all the attributes of perfection which it deserves, and by it the existence of an essence stripped of the attributes of perfection is forbidden.

Therefore the name "God" embraces the essence described by the attributes of perfection. These attributes are not additional to this naming, but rather enter into it; however, they arc additional to the simple essence which is established by the denial of the attributes. Those holding the former view claim that God is simple essence, while those holding the latter position object that the attributes are additional to the essence established by the others. The heart of the matter is that there is no simple essence for which God's attributes are additional; rather, God is the sacred essence described by attributes of perfection, and these attributes enter into being called His names.

———

Paul of Antioch states that "God is not divided or divisible," but this is contradictory to what they have stated in their creed and to the way they have represented it. They represented it by the rays of the sun, but these rays are divided and divisible. Those rays which exist in some particular place are only a part or portion of all of them, and it is possible for some of them to go out of existence while the others remain. If an object is placed in some location on which the rays fall, it divides [the rays] upon the area it covers. The rays which fall on that area come to be above it, and thus are separated from the two sets of rays below. It is clear that the sun's rays are existing on the earth and in the air, and that each of them is divided and divisible. That which subsists in divisibility is divisible, for the state follows upon the nature of that which is conditioned. This necessitates division and partitioning in what subsists in it.

The Christians also claim that God united with Christ, who ascended into heaven and sat at the right hand of the Father. They hold, moreover, that the divinity was not partitioned after its union with the human nature. When he ascended into heaven and sat at the right hand of the Father, the one who ascended—according to them—is Christ, who is human divine nature, completely God and completely man. They do not claim that he who sits at the right hand of the Father is the human nature alone, but rather it is the divine nature united with the human who sits at the right hand of the divinity. What division or partitioning could be greater than this?

This does not come from the words of the prophets so that someone could say, "This has a meaning which we don't understand." Rather this comes from the teaching of their leaders who drew it up and made it the belief of their faith. If they were saying what they didn't understand, then they were ignorant and should not have been followed. Even though they did not understand what they were saying, no one could reason that the divine nature united with the human nature had sat at the right hand of the divine nature free from that union, unless this simple divine nature were separated from the divine nature which was in union with and yet dissimilar to it. It is not connected with it, but its goal is that it be in contact with it. It is even necessary that that which is in contact with the simple divine nature be the human nature with the divine nature united to it, and thus we have the reality of division and partitioning with a separation of one part from the other.

Christians should also be asked whether what is united with Christ is the very essence of the Lord of the Universe or just one of His attributes. If it is the very essence of the Father, then Christ is the essence of the Father, and Christ is the Father himself. Despite its falseness, this is what Christians agree upon when they say "He is God, and He is the son of God," just as God spoke about them;

they do not say, however, "He is the father and the son."

According to them the Father is God, and this is one of their contradictions. They say that what united with Christ is an attribute of the Lord. But the Lord's attribute cannot separate from Him, nor is it possible for it to unite with or dwell in something outside the essence. Moreover the attribute is not itself the Creating God, the Lord of the universe, but it is an attribute. No intelligent person says that the speech of God, the knowledge of God, or the life of God is the Lord of the universe who created the heavens and the earth. Even if it were possible that Christ be himself an attribute of God, he still would not be God, would not be the Lord of the Universe, not be the creator of the heavens and the earth.

Christians say that Christ is the Lord of the universe, the creator of all things. If so, he is the creator of Adam and Mary, although he was son of Adam and of Mary. He is creator of them by his divinity, and the son of Adam and of Mary by his humanity. If it were possible that Christ be an attribute of the Lord, that attribute would not be that of the creator, so how could this be the case when Christ himself is not an attribute of God, but is only created by the word of God, and called the word of God because God made him to be by His word "Be!" (19:34). God called him His spirit, because He created him by the breath of the Holy Spirit in his mother, and not as he created others from a human father (3:45).

If they claim that what united with Christ was some of the divine nature without the rest, they are speaking of division and partitioning. One of two things follows: either their belief is false, or they admit division and partitioning in God despite its falseness.

They say, moreover, "True God from true God, from the substance of his Father, generated not created, equal to the Father in substance, the unique son of God, generated before all ages." They should be asked whether this son, generated, equal to the Father in substance, who is true God from true God, is an attribute subsisting in something other than it, or a self-subsisting entity. If they answer the first, [they should be told that] an attribute is not a god, nor is it a creator. It cannot be said concerning it that it is generated from God, nor that it is equal to God in substance. No one of the prophets or any followers of the prophets ever called the attributes of God a son or a child of His. They never said that an attribute of God was generated from Him. Nor has any intelligent person ever said that an eternal substance was generated from an eternal essence.

Nevertheless they claim that Christ is a god who created the heavens and the earth by the union of his humanity with this son generated before all ages, equal to the Father in substance. All this is characteristic of a self-subsistent entity, such as substances subsisting in themselves. It is not characteristic of attributes subsisting in something else. If this is so, a division and a partitioning are necessary consequents of their view. The view of a natural generation demands that a part goes out from the thing. This is clear in the Qur'an (43:15-19).

This is the meaning which is established by some of the scholars among the Christians which they call generation or sonship, and thus they call it a necessary eternal attribute subsisting in that which is described a son. Sometimes they call it an utterance by the Word, sometimes knowledge, and sometimes wisdom.

They say, "This is generated from God," and "the son of God," but not one of the prophets or their followers ever said this, nor any other intelligent people but these innovating Christians. No intelligent person has ever understood this meaning for the terms "generation" and "sonship."

The prophets never applied the term "son" except to a creature. Yet Christians say God is a Father to Christ by nature, and to others by adoption. The majority of intelligent people and others can only understand by this a reasonable sonship with the separation of a part from the generator, but this their scholars deny. Here they are not following the prophets, nor do they hold what intelligent people understand. In this way they have fallen into error in what they have transmitted from the prophets, and they have caused their followers and the masses to go astray by what they have stated. Even though they have not been saying that God's generation is like the generation of animals in which a thing is created by parturition, they do say that divine generation comes about by the separation of a part of the divinity which descends upon the human nature. They do not understand anything other than this by generation.

They say, moreover, "We believe in the Holy Spirit, the Lord, the Giver of life, who proceeds from the Father and with the Father is worshiped and glorified, who spoke through the prophets." Their holding that the spirit proceeds from the Father and is worshiped and glorified makes it impossible for them to hold that this is the life of the Lord subsisting in Him. His life does not proceed out from Him like other attributes. If there were an attribute subsisting in itself proceeding forth it would be God's knowledge, His power, or other attributes proceeding from Him. The proceeding forth from Him of the word is more apparent than that of His life. Speech goes out from the speaker, but life does not spring forth from one who is living. Were there among the attributes one which proceeds, that attribute would be what they call the son. For them to say, "It is [the attribute] of knowledge or speech, utterance or wisdom" is preferable to their holding that about life, which is more remote from [procession] than is speech.

They say also that the Spirit is "with the Father worshiped and glorified." However, an attribute subsisting in the Lord is not worshiped with Him. They say, "He speaks through the prophets," but an attribute of the Lord does not speak through the prophets. All of this is rather an attribute of the Holy Spirit, which God places in the hearts of the prophets, or an attribute of one of the angels like Jibril. But if this is a proceeding from the Father, and a procession is a going forth, what division and partitioning is greater than this?

If they compare this to the going forth of rays from the sun, this is false from various aspects.

1) The rays are an accident subsisting in the air and on the earth, not a substance in themselves. Among them, however, the Spirit is living and something to be worshiped, and is thus a substance.

2) Procession is unique to the Holy Spirit; they do not say about the Word that it proceeds. If procession were true, it would apply to the speech of God, for speech is more receptive to that than is life.

In all of this the least intelligent person who considers what they say in their creed and elsewhere would find contradictions and error unconcealed from any but its followers. He would find in it, moreover, that which is contradictory to the Torah, the Gospel, and the rest of the books of God, contradictions which also could not be concealed from anyone who considers these things. Finally, he would find in it what contradicts sound reason, and this could be hidden only from those who are either stubborn or ignorant. Their view is internally contradictory, opposed to sound reason and to the sound tradition handed down from all the prophets and messengers.

———

Paul of Antioch states: We hold the incarnation of the creative Word of God in a created man and the birth of both together, i.e., the word with the humanity. The Creator never spoke to any one of the prophets except by revelation or from behind a veil, according to what it says in the Qur'an (42:51).

If those things which are subtle like the Holy Spirit and other things do not manifest themselves except in those which are solid, would the Word of God who created the subtle beings manifest Himself in that which is not solid? Never! In this way Jesus the son of Mary appeared, since mankind is the most exalted of what God created, and thus He speaks to creatures who bear witness to what they see.[2]

This can be answered in various ways.

1) Their statement and claim is that the incarnation of the creative word of God in a created man and the birth of both of them together—that is, the Word with humanity—is what is expressed by the union of divinity and humanity. This is contrary to sound reason. What is known to be impossible by sound reason cannot be spoken by a messenger of God, for the messengers only inform people of what sound reason does not know to be impossible. The prophets are far beyond stating anything which sound reason knows to be impossible.

2) The correct divine message is that Christ is a servant of God, not the creator of the world, and yet Christians say that he is complete God and complete man. Concerning what they have stated we will answer them on several points.

a) Is that which united Christ with the divine essence described by the Word, or is it the Word alone? In other words, is that which united with the human nature the Word with the essence or the Word without the essence? If what became united with him was the Word with the essence, Christ would be the Father, son, and Holy Spirit, and Christ would be all three divine persons. This is false by the agreement of Christians as well as by that of people of the other religions, false by agreement of the divine books, and false by sound reason, as we, God willing, will show.

If what united in him was the Word alone, it must be said that the Word is an attribute, and an attribute does not subsist except in that which it describes. An attribute is not a creating God, but Christ according to them is the creating God.

Their view is false on either basis. If they say that what united with him was that which was described by the attribute, Christ would be the Father, but according to them he is not the Father. If they say it was the attribute alone, the attribute does not exist outside what it describes nor does it separate from it. The attribute does not create or give sustenance and is not God. As for that which unites with Christ's human nature being the Father solely—who is the essence stripped of its attributes—this view is most strongly impossible and none of them hold this view.

b) If the essence united with the humanity of Christ and the humanity of Christ remained after the union of the two essences, they would be two substances as they were before the union, and thus there would have actually been no union. If it is said that they became one substance—as some of them say—like fire united with a piece of iron or milk united with water, then the transformation of both of them necessarily follows, and a disruption of the attributes of each. Even its very nature would be transformed, just as water and milk are changed when they are mixed, or the fire and the piece of iron. It follows from this that the divinity was transformed and its attributes and real nature replaced by something else. This transformation could not occur except by the going out of existence of something and the coming into existence of something else. There follows from this the going out of existence of some [aspect] of the pre-eternal necessarily self-subsistent One. That which was demanded by His eternity is transformed by going out of existence, and what its existence demands, its non-existence forbids.

The eternal being is not eternal except by His being internally necessary; it is obligatory that He be necessary in Himself. This is because if such were not obligatory for Him, but unnecessary [for His nature], He would not be eternal in His eternity. His being necessary in Himself prevents His non-existence, for the denial of what demands something necessarily demands the denial of what is demanded by it.

c) People hold various opinions about the Word of God, but the view of Christians is false according to all the opinions which people hold on this question. By any estimation the falsity of their position is established. The Word of God is either 1) an attribute subsisting in Him or 2) is created and different from Him, or 3) it is neither of these, but rather what is found in men's souls.

This third view is the farthest from the views of the prophets. It is the view of some philosophers and Sabaeans: The Lord has no attributes subsisting in Him, nor is He creator by choice. They hold, moreover, that He does not know particular things, nor that He is able to change the celestial spheres. According to these people His speech is what flows over upon souls, and they might call it a "speech by the tongue of the resider." These people deny speech to God and say that He is not a speaker. They may hold Him to be a metaphorical speaker, but those among them who belong to one of the religions apply it absolutely when the prophets speak by Him, and then they explain it in this way. This is one of the two views of the Jahmites.

The second view is that He is truly a speaker but His speech is created, something He created outside of Himself. This is the opinion of the Mu'tazila and others, and the other view is [properly] that of the Jahmites.

According to this view, God's speech is not subsisting in Him until it unites with Christ or resides in him. It is created, an accident, not God the creator. There are many People of the Book—Jews and Christians—who hold for each of these views.

The first view is that of the *salaf* and the imams of the community, and of the majority of its people. It is the view of many of the *salaf* of the People of the Book and the majority of their people. Either the speech of God is said to be generically eternal (*qadim al-naw'*) with the meaning that He was always a speaker by will, or that it is eternal in its individual manifestation (*qadim al-'ayn*), or that it was not eternal but came into being in time. The first is the well-known view of the imams of the sunna and hadith.

## D. *HULUL*: INDWELLING OF GOD IN CHRIST

> Paul of Antioch states: In this way God became manifest in Jesus the son of Mary, since mankind is the most exalted of what God created. God thus preached to mankind and they witnessed from him what they saw.[1]

If you claim that God's manifestation in Jesus was like His manifestation in Abraham, Moses, and Muhammad, and as He is manifest in His houses which He permitted to be erected in which His name is remembered, that is, by the manifestation of His light and knowledge and the remembrance of His names and the worship of Him, then we agree. In this there is no indwelling of the essence of God in man nor any union with him. This is a matter shared between Christ and others, and nothing peculiar to Christ in it. This also may be called *hulul*. They hold that God descended upon upright men, and this is mentioned among them in some of the divine books, such as in Psalm 4.

David said in his private conversation with his Lord, "Let those who trust in you rejoice forever, and let them be glad. Dwell in them and they will prosper." God stated that He dwelled in the here-mentioned upright persons, and so it is known that this is no special characteristic of Christ. In this way, by their own agreement and that of Muslims, the essence of God Himself does not become united with man and become divine and human nature, like fire and iron, water and milk, or any of those ways by which they represent unity. By *hulul* is meant, rather, the presence of faith in God and knowledge of Him, love and remembrance of Him, worship of Him, and His light and guidance.

This may be expressed as an indwelling of the intellective representation (*al-mithal al-'ilmi*), as is mentioned in the Qur'an (6:3;

30:28). To God belong the highest representations in the hearts of the people of the heavens and the people of the earth. Some of what the prophet Muhammad related about his Lord is of this nature.

He said, "God says, 'I am with My servant when he recollects Me, and his lips move with me'." God informs us that His servants lips move with Him, that is, with His name. In another sound hadith He says:

> "My servant was sick and did not come to Me for treatment." The servant says, "O Lord, how can I come to You when You are Lord of the universe?" He says, "If you knew that My servant was sick and you came to him you would find Me with him."

By "you would find Me with him" is not meant "you would find Me Myself," so that God is with him, that is, in his heart. What is in his heart is the intellective representation.

God spoke in a sound hadith which Al-Bukhari relates from Abu Hu'ayra from the Prophet:

> God says: "Whoever acts as an enemy to a friend of Mine, against him I permit him to wage war. But My servant draws near to Me by performing what I have imposed upon him, and My servant continues to draw near to Me by supererogatory acts so that I love him. When I love him I am his hearing by which he hears, his sight by which he sees, his hand by which he touches, his leg by which he walks."

In another account:

> "In Me he hears, in Me he sees, in Me he touches, in Me he walks. If he asks of Me I will give him; if he seeks My protection I will guard him. I have not hesitated to do anything I might do [for him], like My hesitation to take the spirit of my believing servant. He dislikes death, and I dislike hurting him."

This hadith may have been used as an argument for those who hold for a general *hulul* or a general union, or for the oneness of existence as well as by those who hold a particular *hulul* or *ittihad*, as do those who resemble Christians. Actually, the hadith is a proof against both groups.

He says, "Who acts as an enemy to my friend, against him I permit him to wage war." This establishes three things: a friend to God, an enemy who opposes His friend, and the distinction between God Himself, His friend, and the enemy of His friend. He says, "Whoever acts in enmity to a friend of mine, against him I permit him to wage war." This indicates God's friend whom He has befriended, so that God has come to love what he loves, hate what he hates, befriend whom he befriends, oppose whom he opposes, so that the Lord announces war on those who oppose him, for his opponent has become an enemy to God.

God says, "Now My servant draws near to Me by his performance of what I imposed upon him." There is a distinction between the servant drawing near and the Lord to whom he draws near. He says: "My servant continues to draw near by additional works so that I love him." It is clear that He loves him after he has drawn near by obligatory and supererogatory works.

He says: "If I love him I am his hearing by which he hears, his sight by which he sees, his hand by which he touches, his leg by which he walks." According to those who hold for general *hulul* or *ittihad* or *wahdat al-wujud*, God is his chest, his stomach, his head, his hair. He is everything or in everything before and after the servant's drawing near. According to the people of specific *hulul*, God becomes the person himself, like fire and iron or water and milk.

God says: "In Me he hears, in Me he sees, in Me he touches, in Me he walks." According to the view of these people, the Lord is the one who hears, sees, touches, and walks, and the messenger only says "in me." God says: "If he asks Me, I will grant him, if he seeks protection I will guard him." He makes the servant seeking, asking protection, and the Lord the one asked, sought for. This is contradictory to "union" (*ittihad*). God's saying "In Me he hears" is like His saying "His lips move with Me." By this He means the intellective similitude.

God's saying "God will be in his heart" means His knowledge, love, guidance, friendship. It is the intellective similitude [of God] in his heart which the person hears, sees, touches, and walks.

If a person loves, extols, or obeys another, he says something like this about him. He says, "You are in my heart and in my soul. You remain between my eyes." Or the line of poetry:

> Your image in my eyes, your remembrance on my tongue
> Your abode is in my heart, in what part of me are you absent?

Or again:

> How amazing it is that I long for them
> Whomever I meet I ask for them, but they are with me.
> My eye seeks them but they are in its pupils,
> My heart searches for them, but they are within its chambers.

There are many verses like this, in spite of the knowledge of intelligent people that the person of the extolled beloved as he is in himself is not himself in the eye of the lover nor in his heart.

Still it may be poetically represented in this way. Some mistaken people may even think that the worshiped Beloved is Himself in the person of the worshiping lover.

This is similar to the error of some of the philosophers who think that the essence of what is intellected and known is united with the intellecting knower, so that they make what is intellected, intellection, and intellector one thing. They do not distinguish between the indwelling of the image of something caused and the indwelling of the essence. This is due to the weakness of the intellect and the persuasive power of love and gnosis (*marifa*).[2] Mankind in worship is absent from the object of his worship, absent in his love from the Beloved, in his witness from the One witnessed to, in his knowledge from the One known. The one who [at one time] was not becomes oblivious to his experience of himself as servant. It is not that he himself becomes non-existent or that He who never ceased to be passes away in his experience [of Him].

When a Muslim errs in this area, he may say something like what is attributed to Abu Yazid al-Bistami, "Glory be to me! Glory be to me!" or "There is nothing in my cloak but God." In this regard a story may be mentioned here of a person who loved another. The beloved threw himself in the water and so the lover threw himself in after his beloved. Said the first, "I fell but why did you fall?" Said the lover, "There was a distance, you from me; then I thought you were me." The loving worshiper, when the dominion of love takes possession of his heart, his heart becomes engulfed in his beloved, and his heart does not experience anything other than what is in his heart. He fails to observe his own self and his actions and thinks that he is the same as the beloved. This is even easier for him who thinks that he is the very essence of the beloved.

This thought that one has united with the essence of God or that He in His essence dwells in someone is a mistaken notion into which many people have fallen. They say that Christ or some other human is God or that God is dwelling in him. Their error may be of this kind that when they hear the teaching of some person they decide that God is in the being of that person, and they make the action of this person the act of God. They consider that essential union and indwelling.

What is meant is only that the knowledge of God is in the person, a union of adherence to what God has commanded and enmity to what He has forbidden, as God said in the Qur'an (4:80; 48:10). That is not because the Messenger is God, nor because God Himself has dwelled within the Messenger, but because the Messenger commanded what God had commanded, forbade what He forbade, loved what God loved, hated what He hated, befriended the friends of God, and opposed His enemies. Whoever pledges to hear and obey him has pledged to hear and obey God. Whoever obeys him has indeed obeyed God.

It is the same for Christ and the rest of the messengers. They only command what God commands, only forbid what He has forbidden. They befriend the friends of God and oppose His enemies. Therefore whoever obeys them has obeyed God. Whoever has put confidence in them and received from them what they have made known has received that from God. Whoever befriends them has befriended God, but he who opposes them and wars against them acts inimically to God and wages war against Him.

It must be clear to anyone who considers these matters that the expression *hulul* can be used to express either a correct or a false meaning, and likewise the indwelling of God's speech in the heart. For this reason Ahmad ibn Hanbal was averse to using the expression "the indwelling of the Qur'an in the hearts of believers," as we have mentioned elsewhere.

What makes this clearer is that a thing may have an existence in itself, as well as an existence as a concept in minds, an existence as an expression on the tongue, and an existence in script and illustration—an essential, personal existence, and an intellective, spoken, and written existence. For example, the sun has that which determines it in itself, that is, the sun which is in the sky. The sun may also be imagined in the heart, the word "sun" may be spoken with the tongue, and finally "sun" written with a pen.

What is intended by writing corresponds to the verbal expression, which in turn corresponds to the knowledge of it, and that in turn to that which is known. If someone sees in a book the word "sun" or hears a speaker saying the word, he says, "This is the sun which God made as a gleaming beacon, which rises in the east and sets in the west." He points to the verbal expression he hears and to the writing he sees and knows that the sound and the writing themselves are not what is meant, for those things are not the sun which rises and sets, but knows that what is meant is what was intended by the writing and the sound—that is, the thing indicated which corresponds to them.

The name of God may be seen written in a book, and with it the name of an idol. A person says "I place faith in this and disbelieve in this." What is meant is that he puts faith in God and disbelieves in the idol. He points to the written word and its meaning which is called by this term. Similarly, if someone hears the beautiful names of God mentioned, he says, "This is the Lord of the universe," and what is meant by that is He who is called by those names.

Intelligent people only direct their hearts to the meaning intended without intermediate steps, and express it by expressions which indicate that meaning in order to make their intent manifest. In this way they speak of one who knows the mind of another, or one who gives the commands of another, or the news of another—"This is so-and-so." Therefore if people are seeking information on a matter of obedience to the governor, and then his representative comes presenting his [the governor's] position on the matter, people say, "This is so-and-so himself." That is, what was sought from the absent person is brought by this one. There is a unity of intention between the two which people express by using the name of one for the other. In this way it is said, "'Ikrima is Ibn 'Abbas," or "Abu Yusuf is Abu Hanifa."[3]

Of the same order is what is mentioned about Christ that he said "I and my Father are one; he who has seen me has seen my Father." Similarly we have God's statement which he related about His messenger:

> My servant was sick and you did not treat Me;
> My servant was hungry and you did not feed Me.

Or in the Qur'an, "Those who pay allegiance to you are paying allegiance to God" (48:10). This type of speaking must be understood, for many difficulties can be ascribed to it. This is present in the speech of God, of His Messenger, and in the speech of many creatures of all types; however, its meaning is at the same time clear. Knowledge of the speaker and teacher shows that what is meant is not that the essence of one of the two has become united with the essence of the other.

Even more serious than that is the application of the terms *hulul* and *ittihad*. There is a correct meaning which they can have, as it is said that there is a unity between Smith and Doe, since they are in agreement on what they like, hate, befriend, and oppose. As the desires and goals of the two of them are united, it can be said that they are united, and that between them there is a unity. By this no one means that the essence of one united with the essence of the other, like the union of fire and iron, that of water and milk, or the soul and the body.

The same can be said for the various terms—indwelling (*hulul*), residence (*sukna*), and interpenetration (*takhallul*)—which indicate divine indwelling.

> The way of her spirit mingled with mine,
> In this is the lover called lover.

Their intermingling by way of the spirit is his love for the beloved and the mingling of their feelings, etc., not the indwelling of their very selves.

> The one dwelling in my heart makes it thrive,
> I'll not forget Him; His memory I'll revive.

What is dwelling in the heart is His intellective image, His love, His knowledge. His knowledge and His love dwell in the heart, not His very essence. Similarly, another verse:

> If the stream remain in its clarity,
> Avoiding the movement of the breeze
>
> No doubt the heaven will appear therein
> And the sun appear and then the stars,
>
> So too in the hearts of those who disclose Him
> In their purity is seen the majestic God.

It can be said about someone, "There is nothing but God in the heart of So-and-so," or "He has nothing but God." By that is meant the person has nothing but the remembrance of God, knowledge of Him, His love, fear of Him, obedience to Him, and similar qualities; that is, there is not found in the heart what is in the hearts of other creatures, but in his heart there is only God alone. Similarly it is said that "With Smith there is only Doe" if he is devoted to the remembrance of his friend, whom he prefers above all others.

This is a matter widely understood among speakers and listeners. The one man does not dwell within the other, still less has he united with him. Rather it is as it is said of a mirror which is only turned towards the sun, "There is nothing in it but the sun." What is meant is that nothing appears in it but the sun.

So also with the term *hulul*. Sometimes by it is meant the indwelling of the essence of a thing, and at other times the indwelling of its knowledge, love, and intellective image. This we have already mentioned.

In the prophecies Christians hold that God dwelled with holy men other than Christ and by that it was not meant that the essence of the Lord dwelt within some person. It is rather like saying, "So-and-so lives within me, dwells in me, he is in the depths of my heart, he is in my inmost being, etc." It is only the mental image which dwells in him. If this is so, then it is evident that in a place devoid of someone who knows and worships God the remembrance of God is not found, nor does His worship and His knowledge reside in it. If someone who knows, worships, and remembers God comes to be in such a place, the remembrance of God appears in it and faith is in it. Faith in God, worship and remembrance of Him reside in that place, and it becomes the house of God. It is said, "God is in it," "God dwells in it."

Similarly it is said that God is in the hearts of those who know Him and He dwells in them. By this is meant the presence of knowledge of Him, faith in Him, love for Him. Evidence for this has already been presented. When the Lord is in the hearts of His believing servants—that is, His light and His knowledge—this is expressed by saying that He is dwelling in them. When they are in the mosque, it is said that God is in the mosque, and in this sense He is residing in it. In just this sense one might say, "God is in the heart of So-and-so," and "With So-and-so there is only God." This is as the prophet said in a sound hadith, "You may know that My servant So-and-so is sick; if you treat him you will find Me with him."

What makes all this clear is what occurs when a dreamer sees some individual in his dream. This person may speak to him, command him and forbid him, and bring him news of many matters. Afterwards he says, "I saw So-and-so in my dream and He said such-and-such to me, and I answered him so, he did this, and then I did that." He mentions the kinds of things said and done.

In this there may be knowledge, judgments, and social graces which benefit the dreamer greatly. Possibly the person seen in the dream is living, but he has no awareness that the other person saw him in his dream, much less was he aware that he spoke and acted in the dream. The one seen doesn't know anything about it, nor has he had any awareness of it. This is because that which was seen and which resided in the heart of the dreamer was a cognitive image corresponding to the real existent, just as someone sees in a mirror or in water a person present only at a distance. On the other hand, one of those seen in the dream may be aware that he was seen in a dream, and then he discloses it to the dreamer, just as he may disclose other matters to him, not because the other person himself dwelled within him.

If the vision was accurate, the speech and action in it would correspond to the situation of the person seen in what he customarily said or did in real life. His image is then represented to the dreamer, speaking and acting according to the way the dreamer knows him to speak and act in actuality. The dreamer draws benefit from this, just as someone relates the speech and actions of another to an individual so that from this may be known the same speech and action of the one relating them. There are many things which most people do not know unless a representation is made for them.

In spite of the knowledge that the nature of one is not the nature of the other, when someone imagines that a person he has seen in his dream, whether waking or sleeping, has himself taken residence in him, this is an indication of the stupidity of that dreamer. Many of those seen are living, and they have no awareness of what the other saw. They feel it neither in their spirit nor in their body. It must not be imagined that the spirit of that person has been represented in its bodily form to the dreamer, but what was represented was the image in the dreamer himself which corresponded in body and spirit to the one seen wherever he might have been.

Furthermore the vision may be from God—in which case it is true—or it may be from Satan. This division into these two categories has been established in sound hadith reports. Satan, when he appears in a dream in the form of some person and seen by many people, in this way leads astray those who are not among the people of knowledge and faith. This has happened to many Hindu idolaters and others. After people among them have died, their survivors see them coming to them, demanding unfulfilled obligations, entrusting responsibilities, and bringing information about matters concerning the dead. All of this, however, is Satan taking on the appearance of the dead person. He may come to them in the guise of some of the holy men whom they revere, and say "I am So-and-so." But it is only Satan.

One of the shaykhs may rise up and appoint in his place a person in his likeness who people call the "spiritual nature" of the shaykh and his comrade, but this is one of the jinn appearing in the shaykh's likeness. This has occurred to many of the monks and to others than monks as well as among those who call themselves Muslims. Someone may see while awake a person who says to him "I am Abraham," "I am Moses," "I am Christ," "I am Muhammad," or some one of the Companions or apostles, and he may see him flying in the air. That is only a demon; that form is not the same as the form of the actual person.

The Prophet has said, "Whoever sees me in a dream has truly seen me, for Satan cannot represent my image." Thus the vision of Muhammad in a dream is true. But Muhammad is never seen by the eye of a waking person, nor is anyone of the dead, although many people have seen while awake what they thought to be one of the prophets, either at his grave or somewhere else.

The grave may be seen splitting open, and the form of a person thought to be a dead man rising out of the grave, or that his spirit took flesh and rose from the grave. However, that is only one of the jinn representing the form of that person in order to lead the viewer astray. The spirit is not what is buried under the ground, so that the dirt can split apart over it. The spirit, although it may be connected with the body, has no need for any splitting of the earth. Neither does the ground split apart over the body, but that is a trick of Satan. Things like this have occurred to many of those adhering to Islam, to the People of the Book, and to idolaters.

Many people think that this sort of thing is among the preternatural favors granted to God's upright servants, but it actually belongs to the machinations of the devil. This topic we have more fully treated in other works, such as *Al-Furqan bayn Awliya' al-Rahman wa-Awliya' al-Shaytan.*[4]

————

If by your statement you mean that in Jesus appeared the indwelling of God Himself and His union with Christ or someone else, this is a gratuitous claim without any preceding or subsequent proof. As for man's being the most exalted of what God created, if by this he was suitable for God's indwelling in him, this would not be a matter particularized to Christ. An argument could even be raised for someone other than Christ greater than him, such as Abraham or Muhammad.

God took these two as special friends (*khalilayn*), and there is no rank higher than that of *khalil*. If God were to take up residence in the most exalted of the mankind He had created, which in turn was the most exalted of His creatures, He would have dwelt within the most exalted of mankind, that is, the *khalil* Abraham or Muhammad. There has never been any proof that the body of Christ which he took from Mary, since according to their argument it was not united with the divine nature, was more perfect than Abraham or Moses.

If they say that he never committed a sin, [we answer that] John the son of Zakariah never committed a sin. Moreover, whoever commits a sin and repents of it becomes by his repentance finer than before his sin and finer than him who never committed that sin. Abraham and Moses are finer than John whom they call "John the Baptist."

They say: "And thus He [God] taught mankind." But the one who taught mankind was Jesus the son of Mary. People only heard his voice and none other than his. When one of the jinn resides in a person and speaks through his tongue, it is evident to the hearers that this voice is not human, and when he speaks some message, those present know that it is not a human message.

People did not hear from Christ anything other than what was heard from the messengers like him. If what was speaking through the tongue of his human nature was one of the jinn or an angel, that would have been evident. It would have been obvious that the speaker was not human. How could this not be the case if the speaker was the Lord of the universe? If this were the situation, it would be many times more evident than would be the speech of an angel or one of the jinn on the tongue of a human.

As for the miracles of Christ which people witnessed, they witnessed similar or greater ones from other prophets. Others than he gave life to the dead and gave information of the unseen more than he did. The miracles of Moses were greater and more numerous than his. The miracles worked at his hands gave evidence of his prophethood and his messengership, just as the miracles of others gave evidence of their prophethood. Their messengership never indicated divinity. When Al-Dajjal claims divinity, he will not have his claim verified by the wonders which will be worked at his hands. The claim to divinity is impossible, and the appearance of wonders can never give proof for a matter that is impossible.

———

They claim[5] that Zakariah the prophet said:

> Rejoice, O daughter of Zion! For I am coming to you, I shall dwell within you (*wa-ahull fik*), and you will see Me. God says: Many nations will believe in God in those days. They will bring forth for Him one people. He and they will dwell in you (*yahull huwa wa-hum fik*), and you will know that I am God the Strong One dwelling in you (*ana Allah al-Qawi al-Sakin fik*). On that day God will raise up a king from Judah, and he will rule over them forever.[6]

It should be said to them that they themselves hold that statements like this have been mentioned concerning Abraham and the other prophets, that God manifested Himself to him, disclosed Himself to him, showed Himself to him, and expressions like this. This does not indicate God's dwelling within the prophet. Similarly, at Christ's coming, God did not say "I will dwell in Christ or unite with him." He only said concerning the house of Zion, "I am coming to you and will dwell within you," just as He said elsewhere—according to them—and this did not indicate His indwelling in mankind.

In the same way when God said "You will know that I am God, the Strong One dwelling in you," He did not mean by this expression His indwelling in Christ. Christ did not live in Jerusalem. He was strong, but when he entered Jerusalem, he was overcome and defeated, so that they seized him and crucified him—or so it appeared. When the knowledge of God and faith in Him succeeded in men's hearts, they were calm and peaceful. When the religion of Christ appeared in Jerusalem after his assumption, there occurred in the city this faith in God and knowledge of Him; but this was not present before that.

The sum of all this is that the early prophecies and the divine Books like the Torah, the Gospel, the Psalms, and the rest of the books of the prophets never single out Christ by anything which demands particularizing in him unity with the Godhead or its indwelling within him, as the Christians claim. These books, rather, single him out only in that by which Muhammad singled him out, in God's statement (4:171).

The books of the early prophets and the rest of the prophecies are in agreement with what Muhammad brought, and they confirm one another. All that the Christians call upon as proofs for Christ's divinity from the words of the prophets is paralleled by the same words used in the case of others than him. Their particularizing divinity to Christ without others is false, as is their application of the term "son" to Christ, their specifying the indwelling of the Holy Spirit in him, their calling him "God," [their belief in] the manifestation, *hulul*, or residence of the Lord in him or in his being God's *locus* [on earth].

All these statements and others which resemble them are found as well in the case of others than Christ, as they admit. These others are not thereby divine. However, those who hold for *hulul* and *ittihad* in the case of all the prophets and holy men could possibly argue from these statements.

However, such a belief is false by the agreement of Muslims, Jews, and Christians, as well as being false from reason and revelation. There have been groups of apostates and heretics who call themselves Muslims, Jews, and Christians who hold that. Their confusion arises from the faith in Him, knowledge of Him, His light, guidance, and the spirit from Him which dwell in the hearts of those who know Him, and the exemplary forms and mental representations by which this is expressed.

They think that this indicates the essence of the Lord, just as they think that the very term by name is that which is in the heart, or that the writing itself is the very verbal expression. Some of them think that the essence of the beloved has come to dwell in the essence of the lover and united with him, or that the thing known and understood itself dwells in the intellector, the knower, and by this has united with him. This is in spite of certain knowledge that the beloved or the thing known is dissimilar to the essence of the lover in spirit and body, and by neither element can it dwell in the person of the lover.

Believers know, love, serve, and remember Him and it is said that He is in their hearts (30:27; 43:84; 6:3). What is meant is His knowledge, His love, and His service, and this is a mental representation; what is not meant is His very essence itself. It is just as someone says to another, "You are in my heart; you remain in my heart and between my eyes."

Mosques are the houses of God in which He is manifest, as God said (24:35). 'Ubayy ibn Ka'b said it is like His light in the hearts of believers. Then God says "Light upon light," and then "in houses which God has allowed to be exalted and that His name shall be remembered therein" (24:36). The light of God the exalted is remembered in the hearts of believers, and is remembered in His houses as well, and this is what was stated in the earlier Books.

As for God's coming and manifestation, they have it in their own books that God said in the Torah to Moses, "I am coming to you in the thickness of cloud, so that the people may hear My speaking to you." Then He said, "Gather seventy leading men of the Israelites and take them to the tent of meeting and stand there until I speak to you." In the Book of Numbers when Maryam and Aaron were speaking about Moses:

> Then God manifested Himself in a pillar of cloud, standing at the door of the tent calling, "Maryam, Aaron!" So both of them went out and He said, "Hear My words: I am God in your midst."[7]

And in Chapter 13:

> You brought up this people in Your might from among them, and they will tell the inhabitants of this land. They have heard . . . , that You, O Lord, are in the midst of this people; You O Lord are seen face to face, and Your cloud stands over them and You go before them, in a pillar of cloud by day and in a pillar of fire by night.[8]

In the Book of Deuteronomy Moses said to the Israelites:

> Do not be in dread or afraid of them. The Lord your God who goes before you will Himself fight for you.[9]

In another place Moses said:

> This people is your people. God said: "Moses, I am going to pass before you and depart." Moses said: "Unless You go with us we will

never rise out of here. How can I and this people know that we have found favor before You unless You go with us?"

In Psalm 4 it says:

Let those who speak about you rejoice forever; let them be glad. He will dwell among them and they rejoice.[10]

[In these passages] God informs them that He dwells among all His friends, that is, by His knowledge and light. They agree that the essence of God does not dwell among the faithful friends of God.

Finally in the epistle of John the evangelist: "If we love one another we know that God abides in us"—that is, His love. There are many passages similar to these in their books.

———

The Christians quote from the prophet Amos:

"The sun will shine on the earth, and those astray will be guided by it, but the children of Israel will stray from it." The sun is the lord Christ. Those astray who are guided by it are those Christians of different languages who previously were worshipers of idols and straying from the knowledge of God. When the apostles brought them and warned them of what the Lord Christ commanded them, they forsook the worship of idols and were rightly guided as followers of the Lord Christ.[11]

This is something on which Muslims do not dispute with Christians; they only dispute in matters like this with the Jews who reject Christ, just as they dispute with the believers of the People of the Book who reject Muhammad. Muslims believe in all the books of God and his messengers, and hence believe that Christ shone his light on earth, just as before him shone the light of Moses, and after him the light of Muhammad. God announced this to Muhammad in the Qur'an (33:45-46). God called him an "illuminating lamp," and He called the sun "a fiery lamp." An illuminating lamp is more perfect that a fiery lamp, for the latter has a harmful heat, whereas the former guides with its light without the harmfulness of its fire (7:157; 42:52-53).

Muslims affirm that all those who have followed the unchanged, uncorrupted religion of Christ have been rightly guided by him away from error, and whoever of the children of Israel disbelieved in him was in error and a disbeliever (3:55-57; 61:14). God's statement "The sun will shine on the earth and those astray will be rightly guided by it, but the children of Israel will stray from it" is consistent with His statement in the Torah: "The Lord has come from Mt. Sinai, and shines forth from Sa'ir, His light made known from Mt. Faran." The shining forth of God's light from Sa'ir is the manifestation of His light in Moses, and its breaking forth from Mt. Faran is the manifestation of that same light in Muhammad.

These are the three places by which God swore in the Qur'an:

> By the fig and the olive
> By Mount Sinai
> And by this land made safe (95:1-3).

The land of the fig and the olive is the Holy Land from which Christ was sent; in it lived the prophets of the Israelites; Muhammad made his night journey there, and in that land his prophethood was made manifest. Mount Sinai is the place in which God spoke to Moses the son of 'Imran. "This land made safe" is the land of Mekka from which God sent Muhammad upon whom He sent down the Qur'an.

———

> Paul of Antioch states: "The new law chosen [by God] is that sunna which we have received from the hands of the holy apostles in accordance with what they received from Christ."

It should be said to them: If you were really following the Law, you would not have changed it. It was no use for you to take a stance against it when you rejected the Messenger, the prophet who was unacquainted with the earlier scriptures, who was sent to you and to the rest of creation with another law (sunna) more perfect than the laws (*sunan*) which preceded it. In a similar way it did not benefit the Jews who held fast to the Law of the Torah and did not follow the law of Christ when it was sent to them. Whoever rejects even one messenger is an unbeliever (4:150).

Nevertheless, the law which Christ brought was true, and everyone who was a follower of it was a believer, a Muslim, one of the friends of God and the people of paradise for whom there is no fear and no sadness (2:62; 61:14). Whoever followed Christ was a believer, and he who disbelieved in him was a disbeliever (3:55-57).

However, you Christians had changed and replaced his law before the coming of Muhammad. You became unbelievers by replacing the law of Christ and by rejecting the law of Muhammad, just as the Jews disbelieved by replacing the Law of the Torah and by rejecting the law of the Gospel, and then later disbelieved by rejecting the law of Muhammad.

Christ did not ordain for you the trinity, nor your thinking on the divine persons, nor your doctrine that he is lord of the universe. He did not prescribe for you that you make pork and other forbidden things licit. He never commanded you to omit circumcision, or that you should pray to the east; or that you should take your great men and monks as masters beside God. He did not tell you to commit ***shirk*** by using statues and the cross, or by praying to dead or absent prophets and holy men and telling them your needs. He did not prescribe monasticism or the other reprehensible practices which you innovated. Christ never ordained such things for you, nor is what you follow the Law which you received from the messengers of Christ.

Most of the traditions you follow were invented and innovated after the time of the apostles, like your fast of fifty days in springtime, your institution of the Feasts of Holy Thursday, Friday, and Saturday. Neither Christ nor any one of the apostles ever commanded these or any other feasts of yours, such as that of the Apostles, Christmas, or Epiphany.

It was Helena the Harraniyya, the innkeeper,[12] the mother of Constantine, who innovated the Feast of the Holy Cross. You admit that it was she who uncovered the cross and made the time of its appearance a feast. That occurred a long time after Christ and the apostles because the reign of Constantine came over 300 years after Christ.

It was during that time in which you invented the creed, which is opposed to the texts of the prophets in more than one place. It was then that you announced the permission to eat pork and the lifting of sanctions against those who ate it. At that time you innovated the glorification of the cross and other heresies of yours.

Thus the law codes which you possess, on which you base your tradition and law, contain some material from the prophets and apostles and much of what was innovated after them which was handed down neither from Christ not from the apostles. How can you claim that you follow the tradition and law which Christ followed? This is something known necessarily and by successive transmission to be a clear lie.

## E. QUR'ANIC TEACHING ABOUT JESUS

Paul of Antioch states: In the Qur'an which this man brought it says:

"The Christ, Jesus the son of Mary, is the messenger of God, His word which He sent down upon Mary, and a Spirit from Him" (4:171).

This agrees with our view, since it bears witness that he is a man like us in his human nature which he took from Mary, and the Word of God and His Spirit united in him, except that the Word and the Spirit of God is creative, while we are creatures. It also says:

"They did not kill him, nor did they crucify him; but it seemed so to them" (4:157).

By this statement the Qur'an gives evidence for the divine nature of Christ which is the Word of God, which neither pain nor scorn could touch.

"O Jesus, I am gathering you and causing you to ascend to Me, and am cleansing you of those who disbelieve and am setting those who follow you above those who disbelieve until the Day of Resurrection" (3:55).

"I was a witness of them while I dwelt among them, and when You took me You were the Watcher over them. You are the witness of all things" (5:117).

By this is indicated his divinity, which is that of the creative Word of God, and by analogy with this we say that Christ was crucified and suffered in his human nature; in his divine nature he neither suffered nor was crucified.[1]

This may be answered in various ways.

1) Their claim that Muhammad demonstrated the divine and human natures in Christ, as Christians allege about him, is a clear and evident lie against Muhammad which can be known conclusively from his religion. It is similarly known from his religion that he confirmed Christ and demonstrated his messengership. Thus, were any Jew to claim that Muhammad rejected Christ and denied his prophetic mission, it would be like the claim of the Christians. These people claim that Muhammad said that Christ was the lord of the universe, that the divine nature united with his human nature. However, Muhammad brought what was communicated to men from God and he declared unbelievers people who said such things.

In more than one place the Qur'an clearly contradicts such a view (5:17; 5:72-77; 9:30-34; 43:57-65; 5:116-117). Muhammad taught about Christ that he never spoke to people anything except what God had commanded him to say. He told them to "Worship God, my Lord and your Lord." He was a witness over them while he was with them, and after his death God was the watcher over them. If any one of them erred in transmitting what he said, or in interpreting his message, or intentionally changed his religion, Christ would be responsible for none of that. He is nothing but a clear and great messenger.

God spoke through him as soon as he began to speak, and he sought a blessing upon himself (19:30-33). Christians say: "God's blessing is upon us from him," just as the extremists say about those for whom they claim divinity like 'Ali or the Hakimiyya [Druzes] about Al-Hakim.

2) God did not state that Christ died, nor that he was killed. He said, rather:

> O Jesus, I am gathering you and causing you to ascend to Me, and am cleansing you of those who disbelieve (3:55).

God spoke similarly in other passages (5:117; 4:155-161).

God cursed the Jews for various things. Among them was "their speaking against Mary a tremendous calumny" (4:156), their claiming that she was a fornicator. They are also condemned for their claim "We slew the Messiah Jesus son of Mary, God's messenger" (4:157). God said: "They slew him not nor crucified, but it appeared so to them" (4:157). God attributes this statement to them and curses them for it. The Christians are not mentioned because the ones who assumed responsibility for crucifying the supposedly crucified person were the Jews. Not a single one of the Christians was a witness [to the event] with them. Rather the apostles kept at a distance through fear, and not one of them witnessed the crucifixion. The only witnesses were the Jews who informed people that they had crucified Christ. Christians and others who handed on the story that Christ had been crucified only passed on what they had received from these Jews who were the chosen minions of the powers of darkness. Nor were they such a great number that prevented their colluding on a lie.

God said: "They did not kill him nor did they crucify him, but it seemed so to them." Then He said, "There will not be any of the People of the Book but will believe in him before his death" (4:159). Among the majority of scholars it is believed that this means "before the death of Christ." It may be said to mean "before the death of the Jew," but this is weak. Similarly it is said to mean "before the death of Muhammad," but this is even weaker. If one placed faith in him before death, this act of faith would benefit him, for the repentance of a person is accepted which is not after the moment of death.

It might be said that what is meant by this is the faith which is after the moment of death and therefore of no use. After his death everyone believes in the unknown which he had previously rejected, and so there is nothing special to Christ in this, because God said "before his death," and did not say "after his death." This is because there is no difference between someone's placing faith in Christ and Muhammad. The Jew who dies in his Judaism dies a disbeliever in Christ and Muhammad. Moreover God said: "There will not be any of the People of the Book but *will believe* in him before his death." The verb (*la-yu'minanna*) can only mean the future, and this is an indication that this faith is subsequent to God's informing mankind of this. Had He meant "before the death of the follower of the Book," He would have said, "There is no Follower of the Book but who believes (*yu'min*) in him before his death."

God also speaks of "the People of the Book," which is a general term for Jews and Christians, and this indicates that all People of the Book, Jews and Christians, will be believing in Christ before the death of Christ. When he descends, the Jews and Christians will believe that he is the messenger of God—not rejecting him as do the Jews now, nor claiming that he is God as do the Christians.

God states that they will put faith in him when he descends to earth. It is stated that he was raised up to God when He said: "I am gathering you and causing you to ascend to Me" (3:55). He will descend to earth before the Day of Resurrection and then he will die. By this God has informed us that they will believe in him before Christ's death, as He also says elsewhere (43:59-65).

In the sound hadith reports from the Prophet he said:

> It is impending that the son of Mary will descend among you as a just judge, a righteous *imam*; he will break the cross, kill the pig, and impose the *jizya*.

In the Qur'an (4:157) God has made it clear that He has raised up Christ alive and saved him from death, and that they will believe in him before he dies. This is confirmed by God's saying, "and I am purifying you from those who have disbelieved" (3:55); had he died there would have been no difference between him and others.

The word *al-tawaffi* in Arabic means "completion" and "receiving" and that is of three kinds:

a) the completion of sleep

b) the final completion of death

c) the final completion of soul and body together.

It is in this third meaning whereby Christ went out from the state of the people of the earth who have need of food, drink, and clothing, and he departed from them in matters pertaining to natural functions. God brought Christ to this state of completion; he is in the second heaven[2] until the time he descends to earth, and his state is not like the situation of the people of the earth in eating, drinking, dressing, sleep, natural functioning, etc.

3) For their statement that by his death is meant the death of his human nature it is necessary that they hold as their basis that by his "completion" is meant the death of his human nature. Whether it is said to refer to his death or to his completion in God, he is nothing other than human nature, for there is nothing other than that which God "brings to Himself" (3:55). This "gathering" is his being raised to God. Their view that what is raised is his divine nature would be contrary to the text of the Qur'an, even if it were a matter of his death. So how can that be the meaning when he is not said to die? They can make what is raised up something other than "received, completed," and yet the Qur'an states that what is raised up is "received."

Similarly when in another verse God says, "They certainly did not kill him, but God raised him up to Himself" (5:157-158), He is rejecting the claim of the Jews that "We have killed the Messiah, Jesus the son of Mary, messenger of God." The Jews did not claim to have killed divinity, nor did they concede that God had a divine nature in Christ. Moreover God did not mention their claims to have killed him from the Christians, so that one could say that their intent was the killing of the human nature without the divine. The claim, however, was from the Jews, who only attested to the human nature in Christ.

The Jews had claimed that they killed him, and so God said "They certainly did not kill him, but God raised him to Himself." God thereby attested to His raising up that which they claim to have killed, that is, Christ's human nature. It is obvious, therefore, that God denies that [Christ's] human nature had been killed. Rather, He is assuming it to Himself. Christians admit the assumption of the human nature, but they claim that it was crucified, rose from the grave either after a day or three days, and then ascended to heaven and sat, human nature and divine, at the right hand of the Father.

God said: "They certainly did not kill him." The meaning is that God denies the killing; He is certain about it. There is no doubt about it, in contrast to those who differed because they were in doubt whether or not he was killed. Those who believed it were not certain about it, since they could produce no proof for it.

There was a group of Christians saying that he was not crucified, for those who crucified the crucified man were the Jews, and they had confused Christ with someone else, as the Qur'an indicates. Among the People of the Book also it was held that he was confused with another, and those who wanted to kill him did not know who Christ was, until one of the people said to them "I know him." Only then did they know him.[3]

The view of those who say the meaning of the passage is "They did not kill him knowingly, but rather uncertainly" is weak.[4]

4) God said: "O Jesus, I am gathering you and causing you to ascend to Me, and am cleansing you from those who disbelieve." If that which was raised up was the divine nature, the Lord of the Universe would be saying to Himself and to His word "I am causing you to ascend to Me." Moreover, God said: "But God raised him up to Himself," but according to them Christ *is* God.

It is obvious that His raising Himself to Himself is impossible. If they say that he is the Word, they nevertheless hold that he is the Creator God. They do not make him of the same status as the Torah and the Qur'an, and other speech of God like these about which God spoke "To Him there arises the good word" (35:10). According to them Christ is God the Lord of the universe, the Creator, the Sustainer; the raising up of the Lord of the universe to the Lord of the universe is impossible.

5) God said: "I was a witness of them while I dwelled among them, and when You took me You were the Watcher over them." This indicates that after his being gathered up to God Christ was not a watcher over them, but only God without Christ. This statement is also an indication of the Reckoning; if this and statements like it are true, it is known that after his being taken up Christ is not a watcher over his followers. God is the watcher who observes them, counts up their deeds, and requites them accordingly. Christ is not a watcher; he does not observe their actions; neither does he reckon them up, nor does he reward them.

———

> Paul of Antioch states: On analogy to this we state that in Christ the Lord there are two natures. [There is] the divine nature, which is the nature of the Word of God and His spirit, and the human nature, which he took from the Virgin Mary, and the Word was united with it.[5]

It should be said to them that the explanation of Christians on this matter is muddled, differing, and contradictory. They have no view concerning it on which they agree. Their position is neither reasonable nor indicated by any sacred book. They have divided into sects and groups on this issue, each sect declaring the others unbelievers, as do the Jacobites, Melkites, and Nestorians. The transmission of opinions on this matter from these sects is confusing and with numerous inconsistencies.

It has been said that if you gather together ten Christians, they would split into eleven opinions. Moreover, the belief which they hold on the trinity and the hypostatic union in Christ as it is stated in their creed was never uttered in a single one of the prophetic books. It is not found in the speech of Christ, nor in that of the apostles, nor of any of the prophets. What they have in the books are ambiguities as well as clear-cut statements over the understanding of which they dispute. They affirm their creed, although the generality of Christians today among the Melkites, Nestorians, and Jacobites differ in interpreting it. Their view itself is internally contradictory so that imagining it in the correct sense is impossible.

For this reason each of them has come to hold what he believes to be closer to the correct view than others. Some of them, like the Jacobites, heed carefully the terminology of their creed and declare unbelievers those who disclose its falseness to everyone. Others, like the Nestorians, conceal some of it.[6] Many of them—and these are the Melkites—are between one group and the other. When they innovated their heresy of trinity, divine indwelling, and the like, there were, however, those who opposed them in this.

There exists a delineation of [Christians] according to their differing opinions—that is, according to the opinion of the sect whose view is handed down by its transmittor. The [Melkite] view related by many Muslim observers, which many [Christians] are found to oppose, is that handed down from them and mentioned by Abu al-Ma'ali,[7] his student Abu al-Qasim al-Ansari[8] and others.

They relate about them that life and knowledge are not two attributes existing additional to the essence, but are, rather, two personal (*nafsiatan*) attributes of the [divine] nature. They state that were the Christians to elucidate their position by an example, they would say that according to them the hypostases are analogous to states (*ahwal*)[9] and personal attributes (*sifat nafsiyya*) among those Muslims who affirm these concepts.

Perhaps by expressing the attributes as the Father, the son, and the Holy Spirit, they mean that the Father is existence, the son is Christ and the Word—or they may call knowledge a Word and the Word knowledge—and the spirit is life. By the Word they do not mean speech, for according to them speech is an attribute of action, and they do not call God's knowledge before its clothing itself in Christ and its union with him a son. But they do call Christ with that in which he was invested a son.

It is said that in their view the Word united with Christ and took on his human nature, but they differ as to the nature of this union. Some describe it as an interpenetration and a mixing, and this is the view of the Jacobites, Nestorians, and Melkites. They hold that the Word mingled with the body of Christ and interpenetrated it much as water and wine mix, or water and milk. It is said that this is the [official] view of Byzantium [Rum] and the majority of those who hold this are Melkites. The Word mingled with the body of Christ and that came to be one thing, and the multiplicity disappeared.

A group of Jacobites has adopted the position that the Word totally transformed the flesh and blood. A small group from each sect is said to hold that. What is meant by *ittihad* is the appearance of the divine nature over the human, like the appearance of a picture in a mirror, or the impression in a seal.

There are those among them who say that the manifestation of the divine nature in the human is equivalent to that of God upon the throne according to Muslims. Many of these sects have held that what is meant by divine union (*ittihad*) is divine indwelling (*hulul*).

They are said to have differed as well on the matter of nature and hypostases. The Jacobites and Nestorians have taken the position that the nature is not different from the hypostases. The Melkites, however, have declared that the nature is not the hypostases, and that it is different from them, while the others hold it to be the hypostases.

It is said that Christians have split into sects from another aspect, the Byzantine group going so far as to affirming the establishment of three gods while the Jacobites and Nestorians having prevented that in one respect have made it a necessary conclusion in another. That is, they hold that the word is God, the spirit is God, the Father is God; the three persons of which each person is God is one God.

A small group of Christians is said to hold that Jesus was son of God by way of a special favor; just as Abraham was taken to be *khalil*, or special friend of God, so was Christ held to be a son of God. These are called Arians.

In these reports of Muslims there are things which some, but not all, Christians hold. For example, they report about them that by the "Logos" they do not mean speech, for speech according to them is an attribute of action. This is a view of a group of them as well as of Jews, but many and possibly most of them hold the speech of God to be uncreated, and reject those who say that it is created.[10]

Another group of Muslim scholars, including Abu al-Hasan ibn al-Zaghuni,[11] have reported about them that which agrees with this in a certain respect. They say that groups of Christians have agreed that God is not a body, and agree that He is one nature, three persons, and that each one of the persons is a particular nature. They are joined by the common nature substance and then they are differentiated.

Some of them hold that the persons are opposed in personality but agree in substantiality. Others hold that they are not opposed in personality but merely differ in personality. A group of them holds that each one of the hypostases is neither the other nor different from the other, that is, neither different nor opposed.

They claim that the nature is not different from the hypostases, except what has been already mentioned concerning a group of Melkites who hold that the hypostases are the nature, although the nature is different from the hypostases. They claim that the nature is the Father and the hypostases are life—which is the Holy Spirit—power, and knowledge. They hold that God united with one of the hypostases—who is the son—in Jesus the son of Mary, who thereby became Christ upon the union of the divine and human nature. As such he was carried [in the womb], born, raised, crucified, killed, and buried.

On this union in Christ they differ also. Nestorians hold that Christ is two natures, two hypostases—one eternal, one created in time. The union in him is only in his will, and the will of both persons is one, although he was two natures. However, the Jacobites hold that when they—the eternal nature and the created nature—united, the two natures came to be one nature. In this also they differ. Some hold the created nature to have become eternal.

Others hold that when the two natures united, they became one nature, in one respect eternal, in another created.

The Melkites hold that Christ is two natures but one hypostasis. It is related about still others that Christ is two hypostases but one nature. The Arians held that God has neither a body nor hypostases; that Christ was neither crucified nor killed; that he is a prophet. It is related about some of them that they hold that Christ is not the son of God, and about others that they hold him to be the son of God by appellation and approximation.

They differ concerning the Logos sent down upon Mary. One group says that the Logos took up residence in (*ḥallat fi*) Mary by way of combination, as water combines with milk and thoroughly interpenetrates it. Another group holds that the Logos dwelled in Mary without any mixing, as the features of a person dwell in a mirror or on shiny surfaces without any mixing.

A group of Christians has claimed that the human nature with the divine nature is like a seal with wax on which an impression has been made. Nothing of it remains except the effect, according to this group.

Abu al-Hasan ibn al-Zaghuni and others have confirmed that the Christians differ on the nature of the hypostases, with one group holding them to be substances, another that they are characteristics, a third that they are attributes, still another claiming that they are persons. According to them the Father is the substance comprising the hypostases; the son is the Word who united with the principle of Christ, and the spirit is life. They agree that union is an active attribute, not an attribute of essence.

It is said that their view on divine union differs variously, some of them holding that the union is the Word which is the son dwelling within the body of Christ. This view is said to be that of the majority. Another group among them claims that the union is combination and mixture. A number of Jacobites hold the union to be the Word of God's transformation of the flesh and blood by commingling with it. Many Jacobites and Nestorians claim that the union is that the Word and the human nature have combined and mixed as the mixture of water with wine, or that of wine and milk.[12] Some of them state that the union consists in the Word and the human nature uniting and becoming one edifice.

A group of them hold that the union is like the manifestation of the picture of a man in a mirror, like the impression of a stamp on what is printed, like a seal on wax. Another group claims that the Word united with the body of Christ in the sense that it inhabited him without any contact or admixture. It is as we say that the mind is residing in the soul without mixture with the soul or contact with it. Finally, the Melkites hold that the union is in that the two become one and the multiplicity disappeared.

This is what has been transmitted concerning them by Abu al-Hasan ibn al-Zaghuni, and it is similar to what has been reported by the Qadi Abu Bakr ibn al-Tayyib,[13] the Qadi Abu Ya'la[14] and others.

## F. *ITTIHAD*: UNION OF GOD WITH A CREATURE

> Sa'id ibn Bitriq states: "Through union with that one substratum, the substratum of the creative word of God, Christ was one with the trinity by nature of his divinity and one with the people by nature of his humanity. He was not two, but one with the Father and the Holy Spirit, for he was it [the divine nature], and he was one with all people by combining two different substances—that of the creative divine nature and of the created human nature—by the union in one substance of that of the Word who is son born from God before all ages and that of the one born of the Virgin Mary at the end of the ages without any separation from the Father or the Holy Spirit."[1]

In this passage, and in fact in the whole position which he has presented, there is so much contradiction and falsity that its enumeration and description would take much space. Their view is in itself false; there is no truth in it. They themselves cannot imagine a reasonable meaning for it, and so they say about it that they have been inadequate in their expressing it.

Actually, they are in error and ignorance. They do not imagine what is reasonable, nor do they know what they are saying. They do not even have a belief which they can establish on Christ, but whatever innovations they hold are false. They have admitted that they do not understand what they say.

They say, "This is beyond reason," and "God has united with Christ such that no man can grasp it," but what cannot be grasped or what is beyond reason is not for anyone to believe or to express as his opinion. When the faithful messengers disclose something which the mind of man is inadequate for believing, and if a transmittor were to hand on from them what sound reason knows to be false, it is certain that he has perpetrated a lie against them, either in its text and in meaning, or in one of the two. If someone holds a view the correctness of which he claims to know, or claims that by it he has explained the teaching of the prophets, and yet he cannot imagine what he says nor does he understand it, that person is speaking about God and His messengers that which he does not know. This person has committed the greatest of forbidden crimes, as God Himself has informed us (7:33; 2:169; 4:171-173).

The people of all three religions have agreed that speaking about God without knowledge is forbidden, and God has forbidden them to speak anything but the truth about Him. This is a prohibition against speaking what is false, whether or not they know it to be false. Even if they do not know it is false, they still do not know it to be true, for it is impossible that something which is false be known as true. Even though a believer were to suppose some false belief to be true, that would not be knowledge. No one must speak about God what he does not know.

If they knew it to be false, it would be more proper for them not to hold it. However, the generality of Christians are astray and do not know whether or not what they say is true, but speak about God what they do not know. The point is that there is much in their speech which is false, like their saying, "He came to be through union with that one substratum, the substratum of the creative word of God."

According to them Christ is the name for both the divine and human nature together, the name for the creator and the created, one of which has united with the other. He thus becomes, through union with that substratum, the substratum of the created word of God. Irrespective of whether he means by that that the divine and human natures are the substratum for the divine nature or that the human nature is the substratum for the divine, they cite as an example of this the spirit and the body, or fire and iron. It is as if one were to say that the body and the spirit—or the body alone—are the substratum for the spirit, or that fire and iron—or just iron—were the substratum for the fire.

They should be asked whether that which is created and coming into being in time is the substratum for the eternal creator, who is without beginning and without end. Is something created and made in time which is in need of God in every respect a substratum for the Creator who is supremely independent in every respect? Is this anything but the most obvious and impossible circularity?

It is evident by sound reason and by the consensus of intelligent men that the creature has no subsistence except in the Creator. If the Creator has the creature as His substratum, it necessarily follows that both the Creator and the creature have subsistence through the other; each of the two of them will be in need of the other, since something has a need for whatever serves as a substratum for it.

Moreover, demanding that the creator has a need for His creature—which is clear blasphemy—is clearly forbidden by sound reason. However, this is a necessary conclusion for Christians, whether they hold for the hypostatic union or for the divine indwelling without union, although their three sects have all held a type of union.

In a union each of the two uniting elements must have the other, and is thus in need of the other, just as they represent it in the analysis of the soul with the body or fire with iron. The spirit which is in the body is in need of the body, just as fire in a piece of iron has need for the iron. Similarly with *hulul*, everything that resides in something else has need of that in which it resides.

If some creature were considered to be self-existing and eternal, it would not be a creature. Moreover it is impossible that there be two mutually dependent eternal beings, whether it be supposed that one is a maker of the other or the whole maker of the other, or that the first would be dependent upon the other in some respect.

If the one were dependent upon the other in some respect then he would not be existing except in him. That which exists does not exist except by the existence of those things which are necessary for it, and its existence is not complete except in them. Thus everything which is considered to have a need for something else does not exist except in that other.

If each of the two eternal beings had need for the other, it follows that the first would not exist except by the creation of that in which its need for the other is completed, nor would the second exist except by the creation of that in which its need for the former is completed. The creator would not be creator until he were existent, and he would not be existent except by those things necessary for his existence. It follows that the first would not be existent until the other made it existent, and the second would not be existent until the first made it existent. Since its making the other occurred when its own existence was not complete, its existence would depend upon the other and would not be existent except in it. There is no difference between one of two things having need of the other for its existence and its own existence only being complete in the other. This is an infinite regression forbidden by the agreement of intelligent men.

A "concomitant regression" (*al-dawr al-ma'iyy*) occurs when one thing is not found except with the other, nor is the second except with the first. Examples of this are fatherhood with sonship, some of the attributes of the Lord with others, His attributes with His essence. He is not knowing except with His being powerful, and He is not knowing and powerful except with His being living, nor living except with His being knowing and powerful. His attributes are not existent except in His essence, nor is His essence existing except with His attributes. This kind of regression is possible in two creatures who are in need of a creator to bring them both into being, like fatherhood and sonship; it is also possible with the Lord inseparable from His attributes.

However, if there were supposed two eternal lords acting, it would be impossible that one of them would not be in need of the other, since its own existence would not be complete except by that which its existence needed, and it would not be an agent for anything if its existence were not complete. With the deficiency of each of the two of them in respect to the completeness of its existence, it is impossible that either be an agent upon the other to complete the existence of that other. For this reason no one from any of the religions has spoken in this way except that which Christians have said in their making a creature the substratum for the creator.

This is also more strongly forbidden by sound reason than is the possibility of setting up two creators each as the substratum for the other, although this latter is also impossible. The creature is in need of the creator in all matters. It is impossible that, concomitant with his need for the creator for his existence and for the completeness of his existence, the substratum for the creator be found in him. That would demand that he be a basis for Him and that the completeness of His existence would be in him.

The sum of what is said is that the creator subsists in him. He is from the creator; the creator, who is the creator of every creature, created him; he has no existence and no foundation except in the creator. How can the foundation for the creator be in him?

This is not like substance with its necessary accidents, or like matter and form among those who would claim that form is a substance, since the two are mutually necessary. This latter is of the nature of a "concomitant" regression like sonship and fatherhood, and this type is permissible, as we have previously explained, since the creator for both together is God. With each of the two being creator this is impossible, and with one of the two being creator and the other a creature, this is even more strongly impossible.

The Lord is supremely independent in every respect from everything other than Him, and everything that is not him is in need of him in every respect. This is part of the meaning of His name "Al-Samad." "The Rock" is that to which everything turns (*yasmud*) because of its dependence upon Him. He is supremely independent of everything, does not turn in need to anything, and does not request anything. How could His substratum be in any creature?

This particularized *ittihad* of the Christians resembles in some respects the view of the pantheists and those who claim universal *ittihad*. This is those who hold the view presented by Ibn 'Arabi, the author of *Al-Fusus* and *Al-Futuhat al-Makkiyya*. He states that the essences of creatures subsist in non-existence, and the existence of Truth flows upon them. Thus they are in need of Him from the aspect of general shared existence, and He is their existence; conversely He is in need of them in respect to the essences (*al-a'yan*) subsistent in non-existence. He is that in which every essence is particularized as an essence. This makes both the creator and the creature mutually dependent on the other.

They say that existence is one, and then they establish an enumeration of essences which they claim to be epiphanies (*mazahir*) and manifestations (*majali*). If the manifestation and epiphany is different from the one manifest, then a multiplicity is established; but if He is it, there is no multiplicity. They are thereby forced to a contradiction—much as the Christians are forced to it, when they argue for unity alongside multiplicity. They sing, "He worships me, and I worship Him; He praises me and I praise Him." These people have built their view on two false premises.

1) Essences of contingent beings are fixed in non-existence. It is like those theorists in *kalam* who say, "The non-existent is a thing subsisting in non-existence."[2] This view is false according to the majority of intelligent men. The truth of the matter is that the

non-existent is that by which is meant what is discovered, imagined, spoken, and written about before its existence. It has an existence in the mind, in speech, and in writing, but it has no existence in external reality. Existence is subsistence (*al-thubut*), but there is no subsistence for the non-existent in external objective existence. Its only subsistence is in the mind—that is, the mind intellects it before its existence.

2) They make the very existence of the Lord of the universe—the eternal, the one necessary in Himself—the same existence as that of the contingent, fashioned, governed being, as says Ibn 'Arabi:

> Whoever understands what we hold on numbers and that the denial of them is the essence of proving them knows that transcendent Truth is creation which resembles It (*al-haqq al-munazzah huwa al-khalq al-mushabbah*). The factor that is the creator of the creature, the factor that is the creature of the creator—all of that is of one essence. Rather, it *is* one essence and it is many essences. It is "O Father, do what you are commanded."

Thus, he says "No one has ever slain anyone except himself, nor married anyone but himself." He says:

> One of the Beautiful Names of God is the Most High. Over whom is He high, for what is there but He? What is He higher than when nothing exists except He? His sublimity, then, is in Himself. In respect to existence He is identical with existent things, those things which are called temporal and exalted in themselves; but they are not He.

It was related about Abu Sa'id al-Kharraz[3] that someone said to him, "In what do you know your Lord?" He said, "In His bringing together opposites and in the recitation of His saying, 'He is the first and the last, the manifest and the hidden, and He is knowledgeable about everything'" (57:3). By that he meant that He has brought together in His truth that which is contradictory in the case of others, for the creature is not first and last, evident and hidden.

It is established in a sound hadith report from the Prophet that he said:

> You are the first; there is nothing before You. You are the last; there is nothing after You. You are the manifest; there is nothing above You. You are the hidden; there is nothing beneath You.

Then this apostate comes along and explains the saying of Abu Sa'id to say that the creature *is* the creator. He said:

> Abu Sa'id has said—and he is one of the aspects of Truth and one of the tongues by which He speaks about Himself—that God is not known except by a joining of opposites by which one makes a judgment about Him. He is the first and the last, the evident and the hidden. He is the essence of what is evident, and the essence of what is hidden in the state of its manifestatation. There is nothing one sees but Him, there is nothing hidden from one but Him. He is evident to Himself, hidden from Himself. He is called Abu Sa'id al-Kharraz and other created names.

For this reason a Christian could say to one who claims this or reports it about his shaykhs and says he is a Muslim, "You have declared us unbelievers for our saying 'God is Christ,' but your shaykhs say 'God is Abu Sa'id al-Kharraz.' But Christ is better than Abu Sa'id."

These Christians answer with a retort which shows that these others are greater heretics than the Christians. They say to Christians, "You have particularized Him in Christ, but we say that He is the existence of all things and we do not single out Christ."

For this reason one of them said to 'Afif al-Din al-Tilimsani, one of the wiliest of men, "Are you a Nusayri?" He answered, "Nusayr is a part of me." The Nusayris are followers of Abu Shu'ayb Muhammad ibn Nusayr, who held something similar about 'Ali ibn Abi Talib to what the Christians say about Christ. So also the rest of the extremists about 'Ali or one of the people of his House,[4] the Isma'ilis, the Bani 'Ubayd [the Fatimids], who adhere to Muhammad ibn Isma'il ibn Ja'far, Al-Hakim, and others, or about Al-Hallaj or one of the shaykhs who claim for one of these a union of the divinity in him or His indwelling in him—all of these hold something similar to what the Christians say about Christ.

They hold that *hulul* and *ittihad* occur in time, and that the Eternal One has taken residence in or united with a temporal creature after the two had not been united. These others declare an absolute unity. Those who assert it say that He is the existence of everything, not holding for the union of two existences, nor for the indwelling of one of them in the other. They hold that existence is the subsistence of the existence of Truth and the subsistence of things, and these two, each having a need for the other, unite. The Truth when He is manifest is the human person, and what is hidden in the person is the Lord.

They hold that if the essential manifestation has occurred for you, your worshiping idols and other things would not harm you, for they state clearly that He is at the heart of idols and rivals and that a person does not worship other than Him. Ibn 'Arabi stated something similar to this commending the unbelieving people of Noah [in his comment on the verse "They have plotted a great deception"]:[5]

> Praying to God is a deception on the part of the one praying, for he who had been non-existent at the beginning calls upon the goal—"I call on God" (12:108). This is the essence of the deception. They said in their deception, "Forsake not your gods. Forsake not Wudd, nor Suwa', nor Yaghuth, and Ya'uq and Nasr" (71:23). To the extent they abandoned these gods and turned away from them they would become ignorant of the Truth. The Truth has a face in everything that is worshiped which is known by him who has known it and which is unknown to Him who has been ignorant of it. God said about the Muhammadiyyin, "Your Lord has decreed that you worship none save Him" (17:23). Thus God has only passed judgment on something by what has actually occurred. The gnostic knows whom he worships, and that in every form He is evident so that He is worshiped there. Differentiation and multiplicity are like the various members in a form which is perceived, or the abstract powers in a spiritual form. There is no worship of anything other than God in anything which is worshiped.

This apostate approved Pharaoh in his saying, "I am your Highest Lord" (79:24). He said that because Pharaoh was in the rank of dominion, the master of the age,[6] and he was *khalifa* by the sword, even though in legal terminology he had acted tyranically. Therefore he said, "I am your Highest Lord," that is, although all things are lords in some respect or other, I am the highest of them by virtue of what I have been given in terms of external leadership over you. When the magicians knew the truthfulness of what he said, they did not deny it, but confirmed that for him by what they said (20:72; 20:73), for the government was his. Ibn 'Arabi said that the Pharaoh was correct in saying "I am your Highest Lord," for the Pharaoh was Truth himself (*'ayn al-haqq*).

He also sanctioned the People of the Calf in their worship of the statue, and claimed that Moses was pleased with that. He said that because Moses was more knowledgeable in the matter than Aaron because of his knowledge that God had decreed that we worship only Him, and that nothing occurs but what God had decreed. He reproved Aaron for his dissent, and for his lack of vision. The gnostic is he who sees the Truth in all things; rather, he sees Him as identical with everything.

Among these people there is a group who do not hold for the subsistence of essences in non-existence. They say, rather, that there is no existence but the existence of Truth. They distinguish, however, between the absolute and the specific. They say that He is absolute existence overflowing upon specific existent things, such as the bestial existence specified in every animal, the human specified in every man. This is what is called the natural universal. They call this existence "encompassment" (*al-ihata*), and say that absolute existence is by condition of its freedom from every qualification, and this is called the intellective universal (*al-kulli al-'aqli*).

Among the generality of intelligent men this is said to be found only in the mind and not in external reality. He [Ibn 'Arabi] says about the followers of Plato that they have established these pure ideas of essences in the external world. They speak of eternal, absolute humanity, and eternal absolute animality, and they call them Platonic ideas and suspended images (*al-muthul al-mu'allaqa*).[7]

Their brethren, Aristotle and his party, and the majority of intelligent men, have made a refutation against them. They have made it clear that these ideas are only imagined in minds and do not exist in essences, just as the mind may imagine an absolute number, absolute quantities like a point, a line, a surface, a geometric body, or something like that which the mind imagines, but there is not in that anything of existent beings subsisting in external reality.

These people think that they have established this "absolute with the condition of its absoluteness," and they may call it "encompassment," and it is existence free from any limitations. After this comes unconditioned absolute existence; it is the universal divided into necessary and contingent, into eternal and temporal, and the like, as "animal" is divided into speaking and dumb.[8]

This unconditioned absolute is found in external reality, for the universal name is complete for its kinds and persons, but is only found in external reality limited and specified. Whoever says that it is found in external reality as a universal is wrong. The universal is not universal at all except in minds, and only particular things are found in external reality, if the mere conception of it is assumed to prohibit the participation of any of the same in it. However, the mind grasps the universal factor shared among particular things, and so there is a participated universal in minds. These people make this necessary existence, and they may posit it beyond this, for they say, "This is beyond the necessary."

If it is said that this universal existence does not exist in external reality except as specified, there is nothing existent in external reality except specified existent creatures, personalized by the attributes subsisting in them. Were its existence supposed to be in external reality, it would be either a part or an attribute of specified things. If it were the former, there would not be in the external world an existent being who is the lord of specified existent beings. If the second, the Lord would be either a part or an attribute of existent beings.

It is obvious by sound reason that an attribute of a thing is subsistent in it, not the creator of what is described by it. A part of a thing is likewise not the creator of it, but a part of a thing is merely one of its parts.

Some of these people say that the Lord is in the universe like butter is in milk, oil in sesame seeds, etc. In this way they make Him part of the created universe. Merely imagining this is sufficient to show its falseness in logic. These people say that if you do not abandon reason and religious tradition the certainty which they have achieved will never be yours. They say, "Among us is established by intuitive insight (*kashf*) that which contradicts sound reason."

I say to them that their prophets were the most perfect people in *kashf*. They bring information of what human minds are unable to know, not of what their minds know to be false. They teach the pearls of the intellect, not its absurdities.

If anyone other than them teaches from immediate perception and intuition that which sound reason knows to be false, it may be known that that person's intuition is false. If its falseness is not known, this knowledge may be correct or it may be erroneous, for others than the prophets are not inerrant.

These people hear the name of God and intend to worship and know Him but they stop at His effects—the things He made—and think that [those things] are He. They are like someone who has heard the word "sun," and when he sees its rays spread out in the air and on earth, he thinks that they are the sun, and does not raise his sight and his understanding to the sun which is in the sky. Similarly, these people do not raise the understanding of their hearts to the Lord of the universe who is beyond every thing and dissimilar to his creatures.

The underlying reason for that is that they witness in their hearts a simple absolute existence who has no special name like "The Living," "The Knowing," "The Powerful," nor does it have attributes, nor is one thing distinguished in it from another. This is shared existence. However, this perception is [only] in themselves, and has no reality in the external universe. Many a person with whom they have spoken does not imagine what they have perceived, and they think that that person has not understood what they have witnessed.

I have spoken to more than one of them and have explained to him that this which they have perceived is in the mind according to the proposition that if it were existent in the external universe, it would have to be either an attribute of existent beings or a part of them. Despite their thinking that it is existent in external reality, they do not think that it remains in external reality any different from the way they have experienced it. They conceal from sense perception that which comprehends specific beings; they prevent their minds from imagining them, until they do not distinguish between one existent being and another. They state that there is differentiation in sense perception, and then they witness this absolute existence despite their withdrawal from sense knowledge. They think that this absolute itself is the specified beings and that it is what originally became existent.

It should be said to them that if it were supposed that universal existence were established as universal in the external universe, and that you had witnessed this, it would be evident according to every intelligent person that the existence of the shared universal would not contradict the existence of the specified determined being. Absolute shared animality and humanity do not contradict objectively existent animals and humans, and so the subsistence of objectively existent beings does occur in external reality.

Supposing you were distant from this and did not witness it; a distance from witnessing a thing does not in itself necessitate its non-existence. If a person has not immediately perceived a thing, or has not seen it or known it, if his heart has not trembled with it, nor has he passed away in his experience of it, or been annihilated or absent, it does not follow necessarily from that that the thing in itself would become ephemeral and non-existent, having no reality of its own. There is a clear and evident difference between a thing perishing, vanishing, or being non-existent in itself and a human's lack of immediate experience of it, or his lack of memory or knowledge of it.

These people in their error think that if their immediate experience of existent being passes away that those things themselves are passing away; thus there is no existent being except what they imagine by way of absolute existence. They say that multiplicity and differentiation are in the senses, and if the immediate perception of the heart has passed away from that of the sense, there remains neither differentiation nor multiplicity. They think that sense perception is therefore in error, and it is the mind which witnesses universals and absolutes without the sense. Therefore, if they invalidate what the senses perceive, there only remains with them universal existence.

They think, however, that this is God, and that the Lord remains as a fancy and imagination in their souls, with no reality in the external universe. As Al-Shustari, one of their prominent teachers and the student of Ibn Sab'in, said, "Your imagination is what shows that which is under a thing." And he says:

> Existence is seen as one, and you are it,
> You have nothing more than what is there without you.

I said to one of their leading thinkers: supposing that this absolute existence were subsisting in external reality and that it was the deepest nature (*'ayn*) of experienced existent beings. From where do you get the idea that this is the Lord of the universe who created the heavens and the earth and everything in them? He admitted [my objection] and said, "There is something of a ruse in this."

Unless sense perception—both internal and external (*al-hiss al-batin wal-zahir*)—is joined with reason which distinguishes between what is perceived and what is other than it, it may be deluded by errors of the type which enter upon a dreamer, an insane person, one afflicted with epilepsy, and others who judge by pure sense which has no reason with it. Dumb animals are more rightly guided than these people, as God has said (7:117). Such people clearly state their rejection of both reason and revelation, and are included in God's condemnation:

> Or do you deem that most of them hear or understand? They are but as cattle—nay, they are farther astray (25:44).

They themselves declare the necessity of withdrawing from reason, evident sense knowledge, and revelation, as Al-Tilimsani, one of their most prominent teachers, has said:

> Say to your sense "Remove your attraction,"
> Drive away your delight in it,
> Tell the setting of your mind, "Remain not,"
> Be silent that you see It in you speaking,
> If then you find a tongue speaking—speak.[9]

The views of these people are elaborated elsewhere. The point here is that Christians have claimed that the divinity is in need of the humanity with which He has united, while these people claim that the Lord of the universe is in need of all the essences established in non-existence outside of Him.

Whoever says that the Lord of the universe has united with something other than Him must concede that each of the two uniting is in need of the other despite its impossibility for each of them and the resulting change in God's nature. Furthermore this is not reasonable *hulul*. *Hulul* can only be understood if that which indwells is subsisting in and having a need for that in which it resides. This is the case whether by that is meant the *hulul* of attributes and accidents in things described and in substances, or by it is meant the indwelling of essences. When one of the two bodies is the place of residence for another—like the presence of water in a container—this necessitates the need of the one for the other.

The knowledge of God and faith in Him which resides in the hearts of believers subsists in their hearts and has a need for them.

This is similar to what the philosophers prove about matter and form. They say that matter is a substratum, and along with that they admit that form has a need for matter. Those who speak of *wahdat al-wujud* have made the creator to creatures like form is to matter. Ibn Sab'in indicates this, saying, "He is water in water, fire in fire, and in each thing as the form of that thing." The refutation of these people has been elaborated in other places than this book.

If they say that the Lord resided in Christ as He resided in others, this is the *hulul* found, according to them, in the teaching of David, where he says "You dwell in the hearts of upright persons." This is known to be the indwelling of faith in Him, His knowledge, guidance, light, and the intellective forms—as we have already explained. For this reason it is compared to the appearance and rays which reside in the air and on earth, showing that it is subsisting in them and thus has need for the earth and the air.

The messengers have informed us that God is beyond the universe by various expressions, sometimes saying "He is on high," or "He is the highest," other times saying, "He is in heaven" (67:16; 67:17). By that is not meant that God is in the cavity of the heavens or that God surrounds any created thing. Rather, the speech of each of the prophets confirms the others (37:180-182; 57:3).

It is established in a sound hadith from the Prophet that He said:

> You are the evident; there is nothing above You.
> You are the hidden; there is nothing below You.

He thus informed us that there is nothing above Him. More than one of the *salaf* has said that He descends to the heaven of this earth, but His throne is not devoid of His presence. He does not come to be below creatures nor in their sphere at all. His sublimity above them is a necessary attribute for Him. Wherever a creature is found, the Lord is always above it.[10]

By the prophets' saying that He is "in heaven"—that is, "on High"—is not meant that He is in one of the spheres of the heavenly bodies, but rather the "high heaven." He, if He is above the Throne, is "on high," "the Highest" where there is no creature, so that when the Lord is surrounding some created thing, He is not in any respect created. There is nothing existent except the creator and the creature. The creator is dissimilar to His creatures, elevated beyond them. He is not in any creature at all whether or not that creature is called a direction.

Whoever says that God is in a created direction (*jiha*) above something, surrounding it, or in need of it—in any of its aspects—that person is in error. Similarly anyone who says that there is not a Lord beyond the heavens, or a God is not on the throne, or Muhammad did not ascend it to his Lord, or that the angels do not go up to Him, that the Books do not come down from Him, or nothing approaches Him, or that He does not draw near to a thing—that person is in error also.

He who calls what is beyond the universe a direction, and makes pure void a direction, and says that in this sense He is in a direction, that is, He is beyond every thing, this is the correct meaning. Anyone who denies this meaning by saying "He is not in a direction" is in error.

The path of safety lies in holding that what the messengers have established about God He has proven for Himself, and what the messengers have denied about God He has denied about Himself. The expressions which the messengers have not uttered either by denial or by affirmation, like the expression "direction" (*jiha*), "place" (*ḥayyiz*), and the like, demand neither an absolute denial nor an affirmation until after the clarification of their meaning. Anyone who intends a correct meaning by what he has affirmed is correct in that meaning, although he may have erred in expression. Whoever intends a correct meaning by what he has denied is correct in that meaning, although he may have erred in its expression.

As for the person who has affirmed by his expression both what is true and false, or denied by his expression both something true and something false, both of these are correct in the truth which they intended, and in error in the falsity which they intended; such a person has clothed the truth in falsehood and has joined together truth and falsehood in his teaching.

The prophets are all in mutual agreement on His being in the height. In the Qur'an and the sunna there are close to a thousand indications of that, and in the speech of the earlier prophets an uncountable number.

# IV. FINAL QUESTIONS

## A. THE COMPATIBILITY OF RATIONAL AND REVEALED KNOWLEDGE

This concludes what we have mentioned from the patriarch Sa'id ibn Bitriq, who is highly praised among the Christians. He is their friend and sympathetic to their reports, whose concerns in their religion he has delineated in extolling their religion. Some of the reports suffer from an excess of his putting what they have done in a good light, and many people deny and reject that, as, for example, what he mentioned about the appearance of the cross, the debate about Arius, etc. Many people oppose him in what he has mentioned on these points, and state that the matter of the manifestation of the cross was a counterfeit, a fraud, a deception, and a conspiracy; they state as well that Arius never said that Christ was a creator.

The point is that if one accepts what he has mentioned as trustworthy, it is clear that the greater part of the religion which Christians follow was not taken from Christ, but is rather what one group of them has innovated while others have opposed them on it. It is clear, moreover, that among them there has been enmity and disagreement in their faith and laws which confirm what God has said (5:14).

Christians admit what this patriarch has stated, that the first king to render the religion of Christians victorious was Constantine, and that over three hundred years after Christ. This is half the interval which occurred between Christ and Muhammad, which was 600 or 620 years.

If the Christians admit that what they follow in regards to faith one group of them has produced against the opposition of others, and thus [their teaching] was not handed down from Christ, it is also the case with what they follow by way of permitting what God has forbidden. For example, the killing of those who have opposed their religion is permitted as is the killing of those who forbade pork, despite the law of the Gospel opposing this. Thus too circumcision and the glorification of the cross.

They have mentioned their reliance for that on Constantine's seeing the form of a cross in the stars. Obviously, it is improper to build a *shari'a* on that, for there occur to pagans and star- and idol-worshipers events like this which are even greater than that. It was in ways like this that the religion of the messengers was replaced and people began to engage in idolatrous worship of their Lord and serve idols. It is Satan who deceives people by this and even greater than this.

The cloth which someone may have seen and the voice which he heard[1]—is it possible for any intelligent person to change the law of God with which the messengers were sent by a voice and an apparition like this? Things greater than this have occurred to pagans, star-worshipers, and servants of idols. Although they state this to be from Peter, the head of the apostles, there is [in it] no general permission for everything which was forbidden. He said, rather, "What God has purified do not consider shameful." What God declared shameful in the Torah He made shameful, and did not purify it unless Christ purified it. Pork and other forbidden things were not permitted for the apostles, if, as they believe, Christ's word was inerrant.

Christ did not permit all of what God forbade in the Torah, but permitted only some of that. This is one of the matters described [by Ibn Bitriq] which should induce Muslims to fight the Christians (9:29).

The patriarch had made mention of how some groups of Christians have cursed others in the seven Councils and outside the councils. The description of this is lengthy, and confirms what God has said, "Therefore We have stirred up enmity and hatred among them until the Day of Resurrection" (5:14). When they say "Whom we oppose we curse," it has no effect, for each group of them is both cursing and cursed. In their cursing of those who oppose them there is no establishing the truth or exposing falsehood. Truth is only established by proofs and signs brought by the messengers, as God has said (2:213).

We have previously mentioned that in the information stated by Sa'id Ibn Bitriq a great patriarch of theirs was coming to a church built upon an idol worshiped by the pagans. He acted cleverly to make them worship in place of the idol a creature greater than it, like one of the prophets or angels. For example, there was in Alexandria a temple of the pagans in which there was an idol named Mika'il; the Christians made it a church with the name of the angel Michael, and began to worship the angel and sacrifice to it where they had been previously honoring the idol.[2]

In this Christians are transferring the idolatrous worship of a creature to the idolatrous worship of a higher creature. Earlier peoples had been building their temples and putting in them idols with the names of heavenly bodies like the sun, the planet Venus, etc. The innovators among the Christians changed them over to the worship of some one of the angels or prophets. But God condemned this (3:79-80; 17:56-57).

———

In what we have mentioned [from Ibn Bitriq] there is an answer to Paul of Antioch's statement:

> And on analogy with this we say that in the Lord Jesus Christ there are two natures, the divine nature which is the nature of the Word of

God and His spirit, and the human nature which he took from the Virgin Mary and united with the divine.[3]

It is clear that this is one of the views of Christians, but they have other views which contradict this. Every sect among them declares the others unbelievers, since they have not followed a view which they received from Christ and the apostles. Their inventors have innovated these views, and they thereby have gone astray, as God has stated (5:77). God states that they went astray before the sending of Muhammad, and also that he condemned them to error whose basis is ignorance.

There is never found anyone who is a Christian either openly or secretly who is not ignorant and erring about the object of worship and concerning the origin of his religion. He knows neither Him whom he worships or in what he worships, despite the efforts of some of them who strive diligently in worship, asceticism, and nobility of morals.

Against these people it is said that in their view of "two natures," and their holding also that "he has two wills," and again "he is one person whose number did not increase," they state at the same time "the two of them are united." This is like what they have mentioned in this book of theirs—they do not speak of two persons so that it is not necessary for them to hold for four hypostases.

Some of them say, "the two are two substances," while others, "he is one substance." If they said, "he is one substance," their viewpoint becomes that of the Jacobites, especially if they state, "Mary gave birth to the divine and human natures, for Christ is a name which joins both divinity and humanity since he is completely God and completely man."

If he was one substance, it became necessary for the divine nature to become transformed and changed, and likewise the human nature. If the two became one thing, the second thing was neither pure man nor pure God, but humanity and divinity were combined in it. Moreover man and God are two dissimilar beings—according to their terminology they are two substances (*wa-huma fi istilahihim jawharan*). Therefore, if these two substances became one substance, not two substances, it would follow by necessity that this third thing would be neither pure God nor pure man. It is not two substances—God and man—and these are two substances, not one. It would be a third thing, mixed, combined, and transformed from each of the two. The nature of divinity and that of humanity would have been replaced so that they became this third substance which is neither pure divinity nor pure humanity, as is known in all other types of unity.

In every two things which unite they become one substance,

and thus that transformation must occur in the union of water and milk, wine, and the other things which mix with water. By contrast, water and oil remain two substances as they were, the oil clinging to the water and floating upon it but not uniting with it. Similar to the former is the mixing of fire and iron; the iron is transformed from what it was, and if it cools off it returns to what it was. It is like this also in the union of air with water and dust, so that it becomes a cloud of vapor or dust. To summarize, in all of what people know about union, when two become one and duality has been removed, there must be a transformation of the two.

It may be said that in him there is the nature of the two, and the will of the two, just as in water and milk there is the potency (*quwwa*) of the water and that of the milk. The answer is that in this case there is no doubt that each potency is changed from what it was and breaks the other. As is known from other forms of unity, if one thing unites with another each of them breaks the potency of the other from what it was.

For example, when cold water is united with hot water, the force of the hot and that of the cold are broken from what they were, and the union remains settled midway between pure coldness and pure heat. This is the case with water and milk and other forms of unity.

For this reason it is necessary for the divinity, if it united with humanity, that its power, its nature, and its will undergo change from what it was; the power, nature, and will of the human nature would be distorted from what it had been. There would remain this united being of the divine nature from what it was and a denial of its perfection, just as it would necessitate a perfecting of the human nature from what it was.

Everything by which they describe the human nature's union with the divine demands a diminishment of the divinity, a denial of the perfection which is unique to it, and an invalidation of its perfect attributes in accordance with what occurred to it from that human nature by the act of union. Unless this occurred, there would be no union in any respect. The divine nature would remain as it was and the human nature would remain as it was. In that case they would be two separate things which did not unite one with the other or become one thing.

Moreover, if the substance were one, its will ought to be one and its nature one. If there were two wills, the place of one of the two, being the location for the other with the opposition which is necessary in the two wills, would necessitate the combining of two opposing things in one place.

The human will seeks food and drink and wants to worship, fast, and pray, but it is necessarily impossible for the divine will to desire these things. Its will is that it create, sustain, and put order into the universe, but such a desire is impossible for the human will. If two incompatible wills were subsisting in one place, it would follow that the substance described by these two [wills] would be desiring a thing impossible for it because of its will not desiring it. That would be a joining of contradictories in numerous respects.

It is impossible that in one being there subsist one of two wills resolved on a thing and its contradictory as well, or two incompatible wills determined on a thing and its opposite. An act does not occur except by a will resolving something within its power. Whatever the divine [nature] wills, is, and what it does not will, is not. Whenever it wills a thing with a determining will, it is powerful over what it wills. The human nature does not perform anything of the human prerogatives until it wills that with a determining will. It is impossible that the human nature desire the will of the divine nature and at the same time be incompatible to it. One thing comes to be desirous of a thing with a determining will and capable of it, not desiring it with a determining will and incapable of it.

If the two became one substance who was born, slapped, beaten, crucified, and it suffered and died, it follows that the divinity itself would be beaten and crucified, have suffered and died, as the Jacobites say. This is a necessary consequent for all Christians and is what their creed and their faith requires.

If someone says that they are two substances as well as their being one person with no multiplicity in him, as some Melkites say, it must be answered that this view is internally contradictory. One person in whom there is no multiplicity is one substance, and he is by definition a body. If they liken that to the soul with the body, it follows for them that it be spatially circumscribed (*mahdud*).

Man is, as it has been said about him, one person. It is said that he is one substance in the unity that is between [the soul and the body]. By definition, therefore, he is a sensitive body, he sleeps, moves by his will, speaks. This includes his body and his soul, and to the soul and the body there is one will. Whenever a human wills an act with a determining will within his capability, there is not with him another substance having a will other than his will. If they liken the unity of the divinity and humanity to this, it follows for them that the two be one substance, one will, and this is the view of the Jacobites.

The soul thereby suffers whatever pains occur in the body, and the body—that is, the pineal gland[4]—suffers whatever pains occur in the soul. When the soul suffers, the body's heart and other things suffer as well. Similarly, if the body suffers, and if it is flogged and crucified, if it is slapped and spat upon in its face, if thorns are placed upon it, if it is in agony and dies, all of that is residing in the soul and confers upon the soul the insult of the slapping and the pain of the death agony. They admit that God dwelt in the soul and body of Christ. They are not in disagreement about whether God dwelt in the body of Christ and in his soul. They only disagree concerning whether the divine nature was separated with the soul from the body at death.

According to them the divinity was not separated from the humanity at death, but rather ascended to heaven. Christ, who is fully God and fully man, sits at the right of his father, and thus he will come on the Day of Resurrection. Moreover, the attributes and judgments of the body change depending on whether the soul is in it, and its circumstances are different in its union with or separation from the soul. The attributes and operations of the soul are different when it is in the body.

It follows from this that the human nature of Christ is opposed in attributes and regulations to the rest of human natures, and that the divinity when united to it would have undergone change in its attributes and operations. This is a transformation, an alteration, and a replacement of the attributes of God. At the same time the human nature of Christ is of the genus of human natures. There only appear in it what appear in other natures like it; in other human natures there have appeared more supernatural occurrences than have occurred in it.

In short, any metaphor they produce for union is an argument against them, and the falsity of their view appears in it. If they claim that this is a matter which cannot be understood and is beyond reason, this can be answered from various aspects.

1) A distinction should be made between what the mind knows to be false and impossible and what it is unable to imagine and have knowledge of. The first includes the absurdities of the mind and the second what surpasses it. The messengers have brought information of the second.

No one holds the first except a liar. If it were possible to hold this, it would be possible to say that one object could be white and black in the same situation, or that it could be in two places, or that one thing could be existent and non-existent in one state, or similar statements whose impossibility is known by the mind. The view of Christians is among that which is known by sound reason to be false; it is not among that which the mind is unable to imagine.

What makes this clear is that were someone to say about Mary the mother of Christ that she was "the wife of God and His spouse" because she married Him by an intellectual marriage and that God generated Christ through an intellectual generation, this statement would not be more false than what they say about Christ, as we have pointed out in its proper place. However, they condemn the view of one who says this, and bring an argument of reason against it.

If it is said that this is beyond reason, it cannot be accepted, because each group among them bring an argument *of reason* against the other. When their opponents say "our view is beyond reason," they themselves do not accept this answer. If this were a sound answer, one ought not to investigate anything pertaining to the divine with reason, and every errant fool could speak whatever falsehood he wanted and claim, "My speech is beyond reason." This is what the proponents of *hulul*, *ittihad*, and *wahda* claim; they hold that the existence of the creator is the existence of the creature. They claim that this is beyond reason, and say, "We know this only by intuitive perception (*dhawq*), not by revelation or reason."

2) If the prophets bring information of that which the mind is unable to imagine, it must be accepted from them, for they know what cannot be known by others from human knowledge. Of these views, however, the prophets have never mentioned a thing, although the sects of Christians have stated their opinions and claimed that they have derived these from some of the expressions of the sacred books.

Whoever says this should be asked whether he can imagine what he is saying or not. Can he understand it and can he reason to it? If he answers that he does not imagine what he says, nor understands it, nor reasons to it, he should be told that he has spoken about God what he does not know, and he has followed that of which he has no knowledge.

One of the most hateful and forbidding things in all religions is for someone to give as his opinion about God what he neither imagines nor understands. All intelligent people know that whoever speaks a view which he neither imagines nor understands finds his view refuted and unacceptable, more so if his view is among that which is condemned as false.

If one of them says that he understands what he says and imagines it and can reason to it, he should be told to clarify it for others so that another can understand, reason, and imagine it. He should not say, "It is beyond reason," but "It is a view to which I adhere of which I have knowledge." This distinction is unavoidable for them.

If they have understood what they said and reasoned to it, it follows that it must be reasonable. If, however, they have not understood it nor reasoned to it, it follows that they have spoken about God what they neither understood nor could reason to, a view from their own opinion and mind, not handed down in the words of the prophets. Whoever has handed down the words of the prophets which have been established as being from them, it is not necessary for him to understand and reason to what he says.

We do not demand from someone who has handed down the wording of the Torah, the Gospel, the Qur'an, or the words of the rest of the prophets that he clarify its meaning. By contrast, when one claims that he has understood what the prophets said and expressed that with other words than theirs, it should be said to him, "If you have understood what they said, the meaning is one. They have expressed it by another expression like a translator." This person knows what he says and understands it.

If he says, "I do not understand their speech," or "I have not understood what you have said," he has admitted his ignorance and his error and that he is among those who have not understood the speech of the prophets and does not have knowledge of what they have said. If they say, "We have not understood the speech of the prophets," and are silent, they are on the pattern of those like them who are ignorant of the meaning of the speech of the prophets.

However, when those who have laid down an expression and a formulation which they have innovated command people to follow it by saying, "This is faith and theology," and yet say, "We cannot imagine what we have said, nor do we understand it, nor can we reason to it," these people are among those who speak about God that which they do not know and perpetrate something against God and against the books of God and the prophets of God without knowledge. They speak slanderous falsehood and clear blasphemy, and then they say about that, "We cannot reason to it." This is without doubt the situation of the Christians.

Two groups of people err in this way. The first are the extremists who exaggerate on matters of understanding, until they make that which is not reasonable to be included with the reasonable and have presented it against sense and the texts of the prophets. The second group has shunned reasonable knowledge and presented refutations against matters of sound reason. Against these they have offered what they thought to be religious and sense knowledge. Thus on matters of religious knowledge people are of two kinds, and so on matters of hidden and evident sense knowledge are they of two kinds.

One should know that the truth does not contradict itself, but rather confirms itself, in contrast to falsehood, which is various and contradictory. God has said this concerning those who oppose the messengers (51:7-9). What is known by sound reason is never opposed, either by valid religious information (*khabar*) or correct sense information. What is known by true religious teaching is not opposed by reason or sense, and what is known by the sound senses is not contradicted by what is revealed or reasonable.

Our intention here is the view of those who oppose what is known by reason to revelation and sense knowledge. We say that by the expression "that which is reasoned to" is meant the object of sound reasoning which people know by their natural dispositions with which they are endowed. It does not refer to that which people have received from each other, such as the similitudes they know from those who make them, or the differences of those who disagree. Here I mean the difference of diversity, not the difference of opposition and dissimilarity, for the term "difference" is used for both.

These objects of reasoning are "objects of knowledge," and God has censured those who have opposed them (67:10; 22:46). Many intelligent people take exception to what some call the "objects of reason" (*ma'qulat*), such as the view of the correspondence of bodies and the endurance [in time] of accidents, or that bodies are composed of indivisible atoms,[5] or that they are composed of matter and form, or that something infinite which unfolds itself in succession is impossible of existence,[6] either in the past and future or in the past only, or that universals are self-subsistent substances in external reality, that time or matter is a self-subsistent intelligible substance, or that the existence of a self-subsistent substance for which there is no evidence is possible. Questions like this some thinkers count as established by reason, while others dispute that.

These are not the objects of reason which sense knowledge and revelation ought not refute and to which the forms of human knowledge must return. Rather, the hidden, precise, correct objects of knowledge go back to the first *a priori* principles.

By contrast, the true objects of reason, such as the impossibility of one body being in two places at the same time, are known by the natural disposition with which God has endowed mankind. If there occurs in the sense that which someone supposes to be opposed to sound religious information—as when someone sees on 'Arafat a person who is still in his town which he has not left, or sees someone standing before him while the other is in a different place, or when he sees him giving aid to one who calls to him for help, or when he comes flying in the air with the knowledge that that person is still in his own locality and has not moved from it—

this is only one of the jinn taking on the appearance that person, not him himself. This merely resembles the thing; it is not the thing itself.

Unless reason distinguishes between sense perceptions, the sense will frequently err. This is the case with those who claim "insight," and speak on a matter contrary to sound reason; it can be known that such a person is erring on it. Those who speak of *wahdat al-wujud* say, "I have witnessed within me an absolute existence stripped of names and attributes, no particularization nor limitation to it at all." He does not dispute about this, as some people may dispute it.

He should be asked from where he gets his knowledge that this is the Lord of the universe who created the heavens and the earth. He cannot know by emotional perception (*bi-hiss al-qalb*) that what he experiences in his heart is God. If he claims that he has obtained by mystical intuition what contradicts sound reason, it is obvious that he is in error. The shaykh of these renegades, Al-Tilimsani, has said:

> My friend, you forbid me and you command me,
> But ecstasy is a more faithful prohibitor and commander.
> If I obey you and disobey ecstasy
> I turn back in blindness
> From clear sight to imagined reports.
> The true nature of what you have called me to
> If you examine it closely, neighbor,
> You'll find it forbidden.

In answer I say to him: "Your ecstasy (*wajd*) and intuition (*dhawq*) has only been of benefit to you for witnessing a simple, absolute existence, but what makes you think that this is the Lord of the Universe? From where do you get the idea that this is established as a pure, absolute universal outside of yourself? You only witness it as a pure absolute universal within yourself. You know neither by sense, by reason, nor by religious transmission that this is in external reality."

It is like a dreamer whose false sense witnesses things which are not with him but he is certain that these things are outside himself. When his consciousness returns to him, he knows that this was in his imagination during his dream. So also someone who is drunk, like others whose minds are weakened, witnesses things in his sense, either hidden or open, but his mind has been weakened from perceiving the true nature of that which reaches him. When he regains control of his reason, he realizes that what he has witnessed was only within himself and in his imagination, not outside of that.

Whenever someone has reported something opposed to sound religious transmission or correct reason, one knows that error has overtaken him, even though he is trustworthy in what he experiences in his internal and external sense. The error has occurred in his incorrect thinking, which is opposed to sound reason, not in his pure sense perception. In the senses there is no knowledge of denial and affirmation.

When someone sees a person, there is nothing in his sense but the vision. As for its being Zayd or 'Umar who was seen, the mind must distinguish in this matter between one and the other. Thus for a young child or one who is insane, brutish, drunk, sleeping, etc., they have sense perception, but due to the lack of reason they do not distinguish between one thing and the other in that which is witnessed. They may surmise opinions which do not correspond to reality, as God has said (24:39). Someone dying of thirst sees what he thinks to be water. His sense does not err, but it is his reason which is in error.

The prophets are inerrant; they only speak the truth about God, and only hand down about Him that which is trustworthy. Whenever someone claims something contrary to sound reason in their reports, that person is lying, but among the objects of reason there must necessarily be that which is not correct, and among religious tradition that which is not sound. What is known as certain is that what the prophets have reported cannot possibly be contradictory to reason.

The view of the wayward among Christians and others, whether they are claiming a general or specific divine union, may be known by sound reason to be false. It is impossible that any prophet had taught this. The prophets may teach what the human mind is unable to understand, but not what the mind knows to be false. They teach the pearls of the mind, not its absurdities.

Others than the prophets are not inerrant; there may occur to a person through his insight, sense perception, mystical intuition, and immediate personal experience matters on which he constructs false surmises. If he teaches something like this, its falsity is known by sound reason, and it is known that he is in error. If someone other than the prophets teaches something which the mind of many people is unable to know, it does not follow necessarily that this be untrustworthy or false. We are unable to judge its truthfulness or falseness except by some proof showing whether the probability is that he is in error or whether it is probable that he may have known what others are unable to have knowledge of.

We know someone is in error when he says about that which has come from no prophet and whose falseness according to sound reason is evident, "This is beyond reason," or "This is past the tower of reason and revelation," or "We only know this if we have abandoned reason and revelation," or:

> They have broken the system and burned down the hedge,
> No obligation upon them and no revelation,
> They are madmen, but the secret of their madness
> Is dear to His gates before which the mind falls prostrate.

It is impossible for a prophet to say this, or that a trustworthy person hand it down from a prophet. The sayings of the prophets do not contradict sound reason. How can this be accepted from one who is not a prophet?

If someone should say, as do the Christians and others, that this is indicated by the speech of the prophets, they should be answered by saying that the teaching in the sense of the words which the prophets have uttered is one thing, and the speech which they have misunderstood is another. If it could be supposed that what they and others have mentioned they have understood from the speech of the prophets which is not opposed to sound reason, we would [still] not assert positively that one saying such a thing could imagine what he said, but maybe he misunderstood some element of their teaching contrary to what they meant by it. What shall we say when he himself cannot imagine what he has said? They admit that they have not reasoned to it nor do they understand it. How can this be accepted if that which was said is evidently false according to sound reason?

If someone understood the above-mentioned premises and then said, "I have understood their [the prophets'] speech," his understanding would still not be an argument. How can it be, therefore, if he says, "I do not understand it," or "This is beyond the tower of reason." If he said this, his view would not be a proof, and one ought not to believe that the prophets meant by their speech the meaning which they admit to be beyond the tower of reason. So how can it be permitted as a proof when he admits that that meaning is false, and that it is impossible that an intelligent person—prophet or no prophet—state it?

## B. ADEQUACY OF PHILOSOPHICAL OR PROPHETIC LANGUAGE FOR DISCUSSING THE NATURE OF GOD

Paul of Antioch has stated:

> I said to them: They tell us, "If it is your belief that the creator is one, what prompts you to say 'Father, Son, and Holy Spirit,' so that you cause hearers to imagine that you believe in God composed of three

persons, or three gods, or three parts, and that He has a son? One who does not know your belief would suppose that by that you mean that he is the child of human intercourse and procreation. You bring upon yourselves an accusation against which you must defend yourselves."

However, they also, since their belief in the Creator extols His greatness, holding that He is without a body, bodily organs, and members, and not circumscribed in a place, how can they presume to state that He has two eyes with which He sees, two hands with which He stretches forth, that He walks, that His face turns towards every direction and place, that He approaches under canopies of clouds? In this way hearers imagine that God has a body with members and organs and moves from place to place under canopies of clouds. One who did not know their belief would suppose that they posit a body for the Creator. A group of them has even believed that and have followed that as a sect, and whoever does not affirm that belief of theirs they accuse for being quit of it.

They hold that the reason for their stating this—that God has two eyes and hands, a face, a leg, and a side, and that He approaches under canopies of clouds—is that the Qur'an explicitly mentions this. This is not the evident meaning of the text, and anyone who claims this to be the evident meaning—so that he believes that God has two eyes and hands, a face, a side, members and organs, and that He moves—him they curse and declare an unbeliever. Since they declare unbelievers those who believe this, it is not right for their opponents to hold them to this after they have made it clear they do not believe it.

So also for us Christians, the reason for our saying that God is three hypostases—Father, Son, and Holy Spirit—is that the Gospel has explicitly mentioned that. What is meant by the hypostases is not composite persons with parts and divisions or anything else which would demand ***shirk*** or multiplicity. Similarly, the Father and the Son are not the fatherhood and sonship of marriage and begetting, of sexual union and intercourse.

We condemn, excommunicate, and reject anyone who believes that the three hypostases are three different gods, three identical gods, three united bodies, three distinct parts, three composite persons, accidents, or powers, or any other view which demands participation, multiplicity, divisibility, or anthropomorphism in the divinity. We likewise condemn any view of the sonship of marriage, physical generation, sexual union or procreation, or generation from a wife, a body, angel, or creature.

If we have cursed and declared unbeliever anyone who believes [any of] that, our opponents should not ascribe this belief to us after we have rejected it.[1]

This argument[2] may be answered in various ways.

1) Anyone who believes what the messengers have brought and holds what they held without corrupting it either textually or by interpretation cannot be opposed. This is in contrast to those who have innovated opinions which the messengers never stated and are even opposed to what they held. Whoever has corrupted what the messengers stated, whether textually and by interpretation or merely by interpretation is deserving of being rejected. All the religious groups agree on this.

The basis for the religion of Muslims lies in that they describe God just as He has described Himself in His books, and as His messengers have described Him, without corruption, intellectualization, qualification, or representation. They affirm for Him what He has affirmed for Himself, and deny about Him what He has denied about Himself. In that they follow the statements of the messengers and avoid what opposes the statements of the messengers (37:180-182).

The messengers have described God by the attributes of perfection, and have declared Him transcendent to all deficiencies contrary to perfection. They have established the attributes of perfection in God in a detailed manner while denying Him any representation. In this way they have brought a detailed affirmation with a general denial.

Whoever denies any of the attributes of God which He Himself has affirmed is a "transcendentalist" (*mu'attil*), while anyone who makes these attributes like those of creatures is a "representationist" (*mushabbih*). The former serves a god who is absent, the latter an idol. God has stated, "There is nothing like Him" (42:11), and this is the answer to the representationist; "He is the Hearer, the Seer" (42:11), and this is the answer to the transcendentalist.

The messengers have described Him as living, thus declaring Him to be beyond death, as knowing, and thus beyond ignorance, as almighty, strong, and august, and thus beyond impotence, weakness, ignominy, or fatigue. They have described Him as hearing and seeing and thus beyond dumbness or blindness, as supremely independent and thus beyond dependency, as generous and therefore beyond niggardliness. They have described Him as a gentle judge and thus beyond arrogance, as faithful, and thus beyond falseness, and so on for the rest of the perfections, like their describing Him as affectionate, compassionate, and kind.

He has called Himself the "rock"—Al-Samad. The Rock is the name which includes the affirmation of the attributes of perfection and the denial of deficiencies. He is completely knowing in His knowledge, completely powerful in His might, completely just in His justice.

I have elaborated this in my *tafsir* of this sura[3] and elsewhere in clarifying that it is equivalent to a third of the Qur'an.[4] I have mentioned the views of the Muslim scholars among the Companions and the Followers, and that the generality of what they have said is true. For example, some of them have said "The Rock is that in which there is no hollowness." Others have stated, "He is the Lord whose sovereignty will not end." Still others have held it to mean, "He is the supremely Independent from all that is other than He, while everything else is in need of Him." Similarly, it is said that He is the completely knowing in His knowledge, the completely powerful in his power, and so on for the rest of His attributes.

God has stated in this sura that He is one, and there is nothing similar to Him. By this He has denied that any thing is like Him, and that He is one and has no equal. He has spoken in the same vein elsewhere in the Qur'an (19:65; 42:11; 16:74; 2:22).

The affirmation of the attributes of God which has appeared in the Qur'an and sunna is that which had appeared in the Torah and in the other sacred books like it. It is a matter on which the messengers are agreed, and the People of the Book hold that as well as the Muslims.

If this is so, they [Christians] in their creed do not say what Christ and the prophets held, but rather have innovated a belief not found in the speech of the prophets. In the speech of the prophets, whether in that of Christ or of any of the others, there is no mention of the hypostases of God, either three or more, nor an establishment of three attributes, nor any calling of any one of the attributes God or son of God or Lord, or calling His life a spirit, nor that God had a son who is true God from true God, from the essence of his Father, and that he is creator just as God is creator. This is the case with other opinions comprising forms of disbelief—none of these was ever handed down by any prophet.[5]

Where in the message of the prophets is it stated that any thing of the attributes of God or His creatures is an hypostasis, that he is true God from true God, from the substance of his Father, that he is equal to God in substance, that he is a creator who created everything, that he sits at the right hand of God upon his throne, or that he judges people on the Day of Resurrection? Where in the message of the prophets does it say that God had an eternal son? Which one of them ever called the speech of God, His knowledge, or His wisdom God's offspring or His son? What prophet ever said, "He is generated," and at the same time that he is eternal? Where in their message is it that God has a third hypostasis which is His life, called the Holy Spirit, who is also the living, lifegiving Lord?

If Christians believed in the texts of the prophets like believers have done, they would have no blame. Whenever anyone opposes the texts of the prophets, it is due to the corruption of his understanding and his lack of knowledge. These people have innovated opinions and beliefs not dictated by any one of the prophets; in such views there is clear unbelief and unmistakeable contradiction.

Even if it were supposed that by these they intended a true meaning, they still should not have innovated a wording which no prophet brought and which indicated a contradictory unbelief which opposed both revelation and reason and then say "I only meant by it a correct meaning, but its wording indicates the false meaning." How much more are they in error when what is meant is the false and contradictory position delineated by their explanation?

They have advanced reprehensible opinions and have explained them by an objectionable exegesis and are therefore answered on both sides. In this they are similar to some of the Muslim renegades who believe in the divinity of one of the People of the House or one of the *shaykhs* and who describe God with attributes not stated by the Book. These are the renegades among Muslims. By contrast, the believers are those who have placed faith in God and His messengers, who have believed what the prophets said, and who have not innovated views which the prophets never brought and which they made the basis of their religion.

————

2)[6] It should be said to them that the terms "son" and "Holy Spirit" have been applied by them in the case of others than Christ; according to them even the apostles have said that Christ said to them "God is my Father and your Father." They say, moreover, that the Holy Spirit descended upon them.

According to what you Christians agree to be in the Torah, the Lord says to Moses:

> Go to Pharaoh and say to him, "Israel is My son, My first-born, whom I have sent to serve Me. If you refuse to set free My first-born son, I will kill your first-born son."

When Pharaoh did not release the children of Israel as God had told him, God killed the first-born sons of Pharaoh and his people, from the eldest son of Pharaoh lying on his bed to the oldest children of the people and even to the first-born of their animals. The Torah calls all the children of Israel the sons of God and His first-born and calls the people of Egypt the children of Pharaoh, and even extends this, calling the foals of the animals children of the owners of the animals.

In the Psalms of David He says, "You are My son; ask of Me and I will give you."

In the Gospel it says of Christ, "I am going to my Father and your Father, to my God and your God." He says: "When you pray, say, 'Our Father who are in heaven, holy is Your name, do for us such and such.'"

They state about the saints that the Holy Spirit resided in them, just as he had resided in David and other prophets; according to them God even dwells in all upright men.

If "son" and "Holy Spirit" demanded unity between human and divine natures, each one of the apostles ought to be composed of divine nature and human, and similarly the prophets should have this dual nature. According to you the prophet is the son of God through whom spoke the Holy Spirit, especially when you say in your creed, "The Holy Spirit is glorified, worshiped with Him, and spoke through the prophets."

If this demanded the indwelling of the divine nature in the human or a union with it, it would demand a divine and human nature for other prophets than Christ, even for the apostles and the children of Israel. That which you have made to be the divine nature has descended upon others than Christ and united with them, or dwelt within them, or veiled itself in them, or whatever terms you employ to indicate the indwelling of the divine nature in Christ, such as those of "son" and "Holy Spirit," which terms, according to you, are found in the case of others than Christ.

The miracles which you allege as proof for Christ have existed for others than him. If it were presumed that Christ were more perfect than some of these others—and there is no doubt that Christ was better than the majority of the prophets, more perfect than David, Solomon, the writers of your prophecies, and superior to the apostles—nevertheless this high degree of virtue indicates only his excellence in prophethood and messengership, much as the excellence of Abraham, Moses, and Muhammad did not require their being considered beyond the rank of messengers (5:75).

In summary, our answer is that everything by which you describe Christ—whether his being son of God, or God's descending upon him, or manifesting Himself in him, or dwelling in him, or the Holy Spirit or the Spirit of God dwelling in him, or his being a Christ—all of this is found in your books in the case of others than Christ.

There is nothing peculiar to Christ in a single one of these expressions; his unique status is found only in the expression "the Word" and in his having taken flesh from the Holy Spirit. It is in this that the Qur'an characterizes Christ (4:171). In a sound hadith report from 'Ibada ibn al-Samit, the Messenger says:

> Whoever witnesses that there is no God but God and that Muhammad is His servant and His messenger, and that Jesus is the servant of God and His messenger and His word that He delivered to Mary and a spirit from Him, that person will be taken into heaven by God in spite of the works he had done.

This designation, by which the Qur'an singles out Christ, is the same as that by which the earlier books distinguish him. The Qur'an is faithful to the books which they had, and a guardian of them.

The rest of what is described about him, and what they claim to be his unique characteristics—his being son of God or the Christ, have been applied in the divine books to others than him; others have been called a son of God or a Christ. Similarly the expressions mentioned which they allege to prove divine indwelling—like the Lord's becoming manifest in him, descending upon him, or dwelling in him—these expressions are found in their books in the case of others than Christ.

By contrast the term "union" is not found—in their own books—referring to the prophets, neither in the case of Christ nor that of anyone else. Similarly the term hypostasis is not found among them referring to the prophets; nor is that of trinity, divine nature, human nature or calling God a substance. All of this, rather, is among what they have innovated, just as they have introduced calling the attributes of God "son" and "Holy Spirit." They have innovated expressions not spoken of by the prophets for which they have established false meanings. They have also innovated the use of prophetic expressions against the prophet's intent and have imposed their own intent on them.

The ambiguous expressions by which they have argued for the union of the divine nature in Christ's human nature are found in their own books in the case of others than Christ. In the message of the prophets there is no unique characteristic in Christ that necessitates his being God or son of God. By agreement of Muslims and Christians it is known that the intent of those expressions is to indicate the indwelling of faith in God, knowledge of Him, His guidance, light, and mental image in the hearts of His upright servants. This we have elaborated elsewhere, and in what has preceded.

Some misguided Muslims say, "The Lord has united with or dwelt within the prophets and friends; this is something secret which cannot be divulged." This opinion is the same sort of view as that of Christians about Christ. It is often found in the teachings of many of the shaykhs and propagandists for esoteric knowledge, divine identification, and oneness with God. For those who know God they posit a oneness with Him, so that he who unites becomes Him with whom he unites. Some of them say that God dwells in the heart of the one who knows Him and speaks with his tongue, as a jinni would speak by the tongue of one possessed.

Some of them say that this is the secret which Al-Hallaj and others divulged; according to them this is one of the secrets which the adepts have kept hidden and never divulge except to initiates. Some say that Al-Hallaj was killed only for disclosing this secret, and they sing:

> He who revealed the secret paid the price with his death,
> Vengeance was not taken for him.

In their claims for divine union and indwelling in others than Christ, these people are worse than Christians, for Christ was superior to everyone who was not a prophet, and was even superior to the majority of prophets and messengers. If someone who claims that the divinity united with Christ is an unbeliever, how much more so is he who claims this for someone inferior to him?

This particular union and indwelling is different from the general union and indwelling held by those who say that God dwells in His essence in every place, or is united with everything. The extremists and leading personalities among these people say that God is the essence of existence, or that all existence is one. In this way they make the necessary, eternal creative existence the essence of the existence of the contingent, temporal creature. These are people like Ibn al-'Arabi al-Ta'i, his companion Sadr [al-Din] al-Qunawi, his companion 'Afif [al-Din] al-Tilimsani, Ibn Sab'in and his student Al-Shushtari,[7] 'Abd Allah al-Balabani, 'Amir al-Basri, and other groups.

These people say that the Christians are unbelievers only because they particularize their view to Christ. The reality of the view of these men is a denial of the creator and a neutralizing of Him. It is like Pharaoh said, "What is the Lord of the Universe?" and "I know not that you have a God other than me" (28:38). Pharaoh was not denying this experienced existence of ours, but was denying that it had a maker dissimilar to it whose creation it was. These people are in agreement with Pharaoh in this. But Pharaoh at least made his repudiation and denial manifest; he did not say that created existence is the creator.

These people believe that they hold for the creator, and that created existence is the creator. The argument against these people is elaborated elsewhere than in this book. They have poetry in which they compose verses on their belief, such as Ibn al-Farid's *qasida* called *Nazm al-Suluk*.[8] Similarly, Ibn Isra'il[9] has a section on this in his poetry, for example:

You are nothing but being (*al-kawn*),
Nay, You are its essence,
Who understands this secret
He is the insightful one.[10]

Al-Tilimsani was one of the most insolent of men, and at the same time the cleverest of these renegades. When the *Fusus al-Hikam* of Ibn 'Arabi was read to him, someone said, "This view is opposed to the Qur'an." He replied, "The whole Qur'an is *shirk*; real *tawhid* is found only in our view." It was said to him, "If all existence is one, then why is my mother forbidden to me, but my wife permitted me?" He answered, "Among us everything is *halal*, but those whose eyes are veiled say 'Haram!'; so we say, 'It is *haram*—for you.'"

The view of these people is contradictory, one part contradicting the other. He says, "those whose eyes are veiled," and he says, "We say, 'It is *haram* for you.'" This demands a distinction between him and those who are veiled, between the speaker and the addressee. This is contradictory to *wahdat al-wujud*. If they say that these are merely appearances and manifestations of the truth, it should be replied that that which is manifest is different from the manifestation, that which represents is not that which is represented. This establishes a plurality, and there are two things in existence—that which manifests and that which is manifested. If these people make the two one, their argument fails.

———

It should be said to them, "You say that you follow the sacred books. If this were so, it would not have come about that you inserted into the law of your faith any terms except those brought by the prophets. No one of the prophets ever called God a substance. It was only Aristotle and his kind who called God that. These philosophers were idol-worshiping pagans who had no true knowledge of God. They did not hold God to be creator of heaven and earth, nor that He was over all things knowing, nor over all things powerful. Rather, they worshiped the stars on high, lowly idols, devils, Al-Jibt and Al-Taghut.[11]

"They only became believers when the religion of Christ entered upon them, and that over 300 years after the time of Alexander the Macedonian, the master of Aristotle. They used to call their kings Ptolemies, as the Egyptians called theirs Pharaoh, the Ethiopians Negus, and the Persians Khusraw. They strayed from the path of the prophet and messengers to that of the unbelievers and the transcendentalist idolaters who were in clear error."

In the books of the Christians it states that Paul, when he arrived in Athens—the seat of philosophy in which there was a temple for idols—found written on the door of the house of scholars and idols, "The Hidden God whom you do not know; He is it who created the world." They did not know the Lord of the universe, so how could he[12] deviate from the path of the messengers and prophets of God, like Moses, David, and Christ, to that of these unbelieving transcendentalist idolaters?

The Christians constructed a religion from two religions—from the religion of the monotheist prophets and from that of the idolaters. In their religion it developed that there was a portion containing that which was brought by the prophets and a portion which they innovated from the idolaters by way of opinions and deeds. Thus they innovated the terms of the hypostases, although these terms were not found anywhere in the message of the prophets. Similarly they introduced printed idols in place of bodily idols [icons in place of statues], prayers to them in place of praying to the sun, moon, and stars, and fasting in the spring in order to combine revealed religion and the natural order.[13]

In his book the *Uthulujia*[14] Aristotle did not prove that the Lord is the creator of the heavenly spheres, nor that He is their active cause; he does not call Him the necessary and contingent eternal. It was rather the later philosophers like Ibn Sina who did that. This has been elaborated elsewhere. These later philosophers heard the teaching of the people of the three religions and wanted to correct that teaching and make it closer to what is reasonable so that what was known by sound reason might agree with what was truly revealed.

Thabit ibn Qurra[15] spoke of this and pointed out that there was no constitution (*qiwam*) for a heavenly sphere except by nature, and no constitution for its nature except in its motion, and no constitution for its voluntary movement except in its Mover. They claimed that it was necessary that the Mover be not moved, and proved it by invalid proofs. This we have elaborated elsewhere. They said that He was only mover of the spheres from the aspect of the relation of the sphere to Him, although He had no power over the moving of the spheres and even no cognizance of the sphere in Him.

The philosopher Ibn Rushd and others like him went beyond this and stated that God commanded the spheres to move, and the constitution of the sphere was in its obedience to the command of God. Nevertheless, according to them, He has no will or knowledge of what he commands; rather, the meaning of its being a command is simply that the sphere tries to resemble Him, just as someone's beloved commands that the lover feel love for him, although the beloved has not feelings for him nor any intention of loving him.[16]

Even if it were supposed that He were the Commander, all that would emanate because of His command would be the simple movement of the stars. They compare this to the command given by a sultan to his soldiers. In it they obey him and make movements caused by his words.

By this [reasoning] they do not demonstrate that He created a thing of the heavenly spheres, elements, and secondary effects—neither the intelligences nor the souls. He created neither their essences, nor their attributes, nor their deeds. The limit of His being a commander for them is in a movement similar to that of a king who commands his soldiers. Nevertheless, among them He is not a commander in reality; rather, He does not know a thing of created beings.

The most that Aristotle and his followers claim is that the spheres have a need for Him from the aspect of their imitation of Him. As for His being the necessitating cause for the spheres, it is only some of the latter-day philosophers like Ibn Sina who say this.

It was Al-Farabi who expanded the discussion on this matter. He divided the existent being into necessary and contingent, and made the spheres necessary, but contingent on Him. There is falsity and confusion in this, as we have elaborated elsewhere.

Ibn Sina built his view on the denial of His attributes and upon His being necessary of existence. However, in his book *The Views of the People of the Virtuous City*[17] and other works, Al-Farabi used as his basis the fact of His being the first, and His resembling the first in number. On that they have built their denial of the attributes, so that were we to affirm them, He would no longer be First.

This is in spite of their not establishing a proof for His being first in the sense in which they claim, just as they do not erect an argument for His being necessary of existence in the meaning which they allege. They conceal themselves in general ambiguous expressions which permit both truth and falsehood. It is evident that God is necessary of existence in His essence and self-existent and that He is the First before whom there is nothing; He is the pre-eternal eternal one, who always was and will not cease to be.

These people have made necessary-of-existence to mean that He is not dependent on another and thus has no attribute. His being First is in the sense of the first of numbers in which there is no enumeration. However, it is obvious that the pure number One and the First of all things is only possible in minds, not in external realities. The mind conceives of one, two, three, four, and so on to the rest of the pure numbers. The pure number of what is enumerated is only found in minds, not in external realities. What is existent in the external world are only those essences which are subsistent in themselves or attributes subsistent in others. The first of them is an essence described by his attributes. In essences there is found nothing which is not either subsistent in itself or an attribute subsistent in something else. Moreover, there is not found any essence abstracted from its attributes. These matters are elaborated elsewhere.

We have merely pointed this out here about them because the Christians say:

> We are amazed at this people: they are possessors of virtue, culture, and knowledge. Anyone of this type who has read anything of the books of the philosophers and logicians knows that their conclusions do not deny what we hold.

The view of these Christians includes extolling the philosophers and logicians so that whoever reads their books knows from them the truth of divine things not known by the rest of the followers of the religions.

This indicates the ignorance of these Christians concerning both what the messengers brought as well as what is known by pure reason. As for the first, neither Christ nor his followers, like the apostles and those who followed them, had any among them who extolled those philosophers, nor made use of them, nor paid heed to them. The philosophers were considered to be among the priests of unbelief and leaders of error. Thus it was for Moses and his followers, and thus for Muhammad and his followers.

Among the prophets and messengers of God and among their followers there were none who extolled them or made use of their views. Rather the messengers and their followers were agreed on declaring their error and ignorance.

As for the second point—matters of reason—only he who is among the most ignorant of men in scientific and divine matters would extol the view of these philosophers in the universal and divine sciences. Their view in such things has such ignorance and error in it that can be comprehended only by the Majestic One.

All these people knew was what they had learned of the mathematical and natural sciences like geometry and astronomy and a bit of ethics and civil and domestic politics. This is merely a small part of what the messengers brought.

Christians and Jews, after the abrogation and corruption of their religion, were more learned than these philosophers on matters of divine sciences, ethics, and politics, much less on matters which transcend this. The support given by these Christians to the would-be philosophers shows the depth of their ignorance on matters of religion and reason. This view we have elaborated in numerous places.

In the refutation of the philosophers there is nothing in it specific to Christians. Rather, our view on the matter concerns them in general and anyone from the religions who extols them. It is well known that among those affiliated with Islam are some followers of the philosophers, like Al-Farabi, Ibn Sina, Al-Suhrawardi al-Maqtul, Ibn Rushd, and others like them who are smarter and more learned than the Christians.

The books of the philosophers which came into the hands of the Muslims, such as those of medicine, mathematics, and logic, were cleansed by the affiliates to Islam, who in turn presented their own views which were better than those of the Greeks. Christians and Jews only depended in these sciences on what the affiliates to Islam had laid down. Nevertheless, among the Muslim scholars (*'ulama'*) those men are considered ignorant and erring in divine and universal matters. What stock can be put, therefore, in their inferiors, the Greeks and those Christians and Jews who extol them?

The Greeks only came to know God, to declare His oneness, and to worship Him as believers in His angels, books, and messengers when the followers of Christ came to them inviting them to the religion of God which was sent through Christ. All those who were followers of Christ without changing a thing of his religion before its abrogation were rightly guided Muslim believers, among the God-fearing friends of God and the people of the Garden.

Anyone who thinks that the message of the messengers agrees with these Greeks indicates by this his ignorance of what the messengers brought and of what these people say. Something like this is only found in the teaching of the renegades of the three religions—the apostates among the Jews, Christians, Muslims, and others. I mean, for example, the writers of the Epistles of the Brethren of Purity, and those like them who associate themselves with the Shi'a or with Sufism, like Ibn 'Arabi, Ibn Sab'in, and their kind. In the books held back from those outside his own circle and those like them, a portion of the teaching ascribed to Abu Hamid [al-Ghazali] is of this type.

The point here is that Paul of Antioch states that there is a subtle substance different from crude substance. He likens it to the soul, the mind, or light. He does not erect as proof for that a single argument, and in particular no argument for that from anything in the divine books. The Celestial Soul and the Ten Intelligences were never mentioned in any sacred book or by any messenger. There are, moreover, no rational proofs, for those of the would-be philosophers are weak.

Those, however, who apply the teaching of the messengers to what agrees with the views of these would-be philosophers identify the Inscribed Tablet with the Celestial Soul, just as they identify the Mind and the Pen with the First Intelligence, the Throne with the ninth sphere, etc. All of this has been elaborated elsewhere.

If they cannot erect any religious or rational proof for that which they represent as subtle substances, there is no argument for one who says that "a substance is that which occupies spatial limits (*al-hudud*) and receives accidents." When they compare the soul with the mind, it is evident that they mean the soul of the heavenly sphere. If they meant the human soul, this would be already established, for the messengers and their followers have informed men of that. This is elaborated elsewhere.

## C. SUPERIORITY AND NECESSITY OF ISLAM

Paul of Antioch states:

> We are amazed at these people who, in spite of their culture and the distinction they have earned for themselves by it, do not know that the religious traditions are two: the religion of justice and the religion of grace.[1] Because the Creator is just and generous as well, it was necessary that His justice manifest itself to mankind.
>
> God sent Moses to the Israelites. He laid down the religion of justice and commanded them to act according to it so that it might find a place within them. Since the perfection which is grace would not be imposed except by the most perfect perfection, it was necessary that He be the one who imposes it, since there is nothing more perfect than He. Because He is generous, it was necessary that He act generously towards His creatures.
>
> Among existent beings, there is none more perfect than His Word. Thus it was necessary that He bestow His Word, and that He unite Himself sensibly with it so that His power and generosity be manifest through

it. Since there is nothing in creation more noble than man, He united with a human nature taken from the holy lady, the Virgin Mary, chosen from among all women.

After this perfection there remained nothing to be imposed. All that preceded it was lacking in something, while that which is subsequent to perfection is unnecessary to it. Whatever comes after perfection is bound to be inferior to it, not superior, or else it is derived from it. That which is derived from perfection is superfluous to it, but not necessary.[2]

This can be answered in various ways.

1) Actually there are three religious traditions: the religion of Law alone, that of grace alone, and that religion which combines grace and Law by prescribing justice and exhorting [people] to goodness. This, the most perfect of the three religions, is the religion of the Qur'an, in which are combined justice and grace.

We do not deny, however, that Moses obliged justice and called men to grace, and that Christ did likewise. Moreover, to say that Christ obliged goodness and forbade any oppressed person from avenging himself upon his oppressor or that Moses did not call men to goodness is to shortchange the religion of these two messengers. It may be said, however, that the mention of justice is more frequent in the Torah and that of goodness more common in the Gospel; the Qur'an combines the two to the limit of perfection.

The Qur'an has made it clear that the blessed are the People of the Garden, and these—God's friends—are of two kinds: fair-minded, upright persons and those going beyond this to approach God. The first category comes about through justice, that is, the fulfilling of obligations and the avoidance of forbidden things. The second stage comes about only by grace, and consists in the performance of obligatory and supererogatory acts, and the avoidance of all forbidden and reprehensible things. Thus, as God said, the perfect religion combines justice and goodness.

And if the debtor is in straitened circumstances, then [let there be] postponement to [the time of] ease (2:280).

This is necessary justice; whoever departs from it is deserving of punishment in this world and the next. Then God says:

And that you remit the debt as almsgiving would be better for you, if you did but know (2:280).

This is praiseworthy goodness to which men are invited. God elevates the status of anyone who acts in this way, but someone who fails [to do] this will not be punished for it.

There are many other examples of this found in the Qur'an (4:92; 5:45; 2:237; 16:126; 42:40; 2:261-263; 2:275).

God began the Surat al-Baqara [2] with the origins of faith, beginning with faith in the books and messengers. After having prefaced with that, He stated that the various kinds of people are three: either believers, unbelievers, or hypocrites. He stated the characteristics of the believers, then those of the unbelievers, and finally those of the hypocrites.

God laid down the principles of faith and commanded the worship of God and continued with the signs and benefits of faith. He affirmed the prophethood of His Messenger, and then stated the Last Day and the Promise and the Threat. After this God stated the beginning of the world and the creation of heaven and earth. He mentioned the creation of Adam, the angels' bowing down before him, his expulsion from Paradise, and his descent to earth.

After making general His call to all creation and then specifying it to the People of the Book, He addressed them. He spoke first to the Jews, the sons of Israel, then to the Christians, and then to the believers. He determined for them the pillars of His religion. He stated the origins of the community of Abraham and his building the House, his call to the people of Mecca, and God's assurance to the community of Abraham.

God stated what pertained to the House—Abraham's making it the direction of prayer, his extolling the rites of God which he had, like Safa and Marwa. He stated *tawhid*—his absolute oneness. He mentioned what was permissible and forbidden in the matter of food for all people in general, and then for those who believed in particular. He stated what pertains to killing by way of retaliation and to death by way of wills.

God mentioned the laws of the religion, and mentioned the fast during the month of Ramadan and the devotion which is connected with that. He mentioned all that which is connected with the month of fasting and the seasons of the pilgrimage. God mentioned the pilgrimage and stated the prohibition against killing, both generally and specifically, in the sacred territory. He mentioned prayer, fasting, pilgrimage, *jihad*, and almsgiving, and then what was permitted and what forbidden on matters of modesty. He stated the judgments on intercourse with women—and particularly when they are menstruating—on annulment of marriage, on divorcing and repudiating wives. He stated the laws on children, on nursing, then on the number of wives, their engagement during the waiting period, on divorce before and after consummation. God stated prayers and maintenance for wives and then confirmed the afterlife, and the bringing of the dead to life in this world, which is an indication of the other.

God included in this one sura all that men need to know in religion, both in its principles and its branches. He began the chapter with faith in the books and the messengers, its central part was faith in the books and the messengers, and He concluded it with faith in the books and the messengers. Faith in the books and the messengers is the foundation of faith, its pillar, and its sum.

In this chapter He commanded mankind generally, and after that specifically. In it he stated faith in the Creator and in the signs of His lordship, faith in the afterlife, in the last judgment, and in the good deeds which He commanded. Whoever is following the messengers—believers, and Jews, Christians, and Sabaeans as well—who builds upon these principles, which are faith in God, the Last Day, and in good works, will be happy in the afterlife. Their reward is with their Lord; they need not fear nor will they be sad.

By contrast, those of them who have corrupted the book or have rejected the book are unbelievers. Whoever followed the law of the Torah without changing it before the sending of Christ was among the blessed. Similarly, whoever had been following the law of the Gospel without changing it before the sending of Muhammad is among the blessed. But anyone, like the Jews after the sending of Christ, who corrupted the law of the Torah or rejected Christ is an unbeliever. In the same way the one who changed the law of Christ or rejected Muhammad, as have the Christians after the sending of Muhammad, is an unbeliever.

The ancient Jews and Christians who followed their religion before its corruption and abrogation are among the blessed. However, the Jews and Christians who have clung to a corrupt, abrogated religion, who have ceased to follow the book and the messenger which God sent them and others, they have strayed from the certain path of revealed religion and are unbelievers.

———

People hold two well-known opinions on the matter of God's commands and prohibitions. The first is that these matters go back to pure will, in which it is not said that what is commanded is for the benefit (*maslaha*) of mankind, even though its being a benefit be agreed upon. This is the view of those who say that God neither acts nor judges for a reason—neither through His wisdom nor for a goal. The second, which is the view of the majority of people, is that God only sends messengers to command people that which is for their welfare and will benefit them if they perform it (21:107; 20:123-126).

According to the first view, the question of the wisdom of sending messengers is not asked. According to the second, the laws and benefits obtained through the sending of Muhammad are greater than what pertained to the sending of Moses and Christ, while the probity of the worshipers in this life and the next which came about through his sending is many times that which obtained from the viewpoint of His commanding and creating through the sending of Moses and Christ.

The guidance and true religion which is in the *shari'a* brought by Muhammad is more perfect than what was in the two previous religious laws. By it God made it easy for mankind to follow Him and to be guided by Him in a way which was not easy for those before Muhammad. The superiority of his *shari'a* can be seen from the viewpoint of its own excellence, and from that of its own abundance over what went before it and the perfection of those who received it.

This is in contrast to the law which went before it. Moses was sent to the sons of Israel, but his law met with rejection and stubbornness during the lifetime of Moses and after his death. This is well known, and has been mentioned by the Christians in their books which concern that which had preceded them.

The law of the Torah, unlike that of the Qur'an, is lacking in completeness. In the Qur'an there is mention of the afterlife. It sets up proofs for it and describes it; there are descriptions of the Garden and the Fire which have no parallel in the Torah.

In the Qur'an there is mention of the stories of Hud, Salih, Shu'ayb, and other prophets of which there is no mention in the Torah. In it there is mention of the Beautiful Names of God and His attributes, descriptions of His angels in their various kinds, and the creation of mankind and jinn. Nothing like this is described in the Torah.

In it there is the affirmation of God's absolute oneness with types of proofs for it which are missing in the Torah. In it there is mention of the religions of the people of the earth which are not treated in the Torah. In it are the controversies with the opponents of the messengers and their erecting proofs for the origins of religion. Nothing like this is found in the Torah, although no book ever descended from heaven more full of guidance than the Qur'an or the Torah.

In the Qur'an good things are permitted and disgusting things forbidden while in the Torah many things that are good are forbidden. In the law of the Qur'an the acceptance of indemnity (*diya*)[3] is accepted, but that is not legislated in the Torah. In it there is a lifting of the bonds and fetters of the law which are in the Torah. In the Qur'an there is that which manifests the grace of God upon His people more completely.

As for the Gospel, there is no independent *shari'a* in it, nor any teaching about God's absolute oneness, nor the creation of the world, nor the stories of the prophets and their people. The Gospel refers people to the Torah for most of those matters. Christ, however, permitted for people some of what had been forbidden them, obligated them to goodness, to pardoning offenses, to bearing injuries, and to asceticism in this life. He invented parables to teach these things.

The generality of what distinguished the Gospel from the Torah consisted in noble traits of character, praiseworthy asceticism, and permission of some of what had been forbidden; all of this, however, was in the Qur'an, and in it more perfectly. In the Torah, the Gospel, and the books of the prophets there are no useful forms of knowledge or upright deeds which are not found in the Qur'an, or else there is found that which is better. In the Qur'an there is found guidance and true religion in beneficial knowledge and upright deeds which are not in the other two books.

Christians, however, have not followed either the Torah or the Gospel. Rather, they have invented a religion which was not sent through any one of the prophets. They drew up a creed for Constantine, and composed for him forty books which they called *canons*,[4] in which some things had been brought by the prophets while many other things were opposed to the law of the prophets. They came to accept much from the religion of the pagans who worshiped other gods beside God and rejected His messengers. In this way idolatry came to exist in their religion and the religion of the messengers was altered. Through that which they changed in the law of the Gospel, the religion of the Gospel became mixed, among most Christians, with what was alien to it. They could not distinguish what Christ had abrogated in the law of the Torah from what he had confirmed in it, nor did they know what he had legislated from what was invented after him.

Christ never commanded them to display and honor images, nor did he summon those who fashion such representations to make them according to his likeness. No one of the prophets ever commanded this. No prophet was ever found to command the invocation of angels for intercession, nor the calling on dead prophets and holy men to seek their intercession. Still less did any prophet ever command the invocation of the statues of angels and men for intercession, for this is one of the origins of idolatry to which the messengers put an end.

This was the principle of idolatry among men during the time of Noah. God said about the people of Noah:

> And they have said: Forsake not your gods. Forsake not Wudd, nor Suwa', nor Yaghuth and Ya'uq and Nasr. And they have led many astray (71:23-24).

Many of the scholars including Ibn 'Abbas said that these were upright individuals among the people of Noah, who, when they died, the people devoted themselves to their graves. They fashioned statues of them and then worshiped them. Christ and Christian scholars have also mentioned this.

Christ did not command people to worship him, nor did he say that he was God, nor did he command them to permit all the reprehensible things which God had forbidden in the Torah, such as the eating of pork. They, however, did permit prohibited, disgusting things and changed the religion of the Torah and the Gospel. Christ did not command them to pray to the east, to glorify the cross, to omit circumcision, or to innovate monasticism and the rest of what they invented after him.

Since the corruption of the religion of Christians is so evident, some people like 'Abd Allah al-Razi[5] have come to say, "The practice of the religion of Christ was only manifest among a small group of people before the sending of Muhammad." The religion followed by the majority of Christians was not the religion of Christ.

3) Our third point should make this clear. Supposing the religion of the two books were sufficient, this could only be if this religion were effectively preserved. Such was not the case; rather, many of its features had been effaced.

The People of the Book had differed greatly concerning Christ and other things, as God has told us (5:14; 2:213). At the time when Muhammad was sent there was no one publicly proclaiming what God had sent with the prophets before him. He was sent after a long interval between the prophets when the paths were obliterated and people were in even greater need of a prophet. In a hadith report from 'Iyad ibn Himar according to Muslim, the Messenger said:

> God looked at the people of the earth and despised them, both Arabs and non-Arabs, except for a few of the People of the Book.

People at the time of the sending of Muhammad were either *ummiyyun*—that is, possessors of no sacred book who idolatrously worshiped Al-Rahman as well as serving idols—or they were

People of the Book who had corrupted its meanings and judgments, had changed its permissions and prohibitions, and had mingled its truth with what was false, as we have demonstrated. If someone wanted to distinguish for himself what was brought by the prophets from that which men had invented after them, the majority of people did not know how to do this, but for them all of it had become the same religion.

God sent Muhammad with a book which He revealed to confirm the book which they possessed and to be a guardian over it, so that through it [the Qur'an] truth could be distinguished from falsehood. It was true guidance and integrity from error and sin (5:15-19).

4) The law of the Torah is primarily severity while that of the Gospel is leniency. The law of the Qur'an is moderate, combining both of these qualities (2:43; 48:29; 5:54). God describes His community as acting with mercy and in humility towards believers, but with severity and sternness towards unbelievers.

Muhammad described himself as the most perfect of prophets and the finest of messengers when he said:

> I am Muhammad, I am Ahmad. I am the prophet of mercy, I am the prophet of slaughter. I am the prophet of pardon, but I laugh at fighting [i.e., I fight laughing].

He described himself as the prophet of mercy and pardon, but also as prophet of slaughter who laughs at fighting. In this he is more perfect than someone primarily described as severe and intrepid or principally as lenient.

It has been said that the cause for all this[6] is that the children of Israel had themselves been in a lowly state during the time of Pharaoh's lordship over them and their enslavement by Pharaoh and his people. Thus severity was legislated for them to put an end to that lowliness among them (5:21-23).

The Companions of Muhammad, on the other hand, said to him on the Day of Badr:

> By God, we do not speak to you as did the children of Israel to Moses, "You and your Lord go and fight while we sit here." Rather we fight with you, behind you, at your right and on your left, and with Him who sent you as a prophet in truth. If you presented us with the sea and shook it, we would shake it with you. If you traveled from us to the Birk al-Ghamad[7] we would go there with you.

God sent Christ with pardon and tenderness, with forgiveness to evildoers and bearing with their wrongdoing in order to moderate their morals and put an end to the pride and harshness in them. However, these Christians have gone to excess in laxity so that they have failed to command the good and prohibit what is forbidden. They have failed to do *jihad* in the way of God, and to judge justly between people. Instead of establishing firm punishment [for crimes], their worshipers have become solitary monks.

Nevertheless, the rulers of the Christians display pride and harshness and pass judgment in opposition to what was handed down by God. They have shed blood wrongfully in accordance with what their scholars and believers have told them, as well as against what they have told them. In all that they have shared in [the Qur'anic accusation against] the Jews.

God sent Muhammad with the perfect, just law, and made his community just and good, [a community] who would not corrupt the law in this direction or that. They acted with severity towards the enemies of God, and with leniency towards His friends. They employed pardon and forgiveness in what was for themselves, but they employed vengeance and punishment in what concerned the truth of God.

This was the characteristic of Muhammad as 'A'isha says in a sound hadith:

> The prophet of God never struck a servant of his with his hand, nor did he strike a wife, an animal, or anything except when he was striving in the way of God. Nothing ever received harm from him, nor did he ever avenge himself except if the sacred things of God had been profaned. If these sacred things were profaned, nothing could allay his anger until God should be avenged. Whenever presented with two matters, one easier than the other, he always undertook the easier unless that be sinful. If it were sinful he would be the farthest of people from it.

In the law of Muhammad there is leniency, pardon, forgiveness, and noble qualities of character greater than what is in the Gospel. There is in it, moreover, severity, *jihad*, and setting punishments for unbelievers and hypocrites greater than what is found in the Torah. All of this is to the limit of perfection. Some people say: "Moses was sent with majesty. Jesus was sent with beauty. Muhammad was sent with perfection."

5) God's grace upon His people includes His benefiting and providing for them. This is of two kinds.

a) He protects them from harm and puts an end to their need and poverty, like [His bestowing] their daily sustenance so that if it were not for Him, they would die of hunger, or His granting them victory, so that if it were not for Him, they would be overcome by their enemies, or like His guidance so that, were it not for Him, they would go astray and that would cause them harm in the end. There is no doubt that were people to lose this kind of grace, it would result in their harm, either in this world, in the next, or both. In the Surat al-Nahl [16], which is the chapter of mercy, one can find the principles of God's mercies in which the perfection of mercies is reached.

b) The second kind is those mercies by which are obtained the perfection of graces in the highest degree. On the Last Day people will be of two kinds; the pure companions of the Right and the holy ones who have gone further to approach God, and then there is the other kind—those who have departed from these [upright] people, that is, the people of Hell.

Since grace is of two kinds, mankind was in need of God to send Muhammad from each of these two aspects. These two kinds of grace were obtained through God's sending him, for without him all people, those of the book and those without any book, were ignorant and erring. No one remained of the People of the Book who was a follower of Christ still holding to the religion which brings happiness with God in the afterlife. They had, rather, altered and corrupted that religion.

Even if it were supposed that they had not changed a thing of it, there would still be the perfection of God's graces (*ni'am*) and favors and the highest degree of blessedness in God's sending of Muhammad, which had not been achieved through the first book. His sending was, in fact, the greatest of God's favors of both kinds upon the people of the earth. It will be clear to anyone who examines the affairs of the world that God did not bestow on the people of the earth any favor greater than that which He granted by sending Muhammad. Those who reject his sending are those about whom God spoke (14:28). This is in contrast to the thankfulness of those who have received this grace (6:53; 3:144).

6) When the Christians say, "We are amazed at this people, etc." their view is uncalled-for and ignorant and deserves to be answered. What demands amazement in this—and amazement does not even cease at it—is that every intelligent person wonders at those who know the religion of Muhammad and its goal of truth and then follow something else, knowing that they do that only through an excess of ignorance and error or through an excess in wrong-headedness, as followers of their own whims.

The people of the earth are of two kinds: the People of the Book—i.e., the Christians and Jews—and others like the pagan Arabs, Hindus, Turks, and still others like the Persian Magians and Sabaeans among the would-be philosophers. The People of the Book grant us that everyone other than them derived evident benefit from the prophethood of Muhammad. He called all groups of pagans, Magians, and Sabaeans to be better than what they were, and these were the people most in need of his messengership.

Of the People of the Book, the Jews grant us the need of the Christians for him and that he called them to be better than what they were; the Christians, on the other hand, have granted us the need of the Jews for him and that he called them to be better than they were. There is no group of people of the earth which does not admit that Muhammad called the other groups to be better than they were. This is a witness from all the people of the earth that Muhammad called the people of the earth to be better than what they were.

The witness of groups against each other is acceptable, for they are protective of their interests, and are impartial to Muhammad and his community and impartial to the rest of the communities. Their witness about themselves is not acceptable, for they are its propagandists, and the witness of a propagandist against an adversary is unacceptable.

The philosophers have admitted that the world has not met with a spirit finer than his spirit, and have admitted that his spirit is finer than that of Moses and Christ. They defame other spirits than his, but this is not the place to speak of that. By contrast, not a single one of them has ever defamed the spirit of Muhammad unless one departed from the philosophical precepts of fairness and knowledgeable discourse. Those who adhere to just and knowledgeable discourse agree that the spirit of Muhammad is the finest spirit in the ways of the world. How can someone be in skeptical wonder at a spirit like this?

7) The seventh point is specifically in answer to the People of the Book. One should say to the Jews that they are the lowliest of all peoples. Even if it were supposed that what they hold is the unchanged religion of God, it is, nevertheless, overcome and conquered throughout the world. Can they wonder that God would send a messenger who would guide people to the truth and to the straight path and that He sent him with guidance and the religion of truth to make it victorious over every religion, so that the religion of God with which the prophets were sent and which was revealed in His books has come to be evidently victorious by argumentation and proof, by the sword and spear.

To the Christians it should be said that they have not kept the religion of God which His prophets brought unadulterated by the religion of idolaters and those who make Him unattainable. Rather, they have taken principles of the idolaters and the transcendentalist philosophers and others and have incorporated them into their religion. They do not have, for the most part, either intellectual proof against unbelievers or a conquering hand. Rather they are intimidated and fearful in their hearts towards unbelievers who extol them. They are the weakest of people in argumentation, the narrowest in methodology, the farthest from knowledge and certainty, and the least able to set up arguments and proofs. Sometimes they are afraid of the pagan philosophers and other idolaters and transcendentalists, and either agree with their views or else humbly submit to them. At other times they are fearful of the swords of idolaters and either abandon some of their religion for their sake or else abjectly submit to them.

They are weak in the authority of argumentation and weak in the authority of conquest; therefore it is evident that they are in need of the establishment of guidance and the religion of truth which God sent with His messengers and revealed through His books. What is amazing is how they can turn away from what is manifestly for their happiness in this world and the next to what is for their misery in both worlds.

There is no answer like this for the Muslims, for they have not nor will they cease to be a community founded upon guidance and the religion of truth, conquering by proof and certainty on the one hand and by arm and tongue on the other. God and those who are with Him will inherit the earth. He is the greatest of inheritors, as Muhammad established in a sound hadith reported from him:

> A group of my community will not cease to be founded upon the command of God. Those who depart from it will not harm it nor will those who oppose it, until the Day of Judgment.

It is also reported that he said:

> A group of my people will be victorious until God comes with His command.

8) It is said to the People of the Book—firstly to the Jews—that when they were following the religion of Moses and living according to guidance and the religion of truth, they were victorious. After that, innovations multiplied among them, as they know (5:59-60). The People of the Book admit that the Jews worshiped idols and killed the prophets. God said that it was for this reason they were destroyed twice (17:4-8). The first destruction occurred when Nebuchadnezzar carried them off to Babylon, and that destruction lasted seventy years. The second destruction occurred about seventy years after Christ.

It has been said that this is the meaning of God's statement:

> Those of the children of Israel who went astray were cursed by the tongue of David and by that of Jesus, son of Mary (5:78).

After the second destruction they were scattered throughout the earth, and no king remained for them. Between the two destructions they were under the dominion of unbelieving kings, as they were after Christ.

To Christians one can say that they were continually conquered, overcome, and scattered throughout the earth until Constantine was victorious and established the religion of the Christians by the sword, killing those Jews and pagans who opposed him. However, the religion he made victorious was changed and corrupted and not the religion of Christ.

Nevertheless the lands of Iraq and Persia were still Magian and pagan, as were other regions. As for the lands to the east and the west, they were still [populated by] various kinds of pagan peoples.

When God sent Muhammad, the absolute oneness of God and His service alone with no rivals made such a conquest as no people had ever known, nor had any prophet ever accomplished. Through him He made manifest the Books and the messengers—the Torah, the Gospel, and the Psalms; Moses, Jesus, David, Solomon, and other messengers in a way they had not been manifest, neither among the People of the Book nor among others.

The People of the Book, although they were better than others, were not grounded in the necessary faith in God, His messengers, and in the Last Day, nor in the prescriptions of His religion. They were not, moreover, victorious over the majority of unbelievers, nor were they granted victory over them by God (9:29).

The Jews denigrated and cursed the prophets and mentioned faults beyond which God had elevated them. This is well known. Some of them even say that Solomon was a magician and that David was an astrologer and no prophet. It would take too long to describe all the examples of this. Among them there was disbelief in the prophets the like of which among their ancients was vicious.

Christians, despite their exaggerated devotion to Christ and his followers, treated other prophets lightly. Sometimes they made the apostles equal or superior to Abraham or Moses. At other times they spoke like the Jews, declaring, for example, that Solomon was not a prophet but fell from the rank of prophet. Elsewhere they claimed that what God said about David and others was only intended to refer to Christ.

The text itself, however, does not indicate that, but they have interpreted the books of God simply according to their own whims. Sometimes they hold that anyone of them who obeys God in what they claim is obedience to Him becomes like one of the prophets or even better than him, so that obedience to that person is as necessary as it is to the prophets. In this way they permit people to change the prescriptions of the prophets and to lay down a religion which they have innovated.

Muhammad and his community are grounded in the absolute oneness of God which Abraham, Moses, and the rest of the messengers held. They believe in every Book which God has revealed and in each messenger which He sent. They have established the religion of the Merciful One, which no other religious group has established.

Most of the people of the earth are with Muhammad. Some believe in him both inwardly and openly; they are the God-fearing friends of God, the party of the fortunate, the army of conquerors. Some have surrendered to God in the external order, pious out of fear of His community; these are the hypocrites. Others are peaceably united to Him by treaty, protection (*dhimma*), or truce. These are the peoples of pact and protection throughout the earth, or they may be in fear of His community.

Wherever there is one or a group of His community holding fast to His religion, His light is evident, His certainty is victorious, exalted, and made to conquer. His grace is known upon all. It is a matter known by the people of the earth—pagan unbelievers and the People of the Book—that God characterized Muhammad and his community with guidance and the religion of truth.

They made the religion of the Lord conquer from the eastern parts of the world to the west by word and deed. Can any intelligent person having knowledge and fairness state that there is no benefit in God's sending Muhammad and that he is dispensed from his messengership because of what is held by the People of the Book?

9) They admit that the pagans have benefited greatly from his mission, for they have established the oneness of God and His religion among themselves and they extol Christ and refute the view of the Jews about him. He humiliated them[8] at that time. This was one of the greatest benefits and most glorious accomplishments and greatest favors of God upon His servants.

Nevertheless, he said that God sent him and commanded him to do that. If he were lying—and the liar who perpetrated his deception against God is the worst of unbelievers—the great good the like of which no one of the prophets ever accomplished could never have been derived from him, for he put an end to the religion of the pagans and the religion of the Magians and brought the Jews into subjection. No prophet or messenger before him had any power over any one of these three [peoples].

If a person is truthful, he knows that [Muhammad] reported that he was a prophet of God to the Christians and to the people of other religions. He informed them from God of the unbelief of anyone who did not believe in him. This aspect [of his teaching] is one which he preached to every kind of person.

We say to persons from each of the religions, "You admit that if anyone other than you followed the religion of Muhammad, he would be better than he had been." The Jews admit that if the Christians followed him, it would be better for them than the religion of the Christians, while the Christians confess that if the Jews followed him, it would be better for them than the religion of the Jews. Thus the People of the Book, Jews and Christians, admit that if anyone other than they were to follow him, it would be better for them than what they were following.

The Magians, the pagan Arabs, the black Africans, the Turks, various groups of Khazars[9] and Slavs, and other groups of unbelievers admit that his followers are better than others. Those who are not People of the Book generally admit that the religion of the Muslims is superior to that of the Jews and Christians.

It can therefore be said that it is impossible for someone to hold about the one who brought this religion, to whose superiority all people of the earth attest, that he is among the most unbelieving of men and among the most deserving of God's anger and punishment. Whoever claims that he is prophet of God—if he is truthful—is one of the best people on earth and most deserving of the pleasure of God and His reward. But if he is lying, he is one of the worst people on earth and most deserving of God's anger and punishment.

It is impossible that someone from whom has resulted such goodness, knowledge, and guidance and in which there is benefit for this world and the next greater than what was achieved by all mankind could be one of the most unbelieving of men, deserving the anger and punishment of God. It is necessary, rather, that he be one of the best people on earth and even *the* finest of people on earth and the most deserving of God's pleasure and reward.

10) Before the revelation of the Torah it was the customary practice of God that when one of the prophets was rejected, He would avenge Himself upon his enemies by exacting a punishment upon them. He destroyed the people of Noah with a flood, the people of Hud with a violent wind, the people of Salih with a cry, the people of Shu'ayb with the shadow, the people of Lot with a

storm, and the people of Pharaoh by drowning (28:43). When God revealed the Torah, he commanded the People of the Book to wage *jihad*; some of them withdrew while others obeyed. The object of God's sending a messenger was only attained by knowledge and power (48:28).

The view of these people is that the Torah brought justice, while the Gospel brought grace, and thus there is no need for anything other than the two of them. If this were true, it would only be correct if the two books had not been corrupted but instead were followed in knowledge and act and if the people of the two books were supported by God and granted victory over those who opposed them. How could this be the case when much of what was in both of these books was corrupted and their people were not granted victory over unbelievers? Rather, the unbelievers were overcoming them in most parts of the earth, such as in the Yemen, in the Hijaz and the rest of the Arabian peninsula, in the lands of Iraq, Khurasan, and the Maghrib, in Hind, Sind, and the lands of the Turks. Syria, Egypt, and elsewhere were in the hands of the People of the Book, but even in those areas the Persians had defeated them.[10]

Subsequently God made the Christians victorious over them, but their conquest was a preparation paving the way for the manifestation of Islam. When the Magian Persians defeated Byzantium, it grieved the Prophet and the believers, while the pagans who were more numerous than the believers rejoiced. The People of the Book were closer to the believers than the Magians, while the Magians were closer to the pagans than to the People of the Book. God promised the believers that Byzantium (*Rum*) would conquer after that, and on that day the believers would rejoice in the victory of God.

Later God would send a group of the Companions of Muhammad to Mu'ta,[11] and after that the Muslims went out with him in the year of Tabuk to Syria.[12] His Companions later conquered this land. Thus was the religion of God confirmed and made manifest, while the pagans, Magians, and others were subjected—all at his hands and the hands of his community, not at the hands of the Jews and Christians.

If it were supposed that the religion of these people was perfect with no corruption having occurred in it, but then they were defeated and conquered, God would have sent someone who would confirm and manifest His religion. How much more so, when it was corrupted?

The religion of Ahmad is finer and more perfect than theirs even if it had not been corrupted. Theirs is the corrupted unfavored (*mafdul*) one, his is the uncorrupted, the favored (*fadil*); theirs is the defeated, the conquered; his is the religion confirmed and granted victory. Is not a benefit obtained in some of this from God's sending him?

11) They say, "Since the creator is just and generous, it has been necessary for Him to manifest His justice and generosity." It should be said to them that the generosity of the Generous One does not obligate people to abandon their rights. Since the Generous One is He who does what is good for people, it cannot be He who obligates them to give up their rights.

Yet these people claim that the Law of the Gospel demands that people abandon their rights and that it does not establish the rights of the oppressed against his oppressor. Among them there is no just legal system by which people are judged. The legal system among them is double. There is the judgment of the church, but in this there is no protection for the oppressed from the oppressor. The second is the administration of justice by their kings; this, however, is not a revealed law, but operates according to the opinions of the rulers.

You find them referring people to the judgment of the Law of Islam in cases of homicide, financial matters, and things like that. Even in some of their countries where the king, the military, and most of the people of the land are Christians, and Muslims are but a small group among them, they refer people to the Muslim judge in cases of homicide and financial matters for judgment according to the law of Muslims.

That is because in the case of homicide and financial affairs if it were decided for the oppressed that he should pardon his oppressor in these matters, the judge who decides between people, when he determines that the oppressed should give up his claim, would be judging wrongly and not justly.

Were we to commend the avenger of every slain person not to take vengeance upon the killer, that each creditor should not demand payment but invite it voluntarily, that every person who is struck or slandered should not demand justice from him who did wrong, there would be no deterrent to restrain evildoers, and the strong would oppress the weak and cause corruption on the earth (2:251).

A revealed Law must include a legal system which is just, and must at the same time exhort people to pardon and to act with kindness. The Law of Islam has done this, as we have previously mentioned (5:45; 2:28; 42:40; 16:126; 3:134; 42:41-42; 4:92; 42:43).

Anas said that whenever there was brought before the Prophet a case of something involving retribution, he always advised pardon. He advised pardon, but did not obligate people to it. Once it happened that Barira, the handmaid of 'A'isha the wife of the Prophet, was emancipated, and she determined to dissolve her marriage. Her husband did not want her to part with him, and so the Prophet interceded with her that she not leave her husband. She said, "Do you command me?" He said, "No, I am making intercession." He did not oblige her to accept his intercession.

12) They say, "Where the perfection which is grace exists, it is only possible that what is more perfect than perfection be added to it." It should be said to them that justice and grace are only legislated by God. Only God legislated the law of the Torah; only God legislated the law of the Gospel.

It is clear that God really spoke to Moses from the bush, while Christians in the excess of what they claim about the divinity of Christ hold that God spoke to people through the humanity of Christ, just as He spoke to Moses through the bush. It is evident to every intelligent person that if it is true that God's speaking to Moses was the greatest speech of God to His servants, how could it be said that the law of justice was not legislated by God?[13]

Furthermore, it should be asserted that the Law of justice is more deserving to be ascribed to God than is the Law of grace. The command to pardon and do good can be properly carried out by everyone, but the law of justice and judgment between people is only possible for certain individuals. There are found a great number of those who do good among people through works of charity, but there are but few who do good by making judgments between them in justice.

How can it be said that He who commands by legislating grace is God, without saying also that it is He who commanded by legislating Law? God sent His messengers and revealed His books in order that people practice justice (57:25).

Christ commanded the one who is mistreated to pardon his oppressor, but there is nothing in that to indicate that this is such an obligation whose omission would be deserving of censure and punishment. Rather, it should be something desirable, so that he who does that is deserving of praise and reward.

Moses obligated a justice whose omission is deserving of censure and punishment. At that time there was no inconsistency between the necessity of justice and the desirability of goodness. However, the obligation of justice is associated with threat and warning about its omission, while the desirability of goodness is connected with the hopefulness and attractiveness of performing it. Thus, in the former there is threat present along with some hope, but in the latter there is hope without threat. Christ spoke thusly:

> I was a witness of them while I dwelt among them, and when You took me You were watcher over them. You are witness over all things. If You punish them, lo! they are Your slaves, and if You forgive them [they are Your slaves]. You, only You are the mighty, the wise (5:117-118).

Therefore one can say that Christ came to complete the Torah, for the works of supererogation come after obligatory prescriptions. Otherwise, if it were said that Christ obliged the oppressed person to pardon his oppressor in the sense that he would be deserving of the threat, censure, and punishment were he not to pardon him, it would follow from this that everyone who sought justice from an evildoer would be a wrongdoer deserving of censure and punishment. This is a double injustice upon the mistreated person who has sought justice. First the evildoer wronged him, and then, when he sought justice, he would be wronged a second time. This is unfair to the just person who has sought redress from him who wronged him.

How much better is God's message where He says:

> Now whatever you have been given is but a passing comfort for the life of the world, and that which God has is better and more lasting for those who believe and put their trust in their Lord.
>
> And those who shun the worst of sins and indecencies and when they are wroth, forgive.
>
> And those who answer the call of their Lord, and establish worship, and whose affairs are a matter of counsel, and who spend of what We have bestowed on them.
>
> And those who, when a great wrong is done to them, defend themselves.
>
> The penalty of an ill-deed is an ill the like thereof. But whosoever pardons and amends, his wage is the affair of God. Lo! He loves not wrongdoers.
>
> And whoso defends himself after he has suffered wrong—for such, there is no way [of blame] against them.
>
> The way of blame is only against those who oppress mankind, and wrongfully rebel in the earth. For such there is a painful doom.

> And truly, whoever is patient and forgives—lo! That man is of the steadfast heart of things (42:36-43; 22:60).

This is one of the best, finest, and most just of messages where He legislates justice and says, "The penalty of an ill-deed is an ill the like thereof," and calls to goodness and says, "Whosoever pardons and amends, his wage is the affair of God. Lo! He loves not wrong-doers."

When God calls men to pardon, He states that there is no shame connected with seeking justice. In order that no one suppose that pardon is absolutely prescribed He says, "Whoso defends himself after he has suffered wrong—for such, there is no way against them." It is clear, then, that God's way is only against those who do wrong. Although God does not set His way against those who are wronged, nevertheless He calls them to patience and pardon.

This is the best and most complete legislation. It makes patience, pardon, and doing good totally desirable and mentions the virtues, benefits, and praiseworthy reward in it. It exculpates people who seek justice against those who have wronged them from any blame and offence against justice, and makes it clear that such a person does not depart from the Way when he seeks justice after he has been wronged.

Is it possible that a law come to set the Way against those who justly seek redress, while it does not set it against the evildoer in his injustice? It is known that what Christ commanded was pardon, not so that one who failed to do it would be deserving of blame and punishment, but because such a person would be deprived of the good by way of recompense and reward that would result from pardon. This truth does not contradict the law of the Torah. It also can be seen that the law of the Gospel does not contradict that of the Torah, since it is derived from it and completes it.

Therefore their claim that the law of the Gospel was legislated by God, whereas the law of the Torah was not, is the view of one who is one of the most ignorant and erring of people. This is a conclusion derived from their view of the hypostatic union and that Christ is God. Since that view is false, it renders this absurd view necessary.

# APPENDIX

## THE RELATIONSHIP OF *AL-JAWAB AL-SAHIH* TO *TAKHJIL AHL AL-INJIL*

The textual question of *Al-Jawab al-Sahih* is closely connected with that of the relationship of this work to *Takhjil Ahl al-Injil*,[1] another work written by Ibn Taymiyya on Christianity. In the present state of the textual evidence, *Al-Jawab al-Sahih* consists of approximately 1,400 printed pages[2] and three manuscript versions,[3] while *Takhjil Ahl al-Injil* exists in one unpublished manuscript of approximately 200 folios, the text of which is virtually identical with the final 389 pages of *Al-Jawab al-Sahih*.

In recent times the existence of *Takhjil Ahl al-Injil* as an historical entity separate from *Al-Jawab al-Sahih* has been questioned. Several possible relationships between the two works can be posited: the two titles are merely alternative names for the same book; *Takhjil Ahl al-Injil* is a portion of the other longer work; the existing long work is a composite of two works originally separate; the one was a partial first draft of the other. It is also possible that the two works were individual, separately conceived treatises, one of which—*Takhjil Ahl al-Injil*—has ceased to exist as a separate work except for the Bodleian manuscript. Even though the question cannot be answered at this time, and possibly never will be, it can be elucidated by the textual history of the two works.

Of the 8th/14th century biographers of Ibn Taymiyya, Ibn Kathir and al-Dhahabi[4] mention neither of these works, but the bibliographical lists mentioned by Ibn 'Abd al-Hadi,[5] Ibn Qayyim al-Jawziyya,[6] Ibn Shakir al-Kutubi,[7] and Ibn Rajab[8] bear investigation. The first two of these men, Ibn 'Abd al-Hadi and Ibn Qayyim al-Jawziyya, were students of Ibn Taymiyya, and wrote their biographies in the first decades after his death. Ibn Shakir al-Kutubi (d. 764/1363) represents the second generation of students, while Ibn Rajab, the great Hanbali biographer, died in 795/1393.

It should be noted that none of these authors who have compiled bibliographies of works attributed to Ibn Taymiyya have made any claims to completeness. The most extensive of these compilations, those of Ibn Qayyim and Ibn 'Abd al-Hadi, contain explicit denials[9] of their being exhaustive lists of the shaykh's works. Therefore in studying these bibliographical treatments the absence of a title does not categorically indicate that one should reject its authenticity. In fact a number of works accepted today without question as parts of Ibn Taymiyya's *corpus operarum* are not cited in one or more of these lists.

Ibn 'Abd al-Hadi (d. 744/1344) mentions *Al-Jawab al-Sahih* in his list of the works of his teacher, and calls the work "one of the most illustrious and beneficial of his books."[10]

> It is in two volumes, while some copies of it are in three or more. In many of his long works their copies differ. It includes the establishment of the prophecies and their determination by clear enlightening proofs. It includes the explanation of many verse from the Qur'an and other matters of interest.[11]

In addition to *Al-Jawab al-Sahih*, Ibn 'Abd al-Hadi lists a number of other works on Christianity which have already been discussed—*Al-Sarim al-Maslul* (p. 69), *Iqtida' al-Sirat al-Mustaqim* (p. 83), *Qawa'id al-Kana'is* (p. 78), *Al-Risala al-Qubrusiyya* (p. 71), *Jawab fi Ihtijaj al-Jahmiyya wal-Nasara bil-Kalima.*[12] In addition Ibn 'Abd al-Hadi mentions a work which appears to be lost, *Fi Dhaba'ih Ahl al-Kitab*,[13] presumably a legal judgment elaborating the Qur'anic injunction:

> This day are good things made lawful for you. The food of those who have received the Scripture is lawful for you, and your food is lawful for them (5:5).

*Takhjil Ahl al-Injil* is not mentioned by Ibn 'Abd al-Hadi, a significant omission in such an extensive list.

Almost as extensive is the compilation of Ibn Qayyim al-Jawziyya, although he fails to include the valuable descriptive material appended by Ibn 'Abd al-Hadi to his entries. Like Ibn 'Abd al-Hadi, Ibn Qayyim lists the lost *Ihtijaj bil-Kalima*, although not the work *Dhaba'ih Ahl al-Kitab*. The identity of the above-mentioned work[14] on Christian feasts must also remain an unanswered question. Ibn Qayyim is clearly not referring to *Iqtida' al-Sirat al-Mustaqim*, for he mentions that work elsewhere.

Ibn Qayyim also fails to mention several legal decisions on matters dealing with Christians cited by Ibn 'Abd al-Hadi; otherwise the two lists agree on the works in question. Ibn Qayyim's only descriptive comment about these works is to state that *Al-Jawab al-Sahih* was in two volumes; he thereby corroborates the statement of Ibn 'Abd al-Hadi and confirms the evidence of the early Leiden manuscript that the earliest form of the work was in two volumes.[15]

Ibn Shakir al-Kutubi's list of works is not so complete as the previous two. Listing only *Al-Jawab al-Sahih* (this time in three volumes), and *Al-Risala al-Qubrusiyya*,[16] Ibn Shakir is clearly citing only the most important works of his author. However, his listing of two works on prophecy (*Mu'jizat al-Anbiya' Quwan Nafsaniyya* and *Thubut al-Nubuwwat 'Aqlan wa-Naqlan wal-Mu'jizat wal-Karamat*) provide the first indication that two separate works on prophecy, both of considerable length,[17] were among Ibn Taymiyya's literary legacy. The former title could well indicate the work known today as Ibn Taymiyya's *Kitab al-Nubuwwat*. The absence of a work bearing this title that early indicates that this work, obviously by Ibn Taymiyya, was known in the 8th/14th century by another name.

The latter of these two works on prophecy mentioned by Ibn Shakir describes remarkably well the contents of the Oxford manuscript entitled *Takhjil Ahl al-Injil*, and may provide the earliest indication of this as a separate work. The explicit mention of *Al-Jawab al-Sahih* and *Mu'jizat al-Anbiya'* in the same context emphasizes the existence of three important works of Ibn Taymiyya's *corpus*, of which modern studies have accounted for only two. Thus a question must be raised, even apart from the Oxford manuscript, concerning the identity of this two-volume work to which Ibn Shakir is referring (Ibn 'Abd al-Hadi had previously listed *Taqrir al-Nubuwwat 'Aqlan wa-Naqlan*).[18]

A survey of the lists of works made by the students of Ibn Taymiyya and his earliest biographers nevertheless lays a suspicion that *Takhjil Ahl al-Injil* did not exist as a separate work during the 8th/14th century. Unless it could be identified with one of the works on prophecy cited by Ibn Shakir, the work was not referred to by any of the earliest biographers. Were it not for later evidence to the contrary, one obtaining his information of Ibn Taymiyya's works from these early authors would have no reason to suspect the existence of a work entitled *Takhjil Ahl al-Injil*.

This suspicion is confirmed by an examination of the Leiden manuscript Or 338, the earliest existing manuscript evidence of *Al-Jawab al-Sahih*. This manuscript, dated 730 (1330), just two years after the death of Ibn Taymiyya, is equivalent to the last half of the printed edition, beginning 2:279 until the end at 4:323. There is no indication of a break or any mark indicating 3:275, the point where *Takhjil Ahl al-Injil* begins as a separate work in the Oxford Marsh 299 manuscript. Because the Leiden manuscript claims to be Part 2 of the work, and begins almost exactly at the mid-point of the edition printed from the Hyderabad manuscript, it can be logically concluded that the length of the complete versions of the two manuscripts was the same.

That this was a common, if not the standard, version of the text known throughout its history is indicated by an examination of MS 732 in the Yeni Cami (Istanbul) collection, which exactly complements the Leiden manuscripts, although dated more than three centuries later. Its date reads Saturday 15 Rajab 1094 (1683), and its contents begin with the ***khutba*** on 1:1 of the printed work, and concludes at the bottom of 2:278, the exact point where the Leiden manuscript begins. Beneath the text on the last page it states, "This copy is half the book, but it is also lacking half, so do not . . . [unclear]."[19]

The Indian manuscript is in the Asafiyya library in Hyderabad, the latest (1319/1901) of the existing manuscripts and the only one which contains the whole of *Al-Jawab al-Sahih* as it is known today; it notes neither the break between the halves averted to in the Leiden and Istanbul manuscripts at 3:275. It is solely from this Asafiyya manuscript that both Cairo printed editions were made.[20] The Indian manuscript was apparently produced by adding the Leiden manuscript to the one in Istanbul; however, it may be based on a separate manuscript which is now lost.

Were it not for the Oxford manuscript (Marsh 299 in the Bodleian library), one might think the textual state of *Al-Jawab al-Sahih* not open to question. The evidence offered by this manuscript introduces a number of new, still unanswered, questions. The title page, which Stern has determined to be not an original part of the manuscript,[21] gives the title as *Takhjil Ahl al-Injil wal-Nahj al-Sahih fi al-Radd 'ala Man Baddala Din 'Isa ibn Maryam al-Masih*. The contents, however, as was mentioned above, are identical with the last 380 pages of *Al-Jawab al-Sahih*. The date on the manuscript is unfortunately illegible, but Nicoll suggests that it comes from the fifteenth or sixteenth centuries,[22] which, if correct, would place the manuscript second only to the Leiden manuscript in age.

Fortunately, the manuscript evidence for these works is supplemented by their mention in the works of two 11th/17th-century writers, Kateb Celebi (Hajji Khalifa) and Ludovico Marracci. Hajji Khalifa (1067/1657) gives the first clear evidence of two distinct works when he lists both *Takhjil Ahl al-Injil* and *Al-Jawab al-Sahih* in his *Kashf al-Zunun*. The title Hajji Khalifa gives for *Al-Takhjil* is not identical with that on the Oxford manuscript; his version is *Al-Takhjil li-Man Baddal al-Turah wal-Injil*.[23] The incipit offered by Hajji Khalifa is also different from that in the Oxford manuscript.[24] This could lead one to think Hajji Khalifa was simply referring to a work completely different from that contained in the Oxford manuscript. This suspicion must be tempered, however, with the knowledge that the title page of the Oxford manuscript was not original, and thus both title page and incipit are less likely to be accurate than the original contents.

Hajji Khalifa also lists separately the work entitled *Bayan al-Jawab al-Sahih li-Man Baddal Din al-Masih*,[25] the form in which the title appears in the Leiden and Istanbul manuscripts. He also describes the contents of the book; this is not so helpful as it might have been, for he merely reports Ibn Taymiyya's outline for his six-part reply to Paul of Antioch at 1:20.[26] However, the fact that this six-part refutation ends precisely at the place where the Oxford manuscript begins may be an indication that Ibn Taymiyya's description of his work on 1:20 is a complete outline, and thus he intended the work to end at 3:275. Should this be the case, the work contained in the Oxford manuscript would have to be considered an originally distinct work on the prophethood of Muhammad which, because of the complementary nature of the subject matter, was attached to the end of the longer and more famous work.

The other important 11th/17th-century evidence for this work is that of Ludovico Marracci. In his long *Prodromus* to the Latin translation he made from the Qur'an, Marracci quotes widely from a great number of Muslim authors. The work cited more often by Marracci than any other is not mentioned by name, but is called the "Apologia contra Christianam Religionem pro secta Mahumetana,"[27] by Ahmedus filius Abdohalimi (i.e., Ibn Taymiyya). The work is more frequently referred to as the "Apologia," the author frequently as "Adversarius."

Marracci's practice is to quote the authors he cites first in Arabic, after which he translates the passages in question into Latin. He also cites the page number for some passages, a valuable tool by which his copy of the work in question can be reconstructed.

Nicoll, who had access to the Oxford manuscript but not to any of the Apology against Paul of Antioch, discovered that many of the passages agreed verbally with the contents of the Oxford manuscript, and stated that the work cited and praised so frequently by Marracci was *Takhjil Ahl al-Injil.*

> It is truly the same work which Marracci frequently praises in the *Prodromus*, so much that almost the entire work seems to have been inserted into it (he calls the author Ahmad ibn 'Abd al-Halim, but nevertheless suppressed the title of the work).[28]

Steinschneider accepts Nicoll's statement that it was *Takhjil Ahl al-Injil* which was cited by Marracci, and since he was familiar with Marracci's work, he described the contents of the Oxford manuscript by the citations in Marracci.[29] The passages described by Steinschneider are not in *Takhjil Ahl al-Injil*, however, but in the longer work in portions not found in the Oxford manuscript.

This laid the bases for later errors. Nallino made a study of the sources used by Marracci, but had no access either to the Oxford manuscript or to any of those of the longer work. He therefore repeated Nicoll's statement, and also pointed out that many passages cited by Marracci agreed verbally with those quoted by Di Matteo in his early summary of the argument in *Al-Jawab al-Sahih.*

> Nicoll also had at his disposal at Oxford a manuscript of a similar book by Ibn Taymiyya entitled *Al-Gawab as-sahih li man baddala din al-Masih* which has been well summarized in brief by Msgr. Ignazio di Matteo: *Ibn Taymiyyah o riassunto della sua opera.* I point this out because, without the attestation of Nicoll, it would be possible to think of *Al-Gawab* in which very many of the passages cited by Marracci are also found literally.[30]

Nallino, apparently misled by Steinschneider, who included both *Takhjil Ahl al-Injil* and *Al-Jawab al-Sahih* in the Oxford manuscript,[31] suggested that but for the testimony of Nicoll one might think that the work referred to by Marracci was *Al-Jawab al-Sahih.*

Steinschneider in turn had been misled by an error in the Leiden catalogue of De Jong and De Goeje in which it is stated that in addition to the partial Leiden manuscript of *Al-Jawab al-Sahih* there is another at Oxford.[32] However, the Oxford manuscript was not only not complete, but it contained only a portion of the Leiden manuscript.

At the time when Nallino was writing it was therefore believed that the Oxford manuscript Marsh 299 contained two separate works by Ibn Taymiyya—*Takhjil Ahl al-Injil* and *Al-Jawab al-Sahih.* Evidence of this same error can be seen in Brockelmann's *Geschichte,* where the two works are listed separately in the same Oxford manuscript.[33]

It was not until Stern, who was the first to prove that MS Marsh 299 contained only *Takhjil Ahl al-Injil,* which was in fact identical with the last quarter of *Al-Jawab al-Sahih,* that the question of Marracci's text could be properly asked.

Stern concluded that since all of the citations by Marracci could be found in *Al-Jawab al-Sahih,* while only some of them were in the Oxford manuscript, it should be concluded that the work which Marracci used was the full text of *Al-Jawab al-Sahih.*[34] A closer look at Marracci's *Prodromus* shows that this cannot be the case, and whatever the nature of the work by Ibn Taymiyya used by Marracci might have been, it is highly unlikely that it could have been *Al-Jawab al-Sahih* as we know it today.

The reason is that there is no citation listed by Marracci which appears in *Al-Jawab al-Sahih* before 2:293.[35] From this point until the end of *Al-Jawab al-Sahih* the work is frequently and faithfully cited by Marracci. This alone would make Marracci's work of interest for a study of the text of *Al-Jawab al-Sahih*, for his citations, frequently quoting Ibn Taymiyya *verbatim* for pages at a time, offer textual support and solutions for various problems insoluble solely through use of the manuscripts.

It can be seen that none of these citations fall outside the text included in the Leiden manuscript, and yet fairly inclusively cover the material treated in that part of the text. One would be tempted to conclude that Marracci was working from a copy of the second half of the complete version of *Al-Jawab al-Sahih*. In the final conclusion this may actually have been the case.

There are, however, problems with this. Marracci's paginated citations at first seem to confirm this view, for a hypothetical starting point for Marracci's text can be projected backwards from the paginated citations which would place the beginning of the work reasonably close to the break between parts 1 and 2 reflected in the Istanbul and Leiden manuscripts.[36]

In fact it is easy to see how Nicoll could have felt that it was the Oxford manuscript's *Takhjil Ahl al-Injil* which Marracci was using, for it is this final section of *Al-Jawab al-Sahih* which was of most interest to Marracci. In all of Parts 1 and 2 of the *Prodromus*, Marracci refers only once to a portion of the work preceding that contained in Marsh 299. One gets the impression that Marracci was working his way argument by argument through this final portion of *Al-Jawab al-Sahih* until he approaches the conclusion of Ibn Taymiyya's work at Prod. 3:14.[37]

However, at this point Marracci produces a series of citations from the last part of vol. 2 of *Al-Jawab al-Sahih*, which he describes as coming "in principio partis 2."[38] That these latter citations in Marracci's copy of Ibn Taymiyya's work *follow* those described above is confirmed by one of the passages being located as "pagina mihi 690."[39] This is a clear indication that if this pagination is correct, this section, which according to the present text should have occurred about page 40, actually *followed* the passages listed above.[40]

This citation is neither supported nor denied by the passages around it, none of which mention any pagination. It is possible that the pagination here is incorrect, and it could be assumed that Marracci's text was essentially that of the Leiden manuscript. But even if this paginated citation were dismissed as an error, his noting that the passage *Prod.* 3:17-18 is taken from the beginning of Part 2 would have to be explained.

In conclusion, it appears very likely that the text used by Marracci is not the complete text of 1,400 pages we possess today from the Hyderabad manuscript. It indicates, as does the Oxford manuscript, that different portions and arrangements of the text circulated during its history, and that no final statement can be made on the original nature of the text based on the four existing manuscripts—*no two of which* contain the same text.

Even though it is not possible to make a definitive statement on the nature of the relationship between the two works by Ibn Taymiyya, some of the errors which have appeared in the literature on the works can be rejected. Until the time of Marracci it was not clearly known in Europe that Ibn Taymiyya was to be distinguished from al-Qarafi (in Latin both are called "Ahmedus"). The similarity of their names and the fact of their two refutations of Paul of Antioch left their personalities doubtful to Europeans. Marracci tentatively claimed that they were not the same individual,[41] although in practice he occasionally confused them by calling both simply "Ahmed."

Nicoll, by distinguishing Marsh 299 from al-Qarafi's *Al-Ajwiba al-Fakhira* settled that question finally.[42] Nicoll nevertheless affirmed that Marracci's text of Ibn Taymiyya was simply that of *Takhjil Ahl al-Injil*, which misled Nallino, Brockelmann, and others.

Nicoll never stated that *Al-Jawab al-Sahih*, in addition to *Takhjil Ahl al-Injil*, was contained in MS Marsh 299. This error must be attributed to the Leiden catalogue of De Jong and De Goeje. Steinschneider repeated that error and described the work *Takhjil Ahl al-Injil* by citations from Marracci.

Nallino perpetuated the error that the work of Ibn Taymiyya's used by Marracci was *Takhjil Ahl al-Injil*, but he was also the first to suggest its correspondences with *Al-Jawab al-Sahih* as it was cited by Di Matteo. It was Nallino's pioneer work on Marracci's sources which helped to sort out many Arabic works previously confused in the West.

Brockelmann, in his *Geschichte*, continued the transmitted error and listed two distinct polemical works by Ibn Taymiyya—*Al-Jawab al-Sahih* and *Takhjil Ahl al-Injil*, of which the Oxford manuscript was to have contained both. This listing has in turn misled other scholars up to the present time.[43]

However, Brockelmann also included another incorrect piece of information, that is, that *Takhjil Ahl al-Injil* was summarized by a 10th/16th-century author Abu al-Fadl al-Su'udi in his *Al-Muntakhab al-Jalil min Takhjil Man Harrafa al-Injil*.[44] This work offers a summary, rather, of a work by Abu al-Baqa' al-Ja'fari, as the author himself states in the introduction to his work.

> I have carefully treated what was written by the extremely learned scholar and imam Abu Baqa' Salih ibn al-Husayn al-Ja'fari in his treatise

> *Takhjil Man Harraf al-Injil.* I have plumbed the depths for its pearls, and have gained knowledge from its lights, by which I have been guided to reap the benefit of its learned teachings and harvest its fruits. He is knowledgeable about their Gospels, and the expounder of the real nature of their errors.[45]

Cheikho, in his catalogue of Christian Arabic manuscripts, makes a suggestion about a work by Al-Safi ibn al-'Assal which cannot be accepted.

> The book *Nahj al-Sabil fi al-Radd 'ala Man Qadah fi al-Injil* [The sound method of answering him who slandered the Gospel]. Perhaps he intended the work of Ibn Taymiyya: *Takhjil Man Harrafa al-Injil.*[46]

The conjecture made here by Cheikho that this polemical work by the Christian Al-Safi ibn al-'Assal is written in refutation of Ibn Taymiyya's *Takhjil* is certainly not correct, for Al-Safi ibn al-'Assal died in 664/1263, shortly before the birth of Ibn Taymiyya. I have not seen *Nahj al-Sabil*, but there seems to be no reason to challenge Stern's suggestion,[47] following Graf, that Al-Safi ibn al-'Assal was responding to the above-mentioned *Takhjil* of al-Ja'fari.

Al-Safi ibn al-'Assal was well known to al-Qarafi and was mentioned by him as a prominent Christian controversialist. Given the fact that al-Qarafi's *Al-Ajwiba al-Fakhira* is intended as a comprehensive refutation of Christianity, it is likely that Ibn al-'Assal's polemic provided Al-Qarafi with material for disputation. A careful study of *Nahj al-Sabil* is required, however, for this possibility to be established.

Fritsch repeats the two above errors—Nallino's that Marracci was using *Takhjil Ahl al-Injil*, and Cheikho's that Ibn al-'Assal was responding to Ibn Taymiyya's work.[48] Fritsch's study of *Al-Jawab al-Sahih* centers principally around Ibn Taymiyya's rebuttal against Paul of Antioch, and thus it is not surprising that even if he knew Marracci he would not have seen the correspondences between his citations and the latter portions of *Al-Jawab al-Sahih*.

It was Stern who pointed out many of these errors, principally by being the first to show the identity between the contents of the Oxford manuscript and the final quarter of *Al-Jawab al-Sahih*. Stern, however, did not know the exact contents of the Leiden and Istanbul manuscripts, and thus of the traditional division of the work into two volumes. He does state that until these manuscripts are studied as well as the Oxford manuscript and the printed edition to which he had access, the textual question cannot be resolved.

It is principally in his statements about Marracci's text that Stern's view must be amended. The paginated citations in Marracci's text seem to show irrefutably that he could not have had the whole text of *Al-Jawab al-Sahih*, and the arrangement of the text seems to indicate that his text was not even in the same sequential order as that presented by the four manuscripts which contain some or all of *Al-Jawab al-Sahih*.

It can be seen that the textual and manuscript evidence is inconclusive at best and contradictory at worst for delineating the relationship between *Takhjil Ahl al-Injil* as contained in the Oxford manuscript and *Al-Jawab al-Sahih* as represented by the other three. If the external evidence is ultimately unsatisfying, however, a strong case can be made that originally these were two separate and distinct works by Ibn Taymiyya.

As Stern has noted:

> It can be shown that the volume [in the Oxford manuscript] is not a fragment which we owe its present extent to chance. III:258 [using the first printed edition] is an important turning point in the structure of Ibn Taymiyya's book.[49]

In the 1,016 pages which precede this point Ibn Taymiyya's work is a refutation, page by page, passage by passage, of Paul of Antioch's *Letter to a Muslim*. Ibn Taymiyya makes many digressions, and treats a large number of issues not raised directly by Paul of Antioch; nevertheless, he used the bishop's work to form the structure of his own and continually returns to cite it *verbatim* and then refute it. It is a true polemic in the sense that he allowed his opponent to set the issues for discussion and directed his argumentation to those issues.

The work reflected in the Oxford manuscript and between 2:275-4:323 of *Al-Jawab al-Sahih* is a very different matter. Paul of Antioch is never mentioned nor alluded to in the entire work; neither is any Christian writer, nor are Christians generically mentioned by name.[50] Many of the central concerns of Paul of Antioch, for example—Qur'anic praise of Christ and Christianity and scriptural proofs for the trinity and divinity of Christ—are not mentioned even once in the work.

On the other hand, arguments which are pertinent to the issues raised by Ibn Taymiyya in this work which had also been used in the apology to Paul of Antioch are often repeated at length, as though they had not been previously mentioned. Points elaborately made in the apology to Paul of Antioch are argued again as though for the first time.

The style of this latter work is much different from the Apology to Paul of Antioch. Whereas the Apology is strictly in dialogue form—a quotation from Paul with a rebuttal by Ibn Taymiyya,the work contained in Marsh 299 is a reflective theological treatise which attempts to prove one theological issue: that Muhammad was indeed a prophet, that he was in fact the final Seal of the prophets.

It is in this central theological concern of the Oxford manuscript where the greatest difficulty is found in viewing it as merely a final section in a long apology to Paul of Antioch. Paul of Antioch never denied the prophethood of Muhammad. He denied the universal nature of Muhammad's prophethood, but made it clear that he did not challenge his prophetic call itself; Ibn Taymiyya understood and utilized this distinction extremely effectively. The force of his argumentation is to show that if Muhammad was a prophet, the entirety of his message must be accepted as true and that Muhammad's message included the claim of universality.

It is unlikely that after so exhaustively and consistently treating various issues raised by Paul of Antioch, he would begin a final 400-page discursus on a subject not only irrelevant, but even contrary, to the presumptions and challenges of what preceded. Were it written as a kind of appendix to the longer work, to refute any possible arguments that might be made by unnamed adversaries less conciliatory than Paul of Antioch, then one might have expected at least one reference to Paul or to his own refutation, or that arguments made in the earlier part of the work need not be demonstrated anew.

This is not the impression one receives from this work. It is written as though Ibn Taymiyya had never heard of Paul of Antioch or the specific issues raised by the Christian bishop. It is Ibn Taymiyya's practice to refer to other works of his where one or another subject was discussed at sufficient length so that he need not elaborate the matter in question at that point. He does this often in *Al-Jawab al-Sahih*, and also refers to his *Al-Radd 'ala al-Nasara*[51] in later works. However, nowhere in the work contained in MS Marsh 299 does Ibn Taymiyya acknowledge or refer to his refutation of Paul of Antioch's *Letter to a Muslim*.

In fact, the reverse is true. In the chapter of *Al-Jawab al-Sahih* in which Ibn Taymiyya treats the signs of Muhammad's prophethood which indicate his prophetic nature to one who would deny that, he repeatedly refers to an earlier work of his in which he elaborated the proofs for Muhammad's prophetic character.[52] On the one hand, these references describe well the contents of the work contained in MS Marsh 299 (*Takhjil Ahl al-Injil*), and on the other, there is no other known work of Ibn Taymiyya which fits the description so fully and precisely of the work referred to in *Al-Jawab al-Sahih*.

This leads to the conclusion that the work contained in MS Marsh 299 was probably an earlier work than the Apology to Paul of Antioch, and actually has more affinities in style and content with his own *Kitab al-Nubuwwat* than it does with the Apology. How then did this distinct, important work become in the strongest manuscript tradition merely a long addendum to a very different kind of treatise?

The most likely hypothesis seems to be that Ibn Taymiyya wrote the earlier work to establish Muhammad's prophetic nature and its ultimacy against People of the Book, especially Christians, who challenge that prophethood. Their arguments were that Muhammad did not fulfill their two great conditions of prophethood, that is, he was not announced and that he worked no miracles. Ibn Taymiyya endeavors to show that Muhammad was announced in both Jewish and Christian scriptures, and that the various types of miracles God worked through him—e.g., the revelation of the Qur'an, the miraculous moral effect of his preaching upon Arab life and universal history, his physical miracles of multiplication of food and bringing rain—show him to be not only a prophet but the most illustrious of the line of prophets, their *imam* when they pray, and the one who "seals" and completes the prophetic line. In fact the Oxford manuscript concludes with the phrase "the prophecies are completed,"[53] which in turn reminds one of Ibn 'Abd al-Hadi's early description of the contents of *Al-Jawab al-Sahih*, that the work "includes the establishment of the prophecies."[54] By this Ibn 'Abd al-Hadi may have been acknowledging that *Al-Jawab al-Sahih*, the apology to Paul of Antioch, contained also an earlier work written by Ibn Taymiyya to establish the prophecies and predict Muhammad and his fulfillment of them. Moreover Ibn Shakir's citation of *Thubut al-Nubuwwat*, whose complete title provides an excellent outline of the contents of *Takhjil Ahl al-Injil*, must not be overlooked.

Whether or not this was Ibn 'Abd al-Hadi's intention, the internal evidence, supported in the manuscript tradition by the Oxford manuscript, leads to the following conclusion. Ibn Taymiyya wrote a work to establish the definite prophetic nature of Muhammad *ad extra*, somewhat analogous to the *Kitab al-Nubuwwat* he wrote to deal with prophecy from an internal Islamic point of view. This work possibly carried some version of the title *Takhjil Ahl al-Injil*. When Ibn Taymiyya wrote his longer and subsequently more famous *Al-Jawab al-Sahih*, the earlier work was attached to it because of the similarity of subject matter (in that both were refutations of Christian attacks on Islam). The Leiden manuscript, dated A.H. 730, indicates that this was almost certainly done during Ibn Taymiyya's lifetime, possibly by the shaykh himself. However, the earlier work continued to have a life of its own, distinct from *Al-Jawab al-Sahih*, as attested by Hajji Khalifa and the Oxford manuscript MS Marsh 299.[55]

# LIST OF ABBREVIATIONS

Many of Ibn Taymiyya's works have been published in this century in *majmu'at*—editions of collected works. The following abbreviations refer to these editions of collected works.

MR *Majmu' al-Rasa'il*. Cairo: Al-Matba'a al-Husayniyya al-Misriyya, 1323/1905.

MFK1 *Majmu'at al-Fatawa al-Kubra*. 5 vols. Cairo: Matba'at Kurdistan al-'Ilmiyya, 1329/1911.

MFK2 *Majmu'at al-Fatawa al-Kubra*. 5 vols. Cairo: Dar al-Kutub al-Haditha, 1384/1965.

MF *Majmu' Fatawa Shaykh al-Islam Ahmad ibn Taymiyya*. 35 vols. Riyadh: Matba'at al-Hukuma, 1386/1966.

MRK *Majmu'at al-Rasa'il al-Kubra*. 2 vols. Cairo: Matba'at Muhammad 'Ali Subayh, 1386/1966.

JR *Jami' al-Rasa'il*. Cairo: Matba'at al-Madani, 1389/1969.

MRM *Majmu'at al-Rasa'il wal-Masa'il*. 5 vols. Beirut: Lajnat al-Turath al-'Arabi, n.d.

RDS *Rasa'il Diniyya Salafiyya*. Cairo: Maktabat al-Mutanabbi, n.d.

# NOTES

## Preface

1. This date is taken from one of the manuscripts of the Letter from Cyprus. There is no reason to doubt it, as it fits well with what we know of the circumstances of Ibn Taymiyya's life at that time. The date must certainly be before 721/1321, for Muhammad ibn Abi Talib (cf. below, p. 94) mentions in his *Risala* of that date that Ibn Taymiyya had previously received a copy of the same letter to which he was responding. Ibn Taymiyya himself, in his *Iqtida' al-Sirat al-Mustaqim*, also dated 721/1321, also refers to his earlier refutation of Christians.

2. Cf. below, pp. 370-381, for the relationship between the Letter from Cyprus and Paul of Antioch's earlier work.

3. The word "baddal" means more precisely "to replace (something by something else)." Thus the title bears the meaning "The correct answer to those who replaced the religion of Christ (with one of their own making)."

4. In 1386/1966, a collection of writings by Ibn Taymiyya which totaled 35 volumes was published in Riyadh. This collection, entitled *Majmu' Fatawa Shaykh al-Islam Ahmad ibn Taymiyya*, is not complete, and does not include most of Ibn Taymiyya's longer, multi-volume writings. A complete set of his writings would come to about 50 volumes.

5. Cairo: Matba'at al-Nil, 1322/1905, 4 vols., and Cairo: Matba'at al-Madani. 1383/1964, 4 vols.

## Introduction

1. Ibn Taymiyya's approach to the problem of *ta'wil* (the interpretation of the Qur'an) is important and not yet studied fully. He insists that his view is that of the *salaf*, although this has been recently challenged in a worthwhile study by Mansur Uways, *Ibn Taymiyya Laysa Salafiyyan* (Beirut: Dar al-Nahda al-'Arabiyya, 1970), pp. 7-37. It remains to be ascertained whether Ibn Taymiyya's position on *ta'wil* is consistent with or a departure from the traditional approach of Hanbali scholars.

## Chapter 1. The Polemic Against *Wahdat al-Wujud*

1. That this is not a transient medieval phenomenon within Islam may be seen in the explanation of *tawhid* offered by a contemporary Muslim writer.

Realizing the first *Shahadah* means first of all—"first of all" because this *Shahadah* includes the second in an eminent degree—becoming fully conscious that the Principle alone is real and that the world, though on its own level it "exists" "is not"; in one sense it therefore means realizing the universal void. Realizing the second *Shahadah* means first of all becoming fully conscious that the world—or manifestation—is "not other" than God or the Principle, since to the degree that it has reality it can only be that which alone "is," or in other words it can only be divine.

Frithjof Schuon, *Understanding Islam* (Baltimore: Penguin Books, 1972), p. 17. See also, pp. 60 ff. and 106 ff. of the same work.

2. *Kitab ila Nasr al-Manbiji*, MRM 1:181-82.

3. *Kitab Ibtal Wahdat al-Wujud*, MRM 1:67-68.

4. Ibid., p. 119.

5. In addition to the works listed above (nn. 2, 3), Ibn Taymiyya wrote several other major works wholly or in great part in refutation of *wahdat al-wujud*. The most important are: *Haqiqat Madhhab al-Ittihadiyyin wa-Wahdat al-Wujud*, MF 2:134-285; *Tafsir Surat al-Ikhlas* (Cairo: Dar al-Taba'a al-Muham-

madiyya, n.d.), pp. 56-78; *Bughyat al-Murtad*, MFK1 5:80-140. The first of these, *Haqiqat Madhhab al-Ittihadiyyin*, is closely related to *Fi Ibtal Wahdat al-Wuhud*, and sometimes the texts are verbally identical; elsewhere, however, long passages in one are not found in the other, indicating the possibility of their being separate recensions of the same work.

6. *Jawab Ahl al-'Ilm wal-Iman* (Cairo: Al-Maktaba al-Salafiyya, 1395/1975), p. 65.

7. *Haqiqat Madhhab al-Ittihadiyyin*, p. 297. Cf. also *Fi Ibtal Wahdat al-Wujud*, p. 69.

8. The writers he mentions and then refutes include the following: Najm al-Din ibn Isra'il (cf. below, trans. p. 635, n. 2), Ibn Sab'in, Ibn 'Arabi, Al-Hallaj, Shihab al-Din al-Suhrawardi, Ibn al-Farid, Sadr al-Din al-Qunawi, 'Amr al-Basri, Sa'id al-Faraghani, 'Abd Allah al-Balabani, and 'Afif al-Din al-Tilimsani. He also confronts statements attributed to Rabi'a bint 'Adawiyya, which Ibn Taymiyya denies were ever said by Rabi'a.

9. For Ibn Taymiyya's presentation of the views of the individual *Ittihadis* see *Fi Ibtal Wahdat al-Wujud*, pp. 61-66. His refutation of their statements is found in the same treatise, pp. 76-87.

10. *Bughyat al-Murtad*, p. 85. Cf. also, *Haqiqat Madhhab al-Ittihadiyyin*, p. 185.

11. *Jawab Ahl al-'Ilm wal-Iman*, p. 64.

12. *Fi Ibtal Wahdat al-Wujud*, p. 77.

13. Afif al-Din Sulayman al-Tilimsani (d. 690/1291). This Sufi shaykh and poet was considered by Ibn Taymiyya to be the most extreme exponent of absolute pantheism. Biographical details on al-Tilimsani can be found in EI1 4:766.

14. *Kitab ila Nasr al-Manbiji*, p. 177.

15. Ibid., p. 176.

16. *Fi Ibtal Wahdat al-Wujud*, p. 80.

17. *Kitab al-Nubuwwat* (Cairo: Al-Maktaba al-Salafiyya, 1386/1966), p. 24.

18. *Bughyat al Murtad*, pp. 86-87.

19. *Fi Ibtal Wahdat al-Wujud*, p. 82.

20. *Kitab ila Nasr al-Manbiji*, p. 182. See also *Al-Furqan bayn Awliya' al-Rahman wa-Awliya' al-Shaytan* (Cairo: Maktabat Muhammad 'Ali Subayh, 1378/1958), pp. 104 ff., and *Al-Jawab al-Salih*, 3: 79 ff., trans. p. 245 ff.

21. *Kitab al Nubuwwat*, p. 184.

22. *Fi Tahqiq al-Shukr*, JR, p. 106.

23. *Haqiqat Madhhab al-Ittihadiyya*, p. 185.

24. *Kitab ila Nasr al-Manbiji*, p. 177.

25. *Tafsir Surat al-Ikhlas*, pp. 21-29.

26. *Fi Ibtal Wahdat al Wujud*, p. 101.

27. *Fi al-Jawab 'an-Man Yaqul Inn Sifat al-Rabb Ta'ala Nisab wa-Idafat wa-Ghayr Dhalika*, JR, p. 164.

28. *Kitab ila Nasr al-Manbiji*, p. 172.

29. *Tafsir Surat al-Ikhlas*, p. 56. Massignon believes that Ibn Taymiyya failed to recognize in the work of Ibn Sab'in a philosophically based reaction against monism: His strong Hellenistic background led him to insist, less than Ibn 'Arabi, on the immateriality and the personality of souls; his theory of God, "the supreme principle of indivi-

duation," was not, as Ibn Taymiyya thought, a concession to, but rather a reaction against the monist tendencies of his time (Louis Massignon, "Ibn Sab'in et la critique psychologique dans l'histoire de la philosophie musulmane," *Memorial Henri Basset* (Paris: Librairie Orientaliste Paul Guethner, 1928), 2:124.

30. *Haqiqat Madhhab al-Ittihadiyyin*, p. 241.

31. Sadr al-Din al-Rumi al-Qunawi (d. 672/1274), the disciple and interpreter of Ibn 'Arabi.

32. *Kitab ila Nasr al-Manbiji*, p. 177. See also, *Fi Ibtal Wahdat al-Wujud*, pp. 93-94, and *Jawab Ahl al-'Ilm*, p. 80.

33. *Kitab ila Nasr al-Manbiji*, p. 180.

34. *Al-Futuhat al Makkiyya fi Ma'rifat Asrar al-Malakiyya*, with the *Fusus al-Hikam*, Ibn 'Arabi's most important work. Brockelmann, *Geschichte*, 6: 792.11. *Risala fi Kunh Ma La Budd lil-Mustarshid al-Murid*, in Osman Yahya, *Histoire et Classification de L'Oeuvre d'Ibn Arabi* (Damascus: Institut Français de Damas, 1964), 2:338-352. *Al-Amr al-Muhkam al-Marbut*, in ibid., 1:154.28. *Al-Durra al-Fakhira fi dhikr ma Intafa'tu Bihi fi Tariq al-Akhira*, in ibid., 1:192.105. The work apparently referred to is *Mawaqi' al-Nujum wa-Matali' Ahillat al-Asrar wal-'Ulum*, in ibid., 2:375.443. *Fusus al-Hikam*, in ibid., 1:240.150, and in *Geschichte*, 6:792.12.

35. *Kitab ila Nasr al-Manbiji*, 174-75.

36. "It is a gathering of all the evil in the world. The beginning of their error comes from their not affirming to the Creator an existence dissimilar to the existence of the creature. They take something from the teaching of the philosophers, something from the false teaching of the pseudo-Sufis and *kalam* theologians, something else from the teaching of the Qarmatis and the Batinis. They make the rounds at the doors of the *madhhabs* only to obtain the most miserable of returns." *Fi Jawab 'an-Man Yaqul Inn Sifat al-Rabb Nisab*, p. 167.

## Chapter 2. The Polemic against the Philosophers

1. *Haqiqat Madhhab al-Ittihadiyyin*, p. 175. "Irreligion" or "godlessness" seem to come closest to Ibn Taymiyya's intent as translations of *zandaqa*. The term, which originally meant "crypto-Manichaean," had by Ibn Taymiyya's time come to mean "a godless freethinker." Moreover he is not using the term loosely, for he is convinced that the First Cause of the philosophers is not the Creator and Commander of human destiny revealed in the Qur'an. See George Vajda, "Les Zindiqs en Pays d'Islam," *Revista degli Studi Orientali* 17 (1938): 179-229.

2. *Risala fi Lafz al-Sunna fi al-Qur'an*, JR, p. 52.

3. *'Arsh al-Rahman*, MRM 4:104. The principal targets of Ibn Taymiyya's criticism here are Al-Farabi and Ibn Sina.

4. *Tafsir Surat al-Ikhlas*, pp. 50-52.

5. Ibid., p. 53. The inclusion of Jews among those holding for physical generation in God is surprising,

for Ibn Taymiyya makes clear elsewhere his knowledge that this was not held by the generality of Jews. Possibly it is a gloss in the text, for in the same context immediately preceding and succeeding this statement, the pagan Arabs and the Christians are mentioned, but the Jews are not. If the reference is truly part of the text, his intention is obviously to the Qur'an, 9:30: "And the Jews say, 'Ezra is the son of God.'"

6. *Tafsir Surat al-Ikhlas*, p. 53.

7. *Bughyat al-Murtad*, p. 28.

8. *'Arsh al-Rahman*, p. 135.

9. *Tahqiq al-Shukr*, p. 104. See also, *Tafsir Surat al-Ikhlas*, pp. 82-84.

10. *Tahqiq al-Shukr*, p. 107.

11. Stated in *Al-Alwah al-'Imadiyya*, and in *Al-Mabda' wal-Ma'ad*.

12. *Fi Lafz al-Sunna*, p. 53.

13. *Qa'ida Awwaliyya*, MF 2:86.

14. *Kitab al-Nubuwwat*, p. 168. Trans. and quoted by Fazlur Rahman in *Prophecy in Islam* (London: George Allen and Unwin, 1958), p. 103. Ibn Taymiyya's treatment of the philosophers' view of prophecy is elaborated on pp. 101-105.

15. *Ma'arij al-Wusul*, MRK 1:199.

16. *Tafsil al-Ijmal fi-Ma Yajib l-Allah min Sifat al-Kamal*, MRM 5:74-76.

17. Rahman, *Prophecy in Islam*, p. 101.

18. *Tafsir Surat al-Ikhlas*, pp. 82-83.

19. Ibid., p. 83.

20. *Bughyat al-Murtad*, pp. 31-41. See also, *Tafsir Surat al-Ikhlas*, pp. 151-53.

21. *Dar' Ta'arud al-'Aql wal-Naql*, 2 vols. (Cairo: Matba'at Dar al-Kutub, 1971), 1:222-23. Ibn Taymiyya produces a list of terms adopted by the philosophers which are intrinsically ambiguous, p. 222.

22. Ibid., p. 244.

23. *Tafsir Surat al-Ikhlas*, p. 81.

24. Nasir al-Din al-Tusi (d. 672/1274). A good summary of his philosophical views, with bibliography, can be found in Bakhtyar Husain Siddiqi's "Nasir al-Din Tusi," in M. M. Sharif, ed. *A History of Muslim Philosophy* (Wiesbaden: Otto Harrassowitz, 1963), 1:564-80.

25. Sadr al-Din al-Qunawi died in 672/1274, the same year as al-Tusi. He was Ibn 'Arabi's most illustrious pupil and became the definitive interpreter of his thought. See Annemarie Schimmel, *Mystical Dimensions of Islam* (Chapel Hill: University of North Carolina Press, 1975), pp. 264, 318.

26. *Qa'ida Awwaliyya*, pp. 93-94.

## Chapter 3. The Polemic against Sufis

1. Henri Laoust, *Essai sur les doctrines sociales et politiques de Taki-d-Din Ahmad b. Taimiya* (Cairo: Imprimerie de l'Institut Français d'Archéologie Orientale, 1939), p. 89. See also George Makdisi, "Ibn Taymiya: A Sufi of the Qadiriya Order," *American Journal of Arabic Studies* 1 (1973): 118, for his treatment of the image of Ibn Taymiyya as anti-Sufi in Western scholarship.

2. Donald P. Little, "Did Ibn Taymiyya Have a Screw Loose?" *Studia Islamica* 41: 93-111.

3. For the treatment by recent Muslim scholars on Ibn Taymiyya's attitude towards Sufism, see Salam Hashim Hafiz, *Al-Imam Ibn Taymiyya* (Cairo: Maktabat al-Halabi,

1389/1969), pp. 65-66; 'Abd al-Aziz al-Maraghi, *Ibn Taymiyya* (Cairo: Maktabat al-Halabi, n.d.), p. 69; M. Mahdi al-Istanbuli, *Ibn Taymiyya: Batal al-Islah al-Dini* (Damascus: Dar al-Haya, n.d.), pp. 55-67.

4. Laoust, *Essai*, p. 91.

5. Rahman, *Islam*, pp. 132, 239-40.

6. George Makdisi, "The Hanbali School and Sufism," *Humaniora Islamica* 2 (1974): 61-72. See esp. pp. 65-66 for the spiritual kinship between Sufism and the Hanbali *madhhab*.

7. Idem, "Ibn Taimiya: A Sufi of the Qadiriya Order," pp. 118-29.

8. Idem, "The Hanbali School and Sufism," pp. 68-69. The translation is by Makdisi, and the citation is taken from an unpublished work by Jamal al-Din al-Talyani, "Targhib al-Mutahabbin fi Lubs Khirqat al-Mutamayyizin."

9. Makdisi, "The Hanbali School and Sufism," p. 69. The translation is again Makdisi's, and the citation is taken from Yusuf b. 'Abd al-Hadi's (d. 909/1503) *Bad' al-'Ulqa bi-Lubs al-Khirqa* in which the author quotes an earlier, now lost, work by Ibn Nasir al-Din (d. 842/1438) entitled *Itfa' Hurqat al-Hawba bi-Ilbas Khirqat al-Tawba*.

10. Makdisi, "Ibn Taimiya: A Sufi of the Qadiriya Order," pp. 123-24. It should be noted that the silsila continues through Ibn Taymiyya to include his student Ibn Qayyim al-Jawziyya, the author of *Madarij al-Salikin*, a commentary on *Manazil al-Sa'irin* by the Sufi (and Hanbali) Al-Ansari al-Harawi (d. 481/1089). The silsila concludes with Ibn Rajab, the great Hanbali biographer.

11. *Risalat al-'Ibadat al-Shar'iyya*, MRM 5:83.

12. *Sharh Kalimat li-'Abd al-Qadir fi Kitab "Futuh al-Ghayb,"* MF 10:463. Cf. Thomas F. Michel, "Ibn Taymiyya's Sharh on the Futuh al-Ghayb of 'Abd al-Qadir al-Jilani," *Hamdard Islamicus* 4, no. 2 (1981): 3-12, for a more compete study of this work.

13. Ibid., p. 470.

14. *Kitab ila Nasr al-Manbiji*, p. 162.

15. *Risalat al-'Ibadat al-Shar'iyya*, p. 84.

16. *Kitab ila Nasr al-Manbiji*, p. 162.

17. Fudayl ibn 'Iyad (d. 187/803). Fudayl was a converted highwayman and is called "a typical representative of early orthodox asceticism." Schimmel, *Mystical Dimensions of Islam*, pp. 36-37.

18. Ibrahim ibn Adham (*Adam* in the text of *Al-Furqan* should read *Adham*) (d. c. 173/790). This contemporary of Fudayl's was held in high esteem by al-Junayd and has been an extremely popular figure in mystical circles up to the present time, especially in Indian and Indonesian Islam. Ibid.

19. Abu Sulayman al-Darani (d. 214/830) was one of the early members of the 'Abbadan settlement and a leader of the ascetical movement in Basra. Ibid., pp. 31, 36.

20. Ma'ruf al-Karkhi (d. 199/815) was a younger contemporary of Rabi'a bint al-'Adawiyya. "He was among the first to speak about divine love, and his teaching that one cannot learn love, for it is a divine gift and not an acquisition, has had a great impact on mystical thought." Ibid., p. 53.

There are indications in these lists of Ibn Taymiyya's of a "chain" of early Sufis regarded by traditionalist Muslims of Ibn Taymiyya's time as the transmitters of the orthodox tradition of asceticism and interior striving in religion. Ibn Taymiyya terms them the shaykhs of the early generations of Islam (*shuyukh al-salaf*). The same names reappear, with some additions or omissions, in each of Ibn Taymiyya's lists, and there is a suggestion of a chain of initiation present—e.g., Ma'ruf al-Karkhi was the teacher of Al-Sari al-Saqati, who taught Al-Junayd. Corroborating evidence for this can be found in a predominantly Hanbali chain of Sufi initiation ascending from the 8th/14th century back through 'Abd al-Qadir al-Jilani to include Al-Junayd, Al-Sari al-Saqati, and Ma'ruf al-Karkhi as consecutive links. Makdisi, "L'Isnad Initiatique Soufi de Muwaffaq al-Din Ibn Qudama," in *Louis Massignon* (Paris: Éditions de l'Herne, 1962), pp. 90-91.

21. *Al-Furqan bayn Awliya' Allah wa-Awliya' al-Shaytan*, p. 93.

22. Al-Sari al-Saqati (d. 252/867) was the disciple of Ma'ruf al-Karkhi and the uncle and teacher of Al-Junayd and "was apparently the first to define mystical love 'as real mutual love between man and God.'" Schimmel, p. 53.

23. Hammad al-Dabbas (d. 525/1130) was 'Abd al-Qadir al-Jilani's teacher and figures prominently throughout Ibn Taymiyya's commentary on the *Futuh al-Ghayb*. Ibn Taymiyya's references to him are always laudatory. He is, nevertheless, a rather enigmatic figure, and Ibn Taymiyya's Hanbali predecessor, Ibn 'Aqil—a contemporary of Hammad al-Dabbas, strongly criticized Hammad's Sufi practices. "The Sufi who appears to have been subjected most severely to the criticism of Ibn 'Aqil was Hammad ibn Muslim al-Rahbi al-Dabbas." Makdisi, *Ibn 'Aqil et la Resurgence de l'Islam Traditionaliste au XIe Siècle* (Damascus: Institut Français de Damas, 1963), p. 383, n. 1.

24. Shaykh Abu al-Bayan (d. 551/1156).

25. *Sharh Kalimat li-'Abd al-Qadir*, pp. 516-17.

26. *Al-Furqan bayn Awliya' Allah*, p. 100.

27. *Qa'ida Jalila fi al-Tawassul wal-Wasila* (Cairo: Al-Matba'a al-Salafiyya, 1374/1954), p. 28.

28. *Al-Ihtijaj bil-Qadar*, p. 5.

29. Ibn Taymiyya's criticism of the later Ash'arite equation of God's love with His will, which he saw as tantamount to a denial of the attribute of love, is well treated by Joseph Norment Bell in "The Hanbalite Teaching on Love" (Ph.D. diss., Princeton University, 1971). The relevant section begins on p. 126.

30. *Al-Ihtijaj bil-Qadar*, p. 38.

31. *Haqiqat Madhhab al-Ittihadiyyin*, p. 175. For a further discussion on the development or error from ambiguous passages in the Qur'an and hadith reports, see *Tafsir Surat al-Ikhlas*, pp. 99-100.

32. *Haqiqat Madhhab al-Ittihadiyyin*, p. 340.

33. *Al-'Ibadat al-Shar'iyya*, p. 84.

34. Ibid., p. 91.

35. *Al-'Ubudiyya fi al-Islam*, p. 50. See also *Dhikr Allah wa-Du'a'uhu*, MF 10:553-68.

36. *Al-'Ubudiyya fi al-Islam*, p. 51.

37. *Al-'Ibadat al-Shar'iyya*, pp. 89-90.

38. *Sharh Kalimat li-'Abd al-Qadir*, pp. 508-16; *Mas'ala fi al-Faqr wal-Tasawwuf*, MRM 1:222-24.

39. *Kitab ila Nasr al-Manbiji*, pp. 172-73; *Fi Ibtal Wahdat al-Wujud*, pp. 97-100.

40. *Al-Ihtijaj bil-Qadar*, pp. 38-41.

41. *Mas'ala fi al-Faqr wal-Tas-*

*awwuf*, pp. 220-21.

42. *Al-Fana' al-Ladhi Yujad fi Kalam al-Sufiyya Yufassar bi-Thalathat Umur*, MF 10:337-44.

43. *Al-Risala al-Tadmuriyya fi Tahqiq al-Ithbat li-Asma' Allah wa-Sifatihi* (Cairo: Al-Matba'a al-Salafiyya, 1387/1967), p. 70.

44. *Al-'Ubudiyya fi al-Islam*, p. 46.

45. Ibid., pp. 46-47.

46. *Al-Ihtijaj bil-Qadar*, p. 9.

47. *Al-'Ubudiyya fi al-Islam*, p. 47. The Sufis he mentions here are the same as the ones he mentioned previously: Abu Sulayman al-Darani, Ma'ruf al-Karkhi, Fudayl ibn 'Iyad, Al-Junayd.

48. *Al-Ihtijaj bil-Qadar*, p. 25.

49. *Al-Risala al-Tadmuriyya*, p. 69.

50. *Al-Risala al-Tadmuriyya*, p. 60.

51. Donald P. Little, "The Historical and Historiographical Significance of the Detention of Ibn Taymiyya," *International Journal of Middle East Studies* 4 (1973): 323-25. Ibn Taymiyya's enemies were not limited to Sufis, but included important jurists and judges, especially of the Shafi'i and Maliki schools. Little cites Ibn Hajar al-'Asqalani as asserting that "practically all the qadis, shaykhs, faqirs, ulama, and common people in Egypt were opposed to Ibn Taymiyya" (*Al-Durar al-Kamina*, 1:147). Although this statement of Ibn Hajar's appears to have been an exaggeration, it is clear from other sources that Ibn Taymiyya's opposition was broadly based, and that influential Sufi shaykhs such as Nasr al-Manbiji were prominent in its leadership.

52. *Al-Furqan bayn al-Haqq wal-Batil*, MRK 1:77. The treatise *Risalat al-'Ibadat al-Shar'iyya wal-Farq baynaha wa-bayn al-Bid'iyya* (MRM 5:81-104) entirely concerns itself with this subject.

53. *Risalat al-'Ibadat al-Shar'iyya*, p. 98.

54. Ibid., p. 99.

55. The two most extensive works of Ibn Taymiyya dealing with issues related to local pilgrimages and the visitation of tombs are *Al-Jawab al-Bahir fi Zuwwar al-Maqabir* (Cairo: Al-Matba'a al-Salafiyya, 1395/1975), pp. 1-90, and *Al-Radd 'ala al-Ikhna'i* (Cairo: Al-Matba'a al-Salafiyya, 1346/1927), pp. 1-220. However, the question was a central issue with him, and he treated it often. See also, *Risalat al-'Ibadat al-Shar'iyya*, pp. 97-98; *Ziyarat al-Qubur al-Shar'iyya wal-Shirkiyya* in *Rasa'il Salafiyya Diniyya*, ed. Zakariya Ali Yusuf (Cairo: Maktabat al-Mutanabbi, n.d.), pp. 21-59; *Tafsir Surat al-Ikhlas*, pp. 167-94, contains an extensive and perceptive treatment; *Minhaj al-Sunna al-Nabawiyya*, 1:337-38; *Qa'ida Jalila fi al-Tawassul wal-Wasila*, pp. 23-24; *Al-Furqan bayn Awliya' Allah*, pp. 147-8.

56. Two *risalas* deal primarily with the subject of intercession and mediation. *Qa'ida Jalila fi al-Tawassul wal-Wasila*, pp. 1-175, and *Al-Shafa'a al-Shar'iyya wal-Tawassul ila Allah*, MRM 1:10-24. See also, *Al-Wasita bayn al-Khalq wal-Haqq*, in *Rasa'il Salafiyya Diniyya*, pp. 5-18.

57. For Ibn Taymiyya's treatment of vows, see *Risalat al-'Ibadat al-Shar'iyya*, pp. 103-04; *Tafsir Surat al-Ikhlas*, pp. 161-65; *Risala fi Ahl al-Suffa wal-Abatil Ba'd al-Mutasawwifa fi-him wa-fi al-Awliya'*, MRM 1:55.

58. Ibn Taymiyya's most direct attack on extravagant popular Sufi practices which have little connection with Qur'anic teaching is in a

treatise directed against the Rifa'i *tariqa* entitled *Munazara li-Dajajilat al-Bata'ihiyya al-Rifa'iyya*, MRM 1:121-42, esp. pp. 131-42. See also, *Risala fi Ahl al-Suffa*, p. 39.

59. The aspect of association with demons (*shayatin*) in unlawful religious practices is treated in *Risala fi al-Jawab 'an Su'al 'an al-Hallaj: Hal Kan Siddiq aw Zindiq?* JR, pp. 191-99. Ibn Taymiyya accuses Al-Hallaj of having studied magic in India and Ibn Sab'in of intending to do the same (*Kitab ila Nasr al-Manbiji*, p. 182). Also see *Al-Furqan bayn Awliya' Allah*, pp. 38-39, and *Qa'ida Jalila fi al-Tawassul wal-Wasila*, pp. 25-31.

60. Ibn Taymiyya relates his personal experience of *sama'* in *Risalat fi Ahl al-Suffa*, pp. 38, 56; *Libas al-Futuwwa wal-Khirqa 'ind al-Mutasawwifa*, MRM 1:159-60. He also wrote a treatise specifically against *sama'* and religious dancing: *Fi Hukm al-Sama' wal-Raqs*, MRK 2:293-330.

61. True miracles and deceptive wonders are treated in *Qa'ida Jalila*, pp. 29-30; 159-62; *Al-Furqan bayn Awliya' Allah*, pp. 129-55; *Qa'ida Sharifa fi al-Mu'jizat wal-Karamat*, MRM 1:159-60.

62. *Ra's al-Husayn* (Cairo: Matba'at al-Sunna al-Muhammadiyya, 1372/1953), p. 15. The whole risala deals with questions related to the shrine of Al-Husayn. See also, *Tafsir Surat al-Ikhlas*, p. 192; *Risala fi Ahl al-Suffa*, pp. 58-60.

63. *Minhaj al-Sunna al-Nabawiyya*, 1:332-36.

64. *Al-Jawab al-Bahir fi Zuwwar al-Maqabir*, pp. 20-21.

65. Against the Shi'a, who held that the prophetic *'isma* (which they extended to include the Imams as well) contained the concept of impeccability as well as inerrancy, Ibn Taymiyya argues that one need not hold the prophets to have been sinless. Certainly they could have sinned before their prophetic call, and even after they might have sinned. It is necessary to believe in the repentance (*al-tawba*) of the prophet after his error. *'Isma* means that the prophet could not err in anything which he claimed to have brought from God. *Minhaj al-Sunna al-Nabawiyya*, 2:308-24.

66. *Al-Furqan bayn Awliya' Allah*, p. 73.

67. He usually characterizes Al-Hallaj as one who was deluded by the demons, who manipulated him for their purposes through his pseudo-mystical experiences. He sees Al-Hallaj as becoming in his later years an overbearing, unprincipled charlatan who exulted in his notoriety. Ibn Taymiyya questions his sincerity in these terms: "He manifested among every group of people whatever would lead them to extol him. Among Sunnis he made it known that he was a Sunni, among Shi'a that he was a Shi'i. Sometimes he wore the garment of an ascetic, sometimes that of the military." *Su'al 'an al-Hallaj*, p. 192.

68. Ibid., p. 187.

69. *Fi Ahl al-Suffa*, pp. 33-34.

70. Ibid., p. 34.

71. Abu Hamid al-Ghazali (sometimes spelled al-Ghazzali), *Ihya' 'Ulum al-Din*, 4 vols. (Cairo: Bulaq, 1289/1872). It has been reprinted often.

72. *Al-'Ibadat al-Shar'iyya*, p. 87.

73. *Al-Furqan bayn Awliya' Allah*, p. 56.

74. *Al-Furqan*. This is one of the

traditional epithets of the Qur'an and its usage derives from the Qur'an itself. The Qur'anic usage of the term is not exclusively self-referent, for twice it clearly refers to the Torah or the signs wrought by Moses (2:53; 21:48). However the term elsewhere (2:185; 3:4; 25:1) specifically indicates the Qur'an, and it is in this meaning that the epithet is applied in Islamic tradition.

The import of the term *al-furqan* is that the Qur'an is the criterion by which right and wrong, belief and unbelief, guidance and error are distinguished. Because of its application to the Torah as well, one can conclude that it is as "the Book containing the prophetic revelation" that the sacred book serves to distinguish between truth and falsity in religion. That this aspect of prophetic revelation was of central importance to Ibn Taymiyya may be deduced from his entitling two major works *Al-Furqan bayn al-Haqq wal-Batil* (The Criterion [of discernment] between the True and the False), and *Al-Furqan bayn Awliya' Allah wa-Awliya' al-Shaytan* (The Criterion [of discernment] between the Friends of God and the Friends of Satan).

## Chapter 4. The Polemic against Speculative Theologians

1. Abu Muhammad al-Husan ibn 'Ali al-Barbahari, *Kitab al-Sunna*, included in Ibn Abi Ya'la's *Tabaqat al-Hanabila*, cited by Michel Allard in *Le Problème des Attributs Divins* (Beirut: Imprimerie Catholique, 1964), p. 103.

2. Abu al-Hasan al-Ash'ari, *Al-Ibana 'an Usul al-Diyana* (Cairo: Matba'at al-Muniriyya, 1348/1929), and *Risala fi Istihsan al-Khawd fi 'Ilm al-Kalam*, ed. and trans. by R. J. McCarthy in *The Theology of Al-Ashari* (Beirut: Imprimerie Catholique, 1953).

3. Al-Ash'ari, *Fi Istihsan al-Khawd*, 23.131-132 (Arabic text, 23.95-96).

4. "Ibn 'Aqil and his shaykh Abu Ya'la and those like them have agreed with the Jahmites in denying that God is loved. In that they follow the view of Abu Bakr al-Baqillani and those like him who deny the love of God." *Al-Nubuwwat*, p. 72. On Ibn 'Aqil, the most important works are those by Makdisi, *Ibn 'Aqil et la Résurgence de l'Islam Traditionaliste au XI^e Siècle* and "Nouveaux Details sur l'Affaire d'Ibn 'Aqil," *Mélanges Louis Massignon* (Damascus: Institut Français de Damas, 1956-57), 3:91-126. There is a new study on Abu Ya'la (458/1066) by W. Z. Haddad entitled "Al-Qadi Abu Ya'la ibn al-Farra': His Life, Works and Religious Thought" (M.A. thesis, Harvard University, 1969). A portion of this work has been recently published in Beirut as an edition of Abu Ya'la's *Al-Mu'tamad fi Usul al-Din* with an introduction in English and Arabic (Beirut: Dar al-Mashriq, 1974). It is worth noting that Abu Ya'la, who with his student Ibn 'Aqil would at later times have the reputation of being exceptional as a Hanbali who practiced *kalam*, was during his lifetime the acknowledged leader of the Hanbalis of Baghdad, and was im-

prisoned for anthropomorphism (as would be the later Hanbali scholars Ibn Taymiyya and Ibn Qayyim al-Jawziyya) at the instigation of Ash'arites whose interpretation of the anthropomorphic attributes of God he had attacked. W. Z. Haddad, "Introduction" to *Al-Mu'tamad fi Usul al-Din* by Abu Ya'la ibn al-Farra', pp. 25-27.

5. This is a reference to a *khabar al-wahid*—a hadith report handed on by only one transmitter and yet established as authentic by critical means. The *khabar al-wahid*, like all hadith, was rejected as a basis for theology by the Mu'tazila, but its legal normativeness was accepted by the *fuqaha'* after Al-Shafi'i's defense of it.

6. Muwaffaq al-Din Ibn Qudama, *Tahrim al-Nazar fi Kutub Ahl al-Kalam*, ed. and trans. by George Makdisi in *Ibn Qudama's Censure of Speculative Theology* (London: Luzac & Co., 1962), 81.33 (81.49 in the Arabic text). See also 90.36-37 (90.54 in Arabic).

7. Ibid., 80.32 (80.48 in Arabic).

8. *As'ila fi Usul al-Din*, MFK2 1:444.

9. *Dar' Ta'arud al-'Aql wal-Naql*, pp. 6-7. Ibn Taymiyya interprets Qur'anic references to "the Book and the Wisdom" (Qur'an, 2:129, 151, 231; 3:48, 81, 164; 4:54, 113; 5:110) as indications of the Qur'an and the sunna. This identification of the Qur'anic "Wisdom" (*hikma*) with the prophetic sunna is an interpretation which goes back at least to Al-Shafi'i. See JS. Cf. below p. 232.

10. *As'ila fi Usul al-Din*, pp. 451-52.

11. *Al-Iman*, p. 343.

12. *Tafsir Surat al-Ikhlas*, pp. 61-63.

13. Al-Husayn al-Najjar (d. c. 225/840) was an early anti-Mu'tazili theologian whose views are carefully summarized by Al-Ash'ari in his *Maqalat al-Islamiyyin* (Wiesbaden: Franz Steiner Verlag, 1963), pp. 283-85.

14. Dirar ibn 'Amr (d. c. 194/810). He was an extremely important early *kalam* theologian, who is said to have been the inventor of the notion of *kasb* (human acquisition of the actions of men created by God), which would become a central tenet among later Ash'arites. However, his reputation among later theologians was not good, and he was accused of *ta'til* by later Ash'arites (Al-Shahrastani, *Al-Milal wal-Nihal*, 1:114), although both Al-Ash'ari (*Maqalat al-Islamiyyin*, p. 281) and Al-Shahrastani (*Al-Milal wal-Nihal*, p. 115) approved of his formulation of divine agency of human acts along with their human acquisition. An excellent study of the theology and influence of Dirar ibn 'Amr has been made by Josef van Ess: "Dirar b. 'Amr und die 'Cahmiya,' Biographie einer vergessenen Schule," *Der Islam* 43 (1967): 241-79 and 44 (1968): 1-70. He treats Dirar's relationship to Jahm ibn Safwan and his teaching on *iktisab* on 43:270-79.

15. *Al-Furqan bayn al-Haqq wal-Batil*, MRK 1:75.

16. Laoust mentions that on matters dealing with faith (*iman*) Ibn Taymiyya's preference in theology is for al-Maturidi. See Laoust, *Essai*, p. 81.

17. The relationship between revelation and reason is the subject of one of Ibn Taymiyya's major works: *Dar' Ta'arud al-'Aql wal-Naql* (Cairo: Matba'at Dar al-Kutub, 1971). This work is also known by

an alternate title: *Bayan Muwafaqat Sarih al-Ma'qul li-Sahih al-Manqul.*

18. In addition to referring to both Ash'arite and Mu'tazili views as "Jahmite," Ibn Taymiyya distinguishes each school of thought by its proper names. The Mu'tazila he often refers to as the "Qadariyya." It is occasionally difficult to know specifically who is intended when Ibn Taymiyya uses some terms. In *Fi Ibtal Wahdat al-Wujud* "Al-Hululiyya al-Jahmiyya" means Ibn 'Arabi and his followers (p. 100). The point is that Ibn Taymiyya's application of terminology is often more judgmental than descriptive; his purpose is to indicate the underlying presumptions which he judges a group to be following, or the conclusions to which their beliefs logically lead.

19. W. Montgomery Watt, *The Formative Period of Islamic Thought* (Edinburgh: University Press, 1973), pp. 147-48. For the use of the term "Jahmite" within the Hanbali tradition, see pp. 144-45 of the same work. It should be noted that the term, always one of opprobrium, was applied to other groups as well, such as the Mu'tazila, whose views on *qadar* were diametrically opposed to the "compulsorist" position. See M. Allard, *Le Problème des Attributs Divins*, pp. 252-57.

20. M. Rashad Salim, in the "Muqaddima" to the *Minhaj al-Sunna al-Nabawiyya* of Ibn Taymiyya, 1:3 n. 4.

21. Joseph Norment Bell, *Love Theory in Later Hanbalite Islam* (Albany: SUNY Press, 1979), p. 60.

22. This formulation is actually not very different from that of the Ash'arites, who also describe man as an actor (*fa'il*) who has will and power. Ibn Taymiyya's accusation, however, is that they empty these terms of meaning through their doctrine of acquisition: "Al-Ash'ari agrees with him [Jahm] in that the servant is not an actor nor does he have power which can effect an action. He says he is an 'acquirer,' but most people say they cannot understand the difference between this acquisition which he affirms and the act which he denies" (*Kitab al-Nubuwwat*, p. 142).

23. The reference here is to the Qur'an, 70:19-21: "Lo! man was created anxious, fretful when evil befall him and when good befall him, grudging."

24. *Aqwam Ma Qil fi al-Mashi'a wal-Hikma wal-Qada' wal-Qadar wal-Ta'lil wa-Butlan al-Jabr wal-Ta'til* (MRM 5:113-70), p. 142. This is a fine treatise in which Ibn Taymiyya treats the most essential questions raised concerning causality, predetermination, and the divine will. It is primarily directed against Ash'arite theses, but also refutes Mu'tazili and peripatetic philosophical positions. The other works of Ibn Taymiyya which deal at length with these subjects are *Al-Ihtijaj bil-Qadar* and *Al-Irada wal-Amr.*

25. *Kitab ila Nasr al-Manbiji*, p. 182.

26. *Al-Ihtijaj bil-Qadar*, p. 30.

27. Questions involving the affirmation of divine wisdom in the government of creation are well treated in *Minhaj al-Sunna al-Nabawiyya*, 1:84-99, 315-30.

28. *Al-Irada wal-Amr*, MRK 1:339.

29. *Haqiqat Madhhab al-Ittihadiyyin*, pp. 176-85.

30. Bell, p. 91. Ibn Taymiyya's judgment of *kufr* on Qalandaris and Malamatis will be found in *Jawab*

*li-Su'al 'an al-Qalandariyya wal-Malamiyya*, MF 35: 163-66.

31. Fazlur Rahman, *Islam* (Garden City: Anchor Books, 1968), p. 134.

32. See Richard M. Frank, "The Neoplatonism of Gahm ibn Safwan," *Museon* 78 (1965): 420-21: God, in the system of the ğahmiya, is totally involved in creation to the point of almost becoming one with the reality of creatures, as their act, so that Ibn Taymiyya says that they hold that God "this existence (*wujud*) which is absolute and abstracted from all attributes, is the existence which pervades all things" and compares the teachings of the gahmiya with that of Muhyi d-Din Ibn 'Arabi and Ibn Sab'in, saying that they hold a pantheist doctrine in which "God is the world, existence is one, and the eternally existent creator is the generated and created existent."

33. *Kitab ila Nasr al-Manbiji*, pp. 172-73.

34. *Al-Ihtijaj bil-Qadar*, pp. 35-36.

35. The context clearly indicates that the reference is to compulsorists on *qadar*. He labels them variously as "compulsorist Jahmite determinists" (p. 35), "determinist Jahmites" (p. 37), and "Ash'arites" (p. 38). The term *qadari* in the first two examples cited is used in its technical sense of "proponents of *qadar*," i.e., determinists. Note that in the passage cited here, "Qadarites" carries the popular usage of free-will advocates.

36. The more probable reference here is to Muhammad, the point being that Muhammad, being the best of men, is most worthy of love, and thus God's command to love him can be fulfilled. Were God's love and favor identified with His will, how could one person be more deserving of love than another or—as he continues—one religious community be more favored and loved by God than others?

37. Ibid., p. 36.

38. *Jawab Ahl al-'Ilm wal-Iman*, p. 60. This passage (pp. 60-62) contains an excellent summary of the three usual formulations on the question of the purposiveness and universality of divine agency. Ibn Taymiyya describes as "the two extremes and the median" the voluntarism of the Mu'tazila, the determinism of the Ash'arites, and the position of the *salaf.*

39. *Al-Risala al-Tadmuriyya*, pp. 7-12. The entire *risala* deals with questions related to the divine attributes. See also, *Al-Nubuwwat*, pp. 45-48.

40. Ibid., p. 24. He cites the "pure Jahmites like the Qarmatis" who refuse to affirm either of two contradictory statements about God—e.g., that He is existent or that He is nonexistent.

41. Ibn Taymiyya treats Shi'i adoption of Mu'tazili theses (e.g., their use of the concept of *jawhar* and *jism* and the denial of attributes) in his refutation of the Shi'a in *Minhaj al-Sunna al-Nabawiyya*, 2:73-218; 384-521.

42. *Al-Fatwa al-Hamawiyya al-Kubra*, p. 17. Ibn Taymiyya lists over thirty works which he believes have presented an orthodox refutation of the Mu'tazili denial of divine attributes. The list provides a valuable source not only for discovering who Ibn Taymiyya considered to be exponents of the orthodox view, but for building an estimation of the "library" of Ibn Taymiyya—those works read and used by him and his contemporaries.

43. These anti-Mu'tazili schools

of *kalam* are named after early theologians. 'Abd Allah ibn Sa'id ibn Kullab (d. 239/854). "His chief contribution to *kalam* was his elaboration of the doctrine of the attributes (*sifat*) of God. He asserted that for each descriptive term such as 'powerful,' 'knowing,' 'eternal,' there was an attribute of power, knowledge, or eternity" (Watt, *The Formative Period of Islamic Thought*, p. 287). Abu 'Abd Allah Muh. ibn Karram (d. 264/869). On the questions related to the divine attributes, the distinguishing position of the Karramites was their affirmation that the active as well as the essential attributes of God were eternal (Watt, p. 290). Hisham ibn al-Hakam (d. before 199/815) was an extremely influential early Shi'i theologian and is said to have been among those who introduced much of the technical vocabulary of *kalam* (Watt, pp. 186-88). The distinguishing characteristic of his teaching on the attributes was the assertion of the createdness of the knowledge of God (Wolfson, *The Philosophy of the Kalam*, pp. 143-44).

44. *Jawab Ahl al-'Ilm wal-Iman*, p. 89.

45. *Al-Fatwa al-Hamawiyya al-Kubra*, pp. 15-17. R. M. Frank suggests the probability that Ibn Taymiyya recognized the neo-Platonic associations of Jahmite theology better than did most of its followers. Frank, "The Neoplatonism of Gahm ibn Safwan," pp. 422-24.

46. *Al-Jawab al-Bahir*, p. 22.

47. Wilferd Madelung, "The Origins of the Controversy Concerning the Creation of the Koran," *Orientalis Hispanica* (Leiden: Brill, 1974), 1, no. 1: 513-15, 524-25. Ibn Taymiyya's treatment of questions concerning the Word of God and the uncreatedness of the Qur'an are collected in *Kitab Madhhab al-Salaf al-Qawim fi Tahqiq Mas'alat Kalam Allah al-Karim*, MRM 3:1-165. See also *Tafsir Surat al-Ikhlas*, pp. 58-59, where Ibn Taymiyya tries to demonstrate that the belief in the createdness of the Qur'an was not uniquely a Mu'tazili belief, but was shared by many non-Mu'tazili *kalam* theologians. In *Al-Jawab 'an-Man Yaqul 'an Sifat al-Rabb Nisab wa-Isafat*, JR, pp. 163-69, he refutes the belief that the Qur'an is created and emerges from the soul of the prophet. This belief, which he claims to have resulted from a mixing of ideas and terms of the philosophers and Sufis, Ibn Taymiyya ascribes to al-Ghazali and lists seven works of his in which it is found.

48. *Raf' al-Malam 'an al-A'imma al-A'lam* in *Al-Rasa'il al-Diniyya al-Salafiyya*, pp. 134-76.

49. *Dar' Ta'arud al-'Aql wal-Naql*, pp. 242-43. "This is based on two things: 1) the *usul al-din* are those things which are known by pure reason without revealed religion, and 2) someone who opposes them is an unbeliever." In their *takfir* they are worse than the Kharijites, he states, who at least based their expulsion of others from the community on grounds related to the Qur'an and the sunna.

50. *Ma'arij al-Wusul*, p. 200.

51. The most complete account of Ibn Taymiyya's tribulations and the accusations against him is found in Ibn Rajab's *Dhayl 'ala Tabaqat al-Hanabila* (Damascus: Al-Ma'had al-Faransi bi-Dimashq, 1951), 2:396-403. See also, Henri Laoust, "Ibn Taymiyya," EI2, 3, no. 2: 951-53.

52. See the article by J. Horovitz,

"Umm al-Kitab," in EI1, 4:1012, and "Lawh" by A. J. Wensinck, EI1, 3:19-20.

53. See Fazlur Rahman's *The Philosophy of Mulla Sadra* (Albany: SUNY Press, 1975), pp. 146-63, for a discussion of God's knowledge of existing things. The particular Mu'tazili view in question is treated on pp. 147-48. The Mu'tazila, of course, hold that God has known everything from eternity, and it is on this affirmation that their doctrine of the reality of non-existents is based. Ibn Taymiyya is arguing from their rejection of the hypostatic character of God's knowledge that those things which He knew from eternity would have to subsist in nothingness.

54. The text reads *zulm*—the wrongdoing of God. It should be *'ilm*—the knowledge of God. Cf. p. 176: "They say that the non-existent is a thing established in itself external to the *knowledge* of God."

55. *Kitab ila Nasr al-Manbiji*, pp. 175-76.

56. In this context Makdisi sees Ibn 'Asakir's (571/1175) *Tabyin* and al-Subki's *Tabaqat* as efforts to establish Ash'arism as the theology of the Shafi'i *madhhab* against a minority Shafi'i traditionism which was much closer to the Hanbali tradition. George Makdisi, "Ash'ari and the Ash'arites in Islamic Religious History," *Studia Islamica* 17:37-80 and 18:19-39. The references are to Abu al-Qasim ibn 'Asakir, *Tabyin Kadhib al-Muftari fi-Ma Nusiba ila al-Imam Abi al-Hasan al-Ash'ari* (Damascus: al-Matba'a al-Tawfiqiyya, 1347/1928), and Taj al-Din al-Subki, *Tabaqat al-Shafi'iyya al-Kubra*, 9 vols. (Cairo: Matba'at al-Halabi, 1384/1965).

57. Ignaz Goldziher, "Zur Geschichte der hanbalitischen Bewegungen," *Zeitschrift für Deutsche Morgenlandische Gesellschaft* 62 (1908): 1-28. It should be noted that in Goldziher's treatment the history of Hanbali opposition to *kalam* did not touch on the question of *qadar*. See esp. pp. 15-16, 21-28.

58. Against Ibn Hanbal, Ibn Taymiyya agreed with the Mu'tazila that the Qur'an is temporal. Against them he held that God speaks in its literal meaning and that He does not create His speech.

59. This can be clearly seen in Ibn Hanbal's creeds. In the first creed of Ibn Hanbal's included in Ibn al-Farra's *Tabaqat al-Hanabila* (called "'Aqida I" by Laoust, it is the first of six creeds attributed to Ibn Hanbal which have been extracted from the *Tabaqat* and described by H. Laoust in *La profession de foi d'Ibn Batta* [Damascus: Institut Français de Damas, 1958], pp. xv-xvi), articles no. 6, 8, and 9 affirm the reality of Qur'anic expressions, no. 10 asserts the uncreatedness of the Qur'an. However, article no. 2 is a strong statement on *qadar* against Mu'tazili denial: "*Qadar*, the good and the evil of it, the little and the much of it is from God; no one opposes God's will, nor transgresses his decree, but all men come to that for which He has created them. This is justice from him. Adultery, theft, wine-drinking, murder, consuming unlawful wealth, idolatry, and all sins are by God's determination and decree" (Ahmad ibn Hanbal, cited by Ibn Abi Ya'la, *Tabaqat al-Hanabila*, 1:25).

60. Muhammad ibn Ahmad Abu al-Husayn al-Malati. His *Al-Tanbih wal-Radd 'ala Ahl al-Ahwa' wal-Bida'* is the earliest extant Hanbali book of sects. Biographical infor-

mation on Al-Malati can be found in S. Dedering's introduction to *al-Tanbih*, pp. h-ya. See also Al-Subki, *Tabaqat*, 2: 112.

61. Abu al-'Asim Khushaysh ibn Asram al-Nisa'i, *Kitab al-Istiqama fi al-Radd 'ala Ahl al-Ahwa'*, cited by al-Malati in *al-Tanbih* (Istanbul: Matba'at al-Dawla, 1936), pp. 71-142.

62. Al-Malati, p. 135. Even here the hadith is probably not to be understood as agreeing with the proposition later taken by Ibn Taymiyya. It is likely that it refers to those who held that good comes from God but not evil, and the teaching of the hadith is essentially determinist.

63. Cf. n. 59, above.

64. Ibn Batta al-'Ukbari (387/997), *Kitab al-Sharh wal-Ibana 'ala Usul al-Sunna wal-Diyana*, ed. Henri Laoust in *La profession de foi d'Ibn Batta* (Damascus, 1958), p. 52 (Arabic text).

65. W. Z. Haddad, "Introduction," to Abu Ya'la's *Kitab al-Mu'tamad*, pp. 25-26.

66. Abu al-Husayn ibn Abi Ya'la, *Tabaqat al-Hanabila*, 2:205-06.

67. Abu Ya'la, *Kitab al-Mu'tamad*, p. 131. Questions involving *qadar* are found on pp. 129-31.

68. George Makdisi, *Ibn 'Aqil et la resurgence de l'Islam traditionaliste au XI^e siècle*, pp. 426-33.

69. Henri Laoust, "Hanabila," EI2, 3, no. 1:160.

70. *Al-Ihtijaj bil-Qadar*, p. 46.

71. 'Abd al-Qadir al-Jilani, *Kitab al-Ghunya li-Talibi Tariq al-Haqq* (Cairo: Matba'at Muhammad 'Ali Subayh, 1359/1940), 1:73-74.

72. Ibn Qudama, *Tahrim al-Nazar fi Kutub Ahl al-Kalam*. See n. 6 above.

73. Neither this work nor its author, Abu al-Fadl 'Abbas ibn Mansur ibn 'Abbas al-Burayhi al-Saksaki, are mentioned by Brockelmann or Sezgin. His name and the title of this work are mentioned in *Hidayat al-'Arifin* (1:437) and *Idah al-Maknun* (1:179), where he is called a Shafi'i. However, the only existing manuscript of *Al-Burhan fi Ma'rifat Ahl al-Adyan* clearly calls him a Hanbali. Moreover Ritter lists him as a Hanbali and gives his full name as "Abu al-Fadl 'Abbas b. Mansur b. 'Abbas al-Burayhi al-Saksaki al-Sunni al-Hanbali" (Helmut Ritter, "Muhammedanische Haresiographen," *Der Islam* 28 [1929]: 48).

74. 'Abbas ibn Mansur al-Saksaki, *Al-Burhan fi Ma'rifat 'Aqa'id Ahl al-Adyan* (Cairo: Dar al-Kutub MS 40480, fol. 7b).

## Chapter 5. The Polemic against the Shi'a

1. Laoust, following Ibn Kathir, indicates that Ibn Taymiyya accompanied two military expeditions against the Shi'a of Kasrawan, one in 699/1300 and again in 704-5/1305. He suggests that Ibn Kathir's information on the events of these expeditions may well have been obtained personally from Ibn Taymiyya. Henri Laoust, "Remarques sur les expeditions du Kasrawan sous les premiers Mamluks," *Bulletin du Musée de Beyrouth* 4 (1942): 100-04.

2. Al-Mar'i ibn Yusuf al-Karmi, *Al-Kawakib al-Durriya fi Manaqib al-Imam ibn Taymiyya* in *Al-Majmu' al-Mushtamal 'ala al-Durar al-*

*'Atiyya*, ed. Faraj Allah al-Kurdi (Cairo: Matba'at Kurdistan al-'Ilmiyya, 1329/1911), p. 164.

3. *Jawab 'An al-Rafida al-Imamiyya: Hal Yajib Qitaluhum wa-Yukaffaruna bi-i'tiqadihim*, MF 28:468-69.

4. The Khurramiyya was an Iranian religious and social movement whose pre-Islamic origins are associated with the teaching of the reformer Mazdak. In Islamic times their beliefs evolved into a form of extremist (*ghali*) Shi'ism. Gholam Hossein Sadighi, *Les mouvements religieux iraniens au II^e et au III^e siècle de l'hégire* (Paris: Les Presses Modernes, 1938), pp. 187-228. The Khurramiyya are often associated with the name of their greatest military leader, Babak, under whom they fought the armies of the 'Abbasid caliphs Al-Ma'mun and Al-Mu'tasim. Babak was crucified in 223/838, but his followers, called the Babakiyya by their enemies, were still known in the 5th/11th century. It is likely that it is to this group that Ibn Taymiyya is referring. Cf. D. Sourdel, EI2, s.v. "Babak."

5. In the year 37/658 "some of 'Ali's soldiers repented of having left up to arbitration by neutrals a question—the guilt of 'Uthman—which they felt had already been settled by Qur'anic standards. When 'Ali refused to join them and held to the agreement to arbitrate, they left him to form their own camp, first at Harura' near Kufa. These included some of his most pious followers, notably many Qur'an-reciters; they accused 'Ali of compromising with the supporters of injustice and so betraying his trust, which was to right the wrongs committed by 'Uthman. These extremists, the Shurat, more commonly called Kharijis, elected their own commander, independent of the other Muslims" (Marshall G. S. Hodgson, *The Venture of Islam*, 3 vols. [Chicago: University of Chicago Press, 1974], 1:216-17).

6. *Jawab 'an al-Rafida al-Imamiyya*, p. 476.

7. Ibid, p. 479.

8. That is, the breaking of the fast during the month of Ramadan.

9. Ibid., pp. 479-80.

10. "Risala ila al-Sultan al-Malik al-Nasir," cited in Muhammad ibn 'Abn al-Hadi, *Al-'Uqud al-Durriya*, p. 184. The Sultan al-Malik al-Nasir was, during his three reigns as sultan, consistently a protector of Ibn Taymiyya. For the relations between the two, see Carl Brockelmann, *History of the Islamic Peoples*, trans. J. Carmichael and M. Perlmann (New York: Capricorn Books, 1973), p. 237.

11. Henri Laoust, "Le Hanbalism sous les mamlouks bahrides," *Revue des Etudes Islamiques* 28 (1960): 17-18. Cf. Laoust, *Essai*, p. 60.

12. *'An Hukm al-Durziyya wal-Nusayriyya*, MF 35:161. Cf. *Risala fi al-Radd 'ala al-Nusayriyya*, MR, pp. 96-97. This treatise has been edited and translated by S. Guyard as *Al-Fatwa fi al-Nusayriyya* (Paris: Imprimerie Nationale, 1872).

13. *Radd 'ala Nubadh li-Tawa'if min al-Duruz*, MF 35:162. In the treatise *Al-Radd 'ala al-Nusayriyya*, Ibn Taymiyya discusses the varying opinions of the law schools on the specific points of this ostracism, pp. 99-101.

14. *Al-Radd 'ala al-Nusayriyya*, p. 95.

15. The two versions of this text

which I have seen (MR, Cairo, 1905, and Guyard's Paris, 1872) disagree in many places and sometimes on important terms. As such it seems to be one of the most poorly edited of Ibn Taymiyya's works. My translation, with the exceptions noted, is from the Cairo printing.

"Naturalist" is a translation from Guyard's edition (*al-taba'iyyin*) and seems preferable to *al-ta'inin* in the Cairo text. The usual word for "naturalist" philosophers, however, is *tabi'iyyun* (*-in*), and it is possible that it was thus in the original.

16. *Al-Ilahiyyin*. This term was usually applied to Plato and the later philosophers of his school. According to al-Shahrastani, the Ilahiyyun are those who believe in God but give an entirely rationalistic explanation of religion. Religious traditions are, according to them, creations of public and national interests. The picturesque and mythological language of sacred books as well as the afterlife with its sensate descriptions are equally the product of human needs and desires. Al-Shahrastani, *Al-Milal wal-Nihal*, 2: 93-94.

17. Ibn Taymiyya criticized the Epistles of the Brethren of Purity and denies any link between them and Ja'far al-Sadiq in *As'ila 'an al-Mu'izz Ma'add ibn Tamim*, MF 35:120.

18. *qawl makdhub*, i.e., a spurious hadith report.

19. *hum min a'immathim*. Guyard's edition has *hum min ummatihim*—"They are of their community."

20. *Al-Balagh al-Akbar*. This work, supposedly written after 372/983 by Sharif Akhu Muslim of Damascus, himself a descendant of Muhammad ibn Isma'il, was well known among Sunnis in the centuries previous to Ibn Taymiyya. The work, however, is not Isma'ili, but an anti-Isma'ili forgery. Wilferd Madelung, "Fatimiden und Bahrainqarmaten," *Der Islam* 34 (1958): 68-73.

21. *Al-Radd 'ala al-Nusayriyya*, p. 98. Guyard, *Al-Fatwa fil-Nusayriyya*, pp. 15-17.

22. *As'ila 'an Mu'izz Ma'add ibn Tamim*, p. 120.

23. *Mas'alat al-Kana'is*, MF 28:635-39.

24. *Asila 'an Mu'izz*, pp. 143-44.

25. Al-Hilli's biographical details and his criticism of Sunnism are well summarized by Laoust in "La critique du sunnisme dans la doctrine d'al-Hilli," *Revue des études islamiques* 34 (1966): 35-60.

26. "The arguments which lay the foundation for this obligation of *'isma* go back in a straight line to the political philosophy of al-Farabi and the Brethren of Purity." Ibid., pp. 36-37.

27. This argument from utilitarian or conventional morality was used by Ibn Sina and Al-Ghazali to prove the necessity for the institution of prophecy. According to Al-Ghazali "a legislator is required to determine the rights and duties of individuals vis-à-vis one another in a society necessarily dependent on cooperation but wherein individuals are apt to regard self-interest as the only intrinsic principle." Fazlur Rahman, *Prophecy in Islam* (London: George Allen & Unwin, 1958), p. 97.

28. Al-'Allama 'Ala' al-Din al-Hilli, *Minhaj al-Karama fi Ma'rifat al-Imama*, included in *Minhaj al-Sunna al-Nabawiyya* by Ibn Taymiyya, 1:m93.

29. Al-Hilli, *Minhaj al-Karama*, p. m147. Laoust summarizes Al-Hilli's criticism of the persons and caliphates of Abu Bakr, 'Umar, and 'Uthman on pp. 39-48 of "La critique du sunnisme"; his critique of the 'Ummayad caliphate follows on pp. 48-51, and that of the 'Abbasids on pp. 51-52.

30. Laoust, "La critique du sunnisme," p. 53.

31. Al-Hilli, *Minhaj al-Karama*, p. m83.

32. JS 3:93 ff. *Minhaj al-Sunna al-Nabawiyya*, 1:234-37.

33. Al-Hilli, *Minhaj al-Karama*, pp. m79, m83-m91.

34. Ibid., 1:66.

35. Ibid.

36. *Minhaj al-Sunna al-Nabawiyya fi Naqd Kalam al-Shi'a al-Qadariyya*, 2 vols. (Cairo: Maktabat Dar al-'Uruba, 1382/1962), 2:365.

37. Ibid., 2:359-68.

38. Ibn Taymiyya here refers to the statement of Al-Hilli that the only *ijma'* possible is the consensus of the community that the imam is infallible. Laoust, "La critique du sunnisme," p. 37.

39. *Minhaj al-Sunna*, 1:44.

40. Ibid., p. 47.

41. Arabic distinguishes between pre-eternity (*qidam*, *azal*) and future time-without-end (*abad*). Ibn Taymiyya rejects the theory which he attributed to Jahm ibn Safwan (and hence the Jahmites) and Abu Hudhayl (hence Mu'tazila) that the eschatological abodes, like everything which has come into being in time, must pass away. Ibid., pp. 121-23.

42. Ibid., 2:181-218.

43. Ibid., 1:225.

44. Al-Hilli's accusation that Sunni Muslims hold that God can do evil is answered by Ibn Taymiyya on 1:315-19, his accusation that they believe God acts without purpose or wise design is refuted on 1:320-23, and that they believe that God does not do what is best for mankind, on 1:324-27.

45. Ibn Taymiyya refutes the Mu'tazili position expressed by Al-Hilli which denied hypostatization of the divine attributes in *Minhaj al-Sunna*, 2:383-521.

46. "This is the view of those of the later Shi'a who agree with the Mu'tazila in their position on *tawhid* and justice: God does not create a thing of the acts of living things. These are things which come to be in time, and they come into being without His power or His creation. It is also their view that God cannot guide the erring, nor can he lead astray the rightly guided. The guidance of God for believers and unbelievers is equal. God's favor (*ni'ma*) in religion is not greater for believers than for unbelievers. In summary, the people do not affirm a general will, nor complete power, nor a creation which encompasses every temporal thing. This view they [the Shi'a] have taken from the Mu'tazila" (*Minhaj al-Sunna*, 1:85-87).

47. Ibid., 2:343. Ibn Taymiyya does not specify the extreme Shi'i movements to which he refers. A typical example of those who held beliefs akin to those condemned by Ibn Taymiyya can be seen in the beliefs of the early exponents of *ghali* Shi'ism such as Abu Mansur (d. 122/740) and his followers. Abu Mansur claimed a type of *hulul* for both 'Ali and Jesus, holding that God appeared in their persons. He removed the function of Qur'anic

interpretation from Muhammad and developed a belief in the continuation of prophecy, whereby authoritative interpretation of revelation was made by later infallible leaders. W. Tucker, "Abu Mansur al-Ijli and the Mansuriyya," *Der Islam* 54 (1977): 75.

48. *Minhaj al-Sunna*, 2:346.

49. Ibid., 1:332-33.

## Chapter 6. Ibn Taymiyya's Polemical Writings against Christianity

1. Carl Brockelmann, *Geschichte der arabischen Literatur* (Weimar: 1899/1900 and Supplements), Supp. 2:123. 71. *Iqtida' al-Sirat al-Mustaqim wa-Mujanabat Ashab al-Jahim*. 72. *Takhjil Ahl al-Injil*. 73. *Al-Jawab al-Sahih li-Man Baddal Din al-Masih*. 74. *Mas'alat al-Kana'is*. 75. *Al-Risala al-Qubrusiyya: Khitab li-Sajwas Malik Qubrus*. 76. *Antwort auf eine Frage über den Gründonnerstag*. (This last has been recently printed in Arabic in MF 10:320-28 with the title *Su'al 'an Ma Yaf'aluhu Ba'd Man Yadda'i al-Islam fi 'Id al-Nasara al-Khamis*.)

2. E. Fritsch, *Islam und Christentum im Mittelalter* (Breslau: Verlag Muller & Seiffert, 1930), pp. 25 ff. Henceforward, *Al-Risala al-Qubrusiyya* and *Al-Sarim al-Maslul* will be used in preference to their full titles.

3. Ibn 'Abd al-Hadi, *Al-'Uqud al-Durriyya*, p. 54. Ibn Qayyim al-Jawziyya, *Asma' Mu'allafat Ibn Taymiyya*, p. 22.

4. Dr. M. Rashad Salim treats this subject well in his introduction to *Dar' Ta'arud al-'Aql wal-Naql*. "Al-Muqaddima li-Dar' Ta'arud al-'Aql wal-Naql." (Cairo: Matba'at Dar al-Kutub, 1971), pp. 6-7.

5. Ibn Qayyim, *Al-Asma'*, p. 27.

6. 'Imad al-Din ibn Kathir, *Al-Bidaya wal-Nihaya fi al-Ta'rikh* (Cairo: Matba'at al-Sa'ada, 1358/1929), 13:365. In dating Ibn Taymiyya's writings three sources are used. Sometimes the dates are merely conjectural; at other times, as in the case of *Al-Sarim al-Maslul*, the precise date can be determined. Ibn Kathir's history, *Al-Bidaya wal-Nihaya* is the earliest source used. Fritsch's *Islam und Christentum in Mittelalter* attempts to assign a date to *Al-Risala al-Qubrusiyya* and *Al-Jawab al-Sahih*. Henri Laoust's "Bibliographie d'Ibn Taymiyya d'apres Ibn Kathir" offers possible dates for the other works.

7. Ibn Kathir, *Bidaya*, 13:536.

8. *Al-Sarim al-Maslul* (Beirut: Dar al-Jil, 1965), pp. 4-5.

9. Ibid., pp. 245-46.

10. Ibid., pp. 297-98.

11. Ibid., pp. 369-70.

12. Ibid., pp. 571-72.

13. Laoust, "Biographie," pp. 121-32. Laoust gathered his information from various places in Ibn Kathir's *Bidaya*, vols. 13-14.

14. Ibid., p. 122.

15. Laoust, "Ibn Taymiyya," EI2, 3:951.

16. MF 28:468-501, 553-55.

17. Ibid., pp. 501-08, 508-44.

18. Ibid., p. 480.

19. Ibid., pp. 504-05.

20. Ibid., p. 521.

21. Ibn 'Abd al-Hadi, p. 58. The "Maltese Christians" singled out over against the general term were probably the martial order of the Knights of Malta, who were, of course, not predominantly Maltese.

22. *Al-Risala al-Qubrusiyya*, p. 25.

23. Ibn 'Abd al-Hadi, p. 185.

24. *Al-Risala al-Qubrusiyya*, p. 5.

25. Ibid., p. 6.

26. Ibid., p. 7.

27. Ibid., p. 16. This latter statement seems to have been proverbial among Muslims to describe the Christian rejection of the concept of forbidden foods. It was mentioned by 'Abd al-Jabbar and Al-Qarafi as well.

28. Ibid., p. 24.

29. Ibid., p. 26. In the latter work, *Al-Jawab al-Sahih*, Ibn Taymiyya seems to reject the concept of the *mujaddid*. "Since Muhammad was the seal of the prophets and after him there has been no messenger nor anyone to renew (*mujaddid*), God [Himself] has never ceased to undertake the renewal of the religion" (JS 1:13).

30. *Al-Risala al-Qubrusiyya*, p. 29.

31. Ibid., p. 30.

32. Ibid., p. 38.

33. An extensive compilation of references in the *hadith* literature to Jesus' return and his defeat of Al-Dajjal can be found in A. J. Wensinck, *A Handbook of Early Muhammadan Tradition* (Leiden: E. J. Brill, 1971), pp. 50-51.34. Ibn Kathir, *Bidaya*, 14:18.

35. Laoust, "Biographie," pp. 127-28.

36. *Mas'alat al-Kana'is*, MF 28:634.

37. *'Unwa* land is that obtained by Muslims through military conquest. *Sulh* land is that taken by Muslims through agreement with the local people or ruler.

38. *Mas'alat al-Kana'is*, p. 635.

39. The most famous of several Armenian wazirs in Fatimid Egypt is Badr al-Jamali (d. 487/1094), who governed Egypt under the caliph al-Mustansir, but the one referred to by Ibn Taymiyya is more likely to be Bahram (d. 535/1140), the Christian Armenian wazir to the caliph al-Hafiz. Canard notes that during his governorship a great number of churches were built in Cairo and throughout Egypt. M. Canard, "Un vizier chrétien à l'époque fatimite," *Annales de l'Institut d'Études Orientales* 11 (1953): 100. Cf. also, idem, "Notes sur les Arméniens en Egypte," *Annales de l'Institut d'Études Orientales* 13 (1955): 154-57.

40. *Mas'alat al-Kana'is*, p. 642.

41. *Shurut 'Umar 'ala Ahl al-Dhimma*, MRM 1:227. Bernard Lewis provides an English translation of the *shurut* as obtained from al-Turtushi and al-Shafi'i in *Islam* (New York: Harper & Row, 1974), 2:217-23.

42. *Shurut 'Umar*, MRM 1:227-28.

43. Ibid., p. 229.

44. *Mukhtasar al-Fatawa al-Misriyya* (Cairo: Matba'at al-Sunna al-Muhammadiyya, 1368/1949), p. 511.

45. Ibid., p. 513.

46. *Shurut 'Umar*, MRM 1:229.

47. *Ma Taqul al-Sada al-'Ulama' fi Qawm min Ahl al-Dhimma*, MF 28:658.

48. *Fasl fi Shurut 'Umar 'ala Ahl al-Dhimma*, MF 28:653.

49. *Mukhtasar al-Fatawa al-Misriyya*, p. 512.

50. Ibid.

51. Ibid., p. 514.

52. Ibid., p. 516.

53. Laoust, "Biographie," p. 147.

54. *Tahrim Musharakat Ahl al-Kitab fi A'yadihim*, MRM 1:230.

55. Ibid., p. 232.

56. *Iqtida' al-Sirat al-Mustaqim*, p. 7.

57. "Kitab ila al-Aqarib bi-Dimashq," in Ibn 'Abd al-Hadi, *Al-'Uqud al-Durriyya*, pp. 284-85.

58. *Iqtida' al-Sirat al-Mustaqim* (Cairo: al-Matba'a al-Sharafiyya, 1325/1907), p. 51.

59. Although Memon admits that there is no evidence beyond conjecture for determining the date of this work, he feels that the book can be best linked with the inflammatory situation in Damascus between the years 721/1321-726/1326.

60. M. 'Umar Memon, *Ibn Taymiyya's Struggle against Popular Religion* (Paris: Mouton, 1977). The paginated references will be to an earlier version of the work, a dissertation entitled "The Struggles of Ibn Taymiyya against Popular Religion" (Ph.D. diss., University of California, Los Angeles, 1971).

61. Memon, p. 18.

62. *Iqtida' al-Sirat al-Mustaqim*, pp. 96-97.

63. Ibid., p. 41.

64. Memon, p. 109.

65. *Iqtida' al-Sirat al-Mustaqim*, p. 91.

66. Ibid., pp. 36-37. Ibn Taymiyya cites prophetic hadiths which affirm a manner in which the Jahiliyya continues to exist. "Among my people there are four characteristics belonging to the pre-Islamic period," and as Muhammad said to Abu Dharr, "The Jahiliyya is still with you."

67. Ibid., p. 21.

68. The year 721/1321 was one of intense religious animosity throughout the Middle East. Al-Maqrizi gives a vivid account of the burning of churches, synagogues, mosques, and private homes in Damascus, the Lebanon, Cairo, and throughout Egypt. Taqi al-Din Ahmad al-Maqrizi, *Kitab al-Suluk li-Ma'rifat Duwal al-Muluk* (Cairo: Matba'at Lajnat al-Ta'lif wal-Tarjama wal-Nashr, 1941), 2, no. 1:214.

## Chapter 7. Paul of Antioch's Challenge to Islam

1. Georg Graf, "Philosophische-theologische Schriften des Paulus al-Rahib, Bishofs von Sidon," *Jahrbuch für Philosophie und Spekulative Theologie* 20 (1906): 56. See also Paul Khoury, *Paul d'Antioche* (Beirut: Imprimerie Catholique, 1964), pp. 19-20.

2. M. Horten, "Paulus, Bischof von Sidon: Einige seiner philosophischen Abhandlungen," *Philosophisches Jahrbuch* 19 (1906): 145. See also n. 2, p. 159. Khoury gives references to a hypothesis that believed in the 7th/13th-8th/14th century, n. 8, p. 9. Buffat dated Paul of Antioch at the end of the 7th/13th century. Louis Buffat, "Lettre de Paul, Évêque de Saida," *Revue de l'Orient Chrétien* 8 (1903): 388.

3. Khoury, p. 18. Paul of Antioch could not have lived before c. 1125 because of the earlier writings of both Christians and Muslims which he cites in his treatises. On the other hand, in his work on Christian sects he writes about the Maronites as monothelites, which places that

work prior to the union of the Maronite church with Rome in c. 1180. These conclusions are supported by details of his travels, which presuppose a political situation similar to that existing in the twelfth century.

4. Bulus al-Rahib, *Qawl yadullu 'ala al-Firaq al-Muta'arafa min al-Nasara*, in Khoury, *Paul d'Antioche*, pp. 84-97.

5. Buffat gives the title as *Risala Bulus . . . qad arsalaha li-ba'd ma'arifihi al-ladhina bi-Sayda' min al-Muslimin* [The letter of Paul . . . which he sent to one of his Muslim acquaintances in Saida], p. 413.

6. Erdmann Fritsch, *Islam und Christentum im Mittelalter* (Breslau: Verlag Muller & Seiffert, 1930), p. 30.

7. Bulus al-Rahib al-Antaki, *Risala ila Ba'd asdiqa'ihi al-Ladhina bi-Sayda' min al-Muslimin*, in Khoury, *Paul d'Antioche*, 7:61. (In these citations, the first number refers to the paragraph, the second to the page number in the Arabic text.)

8. Ibid., 12:63.

9. Abu Muhammad ibn Hazm, *Al-Fisal fi al-Milal wal-Ahwa' wal-Nihal* (Baghdad: Maktabat al-Muthanna, n.d.), 1:48-65, 98-224; 2:2-91.

10. Bulus al-Rahib, *Risala ila Ahad al-Muslimin*, 24:68.

11. Ibid., 49:77.

12. Ibid., 54:79-80.

13. The most notable in the Western philosophical tradition is John Scotus Eriugena (d. c. 877), whose approach to the problem is not greatly different from that of Ibn Taymiyya. See Frederick Copleston, *A History of Philosophy*, 2 vols. (New York: Doubleday, 1950), 2:136-37.

14. For a fuller discussion of the translation of the Greek philosophical vocabulary in question into Arabic, see Harry Austryn Wolfson, *The Philosophy of the Kalam* (Cambridge: Harvard University Press, 1976), pp. 128-29, and nn. 88-89. The terms *dhat* and *shay'* are also commonly used by Muslim theologians in respect to God.

15. Ibn Taymiyya, *Al-Jawab al-Sahih li-Man Baddal Din al-Masih*, 4 vols. (Cairo: Al-Matba'a al-Madaniyya, 1382/1964), 1:19. Cf. below pp. 140. The title of Ibn Taymiyya's work, as stated in the Istanbul and Leiden manuscripts and followed by Hajji Khalifa and Steinschneider, is *Bayan al-Jawab al-Sahih*. The title above is that given in the Hyderabad manuscript and the two printed editions. My citations of JS will always be from this, the second, printing.

16. Al-Qarafi, who came originally from Bahnasa, spent his life in Cairo, where he "earned fame as the greatest Maliki jurist of his time." Brockelmann, *Geschichte*, 6:665. A number of al-Qarafi's works of jurisprudence have been published and are considered basic texts of Maliki *fiqh*.

17. Al-Qarafi (682/1283), *Kitab al-Ajwiba al-Fakhira 'an al-As'ila al-Fajira*. In the margin of *Kitab al-Fariq bayn al-Makhluq wal-Khaliq*, by 'Abd al-Rahman Bachche-ji Zadeh (Cairo: Imprimerie Mawsu'at, 1322/1904).

18. Shams al-Din M. ibn Abi Talib al-Sufi al-Dimashqi (d. 727/1327) was imam in Rabwa, Syria. In addition to the *Risala*, he wrote a number of unpublished legal works and a geographical work, *Nukhabat al-Dahr*, which has been published in Paris, and several Sufi treatises. It is possible that the *nisba* "al-Sufi" was part of M. ibn Abi Tal-

ibi's patronymic, rather than an indication of his own affiliation with any Sufi orders. Fritsch, however, following Brockelmann (*Geschichte*, 2:130), believes him to be truly a Sufi. Fritsch, *Islam und Christentum*, p. 36.

19. Muhammad ibn Abi Talib, *Risala li-Ahl Jazirat Qubrus* (Utrecht: Bibliotheek der Rijksuniversiteit te Utrecht, MS 1449).

20. I have treated Muhammad ibn Abi Talib's *Risala* along with the influences upon it from the Islamic polemical tradition in greater detail in my dissertation: "Ibn Taymiyya's *Al-Jawab al-Sahih*: A Muslim Theologian's Response to Christianity," Ph.D. diss., University of Chicago, 1978, pp. 257-67.

21. Called in this study the "Letter from Cyprus."

22. Khoury, p. 10, n. 9. On pp. 19-40 of the same work the author studies the manuscript tradition and the history of the text.

23. Fritsch, p. 30.

24. Bulus al-Rahib, *Risala ila Ahad al-Muslimin*, 15-16:64-65, cf. "Letter from Cyprus" cited in JS 1:362; 2:3, 16.

25. Bulus al-Rahib, *Risala ila Ahad al-Muslimin*, 19:66, cf. "Letter from Cyprus" cited in JS 2:44-45.

26. "Letter from Cyprus" cited in JS 2:231, 236, 237, 238, 239, 241-42, 243, 244, 248, 259.

27. "Letter from Cyprus" cited in JS 2:186-87, 189, 191, 194, 196, 198, 205, 211, 213, 214, 216, 217, 225, 228.

28. Bulus al-Rahib, *Risala ila Ahad al-Muslimin*, 14:64, cf. "Letter from Cyprus" cited in JS 1:296-97. *Risala ila Ahad al-Muslimin*, 38:73, cf. "Letter from Cyprus" in JS 2:279.

29. Bulus al-Rahib, *Risala ila Ahad al-Muslimin*, 33-35:71-72, cf. "Letter from Cyprus" in JS 2:287, 294.

30. JS 2:313-3:4. Al-Hasan's *Risala* does not occupy all of these forty-nine pages, for Ibn Taymiyya occasionally interrupts his quotation with observations of his own.

31. JS 2:313.

32. Al-Hasan ibn Ayyub, *Risala ila 'Ali ibn Ayyub*, cited in *Al-Jawab al Sahih*, 2:340.

33. Al-Hasan ibn Ayyub, *Risala*, cited in JS 2:360.

34. The Islamic terminology adopted by Ibn Bitriq include the following: *munazala*, *'ibad*, *kasaba*, *Iblis*, *al-Khalil*, *islam*, *zakat*, *hawariyyun*, *jahiliyya*, *qurra'*, *sura*, *qibla*, *hanif*. W. Montgomery Watt, Introduction to *Kitab al-Burhan* by Sa'id ibn Bitriq (Louvain: Secretariat du Corpus SCO, 1960), p. iv. See also p. 84.

35. JS 3:5. Cf. *Nazm al-Jawhar*, pp. 93-94. *Annales Euthychii Patriarchae Alexandrini* (Louvain: Secretariat du Corpus SCO, 1962).

36. JS 3:51. Cf. *Nazm al-Jawhar*, p. 161.

## Chapter 8. Ibn Taymiyya's Argumentation against Christianity in *Al-Jawab al-Sahih*

1. Louis Cheikho, "Ibn Taymiyya's wal-Wahhabiyyun," *Al-Mashriq* 22 (1924): 913.

2. Fritsch, *Islam und Christentum im Mittelalter*, pp. 31-32.

3. If "*Takhjil*" is seen as integral

to the original work, the total length of JS in 1,400 pages.

4. JS 1:17, trans. p. 138.

5. JS 3:94.

6. JS 1:18-19, trans. pp. 139-140.

7. JS 1:17, trans. p. 138.

8. JS 1:326, trans. p. 207.

9. JS 1:327, trans. p. 208.

10. JS 1:24, trans. p. 144.

11. JS 1:140, trans. p. 173.

12. JS 1:25, trans. p. 145.

13. JS 1:23, trans. p. 143-144.

14. JS 1:29, trans. p. 147.

15. JS 1:31, trans. pp. 147-148.

16. JS 1:112, trans. p. 155. Paul of Antioch believes the Qur'an to be the composition of Muhammad, while Ibn Taymiyya believes it to be God's speech. For purposes of argumentation he accepts the Christian's categories in order to show that even in his own terms his opponent's arguments are invalid.

17. JS 1:113-14, trans. p. 155.

18. JS 1:112, trans. p. 155.

19. JS 1:51, trans. p. 154.

20. JS 1:57-58.

21. JS 1:59.

22. JS 1:99-100. Ibn Taymiyya claims that in his time a copy of the letter to Heraclius was preserved in the archives of King Alfonso of Castile and that it was a treasured heritage handed on by the descendants of Heraclius (I:95-96).

23. JS 2:83, trans. p. 250.

24. JS 2:82, trans. pp. 249-250.

25. JS 1:49, trans. pp. 152-153.

26. JS 1:127, trans. p. 165.

27. JS 1:155-61.

28. JS 1:161-64, trans. pp. 180-181.

29. JS 1:49, trans. p. 152.

30. JS 1:132, trans. p. 170.

31. JS 1:134, trans. pp. 171-172.

32. JS 1:131-41. This does not imply that Jesus, and later Muhammad, firstly misunderstood the nature of their mission to extend to a limited group and then gradually arrived at a true understanding of its scope. Rather, God sent them only with a mission which was possible to be achieved—firstly to those nearest them and only gradually, as their fame, influence, and power grew, to those distant from them and eventually all mankind. This interpretation can be compared with that of Ibn Khaldun, who explained the local nature of Muhammad's early preaching primarily as a strategy designed to make possible the achievement of the universal goal. Ibn Khaldun, *The Muqaddimah*, trans. by Franz Rosenthal, 3 vols. (New York: Pantheon Books, 1958), 1:188.

33. JS 1:129, trans. p. 167.

34. JS 1:178-79, trans. pp. 190-192. Cf. also 1:37-39, trans. pp. 150-151.

35. JS 1:181, trans. p. 192.

36. JS 1:317-18, trans. p. 199.

37. JS 3:248-49, trans. p. 362.

38. JS 1:356-57, trans. p. 216.

39. JS 1:317, trans. p. 199. "They claim further that miracles occurred at the hands of the apostles and these men; they even claim that raising the dead to life occurred at the hands of some of them. Even if this were true, unless the one who performed the deeds claimed that he was a prophet, this would not indicate that he was inerrant" (JS 1:358, trans. p. 217).

40. JS 1:140-41, trans. pp. 173-174.

41. JS 1:317, trans. pp. 198-203.

42. The passage referred to is probably John 20:19-29. (Another possibility is Luke 24:36-43.)

43. JS 1:321, trans. p. 202. Cf. also 2:58-59, trans. p. 245.

44. JS 1:319, trans. p. 201.

45. JS 1:180, trans. p. 191.
46. JS 1:165.
47. Cf. Appendix, pp. 380-381, n. 52.
48. JS 1:177, trans. p. 189.
49. JS 1:177, trans. pp. 188-189.
50. JS 2:27, trans. pp. 239-240.
51. JS 1:341, trans. p. 210.
52. JS 1:347, trans. p. 213.
53. JS 1:379, trans. p. 229.
54. JS 1:367, trans. pp. 224-225.
55. JS 1:380, trans. p. 230.
56. JS 1:378, trans. p. 229.
57. Ibn Hazm, *Al-Fisal*, 1:197 ff.; Al-Juwayni, *Shifa' al-Ghalil*, pp. 46-47.
58. JS 1:356, trans. p. 215. Cf. also 2:18-19.
59. JS 1:380, trans. p. 230.
60. Ibid.
61. JS 2:11, trans. p. 235.
62. Cf. below, p. 229, n. 4.
63. JS 1:35, trans. p. 149. Cf. also 2:7-8.
64. JS 1:368-69, trans. pp. 225-226. Cf. also 1:378, trans. p. 229, and 2:26, trans. p. 239.
65. Al-Ghazali, *Al-Radd al-Jamil*, p. 8 ff.; Al-Baqillani, *Al-Tamhid*, pp. 95-96.
66. JS 2:186-217. Portions of this section are translated on pp. 298-302.
67. JS 2:191-92, trans. pp. 298-299.
68. JS 2:194-96. An excellent example of this is the interpretation given the passage in the prophecy of Isaiah (9:5-7). Cf. JS 2:213-14.
69. JS 2:75, 4:46, 5:13, 5:41.
70. JS 1:362, trans. p. 220.
71. JS 1:348, trans. p. 214.
72. JS 1:363, trans. p. 221. Cf. the elaboration of this statement on pp. 221-222.
73. JS 2:18.
74. JS 1:114, trans. p. 156.
75. JS 2:230.
76. JS 2:87-88.
77. JS 1:5-7; 1:230-36; 3:240-42. Cf. below, pp. 241-243.
78. JS 3:211, trans. p. 346.
79. JS 2:100, trans. p. 263.
80. JS 1:360, trans. p. 218. He refers here to the creed as the *asl al-din* for Christians, and then again on 1:361, trans. p. 218, he also calls it "the basis of their belief" (*asas i'tiqadihim*).
81. JS 3:123-24, trans. pp. 326-327.
82. JS 3:123, trans. p. 326.
83. JS 1:367, trans. p. 225; 2:15, trans. p. 237.
84. JS 1:313, trans. p. 195.
85. JS 1:365, trans. p. 223.
86. JS 1:366, trans. pp. 223-224.
87. M. ibn Abi Talib, *Risala*, fol. 83a-87b.
88. JS 2:99, trans. p. 262.
89. 'Abd al-Jabbar, *Al-Mughni*, 5:80 ff.; al-Baqillani, *Al-Tamhid*, p. 79 ff.
90. *Ma'arij ul-Wusul*, pp. 200-01. In this *risala* Ibn Taymiyya refers to JS by name and states the proper method for Muslims to refute Christians and Jews.
91. JS 2:90, trans. p. 255.
92. JS 2:95, trans. pp. 259-260.
93. JS 2:120-21, trans. pp. 272-273.
94. JS 2:118, trans. p. 271.
95. JS 2:96, trans. p. 260.
96. JS 2:92, trans. p. 257.
97. JS 2:100, trans. p. 263.
98. JS 2:114, trans. p. 268.
99. JS 2:122-33, trans. pp. 273-278.
100. JS 1:169-72, trans. pp. 183-185.
101. JS 2:133, trans. p. 277.
102. JS 2:99, trans. p. 262-263.
103. JS 2:139, trans. p. 278.
104. JS 2:138-39, trans. pp. 278-279.

105. JS 1:173, trans. p. 186.
106. JS 2:98, trans. p. 262.
107. JS 2:142, trans. p. 279.
108. JS 2:162, trans. p. 288.
109. JS 3:94.
110. JS 3:99.
111. JS 1:172-73, trans. p. 185.
112. JS 2:308-11, trans. pp. 309-312.
113. JS 3:72, trans. pp. 314-315. Cf. also 2:156, trans. p. 282.
114. JS 3:125-32, trans. pp. 327-333.
115. JS 2:175, trans. pp. 288-289.
116. JS 2:175-77, trans. p. 289.
117. JS 2:180-81, trans. p. 293.
118. JS 3:76, trans. p. 318.
119. JS 3:79-80, trans. pp. 321-322.
120. JS 3:216, trans. p. 348.
121. JS 3:218, trans. pp. 349-350.
122. JS 3:130, trans. pp. 331-332.
123. JS 3:133-34, trans. pp. 333-335.
124. JS 3:135, trans. p. 335. Cf. also 3:199-202, trans. pp. 343-345. "Al-Tilimsani was one of the most insolent of men, and at the same time the cleverest of these renegades. When the *Fusus al-Hikam* of Ibn 'Arabi was read to him someone said, 'This view is opposed to the Qur'an.' He replied, 'The whole Qur'an is *shirk*; real *tawhid* is found only in our view'" (JS 3:201, trans. p. 345). See JS 3:81-82, trans. p. 323 where Ibn Taymiyya again cites al-Tilimsani, this time to the effect that one must withdraw from rational and sense perception in order to discover the truth.
125. JS 3:123, trans. p. 326.
126. This epistemological principle is basic, not only to Ibn Taymiyya's approach to questions of *tawhid*, but to his jurisprudence as well. Malcolm Kerr notes: "By denying any conflict between revelation and sound reason or between the outward expression and inner meaning of revelation, while asserting that revelation contained a guide for decision on all occasions, Ibn Taymiyya was able to view *qiyas* neither as the legitimate field for mystic speculations, nor as an exercise in morally sterile pedantry, nor as a debasement of the content of revelation" (Malcolm H. Kerr, *Islamic Reform: The Political and Legal Theories of Muhammad Abduh and Rashid Rida* [Berkeley: University of California Press, 1966], p. 77).
127. Cf. above, p. 92. Cf. also JS 3:138-39, trans. pp. 337-338.
128. JS 3:140, trans. p. 339.
129. JS 3:141, trans. p. 340.
130. JS 3:142, trans. p. 341.
131. Al-Qarafi, *Al-Ajwiba al-Fakhira*, p. 62.
132. JS 3:236, trans. p. 354.
133. Ibid.
134. JS 3:253-58, trans. pp. 365-369.
135. JS 3:255, trans. p. 367.
136. JS 3:238-39, trans. p. 356.
137. JS 3:241, trans. pp. 357-358. Cf. 1:16-17, trans. p. 138 for a summary of the errors of Jews and Christians.
138. JS 3:233, trans. p. 353. Cf. also 1:127, trans. p. 164-165.
139. A typical example is the article by Hassan Saab, "Communication between Christianity and Islam," *Middle East Journal* 18 (1964): 54, where he sets Ibn Taymiyya (severity) and al-Ghazali (leniency) as the two poles between which the literary polemic developed among Muslims since the time of 'Ali al-Tabari.
140. JS 1:312, trans. p. 194.
141. JS 1:310-11, trans. pp. 192-193.
142. JS 3:245-48, trans. pp. 360-362.

143. JS 3:249, trans. pp. 362-363.
144. JS 3:249-50, trans. p. 363. This is exactly what Paul of Antioch had been claiming—that Christians were dispensed from the need to follow Muhammad because of their adherence to Christianity.

# NOTES TO THE TRANSLATION

## I. The Universal Nature of Muhammad's Prophethood

### A. Foreword. The Purpose of Writing *Al-Jawab al-Sahih*

1. *Al-Jawab al-Sahih* is over 1,000 pages long, and in this translation I do not pretend to have made a complete presentation of Ibn Taymiyya's argument against Christianity. I have tried to include those passages which present the principal lines of development in JS as well as those which provide the heart of his argumentation against Paul of Antioch. What has been left out includes the many digressions and repetitions in the book as well as his lengthy citations from the works of Al-Hasan ibn Ayyub and Sa'id ibn Bitriq. Where Ibn Taymiyya uses multiple arguments to prove a point, I have often presented only one or two. Of the many Scriptural passages treated in the section on the biblical prophecies I have included two as exemplary of the rest. The page references are to the second Cairo printing.

2. *min wasawis al-la'in*. That private revelations and inspirations usually had a demonic origin is argued in Ibn Taymiyya's polemic against Sufi practices. Cf. above, pp. 35-36. The passage here reflects Qur'anic verses 7:20, 20:120; 114:4-5. Cf. also below, pp. 202-208; 245.

3. In this summary of the errors of the Peoples of the Book, the first five criticisms are directed against Christians. It should be noted that the list of criticisms of Jews and Christians which Ibn Taymiyya presents is carefully worded to indicate the parallel errors in the Islamic community.

4. A parallel is drawn here with the pre-Islamic peoples who rejected their prophets. After they rejected the warning delivered by God through the prophets, they were subject to divine punishment. This served as a lesson to those to whom Muhammad was preaching. In the same way the admonition has been delivered to the Christians through the Qur'an, and their experience of unbelief serves as a warning to Muslims.

5. *Al-Sahihayn*. The reference is to the two most important collections of hadith reports—those of al-Bukhari and Muslim.

6. Ibn Taymiyya applies the Qur'anic censures of the hypocrites (*al-munafiqun*) to the Batinis, whom he considers to externally profess orthodox Islamic practices and beliefs but who secretly (*fi al-batin*) oppose true Islam. He denies the exoteric-esoteric (*zahiri-*

*batini*) dichotomy in exegesis and practice.

7. "The Balance" (*al-Mizan*) is an expression indicating the role of the Qur'an in the determination of right from wrong and the establishment of justice. "It is God who has revealed the Book with truth and the Balance" (42:17). "We sent our messengers with clear proofs and revealed with them the Book and the Balance that mankind might observe right measure" (55:25).

8. "Bulus al-Rahib Uskuf Sayda al-Antaki." Khoury believes that "al-Rahib" is not part of Paul's name but a designation that he was a "man of religion." As in the Qur'anic usage, the Christian practice of the time was to employ the term "*rahib*" generically to any Christian fully engaged in matters of religion. Khoury, *Paul d'Antioche*, p. 8, n. 3.

9. In his *Risala Mukhtasara 'Aqliyya* (ibid., pp. 1-34 Arabic, 123-46 French), Paul defends by rational argumentation Christian claims to monotheism challenged by Muslims. In his *Sharh al-Hal al-Mujib lil-Umam al-Dukhul ma' al-Yahud fi Din al-Nasraniyya Taw'an* (ibid., pp. 34-59 Arabic, pp. 147-68 French), he attempted to present Christian doctrines in such a way as to encourage Jewish and pagan conversions.

10. "Ila bilad al-Rum wal-Qustantiniyya." Throughout JS it is difficult to determine precisely who is meant by Ibn Taymiyya's use of "*Rum*." Like the earlier Muslim writers he is usually referring to the Byzantine empire and its inhabitants by this designation. But whereas the earlier polemicists seemed almost unaware of the Christianity of Western Europe, Ibn Taymiyya, living after the time of the Crusades, is much better informed. His frequent references to the "Pope of Rome" (*Baba al-Rumi*) in the lists of false prophets (cf. below, pp. 000, 000) are, to my knowledge, unprecedented in a Muslim critique of Christianity.

11. It is possible that Paul's journey, like the dialogue with his Muslim friend, is a literary device rather than a historical fact. Ibn Taymiyya, however, does not challenge the historicity of the trip; Khoury suggests a possible occasion for the voyage, the Third Lateran Council (1179).

12. Ibn Ishaq recounts the story in his *Sirat Rasul Allah*, trans. A. Guillaume as *The Life of Muhammad: A Translation of Ishaq's Sirat Rasul Allah* (Lahore: Oxford University Press, 1967), p. 484.

13. Ibn Ishaq mentions Waraqa ibn Nawfal, the uncle of Muhammad's wife Khadija, as one of the Meccans who had adopted Christianity (pp. 83, 99-100) before the time of Muhammad. The story of Waraqa's response to Khadija on the occasion of Muhammad's first revelation is related in full in the *Sira*, p. 107. Cf. also Fazlur Rahman, who relates Muhammad's Meccan preaching in an atmosphere of Messianic expectation among Christians and Jews in the region of Mecca, and the implications this situation carries for the question of the universality of Muhammad's prophetic claim (Rahman, "Pre-Foundations of the Muslim Community in Mecca," *Studia Islamica* 43 [1976]: 8-12).

14. "After the title and the customary ceremonial formulae, he declares the occasion and the particular genre of this letter. The bishop of Sidon has promised that

upon his return from the voyage he would render an account to his Muslim friend of the idea which Christians have of Muhammad. He thereby withdraws into the role of intermediary, posing to his interlocutors the objections which Muslims are accustomed to make to Christians, and reporting the responses of the Christian scholars. By this is obtained, without dialogue form, an apology for Christianity according to the issues raised by Muslims, not simply an exposition of the announced theme" (Khoury, *Paul d'Antioche*, pp. 52-53).

15. *Al-Masihiyyun*. This is the only time in the entire book in which Ibn Taymiyya calls the Christians "*Masihiyyun*" rather than the Qur'anic term, *al-Nasara*; hence, it may be a gloss.

16. I.e., the Mediterranean.

## B. The Nature of Prophethood

1. Paul of Antioch, *Risala ila Ba'd Asdiqa'ihi al-Ladhina bi-Sayda min al-Muslimin* (par. 4-7, pp. 60-61). In this citation by Ibn Taymiyya, the Letter from Cyprus expands the original work by Paul of Antioch. In later references the Letter to a Muslim by Paul of Antioch will be cited as PA and the "Letter from Cyprus" as LC. The pagination of PA given will be to the Arabic text, but the French pagination can be easily located from the corresponding paragraphing in Khoury's edition.

2. One can know the prophethood of a given messenger from extrinsic circumstances without knowing the specific teachings of the prophet. However, since the teaching of all the prophets is one, the general lines of his teaching (the oneness of God, the wrongness of *shirk* and injustice) can be known. For example, from the teaching of the Qur'an one can know that Salih was a prophet without knowing the specifics of his teaching. Ibn Taymiyya criticizes the Christians for prescinding from the basic question of whether or not Muhammad was a prophet to argue from specific statements and teachings of his.

3. "Musaylima al-Kadhdhab" is a contemptuous diminutive for Maslama, "the Liar," a prophet of the Banu Hanifa contemporary with Muhammad. The fragments of his prophetic utterances are said to resemble the short rhyming oaths typical of early Meccan passages in the Qur'an. Musaylima and his followers were defeated in battle in A.H. 12 by a Muslim army led by Khalid ibn al-Walid. EI1, s.v. "Musaylima." Trimingham feels Christian influence on Musaylima to have been strong (J. Spencer Trimingham, *Christianity among the Arabs in Pre-Islamic Times* [London: Longmans, 1979], p. 286).

4. His proper name is 'Abhala (or 'Ayhala), but is invariably called Al-Aswad al-'Ansi in Islamic literature. He wrested political control of much of the Yemen during the lifetime of the Prophet, and increased his influence by claiming to be a soothsayer and to deliver messages in the name of Allah or al-Rahman. He was killed in an insurrection by his people in the year of the death of Muhammad. Classical accounts of both Al-Aswad al-'Ansi and Musaylima can be found in Abu al-'Abbas al-Bal-

adhuri, *Futuh al-Buldan* (Cairo: Dar al-Nashr al-Jami'iyyin, 1377/1957), pp. 119-21, 146-48.

5. The division of this translation into chapters, as well as the titles of the chapters, is mine. The received text of JS is divided into untitled chapters (*fusul*) of uneven length ranging from a half page to forty pages. In this translation the "*fasl*" divisions will be indicated by a dash "———."

6. *Al-Sarim al-Maslul*, p. 570.

7. Ibn Taymiyya notes that in a variant reading of this verse "and in His Books" (*wa-kutubihi*) is read "and in His Book" (*wa-kitabihi*). The variant reading merely serves to reinforce his statement of the generic application of the term "Book" in the Qur'an to include every revealed Scripture.

8. *Al-muflihun*. The Qur'anic concept of "prosperity" which is promised to believers (*al-falah* includes both spiritual-psychological well-being and material prosperity.

9. The insistence that the native language of Jesus was Hebrew rather than Syriac (Aramaic) is not peculiar to Ibn Taymiyya among Muslim polemicists. Shlomo Pines notes this also in Al-Jahiz, 'Abd al-Jabbar, and Ibn Hazm and suggests a Jewish-Christian influence upon the Muslim writers ('Israel My Firstborn and the Sonship of Jesus," in *Studies in Mysticism and Religion* [Jerusalem: Magnes Press, 1967], pp. 177-90]).

10. His real name was Talha, the diminutive form being contemptuous (cf. above, p. 147 n. 3). Tulayha was an early rebel who after his defeat by Khalid ibn al-Walid in A.H. 11 reaccepted Islam and died a Muslim military hero. His inclusion among the list of false prophets is due to his claim to revelations from Jibril or Dhu al-Nun during the period of his apostasy (V. Vacca, EI1, s.v. "Tulayha b. Khuwaylid").

11. The text is in error here. The sentence must be negative.

12. That is, the company of prophets.

13. Such appraisals of Muhammad's prophetic career can be found in early Christian Arab literature. The Nestorian Catholicos Timothy (d. 207/823) argued for the prophetic stature of Muhammad's mission because of his victorious struggle to establish monotheism. Timothy affirms that Muhammad's zeal in fighting to convert men to godly lives and true worship of God place him firmly in the line of the prophets. A. Mingana, "Timothy's Apology for Christianity," in *Woodbrooke Studies* (Cambridge: W. Heffer & Sons, 1928), 2:61-62.

14. *Al-naql al-mutawatir*. "Mutawatir is applied to a tradition with so many transmitters that there could be no collusion, all being known to be reliable and not being under any complusion to lie" (J. Robson, EI1, s.v. "Hadith").

15. *Al-tabi'un*. The term is used here in its technical sense to mean the second generation of Muslims who succeeded Muhammad and his Companions.

16. In his *Muqaddima* Ibn Khaldun gives the detailed geographical boundaries of each of the zones. He agrees with Ibn Taymiyya that Islam was destined to spread from the third to the fifth climes, and that the people of those climes were physically, intellectually, and morally superior to those of less temperate areas. The third, fourth, and fifth zones are described in the *Muqad-*

*dima*, 1:128-58, while the effects of climatic conditions on physical appearance and moral behavior is treated on 1:167-76 (Ibn Khaldun, *The Muqaddimah*, ed. and trans. Franz Rosenthal, 3 vols. [New York: Pantheon Books, 1958]). Ibn Khaldun's information is taken primarily from Al-Idrisi's *Nuzhat al-Mustaq* (the Book of Roger). The historical development of the designation and description of the seven climes among the Arab geographers previous to the time of Ibn Taymiyya can be found in E. Honigmann's *Sie sieben Klimata und die* πολεις επισημοι (Heidelberg: Carl Winter's Universitätsbuchhandlung, 1929), pp. 160-164.

17. The Muhajirun are those Muslims who made the migration from Mecca to Madina with Muhammad. The Ansar are the Muslims from among the natives of Madina.

18. The reference here is to Abu Muhammad ibn Hisham's (d. 213/828) edition of Muhammad ibn Ishaq's (d. 150/767) *Sirat Rasul Allah*. By Ibn Taymiyya's time the work had already become the standard biography of the Prophet, and he frequently alludes to it simply as "The Biography."

19. The Banu Nadir, along with the Qurayza and to a lesser extent the Qaynuqa', were the most important Jewish tribes of Madina. In A.H. 4 the Muslims defeated the Banu Nadir and exiled them from Madina; the exile is recounted in the Qur'an, 59:2-17.

20. The Qurayza were defeated after the Battle of the Trench in A.H. 5 and were either executed or sold into slavery. The Qur'an refers to the event in 33:26-27.

21. In A.H. 6 those Muslims who had traveled with Muhammad from Madina to make the pilgrimage at Mecca camped at Hudaybiyya, where during the course of negotiations with the Quraysh, they swore allegiance to him under a tree. The pact later came to be called the *Bay'at al-Ridwan*.

22. The allegiance sworn under the tree and the spoils of victory at Khaybar oasis are mentioned in the Qur'an 48:18-20.

23. The argument is unconvincing in that the battles between Muhammad and the Jewish tribes could be explained purely as a struggle for political and military domination. However Ibn Taymiyya's point is that it was not seen this way by Muhammad and his followers. The Qur'an refers to the Banu Nadir as "the People of the Book who disbelieved" (59:2). In what were they disbelieving if not in Muhammad? The victory at Khaybar is seen as a religious as well as a military victory (48:19-20).

24. These letters, which Ibn Taymiyya treats in JS 1:86-105, are cited in full by Al-Tabari, who relates as well the meeting between Heraclius and Abu Sufyan in 6/628 (Ibn Jarir al-Tabari, *Ta'rikh al-Rusul wal-Muluk*, ed. M. J. de Goeje [Leiden: E. J. Brill, 1964] 1:3:1559-74). Ibn Taymiyya took the letters as a model for correspondence with unbelieving monarchs, and consciously patterned his *Al-Risala al-Qubrusiyya* to the King of Cyprus on these early letters. Cf. above, p. 74.

25. Al-Tabari records Muhammad's letter to the Negus Al-Asham (*Ta'rikh*, 1:3:1569) and Al-Asham's response. According to Al-Tabari, the reply of the Negus was the most positive response with which the letters were met. The Negus ac-

cepted Muhammad as Messenger of God, and thanked God for leading him to Islam. He sent a delegation to Muhammad, which was subsequently lost at sea.

26. There follows the text of the Nicene Creed. Ibn Taymiyya does not cite the "*filioque*,"—the phrase "and the son." In no citation of the creed by a Muslim—including those of 'Ali al-Tabari, Al-Qasim ibn Ibrahim, Al-Hasan ibn Ayyub, 'Abd al-Jabbar, Ibn Hazm, and Al-Qarafi—have I ever found any reference to this addition which became the standard in Western Europe after the tenth century, and in some places, like Spain, much earlier. In the east, where most of the above-mentioned writers lived, it is not surprising to find this wording omitted; the omission is more puzzling in the case of Andalusian writers like Ibn Hazm.

27. *Afthitah*. No town of this name is mentioned by Yaqut or Al-Bakri. The usual spelling of "Ephesus" in Arabic is "Afsus" (Yaqut ibn 'Abd Allah, *Marasid al-Ittila' 'ala Asma' al-Amkina wal-Biqa'*, ed. T. G. J. Juynboll as *Lexicon Geographicum* [Leiden: E. J. Brill, 1853], 1:81).

28. Ibn Taymiyya rejects the identification common in his time, and frequently agreed upon by Muslim and non-Muslim scholars today, of Alexander the Great with the Dhu al-Qarnayn mentioned in the Qur'an 18:84-99. Dhu al-Qarnayn is always regarded in Islamic literature as a believer and usually as a prophet. Al-Tha'labi notes that while some scholars considered Dhu al-Qarnayn an upright servant, others considered him "a prophet who was not a *rasul*" (*nabi ghayr mursal*), and it is the latter opinion to which Al-Tha'labi subscribes (*Ibn Ishaq Ahmad al-Tha'labi, Qisas al-Anbiya'* [Cairo: Maktabat al-Kulliyat al-Azhariyya, n.d.], p. 201). From Ibn Taymiyya's perspective, Alexander was a star-worshiping pagan and cannot be identified with the Qur'anic character. The Lakhmid Mundhir (d. 554 C.E.) is sometimes suggested as the Dhu al-Qarnayn mentioned in the Qur'an (Trimingham, *Christianity*, p. 192).

29. The reference here is to the story of Dhu al-Qarnayn in the Qur'an in which he directed the building of a barrier across a mountain pass to prevent Gog and Magog from laying waste the lands of the inhabitants (18:94-98).

30. Dölger also traces the beginnings of the Christian practice of praying towards the east "in the direction of the sunrise" to the influences of eastern solar cults and to attitudes and practices endemic to Graeco-Roman culture (Franz Joseph Dölger, *Sol Salutis: Gebet und Gesang im christlichen Altertum* [Münster: Der Aschendorffsche Verlagsbuchhandlung, 1925], pp. 20-60).

31. It is Ibn Taymiyya's intention to purify Islam from the practice which became popular during Mamluk times of building a tomb adjacent to a mosque on an axis with Mecca (e.g., the tomb-mosque of Sultan Hassan in Cairo, 759/1358), so that those praying in the direction of Mecca would be facing the grave of the deceased as well. He saw the danger of *shirk* in this that the dead person would come to be treated as an intercessor. Muhammad Umar Memon, *Ibn Taymiyya's Struggle against Popular Religion* (The Hague: Mouton, 1976), pp. 46-50. Cf. below, p. 202 n. 2, for ref-

erence to Sufi orders like the 'Adawiyya, who prayed in the direction of their saint's grave.

32. The reference is to Aaron's response to Moses, who had questioned his brother why he had not prevented the Israelites from building the calf. "He answered: O son of my mother! Clutch not my beard nor my head! I feared lest you should say: You have caused division among the Children of Israel, and have not waited for my word." Qur'an 20:94. The explanation for Aaron's action given by many exegetes was that Aaron's concern was for the general good of the community (*al-maslaha*).

33. Ibn Taymiyya's judgment on the philosophers in this passage is unfair; however, he has treated the subject in a more nuanced fashion elsewhere. It can certainly not be said that Ibn Sina denied God's knowledge of particular beings. Rather, he devised an ingenious, although perhaps necessarily ambiguous formula whereby God knows particulars "in as much as they are universal" (*min hayth hiya kulliya*) or "in a universal way" (*'ala nahw kulli*). In *Al-Radd 'ala al-Mantiqiyyin* Ibn Taymiyya does not claim that Ibn Sina denies God's knowledge of particulars, but rather claims that his formulation is internally contradictory.

"Ibn Taymiyya sums up Avicenna's theory as he understands it in the following way: 'God knows particulars in a universal way so that not even the weight of an atom escapes His knowledge in the heavens or on earth.' This, argues Ibn Taymiyya, is a contradiction. To know things 'in a universal way' means to know the universal qualities common to many things. These will never specify the individual. To know the universals, therefore, is not to know any particular thing. Thus to couple universal knowledge with the knowledge of each thing is self-contradictory" (*Al Radd 'ala al-Mantiqiyyin*, pp. 467-77. Michael Marmura, "Some Aspects of Avicenna's Theory of God's Knowledge of Particulars," *Journal of the American Oriental Society* 82 (1962): 303-04).

34. Ibn Sina's teaching on prayer, like that on miracles, is an interpretation of "the Stoic-neo-Platonic doctrine of Sympathy." The two phenomena differ in degree and intensity rather than in kind. Fazlur Rahman, *Prophecy in Islam*, pp. 45-47.

35. The book referred to by Ibn Taymiyya is probably the apocryphal *Revelation of Peter*. The work envisions the last days and recounts the actions by which the saved and the damned will be judged. The work was quite popular in the centuries preceding Muhammad, but the latest manuscript known is from Egypt in the twelfth century. C. E. Hennecke and Schneemelcher, "Offenbarung des Petrus," in *Neutestamentliche Apokryphen*, 2:468-71.

36. This statement is a strong affirmation of the principle of *ijma'* (also cf. below, pp. 162-63), and it appears to give broader scope to the concept than that credited him in references from recent scholars. "Ibn Taymiyya had restricted the validity of *ijma'* to the consensus of the first generation of Muslims in matters concerning the implementation of statements and actions of the Prophet" (Kerr, *Islamic Reform*, p. 144). Cf. also Roberto Mangabeira Unger, *Law in Modern*

*Society* (New York: Free Press, 1976), p. 116.

37. The church of the Holy Virgin of Saydnaya, a village northeast of Damascus, has for centuries been one of the most popular centers of pilgrimage in the Near East, and is mentioned as a Christian center as early as 198 C.E. Habib Zayat, *Ta'rikh Saydnaya* (Harisa: Matba'at al-Qiddis Bulus, 1932), p. 6.

38. The name of the feast is taken from the Latin "Calendas" and the feast, held from January 1-10 was important in agricultural areas of Syria. Yahya ibn Muhammad ibn al-'Awwam, *Kitab al-Filaha*, trans. J.-J. Clement-Mullet (Paris: Librairie A. Franck, 1866), 2:86.

39. The text probably should read "the holiest" (*al-aqdas*) rather than *al-quddas* (the Mass), which makes no sense.

40. Possibly it should read "Pentecost" (*'id al-khamsin*), since the feast of Holy Thursday is mentioned later in the sentence. It was the latter feast which was the frequent target of Ibn Taymiyya's criticism.

## C. Qur'anic Testimony for the Universality of the Prophethood of Muhammad

1. This could be a reference to the *khalifa*, but it seems more consonant with Ibn Taymiyya's thought that it refer to any strong and conscientious military-political leader who defends and promotes Islam.

2. The Qur'anic allusion is to 4:47, but is not cited literally.

3. One of the latest verses of the Qur'an, it was delivered after the first important confrontation between the Muslim forces and Christians at Tabuk. Al-Tabari, *Tafsir al-Tabari*, 6 vol. (Cairo: Dar al-Ma'arif, 1374/1955), 14:200.

4. The Qur'anic reference is to the above-mentioned 3:7.

5. This technical term in Islamic law signifies the concomitants which indicate whether a particular command in the sunna is to be taken restrictively or extensively.

6. His point is that in legal argumentation not only is there no contradiction between a specifying and a generalizing statement of the type cited by PA from the Qur'an, but that such a statement *demands* a generalization before its wider application is permissible. Qur'anic statements of the mission of Muhammad to the Arabs and his mission to all mankind are of this type.

7. The account of the attempt by Muhammad to convert the people of Ta'if to Islam is noted, as well as their disgraceful reception of his mission. Rejected by the people of Ta'if, Muhammad was sitting under a tree and a slave was commanded to bring him food. The boy, a Christian from Nineveh, was astonished to learn that Muhammad knew about Jonah. Muhammad explained, "He is my brother, for he was a prophet, and I am a prophet." The boy recognized him as a prophet, and told his masters that Muhammad had informed him of what is known only by a prophet. Ibn Ishaq's account is found in the *Sira*, p. 193.

## D. Signs of the Prophethood of Muhammad

1. Cf. JS 4:122-28 for fuller accounts of these wonders.

2. The earliest Muslim accounts of the meeting between Muhammad and Bahira seem to have been that in Ibn Ishaq's *Sira* and in Ibn Sa'd's *Tabaqat*. Ibn Sa'd narrates the story that when Muhammad was twelve years old with a trading caravan in Syria, the monk miraculously perceived the sign of prophecy on the boy, and warned his uncle to guard him carefully (Ibn Sa'd, *Kitab al-Tabaqat al-Kabir*, ed. E. Sachau [Leiden: E. J. Brill, 1904], 1:76-77, 99-100). It should be noted that a Christian version of the Bahira (sometimes called Sergius among the Christians) story played an important role in early Christian polemics against Islam. In this version Bahira was said to be a heretical monk who taught Muhammad his knowledge of the Bible. Its polemical interest was to show that all Muhammad taught was but a garbled account of the Christian religion. J. Bignami-Odier and G. Levi della Vida, "Une version latine de l'Apocalypse syro-arabe de Serge-Bahira," *Mélanges d'Archaeologie et d'Histoire* 62 (1950): 128. This article also provides extensive bibliographical references to earlier studies of the Bahira story. It should be noted here that "Bahira" in Aramaic is not a name but a title of respect given to any monk (Trimingham, *Christianity among the Arabs*, pp. 258-59).

3. Ibn Taymiyya recounts these miracles at length in JS 4:186-202. His accounts are taken from hadith reports.

4. *Rajul a'jami*. As Goldziher's article shows, the term "a'jami" was sometimes applied generally to any non-Arab speaker, and at other times specifically to Persians. Cf. Ignaz Goldziher, "'Arab and 'Ajam," in *Muslim Studies* (London: George Allen & Unwin, 1967), 1:106-12.

5. The reference is to the warfare occurring between the Persian and Byzantine armies during the period of Muhammad's preaching in Mecca. In 615-616 the Persian armies to whom the pagan Arabs were sympathetic were threatening Constantinople. Muhammad predicted the tide would change and by 624 the Romans had indeed taken the offensive and entered Persian territory.

6. The following details of Christ's confrontation with Al-Dajjal are taken from hadith reports. See A. J. Wensinck, *A Handbook of Early Mohammedan Tradition*, pp. 50-51.

7. In a long excursus Ibn Taymiyya treats a great number of Qur'anic verses which refer to a particular situation or rule, but which obviously do not preclude a more general or universal application. His point is to show that Qur'anic statements which speak of Muhammad's mission to the Arabs or the revelation of the Qur'an in Arabic are not incompatible with other Qur'anic verses which state a universal mission for Muhammad and a universal message in the Qur'an.

## E. Implications of Denying Muhammad's Prophetic Call

1. Abu Sakhr al-Hudhali (d. c. 80/700). A poet of the 'Umayyad period whose verses are preserved in the *Kitab al-Aghani*. EI2, s.v. "Abu Sakhr."

2. As has been mentioned above (cf. p. 98), Sa'id ibn Bitriq, possibly more than any other Christian author, has incorporated Islamic terminology and ideology into his historical and theological writings. Ibn Taymiyya's reference here is a good example. In elaborating various Christian views on the trinity, Ibn Bitriq states, "There are some among them who hold that Christ and his mother are two gods in addition to God (*inna al-Masih wa-ummahu ilahayn min dun Allah*). These are the Barbaraniyya, and they are [also] called al-Maryamiyyin." Ibn Bitriq's phraseology here is undoubtedly influenced by the Qur'an 5:116 (even to the extent of imitating the Qur'anic wording despite its being grammatically incorrect in Ibn Bitriq's sentence). *Nazm al-Jawhar*, p. 126. It is worth noting further that Ibn Hazm's treatment of the Barbaraniyya is almost verbally identical to that of Ibn Bitriq (correcting only the grammar), so that one might think that Ibn Hazm had used Ibn Bitriq for a source or that both had used a common source (*Al-Fisal*, 1:48). Finally, Ibn Taymiyya's term *al-Marsiyya* is possibly a corruption of Ibn Bitriq's *al-Maryamiyyin*. By contrast, Ibn Bitriq distinguishes this sect from that of Marcion (*Marqyun*) whom he calls "the head of the *hawariyyin* when they rejected Peter the apostle." Although defending a Christian position, this statement also seems to arise from an Islamic conception in alleging an early conflict between the *hawariyyun* (whose spiritual ancestry Muslims claim) and the apostles (whose ancestry Christians claim). A similar story is related by Al-Qarafi, *Al-Ajwiba al-Fakhira*, pp. 174-75.

3. Ibn Hanbal's *Radd 'ala al-Zanadiqa wal-Jahmiyya* is translated in M. Seale's *Muslim Theology* (London: Luzac, 1964), pp. 96-125.

4. Abu Bakr Ahmad ibn Muhammad al-Khallal (3. 310/923). A Hanbali jurist and theologian, his *Kitab al-Jami'* is notable for its attention to the political applications of the *shari'a*. Watt, *Formative Period*, pp. 296-97.

5. Abu 'Umar 'Amir al-Sha'bi (d. c. 110/728). A traditionist whose trustworthiness was accepted by the general judgment of critics. F. Krenkow, EI1, s.v. "Al-Sha'bi."

6. Al-Layth ibn Sa'd (165/782). A Traditionist and independent deliverer of legal judgments. Ibn Sa'd, 7:204.

7. Cf. below, pp. 351-369.

8. M. Abu al-Hudhayl Zufar (d. 158/774) propagated the legal views of Abu Hanifa. Abu 'Abd Allah ibn al-Qasim al-'Utaqi (d. 191/806) was considered the most reliable deliverer of legal opinions of Malik ibn Anas. Abu Ibrahim Isma'il al-Muzani (d. 264/877) was said by Ibn Nadim to be the most learned adherent of the Shafi'i *madhhab*. Ahmad ibn Muhammad al-Athram (d. 286/900) was a legal disciple of Ibn Hanbal. All these men were considered minor jurists in comparison with the four Imams.

9. Al-Akhfash al-Mujashi'i (d. 215/830) and Abu al-'Abbas al-Mubar-

rad (d. 285/898) were grammarians of the school of Sibawayh. By Ibn al-Anbari Ibn Taymiyya is referring to one of three linguistic scholars: Abu Muhammad Qasim ibn al-Anbari, his son Abu Bakr ibn al-Qasim ibn al-Anbari (d. 328/940) or 'Abd al-Rahman ibn al-Anbari. As grammarians none were of the status of Al-Khalil ibn Ahmad, Sibawayh, or Abu Kazariyya al-Farra'.

10. 'Ali ibn al-'Abbas al-Majusi and Abu al-Hasan Masih al-Dimashqi were well-known physicians and authors of medical compendia.

11. Kushyar ibn Labban (d. 400/1010) was an astronomer who compiled *zij*es in the Ptolemaic tradition. Al-Khiraqi was an alchemical and astronomical student of Jabir ibn Hayyan.

12. The argument is elaborated further in JS 3:274 where Ibn Taymiyya's citation of greater and lesser authorities in various fields is more extensive than on p. 187 above. E.g., "It would be like saying that Abu 'Ali ibn Haytham knew much about the science of engineering, but that Euclid did not, or like saying that the moon is an illuminator, but the sun is not an illuminator, that Mercury is a brightly shining star, but that Jupiter is not a bright star, or that Muslim was knowledgeable about hadith but Al-Bukhari was not."

13. The reference is to the rebellion of Abu 'Isa al-Isfahani which was carried out during the reign of the 'Umayyad caliph 'Abd al-Malik ibn Marwan (64/685-86/705). Abu 'Isa claimed Messiahship for himself and affirmed the legitimacy of Christianity and Islam for non-Jews. Abu 'Isa's teachings are pieced together from early sources in "Abu Issa al-Isfahani," by J. N. Simchoni, in EJ 1:623-26. There is nothing unusual in Ibn Taymiyya's calling Abu 'Isa a Dajjal, as Islamic tradition held that there would be a series of Dajjals before the Judgment Day. Elsewhere Ibn Taymiyya states that Al-Hallaj was "undoubtedly one of the Dajjals" (*Su'al 'an Al-Hallaj*, p. 199).

14. Jenkinson has suggested that the hadith be identified with ancient Lydda, the town associated with the St. George legend. Jenkinson attempted to account historically for each detail of the hadith (E. J. Jenkinson, "The Moslem Anti-Christ Legend," *Muslim World* 20 [1930]: 50-55).

15. Nimrod is not mentioned in the Qur'an, but Al-Tha'labi identifies the event in 16:26 with the destruction visited upon Nimrod for failing to believe in Abraham (*Qisas al-Anbiya'*, p. 56).

16. It is not certain who is meant. The most likely possibility is Al-Harith ibn Rashid al-Naji who apostacized to Christianity with 300 of his men during the caliphate of 'Umar. Al-Mas'udi, who relates the incident, does not mention any claims to prophethood by Al-Harith (*Muruj al-Dhabab*, 4:418-19). Another possibility is the rebel Al-Harith ibn Surayj, who, although a pious Muslim, allied himself in his revolt against the 'Ummayad caliph Hisham (c. 105/724) with the pagan tribesmen of Central Asia. Later historians considered him "virtually apostate" by the end of his life for politically rejecting the Islamic *umma* for alliance with the enemies of Islam. Francesco Gabrielli, *Il Califatto di Hisham* (Alexandria: Société de Publications Egyptiennes, 1933), p. 70.

17. That *Baba al-Rumi* refers to

the Pope of Rome seems certain from the fact that historians like Ibn al-Athir (d. 631/1234) had already used this designation earlier than Ibn Taymiyya.

18. Ibn Taymiyya does not claim inerrancy for every utterance of a prophet, but makes this claim only in those statements which the prophet explicitly claims to be reporting from God.

19. This hadith seems to indicate Muhammad's approval either for augury or for the acceptance of omens from natural phenomena, both of which are contrary to Islamic teaching. The dispute revolves around whether Muhammad (like the other prophets) could have erroneously stated something and then corrected himself, or whether one must posit a natural or satanically inspired misunderstanding on the part of his hearers.

20. Text amended from "God sent him with it." The argument is that in the case of a false prophet, one cannot put trust in or argue from those statements of his which happen to be correct.

## F. God's Treatment of Those in Error

1. The reference here is firstly to the Tubba' (ruler of the Yemen in Jahiliyya times) Abu Karib Tiban who accepted Judaism and cleansed the Ka'ba. Cf. Ibn Ishaq, pp. 6-12, for the classical account; cf. also J. Ryckmans, "Le Christianisme en Arabie du Sud preislamique," in *L'Oriente cristiano nella storia della civilta* (Rome: Accademia Nazionale dei Lincei, 1964), pp. 413-53. The second reference is to those Madinan Jews who accepted Islam. The question is asked how these people could be called believers and Muslims when that means accepting all the prophets and they presumably rejected Christ.

2. Abu al-Khattab Mahfuz ibn Ahmad al-Kalwadhani (d. 410/1116). Hanbali jurist, a fellow student with Ibn 'Aqil of Abu Ya'la. Extremely daring in his use of *ijtihad*, Abu al-Khattab is noted by George Makdisi as a leading figure in the Hanbali revival of the 6th/12th century (*Ibn 'Aqil*, pp. 259-63).

3. The printed text has been emended. It reads: "It is not possible for him . . . ," but the sense demands an affirmative sentence.

4. In likening the conscientious Jew or Christian to a *mujtahid* who deserves a reward for his striving irrespective of whether or not he attains truth, Ibn Taymiyya adopts the possibility of their ultimate reward. Their manifest errors make them deserving of punishment, but such punishment is not indicated by the Qur'an, and the matter must be referred back to God. Ibn Taymiyya's position here can be compared with that of Al-Ghazali. He said that a member of any of the religious bodies who believes in God and the Last Day and has earnestly searched for the truth but who is overcome by death before fully attaining Truth (*qabl tamam al-tahqiq*) will also find mercy from God. Abu Hamid al-Ghazali, *Faysal al-Tafriqa bayn al-Islam wal-Zandaqa* (Cairo: Matba'at al-Taraqqa, 1319/1901), p. 78.

5. Thus, even though the apos-

tles and their followers believed something (e.g., the crucifixion and death of Jesus) which was known by Islam to be false, they would not be held accountable for this, since they held it in good faith.

6. The text is ambiguous here. Apparently it is referring to the charge that the small group of Jews who allegedly witnessed the crucifixion lied in affirming that it was Jesus who was crucified.

7. The text should probably read "Abu 'Abd Allah al-Mujahid" (d. 369/980), a well-known student of Al-Ash'ari who taught Al-Baqillani. Ibn Asakir, *Tabyin Kadhib al-Muftari* (Damascus: Matba'at al-Tawfiq, 1347/1928), pp. 177-78.

8. 'Abd al-Malik ibn 'Abd Allah al-Juwayni (d. 478/1085), cf. below, p. 309, n. 7.

9. Cf. above, p. 194, n. 2.

10. Text corrected from "al-Tammi." 'Ali ibn Ahmad al-Nu'aymi (d. 423/1032) was a Shafi'i jurist highly renowned for his knowledge of *hadith*, *fiqh*, *kalam*, and *adab*. Jalal al-Din al-Suyuti (d. 911/1506), *Tabaqat al-Huffaz* (Cairo: Maktabat al-Wahba, 1393/1973), pp. 426-27.

11. 'Abd Allah ibn Ahmad Abu Bakr al-Qaffal (d. 471/1079). Khurasani scholar of the Shafi'i *madhhab*, a Qur'anic exegete and hadith transmitter. Al-Subki, *Tabaqat al-Shafi'iyya*, 5:53-56.

12. 'Ubayd Allah Sa'id al-Sijzi (d. 444/1053) was the author of *Al-Ibana al-Kubra*, a lost work on Qur'anic exegesis and hadith criticism highly praised by Al-Suyuti. *Tabaqat al-Huffaz*, p. 429.

13. Abu al-Qasim Sa'd ibn 'Ali al-Zanjani. The text reads "Rayhani," but "Zanjani" is correct. He was a respected transmitter of hadiths who died in Mecca in 471/1107. Al-Subki, 4:383-86.

14. The prophetic hadith seems to be an elaboration of the Qur'anic verse "So set your purpose for religion as a man by nature upright—the nature of God in which he created man" (30:30). In stating that each person is born "according to the law of nature" (*'ala fitra*) the hadith teaches that the native and proper state for mankind is Islam; it is only through environment and rearing that a child is turned away from Islam and led to adopt an unbelieving religion. Ibn Taymiyya notes that in another account it reads "according to this community (*milla*)." The alternate reading more pointedly offers the same teaching. This belief is reflected in Ibn Taymiyya's argumentation (cf. below, p. 256) where he argues that the natural disposition of Christians is opposed to concepts like the trinity.

## G. Causes of Error among Christians and Those Like Them

1. Ibn Taymiyya's references are to the most popular saints of the time. Shaykh Abu al-Hajjaj al-Uqsuri was a spiritual son of Abu Maydan (cf. below, n. 4) who founded a *zawiya* among the Pharaonic ruins at Luxor, and whose *mawlid* is still among the most important of Upper Egypt. J. Spencer Trimingham, *The Sufi Orders in Islam* (London: Oxford University Press, 1971), p. 47 n. 3.

2. 'Adi ibn Musafir (d. 557/1162). A Sufi from the region of Mosul, his *tariqa* was extremely popular among Kurds and became impor-

tant in Cairo in the 7th/13th century. Tritton's description of the 'Adawiyya in Cairo matches the criticisms which Ibn Taymiyya directed against the Sufis and makes them exemplary of the type of Sufism he deplored. They faced the grave of Shaykh 'Adi when they prayed, and often omitted *salah*. They believed that their shaykhs were not dead, but lived with God, where they could act as intercessors. A. S. Tritton, EI2, s.v. "'Adi b. Musafir." However, Ibn Taymiyya praises Shaykh 'Adi himself as "one of the finest of the upright servants of God and one of the greatest shaykhs who followed [the sunna]" (*Al-Wasiyya al-Kubra*, MRK 1:280).

3. (d. 577/1182). An unlearned Sufi teacher whose entire life was spent in the area of Basra. One of the most important tariqas, the Rifa'iyya, trace their spiritual lineage to him. Ibn Khallikan, *Wafayat al-A'yan*, 1:95-96.

4. This extremely important Sufi teacher died in Tlemcen in 523/1129. Through the influence of his disciple, Abu al-Hasan al-Shadhili, and the Shadhili *tariqa*, Abu Madyan was revered by Sufis as "the Shaykh of the West." (The "Shaykh of the East" was 'Abd al-Qadir al-Jilani.)

5. Dahya ibn Khalifa al-Kalbi was one of the Companions of the Prophet. It is he whom tradition records as bringing the letter from Muhammad to Heraclius. Ibn Ishaq, *Sira*, pp. 655-56. Annemarie Schimmel remarks that the hadith in which Muhammad saw Jibril in the form of Dahya al-Kalbi was used by Sufi teachers and poets to justify the *nazar*, the technique of coming to appreciate divine beauty through contemplation of that in humans. She notes that Hujwiri dismissed the hadith as inauthentic. Schimmel, *Mystical Dimensions*, p. 290.

6. The hadith concludes with the description of Christ descending to earth, killing the Dajjal, breaking the cross, etc., in the same words as in the account on p. 189 above.

7. I cannot identify any book precisely on this topic before the time of Ibn Taymiyya. In the extant Muslim polemical literature, several works devote space to the "tricks of the monks." Notable are 'Abd al-Jabbar's *Tathbit*, 1:202-09, Al-Qarafi's *Al-Ajwiba al-Fakhira*, pp. 6-9, and Al-Khazraji's "Maqami' Hamat al-Sulban," fols. 48a-50b. Al-Khazraji's work formed the basis for a number of later works in the Islamic West which elaborated the false miracles and deceptions of the monks. F. de la Granja, "Milagros españoles en una obra polemica musulmana," *Al-Andalus* 33 (1968): 359-64.

8. Cf. above, p. 163 n. 37.

9. The story of the miraculous fire in the church of the Resurrection in Jerusalem was related much earlier by Al-Jahiz, who, like Ibn Taymiyya, attributed the wonder to fraud. 'Amr ibn Bahr al-Jahiz, *Kitab al-Hayawan* (Cairo: Maktabat al-Halabi, 1356-64/1938-45), 4:483.

10. *Al-Sama'*. Cf. above, p. 36 n. 60.

## II. *Tahrif*: The Corruption of Scripture

### A. Corruption of Scripture before the Time of Muhammad

1. PA, par. 14, p. 64.
2. Surat al-Tawba (9).
3. This was the Qur'anic basis which Ibn Taymiyya used in his condemnation of the Fatimids for their failure to oppose the Crusaders consistently, as well as his accusations of hypocrisy against those who refused to oppose the Christian-Mongol coalition which attacked Damascus in 699/1300.
4. The text reads "Muhammad," but should be "Moses."
5. In Christian Arab usage the term for an apostle of Jesus is *rasul* (or *salih*), whereas the term *rasul* in Islamic usage is nearly synonymous with *nabi* in referring to the inspired prophets. Cf. below, p. 258.
6. Although he was the first to systematically integrate the practice into his polemic, Ibn Taymiyya was not unique in referring errors discovered among Christians to parallel deviations in the Islamic community. Cf. the Qadi Abu Bakr ibn al-'Arabi (d. 543/1149), *Al-'Awasim min al-Qawasim* (Cairo: Al-Maktaba al-Salafiyya, 1396/1976), p. 185; Ibn Hazm, *Al-Fisal*, 2:79-81; idem, "Qasida," in Al-Subki's *Tabaqat al-Shafi'iyya*, 3:219-22; M. ibn Abi Talib, *Risala li-Ahl Jazirat Qubrus*, fols. 57a-58b.
7. The followers of three popular Sufi shaykhs. The 'Adawiyya were followers of 'Adi ibn Musafir, cf. above, p. 202 n. 2.; the Hallajiyya are, of course, followers of Al-Hallaj, cf. above, p. 37 n. 67. The Yunusiyya honor an extremely popular saint of Damascus, Yunus ibn Yusuf al-Shaybani (d. 619/1222). Trimingham, *Sufi Orders*, p. 15.
8. *Ahad*. That is, isolated links in the chain of transmission from the prophet—in this case, from Jesus.

### B. Corruption of Scripture after the Time of Muhammad

1. PA, par. 15, p. 64.
2. The reference here is to the Qur'anic verses 54:9-10, where it is stated that when Noah was repulsed by his people, he cried to God for help and was answered with the flood.
3. Ibn Taymiyya's contemporary, Muhammad ibn Abi Talib, held that the Gospel was a *verbal* revelation to Jesus, not a written book at all. This is in contrast to the written Torah delivered to Moses and the Qur'an handed down to Muhammad (*Risala*, fol. 28b-29a).
4. It has been proposed by W. Cantwell Smith and others that in the structure of Christianity and Islam the role of the Bible in Christianity is parallel to that of the hadith in Islam, rather than to that of the Qur'an. He states: "What corresponds in the Christian scheme to the Qur'an is not the Bible but the person of Christ—it is Christ who is for Christians the revelation of [from] God. And what corresponds in the Islamic scheme to the Bible [the record of revelation] is the Tradition [*hadith*]. (For instance, we believe that the counterpart to Biblical criticism is *had-*

*ith* criticism, which has begun. To look for historical criticism of the Qur'an is rather like looking for a psychoanalysis of Jesus.)" W. C. Smith, *Islam in Modern History* (New York: New American Library, 1959), p. 26 n. 13. See also the article by the same author, "Some Similarities and Differences between Christianity and Islam," in *The World of Islam*, ed. James Kritzeck and R. Bayly Winder (London: Macmillan), p. 52. Also, cf. 'Abd al-Karim al-Khatib's response to this proposal: "Christ is Qur'an, Taurat and Injil," *Muslim World* 61 (1971): 92-94.

5. It is clear from this that Ibn Taymiyya is aware that Christians believe their sacred books to be more than the four gospels. The history of the Arabic translations of the New Testament before the time of Ibn Taymiyya shows the canon to have been well fixed among Christians by his time, particularly through the edition of Ibn al-'Assal (679/1280). Ignazio Guidi, "Le traduzioni degli Evangelii in arabo e in etiopico," *Atti della R. Accademia dei Lincei* 4, no. 4 (1888): 5-33, esp. pp. 18-25.

6. What was abrogated in the Torah and the Gospel, which consisted of only a few legal prescriptions, is of the same order as abrogated verses of the Qur'an. God can abrogate other Qur'anic verses as He can those of the earlier books.

## C. The Extent of Corruption in the Bible.

1. This section is taken from a passage in LC which had greatly expanded and altered PA, par. 15.

2. It is particularly the Gospel accounts of the crucifixion, death, and resurrection of Jesus which Ibn Taymiyya considers to be of this type. The accounts of the death of a prophet could not have been written by that prophet, and when they appear in the book of that prophet must be considered to be of the same status as the unrevealed explanatory notations found in copies of the Qur'an.

"What God handed down is that which they have received from Christ. As for its narration of his situation after he rose, it is like similar ones in the Torah which mention the death of Moses. It is obvious that the information from Moses and Jesus after their deaths which are in the Torah and the Gospel is not among what was revealed by God or what they received from Moses and Jesus. Rather, it is something which they have written alongside that in order to inform people of the situation of their deaths. This is pure information (*khabar*) from those present after the two [prophets] about their state; it is not what God handed down to them, nor something which He commanded them during their lifetimes, nor anything which they reported to people.

"Thus the Companions and scholars commanded the 'stripping' (*tajrid*) of the Qur'an so that in the copies nothing but the Qur'an should be written and that the names of suras, the division into five parts or ten, the amens, and other things like that would not be written. The ancient copies which were transcribed by the people of learning are of this type. There are some copies in which their erasure is recorded; the names of the suras, the division into five and ten parts, the places of stopping and starting are written elsewhere than in the copy to confirm their omission. These things are not part of the Qur'an. Similarly, the information in the Gospel of the crucifixion of Jesus, his death, and his appearance to the apostles after his rising is not anything which Jesus said, but only what those after him supposed. What God handed down is what was heard from Christ who was communicating it from God." *Al-Farq bayn al-Haqq wal-Batil*, MFK 1:79-80.

3. The reference is to the twenty canons passed by the Council of Nicaea on matters of sacramental discipline and jurisdiction. A. E. Burn, *The Council of Nicaea* (New York: Macmillan, 1925), pp. 46-50.

4. LC has greatly expanded the thought of PA, par. 15, p. 64.

5. Al-Juwayni had previously made a careful study of the variations in the text of the Torah used by Jews, Christians, and Samaritans (*Al-Shifa' al-Jalil*, pp. 44-57).

6. In addition to 7:157, the verse 61:6 is often cited as a mention of Muhammad in the Bible. In this verse Jesus announces the advent of a messenger "whose name is Ahmad." Guthrie and Bishop treated the phrase as an interpolation from the Syriac translation of "Paraclete" ("The Paraclete, Almunhamanna, and Ahmad," *Muslim World* 41 [1951]: 251-56). But Schacht (EI2, s.v. "Ahmad") and W. M. Watt ("His Name is Ahmad," *Muslim World* 43 [1953]: 110-17) reject the possibility, and agree in suggesting that "ahmad" is adjectival and the phrase means "a messenger who will come after me whose name is more worthy of praise."

## D. Claims of Qur'anic Approval for Christianity

1. PA, par. 20, p. 66.

2. A *bon mot* in Arabic. "*Jama'u bayn al-zaka' wal-dhaka'*."

3. The Qur'anic reference is either to 9:33, 48:28, or 61:9.

4. Qur'an 1:7.

5. PA, par. 21-22, p. 67.

6. "*Al-mu'minin al-mu'tadilin*." The "moderate" believers in this context means those who are proper, well-balanced, avoiding the extremes of error and keeping to the Straight Path—i.e., Muslims.

7. Al-Qarafi had answered Paul of Antioch by saying that although Christians were unbelievers, they had not been accused of *shirk* in the Qur'an. *Al-Ajwiba al-Fakhira*, p. 40. Ibn Taymiyya holds that because the origin of the Christians' religion is the true prophetic religion which was brought by Christ, they are distinguished in the Qur'an from the followers of the essentially idolatrous religion of the pagan Arabs. However, because Christians engrafted idolatrous practices onto the religion of the prophets, they became the objects of other Qur'anic accusations of *shirk*.

8. In his *Al-Radd 'ala al-Mantiqiyyin* Ibn Taymiyya distinguishes at length between *Al-Sabi'a al-muwahhidun*, who he identifies with the *hunafa'*, the believers in the uncorrupted religion of Abraham, and *al-Sabi'a al-mushrikun*—that is, the star-worshiping Harranians. In his description of the latter he notes the presence in Syria of pre-Christian prayer-halls (*masajid*) with their *qibla* facing the north pole, p. 288. Ibn Taymiyya cites a description of a monotheist Sabaean which is attributed to Wahb ibn Munabbih: "He is one who knows God alone but has no *shari'a* from which to act, and yet he does not speak *kufr*." *Al-Radd 'ala al-Mantiqiyyin*, pp. 287-89, 454-58. The most important Western study on the Sabaeans of Harran is D. A. Chowlson's *Die Ssabier und der Ssabismus*, 2 vols. (St. Petersburg, 1856), in which the author presents, along with the history and beliefs of the Harrainan Sabaeans from the Arabic sources, extensive biographical details of the Sabaeans in Muslim lands. 1:456-623. A number of Chowlson's conclusions about the origins of the Sabaeans, however, have been dismissed in later studies, such as his positing of a common origin for Mandaeans, Sabaeans, and Manichaeans. Cf. Johs. Pedersen, "The Sabians," in *A Volume of Oriental Studies Presented to Edward G. Browne* (Cambridge: University Press, 1922), pp. 383-86. Pedersen, working from the accounts of Al-Biruni, Al-Mas'udi, and Al-Istakhri, shows conclusively that in the centuries subsequent to Muhammad "Sabaeans" indicated a variety of groups whose common factor was a Hellenist gnosticism. Scholars such as Pedersen and Tor Andrae confirm Ibn Taymiyya's identification of the Qur'anic Sabaeans—which Muhammad is himself called—and the *hunafa'*, and Pedersen posits strong influences of this gnosticism on Muhammad (ibid., pp. 386-91). N. A. Faris and H. W. Glidden continue the discussion by positing for "Sabaean" and "*hanif*" in Qur'anic times the meaning of "enlightened Hellenized monotheist" associated with a Nabataean kingdom of North Arabia ("The Development of the Meaning of Qur'anic Hanif," *Journal of the Palestine Oriental Society* 14 [1939-40]: 9-12).

9. 'Amr ibn Luhayy was said to have been the leader of the Khuza'a tribe in Mecca who introduced idols into the Ka'ba and initiated practices condemned in the Qur'an as idolatrous. Very little historical information about him is available. J. W. Fuck, EI2, s.v. "'Amr b. Luhayy."

10. PA, par. 24, p. 68.

11. *Din* is often translated as "religion" and *shari'a* as "law." Inasmuch as Ibn Taymiyya in this context is distinguishing the eternal, unvarying teaching of God through His prophets from the historically limited manifestation of that teaching in belief and practice (which is commonly called "religion"), it seems better to translate the former (*din*) as "faith," and the latter (*shari'a*, *shar'*) as "law" or "legal system."

12. There can be variations in the details of a given *shari'a*. For example, in the details of prayer (*al-salah*) Muslims differ.

13. PA, par. 24, p. 68. The last sentence p. 254 n. 14 has been added in LC.

14. This curious addition to PA in LC marks a Frankish crusader environment in Cyprus as the provenance of the final recension of the Christian work. Cyprus, governed at the time by the Lusignan Henry II, used French as the court language and Italian as that of trade. In M. ibn Abi Talib's citation, the words "according to the view of Bishop Damyan" are added.

## III. Trinitarian Questions

### A. Philosophical Explanation of Trinity

1. PA, pars. 25-30, pp. 69-70.

2. Elsewhere Ibn Taymiyya states that "the attributes of perfection go back to three: knowledge, power, and supreme independence (*al-ghina*). If you want you can say knowledge and power—either the power over an act, that is, the cause, or the power to dispense with [anything else], that is, supreme independence. But the first [way of speaking] is better. In respect to perfection these three [attributes] are applicable only to God, for it is He who encompasses everything by His knowledge, who is powerful over all, and who is supremely independent of the entire universe." *Qa'ida Sharifa fi al-Mu'jizat wal-Karamat*, MRM 5:2. Christian controversialists who identified the Father with existence, the son of knowledge, and the spirit with power claimed a natural predisposition in the nature of God to be described by three such attributes of perfection.

3. Cf. above, p. 218 n. 6.

4. Of course, none of the orthodox Christian theologies ever made that claim. However, since Muhammad ibn Abi Talib alludes to it as well (*Risala li-Ahl Jazirat Qubrus*, fol. 89b) as something Christians state, the view may have been propagated in popular Christian circles of the time.

5. It is certain that Ibn Taymiyya was well acquainted with the Christian writers Yahya ibn 'Adi and Sa'id ibn Bitriq. Ibn Bitriq, in both his *Nazm al-Jawhar* and the *Kitab al-Burhan*, presents such trinitarian formulae. Wolfson notes that the identification of individual hypostases in the trinity with specific attributes of God was peculiar in Christian theology to Arab-speaking theologians (with the isolated exception in Western Europe of Marius Victorinus), and that it developed directly out of debates with Muslims. H. A. Wolfson, *The Philosophy of the Kalam*, p. 122 and pp. 319-22. In the Christian West, except for the condemned theses of John Scotus and Gilbert de la Porree, which implied a real distinction between the essence and attributes of God, it was not until c. 1250 C.E. that Albertus Magnus and Thomas Aquinas questioned whether the attributes of God were distinct from His essence and from each other. Ibid., pp. 350-52.

6. The word *uqnum* comes from the Greek γνωμη "thought, judgment," and became the Arabic equivalent of υποστασεις, "hypostasis."

7. He criticizes the Christian antagonist for making a deduction about eternal realities solely from temporally created data. This reflects the sharp lines he draws elsewhere delimiting the power of human reason alone to arrive at knowledge about God.

## B. The Divine Hypostases

1. Cf. above, p. 156 n. 26. Ibn Taymiyya here cites the Nicene Creed for a second time.

2. The "three kinds" are the formulations describing God as begetting, begotten, or as a son equal to the Father in substantiality.

3. The text reads "father" but should read "son."

4. The grammatical discussion here is meant to distinguish between God's stative or essential attribute of "Living" and the active one of "Life-giving." Unlike God's active attributes, which depend on a creation to which God relates, His essential attributes are not dependent upon the existence of a created universe. Living, states Ibn Taymiyya, like the other stative attributes, cannot proceed forth from God.

5. PA, pars. 30-32, pp. 70-71.

6. PA, par. 30, p. 70.

7. The words for hearing (*sam'*) and understanding (*'aql*) are also the technical terms for revealed and rational knowledge. On this basis, Ibn Taymiyya extends the meaning of the two Qur'anic verses to mean "Had we been wont to follow revealed truth or the proofs of reason, etc." As such, its application is extended to Christians and others whose teachings he considers contradictory to revealed teaching and sound reason.

## C. The Incarnation of the Divine Word in Christ

1. From LC.

2. PA, par. 36, pp. 72-73.

3. "He [Ibn Taymiyya] argued forcefully that the pious ancestors in affirming the uncreated nature of the Koran had never meant to assert its eternity. The speech of God, he maintained, is eternal in its species (*jins*), since God has always spoken when he willed, but not in its individual manifestation (*'ayn*). The Koran was spoken by God in time and therefore uncreated but not eternal. Ibn Taymiyya's doctrine deserves recognition as an impressive effort to provide a consistent synthesis of the early traditionalist views about the speech of God." Wilferd Madelung, "The Controversy on the Creation of the Koran," pp. 524-25.

## D. *Hulul*: Indwelling of God in Christ

1. PA, par. 36, p. 73.

2. *Ma'rifa* is here distinguished from *'ilm* and *'aql*. It is essentially mystical knowledge, one of the

things implanted in the heart by God; like love, however it can err, and its perceptions are not infallible. Cf. Franz Rosenthal, "Muslim Definitions of Knowledge," in *The Conflict of Traditionalism and Modernism in the Muslim Middle East*, ed. Carl Leiden (Austin: University of Texas Press, 1965), pp. 117-26.

3. Ibn 'Abbas, a Companion of the Prophet, was the principal authority in Mecca for hadith traditions from Muhammad. His principal student and spokesman who handed on his traditions was 'Ikrima. The faithfulness and accuracy of 'Ikrima in representing his master's words is reflected in a hadith in which Ibn 'Abbas binds the feet of his pupil and proceeds to teach him the Qur'an, its *tafsir*, and the sunna of the Prophet. Ibn Sa'd, *Al-Tabaqat al-Kubra*, 2:2:133. In an extended sense, therefore, 'Ikrima could be said to "be" his master, Ibn 'Abbas. Similarly, Abu Yusuf was the leading spokesman for the views of Abu Hanifa.

4. *Al-Furqan bayn Awliya' al-Rahman wa-Awliya' al-Shaytan* (Cairo: Maktabat Muhammad 'Ali Subayh, 1378/1958).

5. The Christian opponent claimed that God's indwelling and union in Christ was predicted by the prophets of the Old Testament. The passages cited by him follow a consistent pattern. They are Messianic passages referring either to the son of David or to God's dwelling in the restored Jerusalem. The choice of passages is often made on a verbal basis, with the verbal form of *hulul* or *sukna* prominent as an indication that God does dwell on earth and with(in) His people.

In these passages the divergence between the original work of Paul of Antioch and the amplified work of the Letter from Cyprus is most apparent. This collection of prophetic passages from the Old Testament is not found in PA.

Ibn Taymiyya strives to point out that there is nothing in any of these passages which can serve as scriptural proof for the Christian doctrines of *ittihad* and *hulul*, nor for particularizing any special relationship between Christ and God beyond the characteristics of the prophets in general and those specific to Christ expressed in the Qur'an. One would suppose that the astute controversialist Paul of Antioch would have recognized the apologetic inadequacy of these passages, and it is not surprising to find them only in the later, more popular work composed in Cyprus.

6. Zechariah 2:10-17.

7. Numbers 12:5-6.

8. Numbers 13:13-14.

9. Deuteronomy 1:29-30.

10. This verse is not in Psalm 4, although Psalm 5:11 is similar to it.

11. This passage, not found in PA, is taken from LC.

12. The text should read *al-funduqiyya*, "the innkeeper," rather than *al-qandaqaniyya*. This designation, which may have originated as a slander, was repeated in the biographies of Constantine in both Islamic and Christian literature. Stern traces it to a now-lost pagan Harranian biography of Constantine. S. M. Stern, "'Abd al-Jabbar's Account of How Christ's Religion was Falsified by the Adoption of Roman Customs," *Journal of Theological Studies* 19 (1968): 174-76.

## E. Qur'anic Teaching About Jesus

1. PA, par. 40, but greatly expanded in the LC.

2. The Qur'anic text is cited as basis for the belief in the return of Jesus in 43:61, "He [Jesus] is truly a knowledge of the Hour"—that is, he by whose descent the approach of the Hour is known (G. Anawati, EI2, s.v. "'Isa"). This Qur'anic verse was elaborated by a wealth of detail in the hadith. A. J. Wensinck, *Muhammadan Tradition*, p. 113.

3. This statement raises the question of whether Ibn Taymiyya was acquainted with Christian docetic literature. His source could be 'Abd al-Jabbar's *Tathbit* in which the author made use of an apocryphal gospel in which Judas pointed out the wrong man in the garden and another was crucified in Jesus's place (*Tathbit Dala'il Nubuwwat*, pp. 191-92).

4. The interpretation of the ambiguous "*shubbiha lahum*" has exercised the imaginations of Christian as well as Muslim scholars over the centuries. Nicholas of Cusa (d. 1164) held that the Qur'an did not state that Jesus was not killed, but rather that the Jews did not do it. Sweetman, *Islam and Christian Theology*, 2:1:166-67. R. C. Zaehner undertakes an even more daring interpretation by which he suggests that the meaning is that, contrary to appearances, it was God who caused Jesus to die and then He raised him to Himself. Zaehner concludes that the Qur'anic teaching is substantially identical with the early Christian hymn which Paul incorporated into his Letter to the Philippians 2:6-11 (*At Sundry Times* [London: Faber and Faber, 1958], pp. 212-14). G. Basset-Sani has combined the two theories to posit an identity between Christian and Qur'anic teaching on the matter (*The Koran in the Light of Christ* [Chicago: Franciscan Herald Press, 1977], pp. 168-74).

5. PA, par. 40, p. 74.

6. Elsewhere Ibn Taymiyya held that the Nestorian concealment of credal statements was due to the positive influence of Islam, by which Nestorius reformed Christian belief. *Qa'ida Awwaliyya*, MF 2:85. The relative closeness of Nestorian Christianity to Islam was attested by Muslims and Christians. Ibn Sa'd twice related the Bahira story (cf. p. 174 n. 2) with the name of Nestorius (*Tabaqat* 1:1:83 and 102), while Nicholas of Cusa held that Muhammad, a convert to Nestorian Christianity, simply perpetuated its beliefs in Islam. G. Anawati, "Nicholas de Cues et le probleme de l'Islam," *Nicolo Cusano Agli Inizi del Mondo Moderno* (Florence: Sansoni, 1970), p. 158.

7. 'Abd al-Malik al-Juwayni (d. 478/1085). The noted *kalam* theologian and teacher of Al-Ghazali has no extant treatment of Christian sects, unless it is contained in his unpublished masterwork, the *Shamil*. Louis Gardet, EI2, s.v. "Al-Djuwaini." Were it not for the reference to Al-Juwayni's student, Abu al-Qasim, the reference would appear to be to the *Bayan al-Adyan* of Al-Juwayni's near contemporary, Abu al-Ma'ali al-'Alavi (d. after 485/1092), which contains a detailed delineation of the principal Christian sects. Abu al-Ma'ali, *Bayan al-Adyan* (Tehran: Mu'assasa-

yi-Matbu'at-i-Farahani, 1383/1964), pp. 14-16. One is tempted to think that Ibn Taymiyya confused the two Abu al-Ma'alis.

8. Salman ibn Nasr al-Ansari (d. 511/1117). A pupil of Al-Juwayni, Abu al-Qasim was also known for his work in *tafsir* of the Qur'an. Al-Subki, *Tabaqat al-Shafi'iyya* 5:96-99.

9. This is probably a reference to some Nestorian Christians who explained the trinitarian hypostases by the *ahwal* of Abu Hashim al-Jubba'i. H. A. Wolfson, "An Unknown Splinter Group of Nestorians," *Revue des Études Augustiniennes* 6 (1960): 249.

10. Ibn Taymiyya's concern is to show that the mainstream of thought among the People of the Book was in agreement with the orthodox Sunni view of the uncreated nature of God's speech rather than with that of the Mu'tazili writers cited, who found in Judaism and Christianity support for their view of the created nature of divine speech. It can be strongly questioned whether Ibn Taymiyya was correct in his claim. Jewish scholars, states Wolfson, with one voice agreed with the Mu'tazila in rejecting the hypostatic nature of the attributes (Harry A. Wolfson, "The Jewish Kalam," *The Seventy-Fifth Anniversary Volume of the Jewish Quarterly Review* [Philadelphia, 1932], pp. 555-56).

It would seem to follow that, if the speech was not an attribute eternally subsisting in God, it must be considered something created outside of Him in time. Ibn Taymiyya's observation about Christians that they do not identify the eternal Logos with the individual manifestation of divine speech in the sacred books is correct. However, this made it possible for Christian theologians to stress the nature of the books as historical reports as well as their human authorship, both of which concepts imply, in Islamic terms, that the sacred books are created in time outside the divine essence.

11. (d. 527/1133). Although Ibn Rajab mentions a number of works by Ibn al-Zaghuni on *Usul al-Din* and jurisprudence, he does not list any controversialist work by that author (Ibn Rajab, *Dhayl*, 1:217-18).

12. The text should probably read "water and milk."

13. Al-Baqillani, *Al-Tamhid fi al-Radd 'ala al-Mulhida al-Mu'attila wal-Rafida wal-Khawarij wal-Mu'tazila* (Cairo: Dar al-Fikr al-'Arab, 1366/1948), p. 79 ff.

14. Ibn Abi Ya'la does not list any works about Christianity in his list of his father's writings except a treatise on the *Shurut 'Umar*. He does mention, however, a lost work entitled *Arba' Muqaddimat fi Usul al-Diyanat*, in which he may have elaborated the distinctions in Christian trinitarian formulations. Ibn Abi Ya'la, *Tabaqat al-Hanabila*, 2:205.

## F. *Ittihad*: Union of God with a Creature

1. Cf. Sa'id ibn Bitriq, *Nazm al-Jawhar*, 1:162-63. In addition to his use of Ibn Bitriq's *Nazm al-Jawhar* as a historical source, Ibn Taymiyya undertakes a refutation of the bishop's trinitarian formulation. The

following passage is Ibn Taymiyya's twelfth response to Ibn Bitriq, and treats the heart of Ibn Taymiyya's criticism of all forms of *ittihad* and *hulul*, that is, that any formulation of essential union, contact, or residence with a creature requires a dependence of God upon something created.

2. Cf. above, p. 50 n. 54.

3. Abu Sa'id al-Kharraz (d. 286/899). A Baghdadi Sufi associated with Dhu al-Nun al-Misri and Sari al-Saqati, his *Kitab al-Sidq* is "apart from the writings of Muhasibi, the earliest systematic presentation of the theory of Sufi experience written by a practicing Sufi" (A. J. Arberry, "Preface" to *The Book of Truthfulness* [*Kitab al-Sidq*] [London: Oxford University Press, 1937]). Although the statement cited by Ibn Taymiyya is not found in the *Kitab al-Sidq*, it was well known in medieval times and was cited also by Ibn Khaldun, *The Muqaddimah*, 2:96 and n. 526.

4. *Ahl al-Bayt*. That is, a direct descendant of Muhammad.

5. The deception perpetrated by the people of Noah was to single out their various gods (or ancestors, cf. below, p. 356) for worship to the exclusion of the rest of existence. However, Noah's reproof is also full of deception, for in wanting to prevent his people from following their practices he set up God as an opposing idol. The reality, according to Ibn 'Arabi, is that it is impossible for anyone to worship anything other than God.

6. *Sahib al-waqt*. Among Sufis this term was generally applied to the *Qutb*—the highest in the hierarchy of saints, upon whom the well-being of the universe depends.

7. The two concepts are confused by Ibn Taymiyya. Plato and the later Platonists do not speak of the suspended images; the concept was introduced in Islamic philosophy by Al-Suhrawardi.

8. *Al-mutlaq bi-shart al-itlaq* ("the absolute with the condition of its absoluteness" and *al-mutlaq la bi-shart* ("the absolute without any condition") are technical terms taken from logic. The former relates to the absolute on the condition that it remain absolute, i.e., by its nature it cannot be limited or specified. The latter refers to the absolute with no conditions attached, i.e., it may remain absolute or it may be conditioned. According to Ibn Taymiyya, the former concept does not exist in reality, while the latter exists in external reality only as specified.

9. The Diwan of Al-Tilimsani has unfortunately never been published, but seven manuscript copies are listed by Brockelmann (*Geschichte*, 1:300, 16).

10. This treatment is an important corrective to the accusations sometimes leveled at Ibn Taymiyya of a simplistic, anthropomorphist cosmology. This criticism has been immortalized for both Muslim and Western scholars in Ibn Battuta's questionable account of Ibn Taymiyya's Friday sermon in the Damascus mosque. Cf. Donald P. Little, "Did Ibn Taymiyya Have a Screw Loose?" pp. 93-95.

It can be seen here that Ibn Taymiyya's cosmology is carefully nuanced, and his central point is to preserve the total otherness of God as being in no way essentially connected with the universe. God's "height" is not to be understood in the geographical or locational sense of His being located ("fixed") in a celestial realm or beyond the highest realm, but is meant in a metaphysical sense, that God's nature is dissimilar to, independent of, and thus separate from all created reality. God's being and prerogatives totally transcend those of creation; this is a necessary concomitant of His nature, and in no way prejudiced by His external activities of creation, revelation, and sustenance.

All the messages of the prophets are to be understood in this sense. When God is said to descend to the realm of creation—to create, to speak, to judge—His absolute transcendance, "His height, His throne," is in no way compromised. It is another thing to say that such expres sions of God's height or His "descent" are to be taken metaphorically, and this Ibn Taymiyya rejects. His refusal is based on two grounds. Firstly, the implication of unreality contained in metaphorical terminology; one must not think that the speech of the prophets was not handed down and uttered in full truth. The second reason for his rejection goes deeper. He is rejecting the role of human reason to determine the content of revealed truth. There can be no contradiction between what is known from reason and that which is known from revelation. The prophets can reveal things which would not otherwise be known from reason, but reason is unable to disprove any revealed statement or be incompatible with it. Ibn Taymiyya accused the peripatetic philosophers and the systematic theologians of believing that cases existed in which revealed teachings were incompatible with rational knowledge. In using reason to test revelation, one makes the former, rather than the divine message, become the ultimate arbiter of revealed truth. Only that which was revealed by the prophets can be accepted as infallibly true, and thus there is nothing in its content that reason need reinterpret as metaphorical.

## IV. Final Questions

### A. The Compatibility of Rational and Revealed Knowledge

1. The reference is to Acts 10:1-43 and 11:1-18.

2. Sa'id ibn Bitriq, *Nazm al-Jawhar*, 1:124-25.

3. PA, par. 40, p. 74.

4. "*Al-qalb al-sunburi*." Literally, the pineal heart. The pineal gland was considered in medieval medicine to be the seat of the soul.

5. "*Al-jawahir al-munfarida*." A reference to the atomist theses of the later Ash'arites.

6. The argument used by Al-Ghazali against the peripatetic philosophers that "the infinite actual is absurd." If the world is eternal, held Al-Ghazali, infinite actual is possible. But the infinite actual is absurd. Therefore the universe is not eternal. Abu Hamid al-Ghazali, *Tahafut al-Falasifa* (Cairo: Dar al-Ma'arif, 1392/1972), pp. 99-103.

## B. Adequacy of Philosophical and Prophetic Language for Discussing the Nature of God

1. Paul of Antioch has taken this argument from a "session" (*majlis*) of Ilya ibn Shina, the Bishop of Nasibin (d. 440/1049), with which it is verbally identical. Cf. Louis Shayku (Cheikho), "Majalis Ilya Mutran Nasibin," *Mashriq* 20 (1922): 42. A 7th/13th-century date has been suggested for Ilya, which means he would have taken the argument from PA. However, Shaykhu's evidence for the earlier date is convincing (p. 34).

2. Paul's point is that language is necessarily inadequate in speaking about God and thus passages in the sacred books are by their nature ambiguous. A people's belief means what they say it means and is delineated by what they have excluded as incompatible with that belief. Ibn Taymiyya's first response stresses a return to prophetic religion. That which is incompatible with the intention of the messengers—the question of textual corruption is ultimately irrelevant—is never acceptable.

3. *Tafsir Surat al-Ikhlas* (Cairo: Maktabat Ansar al-Sunna al-Muhammadiyya, n.d.), 200 pp.

4. "Jawab Ahl al-'Ilm wal-Iman Anna, 'Qul, Huwa Allah Ahad' Ta'dul Thulth al-Qur'an," MF 17:5-206.

5. Another citation of the Nicene creed is included here.

6. This is response no. 15 in the complete text of JS.

7. The poet Al-Shustari (d. 668/1269) was the disciple of Ibn Sab'in and followed the *tariqa* of Abu Madyan (cf. p. 202 n. 4 above). "His short *muwashshahat* poems . . . have continued to be popular in Shadhili *hadras* [sessions] until today" (Trimingham, *Sufi Orders*, p. 47).

8. Sharaf al-Din Abu Hafs ibn al-Farid (d. 632/1235). The mystical imagery and poetic structure of *Nazm al-Suluk* are studied by Arberry in *The Mystical Poems of Ibn al-Farid* (Dublin: Emery Walker, 1956). pp. 10-19.

9. Muhammad ibn Sawwar Najm al-Din ibn Isra'il (d. 677/1278). A Sufi poet of the Suhrawardi *tariqa*, Ibn Isra'il was one of the principal targets among Sufis of Ibn Taymiyya's criticism. Biographical information on Ibn Isra'il can be found in Ibn Shakir al-Kutubi's *Fawat al-Wafayat*, 3:383-87. References to other classical biographies are listed in Bernard Lewis's "Kamal al-Din's Biography of Rashid al-Din Sinan," *Arabica* 13 (1966): 257.

10. Ibn Shakir al-Kutubi states that when Ibn Isra'il recited this verse at a prayer session, Ibn al-Hakim shouted, "You have disbelieved, you have disbelieved!" Ibn Isra'il answered, "No, I have not disbelieved; you do not understand, and you're disturbing the session." *Fawat* 3:384.

11. *Al-Jibt* and *Al-Taghut* are mentioned in the Qur'an as objects of belief for "those who have received a portion of the Book" (4:54). The usual interpretation is that these were idols of the pagan Arabs, but as early a commentator as Al-Sha'bi has explained *al-jibt* as magic and Al-Taghut as Satan. Hisham ibn Sa'ib al-Kalbi, *Kitab al-Asnam* (Cairo: Dar al-Qawmiyya lil-Taba'a wal-Nashr, 1384/1965), pp.

108, 110. Ibn Taymiyya's designation of them as idols worshiped by the Greek philosophers does not seem to have any historical basis.

12. A number of Muslim polemicists before Ibn Taymiyya had already discussed the role of Paul as pivotal in corrupting the teaching of Jesus. Abd al-Jabbar, *Tathbit*, pp. 156-58; Al-Isfara'ini, *Al-Tabsir fi al-Din* (Cairo: Matba'at al-Anwar, 1359/1940), pp. 90-91; Ibn Hazm, *Fisal*, 2:70-71; Al-Qarafi, *Al-Ajwiba al-Fakhira*, pp. 172-75. A number of the stories about Paul were the common property of Muslims and Jews and figure prominently in Jewish writing on Christianity as well. Yaqub al-Qirqisani, *Kitab al-Anwar wal-Maraqib* (New York: Alexander Kohut Memorial Foundation, 1939), 1:43. Ibn Kammuna states that most innovated practices and beliefs in Christianity arose from the opinion of Paul (Sa'd ibn Mansur ibn Kammuna, *Tanqih al-Abhath lil-Milal al-Thalath* [Berkeley: University of California Press, 1967], p. 54).

13. This was a criticism which Ibn Taymiyya leveled not only at Christians, but at Muslim and Jewish philosophers as well. He refers to Maimonides, with whose *Dalalat al-Ha'irin* he was acquainted, as being like Al-Ghazali "in commingling the dicta of the prophets and the philosophers and allegorically interpreting the former according to the latter." Shlomo Pines, "Ibn Khaldun and Maimonides," *Studia Islamica* 32 (1970): 272. Among Christians, however, he saw the innovated synthetic religion as having overcome the prophetic religion, while in Islam, at least, its influence was limited to aberrant individuals.

14. The *Uthulujia* is not by Aristotle, but rather a paraphrase with commentary of parts of Plotinus's *Enneads*. The work, which is frequently mentioned in classical Arabic literature and later appeared in Latin translation seems to have been originally written in Syriac. Its extremely complicated history is unraveled by Badawi in *Aflutin 'ind al-'Arab* (Cairo: Dar al-Nahda al-'Arabiyya, 1385/1966), pp. 1-37. Furthermore, Rosenthal has determined the *Uthulujia* and the work of "Al-Shaykh al-Yunani" referred to by Al-Shahrastani, Ibn Miskawayh, and others to have derived from a common source with a recension of the *Uthulujia* (Franz Rosenthal, "As-Sayh al-Yunani and the Arabic Plotinus Source," *Orientalia* 21 [1952]: 467-73).

15. (d. 288/901). A mathematician and astronomer of Sabaean background, his astronomical works in Syriac and Greek have been frequently studied and translated. An extensive, although somewhat dated, bibliography can be found in J. Ruska, EI1, s.v. "Thabit b. Kurra."

16. Ibn Taymiyya is trying to reduce the philosophers' position to absurdity by arguing that it results in God's being understood as a beloved who has no knowledge or feelings for the lover.

17. Abu al-Nasr al-Farabi (d. 338/950), *Kitab Ara' Ahl al-Madina al-Fadila* (Beirut: Al-Maktaba al-Kathulikiyya, 1959).

## C. Superiority and Necessity of Islam

1. "*shari'at fadl.*" *Al-fadl* is difficult to translate. In reference to God's acts it encompasses the idea of God's favor which goes beyond justice, of preference, of grace. On the human side it indicates supererogatory goodness as opposed to strict justice. The word will be translated variously as the sense requires it.

2. PA, pars. 59-64, pp. 81-83. Prior to Paul of Antioch, 'Isa ibn Ishaq ibn Zur'a (d. 398/1008) used the identical argument against Islam presented here in very similar terms. Further study may show some dependence of Paul of Antioch upon the earlier writer. Cf. Ibn Zur'a, *Radd Abi al-Qasim al-Balkhi*, in *Mabahith Falsafiyya Diniyya*, pp. 55-57.

3. Cf. Joseph Schacht, *An Introduction to Islamic Law*, pp. 181-87, for a summary of Islamic legislation in matters of blood money.

4. Cf. above, p. 237 n. 3.

5. 'Abd Allah ibn Abi Ja'far al-Razi was an early transmitter of hadiths in the generation of the *tabi'un*, whose reliability was challenged by later scholars. Ibn Hajar al-'Asqalani, *Tahdhib al-Tahdhib* (Beirut: Dar Sadir, 1326), 5:176.

6. That is, that the Torah was generally severe.

7. A place near the Red Sea, five nights' journey from Mecca (Yaqut, 1:136). Yaqut mentions that it is also said to be a town in the Yemen.

8. The text is ambiguous. It could refer to the pagans, to the Jews, or to both.

9. The Khazars are a people inhabiting the lands to the north and west of the Caspian Sea. Their long history of involvement with Islamic peoples is related in W. Berthold, EI1, s.v. "Khazar."

10. In the middle of the sixth century C.E. the Persians took the offensive against Byzantium, a campaign which resulted in the sack of Antioch in 540 and a threat to Constantinople itself.

11. The first Muslim penetration into the territory of the Byzantine empire. "Theodore the Vicar raised a force of Arab auxiliaries—both Christian and pagan—from the frontier region to the southeast of the Dead Sea. So says the Byzantine historian Theophanes; this is the first time that incidents in the Prophet's life can be taken from a non-Muslim source. The armies met at Mu'ta; the affray was a bloody one" (Maxime Rodinson, *Mohammed* [New York: Random House, 1968], p. 256).

12. Ten months after Muhammad returned victoriously to Mecca, he set out with a large army for Tabuk, a desert town 250 miles north of Mecca. There was no military engagement there, but local rulers—Christians and Jews—agreed to pay tribute to Muhammad.

13. The argument here is that the Christian position implies that the Jewish law was an imperfect and temporary product of human (Moses's) legislation. Ibn Taymiyya responds that the Law of the Torah is as much the result of divine revelation as is that of the Gospel; in fact, it is more worthy than the Gospel of being attributed to God.

## NOTES TO THE APPENDIX

### The Relationship of *Al-Jawab al-Sahih* to *Takhjil Ahl al-Injil*

1. The full title given in Bodleian MS Marsh 299 is "Takhjil Ahl al-Injil wal-Nahj al-Sahih fi al-Radd 'ala Man Baddal Din 'Isa Ibn Maryam al-Masih."

2. The first printed edition is that of Cairo: Matba'at al-Nil, 1322/1905. It is in 4 volumes and 1,422 pages. The second edition is Cairo: Matba'at al-Madani, 1383/1964, four volumes and 1,412 pages. Both printed editions are made from one and the same manuscript, that of the Asafiyya library in Hyderabad.

3. Leiden MS Or 338. Dated A.H. 730, name of scribe illegible, provenance unknown. Contains part 2 of printed ed.

Istanbul Yeni Cami MS 732. Dated Sat. 15 Rajab 1094/1683, in two different hands, neither scribe named, provenance unknown. Contains part 1 of printed ed.

Haydarabad. Asafiyya MS 2 (165/6):1298. The latest of the manuscripts, it is dated 1319/1901. Its text is essentially that of the printed editions, which were made solely from this manuscript.

4. Ibn Kathir, *Al-Bidaya wal-Nihaya*, 14:135. Jalal al-Din al-Dhahabi al-Suyuti, *Tabaqat al-Huffaz* (Cairo: Maktabat al-Wahba, 1393/1973), p. 516.

5. Ibn 'Abd al-Hadi, *Al-'Uqud al-Durriyya*, p. 28.

6. Ibn Qayyim al-Jawziyya, *Asma' Mu'allafat Ibn Taymiyya* (Damascus: Al-Majma' al-'Ilmi al-'Arabi bi-Dimashq, 1372/1953).

7. M. Ibn Shakir al-Kutubi, *Fawat al-Wafayat* (Beirut: Dar al-Thaqafa, 1973), 1:74-80.

8. Zayn al-Din Ibn Rajab, *Al-Dhayl 'ala Tabaqat al-Hanabila* (Damascus: Al-Ma'had al-Faransi bi-Dimashq, 1951), 2:403-04.

9. Ibn 'Abd al-Hadi, "There remain many of his answers and legal judgments of which we have not made mention" (p. 64).

10. Ibid., p. 28.

11. Ibid.

12. Ibid., p. 54. This last work is possibly to be identified with a work mentioned by Ibn Rajab, *Talbis al-Jahmiyya fi Ta'sis Bida'ihim al-Kalamiyya* (Ibn Rajab, *Al-Dhayl*, p. 403).

13. Ibn 'Abd al-Hadi, p. 49.

14. Cf. above, p. 68 n. 5.

15. Shams al-Din Ibn Qayyim al-Jawziyya, *Asma' Mu'allafat Ibn Taymiyya*, JS, 2 vols., p. 19. *Risala fi Ihtijaj al-Jahmiyya wal-Nasara bil-Kalima*, p. 22. *Al-Risala al-Qubrusiyya*, p. 25. *Al-Sarim al-Maslul*, p. 26. *Iqtida' al-Sirat al-Mustaqim*, p. 26. *Risala fi al-Nahy 'an A'yad al-Nasara*, p. 27 *Qa'ida fi al-Kana'is*, p. 28.

16. Ibn Shakir al-Kutubi, 1:76.

17. Ibid.

18. Ibn 'Abd al-Hadi, p. 66.

19. *Bayan al-Jawab al-Sahih*, MS Yeni Cami 732, Istanbul, f. 2316.

20. S. M. Stern, "The Oxford Manuscript of Ibn Taymiyya's Anti-Christian Polemics," *Bulletin of the School of Oriental and African Studies* 20 (1959): 124.

21. The printed edition attempts to minimize the disparity of content and style at 3:275 by adding *wal-Nasara* to the Hyderabad manuscript text. I believe that this

reference, which appears in no manuscript and appears to be a late editor's addition, is the only time that Christians are mentioned by name in the entire work (MS Marsh 299). The impression is that the work was written as a general defense of Muhammad's prophethood.

22. Alexander Nicoll, *Catalogi codicum manuscriptorum orientalium Bibliothecae Bodleianae* (Oxford: E Typographio Academico, 1835), 2:74.

23. Hajji Khalifa, *Kashf al-Zunun 'an Asami al-Kutub wal-Funun* (Istanbul: University Press, 1360/1941), 1:379.

24. Ibid., p. 380.

25. Ibid., pp. 260-61.

26. JS, 1:20, trans. p. 141.

27. Ludovico Marracci, *Alcorani Textus Universus: Praemissus est Prodromus* (Padua: Typographia Seminarii, 1698), 1:5.

28. Nicoll, 2:510.

29. Moritz Steinschneider, *Polemische und apologetische Literatur in arabischer Sprache zwischen Muslimen, Christen, und Juden* (Leipzig: F. A. Brockhaus, 1877), p. 36.

30. C. A. Nallino, "Le fonti arabe manoscritte dell'opera di Ludovico Marracci sul Corano," *Rendiconti R. Accademia dei Lincei*, reprinted in *Raccolta di Scritti*. Citations here are from his collected works. 2:118.

31. Steinschneider, no. 13, p. 33, and no. 16, p. 36.

32. P. de Jong and M. J. de Goeje, *Catalogus codicum orientalium Bibliothecae Academiae Lugduno Batavae* (Leiden: E. J. Brill, 1866), 4:251. "Another [and complete] copy of this work is contained in Cod. Bodl. (Nic. 45)."

33. Brockelmann, 7:123 nn. 72-73.

34. Stern, "Oxford Manuscript," p. 128.

35. Marracci, *Prodromus*, 3:20.

36. Paginated citations in Marracci and corresponding passages in JS are as follows: p. 60 2:358; p. 253 3:292; p. 307 4:51; p. 320 4:71; p. 333 4:92; p. 355 4:129; p. 359 4:133; p. 379 4:165; p. 382 4:172; p. 419 4:227; p. 424 4:236.

37. Passages cited by Marracci up to this point and corresponding passages in JS: 1:5 3:218; 1:12 3: ; 1:15 3:300 "& post multa" 312-13; 1:16 3:406; 1:20 3: ; 1:21 3:318-19; 1:23 3:323; 1:24 3:327; 1:25 3:328; 1:25 3:330; 1:28 4:8; 1:28 3:326-29; 1:29 4:4-5; 1:33 ; 1:44 ; 2:14 ; 2:16 4:161-64; 2:21 ; 2:22 4:129; 2:23-25 ; 2:30 4:172; 2:46 ?:133; 2:49 4:51; 2:50 4:227; 2:51-53 4:237; 2:69 4:71; 2:75 ; 3:17-18 4:236.

38. *Prodromus* 3:17-18 JS 2:309-11.

39. *Prodromus* 3:38-39 JS 2:321.

40. Cf. n. 37 above.

41. Marracci, *Prodromus* 3:32.

42. Nicoll, *Catalogi*, 2:78 and 510.

43. George Makdisi, "Ibn Taymiyya: A Sufi of the Qadiriyya Order," *American Journal of Arabic Studies* 1 (1973): 119.

44. Brockelmann, *Geschichte*, 7:123, no. 72.

45. Abu al-Fadl al-Su'udi (d. 941/1535), *Al-Muntakhab al-Jalil min Takhjil Man Harrafa al-Injil*, ed. and pub. by F. J. van den Ham entitled *Disputatio pro religione Muhammedanorum adversus Christianos* (Leiden: E. J. Brill, 1890), p. 1.

46. Louis Cheikho, *Al-Makhtutat al-'Arabiyya li-Kitabat al-Nasraniyya* (Beirut: Matba'at al-Aba' al-Yasu'iyyin, 1924), p. 12.

47. Stern, "Oxford Manuscript," p. 127.

48. Fritsch, *Islam und Christentum*, p. 25.

49. Stern, pp. 125-26. 3:258 in the first edition corresponds to 3:275 in the second.

50. Cf. above, p. 373 n. 21.

51. For references to his *Radd 'ala al-Nasara*, cf. *Tafsir Surat al-Ikhlas*, p. 43, *Ma'arij al-Wusul*, MRK, 1:201, where he mentions both titles, and *Al-Radd 'ala al-Mantiqiyyin* (Bombay: Al-Matba'a al-Qayyima, 1949), p. 254.

52. Cf. JS 1:141, 149, 167, 176, 177, corresponding to pp. 174, 179, 182, 188, and 189 of the translation.

53. MS March 299, fol.

54. Ibn 'Abd al-Hadi, p. 28.

55. If the two citations by Marracci mentioned above (p. 376 nn. 38 and 39, above) are correct, then one must posit still another form of the work as having existed, where the "Takhjil" formed the central argument, and the passages from JS in which Ibn Taymiyya refutes trinitarian positions and borrows from Al-Hasan ibn Ayyub for his argumentation from the Gospel form either an appendix or a second part of the work. Either this work used by Marracci or that found in the Oxford manuscript would presumably have been the *Takhjil li-Man Baddal al-Turah wal-Injil* catalogued by Hajji Khalifa.

# BIBLIOGRAPHY

## Works by Ibn Taymiyya

"Aqwam Ma Qil fi al-Mashi'a wal-Hikma wal-Qada' wal-Qadar wal-Ta'lil wa-Butlan al-Jabr wal-Ta'til.' In MRM 5:113-70.

"'Arsh al-Rahman." In MRM 4:103-36.

"As'ila fi Usul al-Din." In MFK2 1:444-64.

"Bayan al-Jawab al-Sahih li-Man Baddal Din al-Masih." Istanbul: Süleymaniye Kütüphanesi. MS Yeni 732.

"Bayan al-Jawab al-Sahih li-Man Baddal Din al-Masih." Leiden: Bibliotheek der Rijksuniversiteit. MS Or 338.

"Bughyat al-Murtad." MFK1 5:1-143 (follows 5:296).

*Dar' Ta'arud al-'Aql wal-Naql*. Cairo: Matba'at Dar al-Kutub, 1390/1971.

"Dhikr Allah wa-Du'a'uhu." MF 10:553-68.

"Al-Fana' al-Ladhi Yujad fi Kalam al-Sufiyya Yufassar bi-Thalathat Umur." MF 10:337-44.

"Fasl fi Shurut 'Umar 'ala Ahl al-Dhimma." MF 28: 651-56.

*Al-Fatwa al-Hamawiyya al-Kubra*. Cairo: Al-Matba'a al-Salafiyya, 1387/1967.

"Al-Fatwa fi al-Nusayriyya." Ed. and trans. by S. Guyard in *Le fetwa d'Ibn Taymiyya sur les Nosaires*. Paris: L'Imprimerie Nationale, 1872.

"Fi Ahl al-Suffa wa-Abatil Ba'd al-Mutasawwifa fi-him." MRM 1:25-60.

"Fi-Hukm al-Sama' wal-Raqs." MRK 2:293-330.

"Fi Ibtal Wahdat al-Wujud." MRM 1:61-120.

"Fi Lafz al-Sunna." JR, pp. 47-58.
"Fi Libas al-Futuwwa 'ind al-Sufiyya." MRM 1:147-60.
"Fi al-Mashi'a wal-Hukum wal-Qada' wal-Qadar wal-Ta'lil." MRM 5:113-70.
"Fi al-Shifa'a al-Shar'iyya wal-Tawassul ila Allah bil-A'mal wal-Ashkhas." MRM 1:10-24.
"Fi Tahqiq al-Shukr." JR, pp. 101-18.
"Al-Furqan bayn al-Haqq wal-Batil." In MRK 1:1-172.
*Al-Furqan bayn Awliya' Allah wa-Awliya' al-Shaytan*. Cairo: Matba'at Muhammad 'Ali Subayh, 1378/1958.
"Haqiqat Madhhab al-Ittihadiyyin." MF 2:134-285.
"Al-'Ibadat al-Shar'iyya wal-Farq baynaha wa-bayn al-Bid'iyya." MRM 5:81-104.
*Al-Ihtijaj bil-Qadar*. Cairo: Al-Matba'a al-Salafiyya, 1394/1974.
*Al-Iman*. Cairo: Dar al-Taba'a al-Muhammadiyya, n.d.
*Iqtida' al-Sirat al-Mustaqim wa-Mukhalafat Ashab al-Jahim*. Cairo: Al-Matba'a al-Sharafiyya, 1325/1907.
"Al-Irada wal-Amr." MRK 1:323-90.
*Jawab Ahl al-'Ilm wal-Iman bi-Tahqiq Ma Akhbara bi-hi Rasul al-Rahman min Ann "Qul Huwa Allah Ahad" Ta'dil Thulth al-Quran*. Cairo: Al-Matba'a al-Salafiyya, 1395/1975. Also, MF 17:5-206.
"Al-Jawab an-Man Yaqul Inn Sifat al-Rabb Ta'ala Nisab wa-Idafat wa-Ghayr Dhalika." JR, pp. 153-73.
*Al-Jawab al-Bahir fi Zuwwar al-Maqabir*. Cairo: Al-Matba'a al-Salafiyya, 1395/1975.
"Al-Jawab 'an Su'al 'an al-Hallaj: Hal Kan Siddiq aw Zindiq?" JR, pp. 185-99.
"Al-Jawab al-Sahih li-Man Baddal Din al-Masih." Haidarabad: MS Asafiyya 165/6, 2:1298.
*Al-Jawab al-Sahih li-Man Baddal Din al-Masih*. 4 vols. Cairo: Matba'at al-Nil, 1322/1905.
*Al-Jawab al-Sahih li-Man Baddal Din al-Masih*. 2nd ed. 4 vols. Cairo: Matba'at al-Madani, 1383/1964.
*Kitab al-Nubuwwat*. Cairo: Al-Matba'a al-Salafiyya, 1386/1966.
"Kitab ila Aqaribihi bi-Dimashq." Cited by Muhammad ibn Ahmad ibn 'Abd al-Hadi. *Al-'Uqud al-Durriyya min Manaqib Shaykh al-Islam Ahmad ibn Taymiyya*. Beirut: Dar al-Kutub al-'Ilmiyya, 1356/1938. Pp. 284-85.
"Ma Taqul fi Ha'ula' al-Tatar: Hal Yajuz Qitaluhum?" MF 28:501-44.
"Ma'arij al-Wusul." MRK 1:173-212.
"Madhhab al-Salaf al-Qawim fi Tahqiq Mas'alat Kalam Allah." MRM 3:2-165.
"Mas'ala fi al-Faqr wal-Tasawwuf." MRM 1:218-26.
"Mas'alat al-Kana'is." MF 28:632-46.
*Minhaj al-Sunna al-Nabawiyya*. 2 vols. Cairo: Matba'at al-Madani, 1382/1962.
*Mukhtasar al-Fatawa al-Misriyya*. Cairo: Matba'at al-Sunna al-Muhammadiyya, 1368/1949.
"Munazara li-Dajajilat al-Bata'ihiyya al-Rifa'iyya." MRM 1:121-42.
"Qa'ida Awwaliyya." MF 2:1-133.
*Qa'ida Jalila fi al-Tawassul wal-Wasila*. Cairo: Al-Matba'a al-Salafiyya, 1374/1954.

"Qa'ida Sharifa fi al-Mu'jizat wal-Karamat." MRM 5:2-36.
*Al-Radd 'ala al-Ikhna'i*. Cairo: Al-Matba'a al-Salafiyya, 1346/1928.
*Al-Radd 'ala al-Mantiqiyyin*. Bombay: Al-Matba'a al-Qayyima, 1949."Al-Radd 'ala al-Nusayriyya." In *Majmu' al-Rasa'il*. Cairo: Matba'at al-Husayniyya al-Misriyya, 1323/1905.
"Al-Radd 'ala Nubadh li-Tawa'if min al-Duruz." MF 35:162.
"Raf' al-Malam 'an al-A'imma al-A'lam." RDS, pp. 134-76.
*Ra's al-Hussayn*. Cairo: Matba'at al-Sunna al-Muhammadiyya, 1372/1953.
*Al-Risala al-Qubrusiyya: Khitab li-Sirjwas Malik Qubrus*. Cairo: Al-Matba'a al-Salafiyya, 1394/1974.
*Al-Risala al-Tadmuriyya fi Tahqiq al-Ithbat li-Asma' Allah wa-Sifatihi*. Cairo: Al-Matba'a al-Salafiyya, 1387/1967.
"Risala ila al-Shaykh Nasr al-Manbiji." MRM 1:161-83.
"Risala ila al-Sultan al-Malik al-Nasir." Cited by Muhammad ibn Ahmad ibn 'Abd al-Hadi in *Al-'Uqud al-Durriya min Manaqib Shaykh al-Islam Ahmad ibn Taymiyya*. Beirut: Dar al-Kutub al-'Ilmiyya, 1356/1938. Pp. 182-94.
*Al-Sarim al-Maslul 'ala Shatim al-Rasul*. Beirut: Dar al-Jil, 1395/1975.
"Sharh Kalimat li-'Abd al-Qadir fi Kitab 'Futuh al-Ghayb.'" MF 10:549-68.
"Shurut 'Umar 'ala Ahl al-Kitab." MRM 1:227-29.
"Su'al 'an Ha'ula' al-Qalandariyya." MF 35:163-66.
"Su'al 'an Al-Durziyya wal-Nusayriyya." MF 35:161-62.
"Su'al 'an Al-Mu'izz Ma'add ibn Tamim." MF 35:120-44.
"Su'al 'an al-Rafida al-Imamiyya: Hal Yajib Qitaluhum wa-Yukaffirun bi-I'tiqadihim?" MF 28: 468-501.
"Tafsil al-Ijmal fi-Ma Yajib li-Allah min Sifat al-Kamal." MRM 5:37-80.
*Tafsir Surat al-Ikhlas*. Cairo: Maktabat Ansar al-Sunna al-Muhammadiyya, n.d.
"Tahrim Musharakat Ahl al-Kitab fi A'yadihim." MRM 1:230-31.
"Takhjil Ahl al-Injil wal-Nahj al-Sahih fi al-Radd 'ala Man Baddal Din 'Isa ibn Maryam al-Masih." Oxford: Bodleian Library. MS Marsh 299.
"Tanawwu' al-'Ibadat." RDS, pp. 51-63.
*Al-'Ubudiyya fi al-Islam*. Cairo: Al-Matba'a al-Salafiyya, 1387/1967.
"Al-Wasita bayn al-Haqq wal-Khalq." RDS, pp. 5-20.
"Al-Wasiya al-Kubra." MRK 1:267-322.
"Ziyarat al-Qubur al-Shar'iyya wal-Shirkiyya." RDS, pp. 21-59.

## Works in Arabic and Persian

'Abd al-Qadir al-Jilani. *Kitab al-Ghunya li-Talibi Tariq al-Haqq*. 2 vols. Cairo: Matba'at Muhammad 'Ali Subayh, 1359/1940.
'Abduh, Muhammad Sa'id Isma'il. "Mushkilat al-Jabr wal-Ikhtiyar wa-Ra'y Ibn Taymiyya," in *Usbu' al-Fiqh al-Islami wa-Mahrajan al-Imam Ibn Taymiyya*. Cairo: Al-Majlis al-A'la li-Ri'ayat al-Funun wal-Adab wal-'Ulum al-Ijtima'iyya, 1380/1961. Pp. 759-828.
Abu al-Ma'ali al-'Alavi. *Bayan al-Adyan*. Tehran: Mu'assasayi-Matbu'at-i-Farahani, 1383/1964.
Abu Zahra, Muhammad. *Ibn Taymiyya: Hayatuhu wa-Asruhu wa-Fiqhuhu*. Cairo: Dar al-Fikr al-'Arabi, 1371/1952.

Al-Asadabadi, 'Abd al-Jabbar Abu al-Hasan. *Al-Mughni fi Abwab al-Tawhid wal-'Adl.* 17 vols. Cairo: Al-Dar al-Misriyya lil-Ta'lif wal-Tarjama, 1965.

_____. *Tathbit Dala'il Nubuwwat Muhammad Rasul Allah.* Beirut: Dar al-Turath al-'Arabi, n.d.

Al-'Asali, Khalid. *Jahm ibn Safwan: Makanatuhu fi al-Fikr al-Islami.* Baghdad: Matba'at al-Irshad, 1384.

Al-Ash'ari, Abu al-Hasan. *Al-Ibana 'an Usul al-Diyana.* Cairo: Matba'at al-Muniriyya, 1348/1929.

_____. *Maqalat al-Islamiyyin.* 2 vols. Wiesbaden: Franz Steiner Verlag, 1963.

_____. "Risala fi Istihsan al-Khawd fi 'Ilm al-Kalam." Ed. and trans. by R. J. McCarthy in *The Theology of Al-Ash'ari.* Beirut: Imprimerie Catholique, 1953.

Al-'Asqalani, Ibn Hajar. *Al-Durar al-Kamina fi A'yan al-Mi'a al-Thamina.* 3 vols. Cairo: Dar al-Kutub al-Haditha, 1385/1966.

_____. *Lisan al-Mizan.* 6 vols. Haidarabad: Matba'at Majlis Da'irat al-Ma'arif al-Nizamiyya, 1331/1913.

_____. *Tahdhib al-Tahdhib.* 12 vols. Beirut: Dar Sadir, 1326/1908.

Badawi, 'Abd al-Rahman. *Aflutin 'ind al-'Arab.* Cairo: Dar al-Nahda al-'Arabiyya, 1385/1966.

_____. *Min Ta'rikh al-Ilhad fi al-Islam.* Cairo: Maktabat al-Nahda al-Misriyya, 1363/1945.

Al-Baghdadi, 'Abd al-Qahir ibn Tahir. *Al-Farq bayn al-Firaq.* Cairo: Matba'at Muhammad 'Ali Subayh, 1383/1964.

Al-Baghdadi, Al-Khatib. *Ta'rikh Baghdad.* 14 vols. Beirut: Dar al-Kitab al-'Arabi, 1385/1966.

Al-Bakri, Abu 'Ubayd 'Abd Allah. *Mu'jam Ma Ista'jam.* Ed. by F. Wustenfeld. 4 vols. Göttingen: Deuerlich'sche Buchhandlung, 1877.

Al-Bakri, Muhammad Hamdi. "Ba'd Muhawarat bayn al-Nasraniyya wal-Islam wa-Mulahazat 'alayha." Magisterial thesis, Cairo University, 1934.

Al-Baladhuri, Abu al-'Abbas. *Futuh al-Buldan.* Cairo: Dar al-Nashr al-Jama'iyyin, 1377/1957.

Al-Baqillani, Abu Bakr ibn al-Tayyib. *Al-Tamhid fi al-Radd 'ala al-Mulhida al-Mu'attila wal-Rafida wal-Khawarij wal-Mu'tazila.* Cairo: Dar al-Fikr al-'Arabi, 1366/1948.

Al-Baytar, Muhammad Bahjat. "'Alawa Thaniyya fi Ikhtiyarat Shaykh al-Islam Ibn Taymiyya." In *Ra's al-Hussayn,* by Ibn Taymiyya. Cairo: Matba'at al-Sunna al-Muhammadiyya, 1372/1953. Pp. 115-23.

Al-Biruni, Abu al-Rayhan al-Khwarizmi. *Al-Athar al-Baqiya 'an al-Qurun al-Khaliya.* Ed. by E. Sachau. Leipzig: F. A. Brockhaus, 1878.

Bulus al-Rahib. "Qawl Yadull 'ala al-Firaq al-Muta'arafa min al-Nasara." Ed. and trans. by Paul Khoury in *Paul d'Antioche.* Beirut: Imprimerie Catholique, 1964. Pp. 84-97.

_____. "Risala ila Ahad al-Muslimin." Ed. and trans. by Paul Khoury in *Paul d'Antioche.* Beirut: Imprimerie Catholique, 1964. Pp. 59-83.

Al-Daylami, Muhammad ibn al-Hasan. "Bayan Madhhab al-Batiniyya wa-Butlanuhu." Quoted in *Kitab Qawa'id 'Aqa'id Al Muhammad.* Ed. by R. Strothman. Istanbul: Jami'at al-Mustashriqin al-Almaniyya, 1938.

Al-Dhahabi, Shams al-Din Abu 'Abd Allah. *Tadhkirat al-Huffaz*. 4 vols. Haidarabad: Matba'at Majlis Da'irat al-Ma'arif al-Nizamiyya, 1334/1915.
Al-Dimashqi, Muhammad ibn Nasir al-Din. *Al-Radd al-Wafir 'ala Man Za'am Ann Man Samma Ibn Taymiyya Shaykh al-Islam Kafir*. Beirut: Al-Maktab al-Islami, 1393/1972.
Al-Farabi, Abu al-Nasr. *Kitab Ara' Ahl al-Madina al-Fadila*. Beirut: Al-Maktaba al-Kathuliqiyya, 1949.
Fathi 'Uthman. *Ma' al-Masih fi al-Anajil al-Arba'a*. Cairo: Al-Dar al-Qawmiyya lil-Tiba'a wal-Nashr, 1966.
Al-Fayani, Ibrahim ibn Ahmad. *Nahiya min Hayat Shaykh al-Islam Ibn Taymiyya*. Cairo: Dar al-Maktaba al-Salafiyya, 1395/1975.
Hafiz, 'Abd al-Salam Hashim. *Al-Imam Ibn Taymiyya*. Cairo: Maktabat al-Halabi, 1389/1969.
Hajji Khalifa (Katib Celebi). *Kashf al-Zunun 'an Asami al-Kutub wal-Funun*. 2 vols. Istanbul: University Press, 1360/1941.
Al-Hasan ibn Ayyub. "Risala ila 'Ali ibn Ayyub." In Ibn Taymiyya, *Al-Jawab al-Sahih li-Man Baddal Din al-Masih*. Cairo: Matba'at al-Nil, 1322/1905. 2:312-63, 3:2-3.
Al-Hasani, Abu al-Hasan al-Nadwi. *Al-Hafiz Ahmad ibn Taymiyya*. Translated from Urdu into Arabic by Sa'id al-A'zami al-Nadwi. Al-Kuwait: Dar al-Qalam, 1395/1975.
Ibn 'Abd al-Hadi, Muhammad ibn Ahmad. *Al-'Uqud al-Durriya min Manaqib Shaykh al-Islam Ahmad ibn Taymiyya*. Beirut: Dar al-Kutub al-'Ilmiyya, 1356/1938.
Ibn Abi Talib, Muhammad. "Risala li-Ahl Jazirat Qubrus." Utrecht: Bibliotheek der Rijksuniversiteit te Utrecht. MS 1449.
Ibn Abi Ya'la, Abu al-Hussayn. *Tabaqat al-Hanabila*. 2 vols. Cairo: Matba'at al-Sunna al-Muhammadiyya, 1371/1952.
Ibn al-'Arabi, Al-Qadi Abu Bakr. *Al-'Awasim min al-Qawasim*. Cairo: Al-Matba'a al-Salafiyya, 1396/1976.
Ibn al-Athir, 'Izz al-Din. *Al-Kamil fi al-Ta'rikh*. 14 vols. Dar Sadir, 1965. Reprinted from the edition of C. J. Tornberg. Leiden: E. J. Brill, 1867.
Ibn al-'Awwam, Yahya ibn Muhammad. *Kitab al-Filaha*. Trans. by J.-J. Clement-Mullet. 2 vols. Paris: Librairie A. Franck, 1866.
Ibn al-Farra', Abu Ya'la ibn al-Husayn. *Al-Mu'tamad fi Usul al-Din*. Beirut: Dar al-Mashriq, 1974.
Ibn al-Nadim, Muhammad ibn Ishaq. *Al-Fihrist*. 2 vols. Ed. by Bayard Dodge. New York: Columbia University Press, 1970.
Ibn 'Asakir, Abu al-Qasim. *Tabyin Kadhib al-Muftari fi-Ma Nusiba ila al-Imam Abi al-Hasan al-Ash'ari*. Damascus: Al-Matba'a al-Tawfiqiyya, 1347/1928.
Ibn Batta al-'Ukbari. "Kitab al-Sharh wal-Ibana 'ala Usul al-Sunna wal-Diyana." Ed. and trans. by Henri Laoust in *La profession de foi d'Ibn Batta*. Damascus: Institut Français de Damas, 1958.
Ibn al-Farid, Sharaf al-Din Abu Hafs. Ed. and trans. by A. J. Arberry in *The Mystical Poems of Ibn al-Farid*. Dublin: Emery Walker, 1956.
Ibn Hanbal, Ahmad. "Al-Radd 'ala al-Zanadiqa wal-Jahmiyya." Trans. by M. Seale in *Muslim Theology*. London: Luzac, 1964. Pp. 96-125.

Ibn Hazm, Abu Muhammad. *Kitab al-Fisal fi al-Milal wal-Ahwa' wal-Nihal.* 5 vols. Baghdad: Maktabat al-Muthanna, n.d.

Ibn Ishaq, Muhammad. *Sirat Rasul Allah.* Trans. by A. Guillaume as *The Life of Muhammad: A Translation of Ishaq's Sirat Rasul Allah.* Lahore: Oxford University Press, 1967.

Ibn Kammuna, Sa'd ibn Mansur. *Tanqih al-Abhath lil-Milal al-Thalath.* Ed. by M. Perlemann. Berkeley: University of California Press, 1967.

Ibn Kathir, 'Imad al-Din ibn 'Umar. *Al-Bidaya wal-Nihaya fi al-Ta'rikh.* Cairo: Matba'at al-Sa'ada, 1358/1939.

———. *Kitab al-Nihaya aw al-Fitan wal-Malahim.* 2 vols. Cairo: Dar al-Kutub al-Haditha, 1389/1969.

Ibn Khaldun. *Al-Muqaddima.* Ed. and trans. by Franz Rosenthal as *The Muqaddimah.* 3 vols. New York: Pantheon Books, 1958.

Ibn Khallikan, Abu al-'Abbas. *Wifayat al-A'yan.* 6 vols. Cairo: Maktabat al-Nahda al-Misriyya, 1367/1948.

Ibn Qayyim, al-Jawziyya. *Asma' Mu'allafat Ibn Taymiyya.* Damascus: Al-Majma' al-'Ilmi al-'Arabi bi Dimashq, 1372/1953.

———. "Kitab Hidaya al-Hayari fi Ajwibat al-Yahud wal-Nasara." In margin of *Al-Fariq bayn al-Makhluq wal-Khaliq* by 'Abd al-Rahman Bachcheji Zadeh. Cairo: Matba'at al-Mawsu'at, 1904.

Ibn Qudama, Muwaffaq al-Din. "Tahrim al-Nazar fi Kutub Ahl al-Kalam." Ed. and trans. by George Makdisi in *Censure of Speculative Theology.* London: Luzac, 1962.

Ibn Qutayba, Abu Muhammad 'Abd Allah ibn Muslim. *Kitab al-Ma'arif.* Cairo: Matba'at Dar al-Kutub, 1960.

———. *Kitab Ta'wil Mukhtalif al-Hadith.* Cairo: Matba'at Kurdistan al-'Ilmiyya, 1326/1925.

———. *'Uyun al-Akhbar.* 4 vols. Cairo: Al-Mu'assasa al-Misriyya al-'Amma lil-Ta'lif wal-Tiba'a wal-Nashr, 1964.

Ibn Rajab, Zayn al-Din. *Al-Dhayl 'ala Tabaqat al-Hanabila.* 2 vols. Damascus: Al-Ma'had al-Faransi bi-Dimashq, 1951.

Ibn Rushd, Muhammad ibn Ahmad. *Bidayat al-Mujtahid wa Nihayat al-Muqtasid.* Cairo: Maktabat al-Kulliyyat al-Azhariyya, 1386/1966.

———. *Tahafut al-Tahafut.* Translated by Simon van den Bergh. 2 vols. Oxford: University Press, 1954.

Ibn Sab'in, Abu Muhammad 'Abd al-Haqq. *Al-Kalam 'ala al-Masa'il al-Siqiliyya.* Ed. by M. Sharaf al-Din Yaltqaya. Beirut: Al-Matba'a al-Kathuliqiyya, 1941.

Ibn Sa'd. *Kitab al-Tabaqat al-Kabir.* Ed. by E. Sachau. Leiden: E. J. Brill, 1904.

Ibn Shakir al-Kutubi. *Fawat al-Wafayat.* 4 vols. Beirut: Dar al-Thaqafa, 1973.

Al-'Iraqi, Abu Muhammad 'Uthman. "Dhikr al-Firaq al-Mutabadi'a wa-Ahl al-Ahwa' wa-Madhahibihim." Alexandria: Al-Maktaba al-Baladiyya. MS 6420.

———. "Al-Firaq al-Muftariqa bayn Ahl al-Zaygh wal-Zandaqa." Ed. by Yasar Kutluay in *Sapiklara Dinsizlerin Cesitli Mezhepleri.* Ankara: Nur Matbaasi, 1961.

Al-Isfara'ini, Abu al-Muzaffar ibn Tahir. *Tabsir fi al-Din.* Cairo: Maktabat al-Anwar, 1940.

Isma'il ibn Muhammad al-Babani. *Hadiyat al-'Arifin: Asma' al-Mu'allifin wa-Athar al-Musannifin*. 2 vols. Istanbul: Matba'at Wikalat al-Ma'arif, 1951.

———. *'Idah al-Maknun fi al-Dhayl 'ala Kashf al-Zunun*. 2 vols. Istanbul: Matba'at Wikalat al-Ma'arif, 1364-66/1945-47.

Al-Istanbuli, Muhammad Mahdi. *Ibn Taymiyya: Batal al-Islah al-Islami*. Damascus: Dar al-Hayah, n.d.

'Iyad ibn Musa. *Al-Shifa' bi-Ta'rif Huquq al-Mustafa*. 2 vols. Cairo: Dar al-Kutub al-'Arabiyya al-Kubra, 1329/1911.

Al-Jahiz, Abu 'Uthman 'Amr ibn Bahr. *Kitab al-Hayawan*. 4 vols. Cairo: Maktabat al-Halabi, 1356-64/1938-45.

———. "Al-Radd 'ala al-Nasara." In *Thalath Rasa'il*. Cairo: Al-Matba'a al-Salafiyya, 1382/1963.

Al-Jalayand, Muhammad al-Hay'a. *Al-Imam Ibn Taymiyya: Mawqifa min Qadiyat al-Ta'wil*. Cairo: Al-Ha'ya al-'Amma li-Shu'un al-Matabi' al-Amiriyya, 1393/1973.

Al-Jasir, Hamad. "Mawqi' Suq 'Ukaz." *Majallat al-Majma' al-'Ilmi al-'Arabi bi-Dimashq* 26 (1370/1951): 377-98.

Al-Kalbi, Hisham ibn Sa'ib. *Kitab al-Asnam*. Cairo: Dar al-Qawmiyya lil-Tiba'a wal-Nashr, 1384/1965.

Al-Kharraz, Abu Sa'id. "Kitab al-Sidq." Ed. and trans. by A. J. Arberry in *The Book of Truthfulness*. London: Oxford University Press, 1937.

Al-Khayyat, Abu al-Hussayn ibn Muhammad. *Kitab al-Intisar*. Ed. by S. Nyberg. Beirut: Al-Matba'a al-Kathuliqiyya, 1957.

Al-Kurdi, Faraj Allah, ed. *Al-Majmu' al-Mustamal 'ala al-Durar al-Atiyya*. Cairo: Matba'at Kurdistan al-'Ilmiyya, 1329/1911.

Al-Malati, Abu al-Husayn Muhammad ibn Ahmad. *Al-Tanbih wal-Radd 'ala Ahl al-Ahwa' wal-Bida'*. Istanbul: Matba'at al-Dawla, 1936.

Al-Mar'i ibn Yusuf al-Karmi. "Al-Kawakib al-Durriyya fi Manaqib al-Imam Ibn Taymiyya." In *Majmu' al-Mushtamal 'ala al-Durar al-Atiyya*. Ed. by Faraj Allah al-Kurdi. Cairo: Matba'at Kurdistan al-'Ilmiyya, 1329/1911.

Al-Maqrizi, Taqi al-Din Ahmad. *Kitab al-Suluk li-Ma'rifat Duwal al-Muluk*. 2 vols. in 3. Cairo: Matba'at Lajnat al-Ta'lif wal-Tarjama wal-Nashr, 1941.

Al-Maraghi, 'Abd al-'Aziz. *Ibn Taymiyya*. Cairo: Matba'at al-Halabi, n.d.

Al-Mas'udi, Abu 'Ali ibn al-Hussayn. *Muruj al-Dhahab wa-Ma'adin al-Jawhar*. 4 vols. Beirut: Dar al-Andalus, 1965-66.

Al-Maturidi, Abu Mansur Muhammad. *Kitab al-Tawhid*. Beirut: Dar al-Mashriq, 1970.

Musa, Muhammad Yusuf. *Ibn Taymiyya*. Cairo: Al-Mu'assasa al-Misriyya al-'Ammiyya, 1381/1962.

Muhaqqiq (Mohaghegh), Mahdi. *Faylasuf-i-Rayy*. Tehran: Offset Press, 1352/1974.

Al-Qarafi, Shihab al-Din Ahmad ibn Idris. "Al-Ajwiba al-Fakhira 'an al-As'ila al-Fajira." In margin of *Kitab al-Fariq bayn al-Makhluq wal-Khaliq* by 'Abd al-Rahman Bachche-ji Zadeh. Cairo: Matba'at al-Mawsu'at, 1322/1904.

Al-Qifti, Jamal al-Din. *Ta'rikh al-Hukama'*. Baghdad: Maktabat al-Muthanna, n.d.

Al-Qirqisani, Ya'qub. *Kitab al-Anwar wal-Maraqib*. Ed. by Leon Nemoy.

5 vols. New York: Alexander Kohut Memorial Foundation, 1939.

Al-Razi, Fakhr al-Din. *I'tiqadat Firaq al-Muslimin wal-Mushrikin*. Cairo: Maktabat al-Nahda al-Misriyya, 1356/1938.

———. *Mafatih al-Ghayb*. 8 vols. Cairo: Al-Matba'a al-'Amira al-Sarafiyya, 1324/1897.

Sa'id ibn Bitriq (Eutychius). *Kitab al-Burhan*. 2 vols. Ed. by Pierre Cachia. Louvain: Secretariat du Corpus Scriptorum Christianorum Orientalium, 1960.

———. *Nazm al-Jawhar*. 2 vols. Ed. by L. Shaykhu (Cheikho) as *Annales Eutychii Patriarchae Alexandrini*. Louvain: Secretariat du Corpus Scriptorum Christianorum Orientalium, 1962.

Al-Saksaki, 'Abbas ibn Mansur al-Burayhi. *Al-Burhan fi Ma'rifat 'Aqa'id Ahl al-Adyan*. Cairo: MS Dar al-Kutub. Microfilm Tawhid 49 in Arab League.

Al-Shahrastani, 'Abd al-Karim. *Nihayat al-Iqdam fi 'Ilm al-Kalam*. Baghdad: Maktabat al-Muthanna, n.d.

Shaykhu (Cheikho), Louis. "Ibn Taymiyya wal-Wahabiyyun," *Al-Mashriq* 22 (1924): 905-14.

———. "Majalis Ilya Mutran Nasibin," *Al-Mashriq* 20 (1922): 35-44, 112-22, 267-72, 366-77, 425-34.

———. *Kitab al-Makhtutat al-'Arabiyya li-Katabat al-Nasraniyya*. Beirut: Matba'at al-Aba' al-Yasu'iyyin, 1924.

Al-Sijistani, Abu Sulayman Tahir. "Kalam fi Mabadi' al-Mawjudat." Ed. and trans. by G. Troupeau in "Un traité sur les principes des etres attribué a Abu Sulayman al-Sijistani," *Pensamiento* 25 (1969): 259-70.

Al-Subki, Taj al-Din. *Tabaqat al-Shafi'iyya al-Kubra*. 9 vols. Cairo: Maktabat al-Halabi, 1384/1965.

Al-Suyuti, Jalal al-Din. *Tabaqat al-Huffaz*. Cairo: Maktabat al-Wahba, 1393/1973.

Al-Tabari, Muhammad ibn Jarir Abu Ja'far. *Tafsir al-Tabari*. 16 vols. Cairo: Dar al-Ma'arif, 1374/1955.

———. *Ta'rikh al-Rusul wal-Muluk*. Ed. by M. J. de Goeje. 16 vols. Leiden: E. J. Brill, 1964.

Al-Tahanawi, Muhammad 'Ali al-Faruqi. *Kashshaf Istilahat al-Funun*. 2 vols. Calcutta: W. N. Lees, 1862.

Al-Tha'labi, Ibn Ishaq Ahmad. *Qisas al-Anbiya'*. Cairo: Maktabat al-Kulliyat al-Azhariyya, n.d.

Uways, Mansur Muhammad. *Ibn Taymiyya Laysa Salafiyyan*. Beirut: Dar al-Nahda al-'Arabiyya, 1970.

Yahya ibn 'Adi. "Collected Works." Ed. and trans. by A. Perier in *Petits traites apologetiques de Yahya ibn 'Adi*. Paris: Paul Guethner, 1920.

Yaqut ibn 'Abd Allah. *Irshad al-Arib ila Ma'rifat al-Adib*. Ed. by D. S. Margoliouth. 7 vols. Leiden: E. J. Brill, 1907-27.

———. *Marasid al-Ittila' 'ala Asma' al-Amkina wal-Biqa'*. 6 vols. Ed. by T. G. J. Juynboll as *Lexicon Graphicum*. Leiden: E. J. Brill, 1853.

Yusuf al-Basir. "Kitab al-Muhtawi." Ed. and trans. by G. Vajda as *La démonstration de l'unité divine d'après Yusuf al-Basir: Studies in Mysticism and Religion Presented to G. G. Scholem*. Jerusalem: Magnes Press, 1967.

Zakariyya 'Ali Yusuf, ed. *Rasa'il Diniyya Salafiyya.* Cairo: Maktabat al-Mutanabbi, n.d.

## Works in European Languages

'Abd al-Karim al-Khatib. "Christ in the Qur'an, the Taurat, and the Injil," *Muslim World* 61 (1971): 90-101.

Abel, Armand. "Le chapitre sur les Christianisme dans le 'Tamhid' d'al-Baqillani," in *Études d'Orientalisme Dédiees a la Memoire de Levi-Provençal.* Paris: G.-P. Maisonneuve et Larose, 1962. Pp. 1-11.

———. "Het Geschrift ter Weerlegging van de Drie Christelijke Secten door Abu 'Isa al-Warrak," in *Verslag van het Achtste Congres van het Oosterse Genootschap in Nederland.* Leiden: E. J. Brill, 1935. Pp. 27-31.

———. "La polemique damascenienne et son influence sur les origines de la theologie Musulmane," in *L'Elaboration de l'Islam.* Paris: Presses de l'Université de France, 1961. Pp. 61-85.

Allard, Michel. "Les Chrétiens à Baghdad," *Arabica* 9 (1962): 375-88.

———. *Le problème des attributs divins.* Beirut: Imprimerie Catholique, 1965.

Anawati, G. "Nicholas de Cues et le problème de l'Islam," in *Nicolo Cusano agli inizi del mondo moderno.* Florence: Sansoni, 1970. Pp. 141-73.

Andrae, Tor. *Mohammed.* New York: Harper & Row, 1960.

Arberry, A. J. *The Mystical Poems of Ibn al-Farid.* Dublin: Emery Walker, 1956.

Arnaldez, Roger. *Grammaire et théologie chez Ibn Hazm de Cordoue.* Paris: Librairie Philosophique J. Vrin, 1956.

Asin Palacios, Miguel. *El justo medio en la creencia: Compendio de teológica dogmática de Algazel.* Madrid: Instituto de Valencia de Don Juan, 1929.

———. "Logia et Agrapha Domini Jesu apud Moslemicos Scriptores," *Patrologia Orientalia* 13 (1913): 331-431; 19 (1919): 529-624.

Becker, C. H. "Christliche Polemik und islamische Dogmenbildung," *Zeitschrift für Assyriologie und Verwandte Gebiete* 12 (1926): 175-95.

Bell, Joseph Norment. "The Hanbalite Teaching on Love." Ph.D. diss., Princeton University, 1971.

———. *Love Theory in Later Hanbalite Islam.* Albany: SUNY Press, 1979.

Bignami-Odier, J. and G. Levi della Vida. "Une version latine de l'Apocalypse syro-arabe de Serge-Bahira," *Mélanges d'Archéologie et d'Histoire* 62 (1950): 125-48.

Brockelmann, Carl. "Ibn Gauzi's 'Kitab al-Wafa fi Fada'il al-Mustafa,'" in *Beitrage zur Assyriologie und Semitischen Sprachwissenschaft.* Leipzig: J. C. Hinrich's, 1898. Pp. 46-55.

———. *History of the Islamic Peoples.* Trans. by J. Carmichael and M. Perlmann. New York: Capricorn Books, 1973.

———. "Muhammedanische Weissagungen im Alten Testament," *Zeitschrift für die alttestamentliche Wissenschaft* 15 (1895): 138-42.

Buffat, Louis. "Lettre de Paul Évêque de Saida a un musulman de ses amis demeurant à Saida," *Revue de l'Orient Chrétien* 8 (1903): 388-425.

Cabanelas, Dario. "Federico II de Sicilia e Ibn Sab'in de Murcia: Las 'Cuestiones Sicilianas,'" *Miscelánea de Estudios Arabes y Hebraicos* 4 (1955): 31-64.

Canard, M. "Notes sur les Arméniens en Egypte," *Annales de l'Institut d'Études Orientales* 13 (1955): 143-57.

———. "Un vizier chrétien a l'époque fatimite," *Annales de l'Institut d'Études Orientales* 12 (1954): 84-113.

Caspar, Robert. "Bibliographie du dialogue Islamo-Chrétien," *Islamochristiana* 1 (1975): 125-76; 2 (1976): 187-249.

———. "Le salut des non-musulmans d'après Ghazali," *Revue de l'Institut des Belles Lettres Arabes à Tunis* 31 (1968): 301-13.

Chwolson, D. A. *Die Ssabier und der Ssabismus*. 2 vols. St. Petersburg: Buchdruckerei der Kaiserlichen Akademie der Wissenschaften, 1856.

Copleston, Frederick. *A History of Philosophy*. 8 vols. New York: Doubleday, 1950.

Daniel, Norman. *Islam and the West*. Edinburgh: University Press, 1960.

de Jong, P., and M. J. de Goeje. *Catalogus Codicum Orientalium Bibliothecae Academiae Lugduno Batavae*. 6 vols. Leiden: E. J. Brill, 1851-77.

de Strycker, Emile. *La forme la plus ancienne du Proto-evangile de Jacques*. Brussels: Société des Bollandistes, 1961.

Di Matteo, Ignazio. *La divinità di Cristo e la dottrina della Trinità in Maometto e nei polemisti musulmani*. Rome: Pontificio Instituto Biblico, 1938.

———. *Ibn Taymiyyah o riassunto della sua opera*. Palermo: Tipografia Domenico Vena, 1912. Microfilm Biblioteca Apostolica Vaticana, R. G. Oriente 5, 1316.

———. "Il-Tahrif—Od adulterazione della Bibbia secondo i Musulmani," *Estratto dal Bessarione* 26 (1922): 64-111, 223-260.

Dölger, Franz Joseph. *Sol Salutis: Gebet und Gesang im christlichen Altertum*. Münster: Der Aschendorffschen Verlagsbuchhandlung, 1925.

*Encyclopaedia Judaica*. S.v. "Abu Issa al-Isfahani," by J. N. Simchoni.

———. "Josef ben Abraham Ha-Kohen Ha-Roe," by I. Markon.

*Encyclopaedia of Islam*, 1st ed. (EI1). S.v. "Khazar," by W. Berthold.

———. "Lawh," by A. J. Wensinck.

———. "Musailima," by F. Buhl.

———. "Nahw," by Ilse Lichtenstater.

———. "Al-Sha'bi," by F. Krenkow.

———. "Thabit b. Kurra," by J. Ruska.

———. "Tulayha," by V. Vacca.

———. "Umm al-Kitab," by J. Horovitz.

———. "Wahb b. Muhabbih," by J. Horovitz.

*Encyclopaedia of Islam*, 2d ed. (EI2). S.v. "Abu Sakhr al-Hudhali," by R. Blachere.

———. "'Adi b. Musafir," by A. S. Tritton.

———. "Ahmad b. Habit," by Charles Pellat.

______. "Ahmad," by Joseph Schacht.
______. "Al-Aswad b. Ka'b al-'Ansi," by W. Montgomery Watt.
______. "Babak," by D. Sourdel.
______. "Al-Djarh wal-Ta'dil," by J. Robson.
______. "Al-Djuwaini," by Louis Gardet.
______. "Fatra," by Charles Pellat.
______. "Hadith," by J. Robson.
______. "Hanabila," by Henri Laoust.
______. "Ibn al-Qasim," by Joseph Schacht.
______. "Ibn Dirham," by George Vajda.
______. "Ibn Taymiyya," by Henri Laoust.
______. "'Ilm al-Hay'a," by David Pingree.
______. "'Isa," by G. Anawati.

Faris, Nabih A. and H. W. Glidden. "The Development of the Meaning of Qur'anic Hanif," *Journal of the Palestine Oriental Society* 14 (1939-40): 1-13.

Frank, Richard M. "The Neoplatonism of Ǧahm ibn Safwan," *Museon* 78 (1965): 395-424.

Fritsch, Erdmann. *Islam und Christentum im Mittelalter*. Breslau: Verlag Müller & Seiffert, 1930.

Gabrielli, Francesco. *Il Califatto di Hisham*. Alexandria: Société de Publications Egyptiennes, 1933.

Goldziher, Ignaz. "'Arab and 'Ajam," in *Muslim Studies*. 2 vols. London: George Allen & Unwin, 1967-74. 1: 98-136.

______. "Le denombrement des sectes Mahomentanes," *Revue de l'histoire de la religion* 26 (1892): 129-37.

______. "Zur Geschichte der hanbalischen Bewegungen," *Zeitschrift der deutschen morgenlandischen Gesellschaft* 62 (1908): 1-28.

Graf, Georg. *Geschichte der christlichen arabischen Literatur*. 5 vols. Rome: Biblioteca Apostolica Vaticana, 1944-53.

______. "Philosophische-theologische Schriften des Paulus al-Rahib, Bischofs von Sidon," *Jahrbuch für Philosophie und spekulative Theologie* 20 (1906): 55-80, 160-79.

Guidi, Ignazio. "Le traduzioni degli Evangeli in arabo e in etiopico," *Atti della R. Accademia dei Lincei* 4, no. 4 (1888): 5-37.

Guyard, S. *Le fetwa d'Ibn Taymiyya sur les Nosaires*. Paris: Imprimerie National, 1872.

Haq, Sirajul. "Ibn Taymiyya's Conception of Analogy and Consensus," *Islamic Culture* 17 (1943): 77-87.

Hennecke, Edgar, and Wilhelm Schneemelcher. *Neutestamentliche Apokryphen*. 2 vols. Tubingen: J. C. B. Mohr, 1959.

Hill, George. *A History of Cyprus*. 4 vols. Cambridge: University Press, 1948.

Hodgson, Marshall G. S. *The Venture of Islam*. 3 vols. Chicago: University of Chicago Press, 1974.

Honigmann, E. *Die sieben Klimata und die poleis episemoi*. Heidelberg: Carl Winter's Universitätsbuchhandlung, 1929.

Horten, Max. "Paulus, Bischof von Sidon: Einige seiner philosophischen

Abhandlungen," *Philosophisches Jahrbuch* 19 (1906): 144-66.
Jabre, Farid. *La Notion de la ma'rifa chez Ghazali*. Beirut: Imprimerie Catholique, 1958.
Jenkinson, E. J. "The Moslem Anti-Christ Legend," *Muslim World* 20 (1930): 50-55.
Kerr, Malcolm H. *Islamic Reform: The Political and Legal Theories of Muhammad 'Abduh and Rashid Rida*. Berkeley: University of California Press, 1966.
Khoury, Paul. *Paul d'Antioche*. Beirut: Imprimerie Catholique, 1964.
Laoust, Henri. "La bibliographie d'Ibn Taymiyya d'après Ibn Kathir," *Bulletin d'Études Orientales* 9 (1942-45): 115-62.
———. "La critique du sunnisme dans la doctrine d'al-Hilli," *Revue des Études Islamiques* (1966): 35-60.
———. *Contribution a une étude de la méthodologie canonique de Taki-dDin Ahmad b. Taymiya*. Cairo: Imprimerie de l'Institut Français d'Archéologie Orientale, 1939.
———. *Essai sur les doctrines sociales et politiques de Taki-d-Din Ahmad b. Taymiyya*. Cairo: Imprimerie de l'Institut Français d'Archéologie Orientale, 1939.
———. "Le Hanbalisme sous les mamlouks bahrides," *Revue des Études Islamiques* 28 (1960): 1-71.
———. *La profession de foi d'Ibn Batta*. Damascus: Institut Français de Damas, 1958.
———. "Quelques opinions sur la théodicée d'Ibn Taymiyya," in *Melanges Maspero*. Cairo: Imprimerie de l'Institut Français d'Archéologie Orientale, 1940. Pp. 431-38.
———. "Remarques sur les expeditions du Kasrawan sous les premièrs Mamluks," *Bulletin de Musée de Beyrouth* 4 (1942): 93-114.
Lazarus-Yafeh, Havah. "Is There a Concept of Redemption in Islam?" *Types of Redemption*. Ed. by R. I. Z. Werblowsky and C. J. Bleeker. Leiden: E. J. Brill, 1970. Pp. 168-80.
Lewis, Bernard. "Kamal al-Din's Biography of Rashid al-Din Sinan," *Arabica* 13 (1966): 225-67.
Little, Donald P. "Did Ibn Taymiyya Have a Screw Loose?" *Studia Islamica* 41 (1975): 93-111.
———. "The Historical and Historiographical Significance of the Detention of Ibn Taymiyya," *International Journal of Middle East Studies* 4 (1973): 311-27.
Madelung, Wilferd. "Fatimiden und Bahrainqarmaten," *Der Islam* 34 (1958): 34-88.
———. *Der Imam al-Qasim ibn Ibrahim und die Glaubenslehre der Zaiditen*. Berlin: Walter de Gruyter & Co., 1965.
———. "The Origins of the Controversy Concerning the Creation of the Quran," *Orientalia Hispanica* 1, pt. 1: 504-25.
———. "As-Sahrastanis Streitschrift gegen Avicenna und ihre Widerlegung durch Nasir al-Din al-Tusi," *Akten des VII Kongresses für Arabistik und Islamwissenschaft*. Göttingen: Vanderhoeck and Ruprecht, 1971.
Makdisi, George. "Ash'ari and the Ash'arites in Islamic Religious History," *Studia Islamica* 17 (1955): 37-80; 18 (1956): 19-39.

———. *Censure of Speculative Theology: An Edition and Translation of Ibn Qudama's Tahrim al-Nazar fi Kutub Ahl al-Kalam*. London: Luzac, 1962.

———. "The Hanbali School and Sufism," *Humaniora Islamica* 2 (1974): 61-72.

———. *Ibn 'Aqil et la résurgence de l'Islam traditionaliste au XIe siècle*. Damascus: Institut Français de Damas, 1963.

———. "Ibn Taymiyya: A Sufi of the Qadiriyya Order," *American Journal of Arabic Studies* 1 (1973): 118-29.

———. "L'Isnad initiatique sufi de Muwaffaq al-Din ibn Qudama," in *Louis Massignon*. Paris: Éditions de l'Herne, 1970. Pp. 88-96.

———. "Nouveaux details sur l'affaire d'Ibn 'Aqil," *Mélanges Louis Massignon*. Damascus: Institut Français de Damas, 1956-57. 3: 91-126.

———. "The Tanbih of Ibn Taymiyya on Dialectic." *Medieval and Middle Eastern Studies in Honor of Aziz Suryal Atiya*. Leiden: E. J. Brill, 1972. Pp. 285-94.

Marmura, Michael. "Some Aspects of Avicenna's Theory of God's Knowledge of Particulars," *Journal of the American Oriental Society* 82, no. 3 (1962): 299-312.

Marracci, Luigi. *Fides Islamitica, i.e., Al-Coranus ex Idiomate Arabico Praemissa Brevi Introductione et Totius Religionis Mohammedicae Synopsi*. Introduction by Christianus Reineccius. Leipzig: Sumptibus Lanckisianis, 1721.

———. *Alcorani Textus Universus. Praemissue est Prodromus Totum Priorem Tomum Implens*. Padua: Typographia Seminarii, 1698.

Massignon, Louis. *Essai sur les origines du lexique technique de la mystique musulmane*. Librairie Philosophique J. Vrin, 1968.

———. "Ibn Sab'in et la critique psychologique dans l'histoire de la philosophie musulmane," in *Mémorial Henri Basset*. 2 vols. Paris: Librairie Orientaliste Paul Geuthner, 1928. 2: 119-28.

———. "Notes sur l'apologetique islamique," *Revue des Études Islamiques* 6 (1932): 491-92.

Memon, Muhammad Umar. *Ibn Taymiyya's Struggle against Popular Religion*. The Hague: Mouton, 1977.

———. "The Struggles of Ibn Taymiyya against Popular Religion." Ph.D. diss., University of California, Los Angeles, 1971.

Michel, Thomas F. "Ibn Taymiyya's Sharh on the Futuh al-Ghayb of 'Abd al-Qadir al-Jilani," *Hamdard Islamicus* 4, no. 2 (1981): 3-12.

Monnot, Guy. "Les écrits musulmans sur les religions non-bibliques," *Mélanges Institut Dominicain d'Études Orientales du Caire* 2 (1972): 5-48.

Nallino, C. A. "Le fonte arabe manoscritte dell'opera di Ludovico Marracci sul Corano," *Rendiconti R. Accademia dei Lincei* (1931): 303-49. Reprinted in Nallino's *Raccolta di Scritti*. 6 vols. Instituto per l'Oriente, 1939-48. 2: 90-134.

Nasr, Seyyed Hossein. *Science and Civilization in Islam*. New York: New American Library, 1970.

Nemoy, Leon. "Early Karaism," *Jewish Quarterly Review* 40 (1949-50): 307-15.

Nicoll, Alexander. *Catalogi Codicum Manuscriptorum Orientalium Bibliothecae Bodleianae*. 2 vols. Oxford: E Typographeo Academico, 1835.
Paret, Rudi. "Al-Nazzam als Experimentator," *Der Islam* 25 (1939): 228-33.
Patton, Walter M. *Ahmed ibn Hanbal and the Mihna*. Leiden: E. J. Brill, 1897.
Pedersen, Johs. "The Sabians," in *A Volume of Oriental Studies Presented to Edward G. Browne*. Cambridge: University Press, 1922. Pp. 383-91.
Peeters, Paul. *Evangiles apocryphes*. 2 vols. Paris: Auguste Picard, 1914.
Perier, Augustin. *Yahya ben 'Adi: Un philosophe arabe chrétien du Xe siècle*. Paris: Paul Geuthner, 1920.
Peters, J. R. T. M. *God's Created Speech*. Leiden: E. J. Brill, 1976.
Pines, Shlomo. *Beiträge zur islamische Atomenlehre*. Gräfenhainichen: A. Heine, 1936.
———. "Ibn Khaldun and Maimonides," *Studia Islamica* 32 (1970): 265-74.
———. *"Israel My Firstborn": Studies in Mysticism and Religion*. Jerusalem: Magnes Press, 1967. Pp. 177-90.
Provera, Mario. *Il Vangelo arabo dell'Infanzia*. Jerusalem: Franciscan Printing Press, 1973.
Rahman, Fazlur. *Islam*. Garden City, N.Y.: Doubleday & Co., 1968.
———. *The Philosophy of Mulla Sadra*. Albany: SUNY Press, 1975.
———. "Pre-Foundations of the Muslim Community in Mecca," *Studia Islamica* 38 (1976): 5-24.
———. *Prophecy in Islam*. London: George Allen and Unwin, 1958.
Raïsäanen, Heikki. "Das koranische Jesusbild: Ein Beitrag zur Theologie des Korans." Helsinki: Schriften der finnischen Gesellschaft für Missiologie und Ökumenik, 1971. Quoted, passim, by O. Schumann in *Der Christus der Muslime* (Gütersloh, 1975).
Rodinson, Maxime. *Mohammed*. New York: Random House, 1968.
Rosenthal, Franz. "Aš-Šayh al-Yûnânî and the Arabic Plotinus Source," *Orientalia* 21 (1952): 467-73.
———. "Muslim Definitions of Knowledge," in *The Conflict of Traditionalism and Modernism in the Modern Middle East*. Ed. by Carl Leiden. Austin: University of Texas Press, 1965. Pp. 117-26.
Ryckmans, Jacques. "Le Christianisme en Arabie du Sud préislamique," *L'Oriente cristiano nella storia della Civiltà*. Rome: Accademia Nazionale dei Lincei, 1964. Pp. 413-53.
———. *La persécution des Chrétiens Himyarites au sixième siècle*. Istanbul: Nederlands Historisch-archeologisch Instituut in het Nabije Oosten, 1956.
Saab, Hassan. "Communication between Christianity and Islam," *Middle East Journal* 18 (1964): 41-62.
Sadighi, Gholam Hossein. *Les mouvements religieux iraniens au IIe et au IIIe siècle de l'hégire*. Paris: Les Presses Modernes, 1938.
Schacht, Joseph. *An Introduction to Islamic Law*. Oxford: Clarendon Press, 1964.
Schimmel, Annemarie. *Mystical Dimensions of Islam*. Chapel Hill: University of North Carolina Press, 1975.

Schlumberger, Gustave. *Un empereur byzantine au dixième siècle: Nicéphore Phocas*. Paris: Librairie de Firmin-Didot et Cie., 1890.
Schuon, Frithjof. *Understanding Islam*. Baltimore: Penguin Books, 1972.
Schwab, Moise. "Les non-Musulmans dans le monde de l'Islam," *Revue du Monde Musulman* 6 (1908): 622-39.
Seale, Morris. *Muslim Theology*. London: Luzac, 1964.
Sharif, M. M. *A History of Muslim Philosophy*. 2 vols. Wiesbaden: Otto Harrassowitz, 1963.
Smith, Wilfred Cantwell. *Islam in Modern History*. New York: New American Library, 1959.
______. "Some Similarities and Differences between Christianity and Islam," in *The World of Islam*. Ed. by James Kritzeck and R. Bayly Winder. London: Macmillan and Co., 1959. Pp. 47-59.
Stern, S. M. "The Oxford Manuscript of Ibn Taymiyya's Anti-Christian Polemics," *Bulletin of the School of Oriental and African Studies* 20 (1959): 124-28.
______. "Quotations from Apocryphal Gospels in 'Abd al-Jabbar," *Journal of Theological Studies* 18 (1967): 34-57.
Stieglecker, Herman. *Die Glaubenslehren des Islam*. Paderborn: Ferdinand Schoningh, 1962.
Trimingham, J. Spencer. *Christianity among the Arabs in Pre-Islamic Times*. London: Longman, 1979.
______. *The Sufi Orders in Islam*. London: Oxford University Press, 1971.
Tucker, William. "Abu Mansur al-Ijli and the Mansuriyya: A Study in Medieval Terrorism," *Der Islam* 54 (1977): 66-76.
Umaruddin, Muhammad. "Ibn Taymiyya as a Thinker and Reformer," in *Usbu' al-Fiqh al-Islami wa-Mahrajan al-Imam Ibn Taymiyya*. Cairo: Al-Majlis al-A'la li-Ri'ayat al-Funun wal-Adab wal-'Ulum al-Ijtima'iyya, 1380/1961. Pp. 688-731.
Vajda, George. "La demonstration de l'unitè divine d'après Yùsuf al-Basir," in *Studies in Mysticism and Religion Presented to G. G. Scholem*. Jerusalem: Magnes Press, 1967. Pp. 299-306.
______. "Le témoignage d'al-Maturidi sur la doctrine des Manicheens, des Daysanites et des Marcionites," *Arabica* 13 (1966): 1-38.
______. "Les Zindiqs en pays d'Islam," *Rivista degli Studi Orientali* 17 (1938): 173-229.
van Ess, Josef. "Dirar b. 'Amr und die 'Cahmiya': Biographie einer vergessenen Schule," *Der Islam* 43 (1967): 241-79; 44 (1968): 1-70.
______. *Das Kitab al-Nakth des Nazzam*. Göttingen: Vanderhoeck & Ruprecht, 1972.
Vasiliev, A. A. *Byzance et les Arabes*. 3 vols. Brussels: Fondacion Byzantine, 1968.
Vitestam, Gosta. *Kitab al-Radd 'ala al-Jahmiyya lil-Darimi*. Lund: C. W. K. Gleerup, 1960.
Watt, W. Montgomery. *The Formative Period of Islamic Thought*. Edinburgh: University Press, 1973.
______. "His Name is Ahmad," *Muslim World* 41 (1951): 251-56.
Wensinck, Arent Jan. *A Handbook of Early Muhammadan Tradition*. Leiden: E. J. Brill, 1971.

Wolfson, Harry Austryn. "The Jewish Kalam," in *The Seventy-Fifth Anniversary Volume of The Jewish Quarterly Review*. Philadelphia, 1932. Pp. 544-73.

_____. *Philo: Foundations of Religious Philosophy in Judaism, Christianity, and Islam*. 2 vols. Cambridge: Harvard University Press, 1947.

_____. "Philosophical Implications of the Problem of the Divine Attributes in the Koran," *Journal of the American Oriental Society* 79 (1959): 73-80.

_____. *The Philosophy of the Kalam*. Cambridge: Harvard University Press, 1976.

Yahya, Osman. *Histoire et classification de l'oeuvre d'Ibn al-'Arabi*. 2 vols. Damascus: Institut Français de Damas, 1964.

## GLOSSARY

*ahl al-dhimma*: the "Protected Peoples," i.e., the legal status of Jews and Christians in an Islamic state.
*ahl al-qibla*: neutral term indicating all those who identify themselves as members of the Islamic *umma*.
*'alim* (pl. *'ulama'*): someone learned in the religious sciences of Islam.
*al-amr wal-nahy*: the complex of commands and prohibitions in Islam.
*al-'aql al-fa''al*: in neoplatonic cosmology, the celestial intellect which governs the lower world. Identified with Aristotelian demiurge, fashioner of forms and giver of knowledge.

*batini*: the hidden, inner meaning of scripture.
*bid'a* (pl. *bida'*): unlawful religious innovation against the original prophetic teaching.

*da'wa*: the invitation to accept Islam; calling unbelievers to accept Islam.
*dhat*: the equivalent in Arabic philosophy to the scholastic "essentia."
*dhawq*: intuition/immediate perception—a faculty of knowledge distinct from reason.
*dhikr*: remembrance of God. Sufis developed *dhikr* into forms of prayer which would lead the believer into mystical union with God.
*dhimmi* (pl. *dhimmiyyun* or *ahl al-dhimma*): cf. *ahl al-dhimma*.
*din*: faith in the one, universal, eternal message of all the prophets.

*fana'*: a mystical state in which all things pass away from the believer, even awareness of his own self; all that remains (*baqa'*) is God.
*faqih*: a scholar of Islamic jurisprudence.
*fatwa*: a legal opinion delivered by one versed in Islamic jurisprudence.
*filsuf* (pl. *falasifa*): philosopher, esp. one of the Hellenist tradition.
*fiqh*: Islamic jurisprudence.
*furqan*: one of the names of the Qur'an, indicating its nature as the criterion of discernment between truth and falsehood, right and wrong.

*ghali* (pl. *ghulat*): one holding an extreme position in matters of religion.
*ghayb*: information known only to God and revealed through the prophets.
*ghuluw*: extremism in beliefs or practices. Cf. *ghali*.

*hadith*: an oral tradition relating the sayings, deeds, and decisions of the prophet which, if proven sound, is a basis for belief and practice.
*hajj*: the pilgrimage to Mecca, one of the pillars of Islam.
*halal*: that which is permissible according to Islamic law.

*hanif* (pl. *hunafa'*): an Arab monotheist who rejected the pagan religion but did not join one of the Religions of the Book.
*haram*: something forbidden by Islamic law.
*hawa* (pl. *ahwa'*): human whim, i.e., that which someone would like to believe and is thus tempted to consider the true teaching of his religion.
*hawari* (pl. *hawariyyun*): the Qur'anic term for the disciples of Jesus.
*hikma*: divine wisdom and purposefulness in creation.
*hulul*: the indwelling of God in a human person.

*ijma'*: consensus of the Islamic *umma*, accepted by Sunni Muslims as a basis for law.
*ijtihad*: exercise of one's own efforts to arrive at a legal opinion on problems for which no explicit answer is given in the Qur'an and sunna.
*imam*: among Shi'a, one of the line of 12 (or 7 or 5) infallible teachers after Muhammad.
*'isma*: inerrancy, a characteristic of the prophets in Sunni and Shi'i Islam; Shi'a also consider the Imams inerrant.
*ittihad* (*'amm/khass*): union of God with creation or a created being.
*ittihad 'amm*: the identification of God, essentially or existentially, with the universe.
*ittihad khass*: union of God with a specific person.
*Ittihadiyya*: "pantheist," a pejorative referring to the proponents of *wahdat al-wujud*.

*jinni* (pl. *jinn*): a spirit; may be either good or evil.
*jizya*: tax paid by *dhimmi* in an Islamic state.

*kalam*: speculative discourse on matters pertaining to God, i.e., Islamic theology.
*karama* (pl. *karamat*): wondrous deed performed by a holy person.
*kashf*: immediate, non-rational discovery of Truth, i.e., that existence is one and that is God. Cf. *dhawq*.
*khabar*: neutral term indicating information which may be true or false.
*khabar wahid*: a hadith report transmitted by only one person.
*khalifa*: a successor to Muhammad as head of the *umma*. Sunni Muslims recognize four "rightly guided" *khalifas*: Abu Bakr, 'Umar, 'Uthman, 'Ali.
*khalil*: intimate friend of God, a title reserved to Abraham and Muhammad.
*khalwa*: retreat from active life for a certain period in order to engage in spiritual exercises.
*kufr*: unbelief, rejection of a prophet and the message he brings from God.

*madhhab*: one of the four law schools of Sunni Islam. Also used in the broader meaning of "sect."
*madrasa*: Islamic school.
*malami*: Islamic mystic who lives outwardly reprehensible life so that his true piety not be evident.
*maslaha*: the welfare of the community.
*mawlid*: celebration of the birthday of Muhammad or some other great person.

*al-milal wal-nihal*: heresiographical literature.
*milla*: a socio-religious community in an Islamic state which is governed at least in part by its own religious law.
*mu'attil*: one guilty of *ta'til*, i.e., an extreme transcendentalist.
*mujaddid*: a renewer of religion. Islamic tradition teaches that at the beginning of each century, someone is sent to renew the faith of the *umma*.
*mujtahid*: one who performs *ijtihad*.
*mulamasa*: intermingling of God in creation or in a created person.
*mu'min* (pl. *mu'minun*): believer; term most commonly employed by the Qur'an to indicate the followers of Muhammad.
*murtadd*: an apostate from Islam.
*mushrik* (pl. *mushrikun*): one who commits *shirk*.
*musnad*: religious literature which studies the *hadith* traditions, specifically the chain of transmission.
*mutashabih*: one guilty of *tashbih*, i.e., an anthropomorphist.

*qada'*: the divine decree.
*qadar*: divine determination of human actions.
*qalandar*: itinerant, mendicant Sufis, who often declared themselves "beyond the Law."
*qibla*: the direction of prayer, for Muslims, that of the Ka'ba. Cf. *ahl al-qibla*.
*qiyas*: the use of analogy as a basis for law in Islamic jurisprudence.

*Rafida*: pejorative term for Shi'a ("those who refuse" the leadership of the first three *khalifas*).
*rasul*: a messenger of God; often synonymous with *nabi* (prophet), sometimes distinguished from *nabi* to indicate a prophet who brought a written message, i.e., a Book.
*risala*: a treatise.

*Sahaba*: the Companions of Muhammad; the first generation of Muslims.
*sahih*: a sound *hadith* report. Also, one of the two great collections of sound *hadiths* compiled by al-Bukhari and Muslim.
*sahihayn*: the *hadith* collections of al-Bukhari and Muslim.
*salaf*: the earliest generations of Muslims (usually, the first three generations) whose interpretation of Islamic belief and practice is held to be correct.
*salah*: the ritual prayer of Islam performed five times daily.
*salb*: the theological position which holds that since all human terminology can only be applied analogously to God, one can speak precisely about God only in negative terms (e.g., "God is *not* dead, ignorant, weak, etc.").
*salik* (pl. *salikun*): one who follows the mystical path in Islam.
*sama'*: musically accompanied *dhikr*.
*al-Samad*: "the Rock." A Qur'anic name for God indicating His sovereign independence from all else, and simultaneously the dependence of all things upon Him.

*shahada* (dual, *shahadatayn*): the two-part witness of faith that there is no god but God and Muhammad is His messenger.
*shari'a*: the religious Law that characterizes each prophetic religion.
*shath* (pl. *shatahat*): ecstatic "intoxicated" mystical utterance, often shocking or blasphemous if taken literally.
*shay'*: neutral term indicating any "thing" which exists.
*shaytan*: one of the demons, or Satan (Iblis) himself.
*Shi'i* (pl. *Shi'a*): the party of 'Ali and the Imams. Those Muslims who follow the teachings of Islam transmitted through the infallible Imams.
*shirk*: allowing some creature to participate in the worship due only to God; worshiping God but something else as well.
*sifa* (pl. *sifat*): attribute, characteristic; used as the technical term for the attributes of God.
*silsila*: chain of authority going back to the early teacher. Among Sufis, the *silsila* connects the believer with the founder of the *tariqa* and beyond.
*sira*: the biography of Muhammad, esp. that composed by Ibn Ishaq.
*sukna*: residence, used in the sense of God's taking up residence in an individual or in His people.
*sulh*: land governed by Muslims through treaty with the local people or ruler.
*sunna*: Islamic way of life based on the words and example of Muhammad.
*Sunni*: the people of the *sunna* and community. Those Muslims who follow the Qur'an and example of Muhammad (*sunna*) transmitted through the rightly guided *khalifa*s and confirmed by consensus of the community.

*tabdil*: replacement of beliefs/practices taught by the prophets with innovated, human creations. Cf. *tahrif*.
*tabi'un*: the second generation of Muslims, the "followers" of the *Sahaba*.
*tafsir*: exegesis of and commentary on scripture.
*tafwid*: to refer back to God those things which humans can neither affirm nor deny.
*taghyir*: changing the wording or meaning of scripture. Cf *tahrif*.
*tahrif*: corruption of scripture. *tahrif al-lafz*: textual deformation. *tahrif al-ma'na*: erroneous interpretation of scriptural text.
*tajallin*: a divine epiphany in the existing universe.
*tajassum*: to hold that God has a body.
*tajsim*: to describe God with corporeal attributes.
*takfir*: to declare someone an unbeliever.
*tamthil*: the proper expression of divine immanence which avoids both essential identification of God with creation and His dependence upon it.
*tanazzul*: one of a series of divine manifestations by which the universe continually comes into existence, according to the teaching of *wahdat al-wujud*.
*tanzih*: the proper expression of divine transcendence which preserves God's constant, active relation to creation.

*taqlid*: blind following of the teaching of earlier generations.
*taqwa*: reverential fear of God.
*tariqa*: a mystical path, hence a Sufi order.
*tashbih*: an understanding of divine immanence which makes God essentially united with or dependent upon the created universe.
*ta'til*: exaggerated concept of divine transcendence, which either theoretically or practically denies divine contact with the universe. Raising God to irrelevance.
*tawhid*: the proper expression of divine unity taught by Islam.

*'ulama'*: cf. *'alim*.
*umma*: the Islamic community of believers.
*'unwa*: land governed by Muslims through conquest.
*uqnum* (pl. *aqanim*): Arabic equivalent of the Greek "hypostasis," i.e., a mode of divine subsistence.
*usul al-din*: "the bases of religion." The Qur'an and *sunna* as bases for Islamic belief and practice.

*wahda*: cf. *wahdat al-wujud*.
*wahdat al-wujud*: philosophical/theological system in Islam based on the principle of the unity of existence.
*wahy*: divine revelation communicated to the prophets.
*wajd*: knowledge of the Truth through ecstatic experience. Cf. *dhawq*, *kashf*.

*zahiri*: the evident, exegetically sound meaning of scripture.
*zakah*: the poor tax, one of the pillars of Islam.
*zuhd*: asceticism.

Note: the definitions given in this Glossary are not meant to be inclusive, but merely to indicate how the term is used by Ibn Taymiyya in the passages cited in this book.

## INDEX